Catholic Dogmatic Theology ⁌ A Synthesis

BOOK 3

THOMISTIC RESSOURCEMENT SERIES

Volume 18

SERIES EDITORS

Matthew Levering, Mundelein Seminary

Thomas Joseph White, OP, Pontifical University
of St. Thomas Aquinas

EDITORIAL BOARD

Serge-Thomas Bonino, OP, Pontifical University
of St. Thomas Aquinas

Gilles Emery, OP, University of Fribourg

Reinhard Hütter, The Catholic University of America

Bruce Marshall, Southern Methodist University

Emmanuel Perrier, OP, Dominican Studium, Toulouse

Richard Schenk, OP, University of Freiburg (Germany)

Kevin White, The Catholic University of America

Catholic Dogmatic Theology ✦ A Synthesis

BOOK 3, ON THE CHURCH AND
THE SACRAMENTS

JEAN-HERVÉ NICOLAS, OP

FOREWORD BY JOSEPH RATZINGER

FOREWORD TO THE ENGLISH EDITION
BY ARCHBISHOP ALLEN VIGNERON

TRANSLATED BY MATTHEW K. MINERD

The Catholic University of America Press
Washington, DC

Originally published as *Synthèse dogmatique: De la Trinité à la Trinité*, © Paris: Beauchesne, 1985. Toute demande concernant les droits de traduction, de reproduction, d'adaptation, en quelque langue que se soit, devra obligatoirement être adressé a Beauchesne Editeur, 7 Cité du Cardinal Lemoine 75005 Paris — France, Editeur l'édition originale.

English Translation Copyright © 2024
The Catholic University of America Press
All rights reserved
The paper used in this publication meets the minimum requirements of American National Standards for Information Science—Permanence of Paper for Printed Library Materials,
ANSI Z39.48-1992.
∞

Cataloging-in-Publication Data is available
from the Library of Congress
Hardcover ISBN: 978-0-8132-3852-4
Paperback ISBN: 978-0-8132-3788-6
eISBN: 978-0-8132-3789-3

Table of Contents

Foreword to the English Edition by Archbishop Allen Vigneron — vii

Translator's Preface — ix

Foreword to the Original Edition by Cardinal Joseph Ratzinger — xiii

List of Abbreviations — xv

PART 1. THE CHURCH — 1

1. The Sacramentality of the Church — 5
2. Christ's Presence to the World through the Church — 61
3. The Church's Universal Mediation — 113
4. The Sacraments in the Church — 141

PART 2. BAPTISM AND CONFIRMATION — 237

5. Introduction to the Theology of Baptism — 239
6. The Effects of Baptism — 246
7. Baptism and Faith — 276
8. The Necessity of Baptism — 303
9. The Sacrament of Confirmation — 322

PART 3. THE SACRAMENT OF THE EUCHARIST — 347

10. What the Church Believes Regarding the Eucharist — 353
11. The Eucharistic Sacrifice — 419
12. The Eucharistic Presence of Christ: The Reality of This Presence — 451
13. The Sacramental Action by Which Transubstantiation Is Brought About — 498
14. Christ's Eucharistic Presence: Christ Present to the Church — 513

PART 4. PENANCE AND THE ANOINTING OF THE SICK — 547

15. The Problem of the Sacrament of Penance — 549
16. The Theology of the Sacrament of Penance — 566
17. The Anointing of the Sick — 615

PART 5. THE SACRAMENT OF HOLY ORDERS — 631

18. The Priest in the Church — 635
19. The Character Imprinted by the Sacrament of Holy Orders — 681

PART 6. THE SACRAMENT OF MARRIAGE — 719

20. What Is the Sacrament of Marriage? — 721
21. The Effects of the Sacrament of Marriage — 734

General Conclusion: From the Trinity to the Trinity — 751

Works Cited — 759
Scripture Index — 787
Name/Subject Index — 791

Foreword to the English Edition

ARCHBISHOP ALLEN VIGNERON

———·———

In guiding the work of the Second Vatican Council, St. John XXIII and St. Paul VI made it clear that this epochal event was not for the sake of the Church herself. As their successor Pope Francis might put it: the Council was not "self-referential." The aim of the Council was the renewal of the Church as the sacrament of Jesus Christ, the Light of the Nations—*Lumen gentium*, so that she would be the ever more effective instrument for sharing the Good News. The aim of the Council was to launch the Church once more out into the deep of evangelizing the world (cf. Lk 5:4).

The Council Fathers identified the renewal of theology as a necessary dimension of this more general project of renewal-for-mission. As part of that mandate they explicitly mentioned the role that the theological achievement of St. Thomas Aquinas ought to play in achieving this aim: "In order that they may illumine the mysteries of salvation as completely as possible, sshould learn to penetrate them more deeply with the help of speculation, under the guidance of St. Thomas, and to perceive their interconnections" (*Optatam totius*, 16).

As a bishop, charged, as I am, to do my part to fulfill the Great Commission "to make disciples of all nations" (Mt 28:19), I welcome the publication of the English translation of Fr. Nicolas's *Synthèse dogmatique*, since it makes readily available to students an effective instrument for Aquinas to guide them into a deeper understanding of the saving mysteries of the gospel. And as Cardinal Ratzinger affirms in his foreword to this work, Fr. Nicolas goes about his task of exploring the mind of Aquinas with the conviction that "revealed truths are not only truths. They are principles of life, conversion, and therefore also of preaching." Thus, the deeper penetration of gospel truth that students will achieve by joining with St. Thomas to think about them with the help of Fr. Nicolas will be a blessed resource for the Church on her mission to give an account for the hope that she offers the world in the name of Christ (cf. 1 Pt 3:15).

I first became acquainted with Fr. Nicolas's *Synthèse dogmatique* when I was engaged in teaching theology to seminarians. Since then I had looked for the day when this work would be available to English-speaking students in their own language. Through the considerable efforts of the translator, Dr. Matthew Minerd, with help of those he so generously acknowledges, I have the satisfaction of seeing my long-felt need for this resource met for the good of students and professors alike. To Dr. Minerd and his colleagues I offer my sincere thanks.

A key moment in my own theological studies was when a wise professor observed in passing, "To explain a profound mystery simply you must understand it profoundly." I have made this piece of advice an axiom for my study and for my teaching. I am confident that the appearance of Fr. Nicolas's *Synthèse dogmatique* in English will aid in that profound understanding which yields in students of theology the great good fruit of their being able to offer that clear and compelling explanation of the revealed mysteries which goes by the deceptive name of "simple."

Translator's Preface

This work represents the third portion of Fr. Nicolas's *Synthèse dogmatique*, a formidable pair of tomes which, in English, will be presented as a series of separate thematic volumes. As Fr. Nicolas explains in the first volume of this English-language series of texts, *Synthèse dogmatique* is based upon a sequence of course lectures given over a number of decades. Because of these origins, his written French style can be a bit choppy at times, using formulations that are either fragmentary or idiosyncratic. The voice of the original classroom lecture texts is often obvious in the original French. Furthermore, as will be particularly evident in the fourth volume of this series, Fr. Nicolas's own personal style is quite wordy, often falling into sentences that are a hundred words in length. In most cases, care has been taken to retain Fr. Nicolas's voice. However, upon consultation with Fr. Thomas Joseph White, OP—to whom my work on this project owes a great debt—I decided it best to err on the side of readability, for these texts are destined for use in the pedagogical formation of theologians. When stylistic modification was deemed necessary, this generally required me to present a slightly more paratactic style than the more serpentine forms used by Fr. Nicolas. However, where there is a chance that I have added a nuance, I utilize square brackets (either for my added text or to provide the original language equivalent). Moreover, Fr. Nicolas frequently utilizes a non-standard style of quoting authors, setting off in block quotes even single lines of quotation. I have worked to stylistically integrate these quotations into a standard form conformed to the style sheet of The Catholic

University of America Press. On occasion, he expresses side comments or technical qualifications in small text as well. For the sake of flow, I have moved most of these to footnotes, though, on occasion, I have integrated such asides into the body of the text.

In Fr. Nicolas's original volume, the footnotes were written in shorthand, referencing a single bibliography at the end of the lengthy volume. I have moved all bibliographical references to the footnotes for ease of reference. On occasion, I have had to note what appear to be mistakes by Fr. Nicolas in these notes.

In general, scriptural references have been taken from the Revised Standard Version of the Bible. Where contextual rhetorical concerns did not seem to allow this, I translated the text from the French provided by Fr. Nicolas. All such citations from the Revised Standard Version are marked in the scriptural citation. For example, if a direct citation has been taken from Romans 6:1, it is cited as Rom 6:1 (RSV).

All direct citations from Denzinger are taken from the English translation provided in the 43rd edition published by Ignatius Press. Where available, citations from contemporary non-French works have been taken from authorized translations with the relevant citation details being provided in the appropriate footnotes. All French authors have been translated anew. Because Fr. Nicolas has made slight interpretive nuances to his citations from St. Thomas, I have chosen to translate from his own translation of the Angelic Doctor but have done so with an eye to the original and always with a literal approach to Fr. Nicolas's own rendering. The same holds for his citations of Patristic and scholastic sources.

It remains an *immense* honor to work as the translator of these erudite volumes by the great Dominican theologian. I would, however, be remiss if I were not to note several points upon which I have differences with Fr. Nicolas, specifically in relation to certain points that engage the intersection between the Byzantine East and the Roman Catholic West. On the whole, he takes great pains to charitably interact with Orthodox outlooks, often even adjusting his own vocabulary so as to integrate what he believes is good therein. However, on several topics, I must, for the sake of my own identity as a

Ruthenian Catholic, note the following points, in which I distance myself from Fr. Nicolas's own theological conclusions or the tone with which he addresses the particular topic: the question of the minister of the sacrament of matrimony;[1] his comments concerning baptism and the reception of the Eucharist, and in particular an all-too-brisk and Latin-chauvinistic proclamation of the superiority of the Latin practice of confirmation after the age of reason (though he is, happily, a partisan of the appropriate ordering of the sacraments of initiation); his approach to clerical celibacy is not as dismissive of Eastern practices as certain Roman Catholic authors of late, though he does little to engage with the issue in detail;[2] his treatment of the Epiclesis, though very genteel, leaves room for further debate;[3] and, really, quite sadly, his idea of the "East" is limited only to certain Byzantine Orthodox Churches, not seriously taking into account either the other Churches of the Christian East, nor recognizing the unique Eastern Catholic Churches in union with Rome.

Allow me, however, to be clear: the great thematic "bones" of Fr. Nicolas's work are of immense worth and illumination. There is much, especially in his discussion of ecclesiological matters, that I hope will be received warmly by my Byzantine brethren. And while his presentation of the individual sacraments are somewhat marked by the ritual tradition of the Roman Rite, Fr. Nicolas presents the

---

1. See George Gallaro and Dimitri Salachas, "The *Ritus Sacer* of the Sacrament of Marriage in the Byzantine Churches," *The Jurist: Studies in Church Law and Ministry* 70, no. 1 (2010): 206–34. My citation of (now-Archbishop) Gallaro's work, as well as the works cited in the next two notes, is not necessarily an endorsement of every point found therein. Nonetheless, as an Eastern Catholic, I think it necessary to point out how important it is that these kinds of concerns be taken seriously, for in all these cases, the Byzantine Churches in union with Rome keenly feel their status as second-class citizens at the table, above all in the eyes of many Thomists, not being taken as real theological dialogue partners whose practices might bear witness to important nuances that should be made *within Thomistic theological science itself*. I write this, of course, in a spirit of *immense* filial devotion to Fr. Nicolas's work and to the august *Schola thomae*, in whose service I have spent many hours translating technical works of philosophy and theology.

2. See Adam J. DeVille (ed.), *Married Priests in the Catholic Church* (Notre Dame, IN: University of Notre Dame Press, 2021).

3. For indications concerning a more Orthodox-sensitive approach to these issues, one may consult Christiaan Kappes, *The Epiclesis Debate at the Council of Florence* (Notre Dame, IN: University of Notre Dame Press, 2019).

great principles of these sacred acts of Christ through the Church with such clarity and force that the great majority of what he says is of universal value in the formation of the theological *habitus*, no matter what one's particular Church might be. I consider Fr. Nicolas to be one of my great masters, and it is in a spirit of filial devotion that I have noted the minor concerns above.

Thanks go to Dr. Reinhard Hütter and, especially, Fr. Thomas-Joseph White, OP, for their support in undertaking this project, as well as to Matthew Levering, who offered friendly encouragement through the long hours of working on this volume in conjunction with future portions of Fr. Nicolas's text. Likewise, gratitude is owed to the Thomistic Institute (and a kind donor) for providing funds for the overall project of translating Fr. Nicolas's *Synthèse dogmatique*. Finally, sincerest thanks are owed to all those persons involved in the editorial process without whom this volume would have been significantly more deficient: John Martino, Trevor Crowell, Paul Higgins and Mary Ann Lieser.

This translation is dedicated to my step-uncle Terrence J. Szepesi, who through a long life, and through its many vicissitudes, has retained the flame of his love for the Church, despite the many paradoxes and frustrations he has experienced due to the *chiaroscuro* of her holiness and the sinfulness of her members. Mnohaya lita! May God grant him many blessed years and the eternal bliss he so clearly and ardently desires!

Foreword to the Original Edition

CARDINAL JOSEPH RATZINGER

---·---

We live in an age of excessive specialization. This assertion holds true in the domain of theology, where the number of publications has grown beyond what sight can embrace, thus making it increasingly difficult for one to have an overview of the whole of theology. In this state of affairs, we find ourselves faced with the fact that contemporary overview presentations of dogmatic theology most often are the collective work of many authors. Certainly, in such works, particular points are given thorough treatments. However, the various parts are connected to one another only in an extrinsic manner. Now, given that (according to Hegel's expression) "the Truth is the Whole," theology's current state raises problems that are not merely didactic and pedagogical. Beyond such concerns, this state of affairs also compromises the very task of theology in what is essential to it. In this regard, recall that Irenaeus of Lyon founded Catholic theology in the proper sense of the word by holding that it is based on "the primordial system" (Adv. Haer. IV, 33, 8), on the basis of what is foundational for the unity of ecclesial life. This enabled him to perceive the unity of the Old and New Covenant, of the Creator and the Savior, of philosophy and faith, and what alone can constitute the specific character of theology.

In this regard, the publication of this text in dogmatic theology by Jean-Hervé Nicolas, which matured over the course of many years of teaching, for many reasons represents a theological event of great importance. The Thomist option, which he takes as his point of departure, is not based on Aquinas's authority as such but, rather, on his theological thought, which the author receives by critically rethinking it. What is characteristic of a theology thus situated is that it is, above all, a synthesis between historical knowledge and philosophical reflection. However, it also represents the conjunction of the Church's teaching with critical reflection, as well as that of theory with practice. "Revealed truths," writes Fr. Nicolas, "are not only truths. They are principles of life, conversion, and therefore also of preaching." What strikes me in Fr. Nicolas's book is, first of all, its sure erudition in exegesis and in the history of dogmas. However, I am also struck to no less an extent by the vigor of his philosophical outlook, something that is not encountered very often today in pedagogical volumes on dogmatic theology. This philosophical outlook gives this book its depth, internal unity, and at the same time, a persuasiveness that could never arise from a more or less positivist organization of the various topics discussed therein. The reader who will allow himself to be guided by Fr. Nicolas will perceive that the ecclesiality of theology, if it is authentic, in no way impedes the power and openness of one's thought. On the contrary, it places thought in profound agreement with the great thinkers of all ages. Without such agreement, one falls into individual isolation and, in the end, into skepticism, which represents an impoverishment of the truth. Fr. Nicolas's book can assist us in drawing closer to this "unity in theology." Without such unity, the latter, inasmuch as it is theology, disintegrates. This is why I hope that this text will be broadly received by many open-minded readers.

Rome, Feast of the Exaltation of the Cross [1984/5]

List of Abbreviations

AAS	*Acta Apostolicae Sedis*
CSEL	Corpus Scriptorum Ecclesiasticorum Latinorum
D.-Sch.	Denzinger, *Enchiridion Symbolorum*
In Sent.	Thomas Aquinas, *Scriptum super libros Sententiarum*
OESA	Oeuvres de Saint Augustin
PG	Patrologia Graeca (ed. Migne)
PL	Patrologia Latina (ed. Migne)
SC	Sources Chrétiennes
SCG	Thomas Aquinas, *Summa contra gentiles*
ST	Thomas Aquinas, *Summa theologiae*

PART 1

THE CHURCH

GENERAL INTRODUCTION

{607} In recent years, ecclesiology has undergone such developments that it nearly constitutes a discipline set apart. In any case, it has developed to such a degree that it calls for specialization (or, perhaps, a number of specializations). Does this mean that we must forbid ourselves from discussing it in a general text in dogmatic theology? It is quite certainly part of "the economy [of salvation]," and the dogmatic theologian feels called to reflect on this topic as well. Here, as in other domains of revealed truths, he must present the order that exists among all the various revealed truths, as well as their relationship to "theology" [i.e., the intra-Trinitarian mystery].

However, where should we place ecclesiology in an overall theological synthesis? In St. Thomas's *Summa theologiae*, we do not find a "Treatise on the Church." He ceaselessly speaks about the Church in connection with all of the *Summa*'s treatises. She is the dwelling place and conduit of the Word and of grace. However, today, how could the Church not be treated apart on her own in a theological synthesis? Could we be content with speaking ceaselessly about her though only in relation to other topics, never reflecting on her for her own sake?

Where, however, should such a treatise be placed? If we consider the fact that we believe and theologize in the Church and through her [own activity], she could be omnipresent. Still, if we were to do this, we would thus return to a synthesis in which she would have no special place set apart.

Therefore, we must resign ourselves to constructing a treatise on the Church placed among the other treatises of theology, likewise accepting the fact that this treatise will be incomplete. Today, we find ourselves faced with a host of problems (e.g., concerning the Church's structure, her government, ecumenical problems, and issues related to the relationship between the Church and the world). However, in this synthesis, we will not be able to treat these problems in themselves but, rather, will only be able to treat the general principles involved in resolving them.

Now, where should such a treatise on the Church be placed in a Thomistic theological synthesis? The Church can be considered only in relation to Christ, as His prolongation here-below, His "body" (even if this expression must be examined with care and explained with due precision). Therefore, an ecclesiology like that presented in this text can be nothing other than a continuation of Christology. It is naturally placed after the study of the Word Incarnate and before the study of the sacraments.

However, we should take care to ensure that it has a close connection to sacramental theology. Indeed, if we consider the sacraments not only as sanctifying rites but also as acts that each realize the essential character of saving grace in a partial manner (i.e., if we consider "sacramentality" as such), we will be led to study this sacramentality, which is realized in each of them in a singular way, from another perspective as well: as a general property of the Church herself.

This presupposes a preliminary choice. Among all the images and actions that are proposed for expressing what the Church is, "sacramentality" must be chosen as being the most comprehensive of these images, the one that is most apt to render account of her multiple aspects.

We are invited to make this choice by Vatican II which, from the start of *Lumen Gentium*, presents the Church as "[being] in Christ like a sacrament or as a sign and instrument both of a very closely knit union with God and of the unity of the whole human race,"[1]

---

1. *Lumen Gentium*, November 21, 1964, no. 1.

repeating this affirmation a number of times. This is the first time that we encounter a Magisterial document expressing this way of conceiving of the Church.

However, the idea was not entirely new. Besides its biblical and Patristic sources (where the Church is presented from the start as the visible manifestation of the "mystery of God" and as the anticipated realization of salvation),[2] the very word can be found in a text written by St. Cyprian which is cited by *Lumen Gentium*: "inseparabile unitatis sacramentum."[3] This idea had been retrieved in the nineteenth century by Möhler and Scheeben, the great German precursors of modern ecclesiology, and it was an idea taken up again at the end of the century by the theologian [Johann H.] Oswald.[4] After a long silence, it was taken up by modern theologians like Chaillet,[5] de Lubac,[6] and above all by Semmelroth[7] and Schillebeeckx.[8] If we look further back into the past, we will then discover that, at least according to Congar, one of the fundamental ideas of St. Thomas's ecclesiology is the idea that "the Church as an institution is the sacrament and minister of the Mystical Body, in short, the instrument of the Mystical Body's realization *l'instrument de realization du Corps Mystique*."[9]

Therefore, we can say that there had been preparative steps prior to Vatican II's declarations. Nonetheless, their novelty was a bit surprising. Indeed, though the idea itself was not new, the use of it for characterizing the nature of the Church was.

Therefore, in our first section, we must explain and justify our choice to place this notion at the center of ecclesiology and show how sacramentality can be the organizing principle thereof.

2. See Pieter Smulders, "L'Église sacrement de salut," in *L'Eglise de Vatican II*, Unam Sanctam 51 (Paris: Cerf, 1966), 313–38, at 314n2.
3. See *Lumen Gentium*, no. 9.
4. See Smulders, "L'Église sacrement de salut," 314–15.
5. See Pierre Chaillet, "Introduction" to Johann Adam Möhler, *L'unité dans l'Eglise*, trans. André de Lilienfeld, Unam Sanctam 2 (Paris: Cerf, 1938).
6. Henri de Lubac, *Corpus mystium, L'Eucharistie et l'Église au Moyen Age* (Paris: Aubier, 1949), ch. 6.
7. Otto Semmelroth, *L'Église, sacrament de la redemption*, trans. Germain Varin (Paris: St. Paul, 1963); "Pour l'unité de la notion d'Église," *in Questions théologiques aujourd'hui*, vol. 2, translated by Y-Cl. Gélébar (Paris: Desclée de Brouwer, 1965), 161ff.
8. Edward Schillebeeckx, *Le Christ, sacrament de la rencontre de Dieu*, trans. Augustin Kerkvoorde (Paris: Cerf, 1960).
9. Yves Congar, *Esquisses du mystère de l'Église* (Paris: Cerf, 1941), 59–91.

4   The Church

GENERAL BIBLIOGRAPHY
CONCERNING THE CHURCH

This is not meant to be a complete bibliography, nor even a remotely complete one. Here, I only note some general works that I highly recommend that students read, at least partially and by way of consultation.*

* Louis Bouyer, *L'Église de Dieu* (Paris: Cerf, 1970), is perhaps the best modern introduction to ecclesiology. On this, see Charles Journet, "L'Église de dieu, le livre du Père Bouyer," *Nova et Vetera* 46 (1971): 129–47. See also Yves Congar, "L'Église, une, sainte, catholique et apostolique," in *Mysterium salutis*, vol. 15 (Paris: Cerf, 1970); *l'Ecclésiologie du Haut Moyen Age* (Paris: Cerf, 1968); *l'Église de saint Augustin à l'époque modern* (Paris: Cerf, 1970). Stanley Jaki, *Les tendances nouvelles de l'ecclésiologie* (Rome, 1957). Charles Journet, *L'Église du Verbe Incarné*, vols. 1–3 (Paris: Desclée de Brouwer, 1951–69). Besides being an inexhaustible mine of information, these volumes constitute the always-personal and very profound methodical treatment of the principal problems of ecclesiology. The author has provided a substantial summary of the first two volumes in his *Théologie de l'Église* (Paris: Desclée de Brouwer, 1958). Hans Küng, *Structures de l'Église* (Paris: Desclée de Brouwer, 1963); *L'Église*, trans. Henri Marie Rochais (Paris: Desclée de Brouwer, 1968); see the thorough reviews, which are laudatory though not without reservations and critiques, but by no means [wholly] negative, in Fr. Bouyer in *Civitas* (Luzern) 23 (1968): 933–40. Yves Congar, *Revue des Sciences philosophiques et théologiques* 53 (1969): 693–706. See also Joseph Coppens, "L'Église dans l'optique de Hans Küng," *Ephemerides Theologicae Lovanienses* 46 (1970): 121–30. Gustave Dejaifve, "A propos d'un livre recent," *Nouvelle revue théologique* 89 (1967): 1085–95. Hermann Häring and Josef Nolte (eds.), *Diskussion um H. Küng "Die Kirche"* (Freiburg: Herder, 1971): collection of judgments brought together and ordered by two disciples, with a contribution by Küng and his response to Congar. Marie-Vincent Leroy, "L'Église de H. Küng," *Revue thomiste* (1970): 293–310. Jacques Maritain, *De l'Église du Christe, la Personne de l'Église et son personnel* (Paris: Desclée de Brouwer, 1970). Jean-Guy Page, *Qui est l'Église? I. Le mystère et le sacrament du salut* (Montréal: Ed. Bellarmin, 1982); *II. Qui est l'Église* (Montréal: Ed. Bellarmin, 1979). Gérard Philips, *L'Église et son Mystère au deuxième concile du Vatican. Histoire, texte et commentaire de la constitution "Lumen Gentium"* (Paris: Desclée, 1968); Philips's text is the most authoritative and classic commentary on *Lumen Gentium*. Möhler, *L'unité dans l'Église*. Mattias Joseph Scheeben, *Le mystère de l'Église et de ses sacrements*, trans. Augusin Kerkvoorde (Paris: Cerf, 1956).

1

The Sacramentality of the Church

{608} Before taking on its specific meaning designating the Church's seven sanctifying rites, the notion of a "sacrament" was the equivalent for the Greek word *musterion*. In a very general way, it designates a visible reality, itself belonging to the world of experience, though re-presenting (i.e., rendering present) supernatural realities for man. For this reason, it belongs to the invisible world, making the realities of this latter world enter into our own world (as well as into our awareness): "Every supernatural reality historically accomplished in our life is sacramental."[1]

Only God can take such an initiative in order to enter into our world in this way, for man, by himself, does not hold sway over God. Indeed, a sacrament which would have man as its source would be nothing more than a projection fabricated by human consciousness, thereby being deprived of all true transcendence. (In other words, it would no longer be a truly supernatural reality.) This descent of God into our world is *revelation*.

Still, what is the relationship between revelation and the sacraments? In Himself, God is not conceptualizable. He cannot be grasped by man. (If He can be rendered "graspable," this happens by the human intellect being elevated to Him, implying that it would be wrenched away from itself and from the world.)[2] In this world, God

---

1. Schillebeeckx, *Le Christ*, 30.
2. See §174 in the first volume of this work.

can reveal Himself only by making use of human concepts, which are elaborated on the basis of man's experience of created things. Analogy enables us to transcend them by means of the act of judgment. However, this conceptual knowledge cannot by itself make God enter into our life, for it attains God only as an object. Revelation necessarily involves God's own activity, using realities and events that "represent" Him, introducing these realities and events into our human life and into its history, making Him present to us. In such events, He offers Himself to man, and we can find Him in them. Such realities function as the means by which, and place wherein, man's encounter with God takes place, an encounter which is the very essence of religion.

Thus, sacraments "signify the divine gift of salvation in and by an externally perceptible and ascertainable form, which concretizes this gift—a gift of salvation in a historically visible manner."[3]

This brings to light the twofold dimension of every sacrament. First and essentially, there is its aspect as a sign and symbol. It has this character because, generally speaking, a *sign* is a reality whose very meaning is to direct man to another hidden reality (here, one that is invisible by its very nature). When that sign holds the place of this reality for man, it is a *symbol* or *image* of it. (Concerning this point, the reader should refer to the invaluable considerations found in classical theological authors [*des anciens*] concerning the relationship between man's bodily-spiritual nature and the sacramental sign, a sensible reality charged with a spiritual meaning.)[4] Moreover, if (as we have said) sacraments are the place where man encounters God (and this encounter is what salvation is), a sacrament must be more than a sign that refers to something else. God's mysterious gift to man must be accomplished in it and by means of it. Therefore, if in their essence the sacraments are the sign and symbol of the divine gift, they also are, in some way, the means by which this gift is realized and, indeed, the beginning of its realization, and not only a promise for the future.

Thus, every sacrament is, at different analogical levels, *an efficacious symbol* of God's gift.

---

3. Schillebeeckx, *Le Christ*, 30.
4. See *ST* III, q. 61.

THE SACRAMENTALITY OF THE CHURCH AS THE PROLONGATION OF THE SACRAMENTALITY OF CHRIST

The Sacramentality of Christ

{609} From what we have said, it is clear that Christ is the primordial sacrament, just as the Incarnation is the primordial event of salvation (primordial not only as the source of the others but also as including them in advance). By utilizing topics that we discussed in the second part of this course, we can readily demonstrate Christ's sacramentality.

Persona divina facta est persona humana
Through the Incarnation, the Word has become a human person.[5] Like every human person, He manifested Himself to men in a way that was accessible to their sense powers, taking up His place in the community of men and in history, making Himself foundationally present to all men in His generation solely by the fact that He was virtually related to them by the very fact of His Incarnation.[6]

However, when one of his contemporaries knew and loved this human person, he or she in fact formed a relationship with the Divine Person of the Word, for *this person was the Word*, who revealed Himself as being a Divine Person. Through faith, He was recognized, loved, and adored as such.

Therefore, we are here faced with the culminating point of what sacramentality is. In the case of Christ, we are faced with a visible form that not only refers the mind and heart to an invisible reality but also mysteriously contains the invisible reality within itself and, indeed, is identical with it. (This does not mean that Jesus' humanity is identical with the Word but, rather, that the Word Himself manifested Himself and made Himself present through Christ's human nature.) Here, we have the entrance of a Divine Person into history, His insertion into the world of men. Likewise, Scripture itself uses

---

5. See §314 in the previous volume. [Tr. note: This section must be referred to in whole in order to understand the nuanced position Fr. Nicolas is making, without denying the singular ontological personality of the Word in Christ.]
6. See §227 in the first volume of this work.

the term "mystery" in relation to Christ Himself, in His being, in His entire activity, and in His works: "To you has been given the secret [*mystère*] of the kingdom of God."[7] And this is clear in St. Paul, at least in his later letters.[8]

Consequently, when, through faith, man enters into a relationship with Jesus Christ, he personally encounters the Word.

The visible image of the invisible God

Jesus Christ not only reveals the Word, whom He is. As the Word, He is the image of the Father,[9] His revealer. Therefore, through the Incarnation, He has become the "visible image of the invisible God: He who sees me, sees the Father."

The mystery of the Trinity was *manifested to men* first and foremost through the Incarnation. The manifestations proper to the first and third Persons can truly lead us to them only thanks to the Word's manifestation in Christ. Without this manifestation, how would the Spirit's own, proper manifestations make Him known as a distinct Person? And the primordial manifestation of the Father (without which He likewise would not have been manifested as a distinct Person) is the fact that He sent His only Son.

Christ, "the exegete of the Father"

Finally (and in line with what we have said), there is the revelation of the mystery of God expressed by the Word Incarnate in human language: "No one has ever seen God; the only Son, who is in the bosom of the Father, he has made him known."[10] Jesus Himself is the revealing sign of God's will to save mankind and of this very salvation. He is *revelation*, and we have seen that revelation is sacramental by its essence.

---

7. Mk 4:11 (RSV). See *Lumen Gentium*, no. 5.
8. See Col 1:25–27, 2:2, 4:3; Eph 3:3. See also *Traduction Oecuménique de la Bible*, 574, note b.
9. See §144 in the first volume of this work.
10. Jn 1:18 (RSV).

The Sacramentality of the Church

{610} By the word "Church" we designate (while awaiting further precision) all of the redeemed, of those who have been *called* or *gathered together* and have responded to this appeal, who for this reason alone, are distinct and constitute a distinct, historically discernable human group, as we can see in Acts 3–5.[11]

The Church, included in the mystery of Christ

Already in St. Paul's first letters, and in a more manifest way in the letters written during his captivity, it becomes clear that the "mystery of Christ" (therefore, according to what we have already said, His sacramentality) includes an ecclesial dimension.[12] Let us note that, immediately after having said that Christ is the image of the invisible God, he adds that He is the "head of the body,"[13] and for him the "mystery of Christ" consists in the fact that the Jews and Gentiles are gathered together into a single body, the body of Christ:[14]

What is meant by the apostle's phrase referring to the Church as the mystery of Christ? First, it means ... that the mystery of God's eternal will is manifested in the Church: "to unite all things in him, things in heaven and things on earth."[15] However, we find something else here. By her essence, from the start, the Church is oriented toward the whole of humanity and the entire world ... In speaking of the mystery of Christ, the Apostle has the Church in view, the mystery of the will of God, who raises up all things in peace, who is occupied with all things and who foresees all things.[16]

---

11. See Joseph Schmitt, *Jésus ressuscité dans la prédication apostolique. Étude de théologie biblique* (Paris: Gabalda, 1949).
12. See Lucien Cerfaux, *La théologie de l'Église suivant saint Paul* (Paris: Cerf, 1965). André Feuillet, "L'hymne christologique de l'êpitre aux Éphéiens," *Revue biblique* 72 (1965): 481–506. (Republished in *Christologie paulinienne et tradition biblique* [Paris: Desclée de Brouwer, 1973].) Heinrich Schlier, *Le temps de l'Église*, trans. Françoise Corin (Tournai: Casterman, 1961). Rudolf Schnackenburg, *L'Église dans le Nouveau Testament Réalité et I, signification théologique; Nature et mystère de l'église*, trans. Raphaël Louis Oechslin (Paris: Cerf, 1964).
13. See Col 1:15.
14. See Eph 3:6.
15. Eph 1:10 (RSV).
16. Schlier, *Le temps de l'Église*, 302.

What is the Church a sacrament of?

{612} It is remarkable that the various authors who speak about the Church as a sacrament give this word a different, supplementary meaning. Sometimes one and the same author proposes, without explaining himself further, many different qualifications: sacrament of unity, sacrament of the world or of humanity, source-sacrament (*Ursakrament*), root-sacrament...

Even in the Council's documents, we find at least three qualifications, each employed in a seemingly indifferent way:

Sacramentum seu signum et instrumentum unionis cum Deo.[17] [The sacrament (or, sign) and instrument of union with God.]
Sacramentum visibile salutiferae unitatis.[18] [Visible sacrament of saving unity.]
Universale salutis sacramentum.[19] [Universal sacrament of salvation.]

Is there an ambiguity at work here? It truth, it seems clear that all these various expressions can and must be reduced to a single expression: "The Church is the sacrament of Christ."

First of all, we can easily unify the Council's various expressions. Indeed, what is salvation if not man's union with God? We have emphasized this fundamental point of Christian anthropology many times: man is foundationally ordered to God, and in God alone does he find his completion, the ultimate fulfillment of himself, his "ultimate end." Indeed, this union with God is "salvation" as soon as it is understood as being the goal of a journey of grace whose point of departure is a situation of sin (i.e., a situation of rupture with God and therefore of perdition).

As regards *unity*, if it is that of mankind, it is quite clear that its principle is the union of all men (and of each man) with God. Sin divides. It divides man from God and divides men from each other, for it makes the individual good (*amor sui*) prevail over the universal good (*amor Dei*). Conversely, salvation, which is first of all liberation from sin, is unifying.

---

17. *Lumen Gentium*, no. 1; *Gaudium et Spes*, no. 42.
18. *Lumen Gentium*, no. 9; *Gaudium et Spes*, no. 42; *Sacrosanctum Concilium*, no. 26.
19. *Lumen Gentium*, nos. 48 and 59; *Gaudium et Spes*, no. 45; *Ad Gentes*, no. 5.

Now, "the Savior" is Christ, and He also is "salvation." This is so because man is united to the Trinity in Christ, thus fulfilling our human destiny. (This occurs, first of all, collectively on account of the primordial inclusion of all men in Christ. It then occurs individually through personal faith in Jesus Christ.) Indeed, Christ accomplished salvation through the redemption, so that the expression "the sacrament of redemption" is the same as "the sacrament of salvation."

This is also the case for the expression "sacrament of the Mystical Body." We will see that this means that, on account of her visibility, the Church signifies the mystery according to which she is the Mystical Body of Christ. However, what is the Mystical Body of Christ if not, once again and quite precisely, Jesus Christ with all His members whom He has redeemed?

One might hesitate a bit more regarding expressions such as "sacrament of the world" and "sacrament of humanity." However, given that a sacrament is a this-worldly reality referring to the supernatural mystery and containing it, such expressions can only be understood as stating that the world is the whole of humanity to whom Christ is given, being called to salvation, and indeed being saved in a virtual manner. Thus, the Church who, in fact, is only one part of this humanity remains the sign of the whole of humanity. She is the sign of its salvation, the sign of Christ into whose mystery the whole of mankind is called to enter.

In short, we can and must say that *the Church is the sacrament of Christ*. She is the sacrament of Christ the Savior, of Christ containing the whole of humanity in Himself and uniting it to the Trinity. He does so virtually at first and then actually, to the degree that generations come into existence and to the degree that, in these generations, those who will to do so cling to Christ, actualizing through faith (and the sacraments) their belonging to Him.

Indeed, as we will see, this most certainly brings us back to the great Pauline image (which is more than a mere image) of the Church as the body of Christ: as a person is present to the world by means of his body, so too does Christ remain present to the world by means of the Church.

Why a sacrament of Christ?

{613} The[20] meaning of the Incarnation is to enable men to fully and completely encounter God: God among men, one among them. However, one of the paradoxes of the Incarnation is the fact that it is, and indeed must be, at once *universal* (because it is for men of all eras) and *historical* (and therefore is situated in time and space).

It is clear that in order to be real the Incarnation must be accomplished in such a way that the Incarnate Word would be a human individual, inserted into history. However, this implies that He would be inserted into spatiotemporal limits.

This is where the profound reason for the Church's existence becomes clear. As a prolongation of the Incarnation, she extends it to all places, to all times, and to all men—not only as a past event but as the concrete means for each person to encounter God.

This brings us back to sacramentality. Just as Christ is the sacrament of God because He is the one in whom and through whom God Himself enters into history and, likewise, because He concretely presents Him to men, so too (and as a kind of continuation) the Church is the sacrament of Christ because, here in our world, she is the reality in whom and through whom man can encounter Christ, and God in Christ.

Often today, it is said: the Church is not needed, go directly to Christ. However, from what we have said, this attitude represents an illusory pretense. Christ is not "outside" the Church, in and through whom He manifests Himself and gives Himself. Granted, this clearly poses its own problems, for the Church is not identical with Christ in all ways (just as, in general, a sacrament is not identical in all ways with the sacred reality that it signifies and that is given by means of it). Given that a sacrament, in itself, is an earthly reality used by God in order to manifest Himself and give Himself, it cannot be (and, indeed, is not) purely transparent. By its entire earthly consistency, it veils the very reality that is manifested and given through it. We will study this problem below and will attempt to find the principles of discernment that will enable us to specify what in the Church (such

---

20. See Schillebeeckx, *Le Christ*, 67–73.

as she is present to our experience as an earthly and historical reality) must be overcome, sometimes painfully suffered through, and also judged (with the modesty that is befitting for the simple, fallible, and sinful men that we are)—not in order to discard her, but in order to find in her Christ who gives Himself through her (through and by means of her earthly reality).

How is the Church the sacrament of Christ?

The threefold signification of every sacrament

{614} Because salvation is for the sake of men, it has the mysterious character of embracing the past, the present, and the future. It embraces *the past* because it has been accomplished by acts and events that are historically situated and thus, for us, lay in the past. It embraces *the present*, because these acts are salvific only if man actually participates in them today. And it embraces *the future*, because salvation (for each person and for all together) is brought to completion only at the end of time. It is eschatological.

Hence, because the nature of the sacraments is defined in relation to salvation, every sacrament will necessarily have this threefold ordered signification that St. Thomas noted with regard to the sacramental rites. It signifies the redemptive acts and events *in the past*. It signifies man's current participation in these mysteries *in the present*. Finally, it signifies the eschatological fulfilment of redemption *in the future*, the return of Christ.[21]

This is likewise true for the Church as a sacrament.

How the Church refers to the past and contains it

{615} Here, we have a primordial datum of the mystery of the Church. Not only is she not a human creation constituted by men in each generation, nor a creation begun anew by God in each generation, she is a continuous creation whose originative novelty took place in the past.[22] The same Church left by Jesus on the earth as the sacrament of His presence remains through the generations.

This fact is the basis for the primordial importance of the note

---

21. See *ST* III, q. 60, a. 3.
22. See *ST* III, q. 1, a. 3, ad 3. [1, 3, 3um]

of *apostolicity*, which expresses the unwavering continuity between the Church of today and of all times with the Church of the apostles, thanks to apostolic succession.[23]

How the Church refers to the hidden reality present today and contains it

{616} If the Church only referred to the past, she could only call it to mind. She could perhaps give us the promise that God will save us, but she would not be the sign of this salvation. However, she is the sign and cause of salvation because she is the sign of what God is doing today for those who accept salvation. She is the sign of salvation in the midst of its accomplishment.

This is what is meant by the expression "sacrament of the Mystical Body." She is the sacrament of Christ and of the members whom, by means of her, He joins to Himself in our own day.

Given that Christ saves and joins His members to Himself by the cross, the Church, from this perspective, is more particularly the sacrament of Christ in His sacrifice. She is, in the words of Journet, "the kingdom in its pilgrim and crucified state."[24] The entire Church is currently "crucified with Christ."[25]

How the Church refers to the future and contains it

{617} The Church refers us to Christ who is to come. She announces His return and the fulfillment of redemption. She is eschatological.

In other words, she is not "of this world,"[26] though she exists all the while "in the world."[27] Here we have one of the lofty principles that must illuminate very difficult problems concerning the relationship between the Church and the world. We must never forget that the Church is eschatological, even if this is not sufficient for resolving all the problems involved here.

Thus, the Church-sacrament refers us to Christ resurrected and exalted in glory. Indeed, she contains this reality already. In her hidden depths, she is also the luminous kingdom of God's presence,

---

23. See §648 below.
24. Charles Journet, "Controverse avec Congar," *Nova et Vetera* 38 (1963): 308.
25. See Rom 6:5–11 and Gal 2:10.
26. Jn 17:14.
27. Jn 17:11.

eternal life already begun here-below. This is what Oscar Cullmann called, using an expression that has become classic, the dialectic of the "already" and the "not yet."

Here, we come back to the consideration of the Church in heaven. This is not the object of ecclesiology, for given that she is situated beyond history, she is Christ Himself, the whole Christ. Therefore, she is no longer the sign that makes Him known, while being distinct from Him. Nonetheless, she is the end to which the entire being of the earthly Church is ordered, toward which she tends, through all of the dynamism animating her, an end whose beginning is already realized in her: "The kingdom of God is in the midst of you,"[28] and "we are God's children now; it does not yet appear what we shall be."[29] Therefore, we will not understand the earthly Church if we set aside consideration of her internal ordination to her definitive fulfillment in the heavenly Church.

THE EXPLANATORY VALUE OF THE NOTION OF SACRAMENTALITY AS APPLIED TO THE CHURCH

Therefore, the Church is the sacrament of Christ. However, is she only this? Or, more exactly, are we here faced with one property among others? Or, do we have in this expression, if not a definition (which is impossible), at least the principle that explains all the properties of the Church and which, for that reason, can hold the place of a definition?

From the Sacramentality of the Sanctifying Rites to the Sacramentality of the Church

The problem

{618} The Church's sacramentality and the role that it can play in ecclesiology were at first grasped by a kind of intuition. Originally, there was the successful development of sacramental theology, thanks to which the vast and deep character of sacramentality was

---

28. Lk 17:21 (RSV).
29. 1 Jn 3:2 (RSV).

grasped. This development seized upon the connection between the notions of *sacramentum* and *musterion*. Likewise, it seized on the ecclesial nature of the seven sacraments (in contrast to an individualist conception that had prevailed for too long).

However, discussions remained too connected to questions properly pertaining to the sacramental rites. The elaboration of the concept of sacramentality continued to be elaborated on the basis of discussions pertaining to the seven sacraments. In virtue of the aforementioned intuition, some sought to apply this concept univocally to the Church. Again, the Second Vatican Council said, "the sign and instrument ... of a very closely-knit union with God."[30]

Hence, the enterprise seemed doomed to failure, for the activity by which the Church is the instrument of grace by means of the sacramental rites cannot, without artifice, be considered her only activity. She teaches. She governs. She devotes herself to works of mercy ... and in her depths, she lives with God and "serves" Him through worship. All of this could not be reduced to a purely instrumental activity, as is the case for the action of the sacramental rites.

Therefore, we must recognize that the notion of sacramentality is analogous. However, that does not mean that it is equivocal! Without this realization, it can have no explanatory value. Therefore, we must seek out the commonality that is realized in different manners [in each analogate to which the term "sacrament" is applied]. That is, we must seek out the *ratio analogata*.

The sanctifying rites only partially express the
Church's sacramentality

{619} *The Church's sanctifying rites certainly manifest her sacramentality*. First of all, this is so because the Church herself is the effect of the sacraments: "The Church of Christ is said to be built up by the sacraments that poured forth from the side of Christ upon the Cross."[31] Moreover, this is so because the Church is the one who acts by means of the sacraments and is the one who sanctifies.

Regarding the first point, note that, according to St. Paul, the

---

30. *Lumen Gentium*, no. 1.
31. *ST* III, q. 64, a. 2, ad 3.

Church herself was baptized.[32] If the first nucleus of the Church (i.e., the apostles and the group of people gathered together in the Upper Room) were not baptized,[33] this was because that society as a whole required an act that would constitute it. For the Church, this definitive act was the descent of the Holy Spirit upon the disciples at Pentecost, the Spirit sent by Jesus, in virtue of His promise. However, from that point onward, it is through baptism, the Eucharist, and the other sacraments that the Church gathers new members to herself and brings about the development of those who have already been gathered together within her. In short, through them, she brings about her own development.[34]

Regarding the second point, we must consider the sacraments not as things but as actions.[35] They are sacramental actions, that is, ones that are simultaneously symbolic and efficacious, by which what they signify is realized: *significando causant*, by signifying, they cause. Such an action can be efficacious only through Christ's own activity. It is salvific, and Christ alone is the Savior. It is here that the Church's sacramentality becomes clear. As we have seen, her role and her *raison d'être* are to "represent" Christ in a visible manner. In sacramental action, the minister who acts through it, and through whom it acts, sacramentally holds the place of Christ (as we will see more clearly when we discuss the sacrament of holy orders). Therefore, the Church exercises the sacramental action by means of the power of Christ, whom she represents sacramentally.

Thus, the Church's sacramentality manifests itself primarily in the sanctifying rites that we call the sacraments. Moreover, the idea that the Church as a whole is "the sacrament of Christ" was, in fact, formed on the basis of investigations into these rites from a more broadly ecclesial perspective.

However, they do not manifest the Church in her totality, for as we have already noted, she has other activities that are essential for her, though they lay outside of this "sacramental" activity. If as a whole she is "the sacrament of Christ," her sacramentality must also be

---

32. See Eph 5:25–26.
33. See Schillebeeckx, *Le Christ*, 72.
34. See Schnackenburg, *L'Église dans le Nouveau Testament*, 51–54.
35. See §726 below.

expressed and realized in her other activities, even if this requires us to extend the notion of a sacrament.

The overall sacramentality of the Church

{620} When it is a question of "causing grace" (i.e., of making a believing man become *righteous* and *divinized*), the causality that one attributes to the Church can only be instrumental causality. God alone can, by His own power, remit sins and divinize. The very humanity of Christ can participate in this transformation of man only instrumentally.

To say that it is a form of instrumental causality precludes that the Church (i.e., those through whom she acts) would cause grace by her own, proper power. Therefore, it also precludes that the limitations and shortcomings that can affect her would be communicated to the effect. The grace caused in the recipient is not the grace that the minister has. The effect is wholly attributable to God and to Christ in His humanity. It is limited, like every effect, only by the limitations of the recipient.

Obviously, we cannot apply this schema to the Church's other activities and say that she is a mere instrument of Christ in everything that she does, thus meaning that all the effects of this action would need to be purely and simply attributed to Him.

Here, we find ourselves faced with a new approach to the problem concerning the Church's relationship to Christ. On the one hand, Christ acts through His Church. On the other, the Church acts as distinct from Christ and under her own responsibility. (This will raise the difficult and controverted problem concerning the Church's faults in relation to her holiness.)

In any case, the notion of instrumentality is no longer of use here. However, if we still must say that Christ acts through His Church, we will need to admit that this notion of sacramentality can be at work without implying instrumentality. Even when she acts as a second cause (i.e., as a distinct person), the Church remains the sacrament of Christ. However, this obviously imposes an analogical extension of this notion of sacramentality.

The Threefold Structure of the Church's Sacramentality

The three "structural aspects" of every sacrament

{621} As regards the sacramental rites, in the history of theology, a distinction has been elaborated that touches on the sacramental action in its full dynamism: that which is only a sign (*sacramentum tantum*); that which is still a sign but already is the signified reality (*res et sacramentum*); and finally, that which is only the signified reality (*res tantum*).[36] We must first study this at the level of the sacramental rites. Following this, we will then ask if it holds for sacramentality in general and, specifically, for the case of the Church's sacramentality.

The distinction was first of all concerned with the efficacy of the sacraments, though it is also (and principally) related to their signification.

It had been elaborated by scholastic theologians in reaction to the Berengarian controversy. However, it also enabled them to make sense of the Augustinian distinction between the truth of the sacrament and its fruitfulness. This distinction itself enabled the expression of the definitive solution to the problem concerning the non-repetition of baptism even when it had been performed in conditions that would prevent the remission of sins.

The *sacramentum tantum* is the sacramental sign, the rite, which is understood only in function of the signified reality. The signified reality is the *res* (i.e., salvation itself, *grace*). This calls to mind the Augustinian distinction between *res* and *signa*, repeated quite materially by Peter Lombard as being the ordering principle of theology.[37]

However, the *res* presupposes a personal disposition in the beneficiary: faith, in the full sense (i.e., the acceptance of salvation). This disposition is also signified by the sacrament considered as an undertaking to which the person submits himself. However, that signification is not certain. Such a spiritual undertaking, which is signified

---

36. See Ronald F. King, "The Origin and Evolution of a Sacramental Formula: *sacramentum tantum, res et sacramentum, res tantum*," *The Thomist* 31 (1967): 21–82.

37. See St. Augustine, *La doctrine chrétienne*, OESA 11, bk. 1, ch. 2.

and symbolized by the external action, can fail in a given case. Must we say that in such a case there is no sacrament at all? It would seem that there would be none, for the passion and resurrection of Christ are signified and symbolized only as being participated in today by the beneficiary of the sacrament. The dispute concerning rebaptism highlighted the need to admit that once the sacrament has been given it remains, even when it does not produce its fruit, whether on account of heresy, apostasy, or any other grave sin. Likewise, the Berengarian controversy highlighted the fact that the sacrament of the Eucharist remains even without faith and devotion in those present, including the priest.

Thus, between the *sacramentum* and the *res*, theologians were led to recognize an intermediary and stable terminus of the sacramental signification, a kind of interior sacrament, signified and caused by the sacramental rite but not depending on the faith and charity of the beneficiary, such that this intermediary terminus is always signified by the sacramental sign.

This intermediary terminus is the *res* in relation to the sacramental sign, as it is signified by it. However, it is itself a *sacramentum* in relation to the *res tantum*, for it is completely ordered to grace and to the beneficiary's participation in the redemptive passion. It itself is a sign in relation to this ultimate terminus of the sacramental sign.

A difficulty emerges, however, with regard to this *res et sacramentum*. How can we call a wholly interior and invisible reality a *sign* or a *sacrament*? The response to this question is found in the unfailing bond between the *sacramentum tantum* and this reality. The sacramental rite is an event that one can perceive and record. It is an event that can be assured by the natural means of acquiring knowledge (baptismal registries, ordination certificates, and so forth). As soon as it has been validly confected, we can be certain that the intermediary reality in question has been produced, whatever might have been the subject's spiritual dispositions, which are obviously unverifiable. Therefore, this reality, in turn, is assured of its place. Obviously, it is assured in the eyes of faith, as it is by faith alone that I know the sacramental signification and the sanctifying value of the rite. Nonetheless, it is fully assured for him who believes. Thus, connected again to the visible sign, it is, in turn, a sign of the ultimate reality, grace, which can fail as a result of the subject's resistance to it. However, even if it fails, the sacrament took place and remains. The reality of having been baptized remains permanent and ever-actual.

It quickly became clear that three sacraments were in no way repeatable, for they definitively remain in the subject who has received them: baptism, confirmation (which is a kind of prolongation of baptism), and holy orders. The intermediary reality found in these three sacraments is what has been called their "character," in order to simultaneously emphasize its function as a sign as well as its permanence. We will come back to this in our discussions in sacramental theology. In the Eucharist, it is Christ present under the appearances of bread and wine. The "sacrament" is there, ever-offered, but it can be of profit only for those who receive it with the required dispositions.

We will see later on that such an intermediary reality exists for the other sacraments as well. Is this schema of use universally for every kind of sacramentality? In particular, is it useful for explaining the Church's?

The answer must be affirmative.[38] The notion of a sacrament is defined in relation to salvation. Salvation was accomplished by transitory events, but it is, itself, a stable reality. First of all, the Savior is Jesus Christ, who remains for eternity, and He has given the events of salvation their salvific value. Then, the saved person (i.e., the man who clings to Christ and participates in salvation) does so by transitory acts, but he remains saved during his entire earthly life (unless he himself draws back) and for eternity. During his earthly life, this salvation, this state of "being saved," is realized by the *sacramentum et res* of the sacraments. The Church is the community of the redeemed, of the "saved." She also must have a stable earthly existence, an objective consistency. She must be, in herself, the sacrament of salvation. She must be this in her earthly reality, which is made up, as we will see, of those who compose her, though independent of the unverifiable fluctuations of personal freedom.

However, this cannot be the whole of what the Church is, as this

---

38. See Charles Journet, "Le mystère de la sacramentalité. Le Christ, l'Église et les sept sacrements," *Nova et Vetera* 49 (1974): 182.

earthly existence is ordered to salvation, which is personal and eschatological and indeed begins to be realized on earth. Thus, the mystery of the Church, an object of faith, which is signified and realized by the visible [reality] of the Church, itself exercises signification in relation to salvation itself, which is the ultimate *res*. Therefore, the mystery of the Church is a *sacramentum et res*.

The *res tantum* of the Church-sacrament

{622} This is where we must start, for the *res* is what gives the sacrament all of its meaning. The sacrament is totally ordered to this ultimate reality.

In the case of the Church, the *res* is the Trinitarian life, the infinite communion of Persons in eternity, though communicated to men so that they may be drawn into it and so that they may participate eternally in it.

In her depths, the Church is this communion. The heavenly Church will be this communion in full light. The *res* will be presented by it, but not by means of a sign. The visible Church on the earth is this communion *in mysterio*, for this communion is the deepest reality that she designates and symbolizes, that she creates day after day, and that she contains.

Vatican II, in *Lumen Gentium*, begins by describing this deepest reality of the Church.[39]

As was said above with regard to the Church's eschatological dimension, she has a meaning only as being *she who bears the mystery of eternal life that is to be lived in her by those who are part of her, a gift of eternal life that she offers to all*. This does not exclude her earthly reality and everything that this implies, for the mystery is contained in this earthly reality. However, this prevents us from granting an absolute value to this earthly reality.

The *sacramentum tantum* of the Church-sacrament

{623} We must now consider the earthly reality of the Church, inasmuch as she is the sacrament of this extra-mundane reality.

---

39. See *Lumen Gentium*, nos. 2 and 3. Gérard Philips, "La femme dans l'Église," *Ephemerides Theologicae Lovanienses* 37 (1961): 71–93.

First of all, we must consider the *sacramentum tantum* that will lead us to the *sacramentum et res*. Therefore, we must consider the Church inasmuch as she is visible and perceptible.

We must first observe her traits at the moment when she entered into the world.[40]

The Church—as she appears in Acts, in St. Paul's letters, and also in the Gospels[41]—is presented as being the community of those who believe in Christ, in His resurrection and exaltation, and in the salvation that He brings and gives. (The community quickly becomes a number of communities, though they are intimately united with each other through faith in Jesus Christ, in the celebration of baptism and of the Eucharist, and by the outpouring of the Spirit Himself.) This community has a structure and a constitution that is not only pneumatic and charismatic but also institutional, a structure whose primordial form is the authority conferred on the Twelve by Jesus Himself and which they themselves, already during their lifetimes, communicated to others. This community is aware of coming from on high, of having been constituted by God's eschatological action (i.e., by the outpouring of the Holy Spirit). She is aware of bearing a message of salvation that she must convey to the world. Instead of being turned back upon herself and closed within herself, she is open and missionary. This does not, however, prevent her from having her own proper, interior life constituted essentially by worship, with the Eucharist standing at its center.

This is how the Church presented herself to the world from the start. If we consider her today, the most striking and troubling phenomenon we face is the problem of the multiplicity of communities claiming that they come from Christ, each one trying for its own part to be for the world what the apostolic community was.

Among them all, the Catholic Church considers and affirms herself as being the authentic continuation of the apostolic Church, without, for that, refusing the title and reality of "being Christians" to other communities. A little later on, we will attempt to understand how this can be the case from the Catholic perspective.

---

40. See Schnackenburg, *L'Église dans le Nouveau Testament*, 1.
41. Ibid., 34.

However, we accept this perspective as being something we hold on faith, and the objective of this course cannot be to dispute the foundations for this claim. Therefore, we will not here take up the justification of this position. Nor will we examine, at least directly, the innumerable problems that are posed by the division of churches, along with the paths toward their reunion. The Church whom we consider in dogmatic theology is the Catholic Church, whom we believe (such is our Catholic faith) to be the Church founded by Jesus Christ, the apostolic community continued up to our own day.

(N.B. If we might agree with the profound and very well-founded considerations of Bouyer, we will not separate the Orthodox Church from this consideration. She too considers herself to be one, holy, Catholic, [and apostolic]. Indeed, she is such, without detriment to the Catholic Church, for she has never been totally separated from her, constituting with her, despite such painful dissenting, the one Church.[42] Journet connects this position with that of Soloviev and mentions it sympathetically, although with obvious reservations.)[43]

Traditionally, the Church's self-manifestation as the Church of Christ is considered by means of her four notes: one, holy, Catholic, and apostolic. Taking up a remark used by Congar (who chose to explain these notes in his presentation of the Church in *Mysterium Salutis*), they are mutually present to each other and, indeed, mutually interpenetrating, through a kind of circumincession.[44]

However, can we say that the notes and the fact that they exclusively belong to the Catholic Church are manifestly clearer [than her invisible mystery] (i.e., perceptible to any person who considers the Church without prejudices)? Concerning the apologetic use of the notes, the reader can refer to Congar's own work.[45]

In reality, in order to see that the Church contains a *sacramentum* of a hidden reality, we need, if not faith, at least an inclination to believe, for she cannot be known as a sacrament without us also knowing (or at least suspecting) the mystery of which she is the sign. Here, we are faced with a paradox: as she is experienced in the world

---

42. See Bouyer, *L'Eglise de Dieu*, 628–34.
43. See Journet, "L'Église de Dieu," 142.
44. See Yves Congar, *L'Église une, sainte, catholique et apostolique* (Paris: Cerf, 1970), 266.
45. See ibid., 264–67.

and in history, the Church leads us to this mystery, but she can be known for what she really is only in light of this very mystery.

Therefore, if we are to know the earthly reality of the Church in her mystery, we must consider, in the light of faith, the *sacramentum et res* that is manifested in her and through her.

The *sacramentum et res* of the Church-sacrament

{624} Thus, the *sacramentum tantum* in the case of the Church, this original sacrament (*Ursakrament*), is the visible [character] of the Church, her visible appearance in the world. She is a society having her own structure, laws, and activities, ordered to a definitive end: the proclamation of the salvation brought about by Jesus Christ and the realization of this salvation in those who wish to welcome it, enabling them to live in accord with the new life in which salvation consists. Added to this, we find a host of annexed, though often very conspicuous, activities occasioned by the necessary relationships she has with other societies, as well as by ways that she participates in their own objectives. Such a society can be seen and described, but she thinks of herself, and presents herself, as bearing an unseen mystery. She presents herself as the sign and means of salvation, which (all the while concerning men living on the earth in the midst of other men and with them) is not itself an earthly, perceptible reality.[46]

Now, will we say that there is no intermediary between the Church-society, which is seen, and salvation (i.e., communion in Christ experienced by saved men, a communion with the Divine Persons and among the redeemed themselves), something which is not seen? If this were so, one of two things is possible. *Either* the Church-society would her consistency in herself, independent of her sacramental relation to "supernatural communion." Thus, she would be one society among others "a community of men as visible and tangible as the community of Roman people or the Kingdom of France, or the Republic of Venice,"[47] and the conditions for belonging to her would be purely external, that is, the external profession of the true faith, participation in the sacraments, and the acceptance

---

46. See Jean-Hervé Nicolas, "L'appartenance à l'Église selon la théologie catholique," *Austritt aus der Kirche*, ed. Louis Carlen (Fribourg: Universitätsverlag, 1982), 131–45.

47. Bellarmine, cited in Journet, *L'Église du Verbe incarné*, 2:1182.

of the authority of the Roman pontiff. *Or*, on the other hand, the Church-society would not exist and could not be defined except by the communion of which she is the sacrament. However, given that this communion is by nature invisible, unverifiable, and, moreover, unstable, the Church-society would lose her visibility and her stability, just as baptism would lose its visibility and stability if it were to be defined by the grace of the remission of sins and of divinization, of which it is the sacrament, though which the baptized person can fail to receive (in a case of interior rejection of conversion) and which, in any case, can be lost by him. (Thus, in the case of the Church, this hypothesis would hold that he who is in communion with her today through grace and charity can be excluded from her tomorrow by losing grace, then returning to her if he converts.)

These two hypotheses are unacceptable. Whether one wishes it or not, the first hypothesis would lead one to conceive of two churches. The first "Church" would be invisible, constituted by "communion," and it would be in this communion alone that Christ and salvation would exist. The second "Church" would be a visible Church, but we would face great difficulty in seeing how and why it must be the sacrament of salvation, the universal means of salvation, representing Christ, the unique Savior, on earth. The second hypothesis would reduce the Church to a reality that is invisible, unverifiable, and unstable, and it would be impossible to know who does or does not belong to the Church. On this latter hypothesis, the Church's visibility disappears, and we no longer have a sacrament of Christ the Savior.

Therefore, we must hold that there is an intermediary reality between the *sacramentum tantum*, which is the visible society that is called (and is) the Church, and the latter reality of which this society is the sacrament, an eschatological reality that is, as we have seen, the definitive union of all those who have been redeemed, in Christ, with the Trinity—the kingdom and eternal life.

This intermediary reality is immediately the sign and means of realization of the latter reality. In her and through her, eternal life already begins to be realized on earth in all those who have grace and charity. However, it is not itself constituted on earth by grace and charity. It is constituted by the *real* and *permanent* bonds that are established in believers, first of all through the sacraments, but also through the profession of the Christian faith and the acceptance of the authority of the bishops and the pope. In this way, the believer is united to Christ and to the other members in Christ. These bonds are more than juridical, having a real foundation in the believer, namely, their sacramental characters. They are not yet the interpersonal relations that constitute communion, and they remain submitted to the fluctuations of free choice and, for this reason, are directly unverifiable. However, they are completely ordered to these interpersonal relations.

They are what assure the visibility and objective consistency of the Church. This does not mean that they would be intrinsically visible. Instead, the promise of Christ, on which our entire faith in the Church rests, guarantees for us that the external and visible acts of belonging to the Church-society (e.g., celebration of the sacraments, profession of the Christian faith, acceptance of the Church's authority in its concrete form) signify and cause these bonds, which are internal and, of themselves, invisible. The Church is much more than the visible society and institution that we call "the Church." However, she is nothing without this visible society. We will see that this mystery is not yet fully realized in any of the Church's members. In many, it is realized only in an inchoate manner. In other words, on account of their interior personal refusal, the objective bonds of belonging to Christ, which exist in them through their belonging to the Church, fail to blossom forth into interpersonal relations. In short, we are referring to the problem concerning the existence of sinners in the Church. However, on account of the mystery that she bears in herself, the mystery that she signifies and brings about (i.e., the mystery of how all those who believe in Christ and are baptized belong to Christ), the Church-society is present to the world as the sign and means of salvation, as a sacrament of the active presence of Christ the Savior, not as an ordinary, human society.

And the bonds that are established among her members in reference to Christ, the head of the Church (the hierarchical bonds in particular), are themselves also vitally animated by a sacred character that makes them much more than mere juridical and social bonds. They are vital connections among living organs.

THE COMPREHENSIVE VALUE OF THE NOTION OF THE CHURCH-SACRAMENT

{625} Among the different images and notions traditionally used for expressing what the Church is, the principal ones are the following. First, there is "the People of God," which was placed in high relief by Vatican II. Then, there is "the Body of Christ," a Pauline image that has had a significant history and likewise was taken up by the Council, along with the now-traditional adjective "mystical." As we will see, in order to clarify this image, we must supplement it with the image of "the Spouse [of Christ]." Also, there is "Temple of God," an image that is scriptural as well. Finally, there is "Society and Communion."[48] Although the notion of Church-sacrament cannot be substituted for these notions, it is concretized in each of them and gives them their deepest meaning.

The Church, the People of God

{626} The* second chapter of *Lumen Gentium*, entitled "On the People of God in General," was not found in the initial pre-Conciliar schema. On the initiative of Cardinal Suenens,[49] it had been introduced by the "coordination commission" in order to "capture the Council's current thought."[50]

---

48. See Yves Congar, *Sainte Église* (Paris: Cerf, 1963), 21–44.

* In *Concilium* 1 (1965): 91–100, there is a methodical bibliography with brief comments by Rudolf Schnackenburg and Jacques Dupont. To this, one can add the following texts as well. Yves Congar, "L'Église comme peuple de Dieu," *Concilium* 1 (1965): 15–32. Hans Küng, *L'Église*, trans. Henri Marie Rochais and Jean Evrard (Paris: Desclée de Brouwer, 1967), 153–209. Otto Semmelroth, "L'Église, nouveau people de Dieu," in *L'Eglise de Vatican II* (Paris: Cerf, 1966), 2:395–409. Philips, *L'Église*, 1:37–42 and 127. Bouyer, *L'Eglise de Dieu*, 213–84. Auguste Luneau and Marius Bobichon, *Église ou troupeau? Du troupeau fidèle au people de Dieu* (Paris: Editions Ouvrières, 1972). Francesco Geremia, *I primi due capituli dell "Lumen Gentium." Genesi ed elaborazione del testo concilaro* (Rome: Ed. Marianum, 1971).

49. See Geremia, *I primi due capituli dell "Lumen Gentium."*

50. *Concile oecuménique Vatican II, L'Église*, ed. and trans. M. Garrone (Paris: Le Centurion, 1965), 37.

The roots of this conception in Scripture and tradition

{627} This is a fundamental biblical concept.[51] It was first applied to Israel. Then, in the New Testament, it is applied to all of those who have believed in Christ.[52]

This same idea is also expressed by the image of the flock having God (in the Old Testament) and Jesus (in the New) as its shepherd. It is quite close to the image of a *city* (because the people make up the city) and that of a *temple*, which is joined to it in the aforementioned text from 2 Corinthians (because the temple is the gathering place of the People of God). Finally, it includes the quite biblical (and, in particular, quite evangelical) notion of *kingdom*, for the People of God is the people having God as their king. When Jesus announces the coming of God's kingdom, He announces the true People of God. Israel had been their prefiguration, and Christ will rule over them.

This quite traditional notion of the People of God had perhaps been too neglected in the past. It had been sacrificed to the conception that prevailed for many years after Trent, namely that of the Church as a *society*. The rediscovery of ecclesial characteristics that are more interior and vital led, after the First World War, to emphasis being placed on the notion of the Church as the "Mystical Body."[53] Around the years 1937–42, the notion of the People of God began to appear and spread about, above all in Germany. In 1940, Mannes Dominikus Koster quite aggressively set the notion of the People of God (the only one, according to him, capable of being the basis for a scientific ecclesiology) in opposition to that of the "Mystical Body," which supposedly would have contributed to ecclesiology's remaining in a pre-scientific state on account of the latter notion's merely metaphorical character.[54] His book *Ekklesiologie im Werden* was cri-

---

51. See Pierre Grelot, "Peuple," in *Vocabulaire de théologie biblique*, ed. Xavier Léon-Doufour et al. (Paris: Éditions du Cerf, 1962).
52. See 2 Cor 6:15–18 and 1 Pt 2:9–11. The latter text is cited by *Lumen Gentium*, no. 9.
53. Émil Mersch, *Le corps mystique du Christ. Études de théologie historique*, vols. 1–2 (Paris: Desclée de Brouwer, 1951); *La théologie du corps mystique* (Louvain: Desclée de Brouwer, 1943). See other references in Congar, *Sainte Église*, 466–67, 475–78, 481–83, 488.
54. See Mannes Dominikus Koster, *Ekklesiologie im Werden* (Paderborn: Verlag der Bonifacius-Druckerei, 1940).

tiqued for proposing this kind of opposition between the two notions. Nonetheless, the idea made headway[55] and it was consecrated by being placed in relief in *Lumen Gentium*.

The theological significance of this conception

It emphasizes what all the members of the Church have in common

{628} Before the distinction of offices, ministers, and dignities, all the members of the Church commonly share in this fundamental fact: they belong to the People of God.

In this assertion, we find an intentional reaction to a "hierarchiology" that would identify the Church with the hierarchy. However, the notion of "the People of God" also helps to protect ecclesiology against the inverse temptation to situate the pastors on the margins of the Church, which would be constituted essentially by the laity.

An important Conciliar idea emerges from this: every function in the Church is above all a form of service. (Indeed, it is a service that, when it is a question of the function of authority, consists in directing and commanding, but it remains ordered to the goods of others, not to him who exercises this function.) All belong to the People of God, that is, to the flock having Christ as its shepherd. Certain members, without ceasing to be "led," are also charged with leading others and with cooperating with the head shepherd in this activity.

The continuity of the Church in relation to Israel

Israel was the people chosen by God from among all peoples, the bearer of a promise that must be realized by them for the sake of all the peoples of the world. Moreover, at the moment when this function comes to be fulfilled, it must be expanded to universal dimensions. That is, the New Covenant must succeed upon the Old. The Church is the new People of God, in whom Israel takes on universal dimensions.[56]

In this way, we can more readily explain how the Church is related to various temporal communities. Given her transcendence, she

---

55. See Semmelroth, "L'Église, nouveau people de Dieu," 399.
56. See Grelot, "Peuple."

is not one people among the peoples. Nonetheless, without being identified with any of them (which would alienate her from other peoples), she can intermingle with each, taking her members from among those people while not removing them from their own natural people.

Through her internal energy and missionary vocation, the ecclesial People of God asymptotically tends toward being co-terminous with all of mankind without abolishing the differences among various peoples.

The pilgrim character of the Church

The earthly Church exists "in exile,"[57] on the way toward the Lord. The notion of the People of God helps to better highlight the eschatological dimension of the mystery of the Church. Likewise, it helps to highlight her historical character.

The insufficiency of this notion

{629} With Congar, we must recognize (against Koster) that the notion of the People of God obscures certain aspects of the mystery of the Church and cannot be substituted for the notion of "the body [of Christ]."

It obscures the unique relations of the Church with Christ

Christ is not only the shepherd who externally leads His people. The Church is the fullness of Christ, and Christ is the fullness of the Church.

It neglects the visible structure of the Church

There is another danger to be avoided. The Church belongs to Christ, and all the members of the Church share in common the fact that they are led by the Spirit. However, this must not lead us to forget that various functions exist among the members of the Church (i.e., a stable hierarchy willed by Christ).

---

57. See 2 Cor 5:6.

It does not emphasize the current possession of eschatological goods
The Church is pilgrim in nature. She presses on toward Christ and toward the communion with the Divine Persons in Him. However, these goods are not only something set in the future. They are already possessed in faith. She does not only press on toward the kingdom. She already is the kingdom.[58]

Thus, however useful the notion of the People of God may be for enabling us to grasp what the Church is, it must be supplemented by others.

The illumination of this notion by that of sacramentality

{630} As it stands, the idea of the People of God is certainly quite useful for helping us to approach the mystery of the Church. However, in order for it to be rightly understood, it must be illuminated by the notion of sacramentality.

What we call the People of God is, on the level of appearances, this community (or this unified group of communities) composed of men who profess their faith in Jesus Christ and who think of themselves as being *gathered together* by the Holy Spirit (and, indeed, who say that they are called together in this way). This is what we discussed above.

However, in order to recognize that the People of God (i.e., the people whom Jesus has acquired by the shedding of His blood) is present there, we must go beyond external appearances. Through faith, we must discover what brings about the unity of this immense ensemble dispersed throughout all times and places. In other words, we must discover the meaning of the fact that this people belongs to Christ. Looking upon this community, we must see the community of salvation and believe that this people, who is mysteriously led by Christ, is pushing forward toward the kingdom. In short, we must look on it as being the sacrament of Christ—of Christ saving those who believe in Him, being glorified in them and glorifying them in eternity.

---

58. See Congar, "L'Église comme people de Dieu," 15–32. However, also see his criticism of Journet in *Sainte Église*, 667–68. See also Journet's response in "Controverse avec Congar," 308.

The Church, the Body of Christ

The Church as the "body" and *plérôma* of Christ according to St. Paul

{631} Although in many letters the term *plérôma* (fullness) has a commonplace meaning (fullness of time, the fullness of Jews or Gentiles converted, the fullness of Christ's blessing, and so forth), it is given special emphasis in the letters written during St. Paul's captivity, where it is set in relation to the mystery of Christ, indeed expressing it.[59]

Obviously, in the majority of these texts, the term *plérôma* is closely related to the term *soma* (body). On the other hand, at least in the Letter to the Ephesians, the Church, who is the body of Christ, is therefore His *fullness* and *complement*. This is less clear in the texts found in the Letter to the Colossians.

The image of the body

A first group of texts Here,[60] we are concerned with 1 Corinthians 12:12–27 and Romans 12:4–5. At first glance, it would seem that we only have an application of the Stoic allegory comparing the political state to a body. Were the metaphor developed in this direction, it would lead us to conceive of the Church as being a large social body. Now, such a conception is not wrong, but would very insufficiently express St. Paul's thought, for at this level, the Church's unity would be reduced to moral and juridical bonds. By contrast, St. Paul had a very realistic conception of the Christian's union with Christ through baptism, a union that makes us members of Christ.[61]

If the Church constitutes a single body, this must be understood first and foremost by reference to the individual body of Christ, His resurrected body. Here, certain modern exegetes tend toward a

---

59. The principal texts are Col 1:19 and 2:9; Eph 1:23, 3:19, 4:13.
60. In general, concerning the image of the body, see the following texts. Pierre Benoît, "Corps, Tête et Plérôme dans les épîtres de la captivité," in *Exégèse et Théologie* (Paris: Cerf, 1961), 2:107–53; "L'unité de l'Église selon l'épître aux Éphésiens," *Exégèse et Théologie* (Paris: Cerf, 1968), 3:335–57. Bouyer, *L'Église*, 285–372. Cerfaux, *La théologie de l'Église*, chs. 12 and 15. Mersch, *Le corps mystique du Christ*, first part. Schnackenburg, *L'Église dans le Nouveau Testament*, fourth part. Sebastian Tromp, *Corpus Christi quod est Ecclesia* (Rome: Aedes Universitatis Gregorianae, 1946).
61. See Rom 6:1–12; 1 Cor 6:15–18 and 10:16–17.

realism that is difficult to understand,[62] for this realism would—it seems?—have Christians be members of Christ in a physical manner.* What must be retained from this outlook is the realism of this union, even if we find that we cannot interpret it in terms of a physical union. Likewise, we must retain the idea that the whole man, body and soul, is engaged in it.

What is remarkable in these texts is the fact that Christ's relation to the Church is in no manner expressed through the image of the head. The Church is not a body having Christ as her head. She is the "body of Christ."

To understand this relationship, we must reflect on what the body meant in Semitic thought:

> It is the active manifestation of a living being whose life itself is invisible. Even where St. Paul speaks of the members, its principal meaning is not of a sociological-organic order. Instead, the principal meaning is the idea of a partial manifestation of the action of a living being, Christ, whose complete manifestation exists only in the entire *soma*. In short, the essential reference is always Christological.[63]

A second group of texts {633} A second group of Pauline texts are found in the letters written during his captivity. The theme of "the body of Christ" is no longer evoked in light of some other concern. Instead, it occupies a central place designating the community of the redeemed: "Christ is the savior of the body,"[64] the savior of this body of which we are members;[65] we have been called into this unique body.[66] It is a living, coherent, and hierarchized organism, gathering all Christians into itself.[67] It is the Church.[68] Finally, as we have seen, it is associated here with the idea of *fullness*.

---

62. See Benoit, "Corps, Tête et Plérôme dans les épîtres de la captivité," 114–16.

* N.B. One of the reasons adduced in favor of this "realistic" interpretation is the text of 1 Cor 6:15–18. In this text, St. Paul proposes a comparison with the union of man and women in sexual union. However, this text seems to contradict this interpretation's own intentions, for it is not a question of a physical union making two bodies physically one. Moreover, a specification is provided regarding man's union with God: they are one in spirit.

63. Congar, *Sainte Église*, 29.
64. Eph 5:23.
65. See Eph 5:30.
66. See Col 3:15.
67. See Col 2:19 and Eph 4:16.
68. See Col 1:18–24 and Eph 1:23, 5:23.

In these texts, there are important developments in relation to the first presentation of the image:

1. Christ's relationship with the Church is that of the head to the rest of the body. This point leads to a much more marked personalization of the Church in relation to Christ. The image of the body thus becomes insufficient and is brought to completion by spousal imagery.

2. On the other hand, the concern here is no longer focused solely on mankind to be saved but, rather, is concerned with the whole universe to be "recapitulated."

The image of Christ the head

{634} We could readily believe that the theme of Christ the head was formed as an internal development of the theme considering the Church as being His body. In reality, as we have seen, the theme considering the Church to be *the body of Christ* does not lend itself to such a development.

The theme of *Christ as the head of the Church* appears for the first time in the Letter to the Colossians. It is a question of cutting short the speculations being expressed to teachers among them. We only scarcely understand what these speculations exactly were, but according to what is said in the letter, they seem to have accorded too much salvific importance to spiritual powers (whether good or evil). Against this, St. Paul affirms the primacy and lordship of Christ over all creatures, whether visible or invisible. Quite naturally, he uses the image of "head" to make this affirmation, in order to express that Christ is the head [*chef*] of all creatures.

Therefore, this is the obvious (and, moreover, classic) meaning of the image. Christ is the "head," that is, the Lord, He who has dominion, commands, and directs. In particular, He is the Lord of His Church.[69]

However, it is immediately clear that the combination of two images tended to give the image of *head* its primary sense: the head is a part of the body, the principal part and seat of the vital principle. St. Paul was led to this by the physiological conceptions prevailing

---

69. See Col 1:18 and Eph 1:22.

at that time in the Hellenistic world. Indeed, if Aristotle made the heart the seat of sensations, Plato situated *nous* in the head, and after him, the Stoics did so as well. The medical theories of the age held that the head is the source of the nervous influence that directs all the members and vivifies them. The influence of these theories can be seen in texts like Colossians 2:19 and Ephesians 4:16. Moreover, these theories translate, in a quite obvious fashion, the ideas that we commonly form on the level of non-scientific thought. It is a hegemony belonging to the moral order, though it is naturally extended to the physiological order. Thus, man's life appears as a whole that is unified by a principle that is the source of its energy and vitality.

When this perspective is fully articulated, we see Christ present no longer as the invisible principle having the Church as his visible manifestation on the earth (i.e., the first sense of "body") but, rather, with Him being part of the Church, connected to her through the sacraments, which provide contact with Him and the communication of His life to her. He is no longer only the distant Lord in heaven. He is also and simultaneously the vivifying organ, the "head" giving life to the body.

Obviously, however, the two images do not exactly overlap. The first image of the "body" illuminates the eschatological Christ's invisibility, His "temporal absence." It principally emphasizes the Church's role in assuring His presence and action on earth. Secondarily, it emphasizes her character as a social organism, with many diversified functions. By contrast, it does not emphasize well enough the close union between Christ and the Church, a union that is not only moral but ontological. It seems to place Christ beyond and above the Church as a transcendent and distant Lord. At the same time, it seems to strip the Church of all consistency which would properly be hers, thus making her solely the means by which this distant Lord is rendered present to the world.

The second interpretation of the image of the body, having Christ not only as its head [*chef*] but also as its vital and nourishing principle, an integral part and source of life, illustrates well the continuous, vital, and real union existing between Christ and His Church. However, at first glance, it would seem to imply that Christ is visible, like the Church herself. (The "head" of the body is visible like it.) Given that this obviously is not the case, it leads us to delve deeper into the mystery of the Church. The life of the Church is, at least in part, invisible and secret. The Church herself is, in part, invisible.

The two images do not nullify each other; rather, they complete one another. According to the first image, the Church is visible. According to the second, she is invisible. According to the first, Christ transcends His Church. According to the second, He is intimately joined to her. Thus, we can see how this is explained by the idea of the Church as a sacrament.

The spousal image

{635} However, there is another aspect to the mystery. The second image, *Christ the head of the Church*, attempts to emphasize it without completely succeeding at doing so. What I am speaking of is the proper consistency of the Church and, therefore, her distinct personality. Indeed, if Christ is the *head* and the Church the *body*, they are somehow distinct. Christ gives life and the Church receives it. Christ is a living being, living by a life that is proper to Him. The Church is a living being that lives by a life that is received and participated in. However, the head and the body constitute a single living being, and from this perspective, the first image would be preferable, noting better the distinction between Christ and the Church.

In reality, a third image comes into play for this, namely, the image of the spouse.[70] The Church, the body of Christ, is also His *spouse*. In other words, she is a person who is distinct, though entirely united to Him through marriage bonds, which make one person from two. St. Paul accentuates and pushes to its limits the dependent state of the spouse which, in this case, is in fact total, given that the Lord is *the Savior of the body*. However, the dependence has the character of being a form of interdependence, because *to love one's body is to love oneself*.

It is clear that the bond in question is not physical and that it leaves the two persons in their ontological distinction. In the text of

---

70. See Eph 5:22–32.

Genesis to which St. Paul refers, the expressions "to leave" and "to cleave" are conscious and voluntary acts, expressing an interpersonal relationship. And St. Paul expresses this bond by means of expressions that equally designate such relations: "love" and "obedience." Therefore, rather than a physical realism, we should speak of a "spiritual realism."

The images of *spouse* and *body* are closely connected, as is clear in the text of Genesis to which St. Paul refers: "This at last is bone of my bones and flesh of my flesh";[71] "even so husbands should love their wives as their own bodies."[72] The image of *spouse* introduces the idea of *personal otherness*. The image of *body* is more apt for conveying the idea of *the gathering together of believers to Christ as His members*.[73]

The *plérôma* and body of Christ

{636} The image of *the body of Christ* is suitable only to human persons, calling to mind the bodily dimension of human beings, who must be gathered together to Christ, Himself "bodily," indeed wholly so in His human nature. By contrast, the image of *Christ the head* is used by St. Paul to express his primacy and his dominion over all beings, including invisible beings, the "heavenly powers."[74] According to Pierre Benoît, this is what the term *plérôma* would add to the term "body."[75]

Certain exegetes would like to interpret the expression, "in him all the fullness of God was pleased to dwell,"[76] as referring to Christ's divinity. Faced with gnostic theories (which certain exegetes presume suffused the "thought leaders" in the Colossian community)

---

71. Gn 2:23 (RSV).
72. Eph 5:28 (RSV).
73. See André-Marie Dubarle, "L'origine dans l'Ancien Testament de la notion paulinienne de l'Église 'Corps du Christ,'" in *Studiorum Paulinorum Congressus Internationalis Catholicus 1961* (Rome: Pontifical Biblical Institute Press, 1963), 231–40. Paul Andriessen, "La nouvelle Ève, corps du nouvel Adam," in *Aux origins de l'Église* (Paris: Desclée de Brouwer, 1965), 87–109. Christophe-Jean Dumont, *Les voies de l'unité chrétienne* (Paris: Cerf, 1954). Johann Adam Möller, *L'unité dans l'église ou le principe du catholicisme, avec introduction du Pierre Chaillet*, trans. André de Lilienfeld (Paris: Cerf, 1938).
74. See Col 2:10 and Eph 1:10.
75. See Benoît, "Corps, Tête et Plérôme dans les épîtres de la captivité," 107–53, and his "L'unité de l'Église selon l'épître aux Ephésiens," 345.
76. Col 1:19 (RSV).

holding that the *plérôma* had been composed of a host of intermediary entities, among whom the attributes and energies of the divinity were distributed in a diminished fashion, St. Paul would oppose the affirmation that the entire fullness of the divinity is found in Christ who, for this reason, is above these beings, whatever they may be. Benoît presents considerable arguments against this interpretation. On the one hand, he says that we have no certain knowledge concerning the existence of such gnostic theories at Colossae. Indeed, we know about such theories only from writings dating to the second century, and they were certainly influenced by Christianity. On the other hand, he notes that for St. Paul Christ is God by birth (indeed, by eternal filiation) not by the Father's indulgence.

Instead, what was involved here was a term drawn from Stoic philosophy (*plérôma*) expressing the fact that the divine principle of the world (the *pneuma*) fills the entire universe and is filled by it. By a transposition (given that this principle, in the Stoics, is material and not personal in any way), St. Paul would express the important biblical idea concerning God's presence to the whole world and to each of its parts. By applying this to Christ, he would intend to signify the fact that He mysteriously embraces in Himself not only His individual humanity, and not only the Church, but also the entire universe.

On the other hand, it is difficult to not read an affirmation of Christ's divinity in the formula: "For in Him the whole fullness of deity dwells bodily."[77] The members of this body in which the fullness of the divinity dwells themselves participate in this fullness. This leads to a practical consequence: believers participate in Christ's triumph over the hostile powers, no longer need to submit themselves to them, and no longer need to recognize their dominion.[78]

In the Letter to the Ephesians, St. Paul[79] takes up the same themes, though in a non-polemical way. No longer being occupied with "heavenly powers," he returns spontaneously to the point that was always at the center of his preoccupations: the men for whom Christ died, namely, redeemed humanity. This is found at the roots

---

77. Col 2:9 (RSV).
78. See Col 2:11–15.
79. Or whoever wrote in his name.

of his nearly exclusive insistence on the theme of the Church as the body having Christ as its head. Thus, we see the *plérôma* being identified with the Church, the body of Christ.[80] The idea of the body of Christ undergoing genesis and progress also emerges, progress which will come to its fulfillment only at the end of time.[81]

By combining these various data, we arrive at the following awe-inspiring conception. Christ realizes in Himself the fullness of the divinity. However, He extends this fullness to the Church, His body, who completes Him. She is His *plérôma* and yet He also and simultaneously is her *plérôma*, for He dwells in her and vivifies her. This fullness is also extended, in a way that remains very indeterminate, to the entire cosmos and especially to the nonhuman personal creatures who belong to it and who also have Christ as their head [*chef*]. This is an idea that we find being announced already in 1 Corinthians 15:20–29.

The cosmic Christ

{637} Much discussion is devoted to the cosmic conception of Christ which would supposedly be the outlook expressed in the epistles written during St. Paul's captivity. The meaning of such a cosmic outlook must be specified.

The Pauline Christ certainly is an individual, bodily being, a determinate man. In Him, God has, so to speak, once more taken up His work, the whole of His work.[82] This does not mean that Christ's perfection would be substituted for that of the flawed universe. Rather, it is communicated to the universe in order to grant it, by exalting it, the perfection that had been lost.

Mankind is what Christ first draws to Himself, freeing it from sin, purifying it, and communicating His holiness to it. Then, to the degree that men come to Him (through faith), they are gathered to Him and become His body, that is, the Church.

Whether the redemption would in fact have been the motive of the Incarnation, or whether one prefers to consider the Incarnation independent of sin, in both cases, the universe is joined together to

---

80. See Eph 1:23.
81. See Eph 4:1–13.
82. See Eph 1:9–10.

Christ by the intermediary of man. From this comes the identification, asymptotically, between the *body* and the *plérôma*.

The allegory of the vine and the branches in St. John
{638} It[83] is undeniable that this image corresponds to the Pauline image of the body.

Following St. Augustine, many modern exegetes ("the most customary exegesis," according to André Feuillet)[84] integrate [into the other themes] the Old Testament image designating Israel as Lord's vine[85] as well as the parable of the wicked vineyard tenants in which this Old Testament theme is taken up in the Synoptic Gospels.[86] In all these texts, Israel is presented as being a vine planted by the Lord, one that disappoints Him: the vine of death, not of life. This is why Feuillet (following Marie-Joseph Lagrange) refuses this rapprochement. However, the common exegesis relies on St. John's expression, "the true vine," by which Christ seems to intend to contrast himself to Israel. (The vine, having Him as the vine-stock, is the Church. Thus, we would here have the theme of Israel's effacement before the Church.)

Feuillet proposes another interesting rapprochement (which itself need not exclude the first), namely, a text in Sirach where wisdom is compared to a fertile vine.[87] In this image, commentators generally emphasize that the intention here is to show the consubstantiality of the vine-stock and the branches. By this, we come back to the Pauline image of the body and members: "Therefore, Christ is the true vine inasmuch as the man Jesus Christ is the head of the Church."[88]

Belonging to Christ is the condition for participating in His life and, therefore, for being fruitful in good works (an image that is equally Pauline). This belonging is brought about through faith and

---

83. See Jn 15:1–17.
84. See Andreé Feuillet, "Les thèmes bibliques majeurs du discours sur le pain de vie (Jn 6)," *Nouvelle revue théologique* 82 (1960): 927.
85. See Hos 10:1; Is 5:1–7 and 27:2–5; Jer 2:21 and 12:10–11; Ezek 15:1–8, 17:5–10, 19:10–14; and Ps 80:9–17.
86. See Mt 21:33–46, Mk 12:1–12, Lk 20:9–19.
87. See Sir 24:17–20.
88. St. Thomas, *In Joan*, ch. 15, v. 1, no. 1981.

love: "Abide in me, and I in you."* He is speaking here neither of baptism nor of the Eucharist. However, baptism is presupposed: "Truly, truly, I say to you, unless one is born of water and the Spirit, he cannot enter the kingdom of God,"[89] and there is a striking connection to the Eucharist: "He who eats my flesh and drinks my blood abides in me, and I in him."[90]

More fully than does the Pauline image of the body, the Johannine allegory emphasizes the personal character of belonging to Christ. The Church is presented principally as a communion.

The symbolism of branches that are dried up and thrown into the fire calls to mind the biblical texts concerning the vine of Israel, especially Isaiah 15:1–8 emphasizing that the vine has its worth only in its fruit. The only use the dried branch can serve is to be burned up. However, there is a capital difference here. Israel, the vine, could become entirely wicked and dried up. (Thus, the *remnant of Israel* would be some branches preserved by God, which He will replant.) By contrast, now the vine itself remains indefectibly holy and fruitful. Only the branches that are detached from it are dried out.

From the Pauline image of the body to the theological notion of the Mystical Body

The biblical notion of *body* was theologically translated by that of the *Mystical Body*, which was accepted and placed at the center of ecclesiology by Pius XII's encyclical *Mystici Corporis* in 1943[91] and by Vatican II.[92]

The origin of the expression "Mystical Body"

{639} According[93] to Henri de Lubac's thesis, which has strong historical support, the expression "Mystical Body" would have first

---

* Jn 15:4 (RSV).
89. Jn 3:5 (RSV).
90. Jn 6:56 (RSV).
91. *AAS* 35:193–248. See Jérôme Hamer, *L'Église est une communion* (Paris: Cerf, 1962), 11–34.
92. *Lumen Gentium*, nos. 7–8.
93. See Hamer, *L'Église est une communion*, 71–86. Henri de Lubac, *Les Églises particulières dans l'Église universelle* (Paris: Aubier, 1971), 6. (See this text with the presentations found in Congar, *Sainte Église*, 554–60; Journet, *L'Église du Verbe incarné*, 2:673, no. 1; Marie-Joseph

designated Christ's body in the Eucharist, which *mystice vel sacramentaliter* signifies the *corpus verum*, the Church. Gradually—and, it seems, in particular after the controversy connected with Berengar of Tours—there was need to insist on the reality of Christ's body as present in the Eucharist. The expression *corpus verum* thus gradually passed to the body present in the Eucharist, whereas *corpus mysticum* came to designate the Church. In the thirteenth century, the evolution was brought to its completion and, with St. Thomas, the Church begins to be envisioned in herself, not as signified by the Eucharist. Concerning the conclusions that de Lubac draws from this development, and for criticism of them, see the authors identified in the footnote above.

From the fourteenth century onward, this habit of thus designating the Church separately from her relation to the Eucharist becomes fixed. However, the term "mystical" leads Christian thought toward the idea of a wholly spiritual and invisible Church opposed to the institutional and visible Church. Such was the position of Wycliff and, later on, the reformers. For this reason, Catholic theology had a kind of distrust for this expression, a distrust that was manifested at Vatican I by certain bishops' reluctance to introduce it into the Constitution on the Church that had been prepared.[94]

The theological value of this notion

{640} Whatever may have been the historical and semantic vicissitudes leading the expression "Mystical Body" to be applied to the Church, the notion that was gradually elaborated (and of which it is the expression) is good and fruitful in theology, for it enables us to understand the image of the body in its true sense, which is sacramental.

The visible and invisible Church The Church is not a mystery hidden in a sociological reality that itself would be intrinsically natural and

---

Nicolas, "Théologie de l'Église, Études critiques," *Revue thomiste* 46 [1946]: 383–89.) Tromp, *Corpus Christi quod est Ecclesia*, 98–102. [Tr. note: Fr. Nicolas may have miscited de Lubac here. Fr. Marie-Joseph Nicolas's review article from 1946 is dedicated to de Lubac's earlier work, *Corpus mystium, L'Eucharistie et l'Église au Moyen Age* (Paris: Aubier, 1949).]

94. See Giovanni Domenico Mansi, *Sacrorum Conciliorum nova et amplissima Collectio* (Florence, 1758; Venice, 1799; Paris, 1901–27), 51:738.

perfectly accessible to reason ([i.e.,] the ecclesiastical society that is as visible as the Kingdom of France or the Republic of Venice). Although the Church is indeed a sociological reality, a visible society, she is one that is itself mysterious.

If a visible element (i.e., the bodily dimension) and an invisible element (i.e., the spiritual element) can be found in every human reality (and first of all in every human being), in the case of the society that is the Church, the invisible element is the "mystery," an object of faith. This mystery is Christ present in His Church, and it is the Holy Spirit vivifying the Church. Just as the bodily element of the human reality is itself spiritualized by the spiritual element, so too the bodily element of the Church (by which she is visible) is "Christified" and "divinized" by this divine element.

This is what is perfectly expressed by the adjective "mystical." What it has designated from the start is *the mystery of Christ* hidden in visible realities and manifested by them.[95]

Hence, to say that the Church is the "Mystical Body of Christ" does not at all mean that it is Christ's body only in Christian experience ([i.e.,] in the mystic's experience). Much to the contrary, it means that she offers to this experience the mystery hidden in her, manifesting while veiling it.

This term also expresses what is specific to the Church as a body. She is not a purely moral and juridical "body." However, no more is she (as seems to be Teilhard de Chardin's conception) an organically unified body, in which it would be impossible to see how the personality of her members would be preserved in their distinction.[96] When the word "body" is applied to the Church, this term must be understood analogically, that is, in a sense that is proper to it all the while keeping a kind of community with the meanings that it has in the domain of our experience.[97]

---

95. See Louis Bouyer, "Mystique, essai sur l'histoire d'un mot," *Vie Spiritualle, Supplément* 9 (1949): 5–23, and his *La spiritualité du Nouveau Testament et des Pères* (Paris: Aubier, 1960), 485–92.

96. See Teilhard de Chardin, *Oeuvres* (Paris: Seuil, 1955–76), 9:39–44.

97. See Pius XII, *Mystici Corporis* (D.-*Sch.*, nos. 3809–11).

The Church, society, and communion Given our modern languages and following our habits of thought, the term "body," by itself, would orient us toward the idea of a purely social unity, a group united solely by moral and juridical bonds. The adjective "mystical" intends to orient us toward this more profound, more real, spiritual and supernatural unity that makes the Church into a different kind of society. However, it does so without either devouring the substantive or eliminating the aspect of being a structured society, which is part of the mystery of the Church.

The Church, at once identical with Christ and distinct from Him A kind of complexity still exists in the mystery of the Church.* She is Christ, continuing to live and act in history, but she also is herself, distinct from Christ. She is His spouse.

By its own gravitational pull, the image of the "body of Christ" tends toward identification: a person is his own bodily being. The adjective "mystical" corrects this without abolishing the unity that also exists between Christ and the Church, a unity that is ever expressed by the substantive "body." Hence the expression "the Mystical Body of Christ," expresses the fact that the Church is the realization of the *mystery of Christ*.[98] She is this gathering of all the redeemed, spiritually united to Christ (through faith, love, and the harmony of grace) and bodily (by visibly belonging to the ecclesiastical society), and in Christ they are united to the Trinity. She is a spiritual and visible gathering that makes all believers (actually) and all of humanity (potentially) into a single "mystical" person (i.e., not merely a corporate social unit), namely, the bride of Christ, His body (in the biblical sense in which the bride is "the body of her husband"). She is at once distinct from Him (just as the redeemed person is distinct from the redeemer) and yet is wholly ordered to Him, loved by the Father through Him and in Him, with the very love by which Christ is loved.

---

* [Tr. note: Reading "de l'Église" for "du Christ."]
98. See Eph 3:1–12.

The Church, a spiritual and eschatological reality The Church is a temporal reality, assuring the presence and action of Christ in history. However, she is not "of the world" and of history. She already belongs to the end of time. She is not only pressing onward toward the kingdom. She already is the kingdom of God and of Christ.

Left to itself, the term "body" would express only the temporal reality of the Church, the means of Christ's presence in history. The fact that the Church currently belongs to an entire spiritual domain where there will be neither death, nor sin, nor corruption (despite appearances to the contrary) of any sort is also well noted by the term "mystical." This is forever the Christian meaning of a "mystery": a divine, supernatural, and wholly spiritual reality contained in a temporal, bodily, and human reality which simultaneously manifests and conceals it.

The Church, Temple of God Built Upon Christ

This[99] is another metaphor, one which St. Paul developed in particular, though it is found in other New Testament writings as well: the Church is the temple of God. Christ is its foundation, the cornerstone. However, at the same time, we here again find the theme of fullness, for He contains her and is contained by her.

Jesus, the new temple
{641} Jesus presented Himself as the true temple, putting an end to the ancient arrangement of things,[100] substituting Himself for the Jerusalem temple.[101] (This is one of the most certain expressions stated by Jesus. He will be reminded about it, as an accusation, at His trial,[102] and it will be made into a subject of mockery.)[103] According to this expression, the new temple is the crucified and resurrected body of Jesus. However, already during His earthly life, "something greater than the temple is here."[104] And His words to

---

99. See Yves Congar, *Le mystère du Temple*, first part (Paris: Cerf, 1957), 1.
100. See Jn 4:20–25.
101. See Jn 2:18–22.
102. See Mk 14:57.
103. See Mt 27:39.
104. Mt 12:6 (RSV).

Nathanael[105] contain an obvious allusion to Jacob's ladder. Now, Jacob cried out: "How awesome is this place! This is none other than the house of God, and this is the gate of heaven."[106]

Within the framework of the feast of the dedication of the temple, He solemnly affirms that "the Father consecrated and sent [Him] into the world."[107] During the feast of tabernacles, when the miracle of the water flowing forth from the rock was celebrated, He presented Himself as being the rock from which living water will flow.[108] By this, He identifies Himself with the temple which Ezekiel evokes,[109] from which an abundant and vivifying water must flow forth.

After Pentecost, the new temple is the Church

{642} Here, we have a surprising and characteristic fact. Jesus does not cease to be the temple, but the Church is part of this temple that He is. Again, one finds the same elements that we find in the case of the body. On the one hand, Jesus seems to be a part of the new temple (the foundation and the cornerstone). On the other hand, He is the fullness toward which this temple tends, to the degree that it is built up. We can seamlessly pass from one image to the other.

First, the temple is each Christian. It is each Christian as a concrete person, that is, his body, though considered as a manifestation of the person.

As for the Holy Spirit, it is said that He dwells in us as in a temple. However, it is simultaneously said that Christ dwells in us. The expressions "in Christ" and "in the Spirit" at times seem equivalent, not meaning that Christ and the Spirit are identical but, rather, because Christ sanctifies only through His Spirit.[110]

However, if each Christian is the temple of the Holy Spirit, Christians all taken altogether constitute a single temple: "For God's temple is holy, and that temple you are";[111] "in [Christ] you also are

---

105. See Jn 1:51.
106. Gn 28:17 (RSV).
107. Jn 10:36 (RSV).
108. See Jn 7:37–38.
109. See Ezek 47:1–12 and Rv 22:1.
110. See Ferdinand Prat, *Théologie de S. Paul* (Paris: Beauchesne, 1938), 2:417–25. Schnackenburg, *L'Église dans le Nouveau Testament*, 176–83.
111. 1 Cor 3:17 (RSV).

built into it for a dwelling place of God in the Spirit."[112] The Church is the temple.

Christ is the "foundation" or "cornerstone" of this temple. Simultaneously, He is the terminus toward which the construction of the edifice tends. That is, He is the complete edifice or, for now, the plan that the construction must realize:

> Although Christ is the foundation—that from which and according to which everything must be constructed—He also is the plan and model that must be realized. In all the dimensions making up His fullness, He is the terminus and, as it were, the lofty heights or full breadth of the construction ... Christ is at once the foundation, the point of departure for the construction, and its terminus, the fullness toward which she rises upward and which she must realize.[113]

Therefore, there are two statements of the same mystery. In the Gospel, Jesus Himself is the new temple who is substituted for the ancient one and who assures God's presence and dwelling place among men: "He has dwelt among us." In the apostolic writings, the community of believers constitutes a new temple. However, she is founded *on* Christ, who is the foundation and cornerstone. To phrase it better, she exists *in Christ* who, in relation to the edifice, assumes the role of being a generative and unifying principle. (This idea works in conjunction with the image of a living body that develops itself, thanks to an image that is not very coherent in itself, though it is very expressive, namely, that of "living stones.") The two themes come back together and merge in 1 Peter 2:4–6.

Is there any other way to understand this than by the notion of sacramentality? Because the Church is the sacrament of Christ, she can simultaneously be what He is (e.g., the temple of God), without being distinct from Him, and likewise what she is in a way that is proper to herself:

> From this living stone—which is "the Son of God made flesh" in St. John and "the high priest" in the Letter to the Hebrews—and from all the other living stones that, by faith, are clustered to the first, it is made into a single temple, a unique celebration of filial obedience and praise along with its unique exercise of *agapè*, having as its foundational principle Christ

---

112. Eph 2:22 (RSV). Also, see 2 Cor 6:16.
113. Congar, *Le mystère du Temple*, 191.

Himself, who is substantially one with God. There is continuity between the evangelical proclamation concerning the fact that Jesus replaces the temple, and the apostolic proclamation concerning the community of the faithful, the true messianic temple. At bottom, they are the same proclamation.[114]

Complementarity of the image of the temple

{643} The image of the temple seems to add two supplements to the image of the body of Christ. First, it better emphasizes the Church's character as being, after the ascension, the living sign of God's presence among men, for the Jerusalem temple primarily was this. Second, it shows that she is constructed from materials coming from outside, namely, sinful men, who are integrated into the construction when they become living stones by being brought near (through faith) to Christ, who is the living stone. This is something that cannot be expressed solely with the image of the body.

However, it very poorly expresses the idea of living growth through internal movement. It is also deficient for expressing the role of Christ, who is simultaneously the cornerstone, the architect, and the perfect temple.

Thus, all these images have the goal of drawing us into the mystery of the Church, not by way of explanation, but by making the different aspects of this mystery stand forth, such as it has been willed and revealed to us by God.

The Church as an Institution

The Church as a society is the sacrament of a communion

{644} The notion of a *society* emphasizes the Church's human and visible reality and situates her among the realities of this world. On the basis of this notion, we can draw forth the traits that distinguish her, and those who are part of her, from those who are not part of her. She is not a purely spiritual community but, instead, is a community of men and women with their bodily, earthly dimension. She has a juridical structure that assures her consistency here-below.

However, this notion of a "society" has been critiqued for having

---

114. Ibid., 217.

taken on an excessive importance and having prevailed in ecclesiology in the context of the conflicts faced by the Church, either with temporal powers (on the [natural, political] level where they are situated) or with the movements of "spirituals" framed against the hierarchy and the ecclesiastical order. Thus, it was necessary to affirm the visible and juridical existence of the Church as the subject of rights and as the holder of authority on earth. By the same stroke, however, her mystery, which is invisible, tended to be overlooked.

Thus, the philosophical notion of "society" came to be the generative notion of the entire treatise *De ecclesia*, which thus becomes nearly exclusively a treatise on the public right of the Church. Of course, emphasis is given to the fact that the Church was founded by Christ and that she pursues union with God as her common good (and yet, as regards the earthly Church's responsibility, this union is situated above all in the next life). For this reason, she is a supernatural society in relation to her efficient cause and her end. However, her structure (i.e., her material cause and formal cause) is treated as though it were natural, in accordance with the requirements, burdens, and rights of every society. Consequently, all ecclesiological reality was refused to other religious societies that also profess Christ. It was admitted that the individuals who belong to them, if they are of good faith, belong in some manner (invisibly) to the Church. However, it was said that their community has no title to present itself as the Church, even partially.

Within this outlook, one is led to give priority to the treatment of the Church's authority and, consequently, to the organs of this authority. The Church thus, in practice, came to be identified with the hierarchy. The simple faithful are part of her, though as "subjects" of her power. Membership in the Church is thus conceived principally as a juridical relation, founded on baptism inasmuch as it is an external and public act of entrance into the Church and on the recognition of the duties of obedience that flow from it. (However, obviously, baptism is sanctioned by an internal mark, namely, its sacramental character.)

From this outlook, one has Bellarmine's definition, according to which the Church is a community of men "[as] visible and tangible as the community of Roman people or the Kingdom of France, or the Republic of Venice."[115] We will end up "naturalizing" the Church if we do not see that she is mysterious precisely as a visible society and not only a natural society bearing a supernatural mystery. Jesus Christ is not only the efficient cause of the Church. He is her exemplar formal cause and final cause, as He realizes the fullness toward which the Church tends (without ever being able to attain it).

Once again, we find ourselves faced with the notion of sacramentality. Yes, the Church is a (temporal and historical) *society*. However, she is such a community as a sign and sacrament of a hidden reality: *communion*.

The Church as a communion is realized in ecclesial society

{645} During the Middle Ages and especially in St. Thomas's writings, the Church was readily defined as the *congregatio fidelium*, emphasizing that it is a question of the (mystical) gathering of all the saints from the world's beginning up to its end.[116]

In reaction to the post-Tridentine ecclesiology that is too centered on the notions of "society" and "institution," various thinkers strove to retrieve this conception. The originator of this movement was Johann Adam Möhler at the beginning of the nineteenth century.[117] According to this vein of thought, the social structure of the Church, while indeed being instituted by Christ, would proceed from the internal requirements of the communion of love, which is primary and constitutive. In this line of thought there developed an ecclesiology founded on interpersonal communication, to which the institution is subordinated. It has the obvious danger of neglecting this "institutional" aspect, making it play a secondary role. It also has the danger of separating it off, resulting in a distinction between a "juridical" (or "institutional") Church and a Church of communion.

---

115. See Journet, *L'Église du Verbe incarné*, 2:1181–82.
116. See Congar, *Esquisses du mystère de l'Église*, 69; "Ecclesia ab Abel," in *Ahandlungen über Theologie und Kirche. Festschrift für Karl Adam* (Düsseldorf: Schwann, 1952), 79–108. In the opposite direction, see Tromp. See Hamer, *L'Église est une communion*, 75.
117. On Möhler and his ecclesiology, see Pierre Chaillet, "La Tradition vivante. Hommage à J.-A. Möhler," *Revue des sciences philosophiques et théologiques* (1938): 161–212; Congar, *Sainte Église*; Journet, *L'Église du Verbe incarné*, 1:630–40; Marie-Joseph Nicolas, "Théologie de l'Église, Études critiques," 373–79.

This distinction will be rejected by the encyclical *Mystici Corporis* (and, moreover, was not at all contained in what the theologians of the Tübingen school intended to express).

In order to avoid these excesses, we need to understand that, by its nature, ecclesial communion must be realized in a society, in this society founded by Jesus Christ on the foundation of the apostles, the apostolic Church, to whom He had promised that "the powers of death shall not prevail against it,"[118] and that "I am with you always, to the close of the age."[119] This qualification can be registered without, for all that, neglecting the indispensable counter-weight that the notion of communion brings to that of a society, helping to balance the latter, preserving it from its own excesses, though without placing the ecclesiological notion of society into question and without relativizing it in the least. If it is true that theology, without being reduced to a "supernatural" anthropology (for theology first and foremost strives to know God in the light of His revelation, and not man), does indeed presuppose and imply such an anthropology (for the word of God is addressed to man, first to tell him that he is made in God's image and also that he is called to return to that image and, one day, be it in its fullness), we can find in human existence and in every human being a foundation for this intimate conjunction of the invisible and invisible in the Church.

The soul is that by which man is what he is, transcending the entire material universe. Through it, he is conscious and free, a being who loves, a person. However, the soul is made for existence in a body which it informs and forms, a body that it makes exist. It is made to act in it and through it, to make it act. And this soul is made for this body. Without it, this body would not be a human body, but the soul itself would not exist without this body, utterly cut off from it [*hors de lui*].* And just as the soul, which is invisible and imperceptible in itself, manifests itself in its most spiritual aspects by means of the body, so too the ecclesial communion that is established by grace and assured by the Holy Spirit, as we will specify later on, is present

---

118. Mt 16:18 (RSV).
119. Mt 28:20 (RSV).

* [Tr. note: This is not said to the detriment of the continued subsistence of the soul separated from the body. See §§565–68 in the previous volume.]

to the world by means of this society of which it is the invisible face and active principle. (Indeed, without such a communion, no society, whatever may be its spiritual ambitions and organizational efficacy, would be a Church, the Church.

Obviously, there are considerable differences involved here too, as happens when one seeks to penetrate the hidden depths of a supernatural and Divine Reality, beginning with something experienced in this world and utilizing analogy. The soul exists only in the body that it informs, forms, and makes exist, and nothing can belong to this body (which is visible) unless it does so in a visible way. Now, we will be led to consider an extension of ecclesial communion beyond the limits of the visible society in which it is realized. We will thus need to ask ourselves how it remains true that ecclesial communion on earth is rooted in human existence only in and through the society that it vivifies and that bears it, namely the Church. In her visible aspect, with all its unwieldiness and opacity (which is an ordeal for us and, first of all, for her) the Church is the sacrament, indeed, the unique sacrament of communion.

CHRIST THE LORD OF THE CHURCH IN THE LIGHT OF SACRAMENTALITY

{646} Perhaps the most profound reason that led the Protestant reformers to reject and combat the Catholic conception of the Church is that it seemed to them that the Church, in asserting and exercising her authority over the faithful, claimed that she could evade submitting herself to Christ. Luther wrote: "I do not know what you mean when you call the Roman Church the rule of faith. I have always believed that faith was the rule of the Roman Church and of all the churches." Moreover, Karl Barth critiqued the Catholic conception of tradition, conceived of as the very preaching of the Church, standing as the rule of faith, by saying that this immanentizes the rule within the Church, suppressing its *Gegenüber* [opposite], so that the Church will no longer do anything but carry on a monologue with herself.[120]

---

120. Congar, *Sainte Église*, 131–54. The references to Luther and Barth are on page 136.

The Church's necessary dependence on "her Lord" seems so obvious that one can ask how there could have been an argument concerning this point. Nonetheless, the same reproach was recently registered against the Church by Hans Küng. Indeed, it seems that this denunciation of the "emancipation" of the Church would be one of the master ideas of his book on the Church:

> Given that Christ is the head of the Church and hence the origin and goal of its growth, growth is only possible in *obedience* to his head. If the Church is disobedient to its head and his word, it cannot grow, however busy and active it may seem to be, it can only wither ... The valid movements in the Church are those that are set in motion by God's grace ... The New Testament message gives no basis at all for ideas about the development of the Church which play down or even domesticate the idea of the reign of the Church.[121]

Christ, the Founder and Head of the Church

{647} Christ founded the Church. We need not discuss here the theories of salvation holding that the Church would have constituted herself on her own after Christ's death (and His resurrection, inasmuch as these theories acknowledge it) in order to prolong His memory and His action.[122] Everything that has been said up to this point is founded on faith's affirmation (itself without a doubt founded upon Scripture) that the Church not only responds to something Christ willed, but indeed that she was constituted by Him. She comes "from on high."

Was she founded at the cross or, rather, at Pentecost by the outpouring of the Spirit? The second solution draws our assent, for given that the Holy Spirit is, as we will see, "the soul of the Church," it is not easy to see how the Church could have existed before having received the Holy Spirit whom Jesus had promised. Indeed, there can be no doubt that the Gift and mission of the Holy Spirit took place at Pentecost. Nonetheless, it is quite obvious that the Gift of the Spirit is intimately connected to Jesus' death and resurrection,

---

121. Küng, *L'Église*, 322–32. [Tr. note: Taken from Hans Küng, *The Church*, trans. Ray and Rosaleen Ockenden (New York: Sheed and Ward, 1967), 238–39.]

122. For an overview presentation, see Oscar Cullmann, *Le salut dans l'histoire. L'existence chrétienne selon le Nouveau Testament*, trans. Marc Kohler (Neuchâtel: Delachaux et Niestlé, 1966), 23–58.

as it is the sign, the pledge, and the realizer of the pardon of sins and of the divine filiation (i.e., divinization) which Jesus merited for all men through His sacrifice. The Gift of the Spirit to the Church is the prolongation of this action by the Spirit through which Jesus had been raised from the dead, "being put to death in the flesh but made alive in the spirit."[123] The Church, whom the Spirit brings into existence at Pentecost, is made up of disciples formed by Jesus—the Twelve, then the assembly of the first believers. They have accepted redemption and learned from Jesus what Church He wished to found: "But the Counselor, the Holy Spirit ... will teach you all things, and bring to your remembrance all that I have said to you."[124]

According to Bouyer,[125] the question of knowing whether Jesus founded the Church is a false question for the sure reason that "for Jesus, as for the Jews of His time, the People of God was a reality that posed no problem. As it had existed from the time of Abraham, and as it had developed after that, it would remain one and the same up to the last day, despite all the other possible transformations held in reserve by the future." Indeed, Jesus addressed Himself to this people. Doubtlessly, Jewish believers today have the conviction that they are this People of God. (We will take up this question below.) However, precisely speaking, this conviction includes the refusal to recognize that the Church instituted by Jesus Christ is the People of God. Indeed, this Church does not think of herself as being a People of God differing from that which God chose for Himself in Abraham and even from the beginning of humanity being composed of all the just "since the time of Abel." On this essential point, Fr. Bouyer is certainly and entirely correct.

However, this Church has not always existed, and the essential condition for belonging to her is the belief that Jesus Christ is the Messiah whom the Jews awaited. Indeed, this expectation and preparation for the coming of the Messiah was their *raison d'être* and the principle of their unity as the People of God. There also is the new reality of the sacraments, principally baptism and the Eucharist. Jesus Christ did not always exist as the Incarnate Word, nor has the

123. 1 Pt 3:18 (RSV).
124. Jn 14:26 (RSV).
125. Bouyer, *L'Eglise de Dieu*, 677.

Church (who is His body), nor the sacraments of the New Covenant (by which we are gathered into this body and made a participant in Christ's grace). From this perspective, Christ undeniably gave birth to the Church as the sacrament of His presence to the world and of His saving action. This Church is thus differentiated from ancient Israel and the Israel of today, the former having awaited the coming of the Messiah without knowing it and the latter not recognizing Him as the Messiah.

Quite obviously, He alone was able to found it. Just as the Incarnation results from a purely free initiative on God's part (given that no human effort could enable humanity to bring about the Hypostatic Union) so too the Church cannot arise in her deepest reality (which is the very mystery of the fact that she represents Christ) except as resulting from an initiative undertaken by God in Jesus Christ.

Consequently, Christ is, without any doubt, the "lord [*chef*] of the Church," her "head," as we have seen. If the Church exists only as the sacrament of Christ (though as a living and active sacrament), it is clear that she cannot act and accomplish her mission except in complete obedience to Him and in complete docility in relation to the Holy Spirit (the Spirit of Christ). Christ is and remains the sole shepherd of the sole flock, of the unique People of God.[126] He is and remains the sole "head of the Church."

The Apostolicity of the Church

{648} The[127] essential affirmation that Christ founded the Church necessarily implies another affirmation that is no less essential, namely that the Church of yesterday was, the Church of today is, and the Church up to the end of the ages will be the Church founded by Jesus Christ (i.e., the apostolic Church). This is in no way a question of denying the profound modifications that the Church, which is a historical reality, has undergone and will continue to undergo through the course of history. However, these modifications

---

126. See Jn 10:11–16.
127. See Bouyer, *L'Église de Dieu*, chs. 5 and 6. Yves Congar, *La Tradition et les traditions* (Paris: Fayard, 1963), 182–83. Journet, *L'Église du Verbe incarné*, vol. 1, ch. 10.

can affect neither her nature nor her individuality. (Here, they are the same thing, for the Church, a historical reality, is not the individual realization of a common nature, but rather is the unique realization of God's "project" in Jesus Christ which is unique as well.) This is akin to how the uniqueness and unity of the individual personality of a man is not affected by the numerous modifications that occur through the course of its existence. No genius and no concurrence of human efforts could legitimately make a Church which would be different from that which was founded by Jesus Christ. This is the insuperable limitation to every pretention and every effort to adapt the Church to the world and to the age.

This essential characteristic of the Church is assured by apostolicity, that is, by the transmission of the teaching of faith, of the means of grace, and of the fundamental evangelical orientations (the *sequela Christi*) given by the apostles to men chosen by them from the community and handed on by these latter in their own turn to others, up to the present day and unto the end of the ages. This transmission of powers (not the specific powers of the apostles, namely, the powers needed to found the Church, which strictly speaking could not be transmitted precisely because the Church was founded once and for all) was wonderfully described, at the beginning of the Church's life, by St. Clement of Rome:

> Therefore, Christ came from God, and the apostles came from Christ. These two things arise from God's will in good order ... Preaching through the cities and countrysides, they (the apostles) experienced their first fruits in the Holy Spirit and established them as bishops and as the deacons of future believers ... This is indeed why, in their foresight about the future, they established those whom we have spoken of and then laid upon them the rule that after their death other proven men should succeed them in their ministry.[128]

To say that the Church is apostolic is to say that she is the Church founded by the apostles on the unique foundation that is Christ.

---

128. St. Clement of Rome, *Letter to the Corinthians* [Épître aux Corinthiens], trans. Annie Jaubert, SC 167 (Paris: Cerf, 1971), chs. 40–42.

The Church's obedience to Christ

{649} Here we find ourselves faced with a question mentioned earlier:[129] if the Church does not obey Christ, must we not first obey Christ rather than her and then start her anew [*ensuite la reprendre*]? However, this raises a further question, namely: who can judge concerning this obedience and how is one to judge it? Or, to put it another way: can a believer (even a theologian!) simultaneously hold in his gaze the Church (in any of her actions) and Christ, considering them in relation to one another (*Gegenüber*), thus distinguishing the actions done in obedience to Christ and under the motion of His grace from those that are done independent of Him (or that "domesticate" Him)? Following this path, one thus comes to the Lutheran illusion of *sola scriptura* which holds that Scripture would make us know the Word of God in, as it were, a pure state, in light of which we could judge the Church.[130]

Yes, the Church of Christ can exist, develop, and act only in dependence on her Lord. However, it does not lie in the power of anyone to judge this obedience which, far from diminishing her authority, provides its foundation. If she could really withdraw herself from her dependence on Christ, it would be impossible for anyone to know Him and even to believe in Him (and thus even to be saved by Him), for she is the sacrament of Christ. He can be known only by her and through her. He acts and saves only by making use of her.

However, precisely because she exists only as the sacrament of Christ, she cannot withdraw herself, nor us, from obedience to Christ.

Nonetheless, the Church is distinct from Christ as a subject of existence and of action. That is, she is distinct as a person. This point, which will be expressly considered and explained below, is also implied by the notion of a sacrament, as we saw above.[131] Between the sacrament and the *res sacra* of which it is the sacrament (an individual person or a collective person), the former is distinguished

---

129. See §646. [Tr. note: Correcting "§656."]
130. See Ernest Korn, "Compte-rendu du livre de D. Olivier, Le procès de Luther," *Nova et Vetera* 46 (1971): 312–14.
131. See §613 above.

as a person from the sacred (Divine) Person that is represented by the sacrament.[132] If Christ exercises His saving action (i.e., His lordship) over the world (i.e., over men to be saved) by means of His Church, He thus has introduced between His action as supreme shepherd and men the freedom of the pastors whom the Holy Spirit has established as guardians of the flock, of "the Church of God that He (Christ) acquired at the price of his own blood."[133] As was said above, this requires the shepherds to submit their freedom (in their governance) to Christ's lordship, so that Christ's lordship over the world (for salvation, in the things that concern salvation) may pass through the mediation of Christ's lordship over His Church and, more precisely, His lordship over those who, in the Church, have been established as shepherds. However, if they shirk this lordship and are disobedient, the flock will no longer be led toward their goal. It will go astray and will no longer exist as the flock of Christ, ceasing to be the sacrament of the union of men with God in Christ.

Once again, the solution to this grave aporia can by no means be found in a form of control that could be exercised by particular members of the People of God (e.g., theologians or prophets) over the government of the shepherds. Indeed, they exist as members of the People of God (as theologians, prophets, or whatever else may concern their Christian being and acting) only in and through the Church. Were they to break away from her to judge her, they would lose every right to render such a judgment. Christ promised that He would never abandon His Church and that He would send his Spirit to lead her. We will see that the pastors and all the other members of the flock who, in one way or another, play a role leading the flock, can commit faults, indeed, even grave faults that reverberate over the forward progress of the flock, that slow it, or that make it deviate. However, the Holy Spirit will never allow the Church to be led astray and to lose the direction that Christ impressed upon her, a direction that He does not cease to impress upon her, a direction that is He Himself, for the ultimate end [of the Church's life] is "adulthood in Christ."

---

132. This personal distinction is expressed by the biblical image of the Church being Christ's spouse. See §635 above.
133. Acts 20:28.

Although Küng has, on many counts, registered a number of relevant observations concerning the Church, nonetheless, they are gravely deficient when it comes to devoting sufficient attention to the promised assistance of the Holy Spirit. We will see that this assistance is granted to the whole Church, though especially to the shepherds, not for themselves but for the sake of the flock. Without it, there would be no solution to the problem posed by the ever-possible failures of her shepherds. Not only would it be impossible for the Church to rectify her direction if this assistance were lost (who would bring about such a rectification and how would it be brought about?), but moreover it would be impossible to know with certitude whether the Church is currently on course or whether she has gone astray. In other words, the Church would cease to exist, for if one cannot be certain whether one truly encounters Christ in and through a sacrament, that sacrament loses its very existence as a sacrament.

To believe in the Church does not require us to close our eyes to the faults and errors that she can commit in the very fulfillment of her mission. Instead, such belief requires us to hold that, in virtue of the Holy Spirit's assistance, these faults and errors never have gone (nor ever will go) so far as to make her no longer be the People of God redeemed by Christ's blood, the body of Christ and His spouse, the temple of God on earth, the sacrament (i.e., the sign and means) of the communion of men with the Trinity and with each other in Christ.

2

Christ's Presence to the World through the Church

{650} A classic theological theme, one that is entirely in line with the conception of the Church as the sacrament of Christ, compares the mystery of the Church to the mystery of Christ, understanding the Church as the continuation of the Incarnation. From the perspective of a rigorous and classical ecclesiology, see the exposition of this theme in Journet's *Théologie de l'Église* and in Vladimir Lossky.* A very strong expression of it can be read in Leo XIII.[1] Here again, the great precursor in these matters is Möhler, one of the first to connect ecclesiological heresies to Christological heresies.

The most general thematic consideration of the Church as the continuation of the Incarnation was already classical long before Möhler. We can see a striking expression of it in the words of Bossuet: "The Church is Christ spread out and communicated." Today, it can be found in its most emphatic form—indeed, in a way that is so excessive that it is untenable—in the Teilhardian notion of the universal Christ (the "Super-Christ").

From the outset, we must here distinguish two questions. First

---

*See Charles Journet, *Théologie de l'Église* (Paris: Desclée de Brouwer, 1958), 21–28. [Tr. note: Fr. Nicolas also cites "Lossky, 8, ch. 9." There is no corresponding entry 8 for Lossky. This is likely ch. 9 of *The Mystical Theology of the Eastern Church* (Crestwood, N.Y.: St. Vladimir's Seminary Press, 1976).]

1. See Leo XIII, *Satis Cognitum*, Encyclical Letter, January 29, 1896; cited in *AAS* 28 (1896): 710.

there is the question concerning the way the Church makes Christ present to the world through her very being, through her existence as the Church. Then, there is the question concerning how she extends Christ's saving action to each generation and to each man in particular. Then we find ourselves faced with yet another question, namely, concerning the Church's holiness in relation to the faults that she cannot fail to commit, given her own limitations in comparison with the perfection of Christ whom she represents.

THE CHURCH, THE SACRAMENT OF CHRIST IN THE ORDER OF EXISTENCE

We will examine the theme concerning the structural analogy between Christ and the Church. This will help us to see whether it can enable us to understand more profoundly the mystery of the Church.

The Structure of Christ and the Structure of the Church

{651} At the foundation of this theme, we find the confluence of two elements in the Church (a confluence we have already considered), namely her visible and invisible elements. By means of an obvious analogy with, on the one hand, human beings and, on the other, with every human reality, the expression "the soul of the Church" is used to designate the invisible principle that vivifies her, whereas "the body of the Church" is used to designate her visible reality. Considering a similar duality in Christ (i.e., His two natures), one is led to compare this point of ecclesiology to this case in Christology. Is this legitimate?

Indeed, a lengthy tradition compares the union of the two natures in Christ with the union of soul and body, and it would seem that perhaps this could provide an explanation for the parallelism that we are investigating. In any case, we must first consider in general the comparison made between the two natures of Christ and the union of soul and body.

The Hypostatic Union and the union of soul and body

{652} This theme finds a particularly clear expression in the "Quicumque" Symbol [i.e., the Athanasian Creed]: "For just as the rational soul and flesh are together one man, so too God and man are one, Christ." Obviously, we must avoid understanding this formula in an Apollinarist sense. Indeed, in the text itself, this sense is expressly ruled out: "Perfect God and perfect man, man constituted by a rational soul and a human body."

The metaphor is not directly concerned with *the union*, which in the merely human case is *in natura* and in the case of the Hypostatic Union is *in persona*, but is concerned with *the result of the union*. The human person is a spiritual and bodily whole, composed of a "sensible nature" (i.e., a principle of action, the sense appetite) and a "spiritual nature,"* notwithstanding that this person is a single person. So too, analogically, the Person of the Incarnate Word is "composed" of two natures, the human nature and the Divine Nature, and yet, despite this, He is a single person. The difference lies in the mode of union. Man's two natures make up a single ontological nature, whereas the two natures of Christ do not together make up a single nature.

The fundamental difference between the two cases lies in the fact that there is only one human activity in man, integrating sensible and spiritual elements, whereas in Christ there are two activities, the divine activity and the human activity. However, despite this fundamental difference, we can say that there is a kind of analogy between the complexity of the human person and the complexity of the Person of the Incarnate Word.[2]

The twofold nature of Christ and the twofold nature of the Church

The Church certainly includes an internal and invisible element that assures her life and coherence, as well as an external element that situates her in the world, among the realities of this world. The terminology of *soul* and *body* has been used to describe this duality. It was approved, perhaps for the first time, by Bellarmine.[3] However,

---

* [Tr. note: I have altered the parenthetical structure here. The original French is perhaps corrupted. It reads, "composed of a 'sensible nature' (i.e., a principle of action, the sense appetite and a 'spiritual nature')." It does not make sense to include the mention of the spiritual nature in parentheses. Note also that the original text is missing a closing quotation mark, which hints at the likelihood of such a textual corruption.]

2. See §273 in the previous volume.
3. See Robert Bellarmine, *De Conciliis*, in *Roberti Bellarmini opera omnia*, vol. 2 (Naples:

we have also seen that this internal and invisible element is not only the invisible element that one finds in every human reality, for the Church's invisible element constitutes her as "the sacrament of Christ." Hence, must we not compare it to the divine element that makes Jesus Christ God?[4]

The Church's soul and the body

{653} This distinction formalizes the distinction studied above, namely the distinction between the Church's "society aspect" and her "communion aspect." Just as every human being includes two aspects or two "dimensions," one that is invisible (of which the spiritual soul is the principle) and another that is visible (whose distinct principle is the body), so too "ecclesial communion" exists (on the earth) only as realized and as expressed by the ecclesial society. Meanwhile, the latter is an ecclesial society distinct from every purely human society, only able to transcend them through the communion of which she is the sacrament. These are the two aspects or two "dimensions" of the one Church.[5] We must seek out the two distinct principles that make up this one Church. That is, we must seek out the principles from which these two dimensions proceed.

As regards the Church's "body," it is obviously made up of all the human beings who belong to the Church, of all the bonds of belonging and order that bind them together in the Church-society. Moreover, it is obviously composed of all the visible actions and achievements that this society produces in the world, by which she is established as an earthly and historical reality.

Therefore, the [Church's] soul will be the invisible principle that makes all these men and women live the Divine Life, making them into a single living being. In other words, it will be the invisible principle assuring the communion of all of them with the Trinity and with each other in Christ.

To constitute a single living being, each has become a living

---

Apud Josephum Giuliano, 1857), [bk.] 3, ch. 2. Heribert Mühlen, *L'Ésprit dans l'Église*, trans. Arthur Liefooghe, Marthe Massart, and René Virrion (Paris: Cerf, 1969), 15.

4. See Congar, *Sainte Église*, 69–104. Jean-Hervé Nicolas, "Le sens et la valeur en ecclésiologie du parallélisme de structure entre le Christ et l'Église," *Angelicum* 43 (1966): 353–58.

5. See §655 above.

being having this divinized life. Therefore, we must first consider this living individual and seek out that which is the principle of this new life in him. After this, we will ask how all these living beings are united so as to constitute a single, collective living being.

In order to truly become a living being having this divinized life,[6] the believer must have the source of this life in himself and in his depths (for life is defined as a *motus ab intrinseco*, a movement that pours forth from the living being itself and which is not impressed upon it from without). The source in question is created grace, as well as created charity, which is inseparable from grace. However, this life is the very life of God. Its source is found in God Himself. Not only is it the case that created grace (which is a participation in the Divine Nature, which is the proper source of the Divine Life) can only come from God and can only be caused in the created spirit by God. Moreover, it is also the case that it can be the source of Divine Life only in a subordinate manner, that is, by remaining in vital and continuous contact with its ultimate source.

Formally speaking, the action by which God causes created grace is the paternal love, the love by which God makes the free creature His child. This is why, even though it is produced by the three Persons together (as is the case for every Trinitarian action *ad extra*), it is appropriated to the Holy Spirit, who is personified love,[7] as is the divine action making the believer act in accord with the grace of adoption that he has received: "For you did not receive the spirit of slavery to fall back into fear, but you have received the spirit of sonship. When we cry, 'Abba! Father!'"[8]

However, there is much more than solely efficient causality [*efficience*] involved in this communication of the Divine Life. Rather, efficient causality intervenes as a prerequisite needed for assuring the reality of this communication. Indeed, it is quite necessary that the creature be really and profoundly changed by this love of God which makes him pass from the state of unrighteousness (i.e., spiritual death) to the state of righteousness (i.e., new life). For the adoptive filiation to be real, it is necessary that he who becomes a

---

6. This refers to the fourth section of the first volume of this course.
7. On appropriation, see §§191–99 in the first volume of this course.
8. Rom 8:15 (RSV).

son must be really changed in himself, and this is the role of created grace. However, what does this transformation consist in? It consists in the fact that through grace (and through the theological virtues that emanate from it, principally charity) the Trinity is rendered present to the created spirit.[9] Created grace is the means for the aforementioned living and permanent contact between the created spirit and the Divine Nature, which is the proper source of the Divine Life.[10]

In the Trinity, the Holy Spirit is the personified Divine Life (because He is personified Love, the expression of the infinite friendship that is the Trinitarian life).[11] Thus, this communication of the Divine Life to the created spirit is the communication of the Holy Spirit. It is a communication that makes the Father and Son present to the created spirit, the Holy Spirit proceeding from them without any separation. This is the invisible mission of the Holy Spirit.

Thus, the Holy Spirit is the fontal principle of the Divine Life in each "adoptive son." By appropriation, we attribute to Him the activity of causing created grace in the believer. However, this created grace in the believer is a source of Divine Life only because it places him in living and personal contact with the Father and the Son in the Holy Spirit.

Now, although the Church is the body of Christ, His spouse, she is not the mere gathering of the "adoptive sons" who compose her. Rather, she is a distinct being living through the Divine Life. What is the principle of this life in her? "What the soul is to the body of man, the Holy Spirit is to the body of Christ, the Church. The Holy Spirit does in the whole Church what the soul does in all the bodily members of a single body."[12]

An utterly traditional theme holds that the Holy Spirit is the soul of the Church. It may equally be explained by way of theological reflection. Indeed, if He is the principle of the Divine Life in each of the "justified," principally inasmuch as the believer, through created

---

9. See §217 in the first volume of this course.

10. On created grace, see Jean-Hervé Nicolas, *Les profondeurs de la grâce* (Paris: Beauchesne, 1969), 126–60; "Grâce et divinization," in *La Teologia morale nella storia e nella problematica attuale: miscellanea P. Louis Bertrand Gillon* ([Milan]: Massimo, 1982), 38–50.

11. See §150 in the first volume of this course.

12. St. Augustine, *Sermones*, PL 38, serm. 267, no. 4.

grace, is united to Him and in Him to the Father and to the Son, it is easy to see how He is the unifying principle of the Church. All the justified are "divinized" through their union with the same Spirit. Moreover, we can simultaneously see how He is their vivifying principle, for the Divine Life of which He is the unique and common principle in all the "righteous" is one for this reason, one and the same in all of them and in each.

Because of this common principle of the divinized life, it is possible to overcome the great difficulty that was encountered when one sought to rigorously develop the analogy of the soul and the body so as to theologically interpret the mystery of the Church. Indeed, in man, the soul unifies and vivifies a single living thing, the body. The parts of this body do not live for their own sake and are not distinct living beings. The same is not true in the case of the Church. She is made up of distinct living beings and nonetheless gathers them together into a single "body." On the one hand, they are bodily persons. On the other hand, the life by which each one of them lives is the Trinitarian life communicated to each of them by one and the same Holy Spirit.

This is also why it does not seem possible (despite the weighty authority of Cardinal Journet[13]) to speak of a "created soul of the Church," which would be created grace and created charity. Certainly, we must absolutely maintain that the Holy Spirit is the vivifying principle of the Church only by means of the created grace that He arouses in the men and women who compose the Church. Therefore, if He is the soul of the Church, it is not by being part of the Church, entering *ontologically* into composition with the "material cause" of the Church (i.e., either with the men and women who compose her or with the society in which they are externally and interiorly united, as is the case for the human soul that enters into composition with matter in order to form a living body). Rather, He causes this created grace in each of the "righteous." In other words, in and of itself, created grace is multiple, and in each of its realizations, it vivifies only this particular "righteous man." Therefore, it cannot be the unifying and vivifying principle of the Church. All

---

13. See Journet, *L'Église du Verbe incarné*, 2:534–79.

these individual graces (and therefore all the beings living by this Divine Life which these individual graces establish) are, of themselves, multiple, and the Holy Spirit makes a single life out of all these individual lives. From all these distinct living beings, He makes a living being in whom they are included without being merged together, namely, the Church.[14]

The co-extensive character of the Church's soul and body

{654} One[15] might be tempted to say that the soul could extend beyond the body (in order to embrace the "righteous who are outside," who according to a ruinous apologetic would belong to the soul of the Church and not to her body). Likewise and conversely, one may also be tempted to say that the body could extend beyond the soul (so as to embrace the sinners who are members of the visible Church without partaking in invisible communion, and who, according to the same apologetic, would be part of the Church's body without belonging to her soul). However, to assert such a theory leads one to empty the soul-body analogy of its meaning, destroying all of its explanatory value. Indeed, it is clear that in a human body every element that the soul informs is part of the body and that every element not informed by the soul is outside the body (even if it is externally connected to it).

Moreover, this would bring to ruin everything that we established above concerning the Church's sacramentality. It would imply that the portion of the Church's soul extending beyond the body would be an invisible Church. It would likewise imply that the portion of the body extending beyond the soul would be a purely visible Church, not referring to an invisible mystery. Therefore, we would be led to distinguish the visible from the invisible as two distinct Churches, no longer making such a distinction only with regard to two aspects or dimensions of the one Church.

Likewise, this perfect coincidence between the Church's body

---

14. See Jean-Hervé Nicolas, "Le Saint-Esprit principe de l'unité de l'Église," in *Credo in Spiritum sanctum: atti del Congresso teologico Internazionale di pneumatologia in occasione del 1600e anniversario del Concilio di Efeso, Roma, 22–26 marzo 1982* (Vatican City: Libreria editrice Vaticana, 1983), 1359–80.

15. See Journet, *L'Église du Verbe incarné*, 2:950–58.

and soul is a traditional conception, as can be seen in the following characteristic texts:

God's Spirit does not cease to pour faith into the Church as into a beautiful vase. It is there like a precious liquid ceaselessly and overflowingly rejuvenating the vase that contains it. It is a gift that God entrusts to the Church in order to inspire her and inform her, rendering her capable of vivifying all those who are her members. In her, that which Christ came to communicate is offered to us, namely the Holy Spirit, the pledge of incorruption, the support of our faith, and the cause of our ascent to God. Indeed, as the Apostle says,[16] God has arranged in the Church apostles, prophets, teachers, and also the whole of the Spirit's activity. No part in this activity is had by those who, instead of rushing to the Church, withdraw from her life foolishly through a fatal course of action. Indeed, where the Church is, the Spirit of God is present, and where the Spirit of God is present, there is the Church and all grace: the Spirit is truth. Those who do not participate in the Spirit are not given life-giving nourishment at the breasts of their mother and they do not know the pure fountain that flows forth from the body of Christ. They dig cracked cisterns and drink the foul water of cesspits and swamps. They flee from the Church's faith out of fear of being guided and reject the Spirit out of fear of being instructed.[17]

And St. Augustine:

What our spirit (i.e., our soul) is to our bodily members, the Holy Spirit is to the members of Christ, to the body of Christ, the Church. And this is why the Apostle, after having written, "There is only one body,"[18] does not allow us to believe that this body is dead.—Does this body live?—It lives?—By what?—By a single Spirit. Therefore, the Apostle adds, "And there is only one Spirit." My brothers, take care of the body that is ours and pity those who have removed themselves from the Church. If it is a question of our own bodily members, inasmuch as we live in good health, each member has its function. Inasmuch as this member is in the body, it can suffer. It cannot expire, for what does it mean to expire if not to be deprived of the spirit? However, if a member is removed from the body, does the spirit remain in it? Without a doubt, one still recognizes what this member is. It is a finger, a hand, an arm, an ear. When it is detached from the body, it retains its form, but it lacks life. This is what the man separated from the Church is like. One still finds in him the sacrament, baptism,

---

16. See 1 Cor 12:28.
17. St. Irenaeus of Lyon, *Contre les hérésies*, bk. 3, 24.1, in SC 34; bk. 4, SC 100 and 100bis; bk. 5, SC 152 and 153.
18. Eph 4:4.

and the apostolic symbol. Yes, behold the external form. It is in vain that he takes glory in it if he is not internally vivified by the Spirit.[19]

And again:

The Catholic Church alone is the body of Christ. Christ is her head and the Savior of His body. Outside this body, the Spirit vivifies nobody, for according to the Apostle, "God's love has been poured into our hearts through the Holy Spirit which has been given to us,"[20] and nobody participates in charity if he is the enemy of unity. Therefore, those who are outside the Church do not have the Holy Spirit. And those who seem to be in the Church no longer have Him either.[21]

However, how can we resolve the twofold problem concerning the fact that the "righteous on the outside" and "sinful members" belong to the Church? We will examine the reasons and conditions for such belonging later. From what we have said, it follows that, if they are part of the Church, they belong both to her soul and her body. But how?

Sinners, who continue to be part of the Church's body (i.e., of the Church-society), do not entirely cease to belong to her soul, even though they are no longer vivified by the Holy Spirit, given that they are deprived of grace and charity.[22] They still have supernatural gifts: sacramental characters, faith, and hope. These "gifts" do not suffice to assure that they have the vivifying presence of the Holy Spirit in them. Nonetheless, they are intrinsically ordered to grace, and through them, this member of the Church is ordered to the Holy Spirit, vitally connected to the body of Christ, which is traversed and animated by the sap of the Holy Spirit. If this sap does not reach them, this is because of their personal resistance. However, it is at the door, pressing upon them, and if the obstacle posed by this resistance is removed (something which will occur by the triumph of this very pressure), they will be pervaded with this sap.[23] Although the Holy Spirit is only virtually and not actually their

---

19. Augustine, *Sermones*, serm. 268, no. 2.
20. Rom 5:5 (RSV).
21. See St. Augustine, *Epistolae*, PL 33, ep. 185, no. 50.
22. See §697 below.
23. See *ST* III, q. 8, a. 3, co., and ad 2; q. 69, a. 10.

vivifying principle, He remains their unifying principle. By Him they are still united to the Church.

The "righteous on the outside" who, conversely, are vivified by the Holy Spirit without belonging to the Church-society, are part of the "Body of the Church," although imperfectly. Their belonging is imperfect first of all because this body is the "place of grace," so that through their grace (unbeknownst to them and despite whatever they may think about the Church in their clear awareness) they completely tend toward her and do so all the more intensely as their participation in her life, through the Holy Spirit, is more intense. Now, they are not "souls," but rather are spiritual-bodily human persons. Therefore, the life of grace existing in them is expressed and manifested through external acts and visible deeds. All this, to the degree that it is truly inspired by the charity that is found in them, by which they participate (without always willing it) in the vivifying action of the Holy Spirit in relation to the Church, belongs to the Church's "body."

However, we must recognize that this "bodily" dimension of their grace does not play the role of the *sacramentum tantum* that we recognized in the case of the Church's "body" (or does so only in an obscure way), for it does not clearly refer to the mystery of communion realized in the Church. In the case of non-Christians, this "bodily" dimension cannot refer to Christ explicitly. One could say that for them, in contrast to the preceding case, the Holy Spirit, who fully performs His role as the vivifier, here only imperfectly performs His role as unifier. Obviously, this is not because of a deficiency on His part, nor, as in the preceding case, through a (culpable) resistance on theirs. Rather, it is on account of obstacles that are independent of their will, separating them from full Catholic unity, in which they nonetheless take part tendentially, "by a kind of desire and unconscious wish," as is said in Pius XII's encyclical *Mystici Corporis*. Thus, instead of saying, "they are only part of the Invisible Church," we must say: *They are invisibly part of the One Church which is at once visible and invisible.*[24]

---

24. See Jean-Hervé Nicolas, "L'appartenance à l'Église selon la théologie catholique," 156–61.

The Church, the prolongation of Christ's humanity over the earth

{655} Hence, what are we to make of the parallel that some have wished to draw between the "structure" of Christ (a Person "composed" of a divine, invisible nature and a visible, human nature) and that of the Church?

Christ is one through the union of two natures, and He is one in both of them. In the same way, His mystical body is the true Church only on the condition that her visible parts draw their power and life from the supernatural gifts and other invisible elements. It is from this union that the proper nature of the invisible parts themselves result.[25]

We must first observe that human nature, in Christ as in ourselves, is not only visible. It includes an invisible element (indeed, as its principal element). It is the soul and the properly spiritual life which the body expresses, manifests, and refers to. On the other hand, how is Christ "one"? He is a single Person in two natures that are not mixed together. How is the Church one? As we will see, she is one as a Person. (Indeed, this is already implied by what we said concerning the image of the spouse and the image of the body.) However, can we say that this Person is one in two natures? We have seen, on the contrary, that the two constitutive elements of the Church are related as body and soul. That is, they are related as constituting a single nature. This is not at all akin to the use of this analogy for interpreting the Hypostatic Union,[26] for the Divine Nature does not inform [Christ's] human nature, thus constituting a composite with it. The "communion" created by the Holy Spirit (in the way explained above) is immanent within the Church-Society, composing with her a single "body of Christ, which is the Church."

Moreover, Jesus' humanity is also the dwelling place of the Holy Spirit, who arouses created grace and charity in it. It is a

---

25. Leo XIII, *Satis cognitum* in Texts, *AAS* 28:710. [Tr. note: I have taken this from the French because of the reference there regarding the "invisible parts" fitting Fr. Nicolas's discussion. The official English translation reads: "[Christ] is one, from and in both natures, visible and invisible; so the mystical body of Christ is the true Church, only because its visible parts draw life and power from the supernatural gifts and other things whence spring their very nature and essence."]

26. See §652 above.

supernaturalized nature, from which and in which, as we have seen, the Church herself is also supernaturalized, divinized by the gift of the Spirit.[27]

Consequently, the Church's structure must be compared to the structure of Christ's humanity, assumed and divinized by grace, and not to the structure of the Incarnate Word.

If the Church prolongs the Incarnation in the world, this cannot be interpreted as being a kind of new Incarnation (as could be suggested by the idea that she reproduces the structure of the Incarnate Word). No more can it be interpreted as meaning that the assumed humanity would be augmented by the humanity of the redeemed and, gradually, by the entire universe (in a Teilhardian sense). This is so because the Incarnation was accomplished once and for all, and if *development* did take place in the Incarnation during Jesus' earthly life, this is because the assumed humanity developed in accord with Jesus' individual destiny through the growth of His body and soul, up to consummation in glory. Instead, this prolongation must be understood as meaning that, although perfectly conformed to Him according to His humanity and nonetheless distinct from Him (being visible and part of historical, worldly realities), the Church makes visible His presence and salvific activity, which has become invisible from the time of the ascension onward.

To say that she is distinct from Him means that she is a different Person, though she is one with Him in faith by love. In what does this personality of the Church consist?

The Personality of the Church

{656} It[28] is *de fide* that all believers together constitute a new man in Christ. Each retains his personality, and nonetheless, all these personalities constitute a collective personality. This means that the

---

27. See §340 in the second volume of this course.
28. See Bouyer, *L'Eglise de Dieu*, 601–6. See also Congar, *Sainte Église*, 69–104; "La Personne-Eglise," *Revue thomiste* 71 (1971): 613–40; "La croix de Jésus, du P. Chardon," *Vie Spiritualle, Supplément* 51 (1937): 42–57. François Florand, "Introduction" in Louis Chardon, *La croix de Jésus* (Paris: Cerf, 1937), lxxv–lxxxv. Journet, *L'Église du Verbe incarné*, 2:187–228. Jacques Maritain, *L'Église du Christ, la personne de l'Église et son personnel* (Paris: Desclée de Brouwer, 1970). Heribert Mühlen, *L'Éspirit dans l'Église*, trans. Arthur Liefooghe, Marthe Massart, and René Virrion (Paris: Cerf, 1969). Nicolas, *Les profondeurs de la grâce*, 306–80.

Church involves a shared personality and subsistence. It is called "mystical" in the sense specified above, namely, mysterious and supernatural.

On the other hand, it is *de fide* that this shared personality is related both to Christ's personality (as believers are "one in Christ") and to the Holy Spirit's personality (as this unity is His work).

The problem and various solutions

A first solution: Christ, the hypostasis of His Mystical Body

This is the solution presented by Cajetan as well as by various ancient theologians, taken up and vigorously exposited by Louis Chardon.[29]

The fundamental criticism registered against this doctrine is that it does not preserve the personal distinction between the Church and Christ.

From the ecclesiological perspective, it renders irresolvable the question of faults, errors, and even omissions committed in the name of the Church. The only way that it can resolve this issue is by saying that every time that there is an error or fault the Church is not the one acting. However, this would lead directly to the notion of a [solely] invisible Church.

A second solution: The Holy Spirit, the hypostasis of the Church

This is Mühlen's solution. It is connected with the opinions of Petavius and those who follow him concerning the particular union of each of the righteous with the Person of the Holy Spirit. It runs into the difficulty already noted above with regard to the created soul of the Church: in short, the Holy Spirit is not a constitutive part* of the Church. Also, were one to push this position to its logical conclusion, it would lead one to abolish the Church's distinct personality.

Moreover, this way of simultaneously saying that the Holy Spirit is the Church's soul and her personality would curiously tend to reduce the Church's personality to her soul.

---

29. See Florand, "Introduction," lxxv–lxxxv. In the opposite direction, see Congar, "La croix de Jésus, du P. Chardon," 42–57; also, Nicolas, *Les profondeurs de la grâce*, 306–80.

* [Tr. note: That is, as a quasi-metaphysical constitutive, like the intrinsic form-soul in relation to the body.]

A third solution: The Holy Spirit, the extrinsic personality of the Church

This is Journet's position.[30] Through His activity, the Holy Spirit unifies, vivifies, and leads the Church. In this sense, He causes her personality, her unity of life and action. However, can we hold that "to cause a personality" is the same thing as "to be that personality"? The expression "extrinsic personality" is odd, for nothing is as immanent as personality.

Indeed, the most penetrating and most completely accepted divine motion (as was the case for the Virgin Mary) does not suffice for making God the *quod est et quod operatur* (i.e., the principle of attribution for actions and passions when He moves the created person).

A fourth solution: The Church has a created ontological personality

This is the solution proposed and developed by Jacques Maritain,[31] and it is the illuminating and organizing principle of his ecclesiology. For him, the Church is a Person in the metaphysical sense of the word, having a proper "subsistence" distinct from that of her members:

> The Church has a twofold subsistence. One is a natural subsistence like every human community (that of the human persons who are her members). If all Christians were killed off, there would no longer be a Church here-below. On the other hand, inasmuch as she is the unified and universal whole made up of the organized multitude of those who live by her life, she has a supernatural subsistence. The latter presupposes but transcends the natural subsistence of the individual persons who are her members.[32]

However profound and essential the differences between the two cases may be, she is a (common or collective) person just as Peter or Paul is (an individual) person.[33]

The individuality of the image of Christ borne by the Church is analogous to the individuality of the substantial nature possessed by each of us. And just as, in calling Peter or Paul into existence, God confers to a given individual nature the subsistence that constitutes it as a subject or a person, so too in calling His Son's Church into existence, God confers on her,

---

30. See Journet, *L'Église du Verbe incarné*, 2:187–228.
31. Maritain, *L'Église du Christ*.
32. Ibid., 39.
33. Ibid., 40.

through this image that He sees in her, a subsistence that constitutes an entire multitude of human beings into a subject or a person.[34]

Reflecting on the apparently irreconcilable conceptual conflict involved in this conception, Maritain sees this as being the mark of the mystery. Such a conflict exists for the Trinity too, as well as for the Incarnation. This mysterious character comes from the fact that these objects are transcendent by their very essence.[35]

A very important point must be noted. The Person of the Church thus conceived embraces the heavenly Church (the mother of God and the elect) as much as (and indeed more than) believers living on the earth. This is what Maritain calls the Church in her integral fullness:

> The ontological personality of the Church—a supernatural personality received on account of the image of Christ that the Church bears within herself—knows no interruption. The person of the Church is one and the same person, in the wayfaring state here-below and in the state of eternal glory [in heaven].[36]
>
> And, on the last day ... this duality of states will come to an end. The heavenly Jerusalem will descend to earth, souls will rejoin their resurrected bodies, and to the immense multitude of the resurrected there will be reunited the small flock of witnesses to the faith still alive on earth, who will pass into glory without having experienced death.[37]

Maritain draws significant consequences from this. This Church-Person expresses herself through her members who constitute the hierarchy (the pope speaking *ex cathedra* and the bishops with the pope gathered in a council) when a truth of faith is infallibly proclaimed. Thus,

> it is the person of the Church who proposes the truths of the faith to us. It is the person of the Church who is constantly assisted by Christ and the Holy Spirit.[38]

The assistance of the Spirit and the authority of Christ thus pass through the person of the Church, herself speaking to us through the

---

34. Ibid., 43–44.
35. See ibid., 44.
36. Ibid., 88.
37. Ibid., 94.
38. Ibid., 45.

Christ's Presence to the World through the Church

instrumentality of those of her members who have the mission of teaching us.[39]

And this Church-Person is absolutely and completely infallible, "since she is fixed in the beatific vision and since the teaching that is given by her is an illumination of spirit to spirit in God's light."[40]

However, what is the relationship between the personality of the members of the Church and the personality of the Church? Maritain employs the notion of "investing":

> (The Church's) personality is the supernatural personality that is conferred upon her on account of the image of Christ impressed upon her. It seals her soul and the organism with the multiple joints designated as being her body with a unity as perfect as though they formed a single individual substance. It invests each of her members to the same degree that Christ's grace vivifies the being and action of the body, whereas everything that is related to evil and sin withdraws itself from this supernatural personality. The frontier of the Church's personality passes through the heart of each person.[41]

Cardinal Journet presented this solution in a very seductive manner and made it his own, though it is quite different from what he himself had retained.[42] On the contrary, while Fr. Congar presents it sympathetically,[43] he does not fail to critique it. Indeed, it is quite susceptible to critique and can by no means be retained, even if with this intrinsically defective key Maritain manages to open up interesting perspectives in his book. By using the concept of "subsistence" in all of its metaphysical rigor, he places us before a conceptual conflict which appears to be unquestionably contradictory, for what is proper to "subsistence" is the fact that it renders incommunicable the nature that it brings to completion. That is, it constitutes a concrete subject, a being, in which this nature is realized, a subject which is really distinct from every other concrete object [sic] and every other being.

---

39. Ibid., 95.
40. Ibid., 94.
41. Ibid., 67.
42. See Charles Journet, "La sainteté de l'Église: le livre de Jacques Maritain," *Nova et Vetera* 46 (1971): 1–33.
43. See Yves Congar, "La Personne-Église," *Revue thomiste* 71 (1971): 633–34.

Now, he likewise tells us that this Church-Person "invests" the human persons who compose it. Therefore, she communicates herself to them! The idea of a Person who is ontologically subsistent and multitudinous (therefore embracing, without absorbing, a multitude of persons) is contradictory. The danger is that one will situate this Person-Church outside the particular persons making up the Church. Indeed, this is what the expression "the 'Person' of the Church" suggests, as well as the idea of an instrumental action that the Church-Person would exercise on the person of the pope or that of the bishop. But, then, where does this person exist? Through such a magnification of the Church, does one not tend to relegate her to a perfect but unreal Platonic heaven? And how are these persons (the "personnel") part of the Church?

A proposed solution

The personality of Christ is the exemplar, formal principle
of the Church's personality

{657} The Church's personality is made up of all the personalities that compose her. She draws from them her ontological reality, as well as her distinction from Christ's Person.

How do all these various personalities together constitute one person? Obviously, it cannot be according to their natural being, for this would only be a moral and juridical person. Instead, it must be according to their grace-being [*être de grace*], for it is on account of their grace-being and to its measure that they belong to the Church and constitute her.

This grace-being properly and distinctly belongs to each person. Each person within the single Christian vocation has his particular vocation. Each person receives the one Spirit in a way that is proper to him. However, through his grace-being, each person is ordered to Christ as to his exemplar. Each person is conformed to Christ, the holy One of God, to Him in whom grace-being is realized in an absolute manner. Thus, every grace given to men is a participation in His grace.[44]

In the order of grace, without ceasing to be himself, the person of

---

44. See §340 in the second volume of this course.

the Christian thus really takes on the Person of Christ. The Christian passes into Him all the more completely as he is penetrated by grace, and when he reaches the consummation of his state of grace, he will have wholly taken on Christ. Similarly, all the redeemed are found in Christ as "one," while remaining distinct, each one preserving his particular personality and his own grace-being, for they are all together conformed to the same Christ. They are totally conformed to him in what concerns them (i.e., according to their whole person). However, they are only partially conformed to Him in what concerns Christ, for they will only ever imperfectly resemble Him, only partially reproducing His infinite perfection. We can compare this to the unity of the universe, composed of beings that are different inasmuch as they are beings, though united in the fact that each one, according to everything that it is, imitates the infinite and simple Being.

The Church's personality is constituted by the ensemble of the personalities of the redeemed inasmuch as they are one through each person's conformity to Christ. She herself is one, single person with Christ (*una persona mystica*, in the words of St. Thomas[45]) because, on account of their union with Christ (an intentional union of knowledge and love) all these persons constitute *one single man in Christ*.

In other words, the unity of this personality is dynamic, not static. (Therefore, it is not analogous to "subsistence.") It does not belong to the order of being but rather belongs to the order of the good. (The ontological support without which the good would be real is furnished by the human persons who make up this personality, and the unifying principle is the Person of Jesus Christ, the ultimate goal of the activity by which all these distinct persons strive to conform themselves to Him.) Here we see the difference between this position and that of Jacques Maritain.

Thus, Christ's Person is the principle of the Church's unity. He is a transcendent principle, not an immanent one, for the latter would destroy the proper personality of the redeemed persons. Christ's Person is distinct from the unity that He procures, procuring it by

---

45. See *ST* III, q. 19, a. 4; q. 48, a. 1; q. 49, a. 1.

the foundational tendency of all the parts toward Him. Thus, He is not a purely external principle. Instead, He is an interior principle in the sense that He is rendered present to all the parts and to the whole by this very tendency.

Understood in this way, the Person of the Church is at once distinct from that of Christ and united to His Person (*spiritualiter conjuncta*, says St. Thomas[46]), like the person of a wife in relation to the person of her husband.

The personality of the Holy Spirit is the source of the
Church's personality

{658} In no way does this minimize the role of the Holy Spirit. The grace and charity by which Christians are conformed to Christ about have their source in Him. Thus, He is indeed the one who unifies the Church and vivifies her. However, this life is that of Christ. This unity is taken in relation to Him.

The realism of this solution

{659} The ordering of a person to his end is eminently real, given that the person finds his fulfillment by attaining his end. Consequently, the communion of many persons in the same end, pursued together and possessed together, is eminently real.

This communion is neither substantial nor accidental, for these categories are useful only on the level of being (i.e., of first act). This communion is operative and dynamic, uniting the persons (who are distinct as regards their being) inasmuch as they are principles and focal points of spiritual life. There are many living beings but only one life.

The Person of the Church exists concretely (though partially) in each of the persons who are part of the Church, inasmuch as they are part of her (i.e., inasmuch as they personally participate in the communion having the Holy Spirit as its principle). In another way, which we will need to specify and examine, the Church-Person exists in those of her members who are authorized to act concretely in her name through some determinate action. Moreover, she exists in

---

46. *In IV Sent.*, d. 49, q. 4, a. 3, ad 3.

Christ's Presence to the World through the Church 81

the united whole of her members because she exists only inasmuch as the communion or society is (actually) concretized in it.

Therefore, we cannot speak of an instrumental activity exercised by a person who is a member of the Church, performed by the Church-Person, with the latter making use of the former, for each time that the former acts on behalf of the Church, that person is identified with her, though only for this action.

The Church exists only as Christ's spouse

{660} Let us register one final specification. The Church is not a this-worldly reality which Christ would have chosen and taken as His spouse. Prior to his or her calling and conversion, the human person indeed exists, though not as a member of the Church (except virtually, on account of the primordial inclusion of all humanity in Christ[47]) so that Christ, by purifying His spouse,[48] makes her exist. He makes her exist from Himself, as Eve, in the Genesis narrative, is made from Adam.

CHRIST'S CONTINUATION IN THE ORDER OF ACTION BY THE CHURCH

Having returned to the Father, Christ does not cease to be the world's Savior, indeed its only Savior. Just as He continues to be invisibly present to the world by means of the Church, so too through her does He exercise His saving action upon it until the end of time.

In this too, the Church is the sacrament of Christ. She acts in a real manner, through an action that is her own. However, this visible action bears in itself the invisible action of Christ, of which the visible action is the sign and the means, doing so through intricate relations, which we must now attempt to analyze.

Preliminary Distinctions

In this activity exercised by the Church, we must distinguish the following: immanent activities (the theological and moral virtues,

---

47. See §§434–35 in the second volume of this course.
48. See Eph 5:25–28.

prayers, sufferings, and so forth); and external activities (which produce an external effect), which in turn are distinguished into sacramental activities and juridical activities.

The Person of Christ and the Immanent Activities of the Church

{661} Grace is the principle of these activities. Grace comes from the Holy Spirit and conforms the redeemed person to Christ, making him one person with Him (i.e., according to an intentional manner of being). Therefore, the activities of grace are at once from Christ and from the human person, as from two ontologically distinct persons who, nonetheless, are spiritually united through mutual knowledge and love.

Now, in the case of an individual human person [*une personne privée*], it is clear that all his activities do not proceed from grace. Moreover, when some activity does proceed from grace, it finds itself mixed together with many remnants coming from "the old man." It is only to the degree that such a person acts in accord with grace that his activity comes forth from him as united with Christ. Therefore, it also is only to the degree that he acts in accord with grace that this action comes forth from Christ. Christ loves God, praises Him, and so forth, with him and in him.

Now, in the case of the Church, given that the redeemed person is part of her only according to his grace-being, we must equally say that such a person's activity involves the Church only to the degree that this activity proceeds from grace. That is, while sin introduces (even into the believer's spiritual activity) a disjunction between him and Christ, to whom he is imperfectly united, such a disjunction does not exist for the Church.

Therefore, we can say that for all of her spiritual activity, the Church acts only inasmuch as she is united to Christ, constituting *una persona mystica* with him. Through this activity (and its external manifestations), she prolongs Christ's activity throughout the world and throughout history, communicating His love for the Father and for man, His prayer and His sacrifice.

However, who exercises this activity? Obviously, members of the

Church, individually and collectively. However, they do so only to the degree that their action comes from the Holy Spirit.

The Person of Christ and the External Activities of the Church

{622} Here, I adopt the bipartite division of the Church's powers, a division that was defended by Journet[49] and critiqued by Congar.[50] However, against Journet, I recognize Congar's distinction between the Church's power in the speculative order and her power in the practical order as being an essential distinction. Conversely, with Journet, I hold that the distinction between the power that is infallibly assisted and that which is only prudentially assisted is an accidental distinction.

Christ and the Church's sacramental activities

{663} The act of conferring a sacrament (i.e., the sacramental action inasmuch as it is a moral action performed by her minister or ministers), considered in its morality, belongs to the Church's immanent activities. It can be holy, mixed, or sinful. In this regard, it engages Christ and the Church only to the degree that it is holy.

This same action, considered as commanded and ruled by the Church, belongs to her juridical power. The Church is engaged in it only to the degree that the act is obediently performed in communion with her. Christ is engaged in it to the degree that He is engaged in the juridical acts of the Church. (See our discussion of this topic below.)

It is only when we consider the act in its immediate signification and its efficacy that it is grasped an act of Christ acting instrumentally by means of His Church, being represented by the minister. It is an act of Christ's power and also of His love inasmuch as it is the concrete realization of Christ's will instituting the sacraments out of His love for man. This is all the more the case inasmuch as the sacrament always signifies the mystery of Christ suffering, death, and

---

49. See Journet, *L'Église du Verbe incarné*, 1:173–216.
50. Congar, *Sainte Église*, 492, 567–70, 621–22. Also, see the discussion in Journet, "Controverse avec Congar," 308.

resurrection for the salvation of men (no matter how perverse the intentions of those who perform the sacramental action might be).

However, we must say that the Church (through her minister) acts here as a distinct Person (instrumentally used by Christ's Person) because the sacramental action (as we will later see more fully) is necessarily a human act and, therefore, a personal act—in other words, because the minister is a living [*animé*] instrument, indeed animated by an intellectual soul. However, she does not act "inasmuch as she is a distinct person," for her personal activity in no way modifies the signification and efficacy of the sacramental action. She brings Christ's action into existence.

Here, the Church's sacramentality comes fully into play. (In relation to the sacraments, she is the original sacrament, the *Ursakrament*.) However, this is so only at the price of the total effacement (though not, however, the abolition) of her personality.

Christ and the Church's juridical activities

Here, the Church acts as a secondary cause.

With Journet, I distinguish *Magisterial power* from *canonical power*. The Church's Magisterial power is the power to speak the truth in the entire domain of revealed truth. Therefore, it is the power of saying what is in conformity with divine revelation (i.e., that which is absolutely true and is the object of faith). The Church's *canonical power* is her power to authoritatively prescribe what must be done (or not done) in order to act in accord with the revealed truth (i.e., so as "to do the truth").[51]

Christ and the Church's Magisterial actions

{664} Through her Magisterial actions, the Church determines what is true and must be believed because it has been revealed by Christ.[52]

She does this not by means of a new revelation but, rather, by

---

51. See Jn 3:21.
52. On the Magisterium and its exercise, see Bouyer, *L'Eglise de Dieu*, 401–48. "Études et recherches de Foi et Constitution," *Istina* 23 (1978): 5–55. Congar, *La Tradition et les traditions*, 2:137–82. Charles Journet, *Le message révélé, sa transmission, son développement, ses dépendances* (Paris: Desclée de Brouwer, 1963). Edmund Schlink, "Écriture, tradition et magistère dans la constitution Dei Verbum," in *Vatican II, la Révélation divine* (Paris: Cerf, 1968), 499–511. Hans Küng, *Infaillible? Un interpretation*, trans. Henri Rochais (Paris: Desclée de Brouwer, 1971).

further explicating the tradition which is, as it were, her supernatural memory, the Word of God living in her from her beginnings. Certainly, Scripture spoke this Word, though not as a dead letter that would be external to the Church. Rather, this Word has been spoken as expressing the doctrine that she receives and that lives in her.

Obviously, she does this with the particular assistance of the Holy Spirit. This assistance assures her infallibility with regard to her orientation (her forward march toward the kingdom), though it leaves a margin for possible error with regard to the particular object of this decision, in a non-necessary matter, without the fundamental orientation being able to be compromised.

In both cases, the Church acts as a person. That is, those who have power to act in her name and through her authority do so with their intellect and its limitations, nay even its deviations, as well as with their heart and their character. In a necessary matter, we are assured that the that the Church is not deceived in defining a given doctrine, in imposing a given line of conduct as being required for fidelity to Christ. However, it is not at all certain that the formulas chosen would be the best possible. (Moreover, there is no such thing as a "best possible formula.") Nor is it at all certain that it was opportune to define this particular thing when it was defined, in the context when it was defined. Nor is it at all certain that at each moment of her history the Church (even in a necessary matter) would make the decisions that it would be good for her to make. The human persons who at this moment exercise the Church's authority intervene in the preparation, choice, and ultimate determination of the decision. The Holy Spirit's assistance prevents them from erring, but it does not substitute for their own judgment, which is their own work and bears the mark of their personality, with both its positive qualities as well as its defects, its values and its limitations. In a necessary matter, the very determination can be tainted by error, though in such a way that the Church's orientation toward the kingdom would not be called into question (and consequently in such a way that in accepting it and submitting themselves to it, the People of God do not depart from the path leading to life).

Jean-Hervé Nicolas, "Liberté du théologien et authorité du magistère," *Freiburger Zeitschrift für Philosophie und Theologie* 21 (1974): 139–58.

In order to obey, one does not need to be certain that the superior is not deceived. Rather, one must only be sure that his potential, contingent error does not touch upon what is essential to the Christian message.

Thus, in the exercise of her Magisterial power, the Church speaks in her own name, making the voice of the bride heard. However, it is also the voice of Christ, given that she speaks in Christ's name and by His authority and that the foundational rectitude of the determination (as well as its obligatory character for salvation) emanates from Christ, through His Spirit. Whatever is erroneous or lacking in it does not come from Him but, rather, from human freedom and limitations.

Christ and the Church's canonical activities

{665} Here, we are concerned with the acts by which the Church organizes the Christian life on earth, prescribing or forbidding this or that act for believers, as well as establishing punishments. They are subject to the virtue of prudence, which is itself dependent on the right willing of the Church's end, namely, the establishment and preparation (in faith) for the coming (in glory) of the kingdom of God in Christ.

In these actions we must also say that the Church is assisted by Christ's Spirit in such a way that she does not lead the People of God to turn aside from the ultimate end through the exercise of her authority. Likewise, she is assisted in such a manner that the forward progress (at least of the whole of the People of God) would be assured in what is essential to it.

The more that the prescription touches upon a contingent matter, to that degree it is more distant from this assistance. To say that one obeys Christ when one obeys the Church does not mean that this decision emanates from Christ and that He is the one who wills this. Instead, it means that the Church, who prescribes this decision, receives her authority from Him and that He wills that the believer obeys it if all the conditions of obligation are realized. If, as often happens (and as cannot fail to happen), a new superior reverses his predecessor's decision, the decision obviously ceases to obligate, without this meaning that Christ would have changed.

[This can be summarized schematically as follows:]

Christ's Presence to the World through the Church

Figure 1. Christ and the Church's Actions

The various manners in which Christ is personally engaged in the Church's actions

THE CHURCH ACTS …

By her immanent acts (Faith, Hope, Charity, Religion, and also the extrenal manifestations of this activity, e.g., Prayer, Profession of faith, Works of charity, and so forth)			▶	*As a distinct person, indefectibly united to Jesus Christ*
	Sacramental activities (Participation in Christ's priesthood through the power of Orders)		▶	*As a distinct person* (instrumentum animatum anima rationali), *but not precisely inasmuch as she is a distinct person*
By her external activities		*Magisterium* (So as to speak the truth in the domain of Revelation with authority. This is formally addressed to the speculative intellect.)	*Inasmuch as she is a distinct person*	*In a necessary matter* (formally revealed truth or an immediately application of it): she is indefectibly united to Christ by infallible assistance
	Jurisdictional activities (Participation in Christ's illuminative role)	*Canonical power* (To command what is to be done on account of the requirements of revealed truth. This is formally addressed to the practical intellect.)		*In a contingent matter* (truths or practices that are more or less implied by Revelation): she can be dissociated from Christ with regard to the object of the act but not with regard to its tendency toward the ultimate end

THE CHURCH'S HOLINESS AND HER FAULTS

{666} In this matter, we are faced with an extremely complex problem. The most ancient tradition expresses the idea that the Church is holy. It is condensed into the formula, "Credo ... Sanctam ecclesiam," which is found in the most ancient of Creedal symbols of the faith (e.g., see the first ten entries in Denzinger), taking their origin from the well-known text of Ephesians 5:27 (RSV): "... that he might present the church to himself in splendor, without spot or wrinkle or any such thing, that she might be holy and without blemish."

On the other hand, one can object not only that many sins are committed by the members of the Church (all are sinners) but also that many acts performed by the official representatives of the Church, acting precisely in their authoritative capacities and certainly involving the Church, can be critiqued, or even blameworthy and incompatible with the idea that the Church, if she is indeed responsible for these acts, is holy. However, how could she not be responsible for them? The Church presents herself as being penitent and weeping for her sins. Therefore, must we say that the Church is sinful? However, how could she be sinful if she is the "holy Church of Jesus Christ?"

The State of the Question

A summary history of the problem

{667} According[53] to Scripture, it is clear that there is a fundamental difference between the first People of God, Israel, and the new People of God, the Church. Israel is a sinful people who departs from God, returns to Him, excites His anger, and obtains His pardon. The Church herself is never the object of God's wrath. She does not turn away from God.

According to the Fathers, the Church purified by Christ, receiving all her light from Him, is holy. However, she is made up of sinners, and her members continue to sin. It is here that we find an

---

53. See Hans Urs von Balthasar, *Sponsa Verbi* (Einsiedeln: Johannes Verlag, 1960); Yves Congar, *Vraie et fausse réforme dans l'Église* (Paris: Cerf, 1969), 71–89; Journet, *L'Église du Verbe incarné*, 2:1115–29; Tromp, *Corpus Christi quod est Ecclesia*, 102–66.

ambiguity. St. Ambrose wrote, "Ex maculatis immaculata," made up of those who are unclean, though herself spotless, and seeing in Mary Magdalen the type of the Church. He said that in her the Church took on the externals of a sinner, as Christ Himself took on the external appearances of sinful man.[54] However, he also said that the Church must do penance and touch the fringe of Christ's cloak so as to be cleansed: "behold the Church who confesses her wounds and desires to be cleansed."[55] Only, the Church is wounded in us, not in herself.[56]

Another hesitation bears on the question of knowing whether the Church's holiness is a present reality or one that is eschatological. This is especially marked in this retraction written by St. Augustine:

Each time that I have recalled in my books the idea that the Church has neither spot nor wrinkle, one must not think that she already exists in that way, but that she is currently prepared to be so when she will appear in her glory. Currently, on account of her members' particular forms of ignorance and weaknesses, she must say each day, "Forgive us our debts."[57]

However, the Fathers are visibly loathe to say that the Church herself is sinful. They hesitate only to call her holy and nothing more, on account of the sinners who are in her, on account of the penance they attributed to her formally, and also on account of the fact that the Church, from one perspective, is in the midst of making herself (or of being made) and therefore on the way toward holiness rather than having reached the consummation of holiness.

In the medieval theologians, we can find a very strong tendency to accentuate the Church's note of holiness by minimizing sinners' belonging to the Church, as well as the responsibility of the Church as such in these sins. This tendency, having become aberrant, will come to find its exaggerated form in the position of the reformers saying that the Church is made up only of those who are justified or even only of the predestined. This gave rise to the quite sensible reaction that occurred among the theologians of the Counter-Reformation. There would then be a tendency to exclude sinners from the Church

---

54. Congar, *Vraie et fausse réforme dans l'Église*, 79–80.
55. *De Poenitentia*. [sic]
56. See *De Virginitate*. These two texts are cited in Journet, *L'église du verbe incarné*, 2:1116.
57. St. Augustine, *Retractions* (*Les Révisions*), OESA 12 (Turnhout: Brepols, 1964), 18.

on account of their sins. They retorted by including sinners with their sins in the Church, which has the consequence of having their sins affect the Church herself.

Solutions proposed by various contemporary theologians

The Church is simultaneously holy and sinful

{668} The[58] Church is sinful, but she simultaneously is holy. By so expressing the matter, one wishes to overcome the enormous difficulty experienced in affirming the Church's perfect holiness as soon as, on the one hand, one maintains the identification of the Catholic Church and the Church of Christ, and on the other hand, one is led to recognize the historical faults of the Catholic Church (as well as the scandals that besmirch her through the course of history and in every age). To this is added a concern for authenticity. Is not the distinction between the Church and her members a form of subterfuge?

Moreover, one merely poses the problem and does not furnish a solution when it is said that the Church is sinful, immediately saying thereafter that she is still holy.

The Church of sinners

{669} According to Bouyer, Scripture presents the Church as being the fiancé of Christ,[59] whereas the nuptials of the Lamb are situated at the end of history.[60] This would mean that, "to the extent of our faults, our infidelities, our failures, the Church remains a Church of sinners, doubtlessly on the way toward sanctification, but far from fully having it and definitely attaining it."[61]

Obviously, he is not unaware of the image of the spouse,[62] but he evokes it solely in order to emphasize the personal distinction between Christ and the Church.[63]

---

58. See Bouyer, *L'Eglise de Dieu*, pt. 2, ch. 11. Küng, *L'Église*, 449–82. Karl Rahner, "Le péché dans l'Église," *L'Eglise de Vatican II* (Paris: Cerf, 1966), 373–94, and "Die Kirche der Sünder," *Stimmen der Zeit* 140 (1947): 163–77.
59. See 2 Cor 11:2.
60. See Rv 21 and 22.
61. Bouyer, *L'Eglise de Dieu*, 607.
62. See Eph 5:22.
63. See Bouyer, *L'Eglise de Dieu*, 198.

Nonetheless, he refuses to apply to the Church Luther's expression "Simul peccator et Justus," simultaneously a sinner and just.[64] First of all, he contests that this expression is justly applied to the individual Christian. Despite all the individual Christian's sins and the evil that exists in him, Christ is the one who is established at the deepest roots of his being, at least so long as he has not lost faith, whereas the sinner who no longer is touched by salvation is already under the rule of the spirit of evil. Moreover, he notes a capital difference between the individual and the Church, although, according to him, "Everything that we just said holds for each Christian must indeed be understood as applying to the whole of the Church."

This difference consists in the fact that the Church is "indefectible" and is assured of arriving at eternal life: "Here, we find that not only the human element, but also our humanity inasmuch as it is fallen, even though it is still in the process of being raised up to the incorruptible humanity of Christ, already participates, in some way, if not in His inability to sin, at least in His victory over sin."* Consequently, at the end of his highly interesting analyses, he refrains from saying that the Church is sinful, although

she nonetheless remains (and will remain), up to the last day, stained by the numberless sins of her ministers and her faithful, indeed, betrayed by the ever-possible defection not only of her individual members taken individually but also that of all the particular Churches taken individually, outside of which she nonetheless does not have any existence.[65]

This reticence should be noted, for if he truly thought that the Church as such is stained by the sins of her members, what would prevent him from saying that she is sinful? Do we not say that a Christian is a sinner if he is stained by sin, even if we must say at the same time that He is a saint and is divinized by grace?

We must also critically analyze the notion of "indefectibility" as it is utilized here. What is in question is the certitude that we can have that the Church will not be entirely lost and that she is assured of her eventual arrival at eternal life:[66]

---

64. See ibid., 607–9.
* [Tr. note: No citation attached to this paragraph.]
65. Ibid., 612.
66. Ibid., 608

Despite everything, it is an unshakeable element of the Christian faith that the entire Church, in whatever age of her development, cannot fail in this manner. Even if this would be only in some faithful people, united around a handful of Bishops, the Church, one Church, will remain faithful to Christ to the end of the ages. Even if it were only so small a flock that her existence and survival would seem to be insignificant, she will never lose the faith.[67]

It seems that, underneath these explanations, we find ourselves faced with the idea that the earthly Church is holy in the manner of a "saint "on earth, that is, in such a way that her holiness would not exclude venial sins. Juan de Torquemada expressed this idea,[68] and it was recently taken up by Georges Bavaud.[69]

The assertion that "the Church can commit venial sins but not mortal sins" is somewhat strange. Sins, whether venial or mortal, obviously can be "committed" only by particular persons, not by the Church-Person as such. What is meant is that when a member of the Church (a "saint," in other words, someone who is reconciled to God through sanctifying grace and is filially adopted) commits a venial sin, the Church herself is stained by this sin:

> Instead of dividing up the righteous into that which is holy and that which belongs to the venial sin in them, they are entirely included in the Church's holiness, including their sins. Given that holiness prevails in them over their sins, one thinks that they can be included together with her [*bloqués avec elle*], and one enclose all of them in the Church inasmuch as she is holy.[69bis]

In this explanation, the case of mortal sin is different. Those who commit them would be excluded from the Church inasmuch as she is holy. However, at the same time, they are still recognized as belonging to the Church. This would lead us to say that the Church "inasmuch as she is holy" is only one part of the Church, the nucleus constituted by the "saints." Therefore, this explanation ultimately

---

67. Ibid.
68. See Journet, *L'Église du Verbe incarné*, 2:1122–24.
69. Georges Bavaud, "Le pécheur n'appartient pas à l'Eglise. Réflexions sur un thème augustinien," in *Oikoumene: Studi paleocristiani publicati in onore del Concilio Ecumenico Vaticano II* (Catane: Centro di studi sull'antico cristianesimo, Università di Catania, 1964), 47–53; "Le mystère de la sainteté de l'Eglise. S. Augustin, arbiter des controversies actuelles," *Recherches augustiniennes* 3 (1965): 161–66.
69bis. Journet, *L'Église du Verbe incarné*, 2:1123.

means: the Church would be holy because she includes and ever will include within her bosom, constituting her priceless core, her constitutive "nucleus," the saints, that is, the men and women who actually live by God's grace.

Does this suffice for one to say, purely and simply, that the Church is holy? If, as we have seen, one must recognize that she has a personality that is distinct from the sum of the persons who compose her (even though she is collective, resulting from the personalities of all her members unified by the convergence of their ordination to Christ, a convergence assured by the Holy Spirit who animates all of them to some degree), how could one sustain that the Church-Person is holy if she is holy only in one part of herself while being sinful in another? Holiness and sin pertain to the person, and the person is one. A person stained by sin is a sinner, even if "parts" of holiness remain in him.

Hans Urs von Balthasar could be criticized as holding Fr. Bouyer's views regarding these matters.[70] In the Church, he makes a distinction between the body of Christ (i.e., the portion of humanity incorporated into Christ and hence completely holy) and the bride (not distinguishing between the "bride" and the "fiancé," as Bouyer does) who is made up of sinful men, is called to holiness, and is submitted to the sanctifying action of Christ, while she still remains sinful. One will note that in saying that the Church is completely holy inasmuch as she is the "body of Christ" the problem is merely moved, for the Church is the body of Christ made up of the men who compose her. Therefore, we still must explain how these same men who, with their sins, constitute the Church-spouse can, without their sins, simultaneously constitute her immaculate body. Thus, we find ourselves oriented in the direction of a solution that says that the Church is holy but is composed of sinful members.

The Church is utterly holy, but her members are sinners

{670} Here[71] we first distinguish the Church as *a subject of holiness* from the Church as *a cause of holiness* through her sacramental and jurisdictional powers.

---

70. See von Balthasar, *Sponsa Verbi*.
71. See ibid., 893–934. Also, see the excellent summary in Journet, *Théologie de l'Église*, 235–64.

As a subject of holiness The Church, composed of sinners, is completely holy because a man belongs to the Church only to the degree that he participates in her grace and holiness. Indeed, whoever sins thus betrays the Church, betraying her will, her inspiration, and so forth. The righteous person (i.e., he who personally has grace and charity) belongs to the Church only by that part of himself which is under the sway of charity. When this same person sins (venially, for otherwise he would cease to be righteous), he does not act as a member of the Church and therefore does not involve the Church [in his sinful act]. The sinner cannot engage the Church according to his sinful being but only inasmuch as he acts according to the ecclesial being that remains in him (his sacramental character, unformed faith and hope, membership in ecclesiastical society, and so forth). Moreover, he is moved (externally) by the Church's charity in all the holy activity that he preserves (e.g., voluntary participation in worship, acts of mercy, and so forth). However, this holy activity in him is not formally holy, for it is not informed by charity.[72]

The Church does penance. Indeed, penance is inspired by charity (though sometimes distantly, at the beginning of conversion). Therefore, it is holy. If man does not sin precisely inasmuch as he is a member of the Church, he does do penance inasmuch as he is a member of the Church.[73]

The Church is in some way soiled by the sins of her members, in the sense that the world holds her responsible for them, even though this is unjust.[74] We could say the countenance that she presents to the world bears the stains of her members' sins. However, her beauty is not really affected by this.

---

72. N.B. Hans Küng critiques this solution, opposing to it the fact that the human person is indivisible, thus making it impossible for one to separate one's sinful self from one's righteous self. (See Küng, *L'Église*, 454.) However, this is not what is in question. It is a question of knowing what are the grounds on which this person is part of the Church. The renunciation of sin is a primordial condition for one's entrance into the Church. In the human person, who is at once unified and complex, this renunciation, even when it is sincere, is not total. What Journet says is that, to the degree that the person still remains under the grip of sin, he does not belong to the Church. However, to the degree that he really renounces it, he belongs to her.

73. See Journet, *Théologie de l'Église*, 240.

74. See ibid., 244.

As a cause of holiness Her sacramental actions bear Christ's grace, and while the subject's dispositions are necessary, they are not what render the sacraments holy.[75] Her juridical actions bear holiness on account of the assistance provided by the Holy Spirit, who assures its essential rectitude and benevolence (in relation to men's salvation). Erroneous or even unjust measures are not an obstacle to the Church's holiness, for they are repudiated in advance.[76]

Finally, the Church's holiness is a mystery, only knowable by faith. There are signs of it, but the Church's holiness cannot be discovered through a merely historical investigation, even though the historian can see the Church "as a reality that is holy and beneficial for humanity."[77]

To many, this solution seems too formal and a bit unreal in relation to what the Church concretely represents for most men, even believers. Likewise, it seems too formal and unreal in relation to the way that the effects of the failures and faults that are rightly or wrongly attributed to her (but certainly not always wrongly) are felt by those who experience them. We will attempt to correct this impression, placing this solution, which is essentially our own, in its existential context. Here, it suffices to recall that the Church is a mysterious reality, though one that is present in the world. If we do not take her mystery into account, can we render a correct judgment concerning her?

The Church is holy in herself, but sinful in her members

{671} Here,[78] we first distinguish *the Church's objective holiness* (consisting in the ensemble of means of holiness that Christ provided for the Church in instituting her, a holiness that is indefectible) from *the holiness of her members* (which can affect only the persons who are part of the Church). This distinction is related to the twofold sense of the expression *communio sanctorum*: first, the communion of the *sancta*, without any stain; second, the communion of the *sancti*, the sanctified persons are still stained. Moreover, one dis-

---

75. See ibid., 248.
76. See ibid., 252.
77. See ibid., 242–43.
78. See Congar, *Vraie et fausse réforme dans l'Église*, 89–122.

tinguishes *personal faults* (or, sins properly so called) from *historical faults*.

For the first, Congar's solution is very hesitant: "Those who are tempted and sin are the persons in the Church, not the Church herself as a community."[79] But, immediately afterward, he states: "The Church, as the collection of members who compose her (namely, the individuals and hierarchical persons) is subject to temptation and sin and is bound to do penance." Then, further on, "Weaknesses are not part of the Church Herself, but are part of her members."[80]

He attributes the *historical faults* of the Church expressly to her, though in the restricted sense whereby the "Church" means "the Church officials." However, he opposes the weakness of Churchmen to "the purity of the Church herself."[81]

Finally, considering the "concrete" Church in her unity as a communion and an institution, a mystery and a historical reality, he proposes a comprehensive solution that admittedly remains a bit disappointing. His solution is that the Church is holy through her divine part (through that part of her that comes from Christ) and is defective and lacking on account of what falls to her from human freedom. This "human part" is within her, such that "the human matter that enters into her concrete structure is fallible and introduces sin into her, without, for all that, defiling her herself."[82] And he takes up St. Ambrose's formula: *immaculata ex maculatis*.*

---

79. Ibid., 104.
80. Ibid., 107.
81. Ibid., 119. [Tr. note: In the original, this is presented as being as though it were a longer quotation. Here, the text is corrected in line with Congar's original text.]
82. Ibid. 120.

* N.B. The only real difference between Congar and Journet pertains to *historical faults*, i.e., those which the historian as such (namely, the person who has an external perspective concerning the Church) attributes to the Church, for, on the level of historical realities, they have been committed by the "Church" as a society. Congar thinks that this attribution, on this level, is justified, whereas Journet thinks that it is unjust. It seems that in the end Congar, like Journet, attributes *sins properly so called* to the members of the Church and not to the ecclesial community as such. However, failing to accept the notion of partial belonging to the Church (a belonging through what is saved and sanctified in man), he does not succeed at providing a clear explanation for how the Church as such would not be the subject of her members' sins.

The data of the problem

The Church in her mystery and in her historical reality

{672} The mystery of the Church is realized only in the ecclesial society. This is one of the principal points of the encyclical *Mystici Corporis*, which was taken up by Vatican II.[83] Nonetheless, must we not distinguish the Church as she appears (by which I mean the real Church as visible and as seen, not "the appearance" of the Church) from the Church in her hidden reality, which is accessible to faith alone? Thus, Christ was visibly a man, a man of His country and His era. However, invisibly, this man was the Word. The difference is that the Church's mystery consists not in the Person of the Word but, instead, in a created (though hidden) personality. Her visible side is made up of the personalities of those who compose her, having a kind of autonomy in relation to her personality. Thus, a disjunction can exist between her "dynamism" and theirs, between her behavior and theirs. However, her dynamism is recognized only by theirs, and her behavior exists only in theirs. (This is what leads one to rework quite profoundly Maritain's distinction between the Church's Person and her personnel. The Church-Person exists and acts only in the people who make up the Church and does so only through their action.)[84]

Objective holiness and personal holiness

{673} God alone is holy. If the creature can be called holy, this is so inasmuch as it participates in God's holiness.

"Holiness" evokes the idea of "separation" or "being set apart" [*ségrégation*] (in the sense that God's holiness is His majesty and His transcendence, by which He is "separated" [from all things]). From this perspective, the creature participates in God's holiness by becoming "sacred." In other words, such a creature is set apart and reserved for God, rendering testimony to the Divine Majesty among men. These are all signs of the presence of the "thrice holy" God. This is what we can call "holiness of things."

---

83. See *Lumen Gentium*, no. 8.
84. See §656d above.

However, although God is elevated on account of the fact that He is above all creatures, He is united to them through His activity, which is love (or what is inspired by love). Thus, in the creature, holiness designates communion with God, namely, participation in His life and in all the activities or principles of activity that lead to Him—the Holy Spirit and His presence in the righteous. This is "personal holiness."

Here, it is not a question of two irreducible forms of holiness—action follows on being. God expresses His majesty through love. He manifests Himself only in order to unite His free and personal creature to Himself.

If it is a question of nonpersonal beings, they are not susceptible to participating in the divine holiness except in the form of the objective holiness of things. Moreover, they cannot divest themselves of this participation if God gives it to them. However, if it is a question of personal beings, inasmuch as they also are "things" (i.e., created beings), they are also susceptible to this objective holiness. However, just as God's unique holiness is constituted by his holy love and holy majesty, so too in the divine intention, objective holiness in a personal and free creature is ordered to his personal holiness and to communion with God (for others but also for one's own sake).* Granted, objective holiness can be found in a person without personal holiness (a corrupt priest, for example). However, this comes from this person's own resistance, not from the fact that God would have conferred on him a holiness that is exclusively objective.

Given that the Church is an eminently personal being, the distinction between objective holiness and personal holiness, while remaining certainly worthwhile and important (for, indeed, the Church is, on earth, an objectively holy reality), cannot suffice for resolving the problem with which we are now occupied. If the Church were objectively but not personally holy, she would lack the holiness that a person should have in the economy of salvation. Purely and simply, she would be non-holy (i.e., sinful).

---

* Here, we must recall the principle that God never makes use of a creature that is a person without ordering him to personal participation in the good of which he is the intermediary.

The Church's holiness and the holiness of her members

{674} The aforementioned distinction between the Church's personality and the personalities of the humans that compose her indicates that we must distinguish these two forms of holiness. But how? In reality, the Church is not a Person purely and simply distinct from the persons who compose her. Such a distinct person would be an abstraction. If she is personally holy, she can only be holy in her members. To say that she is holy in herself and sinful in her members is to reduce her personal sanctity to nothing.

Personal faults and collective faults

{675} This distinction holds true for every kind of group. Nonetheless, the matter is very delicate. A "collective" fault is always the fault of one or of several individuals. However, sometimes this responsibility cannot be discerned when something hinders the common conscience or the intellectual thoughtlessness of the members of the group as a whole. From the perspective of individuals, an immense role is played by sins of omission, and it is quite difficult to discern a sin of omission.

Is there [such a thing] as collective responsibility [in matters pertaining to the Church]?[85] Congar rejects the idea of a "collective culpability," but extends quite far to the personal participation of individuals, including to collective faults, which thus become, to this degree, personal sins. His analysis, which is very profound, seems to be just. Journet, citing Maritain, inclines toward the idea of a collective culpability from which individuals could be free only by dissociating themselves from these faults. The opposition is not absolute, but the participation of individuals is only extended to omission (not only the omission consisting in allowing the fault itself to come about but also the omission concerning the judgment and condemnation of the collective fault).

It seems that the difference between the two theologians can be reduced to the following. According to Journet, such a collective

---

85. See Congar, *Vraie et fausse réforme dans l'Église*, 524–38. Journet, "Controverse avec Congar," 303–4.

culpability cannot affect the Church because the collective fault is made up of the faults of the members, in which she does not participate. According to Congar, she is united with it.[86]

Penance and sin

{676} Penance is the act by which the sinner repudiates his sin. The penitent as such is no longer a sinner.

Would he himself need to have been a sinner, such that penance would testify to the sinful condition of the penitent, at least in the past, as well as in the present, to the degree that the penance is not total?

Here, we are faced with the unique case of Christ. He bore sinful men in Himself and personified them without participating in their sin in any way because, on the contrary, men are freed from sin to the degree that they are in Christ. However, He did penance for them, personifying their return to God.[87] Men return to the Father "through Him, with Him, and in Him."[88]

The case is different for the Church. In her case, as is expressed by the Patristic images of the sinful woman who is purified and espoused, she is made up of sinful men, Jews and Gentiles. However, as we have seen, she exists as the Church, in her own, proper personality, only through the action of Christ who saves her, purifying and sanctifying these men. ("He is the savior of the body.") In other words, the act that constitutes the Church is quite precisely the act by which the men who compose her are freed from their sins and cease to be sinners.

However, to cease to be a sinner is to begin to be a penitent person. Also, if one cannot say without reservation that the Church is a community of sinners, we can and absolutely must say that she is a community of penitents. (We cannot say without reservation

---

86. See Congar, *Vraie et fausse réforme dans l'Église*, 120–21.
87. On the topic of Christ's penitent love, see §492 in the previous volume.
88. N.B. According to Journet (see Journet, *Théologie de l'Église*, 240), the Savior, who was without sin, could not, properly speaking, do penance. The reason for this is that, although penance is virtuous and good, and even though it has a "grandeur," it is born from a misery, sin, from which Jesus was always exempt. Nonetheless, is there not a kind of inconsistency in refusing Christ's penance and attributing it to the Church when, at the same time, one affirms that the Church is and will always be exempt from the misery of sin?

that she is a community of sinners because she is made up of men who were sinners before being incorporated into the Church but who are no longer sinners, even though, for all that, they are not fully of the Church.)

But, what should we say about the sins that her members commit after they have been gathered together into her? They do not commit them inasmuch as they are members of the Church. To the degree that they are still sinners, they are the matter from which the Church draws her members, not the matter from which the Church is made. When they do penance, they do so inasmuch as they are members of the Church. In them and through them, the Church does penance. Moreover, the Church does penance for all her sinful members, even for those who are not currently penitent because they prefer to remain in their sins.

Present holiness and holiness in the making

{677} To say that the Church is constituted by the activity of Christ who frees His members from their sin is not to say that she is established in a consummated state of holiness. Like the individuals who compose her, the Church passes from an initial state of holiness (which is complete innocence but also is the point of departure for progress, of itself indefinite, in her participation in Christ's holiness) to consummated holiness, which is eschatological.

This means that one must avoid confusing "lesser in holiness" (or "an inferior state of holiness") with "lacking in holiness" (or "a state of sin"). The little baptized child lives in a state of holiness without a shade [of sin], but this state is an inferior one. The beginner in the spiritual life, even if he has not committed any sin, would still be a beginner.

Does this distinction justify reserving the title "bride" for the eschatological Church, thus leaving the pilgrim Church to be only a kind of "fiancé"? Scripture does not truly seem to favor this interpretation, for St. Paul is indeed speaking of the Church here-below when he says that she is the bride of Christ.[89] Moreover, it is not clear why the idea that the earthly Church continuously progresses

---

89. See Eph 5:21–32.

in holiness would be incompatible with the prerogatives of a bride, so long as this progress is understood in such a way that it does not imply any sin from her start, nor in the course of her development. Given that every sin is a form of infidelity, she who from her birth is perfectly a bride cannot sin. But nothing is opposed to the idea that she could make forward progress in love.

Moreover, we must consider that the Church constituted by Christ's redemptive act (doubtlessly constituted at Pentecost, for the sending of the Spirit by the Son is the global effect of the redemptive act, including all the other effects of this) is the instrument used by Christ in then freeing human persons from their sin. Therefore, we must admit that, at the foundation of the Church, the men who composed the very first ecclesial community (the apostles first, and the others present in the Upper Room) were immediately sanctified by Christ. The Church's mediation was then exercised by them on other men whom they brought into the Church. Moreover, it was also exercised on themselves, precisely to the degree that Christ's redemptive, purifying, and sanctifying action could continue being exercised on them in order to lead them to consummated holiness.[90]

From the moment when she exists in the very first community, the Church, through the power of Christ and of the Spirit, draws her members from sinful men, making them participate in her holiness, and likewise makes her members who are still sinners (and therefore, in this, still outside her) members who are ever more holy (thus being evermore drawn into her).

This means that the holiness of the Church "in the midst of making herself" progresses through her own, proper action (which does not prevent every form of growth from being a gift).[91]

---

90. N.B. On this question concerning the Church's anteriority to her members, it does not seem that we can retain Congar's idea (see Congar, *Vraie et fausse réforme dans l'Église*, 91–94) that the Church would have been instituted before the communities of the faithful so that she would have begotten in Christ the members of the very first community as well. Indeed, it is not clear how the Church would have been able (at whatever moment of her history one may imagine) to exist and act other than through the men and women who would currently be her members.

91. N.B. This holds proportionally for the case of individual persons. Once an individual person is constituted in holiness through the gift of grace and charity, he cooperates with the action of the Spirit who sanctifies him. The difference is that the Church cooperates in sanctifying and freeing from sin the person who is not yet constituted in holiness and is outside

Suggestions for a Solution to the Problem

The Church exists and acts only in and through her members. Holiness concerns being (i.e., objective holiness) and activity (i.e., personal holiness).

The Church's objective holiness

{678} The Church is holy because she is the "body of Christ," the means of His presence to the world and history from the time of the ascension onward. This holiness is complete because it does not depend on the holiness of her members, but rather on the holiness of Christ whom she renders present.

Nonetheless, we cannot say that her holiness is completely separate from the holiness of her members. Indeed, the Church is not a thing but, instead, is a person. Indeed, she makes Christ present to the world in a personal manner, not like a kind of thing (e.g., a shrine or a crucifix). She cannot be a sign of Christ's holiness without herself being holy.

A baptized person, a priest, a bishop, or a pope can be stripped of personal holiness. Nonetheless, for all that, on account of their consecration, they cannot cease to represent Christ. However, it is not conceivable that at some particular moment of her history the Church would be stripped of [all] personal holiness in her members, for objective holiness is by its very nature ordered to arouse and manifest personal holiness and does not exist if it is cut off from it. A Church that is stripped of all holiness would be a dead sign, a sign cut off from what it signifies. (Such would be a material church abandoned in a completely dechristianized region, in which nobody, absolutely nobody, would be able to see in her anything but her architecture or her ornamentation, unable to make any religious use of them.)

Can the Church's objective holiness grow? It seems that it can do so in two ways. It can grow quantitatively to the degree that the Church spreads through the world and can qualitatively grow with

---

grace. However, she does not do this outside of Christ, as all of humanity is contained in Him from the moment of the Incarnation (see §§434–35 in the previous volume).

regard to the clarity and power of her testimony. From this perspective, there are doubtlessly phases of progress and of regression, according to times and places.

The Church's personal holiness

{679} Congar distinguishes between *personal faults* (or, "sins properly speaking") and *historical faults*. For the sake of clarity, it is useful to add a third category between these two, namely, *those committed by the legitimate representatives of the Church in the exercise of their functions*.

The Church is in no way sinful

{680} On this point, I unreservedly agree with Journet's thesis: each time that a member of the Church sins, to the degree that he sins, he separates himself from the Church and, simultaneously, from Christ.

This separation comes in degrees. With the exception of schism or heresy, the separation is not complete, and the sinner continues to belong to the Church, as we will see. However, if someone is a member of the Church, this is not on account of his sins. Nor is he even such with his sins. Instead, he is a member of the Church despite his sins.

Journet proves this by means of the immense and important fact that the Holy Spirit is the uncreated soul of the Church. Obviously, it is inconceivable that someone would sin inasmuch as he is vivified and moved by the Spirit of God. This is just as true for venial sin, for whatever is in accord with the Spirit of God cannot simultaneously be a sin of any degree whatsoever.

One can also prove this by means of the definition of the Church's personality which I strove to establish above. Indeed, if the Church's personality is made up of the personalities that compose her, provided that they are conformed to Jesus Christ, it is clear that their sin does not engage the Church's personality. On the contrary, by sinning, they "betray" her. If they do not, properly speaking, "betray" her when they venially sin, they nonetheless distance themselves from her.

A question remains concerning the attribution of these sins to the Church. The Church's personality is a mystery that is manifested only by means of the human personalities that compose her. The clearer the bond between a human person and the Church, it is all the more difficult for someone looking on this person from the outside to perceive, comprehend, and admit this dissociation between the personality of the Church and the personality of this member who sins. Here, we are faced with the entire problem of the scandal given by the counter-witness of Christians. This scandal is not that of the Church. However, it reflects back on the Church, implicates her, and is made graver by this fact.

We must say that the Church is not the cause of these scandals but, instead, their victim. And nonetheless, she is the one who in fact (though, without this being her own fault) "causes scandal."

The Church is responsible for the "historical faults" that taint her action

{681} Nobody can deny that many of the acts performed in the course of history by the Church as such, acting through her appointed representatives, in her name and by her authority, are "faults." (These can also be acts performed by one representative part of the People of God.) It would be artificial and, in the end, untenable, to claim that the responsibility for these acts does not ultimately belong to her in some way, for her authority was involved and, indeed, these acts would not have had their historical existence if they had not involved that authority. (For example, the Inquisition could not have been what it in fact was if it had been done only by individuals, acting on behalf of non-ecclesial groups or if it had been disavowed by the Church's authorities, whereas, it was in fact encouraged by them.)

How can one hold that these faults do not "defile" her and do not make her a sinner? Here, it is necessary (and perfectly just) to distinguish "fault" from "sin." Obviously, every sin is a fault, but the converse is not true. Sin is a failure of the free person in the exercise of his freedom with regard to God as the Final End. Many human acts are "faults" in relation to a particular end (e.g., a given "work of art" in comparison to the end of art, namely, beauty) which are not faults in relation to God. Take as an example a given piece of poetry into which a saint has simultaneously placed all of his charity, all his faith, and all of the bad taste of his surrounding culture along with his own bad taste. As another example, there might be an error, even one that is grave, in temporal administration. Indeed, let us go even further still. An error, indeed even one that is grave, in missionary activity (e.g., inattention to and lack of respect for native cultures) is not necessarily a sin. And if, in the two preceding cases, there is sin, this is not on account of the gravity of the error committed in relation to the temporal end and its consequences. Rather, there is sin in relation to the moral responsibility of the person who committed it. In this sense, we cannot avoid saying that the Church has committed (and every day commits) "faults," but this does not imply that she would have committed sins.

Certainly, a host of sins, properly speaking, whether by commission or omission, are involved in constituting a collective fault. From this perspective, collective fault falls under the solution proposed for the sins which the members of the Church commit.[92]

However, not only sins are involved here. There also are human nature's inherent limitations. Every man is simultaneously enriched by his individual and common culture while likewise being a prisoner of this same culture. He develops himself along the lines of his character and spirit. But by the same token, other possible developments remain foreign to him. Genius is necessary for one to push beyond the limits of a collective mentality, indeed, moreover, a genius that is oriented in the direction of overcoming these limits. It is not a sin to be lacking in such genius or to have a genius oriented in such a way that many human values remain foreign (or, at least, not very familiar) to oneself.

"Collective fault" or *historical fault* is the result of this ensemble of faults and limitations. Inasmuch as it is collective, it is not a sin. Consequently, we must not consider it to be something opposed to the Church's personal holiness, placing her in a state of sin, but rather, hold that it is something determining this imperfect state of holiness of which we spoke earlier.

Let us take an example. A very holy person, who is quite rightly

---

92. See §678 above.

venerated for his holiness, can present manifest lacunae in his conceptions, as well as in his character and in his stances, without requiring us to judge that such lacunae are contrary to his holiness though they do indeed have bad effects for his witness and action (and likewise for the Church's witness and action, to the degree that he represents her).

Consummated holiness will exclude such lacunae and such limitations, for at this ultimate terminus, the heart and mind converge in perfect participation in the knowledge and love of God.

Here again, those who look on the Church externally can reproach her for these limitations and historical faults, just as one can ridicule a true saint who has certain conceptions that are worthy of criticism as well as certain absurd behaviors. Such reproaches are not completely unjust. (As we will see, the Church ought to reproach herself for such things.) However, it is unjust to make them reflect back on Christ and the Gospel. By representing Himself on earth by means of men, Christ accepted these limitations and faults, only preventing them, by His Spirit, from compromising the Church's personal holiness.

By His Spirit as well, He urges her to reform herself, as we will see.

The powers of the Church are holy, despite the faults committed
in the exercise of her authority

{682} Without a doubt, this is the most difficult case.

When an authentic representative of the Church, acting *ex officio* and legitimately, commits a fault (sometimes bringing about an injustice, a misstep [*maladresse*], or an error), one can and must distinguish the moral fault (of commission or omission) which perhaps had been committed by the person or persons responsible for this act from the "objective" fault that this decision constitutes (e.g., the condemnation of Galileo, the excommunication of the Patriarch of Constantinople, Cerularius, by the legate of Pope Humbert on July 16, 1054, many scientifically untenable positions of the Pontifical Biblical Commission, and so forth). As was said above, we must say that the moral fault concerns not the Church but this member of the Church who, by sinning, has acted against the Church. However, how can we really say that the "objective fault" is not committed by the Church?

The particular difficulty of this case is not related to the personal holiness of the Church. Rather, it is related to what Journet calls the tendential holiness of her hierarchical powers.[93] How can one claim that such actions are sanctifying?

The powers of the Church are sanctifying not only because they are given to her by God in view of the sanctification of men, but also because, in their exercise, the Church is preserved, by the assistance of the Holy Spirit, from deviating and making the People of God deviate in relation to true holiness, the kingdom of God. However grave and detrimental these faults may be, they are errors in the application of perfectly right and just directive principles. Thus, the condemnation of Galileo was a fault—indeed a very unfortunate one, for a real opposition did not exist between the scientific theory of heliocentrism and the biblical narrative of creation. However, the sovereignty of the Word of God, and the human mind's duty to submit itself to it in the investigation of the truth, is a directive principle that one cannot put aside without putting aside the kingdom of God and holiness. Humbert committed the greatest of faults in excommunicating Cerularius, but he was right to affirm the authority of the bishop of Rome over all the Church.

In light of this explanation (i.e., having taken into account the certain fact that the power that is abused is sanctifying in itself and never ceases at all to be such, despite this abuse), we can understand and greatly extend what St. Augustine says with regard to unreasonable excommunications:

> Sometimes, even Divine Providence allows that, as a result of grave partisan violences on the part of carnal men, even just men may be driven out of the Christian community. If the victims of this unjust affront bear it in all patience for the peace of the Church, without fomenting either heretical or schismatic movements, they will give to all the example of right sentiment and of pure charity, which one must have in the service of God. Therefore, the intention of such men is to return to port once the storms come to an end. Or indeed, if they cannot do so (either because

---

93. See Journet, *Théologie de l'Église*, 247.

the tempest is prolonged or because they fear that their return would arouse something similar or more furious), they maintain the intention to provide for the salvation of those very persons whose seditious conduct required them to leave, without isolating themselves and without forming cliques for themselves, defending the faith to their death and serving it through their testimony, the faith which they know that the Catholic Church preaches. They receive their crown in secret, from the Father who sees in secret. Such a case is rare, but, nonetheless, examples of it are not lacking. It is even more frequent than is commonly believed.[94]

Certainly, many are far from the Church and distance themselves from her because of these faults, either because they have been the victim of them or because they have rebelled against them, or quite simply have had an insurmountable defiance engendered in themselves by them. God alone judges consciences and one's ultimate personal motivations. Objectively, these faults do not justify one in ceasing to believe in the Church, that is, in the sanctifying value of her authority and, therefore, also the sanctifying value of the recognition of this authority and of obedience to it.

According to Journet, when the contradiction between this particular decision and the directive principle claiming to be applied in this decision becomes obvious, it ceases to obligate.[95] If this contradiction is clear only to this or that person (and in this case, each must also believe oneself to be fallible and not speak flippantly about the evidence), only one of two things is possible. Either, on the one hand, the prescribed act is not a sin but only is an "objective fault," or on the other, it would be a sin for him to whom it is prescribed. In the first case, one must submit oneself, at least if one cannot disobey without simultaneously rebelling, for the act of placing the authority of the Church into question would be a graver error than this particular error. (Moreover, most often, it is not certain that it is an error.) In the second case, the objection of conscience must hold, but in such a manner that, without rebelling, one accepts all the personal consequences of disobedience.

---

94. St. Augustine, *La vraie religion*, OESA 8, 7.11.
95. See Journet, *Théologie de l'Église*, 252–53.

To be fair to the Church

{683} The theologian cannot shrink back from the problem posed by the Church's faults, which are an affront for every member of the Church who reflects on her, indeed, sometimes to the very degree of one's love for her, whether in his personal life or in the testimony that he tries to render concerning her. Nonetheless, one must guard against the grave temptation—one that is so modern in its tenor—to blacken over the picture and not see in the Church anything other than these "faults" committed by her or even sins and crimes that she in no way has committed, even though she painfully bears their weight and hatred before men, who do not know the depths to which she herself is wounded by them.

Between, on the one hand, a naïve apologetic that strives to show that everything the Church has done is admirable and, on the other, a reaction that consists in pitilessly accumulating reproaches and condemnations against her, without welcoming the least attenuating circumstance (disdainfully rejecting every good and often admirable thing that she has done), there is room for an equitable judgment that, lucidly assessing her as a historical reality, recognizes her grandeur and beneficence. Does any other human institution exist which has not committed incomparably more evil than she has done, having itself done incomparably less good than her? From the perspective of good and evil, what kind of figure is struck by whatever nation that there is, in whatsoever of our homelands? If we say that we judge her severely because we love her, we must indeed fear hypocrisy. If true love does beget severity, it is a painful severity, guarding itself against every form of injustice. If we say that we do not judge her, not only for what she has done, but also in function of her claims to sanctity, we have nonetheless striven to say why and how these claims do not imply any smugness on our part, nor any ignorance concerning her weaknesses. The actual attitudes of her highest officials make this clear this in a thousand ways.

The apostle Peter said of Christ: "He went about doing good."[96] We must understand this as meaning, "Only doing good." Alas, this

---

96. Acts 10:38 (RSV).

cannot be said of the Church! She does not pass throughout history only doing good. However, we can truly say that she has gone about doing good, above all this incomparable good: she has not ceased, does not cease, and will not cease to make the Savior known to the world and to communicate His salvation. And if she is primordially mandated and authorized to communicate eternal salvation to men, through words and sacraments, she has never neglected to contribute efficaciously also, in turn, to their temporal salvation, through her innumerable works of mercy as well as through her teaching. If, undoubtedly, in the course of her long history, she has committed innumerable faults, some that are very substantial, the balance sheet of her benefits (even those that are merely temporal) and her shortcomings is largely positive in the end. None of her members is justified in blushing because of her, even if sometimes he is afflicted at not seeing her sanctity shine forth as it ought.

Ecclesia semper reformanda et purificanda
{684} As should be clear, this conception of the Church's holiness does not exclude the need for reforming the Church. The Church has often felt this necessity through the course of her history. In particular, there was the Gregorian Reform. Then, there was the Counter-Reformation, which does not directly designate the battle of the Catholic Church against the Protestant Reformation but, rather, the "Catholic Reformation."

Indeed, it is clear that if (individual or collective) objective faults are not the Church's sins, they are an evil that diminishes her radiance and the accomplishment of her mission. It is up to her to correct such evils by eliminating the results of these faults in her (e.g., bad organization, various errors, and so forth) and by giving her members, to varying degrees, the possibility of a better formation.

However, we can also speak of purification, for while the sins committed by the members of the Church are not sins of the Church, it remains the case that her role is to purify her members from their sins. And just as the Church does penance in her repentant members (even though she herself does not sin in these sinful members), so too she is purified to the degree that she purifies her members. We could say that she is not really defiled by the defilements of her members, but she does become more intensively pure when her members purify themselves of their faults.[97]

CONCLUSION

{685} The Church's holiness is part of her mystery, which is an object of faith. If one considers the Church in a purely external manner, like a reality of this world, the distinctions that we have made will be meaningless. However, in that case, the very notion of holiness loses its meaning.

The believer can never look upon the Church only externally, except from a purely methodological perspective in order to attempt to render account of how the Church might appear to those who consider her in this way.

Many false and offensive things are said today about the Church by her members and even by theologians under the pretense of authenticity and loyalty. Many of these things are not acceptable because they are based on a willingness to consider the Church externally, as though she were not, beyond what her appearances may be, a mystery of faith, and as though this mystery did not give the true meaning to those appearances. Moreover, such people act as though the believer could place himself outside the Church so as to judge her, without thereby losing his own, proper Christian existence.

---

97. See Bouyer, *L'Eglise de Dieu*, 612–26. Jean Jacques von Allmen, *Une réforme dans l'Église, possiblités, critères, acteurs, étapes* (Gembloux: Duculot, 1971).

3

The Church's Universal Mediation

If Christ continues His redemptive action in the world through the Church, who is "His body," it follows that, in the economy of salvation instituted by God, men cannot be saved except by means of the Church, just as they cannot be saved except through Christ. However, this assertion poses many problems.

NO SALVATION OUTSIDE THE CHURCH

Historical Points

{686} The[1] formula *extra ecclesiam non est salus* [sic] comes from St. Cyprian.[2] It meant that baptism conferred outside communion with the Catholic Church was worthless. The Church did not follow

---

1. For a methodical bibliography, see Boniface Willems, "La nécessité de l'Église pour le salut, aperçu bibliographique," *Concilium* 1 (1965): 101–11. There, see in particular (or, add where they are not present) the following. Louis Caperan, *Le problème du salut des infidels, Essai historique* (Toulouse: Grand séminaire de Toulouse, 1934), and *L'appel des non-chrétiens au salut* (Paris: Éditions du Centurion, 1961). Congar, *Sainte Église*, 417–34. Riccardo Lombardi, *The Salvation of the Unbeliever*, trans. Dorothy M. White (London: Burns & Oates, 1956). Jean-Hervé Nicolas, "Universalité de la mediation du Christ et salut de ceux qui ne connaissent pas le Christ," in *Acta del Congresso internazionale Tommaso d'Aquino nel suo settimo centenario* (Naples: Edizioni domenicane italiane, 1976), 4:261–73. Karl Rahner, "L'appartenance à l'Église d'après la doctrine de l'encyclique Mystici Corporis Christi," *Ecrits théologiques*, 2:9–112. Gustave Thils, "Ceux qui n'ont pas reçu l'Évangile," *L'Eglise de Vatican II* (Paris: Cerf, 1966), 669–79.
2. See St. Cyprian, *Correspondance*, trans. Louis Bayard (Paris: Société d'édition "Les Belles lettres" / Budé, 1925), Letter 4, §4, and *De catholicae Ecclesiae unitate*, trans. Pierre de Labriolle (Paris: Cerf, 1942), ch. 6.

him in this, and with the Donatists later having claimed St. Cyprian's patronage, St. Augustine, in his *De baptismo*, had to elaborate the distinction between the validity of a sacrament and its fruitfulness. However, St. Cyprian's formula endured.

The idea is found in the most ancient Fathers and, in a certain sense, already in Scripture.

If development regarding this formula occurred slowly in the teaching of theologians and of the Catholic Church, it was in the direction of greater attention to the persons [involved in the meaning of the dictum]. As used by the Fathers, the formula intended above all to highlight the fact that the Church is the universal and necessary means through which redemption passes. However, thinkers gradually became aware of the immense number of people who did not have the real possibility of knowing the Church and of placing themselves under her influence. (An important development concerning this matter was the discovery of the New World and also the activity of missionary expansion, thus leading to the appearance of entire civilizations which had a striking beauty and, sometimes, a quite developed religious sense, constituted entirely outside the Church and independent of her.)

Moreover, there has been the phenomenon of the de-Christianization of formerly Christian countries, as well as the problem of "good faith" in some matter of faith, or of the refusal to believe. In short, since the nineteenth century, the Magisterium has been increasingly precise in its declarations admitting the excuse of ignorance and, in the name of God's universal salvific will, recognizing that those who do not belong to the Church, if they are of good faith, also receive the graces of salvation. In the twentieth century, the doctrine was specified in the decision of the Holy Office concerning Leonard Feeny,[3] then in *Mystici Corporis*, applying to membership in the Church the distinction admitted by Trent for baptism, namely, the distinction between belonging *in re* (in fact) and *in voto* (in desire), a *votum* that can be very implicit. Finally, we find a very clear affirmation in Vatican II concerning the possibility of salvation for those who "through no fault of their own do not know the Gospel of Christ or His Church."[4]

---

3. See Willems, "La nécessité de l'Église," 105n5.
4. Vatican II, *Lumen Gentium*, no. 16.

If no contradiction exists between these modern and ancient positions, this is because the perspective has changed. The necessity of the Church for salvation is maintained just as firmly today as in the past. However, today's preoccupation is turned to those who cannot know this necessity. Thus, the contemporary perspective looks into the ways by which the Church could exercise her action on these men *for whom Christ also died*.

The Twofold Data of Faith

{687} *On the one hand*, the Church is the universal means of salvation. She is at once the cause that Christ makes use of in exercising the saving action of His passion, death, and resurrection in all generations and in each man and also is the community of the redeemed, those who have been touched by this action and have consented to it.

Now, as we have seen, the Church is the ecclesial society in whom the mystery of the "body of Christ" is realized. Her unity lies not only in the fact that she is a communion but also in the fact that she is a society. However, considered as a society, as a reality in this world and historical in nature, she has a partial character in relation to the ensemble of mankind. She is a Christian church in relation to other Christian churches and a religious society in relation to other religious societies. When we profess that she is the necessary means for salvation, does this not exclude from salvation all the men who do not recognize her as such?

On the other hand, another datum, one that is rooted in Scripture and the Church's tradition, is that Christ died for all men. He is related to humanity in the order of salvation as Adam is related to it in the order of perdition. This is expressed in His universal salvific will, affirmed in proper terms by St. Paul in 1 Timothy,[5] underlying his entire soteriology.[6] The same can be found in St. John.[7]

Here, we are faced with a grave theological aporia which discloses itself to us to the degree that we realize more fully the material, moral,

---

5. 1 Tm 2:4.

6. See Prat, *Théologie de S. Paul*, 1:284. Ceslas Spicq, "Médiation dans le Nouveau Testament," *Dictionnaire de la Bible*, 5:1040–41. Schnackenburg, *L'Église dans le Nouveau Testament*, 152–57.

7. See André Feuillet, *Le prologue du IVe évangile* (Paris: Desclée de Brouwer, 1968), 162–77; *Le mystère de l'amour divin dans la théologie johannique* (Paris: Gabalda, 1972), 35–38.

and psychological obstacles that, in fact, render explicit belief in the Church and even in Christ impossible for a host of men. How can one speak of a divine willing of salvation for these men who, without any fault on their part, would be unable to make use of the sole means of salvation instituted for men by God? This is only possible if we can discover a way by which the use of this means would be possible also for those who do not recognize her, as well as for every man whatever may be his situation in relation to the Church as a society.

The Necessity of Personal Adherence to the Church

{688} A first solution to the aporia would be found in the idea that humanity as a whole already exists "in Christ" on account of the Incarnation and on account of the universally applicable redemptive act. This is the famed Rahnerian notion of "anonymous Christians."[8] In this case, on account of the Incarnation and the Redemption, man would be "naturally" (with "naturally" meaning "natively") a member of the Church. An act of rejection would be needed in order for one to no longer be a member of the Church; not an express rejection of the Church but, instead, man's rejection of his concrete human nature which includes among its elements this initial membership in the Church.

This does not seem acceptable. First of all, Scripture manifestly makes salvation (and membership in the Church, the community of the saved) depend on a personal act performed by man: faith and baptism. This seems to be an essential datum of the mystery of salvation: it is not imposed on anyone and must be accepted. One is not born saved. On the contrary, one is born a "son of wrath" and comes to salvation through faith.

On the other hand, theologically, the utterly just and true principle of all men's initial belonging to Christ does not allow for this consequence. This is so because it is a question of native membership as part of nature, a belonging that does not suppress solidarity with the

---

8. See Rahner, "L'appartenance à l'Église," 91–112; Edward Schillebeeckx, "L'Église et l'humanité," *Concilium* 1 (1965): 57–58 and 66–73. For a vigorous critique, see Hans Urs von Balthasar, *Cordula ou l'épreuve decisive*, trans. Bernard Fraigneau-Julien (Paris: Beauchesne, 1969), 79–90 and 120–22. A good summary exposition of the theory can be found in Willems, "La nécessité de l'Église," 110.

old Adam in sin and in perdition. Our initial belonging to Christ must be personalized, and it cannot be so without a personal act. To freely accept one's concrete nature does not only mean that one accepts one's initial belonging to Christ. It also means that one accepts one's solidarity with the sinful Adam. (Indeed, we could ask to what degree this acceptance of one's concrete nature is not implied in every act of freedom and therefore whether a refusal would even be conceivable.) And if the act implying this acceptance is made in imitation of Adam's transgression, the latter solidarity (i.e., the first in the order of succession) prevails. Therefore, we cannot commit ourselves to the idea that we would be born with a sort of native membership to the Church. Instead, the path forward is found in the notion of implicit adherence.

The Idea of an Implicit Adherence to the Church

{689} One adheres internally to Christ and the Church through faith. Salvation is attained in this way. Normally, faith is at once a submission of mind and heart to Christ the Savior and illuminator, as well as the acceptance of the truths that He teaches (concerning the mystery of God, Himself, and salvation). These are the two components in a single process. The first is the most important because it entails the second. This process is brought about under the interior action of grace, which is a light for the mind and an impulse of the heart toward Christ. Also, it normally requires an objective presentation of the master and of His teaching.

Implicit faith

{690} Indeed the objective content of the act of faith and its subjective intention do not completely coincide. He who believes is open to the whole of the Person of Christ and of His message. However, he does not necessarily know all the truths that this message contains. Thus, when the Ethiopian requested baptism,[9] he did not yet know the entire doctrine of Christ. He believed only *in the good news of Jesus*. It can even happen that Jesus, the source of revelation, may not yet be known as such. As Israel believed in Christ in ad-

---

9. See Acts 8:36–40.

vance without knowing Him, so too a given man may have a heart that is open to revelation but be prevented from knowing that Jesus is the Christ because of the existential conditions wherein he finds himself.

What is not known clearly and in full awareness by the believer is implied in what he believes, even if the objective content of his faith is reduced to very little. This is so because the essence of faith consists in a willed openness to God, a complete, interior acceptance of God, who is the truth.[10]

The "faith" of non-Catholic Christians

{691} Obviously, the faith in Christ found in all Christian religions implies acceptance of all revealed truths, even if this or that one is expressly denied in this or that particular religion, for it is clearly not denied as being taught by Christ. What is denied is that it is part of the teaching of Christ, and it is denied in good faith by the believers formed in this particular religion.*

The "faith" of non-Christians

{692} However, in other religions as well, some teachings are received as coming from God. These teachings contain authentic religious truths. Sometimes, they come from revelation itself (i.e., the Jewish religion of today). Sometimes, they have been drawn from revealed religion (i.e., Islam). In other cases, they participate in the common depths of humanity, without one necessarily needing to preclude a special action by the Holy Spirit on the founder or founders of this religion in the choice of these truths, as well as in the insistence with which they are instilled into their disciples. Thus, Vatican II stated:

---

10. See Karl Rahner, "Essai sur le martyre," in *Ecrits théologiques* (Paris: Desclée de Brouwer, 1963), 3:181–82.

* N.B. The same cannot be said for him who, having received this truth in the Catholic Church as something coming from Christ, then rejects it for the sake of personal, intellectual, or moral expediency. Such a person makes a choice (*airesis*) within the teaching of Christ and for this reason no longer adheres to Christ the illuminator, thus no longer believing "upon His word." It is a different question, however, to ask whether some can, *in good faith*, exclude a particular truth from the teaching of the Church, thinking that the Church is deceived in attributing it to Christ.

The Catholic Church rejects nothing that is true and holy in these religions. She regards with sincere reverence those ways of conduct and of life, those precepts and teachings which, though differing in many aspects from the ones she holds and sets forth, nonetheless often reflect a ray of that Truth which enlightens all men.[11]

Such a teaching provides a sufficient objective for a man, illuminated by the internal light of faith, to be able to accept God and Christ without knowing them. In Christ (and, of course, in just as unknown a manner as holds for such a case of implicit faith in Him) the Church is accepted as the universal means of salvation.

The "faith" of atheists

{693} Can we push this investigation further, all the way to the case of those who, denying the existence of God, seem to be deprived of the minimum objective content needed for faith, thus meaning that the interior light of faith would not have any truth to take hold of in man's mind [*esprit*]? However, can we today deny the existence of atheists of good faith, even a good number of them? Can we exclude them from salvation or think that God's grace for leading them to faith necessarily requires them first to explicitly acknowledge God's existence?

This was the position of Riccardo Lombardi,[12] which was critiqued by Congar.[13] Vatican II is certainly more open to it, even though its text is not completely clear: "Nor does Divine Providence deny the helps necessary for salvation to those who, without blame on their part, have not yet arrived at an explicit knowledge of God."[14]

St. Thomas, in a context that is absolutely different from that of our question, set forth an idea that can be very fruitful in this matter.[15] According to him, when the unbaptized child awakens to the use of reason, he is led before all things to *deliberare de seipso*, that is, to pose to himself the question of the meaning of his existence. (Obviously, he does not envision that this child has been instructed in

---

11. Vatican Council II, *Nostra Aetate*, no. 2.
12. See Lombardi's *The Salvation of the Unbeliever*, cited at the start of this chapter.
13. See Congar, *Sainte Église*, 433–34.
14. *Lumen Gentium*, no. 16.
15. See *ST* I-II, q. 89, a. 1.

the Christian religion, though no more does he envision that he has had preliminary instruction concerning God and His existence.) At this moment, "if, aided by grace, he orders himself to the end that is assigned to him (by God), he will obtain the remission of original sin."

Jacques Maritain made use of this text (in a way that St. Thomas obviously never dreamed of using it) to open up the way for a solution to the aporia born of the recognition of a kind of good-faith atheism, faced with the certitude that God wills the salvation of all and that nobody will be excluded from salvation except through his refusal to be saved.[16] According to him, in so concretely and existentially ordering oneself to the end assigned by God, which at the same time is God Himself (i.e., the sovereign Good), the person in question knows Him already in some manner as the supreme rule of his freedom and therefore as the Creator. Such a person knows God as his Good and therefore as He who gives Himself. This knowledge is purely practical and in no way theoretical. It is "volitional," that is, unable to be separated from the act of will that it rules. Therefore, it is compatible with some kind of denial of God on the theoretical level (a denial of the false God that has been presented as being the only God, though no other is known).[17]

Existing in the depths of the person whom God penetrates with His loving glance, such knowledge seems to provide a sufficient objective content for the light of faith (which is a grace, though nobody is excluded from it *a priori*) to be able to "take hold." Hence, man's adherence to God the revealer and, *implicitly*, to revelation as a whole (therefore to Christ and the Church) is possible without the intellect necessarily (and, above all, immediately) being freed from one's speculative atheism.

The difference between this solution and the Rahnerian "anonymous Christian" is that for Maritain, it is a question of a personal act, one that is a true conversion, by which man is delivered (and

---

16. See J. Maritain, "La dialectique immanent du premier acte de liberté," in *Raison et raisons* (Fribourg: Egloff, 1947).

17. See Nicolas, *Les profondeurs de la grâce*, 478–86; "Universalité de la mediation du Christ et salut de ceux qui ne connaissent pas le Christ," in *Acta del Congressso internazionale Tommaso d'Aquino nel suo settimo centenario* (Naples, 1976), 269–73.

simultaneously delivers himself) from solidarity with the old Adam in sin. By contrast, in the Rahnerian solution, man is held to be born in Christ and in the Church and can exist outside of her only through an act of rejection.

Obviously, St. Thomas's analysis of the first act of freedom could equally be applied to other acts of freedom performed by adults, for man can *deliberare de seipso* at any moment of his existence. Therefore, these insights enable us to admit that there is a possibility that an atheist may "convert himself" to the living and true God, "abandoning idols"[18] without, for all that, ceasing to be an atheist with regard to his purely intellectual positions.

BELONGING TO THE CHURCH

{694} Therefore, the principle *extra ecclesiam non est salus* means that the Church of Christ (the sole Church of Christ which, according to our faith, is the Church governed by the bishop of Rome) is the universal means and place of redemptive grace. This poses a twofold problem. First, *from the perspective of individuals*, we are led to wonder how one can belong to the Church and benefit from her saving mediation without recognizing the latter. Second, *from the perspective of ecclesial communities* that are separated from the Catholic Church, we can ask: "If the Catholic Church is the sole Church of Christ the Savior, what is their meaning and value for salvation?"

Various Individual Situations in Relation to the One Church's Mediation

{695} Given that such belonging to the Church is necessary for salvation, we are here concerned with discerning and defining the different ways one may belong to the Church in a way that takes heed of two fundamental data. On the one hand, we must not exclude from salvation men of good will who do not know her or who do not recognize her as mediating salvation. On the other hand, we must note that merely knowing her as such does not suffice for salvation.

---

18. 1 Thes 1:9.

Full belonging to the Church

{696} We have seen that the Holy Spirit is the soul of the Church and likewise have seen how He is such—not as a constitutive principle but as the "fontal principle" of created grace, by which each member of the Church participates in her life, which is communion with the Divine Persons, eternal life. With Journet, we must specify that this grace is Christ's grace, redemptive grace. It is "sacramental," that is, conferred to men in virtue of the passion, death, and resurrection of Christ, whose power is actualized in and through the sacraments. It is "oriented." That is, in submitting the believer to the sole shepherd, Jesus Christ, this grace submits him by the same stroke to the earthly Church that He established, by means of which He exercises His mission as universal shepherd.

Therefore, full belonging to the Church includes these various elements. It is a participation in grace inasmuch as it is sanctifying (i.e., the presence of the Holy Spirit and therefore personal participation in Christ's grace and charity). It is a participation in grace received, increased, and preserved by means of the sacraments established by Christ and entrusted to the Church. It is a participation in grace lived in recognition of the pastoral authority of the Church (i.e., in obedience to her legitimate shepherds).[19]

This belonging is called "full" because it is a personal participation in the life of the Church, which is essentially a communion, in Christ, with the Divine Persons and a personal participation in her missionary activity. Nonetheless, it is not complete because of the venial sins that indicate that some part of the person evades this participation. Still, such a person's "center of gravity" is within the Church.

Manifest, but deficient, belonging to the Church: Sinners in the Church

{697} This is an ancient and difficult debate. We have gathered together the data concerning it for reference below in a note.[20]

---

19. See Charles Journet, "Qui est membre de l'Église?," *Nova et Vetera* 36:193–203. This essay was revised and improved in *L'Église du Verbe incarné* (2nd ed.), 2:1304–14. Nicolas, "L'appartenance à l'Église selon la théologie catholique," 131–45.

20. See Pius XII, *Mystici Corporis*, gathered in *AAS* (1943): 203–4. Congar, *Vraie et fausse*

The Church's Universal Mediation 123

Remembering that we hold the position that the Holy Spirit is the soul of the Church, we must say that the sinner does not fully belong to the Church because he does not participate in her life. He has closed himself off to the gift of the Holy Spirit.

However, he is part of the Church as a society. If we admit the complete identification of the Church as a society with the Mystical Body, we must say that sinners are part of the Mystical Body, though in a deficient manner.

They are part of her because they continue to participate in certain elements of her life. Such elements are not living *in them*, for they are not enlivened by charity. Nonetheless, they connect them to the soul of the Church and could revive them if charity is bestowed upon them. Such elements include their sacramental characters, unformed faith and hope, voluntarily preserved Christian habits, and so forth.

They are also part of her because they collectively participate in the Church's charity, in which they have ceased to personally participate. This charity of the Church dictates some of their behaviors (though, as it were, only externally). For example, there are the virtuous behaviors that they preserve and perhaps develop, [as well as] behaviors that are "natural" in themselves but which themselves too call out to be animated by charity. This does not take place without grace and therefore without the action of the Holy Spirit, though it is a grace that acts on this believer externally, as it were:

> It falls to sanctifying grace to be that by which the Holy Spirit dwells (in Him whom such grace enriches), whereas it falls to the grace that is called "gratis data" (which today one would call "charismatic" grace) only to be that by which the Holy Spirit is manifested, as the interior movement of the heart is expressed by the voice ... Through graces of this kind, the *Holy Spirit* manifests Himself in two ways. On the one hand, he does so inasmuch as He dwells in the Church, instructing her and sanctifying her (as when a sinner, in whom the Holy Spirit does not dwell, performs miracles that show that the faith of the Church which He preaches is true) ...

---

réforme dans l'Église, 99–124. Journet, *L'Église du Verbe incarné*, 2:1103–06; "Qui est member de l'Église?," 193–203 (revised and improved in *L'Église du Verbe incarné* [2nd ed.], 2:1304–14). Nicolas, "L'appartenance à l'Église selon la théologie catholique," 149–51. Rahner, "Le péché dans l'Église," 373–94, and "Die Kirche der Sünder," 163–77.

However, it also happens that through these graces the Holy Spirit manifests Himself as dwelling in him to whom they have been granted.[21]

Here, St. Thomas speaks of charismatic graces properly so called, namely, those that move one to an extraordinary act. We can extend what he says here to the actual graces (which can be non-charismatic) by which the Holy Spirit moves a sinner to perform good acts. These acts, of themselves, call to be inspired and elevated by charity. It is the lack of charity, as the normal relay between the Holy Spirit's action and such acts, which leads them to be not ordered to the final end which is good and meritorious for eternal life. However, their moral goodness in a "Christian" makes them belong to the order of salvation, that is, to the order of faith in Jesus Christ. Consequently, such moral goodness denotes the action of the Holy Spirit: "no one can say, 'Jesus is Lord,' except by the Holy Spirit."[22]

Finally, they are part of her because they continue to participate in the Church's action (e.g., in giving the sacraments, preaching the Gospel, and guiding the flock). Their participation is not full, for they do not participate in charity, which is the principle of this action in the Church, bestowing it with meaning. However, the Church is who acts through them. (Indeed, to the degree that it is a question of an action to which they personally devote themselves, they work for the salvation of souls under the external influence of charity.)

Solely apparent belonging to the Church: Hidden heretics

{698} Here we are faced with a debated question. If someone externally makes a profession of belonging to the Church but has internally ceased to believe in her and in her teaching, is such a person still a member of the Church?[23]

The principal reason for an affirmative response is that if such heretics are endowed with authority in the Church, they continue to exercise it: indeed, validly. It seems impossible that someone who

---

21. See Aquinas, *In I Cor.*, 12:7, lect. 2.
22. 1 Cor 12:3 (RSV).
23. For the affirmative side, see Rahner, "L'appartenance à l'Église," 24–25. Semmelroth, *L'Église*. Willems, "La nécessité de l'Église," 290. On the negative side, see Hamer, *L'Église est une communion*, 92–95, and Journet, *L'Église du Verbe incarné*, 2:821 and 1063–65.

is not a member of the Church would have authority in the Church. To this, certain theologians respond that, in fact, their acts are illegitimate, but that, insofar as their heresy is not manifest, the Holy Spirit supplies. This seems rather artificial. Journet thinks that they retain a true juridical authority so long as it is not expressly taken from them. Indeed, the sacramental efficacy [of holy orders] remains, and it is not clear why someone who is no longer really a member of the Church (though, without it being known) would not retain the authority that was entrusted to him, as long as such authority has not been withdrawn from him or as long as he himself has not publicly withdrawn himself from the Church.

The essential reason for the negative response is that membership in the Church can be brought about only through a personal act and that this act is essentially faith. He who rejects the faith, even interiorly, thereby totally stops belonging to Christ and, therefore, to the Church. Indeed, two cases must be distinguished. First there is the case (discussed above) of the person having a faith whose objective content is very minimal, while nonetheless sufficing so that the entire divine teaching may be implicitly contained in it (including salvation by Christ as well as the mediating role of the Church). This first case must be distinguished from that of the person who, having already believed explicitly in Christ and the Church (or, having been placed in sufficient conditions to believe in them explicitly) refuses to believe. In this case, we cannot speak of implicit faith. Rather, the truths that one is pleased to preserve are no longer the objective content of an act of faith because he does not accept them "by faith in the Word of God" but, rather, for purely subjective reasons. In rejecting faith, he rejects Christ, and in rejecting Christ, he rejects the Church (unless, as is more often the case, the reverse happens: he rejects the Church and, then, Christ with her). Hence, he no longer really belongs to the Church but only does so in appearance.

Hidden and unconscious belonging to the Church:
The "just who are outside"
This also is a very delicate problem, both from the perspective of Catholic theology and from the perspective of the religious aware-

ness and teaching of the persons concerned (which must be considered from an ecumenical perspective).

From the perspective of Catholic theology

{699} According to what we said above, whoever believes in Christ (through a living faith, including the movement of his heart toward Him, along with the foundational rectification of one's life) under the (often very distant and indistinct) form by which Christ presents Himself and is present to one's awareness, thereby belongs to Christ. Therefore, such a person belongs to His body, the Church. That is, such a person belongs to the religious society that He founded and in which His body is realized.

The encyclical *Mystici Corporis* speaks of a tendency toward the Church rather than belonging to the Church. To avoid seeing this as representing an exception to the principle, "No salvation outside the Church," we must interpret this notion of "tendency" as meaning a real belonging (just as the justification obtained thanks to the *votum baptismi* is a real form of justification). With Journet,[24] we can speak of a belonging to the Church that is impeded and tendential as well as of an invisible, secret, and inchoative belonging.

Ecumenical perspective

{700} Obviously, it is impossible to force a non-Catholic to accept this idea that he is invisibly a member of the Church (whether he be a Christian, a Jew, a Muslim, someone belonging to a non-monotheistic religion, or an atheist). Such a person is aware of not belonging to the Catholic Church and of not wishing to belong to her. To the degree that such a person is attached to his religion (or simply to the idea that he has formed of himself in relation to the world, to others, and to God), he can consider this Catholic position to be offensive, for it seems to suppose that he himself does not know what he is and what he truly wishes, at least religiously speaking.

On the other hand, the Catholic cannot, without renouncing his own faith, abandon the idea that the Church of Jesus Christ is the universal and necessary means of redemptive grace. Nor, can he

---

24. See Journet, "Qui est member de l'Église?," revised and improved in his *L'Église du Verbe incarné* (2nd ed.), 2:1304–14.

abandon the idea that the Church of Jesus Christ is the one that recognizes the pope as her head, as well as all the teaching that is stewarded by the pope, with the episcopal college gathered around him, and the sacraments that are dispensed by this Church.

It seems that, on the level of ecumenical dialogue, we must strive to present this Catholic position as being a Catholic interpretation of the adage, "No salvation outside the Church," without claiming, for all that, to impose this outlook. As regards the "offense" that might be felt by the non-Catholic, such offense can be avoided by emphasizing that, from the Catholic perspective, it is a question of the contradiction that can be found (even in the most mindful and lucid man) between his deepest intention (i.e., his *willing will*) and the ever partially constructed form that he gives to the object and ideal toward which he tends (i.e., his *willed will*).

Communities' Membership in the Church

Up to this point, we have spoken of the members of the Church who are individual persons. However, the Church is also made up of communities. We must consider the conditions for these communities' belonging to the Church.

Local churches and the universal Church

{701} What the apostles founded were "local Churches," complete ecclesial societies, each constituting "the Body of Christ." Hans Küng writes: "In 1 Corinthians and Romans the body of Christ is the individual community."[25] However, at the same time, the Church of which St. Paul speaks in the letters written during his captivity is certainly the universal Church.[26] On the other hand, the term "Catholic Church," which appears for the first time in St. Ignatius of Antioch,[27] designates from the beginning of the tradition the universal Church spread out over the earth, formed of men of all races and nations.[28]

---

25. Küng, *L'Église*, 317. [Tr. note: Taken from Küng, *The Church*, 230. Note that the text reads in the French of Nicolas: "For the first Letter to the Corinthians, and for that to the Romans, the body of Christ is the particular Church."]

26. See ibid. On St. Paul's teaching and its evolution, see Cerfaux, *La théologie de l'Église*, 163–78 and 249–56.

27. See Ignatius of Antioch, "Letter to the Smyrneans," 8.2.

28. See Gustave Bardy, *La théologie de l'Eglise de S. Clément de Rome à S. Irénée* (Paris:

On the question concerning the relationship between local churches and the universal Church (and, in connection with this, that concerning the relationship between the primacy of the pope and the authority of the bishops), the reader can consult the works contained in the note below.*

It is certain that local churches are, as ecclesial communities, members of the universal Church, which is therefore insufficiently defined if one speaks only of the gathering of the faithful under the authority of the pope. However, can one likewise say that "the Church is a communion of Churches, together forming the Catholica?"[29]

Such a position forgets that although communion is primordially established through charity, it also includes unity of faith and discipline, which have charity as their principle though needing a visible and external bond. In other words, what we said above about person-members of the Church (namely that their communion, in which the mystery of the Church consists, exists only as incarnated in a visible and hierarchical society) is true also (and for the same reasons) of the communion of churches. It must be incarnated in a universal "catholic" society characterized by a central government.

Cerf, 1945), and *La théologie de l'Eglise de S. Irénée au concile de Nicée* (Paris: Cerf, 1947). Louis Bouyer, *L'Eglise de Dieu*, 21–22. N.B. Küng's method of privileging the "great letters" in St. Paul's teaching as being more certainly authentic and, in any case, as reflecting a more ancient state of affairs, has been critiqued as an unjustified bias on behalf of archaism. Equally, his deliberate misunderstanding of the tradition has been seriously subjected to critique.

* *For the positions of the Magisterium:* André Marie Charue, "L'enseignement de S.S. Pie XII et de S.S. Jean XXIII sur l'épiscopate," in *L'épiscopat et l'Église universelle* (Paris: Cerf, 1962), 7–16. Gustave Dejaifve, "Primauté et collégialité au premier concile du Vatican," in *L'épiscopat et l'Église universelle* (Paris: Cerf, 1962), 639–60. Gustave Thils, *Primauté pontificale et prérogative épiscopale.* "Potestas ordinaria" au concile du Vatican (Louvain: Warny, 1961), and *L'Église et les Églises* (Paris: Desclée de Brouwer, 1967), 47–74.

For history: Bardy, *La théologie de l'Eglise de S. Clément de Rome à S. Irénée* and *La théologie de l'Eglise de S. Irénée au concile de Nicée.* Yves Congar, "De la communion des Églises à une ecclésiologie de l'Église universelle," in *L'épiscopat et l'Église universelle* (Paris: Cerf, 1962), 227–60. Joseph Hajjar, "La collégialité dans la tradition orientale," *L'Eglise de Vatican II* (Paris: Cerf, 1966), 847–70. Othmar Perler, "L'évêque représentant du Christ selons les documents des premieres siècles," in *L'épiscopat et l'Église universelle* (Paris: Cerf, 1962), 31–66.

For theology: Bouyer, *L'Eglise de Dieu*, 449–94. Congar, "De la communion des Églises," 227–60. De Lubac, *Les Églises particulières.* Karl Rahner, "Quelques réflexions sur les principes constitutionnels de l'Église," in *L'épiscopat et l'Église universelle* (Paris: Cerf, 1962), 541–64.

For a Protestant perspective: Oscar Cullmann, *Saint Pierre, disciple, apôtre, martyr* (Neuchâtel: Delachaux et Niestlé, 1952). Jean Jacques Van Allmen, *La primauté de l'Église de Pierre et de Paul* (Fribourg: Éditions universitaires, 1977).

29. See Leo-Joseph Suenens, *Interview dans I.C.I.* no. 336, 15 May 1968, sup. pp. II/III.

The very delicate problem of the divine right of the episcopate and of collegiality (which we will study in relation to the sacrament of holy orders) lies in understanding how this central government relies on the government proper to each particular church (and does not at all abolish it or absorb it) and also confirms it, assuring the presence of the Catholic Church in each particular church (in accord with the formula, "the Church of God which is 'at Ephesus' or 'at Corinth,'" and so forth).

The Church of Christ and Christian churches

{702} Ecumenism poses many problems today, giving rise to so many studies and conferences that it is quite impossible in a course on dogmatic theology to provide it with the place that its importance demands. These problems are studied for their own sakes in courses, exercises, and meetings of specialized institutes in theological faculties and centers of study. Nonetheless, even in a course in dogmatic theology, they cannot be entirely passed over in silence.

The immense progress made in Catholic doctrine brought about by Vatican II in the domain of ecumenism consists in the fact that meaning, value, and efficacy in the mystery of salvation were acknowledged for the various ecclesial communities in which one finds faith in Jesus Christ, the Word of God, and other visible elements. The title of "church" is not refused to them, although it "contradicts the Catholic sense to use (this word) in the plural, except to designate the local churches over which a bishop presides."[30]

Nonetheless, the decree does not dissimulate and neither does it lessen the Catholic doctrine according to which the Church founded by Jesus Christ is the Catholic Church.[31] From the perspective of Catholic theology, the entire problem of ecumenism is that of arriving at a union of Christian Churches such that, while recognizing the claims of the Catholic Church in calling herself the Church of Christ (i.e., the Church governed by the authority of Christ, in His name, with the assistance of His Spirit, by the bishop of Rome), she would respect the ecclesial specificity of other confessions that also

---

30. Yves Congar, "Introduction au Décret sur l'oecuménisme," in *Concile oecuménique Vatican II* (Paris: Centurion, 1965), 172.
31. See *Unitatis Redintegratio*, no. 3.

claim faith in Christ. Thus, the mere fact of posing the problem presupposes a postulate, namely, that the various Christian confessions do not diverge from each other as regards their authentically Christian character but, rather, as regards the limits (indeed, the deviations) that each, through the course of the centuries, has brought to this authentic tradition.[32] Even in the case of the Catholic Church, nothing prevents, as we have seen, one from speaking of limits and even particular deviations. However, we believe that she has not deviated in the fundamental direction impressed upon her by Christ because Christ, in accord with His promise, is in her and acts upon her, through her, and through the Holy Spirit whom He has sent to her in order to assist her indefectibly, despite the very real and very numerous faults committed through the ages (as well as the errors of her members, particularly of her shepherds).

Israel and the Church

Here we are faced with a vast and difficult problem which cannot be treated in all of its dimensions.[33]

Israel was the People of God, chosen from among all peoples. The Church is the new People of God. Must we think that the promises made to Israel have become null and void? Scripture expressly forbids this. Thus, must we think that Israel continues to be the People of God alongside the Church (therefore, the Israel who refuses to recognize Christ), thus playing a specific role in salvation history? No, for the promises made to Israel have been realized in Jesus Christ and in the Church, who is His body.[34]

Therefore, we must say that Israel has passed over into the Church, first personally in the Jewish people who constituted the apostolic community, and then in the first Christian community: "God has not rejected his people whom he foreknew ... So too at the present time there is a remnant, chosen by grace ... What then? Israel failed to obtain what it sought. The elect obtained it, but the

---

32. See Journet, *L'Église du Verbe incarné*, 2:708–63.
33. See Gregory Baum, "Notes sur les relations d'Israël et de l'Eglise," in *Le diacre dans l'Église et le monde d'aujourd'hui* (Paris: Cerf, 1966); *Les Juifs et l'Evangile*, trans. Jacques Mignon (Paris: Cerf, 1965). Pierre Benoît, "Compte-rendu du livre de Gr. Baum, 'Les Juifs et l'Evangile,'" *Exégèse et Théologie* (Paris: Cerf, 1968), 3:397–99. Küng, *L'Église*, 153–209.
34. See Gal 3:29.

rest were hardened, as it is written."³⁵ In what follows in the same chapter, it is clear that these Israelites who did believe in Christ were "cast aside"³⁶ and will be reintegrated: "And even the others, if they do not persist in their unbelief, will be grafted in, for God has the power to graft them in again."³⁷

Thus Israel as a chosen people was not replaced by the Church. It furnished the Church with her initial nucleus, from which she spread forth to all peoples of the earth. She is the People of God, at once old and new.

As for those who continue to serve God in Judaism, while believing in good faith that Israel still remains the People of God, their case is that of the "righteous outside." As regards Israel itself, it still possesses means of salvation for its good faith members. In this case, one can say that it has a role to play in salvation history. However, it is an "accidental" role, namely, the persistence of an economy of salvation that is historically obsolete (though it remains of value for some).

MARY AND THE CHURCH

{704} The theme of the mutual relationship between Mary and the Church is very ancient. We can even say that it is the point of departure for what later became Mariology.³⁸ However, it had become progressively abandoned, leaving Mariology to develop according to its own law and in a way that, despite undeniable successes, very often went astray into venturesome fabrications. It suffered from being pressed toward a kind of maximalism that, on the pretense that one can never sufficiently glorify the mother of God, ultimately rendered her unreal by setting her wholly apart in salvation history. This is opposed to the truth of the matter, namely, that she draws all of her meaning and true grandeur from the place that she holds in this history.

35. Rom 11:2–8 (RSV). Also, see *Traduction Oecuménique de la Bible*, in loco, note x.
36. See Rom 11:15 (RSV).
37. Rom 11:23 (RSV).
38. See Hervé Coathalem, *Le parallélisme entre la Vierge et l'Église dans la tradition latine jusqu'à la fin du XIIᵉ siècle* (Rome: Apud aedes Universitatis Gregorianae, 1954). Alois Müller, *Ecclesia-Maria. Die Einheit Marias und der Kierche*, Paradosis 5 (Fribourg: Ed. universitaires, 1955).

This ancient theme was renewed in contemporary theology[39] and received a resounding confirmation at the Second Vatican Council. Indeed, after long deliberations and passionate discussions, the Council Fathers decided (granted, by a very weak majority) to integrate the schema that had been prepared on the Virgin Mary into the constitution on the Church. Considerably refashioned because of this manner of presenting things, the text on Mary became the eighth chapter of *Lumen Gentium*: "The Blessed Virgin Mary, Mother of God, in the mystery of Christ and of the Church."[40]

Far from impoverishing Mariology, as was thought by the adversaries of such integration into *Lumen Gentium*, the Council's highlighting of this theme has shown itself to be very fruitful for contemporary theology concerning the mother of God and has opened the way for a balanced and just resolution to the "Marian question."[41] In this, theology has received an acquisition that can be considered irrevocable.

This theme can be reduced to three great orientations.

Mary, Member of the Church

She is among those who are redeemed

{705} Although she is redeemed *sublimiori modo*, in a loftier way, "from the very start," she is wholly redeemed by Christ and His unique sacrifice.[42] We can entirely subscribe to Lossky's observation (despite the fact that he directs the point against the dogma of the Immaculate Conception, though on account of an interpretive error):

She was holy and pure from her mother's womb and, nonetheless, this holiness did not place her outside of the rest of humanity before Christ. At the moment of the Annunciation, she was not in a state analogous to

---

39. "Marie et l'Église," *Etudes Mariales* (Paris: Lethielleux, 1951–53). Vladimir Lossky, "Panhagia," in *À l'image et à la resemblance de Dieu* (Paris: Aubier, 1967), ch. 11. Marie-Joseph Nicolas, *Theotokos, le mystère de Marie* (Paris: Desclée de Brouwer, 1965), 191–213. Philips, *L'Église*, 2:208–86, and "Perspectives mariologiques: Marie et l'Église," *Marianum* 15 (1953): 436–511. Hugo Rahner, *Marie et l'Église*, trans. Bernard Petit and Jean-Pierre Gérard (Paris: Cerf, 1955). Otto Semmelroth, *Marie archétype de l'Église* (Paris: Fleurus, 1965). [Tr. note: Fr. Nicolas cites an entry that does not exist for Lossky. He seems to mean the text cited above.]

40. Antoine Wenger, *Vatican II. Chronique de la deuxième session* (Paris: Centurion, 1964).

41. See René Laurentin, *La question mariale* (Paris: Seuil, 1963).

42. See §§464–69 in the previous volume.

that of Eve before sin ... The Second Eve chooses to become the Mother of God and hears the angelic salutation in the state of fallen humanity.[43]

However, we must add: "... fallen and redeemed."[44]

Therefore, we must resolutely set aside every form of Mariology that would claim to situate Mary between Christ and the Church. She is part of the world to which the Father sends His Son in order to save it and divinize it. She is part of the Church, made up of the world who received her Son, and she allowed herself to be saved by Him.

The first among the members of the Church
Christ's holiness was communicated to her in fullness:

> Although the members of the Church can become members of the household of Christ, His "mother, brothers, and sisters" to the degree that their vocation is fulfilled, only the Mother of God through whom the Word was made flesh could receive the fullness of grace and attain a limitless glory, realizing in her person all the holiness that the Church can have.[45]

However, this holds only for the Church in fullness and for the earthly Church during the time when Mary lived on the earth prior to Pentecost, inasmuch as the latter is a transitory realization of the former (i.e., in the order of love and of holiness and not according to the visible and sacramental hierarchy). Nothing in either the Gospel or tradition enables us to imagine that Mary played a hierarchical role in the early Church. (In the narrative of Pentecost in Acts 2, Mary is named only among the women, after the apostles.) Her role in salvation history is not to represent Christ the priest and shepherd in a sacramental manner. Rather, her role is found in cooperating in the Incarnation itself and in the Redemption.

Mary, the "Type" or "Icon" of the Church

{706} Faced with the annunciation, Mary is the spiritual personification of Israel, the perfect realization of its proper grace and its

---

43. See Lossky, "Panhagia," 201. [Tr. note: As noted above, this seems to be the text to which Fr. Nicolas is referring in his original footnote shorthand.]

44. Jean-Hervé Nicolas, "L'innocence originelle de la Nouvelle Eve," in *Etudes Mariales* (Paris: Lethielleux, 1958), 15–35.

45. See Lossky, "Panhagia," 205. [Tr. note: As noted above, this seems to be the text to which Fr. Nicolas is referring in his original footnote shorthand.]

holiness.⁴⁶ In particular, she is the ultimate personification of the "remnant of Israel" and, at the same time, gives a heart and voice to Israel's expectation. On this head, as we have seen, she can represent "all of mankind" at the annunciation in her free consent to the "Grace" that is the Incarnation.⁴⁷

From this moment, Mary (and she alone), united to Christ through her consensual maternity, finds her place in salvation history within the context of the first coming. She continues to represent humanity, and this is the meaning of her presence at the foot of the cross and of her participation in Christ's sacrifice.⁴⁸ At this moment, Mary is the anticipated personification of the Church, realizing in herself the purely created, perfect holiness that Christ, through His redemptive act, will gradually bring about in the Church. Likewise, her Assumption can be explained theologically as the realization in advance, in herself, of the redemption in its full perfection, which will be realized a second time for the Church only at the end of time.⁴⁹

In Mary, the passage from Israel to the Church takes place, as it were, in its first stage, for during the phase of salvation history now being considered (i.e., the phase of Christ's first advent, between the Incarnation and the Ascension), Israel has already brought forth its fruit. What it was awaiting is here, and it mysteriously is effaced before Him. However, at the same time, the Church, who must fill the entire phase of salvation history between the realized redemptive mystery (Christ's life, death, resurrection, and exaltation) and its consummation in the Parousia and the resurrection of the dead, does not yet exist. Mary is there, representing before Christ the humanity for whom He dies and rises again, the humanity whom He saves and sanctifies through His sacrifice. She is at once the first fruits of saved humanity as well as a figure and type of the Church that will be born at Pentecost from the outpouring of the Spirit sent by Christ and constituted by redeemed mankind, to the degree that

---

46. See René Laurentin, *Court traité sur la Vierge Marie* (Paris: Lethielleux, 1967), 112–17.
47. See §522 in the previous volume.
48. See §523 in the previous volume.
49. See Journet, *L'Église du Verbe incarné*, 2:382–453. Also, from another perspective, see Lossky, "Panhagia." [Tr. note: As noted above, this seems to be the text to which Fr. Nicolas is referring in his original footnote shorthand.]

they are redeemed (as we have seen). This Church's destiny is fulfilled in her in advance. As she was the first of the redeemed, she is also the first of the resurrected, thus becoming, in the beautiful expression used by Bouyer, "the eschatological icon of the Church."[50]

However, from the time that the Church was constituted at Pentecost, it is quite clear that Mary becomes a member of this Church, indeed, her most eminent member. Moreover, the Church is constituted on the basis of her, not (as we have seen) in the order of sacramental and hierarchical powers, but instead in the essential and eternal order of holiness, wherein she holds utter primacy, the physical person in whom the Church-Person finds its exemplary realization:

> Given that the Church's personality is of the mystical order and not of the physical order, it needs to be expressed, incarnated, and personalized in her real members. The humblest Christian, in his prayer and relationship with God, is a kind of personalization of the Church, although an incomplete one and sometimes barely aware of it. However, Mary's person is perfectly, completely, and totally the personification of what the Church will be in eternity and not merely what the Church is in time.[51]

The Spiritual Maternity of Mary in the Church

{707} In relation to the Church, Mary does not only play a role that one could call "representative." If the grace of the Church is indeed realized in her in an eminent and complete manner, this is not only in order for her to be honored and glorified by this. It is also for the sake of her playing an equally eminent role, indeed one that is wholly singular, in the Church's salvific activity (i.e., in her mediation).

We have already spoken about Mary's mediation and have attempted to show how it is understandable only in relation to Christ's mediation, such that He remains the sole mediator without precluding real, subordinate forms of mediation but, rather, making use of them. Among these latter, there is that of the Church and that of Mary. Concerning these, we have equally tried to see how, far from impinging on one another, they mutually envelop each other.[52] At

---

50. See Louis Bouyer, *Le culte de la Mère de Dieu* (Chevetogne: Éditions de Chevetogne, 1955), 33.
51. Nicolas, *Theotokos, le mystère de Marie*, 209.
52. See §§533–39 in the previous volume.

the Second Vatican Council, weighty discussions were undertaken concerning the very legitimacy of using the title of "mediatrix" for Mary and, above all, the danger that this title (even when specified with the greatest exactitude) would be wrongly understood by non-Catholic Christians, uselessly adding a new difficulty to rapprochement among the Christian churches.[53] On the other hand, were the Council not to give her this title, which had become so common in the Church's own teaching, it would thus withdraw it from her, that is, would judge that it was not only inopportune but even falsely attributed to her. In the end, the Council took the middle way, which consisted in giving this title to Mary in the midst of other titles that explain and properly contextualize it:

> By her maternal charity, she cares for the brethren of her Son, who still journey on earth surrounded by dangers and cultics, until they are led into the happiness of their true home. Therefore the Blessed Virgin is invoked by the Church under the titles of Advocate, Auxiliatrix, Adjutrix, and Mediatrix. This, however, is to be so understood that it neither takes away from nor adds anything to the dignity and efficaciousness of Christ the one Mediator.[54]

Therefore, we see that Mary's mediating role is expressly connected to the role that she played in salvation history: her maternity. This maternity has two aspects. On the one hand, there is maternity properly speaking (i.e., physical maternity, though voluntarily accepted and thereby spiritualized) in relation to Jesus, the Incarnate Word. On the other hand, there is her spiritual maternity in relation to believers (though this is in continuity with the maternity properly so called that is her very grace-being).[55] Thus, regarding Jesus' words, "Who are my mother and my brothers?," St. Augustine wrote:

> By doing God's will, Mary is the mother of Christ only in a bodily way, whereas spiritually she is sister and mother ... She is mother according to the spirit, certainly not of our head, who is the Savior Himself, from whom she is, rather, spiritually born (since all those who have believed in Him, among whom she is ranked, are justly called sons of the Bridegroom),

---

53. See Wenger, *Vatican II*, 91–121.
54. *Lumen Gentium*, no. 62.
55. See §451 in the previous volume.

but she is truly mother (according to the spirit) of His members (among whom we are numbered), for through her charity, she has worked (with Christ) to bring to birth the faithful in the Church (i.e., those who are members of this head).[56]

How is this spiritual maternity exercised? Some Mariologists have judged that reducing this exercise to prayer alone would be to minimize it unduly.[57] Indeed, they advanced the idea of a kind of instrumental action analogous to what St. Thomas recognized for the case of Christ's humanity in the bestowal [*collation*] of graces and everything subordinated to it. We cannot take part in this discussion here.[58] Let us only say that the *raison d'être* for such an instrumental power is not immediately evident. It is recognized for the case of Christ's humanity for two reasons. On the one hand, this grace which He confers is that which He merited on the cross. On the other hand, He received it in fullness so that every grace conferred to men after the resurrection flows from His own. If St. Thomas likewise attributed this role to the Church on earth, this is on account of the Church's sacramentality and the divine arrangement according to which Christ's sanctifying action (in itself invisible from the time of His return to the Father) must be rendered visible in a human action through which Christ's own action passes. It is not clear what reality would be added to Mary's mediation by a power whose exercise would be as invisible as Christ's and could not confer on her any supplementary efficacy, but on the contrary, would remove even the unique and proper efficacy that it could have.

Moreover, this position is based on an insufficient estimate of the power of prayer. If we happen to think that merely praying for someone represents an insignificant action, this is because our prayer is poor, hesitant, and undetermined. We do not know what we must ask for, and we ask in a very intermittent manner. Mary's prayer is all-powerful, based on her loving and unqualified participation in the work of salvation. It is concerned with the authentic needs of

---

56. See St. Augustine, *De virginitate*, PL 40, c. 399.
57. This was suggested at the Council itself. See Wenger, *Vatican II*, 111.
58. See Jean-Hervé Nicolas, "Médiation mariale et maternité spirituelle," in *La maternité spirituelle de Marie, Actes du VIIIe congrès marial national, Lisieux 5–9 July 1961* (Paris: Lethielleux, 1962), 67–88, at 82–83.

the person for whom she prays and whom she knows to his or her depths in the light of God. It is continuous. For its efficacious exercise, Mary's maternal action over the faithful has no need of any other power than prayer. What she requests and obtains through this prayer is essentially grace in the form of a disposition to receive God's gift, for God wills to give grace without man's asking for it, for each and every human person. Moreover, He has given it to them in giving Christ to them. However, such grace is received only by those who welcome it, and through his own sin, man closes himself off to it. Inasmuch as it is the misdirection of the free creature into aberrant ways leading him into blind alleys, sin is a *misery*, and by this he draws God's mercy. On the other hand, inasmuch as it is a *counterlove*, it drives away mercy, which is love. The mystery of grace is that grace itself opens a path in man's spirit, disposing him for the reception of God's gift. For his own part, man only can close himself off. Through her prayer Mary's role is to obtain this grace which, opening man to the grace of pardon, reconciliation, and divinization, enables mercy to be exercised: "Formally speaking, Mary's prayer plays the role of being a universal dispositive cause. It is presupposed for every grace. It is maternal in the sense that what it requests and obtains belongs to the vital exercise of the Christian life [*est de l'ordre de la vie*]."[59] Yet it is still God's mercy that arouses Mary's own prayer.

This does not mean that this prayer always obtains what it asks for. When discussing Christ's own prayer, we were led to reflect on man's mysterious ability to place an obstacle before grace and to remain obstinate in his rejection.[60] Mary's prayer is all-powerful. Christ's omnipotence passes through it. However, as also holds true for the activity of the incarnate Christ and for the Triune God Himself, this omnipotence runs into created freedom's rejection when the latter asserts itself and rigidly closes one off to grace.

This spiritual maternity of Mary is not adequately distinguished from that of the Church. Properly as her own, at least during the earthly phase of the Church's life, the latter has the visible means of the sacraments and the preaching of the Word. Mary's maternity

---

59. Marie Joseph Nicolas, "La maternité spirituelle de Marie," *Etudes Mariales* 3 (Paris: Lethielleux, 1961), 52.
60. See §515 in the previous volume.

finds its particular character in the fact that it is situated in continuity with her divine maternity. However, if it is already the case that in each of her members the Church praises God, blesses Him, and prays to Him, for all the more reason is Mary's prayer the loftiest and purest expression of the Church's prayer, just as the communal personality of the Church is in some way condensed and realized in her unique personality.

Mary, Mother of the Church

{708} However, it is well known that Pope Paul VI was not content with the traditional title "mother of the faithful" that was taken up by the constitution *Lumen Gentium*. Through the course of the Council, though not unaware of the hesitations and reticence of the theological commission, he insisted on solemnly proclaiming Mary "mother of the Church." This is not the place to retrace the history of the debates that led to this conclusion.[61] Let us merely note that if this is not a question concerning a conciliar decision, it was proclaimed in the very Council hall by Pope Paul under the applause of the majority of the Council fathers.

What the expression means is not only that Mary is the "mother of the faithful," but that she also plays a role (symbolized by her maternity) in the very birth of the Church. Theologically, this can be understood to the degree that one recognizes that Mary plays a role in the Redemption itself. Indeed, at the moment when salvation is accomplished on the cross, the Church does not yet exist, but instead, comes to be born, according to the traditional image, from Christ's open side. (This is not to be understood as implying that it would have begun at the moment of Christ's death. However, even though it was truly born at Pentecost under the movement of the Spirit who came into her and never ceases to animate her, it was the resurrected and exalted Christ who sent the Spirit from the Father.) By His outpoured blood, He acquired for Himself this Church, whom He made His body and bride. Mary stands there at the foot of the cross, prefiguring the Church, accepting the grace of redemption on behalf of her and of all of redeemed humanity. If she

---

61. See Philips, *L'Église*, 2:213–24 and 287–89. Wenger, *Vatican II*, 113–21.

played a role in the Redemption itself through this acceptance and personal participation (as we have suggested, following a number of theologians[62]), one can better understand how she thus participated in the birth of the Church. Let us recall that this presupposes that we recognize at once that she herself is redeemed and that this very role that she plays (at the foot of the cross) is an effect of redemptive grace.

If one were to object that Mary cannot be the "mother of the Church" because she is a member of the Church, one would thus make a rigid and univocal use of a metaphor, contrary to its own, proper fluidity, above all in religious symbols.

However, what is the interest and meaning of this expression? It is of interest because it makes clear that Mary's action extends not only to all the faithful (including those who have functions, even the highest, to be fulfilled in the Church) but also to the Church as such, to this Church-Person whose nature and role we strove to determine in our discussions above. In order to prevent the symbol from becoming incoherent, we doubtlessly must say that Mary is the mother of the Church-Person in the Church's earthly realization. In the eschatological universe where the glorious and perfect Church (the body of Christ brought to completion and his bride having arrived at her perfection) is progressively constituted by the elect of each new generation, she is the singular person in whom the personality of the Church, embracing all people who are definitively saved and holy, finds its concrete expression, that is, its hypostasis.

62. See §523 in the previous volume.

4

The Sacraments in the Church

{709} As we have seen, the Church is the sacrament of Christ in her very being and in all of her activity. However, among her various activities, there is one in which such sacramentality is fully exercised, in the strongest sense, for there she completely fades away before Christ who acts through her, retaining nothing properly as her own except for her visibility and her instrumentality. For this reason, such activity is rightly called "sacramental." It is the action that she exercises through her sacraments. We now must study it for its own sake and separately, not only because this activity poses specific problems but also because it is where we find the most powerful manifestation of the nature of the Church's sacramentality.

THE SACRAMENTAL ORDER

Summary Exposition of the Data of Scripture and Tradition

{710} In order to find a theological treatise on the sacraments in general we must turn to the twelfth century and the scholastic period, finding such a discussion first in Peter Lombard and then in Hugh of St. Victor. Neither Scripture nor the Fathers discuss the sacraments in themselves. It is principally in relation to baptism and the Eucharist that they furnish the data that will later make up sacramental theology.[1]

---

1. See Yves Congar, "Introduction générale aux traités anti-donatistes de S. Augustin," OESA 28 (Paris: Desclée de Brouwer, 1963), 94.

Sacraments and faith

The contrast between faith and the sacraments dates from a later era (in particular, the Reformation) and does not exist in the New Testament. For the New Testament, salvation requires one to believe and be baptized.[2] The doctrinal teaching that flows from all of this could be formulated as follows.

The gift of divine life resulting from the Son of God's advent into the world and from His death on the cross is transmitted to men by two interconnected means. On the one hand, it is transmitted through the objective sign of water, to which the Spirit, He who is the transcendent agent of "birth from on high," is mysteriously connected. On the other hand, it is transmitted through the subjective means of faith, which gives access to life, salvation, and light.[3]

This observation refers to John 3. However, the author draws similar conclusions regarding other books of the New Testament.

Participation in the event of salvation through baptism and the Eucharist

[The idea that we participate in the event of salvation through baptism and the Eucharist] is quite vigorously noted by St. Paul in particular, above all as regards baptism,[4] though also as regards the Eucharist.[5]

The Church is constituted through baptism and the Eucharist

Through baptism, the believer not only adheres to Christ and enters into the mystery of His death and resurrection but also *is joined to the company of His disciples*.[6] That is, he is gathered into the Church. The ecclesial community is constituted through baptism.

The Church herself is said to be "sanctified" and "purified" by Christ through "the washing of water with the word."[7]

---

2. See Louis Villette, *Foi et sacrement*, vol. 1 (Paris: Bloud et Gay, 1959), ch. 1.
3. Ibid., 82.
4. See Rom 6.
5. See 1 Cor 10:14–22 and 11:17–33. See Villette, *Foi et sacrament*, and Albert Michel, "Sacrements," in *Dictionnaire de Théologie Catholique*, 14:485–644.
6. See Acts 2:41–44.
7. Eph 5:26 (RSV).

The Sacraments in the Church 143

The symbolism of the sacraments
Baptism and the Eucharist are external rites to which efficacity and signification are attached in relation to the reality of salvation, which itself is interior. Such symbolism would seem most pronounced in St. John: rebirth in water, the bread of life, and blood poured out. However, the symbolism of water (absolution and remission of sins or purification) is clear in St. Paul.

A brief history of the notion of a sacrament
In[8] Scripture, the Greek term *mysterion* designates a secret thing, hidden in God, namely, the very object of revelation and faith.[9] The same sense is found in the writers of the second century.

The origins
{711} In Clement of Alexandria and Origen, the word begins to designate the ensemble of Christian truths and practices, likely in contrast to the "pagan mysteries." Thus, generally speaking, a mystery is something that is simultaneously revealed and hidden through an event or a visible rite. Thus, St. John Chrysostom stated:

We find ourselves faced with a mystery when we consider things as being different from what we see ... Here, the judgment of the believer and the unbeliever differ. For my part, I hear that Christ was crucified and

---

8. See Ferdinand Cavallera, "Le décret du concile de Trente sur les sacrements en général," *Bulletin de littérature ecclésiastique* (1918): 170–75. Congar, "Introduction générale aux traités anti-donatistes de S. Augustin," 48–125. Charles Couturier, "Sacramentum et mysterium dans l'oeuvre de S. Augustin," in *Études augustiniennes* (Paris: Aubier, 1953), 161–332. Joseph de Ghellinck, *Pour l'histoire du mot Sacramentum* (Paris, 1924), and "Un chapitre dans l'histoire de la définition des sacrements au XIIIe siècle," in *Mélanges Mandonnet* (Paris: Vrin, 1953), 79–96. Michel, "Sacrements," 485–644. Christine Mohrmann, "Sacramentum dans les plus anciens textes chrétiens," *Harvard Theological Review* 47 (1954): 141–53. Pierre Pourrat, *La théologie sacramentaire, étude de théologie positive* (Paris: Gabalda, 1907). Damien van den Eynde, *Les définitions des sacrements pendant la première période de la théologie scolastique (1050–1240)* (Rome / Louvain: Antonianum / Nauwelaerts, 1950). William A. van Roo, *De sacramentis in genere* (Rome: Apud aedes Universitatis Gregoriana, 1960), 1–70. Villette, *Foi et sacrement*. Manuel Useros Carreteros, *"'Statuta Ecclesiae' y 'sacramenta Ecclesiae'" en la eclesiología de St. Tomás de Aquino: reflexión tomista sobre el derecho de la Iglesia en paralelismo a la actual temática eclesiológico-canónica* (Rome: Pontificia Universitas Gregoriana, 1962). [Tr. note: Fr. Nicolas also includes a reference to "Coll." without providing adequate bibliographical information regarding the particular collected text to which he is referring.]
9. See Mt 13:11; Mk 4:11; Lk 8:9; 1 Cor 2:7–10; Rom 11:25 and 16:25–26; Col 1:26; Eph 3:9.

immediately admire His love for men. The unbeliever also hears it and believes that this was folly ... When the unbeliever comes to know of baptism, he thinks that it is only water. For my part, since I do not consider simply what I see, I contemplate the purification of soul brought about by the Holy Spirit. The unbeliever thinks that baptism is a simple bathing of the body. For my part, I believe that it also renders the soul pure and holy. In a similar way, my thought is drawn to the tomb, the Resurrection, to sanctification, justice, redemption, filial adoption, the heavenly inheritance, the kingdom of heaven, and to the gift of the Holy Spirit ...[10]

St. Ambrose's *De mysteriis* contains a sacramental theology that is already rather elaborate. Through this text, the Greek tradition penetrated into Latin theology. In it, we find an idea that had already been expressed by St. Gregory of Nazianzen and St. Cyril of Jerusalem, namely that the sacrament, which is composed of a visible element and an invisible element, corresponds to man's nature. The sacrament is efficacious not by itself but through the activity of the Godhead and cross of Christ: "Indeed, what is water without the cross of Christ? It is an ordinary element, deprived of every kind of sacramental efficacy. Nonetheless, the mystery of regeneration is not produced without water."[11] Moreover, baptism is clearly marked out as being dually composed of washing and the invocation of the Trinity: "If the catechumen has not been baptized in the name of the Father, the Son, and the Holy Spirit, he can neither receive the remission of sins nor draw from the gift of spiritual grace."[12]

The passage from *mysterion* to *sacramentum*

{712} Tertullian is often credited with the creation of the term "sacrament" for designating the sanctifying rites. Christine Mohrmann has shown that, prior to Tertullian, the word *mysterion* had been translated as *sacramentum* in the ancient Latin translations of the Bible in Africa. Perhaps this was done for the sake of avoiding any possible confusion with the pagan mysteries.

Tertullian also employs the word in a quite broad sense in order to designate the idea of a mystery, a hidden truth. However, in a

---

10. See St. John Chrysostom, *Homélies sur l'épître aux Hébreux*, PG 63, no. 7, ch. 55.
11. See St. Ambrose, *De mysteriis*, ed. and trans. B. Botte, SC 25bis (Paris: Cerf, 1961), IV.
12. Ibid.

stricter fashion, he uses it to designate the rites themselves. He applies it in this latter sense principally to baptism, though he also uses it for the Eucharist and confirmation. He primarily insists, in a fairly materializing manner, on their efficacy and quite strikingly connects such efficacy to signification:

The flesh is cleansed so that the soul may be detached [from the passions]. The flesh is signed so that the soul may be fortified. The flesh is darkened by the imposition of the hands so that the soul may receive the Spirit's illumination. The flesh is nourished by the body and blood of Christ so that the soul may be filled with God.[13]

On the other hand, he expressly attributes the sacraments' efficacy to the Divine Power.[14]

Donatism and the controversies to which it gave rise led the theologians of both camps to deepen these notions, for what was at stake was the question of knowing whether the sanctifying value of the rites depended on the holiness of the person who conferred them as well as on the authenticity of the ecclesial community in which they were conferred.

The Donatists faulted the "Catholics" with celebrating the mysteries to the ruin of those wretched and in need of them: "When a sacrilegious person erects an altar, it is a layman who celebrates the rites and a soiled person who purifies."[15]

Even before St. Augustine, Optatus of Milevis had responded to this problem by emphasizing the purely instrumental character of the minister:

You ceaselessly ask, "How can one give what he does not have?" However, see that it is the Lord who gives. See that it is only God who purifies each one. Indeed, who can wash away spiritual stains and defilements if not God who made the spirit?[16]

He accords great importance to the invocation of the Trinity (in baptism) and also to the faith of the subject, which is faith in the Trinity

---

13. See Tertullian, *De resurrection carnis*, PL 2, 852B.
14. See Tertullian, *Traité du baptême. Texte latin. Introduction and notes by F. Refoulé*, trans. in collaboration with Maurice Drouzy, SC 35 (Paris: Cerf, 1953), ch. 3.
15. On Donatism, see Congar, "Introduction générale aux traités anti-donatistes de S. Augustin," 48–125.
16. Optatus of Milevis, *De schismate donatistorum*, PL 11:1053.

who has been invoked and in the rite thus conferred. This importance is so great that he thinks that baptism conferred by a heretic has no value. However, by contrast, he recognizes the value of baptism conferred by schismatics: "Therefore, one cannot deny that you, schismatics, have them (i.e., the sacraments), for with us, you partake in the true sacraments."[17]

The sacramental doctrine of St. Augustine

{713} St. Augustine played a predominant role in the formation of scholastic theology in this domain, as well as in the doctrine retained by the Church's Magisterium. It is very dependent upon tradition, though also on properly Augustinian insights concerning signs and the signification of visible things in relation to invisible ones.[18] This doctrine can be summarized as follows:

1. St. Augustine extends the term "sacramentum" to all sacred signs, that is, to all those visible realities that, by divine institution, lead the mind to invisible things (either so that we may know them or so that we may obtain them and be united to them). However, he also employs the term in a more precise sense to designate the rites of the Church by means of which the believer obtains salvation and grace.

2. In this more precise sense, all the sacraments signify Christ, the sole Savior. The sacraments of the Old Law signified Christ who was to come. The sacraments of the New Law signify Christ who has already come.

The sacraments of the New Law have a threefold signification. They signify Christ who has already come (i.e., the first coming), as well as His saving mystery (i.e., His passion, death, and resurrection). Likewise, they signify the sanctification and salvation of which they are the means for the person who receives them (i.e., the remission of sin and union with Christ). Finally, they signify Christ's second coming (i.e., the definitive consummation of salvation):

---

17. Ibid., 907.
18. See Charles Couturier, "Structure métaphysique de l'être créé d'après S. Augustin," *Recherches de Philosophie* 1 (1955): 57–84; Villette, *Foi et sacrement*, vol. 1, ch. 4.

For if every sacrament of the new life must not be taken from us because the resurrection of the dead still lies in the future for us, nonetheless, it was necessary that [the ancient sacrament of circumcision] should be changed into a better one. Baptism was substituted for it because something completely new has been effected. In the resurrection of Christ, we have been offered an embodiment of the realization of the eternal life to come.*

3. The sacraments not only signify the salvation of the person who receives them.

They also effect it: "Whence comes to the water this lofty power which, by touching the body, cleanses the soul?"[19] On this point, there is a notable difference between the sacraments of the Old Law and those of the New Law: "The sacraments of the New Testament confer salvation. The sacraments of the Old Testament promised the Savior."[20] Does this mean that, according to St. Augustine, the sacraments of the Old Law had no efficacy? According to Couturier, it would be a question of a lesser form of efficacy.

4. The sacraments produce their saving effect only thanks to the "word."

However, what is this "word"? Is it the sacramental formula or the preaching that must be received in faith? In the text cited,[21] St. Augustine writes: "If you suppress the word, what is the water without the word? The word comes to the elements and the sacrament is itself a kind of visible word." From this remark, he then passes on to the necessity of belief for being purified and saved (and, hence, to the necessity of preaching). This led Calvin to draw the conclusion that the sacrament is nothing without the preaching of faith: "Now, we see how, in the sacraments, he requires preaching from which faith ensues."[22]

In reality, St. Augustine always connected the "fruitfulness" of the sacrament to faith and to the true Church, who is the guardian and preacher of that truth. Without this, the sacrament is of no

---

* [Tr. note: Fr. Nicolas includes no citation here.]
19. St. Augustine, *Homilies on the Gospel of St. John*, PL 35, tract. 80, no. 3.
20. St. Augustine, *Enarrationes in Psalmos*, PL 36 and 37, In Ps. 73.
21. See note oo above.
22. John Calvin, *Institution chrétienne* (Genève: Labor et Fideles, 1967), 4.14.4. [Tr. note: No date provided by Fr. Nicolas.]

use for salvation. However, at the same time, he definitively established that the sacrament exists outside of these conditions and preserves its sanctifying value, even when given *per adulteros* and found in *adulteris*.[23] The passage from the "sacramental word" to the word that begets faith is natural and is a matter of great importance. However, according to him, the sacramental word is what is both necessary and sufficient for the *elementum* to become the *sacramentum*.

5. St. Augustine applied this notion of a sacrament expressly to baptism, the Eucharist, and to the rite by which a Christian is established as a *dispensator verbi et sacramenti*.[24] For our other sacraments, if he speaks of "anointing" (confirmation), he is not sure that he sees a distinct sacrament in it. He is aware of a rite of reconciliation, which he calls *impositio manuum*, and is also aware of a rite of extreme unction. However, he does not expressly designate them using the term "sacraments," thereby indicating that they are sanctifying rites.

From St. Augustine to St. Thomas

{714} At the beginning of the fourth book of Peter Lombard's *Sentences*, we can find definitions of the sacraments that had already become classic. Two of them were claimed to be from St. Augustine (though the second of them was, in reality, from St. Isidore of Seville). Another had been given by Hugh of St. Victor in order to correct and complete the Isidorian definition, and the last was from the *Summa Sententiarum*.

In all of these definitions, emphasis is laid on the nature of what a sign is, which is thus definitively recognized as belonging to the nature of the sacraments. However, the sacrament's efficacy is [also] increasingly emphasized. In Peter Lombard, it becomes part of the definition, so that those rites that do not cause grace (in particular, according to Peter Lombard, the rites of the Old Law) are not sacraments but instead are *signa sacramentalia*. Efficacy is already attributed this essential role by the *Summa sententiarum*: "The sacrament is not only the sign [*figure*] of the sacred thing but also is the cause of it."

---

23. See St. Augustine, *De Baptismo*, PL 29 (1964), 3.15.
24. See Couturier, "Structure métaphysique de l'être créé d'après S. Augustin," 184.

Peter Lombard distinguishes "sacramentals" (*signa sacramentalia*) from sacraments properly so called by the absence of efficacy in the first group. Before him, Abelard had distinguished *sacramentalia spiritualia* (or *sacramenta majora*) from *sacramenta minora*.[25] The *spiritualia* efficaciously bring about salvation. (In analogous terms, St. Thomas will come to say that they lead to the effect of the sacrament, namely the obtaining of grace.)[26] However, Abelard named only five of our septenary as being *sacramenta majora*, mentioning neither penance nor holy orders. Hugh of St. Victor did not seek to enumerate the *sacramenta majora*. It seems that our sequence of seven sacraments is found for the first time in the *Summa Sententiarum*. However, it is not found in the form of an enumeration. Instead, after having treated the sacraments in general, the author successively treats each of the sacraments. Having arrived at holy orders, he mentions it only briefly, but the work is unfinished. A disciple completed it with a treatise on marriage.

Peter Lombard gives us the complete enumeration for the first time.[27] He does so confidently, as expressing something given, without referring to any author. From this time onward, this enumeration is admitted without question or divergence. The great scholastics of the thirteenth century sought to explain this number by means of reasons of fittingness. However, they did not in any way write as though they were seeking to establish its legitimacy.

At this same time, the septenary came to be introduced into the acts of the ecclesiastical Magisterium. At first, it is introduced without great precision. At the Third Lateran Council, we find the following: "It is very deplorable that in certain churches [...] for the enthronement of bishops, and of abbots [...], for the funerals and burial of the dead, for nuptial blessings and the other sacraments..." (The text here, with its punctuation, is that of R. Foreville,[28] but we cannot know with certitude whether the addition "and the other

---

25. On the traditional character of this distinction, see Yves Congar, "L'idée de sacrements majeurs out principaux," *Concilium* 3 (1968): 25–34.

26. See *ST* III, q. 65, a. 1, ad 6.

27. Peter Lombard, *Sententiae in IV Libros distinctae* (Rome: Collegii S. Bonaventura ad claras aquas, 1971), bk. 4, d. 2.

28. See Raymond Foreville, *Latran I, II, II, and Latran IV, HCO* (Paris: Éditions de l'Orante, 1965), 6:213.

sacraments" refers solely to marriages, which are mentioned immediately before, or to the entire ensemble.) To find the first case of the list of the seven sacraments in an official document, we must look to the profession of faith imposed by Pope Innocent III upon the Waldensians who wished to return to union with the Church.[29] It then becomes canonical. It is found in the Council of Florence's *Decretum pro Armenis*,[30] and the septenary is defined as being held *de fide* in the first canon of Trent's *Decretum de Sacramentis*.[31]

How should we explain this development? The Church lived the sacraments before formulating a theory concerning them. Gradually, she disengaged the notion of the sacraments, starting with baptism and the Eucharist, as well as holy orders (because of the problem of reordinations). It was first extended to all the rites contributing to sanctification. Then, the notion of a sacrament was restricted within a group of rites—like the rites of baptism, for example. The other rites were considered as being preparatory, not sanctifying. Thus, the seven rites that were, properly speaking, sanctifying emerged in clarity gradually, while the others (according to Peter Lombard's terminology) were designated as being *signa sacramentalia* (or, sacramentals).

We must also note a precious point of illumination of equal importance, namely the distinction of the three elements of every sacrament: the *sacramentum tantum* (the rite), the *res et sacramentum* (the sanctifying of the beneficiary or, in the case of the Eucharist, of the matter), and the *res* (the grace caused and signified by the sacrament).[32]

Finally, the theory of sacramental hylomorphism was elaborated, translating the classical composition of *verbum-elementum* into Aristotelian terms. It seems that we must attribute its origin to William of Auvergne. In the thirteenth century, it was universally received and since then has entered into official expositions of the Church's teaching, at least terminologically.

---

29. See D.-*Sch.*, no. 793–94.
30. See D.-*Sch.*, no. 1310.
31. See D.-*Sch.*, no. 1601.
32. See King, "The Origin and Evolution of a Sacramental Formula."

The notion of sacrament according to St. Thomas

{715} When we attentively read the *Scriptum*[33] and then the *Summa theologiae*,[34] we can see that St. Thomas, at the beginning of his career, fully accepted the notion proposed by Peter Lombard in which the Augustinian concept of the sacrament (a sign of salvation accomplished in him who receives it) is, as it were, weighed down by the introduction of causality into the very notion of the sacrament.[35] In the *Summa theologiae*, by contrast, he rigorously holds to the notion of a sign, not making [efficient] causality an element of the definition but, instead, a property of Christian sacraments. However, he specifies that it is not a question of any kind of sign whatsoever but instead is a question of the sign *rei sacrae prout sanctificat homines*, a sign of a reality that is not only sacred but also one that sanctifies the person who makes use of it.[36]

There is another development as well. Increasingly, the theologians of the Middle Ages defined the sacraments as remedies against sin (e.g., for Hugh of St. Victor, the sacrament is like a vial containing a remedy) and classified the sacraments according to the different wounds caused by sin. In the *Scriptum*, St. Thomas seems to accept this outlook. In the *Summa theologiae* (but also already in the *Summa contra gentiles*),[37] he nuances it in a notable way. He explains the necessity of the sacraments first by man's nature and only secondarily by the idea of a *medicina spiritualis*. He speaks of the necessity of Christ for being *sanctified*. He does so, doubtlessly, from within our context pursuant to sin, though not only because of sin.[38] He distributes the sacraments first on the basis of the life received from Christ and only secondarily on the basis of the healing of sin that they bring about.[39]

---

33. See *In IV Sent.*, d. 1, q. 1, a. 3.
34. See *ST* III, q. 60, aa. 1–3.
35. In particular, see *In IV Sent.*, d. 1, q. 1, a. 1, ad 4 and 5 (ed. Moos, 83–90).
36. See Hyacinthe François Dondaine, "La définition des sacrements dans la Somme théologique," *Revue des sciences philosophiques et théologiques* 31 (1947): 213–28; Aimon-Marie Roguet, *Les sacrements*, in *Saint Thomas d'Aquin. Somme théologique* (Paris: Cerf, 1955), 262–69.
37. See *ST* III, q. 61, a. 1; *SCG* IV, bk. 58.
38. See *ST* III, q. 61, a. 1, ad 3.
39. See *ST* III, q. 65, a. 1.

The Nature of the Christian Sacraments
The sacrament as a sign of the redemptive mystery in action
The sacraments are signs

{716} Christ[40] is the sole Savior, and He saved men through His passion, death, and resurrection. There is no other salvation for man except through participation in this "redemptive mystery."

Because the sacraments are means of salvation, we cannot think of them as though they were means of salvation merely superadded to the redemptive mystery itself. Thus, they can be "saving" only if they are in some manner the redemptive mystery itself.

Only one notion can render an account of such an identification between things that are ontologically, spatially, and temporally distinct: *the notion of signs*. "Indeed, a sign is a thing that, beyond the appearance that it impresses upon sense knowledge, introduces to knowledge something other than itself."[41] "A sign is that which presents to a knowing faculty something other than itself, whose place it holds."[42]

Therefore, it is a question of an intentional identification (i.e., according to the form spiritually possessed) and not a "real" one (i.e., according to the form "existentially" possessed).* In other words, the

---

40. See the following: Louis Bouyer, *Le rite et l'homme* (Paris: Cerf, 1962). Cajetan, *In ST III*, q. 60; Henri Denis, *Des sacrements et des hommes: dix ans après Vatican II* (Lyon: Chalet, 1976). John of St. Thomas, *Cursus philosophicus*, vol. 1, ed. Beatus Reiser (Turin: Marietti, 1930), pt. 2, qq. 21–22, and *Cursus theologicus*, vol. 9 (Paris: Vivès, 1886); *De sacramentis*, d. 22. Bernard Leeming, *Principles of Sacramental Theology* (London: Longmans, 1960). Eugène Masure, *Le Signe: le Passage du visible a l'invisible; Psychologie, Histoire, Mystère; le geste, l'outil, le langage, le rite, le miracle* (Paris: Bloud et Gay, 1954). Colman E. O'Neill, *Meeting Christ in the Sacraments* (New York: Alba House, 1964), and *Sacramental Realism: A General Theory of the Sacraments* (Dublin: Dominican Publications, 1983). Karl Rahner, *Église et sacrements*, trans. Henri Rochais (Paris: Desclée de Brouwer, 1971). Aimon-Marie Roguet (ed.), *Les sacrements* (Paris: Société Saint Jean l'Évangéliste, 1951). *Collegii Salmanticensis cursus theologicus* (Paris: Palmé, 1897), tr. 22, d. 1. Edward Schillebeeckx, *De sacramentele heilseconomie* (Antwerpen: H. Nelissen, 1952) (at 665–72, this text contains a summary in French by the author), and *Le Christ, sacrament de la rencontre de Dieu* (Paris: Cerf, 1960), and "Pouvons-nous nous passer de symboles?," *Concilium* 31 (1968). [Tr. note: Fr. Nicolas also includes among the works scited a reference to Jean-Hervé Nicolas, "Compte-rendu du livre de Febrer M., El concepto de persona y la union hipostatica," *Revue thomiste* 55 (1955): 186–88. He may have meant to refer to Jean-Hervé Nicolas, "Réactualisation des mystères rédempteurs dans et par les sacrements," *Revue thomiste* 58 (1958): 20–54.]

41. St. Augustine, *La doctrine chrétienne*, OESA 11, bk. 2, ch. 1.

42. John of St. Thomas, *Cursus philosophicus*, 1:9 and 646.

* [Tr. note: Because this very brief, scholastic vocabulary used by Fr. Nicolas risks being

identification is produced only on the level of knowledge: *it exists only for a knower.* That is, in the case of the sacraments, it exists only for the believer. We have already encountered this outlook in the tradition.

However, does this not deprive the sacraments of all objective value? No, for a sign is a sign, even if someone cannot decipher it, and even if it is not known to be a sign. Let us say that the value of the sign (i.e., its "signification") is connected to a thing or a deed as soon as this thing or this deed is chosen to signify a given reality and as soon as those to whom they are addressed can possibly know what signification is thus given to the sign.

The sacraments are conventional signs

{717} A natural sign is a thing that, by its structure or its appearance, naturally refers the mind to something else. For example, an effect is naturally the sign of its cause. Thus, according to St. Augustine, visible creatures are the sign of God's invisible attributes.

A conventional sign is a thing or a deed to which a determinate signification is attributed by an act of will. Only those who know the convention can know this signification.

What characterizes a conventional sign is, above all, the fact that it is a kind of "language." (For this reason, according to St. Augustine, it belongs principally to signs to signify, and things or deeds charged with a given signification are themselves visible words.) A conventional sign is a word addressed by one person to other persons. It is the means of interpersonal communication. Therefore, it presupposes a being who signifies both from the start (for the establishment of the relation of signification) and in what follows (for the use of the sign in the group that retains this convention). In other words, it presupposes someone who has made this deed or word mean something determinate and someone who actually makes use of the sign to designate this.

---

misunderstood, I have added the quotation marks around "real" and "existentially" for the distinction between objective-intentional being and subjective-existential being. In the discussion of the Eucharist, Fr. Nicolas seems to approvingly cite Fr. Anscar Vonier's *A Key to the Doctrine of the Eucharist*, which deals with this topic very well and should be consulted to understand Fr. Nicolas's point here.]

The sacraments are practical signs

{718} By means of language, one can express to others either pure knowledge (speculative knowledge) or knowledge ordered to action or making (practical knowledge). All the signs that express this second kind of knowledge are called "practical signs": a contract, an order, a pledge, and so forth. In the case of man, a sign is not practical in the sense that it would of itself bring about what it signifies. Instead, it is practical in the sense that it is destined to order the will of the person who receives it to bring about what is signified. When He who signifies is God, His word is efficacious.

The Gospel is "the Divine Power for salvation." The sacraments are not only the preaching of the Gospel but, rather, are the Gospel (the good news of salvation through Christ) exercising its saving power on the person who receives the sacrament.

In this way, they are distinguished from Scripture and from preaching, all the while implying them, for practical knowledge is founded on speculative knowledge. One cannot receive the saving word without knowing that Christ has saved men and how He has saved them (taking into account, however, what was said earlier concerning the possibility of a merely implicit adherence to the Church and to her teaching).[43]

The sacraments are signs of salvation brought about today by Christ in the beneficiary as well as the sign of its future fulfillment

{719} The sacraments are signs representing the saving mystery: Christ's passion, death, and resurrection. However, they do not exist simply to make them known. Through them, in a way that we still must explain, the saving mystery exercises its saving action on the person who receives the sacrament, and through this action, the believer is conformed to Christ. (We will see that the diversity of sacraments arises from the various aspects and modes of this conformation.) Therefore, a sacrament likewise is a sign of this conformation of the believer to Christ by grace. In other words, it is a sign

---

43. See §690 above.

of the fact that Christ acts within the believer through the sacrament, applying to him the power of His redemptive passion.

However, this order of signs is not only turned toward the past. It also announces what is to come, the full accomplishment of the Redemption by Christ's return. "For if we have been united with Him in a death like His, we shall certainly be united with Him in a resurrection like His."[44] The beneficiary of this ultimate and perfect assimilation is at once completely dependent on what has taken place in the past (the redemptive passion) and completely tends toward the fulfillment in the future that will, with the resurrection, bring all signs to an end.

The sacraments are sign-symbols

{720} A sign can make known the signified reality in virtue of a simple convention without being an image of it (e.g., a word). However, it also can represent what is signified on account of its own form, being a more or less lively image of the signified reality. In this case, the sign is also a *symbol*. The passage from the symbol to the symbolized reality is more complex than that from a sign to the signified. Through the very form [*forme*] that it gives birth to in the knower, the symbol evokes in him a reality (often an abstract and sometimes mysterious one) not through a material likeness but, rather, through the unfolding of an analogy. Affective elements are involved in this analogy. (The reality is a reality for me, one that has a meaning for me.) Thus, the lily symbolizes purity and the flag symbolizes one's country.[45] "Indeed, if the sacraments did not have a particular resemblance with the things of which they are signs, they would not be sacraments."[46] The sacraments symbolically represent this mysterious participation by the beneficiary in the passion of Christ, a participation that is brought about through the sacraments. Below,[46b] we will consider the essential role played by this symbolic function of the sacraments.

44. Rom 6:5 (RSV).
45. See Jacques Maritain, "Signe et symbole," in *Quatre essais sur l'esprit dans sa condition charnelle* (Paris: Desclée de Brouwer, 1939), 63–127. Jean-Hervé Nicolas, *Dieu connue comme inconnu* (Paris: Desclée de Brouwer, 1966), 161–69.
46. St. Augustine, *Sermones*, PL 38, ep. 108, no. 9, ch. 363.
46b. See §717 below.

The sacrament, sign of the faith of those who are redeemed

{721} Nobody is saved except by faith. Faith is the fundamental process by which man opens himself to Christ's redemptive action, and without it, he remains outside of redemption, even though Christ died for all and for each person. This is so because the human person can be saved only by personally accepting salvation, which is lost through a voluntary refusal.

Moreover, the sacraments cannot be separated from faith.[47] However, does this not render them useless? According to Scripture, faith is not only an indispensable element of salvation. It is also sufficient for it.[48] Nonetheless, the sacraments are not rendered useless by the sufficiency of faith *precisely because they are signs of faith*.

Signs of the beneficiary's faith

{722} It is natural for man to express through bodily means an activity that in itself is spiritual. Faith is one's approach to Christ, who suffered, died, and rose again for me. It is an acceptance of His will and His redemptive work. How is one to "realize" and "concretize" this activity? Christ is no longer visibly and historically present, and His death lies in the past. However, the sign remains, quite precisely the sign in which and by which the redemptive mystery is represented and symbolized as applying to me.

Thus, considered from the perspective of the person who receives it, the sacrament is a truly personal activity. It is a bodily action that does not add anything to the spiritual act performed through faith, just as the bodily deed, in general, does not add to the thought or sentiment that it expresses. It is a single spiritual and bodily act performed by the human person, through which he approaches Christ. It is a significative and symbolic activity whose "mysterious meaning" is furnished by the faith of the person who performs it, that is, through his "intention" (i.e., his intention to let himself be saved today by Christ in this sacrament).

---

47. See Villette, *Foi et sacrement*, vol. 1.

48. See Gaston Deluz, "Nécessité des sacrements," in *La Saint Cène, Cahiers théologiques de l'actualité protestante* (Neuchâtel: Delachaux et Niestlé, 1945).

However, whereas the relation of the sign to the signified reality is indefectible when it is a question of the signified reality that is a saving mystery, it can sometimes happen that no spiritual action corresponds to the bodily action. Thus, through man's own fault (and inasmuch as it is a deed performed by him), the sacrament becomes a deceptive sign.

Sign of the Church's faith

{723} Without faith, the sacrament would not exist. It is not the beneficiary's faith that makes the sacrament exist as a sacrament. It is the Church's faith that does this, for the sacrament is also an act performed by the Church, extending, in accord with her mission, to the believer who presents himself to her to be redeemed, the Redemption brought about by Christ. Through this activity, the Church proclaims her faith in Christ the Savior and in the efficacy of His Redemption.

Could a defect also exist on the side of the Church? The Church is concretely represented by the minister. Yes, but it is not the faith of the minister as such which makes the sacrament exist. It is sovereignly fitting that the minister actually participate in the Church's faith and that in bestowing the sacraments he simultaneously proclaims his faith and that of the Church. However, if he personally separates himself from it (whether because he refuses to believe or because he does not participate in the movement of confidence and love that is included in faith in its full sense, namely, formed faith) the deed that he performs in the name of the Church and according to the Church's ritual form continues to signify the Church's faith which itself cannot fail.

The place and means for the encounter with Christ is
found in the Church

{724} Thus, the sacrament is not (as it is too often represented) an action by the Church, having Christ in some manner as its object (an action consisting in giving Christ's grace, in giving Christ) and whose beneficiary would be the "patient." Rather, it includes three elements. First, there is the saving act of Christ, rendered mysteriously present for the beneficiary through the sacramental sign. Second, there is the Church's own action bringing about this active presence through the sacramental action. Then, finally, there is the beneficiary's own agency, freely submitting himself to this action and allowing himself to be conformed to Christ. In other words, because it is a question of a dynamic conformation to Christ, the beneficiary freely approaches Christ in faith through such activity.

In the sacrament, the Church plays her role as a mediator in an eminent manner. She brings about the personal encounter between the believer and Christ, as long as the believer wills it, that is, as long as he acts as a believer.

The Structure of Sacraments

Signification is a relation, indeed a rationate relation [i.e., a *relatio rationis*]. It is a relationship established by reason between the reality currently present to knowledge (the sign) and the absent or mysterious reality (the signified thing). Objective consistency is conferred by the fact that, before being established by the reason of the person who perceives the sign as such, this connection was established by another person (the signifier) in a way that is stably knowable by all those involved in the use of this sign.

A relation can exist only in a subject. Here, the subject is the rite, bestowed with sacramental signification by Christ and the Church. We must examine the sacrament from this perspective.[49]

Sacramental hylomorphism

{725} All the sacraments have in common the fact that the sacrament consists in words and bodily realities. The words that make these realities sacred are called the forms of the sacraments. Thus, the realities rendered sacred are called the matters of the sacraments ... Moreover, in every sacrament the person of the minister plays a necessary role.[50]

---

49. The word "subject" is not here used in the modern sense, designating the person in his opposition to the world (the self in contrast to the non-self). Instead, it is used in the scholastic sense, designating the *suppositum*, the concrete being determined and qualified by accidents. In this sense, the subject of a relation is the reality referred to a terminus by this relation.
50. See St. Thomas, *De articulis fidei et ecclesiae sacramentis* (Leonine edition, vol. 42), 253.

To what degree is the Church's faith bound by sacramental hylomorphism?

Hylomorphic language passed over into the ordinary formulation of sacramental theology, even into the Church's own official documents. Clearly, this does not commit one to taking any philosophical stance concerning hylomorphism, nor to taking any theological position regarding how this notion can serve in explaining the sacramental reality. It is used as a matter of convenience, as such language is used in ordinary language (as when, in judging a literary work, one speaks of its substance [*fond*] and its form). Thus, the terms are used to say this, which is something *de fide*: every sacrament includes a *res corporalis* and determinate words, a "formula." (We must understand the notion of *res corporalis* in a multiform sense. This can be merely a thing as is the case in the Eucharist alone. It is a deed using determinate things in the case of baptism, confirmation, anointing of the sick, and holy orders. Finally, it is a human act concretized in word and deed, as we find with contrition in penance and consent* in marriage.)

How should one understand sacramental hylomorphism?

The problem is to see how we can understand the "composition" of the *res corporalis* with the words.

We must exclude the idea of scholastic theologians seeking a "physical composition," an idea that is realistic to the point of being "reified." Such a composition is completely unthinkable. Moreover, it "reifies" the sacrament, making it into an absolute reality, which God would utilize in order to make a sign in addition (whereas the sacrament as such has no other existence than its being a sacred sign).

If we examine St. Thomas's texts closely,[51] his position is that the composition in question is not physical in any way. Instead, it is completely intentional, exclusively concerning the signification which, as we have said, affects the thing only as an object of knowledge:

---

* [Tr. note: Regarding the Byzantine East and this matter, see the translator's note at the start of this volume.]

51. See *In IV Sent.* [*sic*] and *ST* II, q. 60, a. 6, co. and ad 2; a. 7, ad 1; a. 8, ad 2.

Although words and bodily realities belong to different genera with regard to real nature, they have in common the fact that they are endowed with signification. Such signification is found more perfectly in words than in other things. Consequently, one unified reality results from words joined to realities, like form and matter, inasmuch as the signification of bodily realities is determined by the words.[52]

Because the sacrament exists only as a sign, the "matter" and the "form" are united only in order to compose the sacramental sign (or, the support of the sacramental signification). What does "matter" mean in hylomorphism? Essentially it means *the determinable element*, whereas the form is the *determining element*. If this basic meaning is transposed to the case of the sacraments, we have a bodily deed that is undetermined of itself (e.g., washing can signify purification, refreshing, bodily cleaning, and so forth) and the words that specify the signification of the deed, lifting it out of its indetermination.

Thus, words are required, not as a magic formula, but as something necessary for expressing the sacramental signification. However, the bodily deed is also necessary, for the words are related to it: "this" (which I hold between my hands, which was bread when I took hold of it) "is my body," and, "I baptize you," words that would be meaningless if I did not simultaneously baptize with water the person whom I am addressing.

Thus, because this composition is brought about in the mind, there can be a temporal succession involved between the matter and the form (in penance and marriage). This does not eliminate the reality of the composition. Thus, for example, time is real, even though it exists completely [as a single united reality, uniting past and present] only through an act of the mind.

Sacramental hylomorphism and physical hylomorphism

Hylomorphic composition pertains to sensible (or, material) substances. The sensible substance is composed in its very being as a substance, for experience shows that it can be "decomposed." In every ontological composition, the unity of the composite can result only from an act-potency relationship (i.e., a relation of the deter-

---

52. *ST* III, q. 60, a. 6, ad 2.

mining to the determined) between the two components. When this analysis is applied to material beings, it leads to the idea of prime matter (or, pure matter). Such an ontological element is completely undetermined and therefore unable to exist separately. However, it is determined by a form, constituting with it a given material being or substance (the *physis*). It cannot exist separately, but its existence is not necessarily bound to this form, which actually determines it. Under the action of different physical factors, it can be disengaged from the sway of this form, passing under the sway of another. Such is the process of corruption and generation that has matter as its theater (but also as its principle), for because of its complete indetermination and openness to every form of determination, matter is a principle of instability in the material composite.

"Matter" in the proper sense is this principle. (Through it, the composite is called "material.") However, if I consider its indetermination and determinability, I can extend the notion outside of *physis*. This is so because composition between a determined element (therefore one that is determinable in itself) and a determining element (giving the composite its own proper form in the domain considered) is found in many domains.

First of all, there is the composition of a substance with its accidents, in which the substance plays the role of matter, although it is much more ontologically perfect than are such accidents. However, when it is determined by accidental forms, it is more perfect than it itself was without this determination. Through this determination, it is ontologically brought to its completion.

Next, there is the work of art. The artist realizes his "idea" by giving a "form" to a matter on which he works (e.g., clay, paint, and also sound, though in this last case the extension is even greater, for in the musical work the sounds exist only as organized by the artist).

Next, we have, in the domain of logic, composition between the genus which is variously determinable ("animal" is an incomplete notion needing to be "specified" by another notion in order that it be applied to this or that "nature") and the specific difference, which is this necessary determination. Purely as such, an *animal* does not exist, for every animal realizes animal life in a determinate manner.

In this case, we see quite well that the term "matter" can no longer have anything but a metaphorical meaning as what we are here discussing are concepts [*notions*], which are obviously purely intelligible and in no way material.

Sacramental hylomorphism has its own unique character. It has in common with substantial hylomorphism the fact that the composite is a being endowed with its own proper essence. We speak about the "substance" of a sacrament (i.e., about what essentially constitutes it, as moralists speak about the "substance" of a human act). However, it is distinguished from the material substance in the fact that the composition is intentional and not real.

It has this latter point in common with logical hylomorphism, but here the difference is found in the fact that the elements that enter into composition in the sacrament are real. The sacrament is not a logical being, for it is constituted by things, deeds, and really pronounced words.

Given that these elements constituting the sacrament are united only through a human action and in accord with his idea, the composite is an *artefactum*, like a work of art. However, here again, what is proper to it is the fact that the very composition is intentional, not real.* It exists only for a mind and through the mind's activity.

In these conditions, we can hold that the expressions "matter" and "form," which designate the constitutive elements of each sacraments, are used metaphorically. What remains is the relation of that which is determined to that which determines it.

Sacrament-thing or sacrament-action

{726} The sacraments are ordinarily spoken about as though they were things, as though they were something static, a completely prepared instrument used by the Church to sanctify those who present themselves at an opportune time.

However, this is incorrect. All the sacraments (except, in a unique way, the Eucharist) present themselves as being actions. In them, deeds accompany the words that are pronounced. The term "matter"

---

* [Tr. note: As noted above, the scholastic vocabulary here needs to be understood aright, lest *ens rationis* (and, here, *ens sacramentale*) be reduced to a kind of "nonbeing" or, as some later scholastics would say, "the shadow of being." See the work of Anscar Vonier cited above.]

is usually used for the thing utilized in conferring the sacrament. However, the true "matter" is the deed that makes use of this thing in accord with the rite.[53]

The case of the Eucharist is somewhat different. What is characteristic of it is the fact that it really contains Christ, the holy One and source of all holiness. Therefore, it is "sacred" and a "sacrament" prior to any use by the believer.[54] Nonetheless, it also is ordered to such use by the believer (i.e., to "manducation"). It is not something static. If Jesus is really present in the Eucharist, it is in the form of nourishment and in order to be eaten. He is given in order to be eaten.[55]

The person of the minister and his "intention"

As soon as one perceives that the sacrament is an action, one understands that the person of the minister enters into its very structure, for action implies an agent proportioned to it.[56]

The sacrament is a human act

{727} It is clear that, on the part of the minister, the act of conferring the sacrament is a personal and free act. It is also a moral or immoral act which must be informed by charity and submitted to the regulation of different virtues.

Considered as a human act performed by the minister, the value of the sacramental action is "subjective," completely dependent on the end pursued by the subject and upon its moral regulation. (From this perspective, an "invalid" sacrament can be an act of great virtue and charity if the invalidity is due to an involuntary defect on the part of the minister.) By contrast, however, as an act of the Church, its value depends solely on Christ's institution and on the Church's regulation, for she has the power to fix the rules of validity herself, at least in certain cases. Thus, a perfectly valid sacramental action that is sanctifying for those who benefit from it can be, as a human act, a grave sin for the minister.[57]

---

53. See *ST* III, q. 66, a. 1.
54. See *ST* III, q. 73, a. 1, ad 3.
55. See §904 below.
56. See Jean-Marie-Roger Tillard, "A propos de l'intention du minister et du sujet des sacrements," *Concilium* 31 (1968): 101–12.
57. See §663 above.

Thus, the human act of conferring the sacrament and the sacramental action are one and the same act considered from two different perspectives, for to confer a sacrament is nothing other than to perform the sacramental action upon a believer. (This does not exactly hold true for the case of the Eucharist, for the accomplishment of the sacramental action is one thing, namely the consecrating of the matter, and the conferring of the sacrament is another, namely the giving of communion. However, it remains true that the act of consecration is at once the human act of the priest and a sacramental action.)

This means that the sacramental action includes in its very structure the minister's intention as well.[58] Indeed, a human act is first of all and principally an act of will, whether elicited or commanded. Where the voluntary character is missing, we no longer have a human act. Is it conceivable that an act that would merely be one performed by a man (an *actus hominis*) and not a voluntary, human act (an *actus humanus*) could be a true sacramental action if it is performed in accord with the rite? Obviously not. The sacramental words always express a decision and a willing. Indeed, just as to say, "I baptize you," without performing the corresponding deed would be the speaking of empty words, so too if an expression did not express the intention to baptize it would be vain and meaningless.

Therefore, the intention is not an extrinsic condition or even a merely indispensable element. It is much more than this. It is a constitutive element of the sacrament.

What intention is required

{728} Here, we must recall the results drawn from the analysis of human acts.

Through the action that he performs, every man pursues many ends in accordance with a particular ordering. Therefore, he has many organized "intentions," not a host of mutually unrelated designs.

This organization can be either objective or subjective. *The objective order* of ends is the ordering which is inscribed in the very object of the act. For example, the act or acts of thinking up a house in

---

58. See note oo above.

which to live, of designing a plan for it, of ordering its construction, and so forth, are all ordered to each other and objectively ordered to the house, which itself is ordered to inhabitation, which is ordered to the organization of man's life, and so forth.

Subjective ordering among ends is established by the agent on account of his own particular ends. The architect can construct the house in order to earn money, to obtain a sum that will enable these or those personal advantages for him, advantages that are perhaps utterly unrelated to architecture itself. (Some claim that Racine wrote his masterpieces so that he may obtain the status of being a nobleman of the king. Having obtained that honor after *Phèdre*, he would have abandoned the theatre!)

If I consider a human act and one of the ends to which it is ordered, the intention of this end can be either *subjective and objective, subjective and not objective,* or *objective and not subjective*. It is *subjective and objective* if the agent deliberately pursues the end to which this act is ordered of itself. It is *subjective and not objective* if it is a question of an end to which the act is not ordered of itself, though which the agent pursues in doing this act. It is *objective and not subjective* if it is a question of an end to which the act is ordered of itself, though in which the agent has no interest.

What intention is required for an act to be a human act? It only requires the intention to perform this action, which presupposes that one is aware of what one is doing. Of course, the agent will always have many subjective intentions (because he always and ultimately acts for his final end). However, it is not at all necessary that the end to which this act is objectively ordered be the object of his intention. Indeed, he can have contrary intentions. In fact, the "voluntary" character without which an act of man is not a human act has as its immediate object the external act itself.[59]

The sacramental action was instituted by Christ for man's salvation and for God's glory. These are the objective intentions inscribed upon the sacramental action. The Church espouses them fully on account of her holiness. The minister, from whom a fully personal collaboration is required, must normally espouse them as well.

---

59. See *ST* I-II, q. 20, a. 1, ad 1.

However, given that his holiness is not a sure thing, it is possible that he may not espouse them. In such a case, the only absolutely necessary intention for the sacramental action to exist as such is that it itself be willed.

What could prevent this from being the case? First of all, the minister may be unable (either momentarily or enduringly) to perform a human act. But what are we to think of an intentional defect in the minister if his intention is not directly oriented to the sacrament itself?[60]

What is required is "at least the intention to do what the Church wills to do."[61] St. Thomas explained this claim in the following way:

> ... the minister of the sacraments acts in the person of the entire Church, for he is at her service. In the words that he speaks, the Church's intention is expressed, which suffices for there to be a sacrament, unless the contrary (i.e., the rejection to follow the Church's intention) would be externally signified either by the minister or by the recipient.[62]

This does not require faith, for the minister acts in the name of the Church. She is the one who acts through him. Nonetheless, for the reason just explained, it does require his internal intention and not only the intention that is purely externalized by the action itself.

However, in the text just cited, St. Thomas seems to require that the rejection of the intention be externalized in some manner. In *ST* III, q. 64, a. 10, on the contrary, he expressly says that the rejection of the intention itself renders the sacrament invalid.

Now, how should we conceive of the possibility of such a rupture between the action and one's intention? This is inconceivable for every ordinary kind of action. If someone performs an action, he cannot simultaneously will to not do it.[63] (This would be a "velleity.") However, the sacramental action exists on two levels. On one level, there is the fact of being a rite. However, beyond this, there is the level of its sacramental signification (i.e., the encounter with Christ, participation in His passion, and so forth). The sacramental action

---

60. See Schillebeeckx, *Le Christ*, 133–37.
61. See Trent, session 7, c. 11, in D.-Sch., no. 1611.
62. *ST* III, q. 64, a. 8, ad 2.
63. This is so even in the case of constraint, for under constraint man wills what he would not do otherwise (e.g., to hand over the key to his coffers).

cannot be performed by a man enjoying his faculties without being willed on the factual level. However, it is possible that this same man could decide not to will it on the level of sacramental signification. (For example, this would be the case, indeed a plain and simple one, when one repeats a ceremony.)

Could there be a case of a priest giving the sacrament out of jest or mockery of the rite? St. Thomas leads one to believe that, in such a case, the external signs could warn those assisting. However, it is not absolutely impossible that the priest, for reasons that are indeed difficult to imagine, *could withhold his intention*. Certainly, in this case, there would not be a sacrament. However, this is such an aberrant behavior that it can only be a rare case and too accidental for it to be taken into consideration on the level of theological reflection. On the existential level, we can be sure that, in such a case, the Lord would immediately produce sacramental grace in the good-faith recipient.[64]

N.B. *Let us note a point regarding the intention of the person who receives the sacrament.* As we have seen, the sacrament implies an action by the person who receives it. This also must be a human act, animated by an "intention." What we said about the minister's intention applies here too. What is absolutely required (the minimum request) is the intention to receive what the Church means to give and to receive the sacrament. If this intention, in the limit case, can exist without faith, it nonetheless precludes the internal rejection of the religious signification of the rite. (Such would be possible if someone were constrained, physically or morally, to receive baptism or the Eucharist, while rejecting it with all his will, even if this rejection were not made manifest.)

The sacralization of the person of the minister

{729} To say that the person of the minister enters into the structure of the sacrament means that the minister himself, inasmuch as he performs the sacramental action, is sacramental.

Because of the necessity of the sacrament of baptism, any human person whatsoever, even someone who himself is not baptized,

---

64. See *ST* III, q. 64, a. 8, ad 2.

can perform this sacramental action. Therefore, a prior sacralization is not absolutely required. In the case of marriage, if the spouses are baptized and exchange their consent in forms fixed by the Church, they themselves are the "ministers of the sacrament."

However, for all the other sacraments, the person of the minister must be sacralized prior to the action. This is brought about through a special sacrament, namely holy orders, which gives the power to confer the sacrament. As regards this sacrament, we will see that its role is to designate a given Christian among the others as the agent of sacramental actions. Without this sacrilization, there is no sacrament, even if the rite is performed in accord with all of the Church's sacramental regulations. It lacks an essential element needed for this rite to be a sacramental sign.

The three structures of the sacrament: *sacramentum tantum*, *sacramentum et res, res tantum*

{730} This[65] distinction is first of all concerned with the efficacy of the sacraments, although it also plays a role in the analysis of their complex reality. As we have seen, it was elaborated by scholastic theologians in response to the Berengarian controversy. However, it also enables us to render an account of the Augustinian distinction between the truth of the sacrament and its fruitfulness. This is a distinction that itself enabled the definitive resolution to the problem concerning the non-repeatability of baptism, even when it is performed in conditions when it could not bring with it the remission of sins.

The *sacramentum tantum* is the sacramental sign (i.e., the rite). We have seen that it is understood only in function of its significate and, indeed exists only as a relation to this significate. The signified is the *res*. We analyzed this above.

However, the *res* presupposes the beneficiary's personal disposition, namely, faith in the full sense, the acceptance of salvation. This disposition is also signified by the sacrament, considered as something undergone by him who submits himself to it. However, we have also seen that this signification was not always certain.

---

65. See §621 above.

The spiritual undertaking that the external undertaking signifies and symbolizes can be lacking in a given case.⁶⁶ Must we say that there is no sacrament at all in this case? This question is legitimate, for Christ's passion and resurrection are signified and symbolized only inasmuch as they are actually participated in by the beneficiary of the sacrament. The dispute *de rebaptizatione* brought to light the need to admit that a sacrament remains once it has been given (even without producing its fruit or if this fruit is lost through heresy, apostasy, or any other grave sin). Likewise, the Berengarian controversy brought to light the fact that the sacrament of the Eucharist remains even without faith and devotion on the part of the priest and those assisting.

Thus, theologians were led to recognize that between the *sacramentum* and the *res* there is an intermediary and stable terminus of sacramental signification, a kind of "interior sacrament" signified (and, as we will see, caused) by the sacramental rite, though not depending upon the beneficiary's faith and charity. Thus, this intermediary terminus is always signified by the sacramental sign and therefore is always given, except in the unique and extreme case when either the minister or the beneficiary would "withdraw his intention," as we saw above.

This intermediary terminus is a *res* in relation to the sacramental sign, as it is signified by it. However, it itself is a *sacramentum* in relation to the *res tantum*, for it is completely ordered to grace and to the beneficiary's participation in the redemptive passion. It itself is a sign in relation to this ultimate terminus of the sacramental sign.

The Institution of the Sacraments by Christ

{731} The Council of Trent defined⁶⁷ the seven sacraments as having been instituted by Christ. In the decree on the Eucharist, we must note this declaration with regard to the Church's power:

Furthermore, <the Holy Council> declares that, in the administration of the sacraments—provided their substance is preserved—there has always been in the Church that power to determine or modify what she judged

---

66. See §722 above.
67. Council of Trent, session 7, c. 1, in D-*Sch.*, no. 1601.

more expedient for the benefit of those receiving the sacraments or for the reverence due to the sacraments themselves—according to the diversity of circumstances, times, and places.[68]

From what we said earlier concerning the role of the signifier in the establishment of the sign,[69] it is clear enough that the sacraments could be instituted only by Christ. If the sacraments are the signs of sanctification brought about in those who receive them by Christ dying and rising from the dead for them, it is clear that because Christ is man's only savior and the sanctifier of man, He is the only one who can attribute this salvific signification to a rite.

However, this general principle raises grave historical difficulties.[70] We must seek to reconcile the theological-dogmatic principle concerning the sacraments' institution by Christ with the historical facts by undertaking a fair and nuanced interpretation of the *salva eorum substantia* of Trent. We must seek out this reconciliation while addressing the historical facts which lead us to recognize, on the one hand, the great incertitude that besets us regarding the origin of certain sacraments and, on the other hand, the notable ritual variations which have existed through the course of the centuries and which indeed still exist between the Eastern Church[es] and the Latin Church.

If we consider a sacramental rite in its totality, it clearly presents itself as being a complex liturgical ceremony that, for a considerable part, is a work of the Church and is subject to variation. What in this ensemble must we hold to be the "substance of the sacrament" (i.e., that which does not vary)? We cannot give a uniform response that would apply to all the sacraments indifferently. For baptism, there is ablution with water, for this is what baptism was when Christ instituted it as a sacrament. However, the fact that the rite varies regarding whether this ablution would be performed through immersion or through sprinkling shows that we are here faced with something that does not belong to the "substance" of the sacrament.

For the Eucharist, Jesus told the apostles to "do this," namely

---

68. Council of Trent, *Decree Concerning Communion Under Both Kinds and by Infants*, July 16, 1562, ch. 2 (D.-*Sch.*, no. 1728).
69. See §717 above.
70. See Michel, "Sacrements," 536–77.

what He had just done, taking bread and wine and pronouncing the words. Thus, it seems that the invariant element consists in the repetition of the words over the bread and wine, thus excluding, for example, the possibility of changing the matter or the words. For the other sacraments, we nowhere see Jesus Himself instituting a rite. Here, it seems to suffice that He would have bestowed the Church with a particular sanctifying power so that she, on account of her "visibility," would have herself been led to establish the rite by which she would exercise this power. (This represents a still-vague solution that is connected to the idea of the Church's sacramentality.) Thus, the Church certainly received the power to remit sins committed after baptism. The way she implemented this power, from the imposition of hands upon those who returned from heresy and upon repentant *lapsi*, passing through various forms of public penance, up to the current practice of auricular confession (and perhaps, later to other forms that are being studied), constitutes the determination of the rite bearing the sacramental signification willed by Christ, not the creation of the sacrament of penance.

The Efficacy of the Sacraments of the New Law

How to understand: "The sacraments bring about what they signify"

{732} From what we have said, it is sufficiently clear that the sacraments are essentially signs of man's sanctification, brought about today by Christ in virtue of His redemptive sacrifice.

However, they are not only signs. They are also the means by which this sanctifying action of Christ is exercised. They are means entrusted to the Church, who acts visibly through them for man's sanctification, whereas Christ acts invisibly and produces this sanctification. What the sacrament signifies is precisely this invisible action by Christ and its effect in the beneficiary.

Sanctification consists in the divine adoption through which the beneficiary is conformed to Him who is the Son by Nature, Jesus Christ. It also consists in the "divinization" through which he is rendered (though, in Christ) a participant in the Divine Life. Likewise, it consists in the remission of sins brought about by the Holy Spirit whom Jesus Christ has sent, a remission that was first merited by Him. In short, sanctification consists in the gift that the Divine Persons make of themselves to the believers in and through Jesus Christ.[71]

It is clear that the sacraments cause neither Jesus Christ, nor the Divine Persons, nor the act by which they give of themselves in Jesus Christ. Much to the contrary, it is Jesus Christ who gave the sacraments to the Church and who acts through them. As we have seen, "created grace" is the only means by which the gift of God is given to the creature.*

If the sacraments are means of sanctification, this can be only by contributing in some way to the divine action by which created grace is "produced" in the soul. Such a contribution cannot be anything but instrumental, for God alone, who created the spiritual being, can "recreate" it and make it like unto Himself. He alone can "divinize" it.

The Council of Trent defined this as follows: "Grace is given by means (*per*) of the sacraments always and to all those who receive in accord with the rite, at least as far as God's part is concerned." Note that this restriction means that there can be an obstacle to this gift of grace on the part of the recipient. Likewise, the same Council states: "Grace is conferred by means of the sacraments of the New Law *ex opere operato*, without one being able to say that mere faith I the divine promise suffices for obtaining grace."[72]

In these two canons, we must not see any intention to define the

---

71. Concerning the divinization of the believer by the sending and gift of the Divine Persons by means of grace, see the fourth section of the first volume of this course.

* Let us succinctly recall that "created grace" must not be conceived of as being a thing [*réalité*], a kind of "spiritual liquid" that would be poured into the soul from outside. It is a *habitus* (or, rather, by including within itself the theological virtues, an ensemble of *habitus* which are nonetheless rooted in the fundamental *habitus* of "sanctifying grace" and flowing from it). In other words, it is a quality produced in the soul, though founded upon the soul itself. (It calls to mind the form that the artist confers upon matter in order to make a work of art with this matter. This form does not come from outside. It is an arrangement of the matter, though it is an arrangement that the artist has produced by acting on it.) God alone can act upon the soul in order to enrich it in this way, enabling it to know Him as He is and to love Him with a love of intimacy and communion. Created grace is produced in the soul by God, though on the basis of the soul itself and on the basis of its spirituality, which renders it radically capable of this prodigious elevation.

72. Council of Trent, session 7, *Decree on the Sacraments in General*, chs. 7 and 8, in D.-Sch., nos. 1607–08). [Tr. note: These texts are re-rendered by Fr. Nicolas into a positive form, whereas they were anathemas in the original Council texts.]

way that the sacraments contribute to the bestowal of grace but only the affirmation that the sacraments' efficacy comes from the divine action always occurring as soon as the sacramental action (*opus*) is ritually exercised (*operatum*) and not from the faith of those who receive them.

How should we conceive of the role conceded to the sacraments in contributing to the gift of grace, in the bestowal of it, and in its production by God?

Recoiling from the idea of a true efficient causality
exercised in the sacraments

{733} The obvious meaning of the formula "[they] bring about that of which they are the sign" is that the sacraments are, instrumentally, causes of grace. Indeed, God produces created grace through efficient causality. To say that He does this *per sacramenta* seems to mean that the sacraments contribute in this production, that they are instruments of it, and that God uses them by super-elevating them.

The significant difficulty involved in conceiving and explaining such causality (even instrumentally understood) by material realities in relation to the wholly spiritual reality of grace has dissuaded (and continues to dissuade) a great number of theologians from holding this conception of sacramental causality, which in their opinion seems to materialize it.[73]

Recourse to occasional causality

Thus, recourse has been made to the idea of a kind of occasional causality. On the occasion of the performing of the sacramental rite, God would produce what this sacrament signifies. St. Thomas was aware of this explanation and refuted[74] it by saying that in this case, the sacraments of the New Law would be nothing more than signs of grace. One could not say that God makes use of them to confer grace. Later on, this occasionalist explanation was perfected along the same lines in an attempt to safeguard a true causality exercised

---

73. See Jean-Hervé Nicolas, "La causalité des sacrements," *Revue thomiste* 62 (1962): 547–52.
74. See *ST* III, q. 62, a. 1.

by the sacraments. Thus, Scotus saw in the sacrament a human activity to which God has attached the bestowal of the grace corresponding to this sacrament. If a man performs this particular rite (e.g., if he submits himself to the baptismal rite), God would then bestow upon him the grace of the remission of sins and of regeneration. We will see later the great importance involved in affirming the fact that the sacrament's beneficiary also plays a role in the saving action (meaning that it is not merely an action of Christ exerted upon him). However, grace is the effect of a given action performed by God, through Christ, in the beneficiary, and it is not clear how Scotus's explanation can in fact articulate how the sacrament efficaciously contributes in this action so that we could grant the full meaning of the affirmation that God causes grace by means of the sacraments.

Recourse to moral causality

{734} Later on, in the sixteenth century, various theories of moral causality were articulated. On the whole, they consist in saying that inasmuch as the sacraments signify Christ's redemptive passion, His sacrificial death, and His resurrection, they are causes of the bestowal of grace by presenting God the merits and satisfaction of Christ, which are the reason why (and in virtue of which) God bestows His grace. Theologians noted, in this case, that the true moral cause is not the sacrament itself but, rather, the Redemption brought about by Christ. Therefore, they perfected the theory, thus amplifying it, saying that, inasmuch as they are performed by the Church, the sacramental actions are acts that please God (certainly in virtue of Christ's passion, which they represent, but also in themselves). They are said to be "the infallible prayers of the Church" in virtue of which God gives, *hic et nunc*, the grace merited by God on the cross.

However, here again, can we truly speak of causality? Inasmuch as they are acts of the Church, the sacraments can be meritorious works and prayers. However, the moral causality that they thus exercise is in no way added to that of Christ's work, the only work that pleases God and that is found in every other work brought about by the Church. Moreover, in itself and by itself, Christ's work contains in itself the fullness of its moral efficacy so that the sacraments would not be, in this case, the means that God would utilize for conferring grace. In short, it is not clear what place one should give to an instrument in the framework of moral causality, which is exercised upon God Himself (given that the moral cause is the motive for which God confers grace). It is not clear whether an inferior intermediary can be introduced between the sacrificial death of Christ (which is an absolutely sufficient moral cause) and God's heart upon which it acts so that He may save those for whom His Son gave His life. Could signs be introduced? However, signs are not addressed to God. Man, not God, stands in need of signs and knows by means of signs. Christ's sacrificial death is ever present to God by itself.[75]

The idea of a real-intentional causality

{735} In reaction to these theories but still refusing to accept efficient causality in the sacramental action in the production of grace, Louis Billot elaborated a famous theory which still has numerous partisans, namely, that of "intentional causality."

On the basis of a fact that we ourselves also entirely agree with, indeed, one that we strove to establish above,[76] namely that the sacrament has its being and unity only as a sign, Billot sought out a kind of efficient causality that would belong to signs as such.[77]

He believed that he found it in the practical sign, at least in certain forms. Indeed, practical signs belong to the order of action, being the work of the practical intellect, which, as part of its fundamental tendency, inscribes its conceptions upon reality. However, it does not inscribe them through its power alone and therefore must deploy causes that are external to the intellect: our bodily members, material instruments, and so forth. If it makes use of signs, this will not directly be to realize this conception itself. Instead, in such a case, it will make use of signs in order to deploy and direct the physical action of another intellectual being (and also of an animal by way of its conditioned reflexes, though there cannot be a question

---

75. See Nicolas, "La causalité des sacrements," 520–30.
76. See §725 above.
77. See Nicolas, "La causalité des sacrements," 530–38.

of this with regard to the sacraments). Billot's original idea is that, in certain cases, by expressing its knowledge through signs to other practical intellects and without recourse to some external action, the practical intellect by this very fact modifies, if not material things, at least the relations between persons and of persons with things (e.g., contracts, judicial verdicts, official nominations, and so forth). Here, there would be an intentional causality, that is, a causality whose effect does not exist outside of the intellects of the members of the community. Nonetheless, it is a real causality because it is objectively imposed and entails real consequences within this community.

Doubtlessly, this is where the explanation betrays its essential defect. This defect is found in the fact that what is formally modified by the sign is not reality itself but, instead, the relations that the persons conventionally cultivate among themselves as well as with reality. It suffices that the social convention uniting a community be placed into question and rejected for a given designation or a given decision concerning the persons involved to become unreal. This is because it was unreal of itself.

And how can this kind of causality be used for explaining the causality of the sacraments? According to Billot, who held that sacramental grace and sacramental characters are real, what is caused by the sacrament is not this real modification of the recipient. Instead, it is a disposition to receive the divine action. Hence, the question returns to the insufficient nature of solely moral causality. Indeed, in human things, to designate someone (through a denomination or through an election) to exercise a given function is to designate that person as holding an authority, thus obligating those who depend on this new authority to collaborate with him in the exercise of this function in accord with his decisions.

However, in the case of the sacraments, who would be concerned with this designation? It would be God Himself, as the action of conferring the character and grace can only be produced by Him and because those holding this theory refuse to associate any creature whatsoever in it. However, a sign is never addressed to God. In order that He may act, God does not need any kind of designation concerning the person upon whom He will act. Therefore, we would need to say that the sacrament would designate in the Church the person on whom God simultaneously acts in order to produce in him what the sacrament signifies. The truth and primordial importance of this aspect of the sacrament will be clear for us very soon. However, this has nothing to do with real causality. God could not sanctify by means of the sacrament itself. It would only designate, by the Church's minister, him whom God sanctifies. Thus, the position does not escape being reduced to a form of moral causality.

However, can we in truth go beyond such moral causality and assign a role to the sacraments in the realization of that of which they are signs, namely, man's sanctification?

Explanation of the sacrament's efficient causality by the (instrumental) efficient causality of the minister

As regards the notion of instrumental causality, we refer the reader to what we said in the second part of this course.[78]

The minister's role

{736} We ordinarily speak about the sacraments as though they were causes. St. Thomas himself often does so. However, they are not causes. They are causal actions, and the true instrumental cause is the minister. Thus, in reality, the problem of the causality of the sacraments is concerned with the causality exercised by the minister in performing the sacramental action.

St. Thomas expressed this participation by the minister in the causality of the sacraments in very clear terms from the beginning of his teaching up to its end. Without claiming here to undertake an exhaustive study of his thought, which by itself would take up a lengthy article, we will first note that in the *Scriptum* as in the *Summa*, as regards each sacrament, St. Thomas dedicates a special question to determining who the minister is for the sacrament under consideration. In the *Scriptum*, this question in relation to baptism begins with an article dedicated to the general problem concerning the possibility of man's cooperation with God in the work of sanctification. In conformity with the position that he adopted at that point

---

78. See §§397–99 in volume 2.

of his career, the Holy Doctor (who at that time did not yet admit that a creature could concur in the production of grace other than by disposing the soul for it) limits man's role to that of being a dispositive, instrumental concurrence. However, within these limits, he admits that God would have been able to confer to man the power of cooperating in the work of sanctification directly, as, in fact, He had enabled man to act by means of the sacraments:

> And such cooperative action with God in this manner for interior purification by way of disposition, as some say, could have been bestowed upon man in way that could be accomplished without the sacrament, as in fact he does by performing the sacramental rite.[79]

This text is of interest in that it shows that when St. Thomas speaks of the causality of the sacraments (as he did at length in the same work as regards the sacraments in general), he does not separate the personal power of the minister from the power of the sacrament.

He even comes to distinguish them expressly and to proclaim the necessity of their conjunction so that instrumental causality may be exercised:

> The instrumental power for realizing the conversion that is spoken of here is not found solely in the words but also is found in the priest. The power is found in both incompletely, for neither the priest without the words, nor the words without the priest, can bring about the sacrament.[80]

Already seeking to define the sacramental character, he held that it is, precisely speaking, a power received sacramentally, making him who bears that character the principle of sacramental actions:

> Just as the sacraments instrumentally cause grace, as was said earlier, so too those who receive the character bring about divine things by way of a service. Indeed, the servant is, as it were, the instrument of the person who makes use of him ... Therefore, like the efficacy of the sacrament itself, the character in the minister is instrumental.[81]

In the *Summa theologiae*, we find these same ideas again. The sacramental character is a power that capacitates the Christian to

---

79. *In IV Sent.*, d. 5, q. 1, a. 3, q. 1.
80. *In IV Sent.*, d. 8, q. 2, a. 3, ad 9.
81. *In IV Sent.*, d. 4, q. 1, a. 1.

perform or receive certain sacramental actions. The sacrament is an action performed by the minister. Its efficacy does not only depend on its institution by Christ, who made it be an efficacious sign of salvation, but also depends on the sacramental power that is possessed or not possessed by the person who confers the sacraments.

However, certain texts seem to exclude this role for the minister, at least in some cases. First of all, there is what we find in *De veritate* with regard to baptism: "In these sacraments, the efficacy of the sacrament in no manner involves the minister."[82] In the *Summa theologiae*, on the contrary, he invariably says for baptism: "There is a twofold cause in baptism. One is the principal cause … The other is instrumental, namely the minister who visibly confers the sacrament."[83]

And if we look into the context of the first text, we will see that St. Thomas is preoccupied with theologically explaining how the sacrament of baptism can be conferred by anyone, even by someone who is not baptized. Thus, he comes to this rapid solution: the minister here is of no importance because he plays no role. In the *Summa theologiae*, faced with the same difficulty, he will respond in a much more nuanced way, saying that Christ can use any man whatsoever as His minister. This response restores the necessary role to the minister: "Thus, he who is not baptized acts as the minister of Christ, whose power's efficacy is not restricted to working solely through the baptized, just as it is not restricted to the sacraments."[84]

In the *Summa theologiae*, however, we can find a similar idea regarding the Eucharistic consecration. This is an important text for our current purposes, for it forcefully affirms that the sacrament is an action performed by the minister whose personal intervention is expressed by the sacramental formula. However, this personal intervention is justly denied in the case of the Eucharistic consecration, the minister being completely effaced before Christ, merely repeating the sacred words as they were pronounced by the Lord at the Last Supper: "The formula of the sacrament is uttered (by the priest) as by the very person of Christ (it is He who speaks), so that the

---

82. *De veritate*, q. 27, a. 4, ad 18.
83. *ST* III, q. 66, a. 5.
84. See *ST* III, q. 67, a. 5, ad 2.

minister, in bringing about this sacrament, does nothing other than utter Christ's words."[85]

This is an insight to which St. Thomas obviously attaches much importance in his treatise on the Eucharist, for he returns to it often, emphasizing that in this sacrament the priest acts "in the person of Christ." Must this be understood as entirely excluding the minister's causality in this case? An expression written by St. Thomas in this same article could lead the hurried reader to believe that this is so: "In this sacrament, the consecration of the matter consists in a miraculous change of the substance that can be brought about only by God."

He attributes the aforementioned instrumentally efficacious power to the words, the minister still having nothing other to do than to repeat them:

> Indeed, when these words are uttered as coming from the very person of Christ, by his order, they receive from Christ an instrumental efficacy ... On account of Christ's infinite power ..., as soon as these words were uttered by Christ, they received a consecratory efficacy such that, no matter what priest they may be spoken by, it is as though Christ Himself uttered them today.[86]

The fact that St. Thomas most certainly affirms that a sacramental power exists in the minister prevents us from interpreting this importance bestowed on Christ's words as though it ultimately implied that the priest plays no active role in the consecration. Were this not the case, Christ's own words at the Last Supper would be stripped of their efficacy:

> During his ordination, the priest has conferred upon him the power to consecrate this sacrament as acting in the person of Christ. By this, he is established at the rank of those to whom the Savior said, "Do this in memory of me." This is why we must say that it is proper to priests to confect this sacrament.[87]

And such instrumental power does not only belong to the words. It also belongs to this sacramental power: "This means that the

---

85. *ST* III, q. 78, a. 1.
86. *ST* III, q. 78, a. 1, a. 5.
87. *ST* III, q. 82, a. 1.

consecratory power does not consist only in the words themselves but also includes the power that was conferred upon the priest at the time of his consecration or ordination."[88]

Therefore, we cannot say that St. Thomas held that the act of consecration would not be a personal act of the priest, with the pronounced words having of themselves a quasi-magical power. If this action [*intervention*] by the priest is not expressed, this is perhaps because it essentially consists in the fact that he allows Christ to act through him, by giving Him his voice. However, this same action is a voluntary and free act, a personal act, and it can be performed only by the person who has received the power and who, in virtue of this power, gives efficacy to the words.

That this is imposed on theological reflection (not only for the Eucharistic consecration but for all other sacramental actions) is sufficiently proven by the need for a power on the one hand and the minister's intention on the other. From the perspective of theories of moral causality and, in truth, that of intentional causality, this power could be reduced to a mere sign that designates a man as being empowered to perform the sacramental rite, to which God would have attached the bestowal of grace. However, if one is convinced that these theories are false [*fallacieuses*] and that sacramental causality is nothing if it is not efficient causality, then we absolutely must admit that the power of the priest is a principle of efficient causality in him.

Thus, we must admit that it is not merely a question of him implementing a cause that is external to him (like someone who would trigger off the movement of a machine and would apply it in some way to a given object) but, rather, is a question of being a cause himself by rendering the sacrament efficacious, a cause that, moreover, obviously remains the necessary means for this efficacy. The sacramental action is inseparable from the sacramental agent. If it is an action of efficient causality, it can be exercised only through him. This is confirmed by the necessity of the minister's intention, which shows that the sacramental action must be a human act, engaging the minister's will, for the sacramental rite itself is the same with or

---

88. Ibid., ad 1.

without the intention. Indeed, if the intention is required for this efficacy, this is because the intention does not only depend on the external and signifying action but also depends on the minister's will.

Thus, we must avoid isolating the sacramental rite as though it consisted in some kind of self-sufficient thing. In reality, the sacrament includes not only the rite but also the minister who performs it, as well as the subject who is subject to it. These three components are all sacramental. In other words, they concur in the sacred signification and in the sanctifying efficacy. The minister does so inasmuch as such a person belongs to the sacramental order either in a fixed manner (through the priestly character) or in a transitory manner (as when a layperson or even a non-baptized person performs a baptism). The rite is the sacrament itself, instituted by Christ to signify holiness and, at the same time, to cause it. Finally, the subject must belong to the sacramental order through the baptismal character. In the case of the sacrament of baptism, which by definition does not presuppose another sacrament, its first effect is precisely to place the subject into the sacramental order by marking him with the baptismal character. In this way, it makes him the agent of sacramental actions, including that of baptism whose further, principal effect is the sacramental grace of justification.

The minister's intention

{737} If the minister is God's instrument in the production of grace by means of the sacrament, we must ask ourselves, as we do for every instrument: "What is this instrument's own proper activity?" The response is obvious and follows from what we have said heretofore. It is the sacramental action, accomplished intentionally (i.e., as a human act whose principle is the will).

However, toward what is this intention directed? As soon as we enter into the domain of human acts, we are led to consider the ends that the agent pursues, and first of all his ultimate end, the final end. This is a primordial consideration when we are concerned with the question of morality, which is immanent and related to the person's good. However, we are not here concerned with the question of morality. Instead, we are concerned with the question of efficacy, which is turned outward and is related to an effect to be produced.

The sacramental action is infallibly efficacious in relation to a determinate grace. As it must be a human act, it requires an intention, a willing. Quite precisely, it requires a willing that makes this act voluntary, not necessarily one that renders it morally good. Therefore, what is simply necessary is that the minister wills to perform this action.

However, this is a sacramental action, that is, one that is significative and (instrumentally) efficacious in relation to grace. It can only be willed as being such [i.e., as being a sacramental action]. Moreover, this presupposes that it be known as such, and this is possible only by faith.

Does this mean that, strictly speaking, the minister would need to have faith? If he were immediately the instrument of Christ, who is invisible, this consequence would follow necessarily, for in that case he could not be united to Him except by his own faith. However, the universal minister of the sacraments, to whom Christ entrusted His priesthood, is the Church. The minister who is present, conferring this sacrament, acts as someone representing the visible Church, performing the sacramental action in her name and through her power. If he wills "to do what the Church does," that is, to perform this action in accord with the meaning that the Church attaches to it, even if he himself, not having faith, is incapable of recognizing this meaning, the sacramental action, inasmuch as it is sacramental, is a human act. This suffices for the power with which he is endowed (whether in a transitory or permanent manner) to be deployed in and through this particular action. Therefore, this suffices in order for him, a minister who is blind and unconscious of what he is doing, to be the instrumental efficient cause of the sanctification that the sacrament brings about.

However, if the sacramental action is an efficient cause of grace inasmuch as it is a human act (i.e., inasmuch as it is voluntary), this is not according to its material conditions, which are indifferent to the presence or absence of intention. However, this is what is efficient because what is efficacious is the willing of its ritual performance. Nonetheless, it is efficient precisely inasmuch as it is part of the minister's human act, the other part being the willing that actually makes it into a human act.

Therefore, inasmuch as it is sacramental, the external act makes up a single human act along with the interior act. It is the commanded act, playing a role in relation to the *imperium* that is analogous to that played by the body in relation to the soul.[89]

In other words, it first of all depends on it in sacramental being, as we have seen, and the necessity of the intention comes from this fact. However, the intention also depends on it, for it takes on its reality and consistency in the external act. On the other hand, given that it is intentionally assimilated to it, as to its realization, being visible while the intention is invisible, it is the natural expression of the intention, signifying it, as, indeed, the body is the expression of the soul.

This spiritual power, which we have seen must be recognized in the sacrament, is precisely the minister's will, which thus passes into the bodily action:

> For in the other sacraments, the consecration of the matter consists only in a blessing, from which the matter thus consecrated holds a kind of spiritual efficacy, which can come upon inanimate instruments through the intermediary of the minister who himself is an animated instrument.[90]

St. Thomas specifies this notion of an animated instrument in relation to the instrumentality of Christ's humanity. Indeed, according to him, what characterizes such an instrument and distinguishes it from others is precisely the fact that the principal cause exercises its elevating motion on his will:

> As regards an instrument that is animated by a rational soul, it is moved by the intermediary of his will, as the slave is set in motion to do something by his master's command. Thus, Christ's human nature was the instrument of His divinity in such a way that it was moved by its own, proper will.[91]

And he makes use of this notion in order to define the minister's role in the sacraments:

> An animated instrument, like the minster, is not only moved but also moves himself in some manner, inasmuch as through his will he moves his members to act. This is why his intention is required. By means of it,

---

89. See *ST* I-II, q. 17, a. 4.
90. *ST* III, q. 78, a. 1.
91. See *ST* III, q. 18, a. 1, ad 2. See §400 in the previous volume.

he places himself under the movement of the principal agent (i.e., by intending to do what Christ and the Church do).[92]

Thus, through his internal intention (i.e., through the practical intellect's act known as the *imperium*, having the sacramental action as its object and being realized in it) the sacramental minister, an animated instrument, cooperates instrumentally in God's sanctifying action. Therefore, the problem is reduced to this: "How can this internal act be elevated by God and rendered efficacious in relation to sacramental grace?"

The efficacy of the minister

{738} The first question to be posed is that of knowing if this interior act has the minimal required efficacy which, as we have seen, is required of an instrumental cause. It is tempting to doubt that it does, as it is a question of an immanent act. Nonetheless, we must, on the contrary, recognize that the will has an efficacious character. In the intelligent being, it is the principle of all the efficacy that it can exercise on the world. God creates by His will. An angel can act on the material world by his will. Finally, by his will, man moves himself and moves things, realizing an external work.

Certainly, solely by his will, man does not have the power to bring about the work that he has conceived and willed. He must set into motion his executive powers, his bodily members, and a host of instruments, doing all of this over the course of an extended temporal duration. However, the will is at the root of all this movement. It is not there as presenting the ideal to be realized but, rather, is there as an efficacious energy impressing its impulse on man's powers. Even though this impulse is only immediately exercised on man's [internal] powers and, through them already, on his muscles, it nonetheless is an action, one ordered toward the conceived work as toward its terminus.

This action is what God's omnipotent willing super-elevates. God's will immediately realizes what it wills: *dixit et facta sunt* [He spoke and they came into being]. If He penetrates and super-elevates the human will, He realizes by it and with it what it wills with Him,

---

92. ST III, q. 64, a. 8, ad 1.

through a willing that would, by itself, be impotent (and doubly so, as we are here concerned with a supernatural work) but which He renders capable of performing this act and indeed actually makes it realize that object.

This is the solution that St. Thomas proposed for the case of a miraculous deed. The wonderworker would present the divine *imperium* to creatures, even material ones. Obviously, this presentation would be something different than the mere transmission of a message as, precisely speaking, it is a question of material creatures, which are incapable of hearing a message and of being conformed to it. It can be understood only as man's practical intellect participating in God's efficacious *imperium*. Moreover, in the *Summa theologiae*, it is expressly mentioned that God can use one of man's internal acts in order to perform a miracle.[93]

Can we justly extend human instrumentality conceived along these lines to the production of grace? It is not clear that there is anything that would be opposed to it.

In willing to perform the sacramental action, the minister more or less consciously wills to sanctify the person on whom he acts in accord with the proper grace of this sacrament. In the case of the words of consecration, he wills to change the bread and wine into the body and blood of Christ. It is clear that wholly by itself this willing would be perfectly inefficacious. Nonetheless, it exists and is at least realized in the uttering of the words and through the accomplishment of the ritual actions. By taking possession of all this, the Divine Omnipotence renders it efficacious. That is, it renders the sacramental rite efficacious, according to its signification. The sacramental action receives from the minister's will the spiritual energy that the sacramental action by itself must have so as to be superelevated and rendered instrumentally efficacious for bringing about a spiritual effect.

However, did St. Thomas have some idea about this kind of transposition? A number of scattered remarks lead us to think that the idea is at least not foreign to his thought. With regard to the form of baptism, in responding to the objection that it is directly

---

93. See *ST* II-II, q. 178, a. 1, ad 1.

addressed (*ego te baptizo*) someone who most often can neither hear nor understand the words is a rather useless action, he responds in a way that curiously recalls what he says about the case of miracles:

> One must say that the words uttered in the sacramental formulas are not pronounced only so as to signify but also so as to bring about [what they signify] inasmuch as they hold their efficacy from the Word through whom all things were made. Consequently, it is perfectly suitable that they be addressed not only to men who are capable of understanding them but also to creatures that are deprived of knowledge, as when one says, "I exorcise you, O creature, salt."[94]

However, it is above all in relation to the words of the Eucharistic consecration that he makes use of this kind of explanation. Seeking to know how they are "true," he appeals to the truth of the practical intellect. Given its efficacious character, the practical intellect renders true the thing that it expresses by making it to be precisely what it has said that it is:

> Just as the conception of the practical intellect does not presuppose that the conceived thing exists but instead makes it exist, so too for the uttering of these words to be true, there is no need that the signified thing first exist. Instead, the uttering makes it exist. This is how the Word of God is related to things made by His intermediacy.[95]

And we may not say that this is particular to the Eucharistic conversion [of bread and wine into the body and blood of Christ], which is a miracle, for St. Thomas affirms the instrumental efficacy of the words of consecration by specifically referring to the general theory of the causality of the sacraments.

Finally, there is another text, one that is rarely noticed, in which sacramental efficacy indeed seems to be attributed expressly to the *imperium*. Here, it is a question concerning the "power of excellence" that Christ has over the sacraments inasmuch as He is a man. St. Thomas describes this power, which is still instrumental, by means of four properties, the last of which consists in not being bound to the sacramental rite so as to cause the sacrament's grace: "Christ

---

94. *ST* III, q. 66, a. 5, ad 3.
95. *ST* III, q. 78, a. 5.

could produce the effect of the sacraments without any sacramental rite."⁹⁶

Then, he asks himself whether such a power could have been communicated to the apostles. His response is that He did not in fact communicate it, though He could have done so. Thus, he takes up the four aforementioned properties which the apostles would have enjoyed in this case. Here, he gives precision regarding the fourth: "namely, by granting them such a fullness of grace ... that they would have been able ... to confer the effect of the sacraments without any rite *solo imperio* (by their willing alone)."⁹⁷

Without twisting the text at all but, on the contrary, by taking it in its obvious sense, one can understand that it is always in virtue of the *imperium* that the sacramental minister causes grace but that, not having the "power of excellence," his *imperium* is made instrumentally efficacious by the Divine Omnipotence only as being expressed, exteriorized, and measured by the ritual action in conformity with Christ's institution [of the sacrament].

Christ's role

{739} However, it is not only by instituting the sacrament that Christ intervenes in the production of grace. As we will see, the role of the sacraments is to place man, who is justified by them, into contact with the mysteries of salvation, Christ's redemptive acts.⁹⁸ This active presence of the mysteries (which lay in the past inasmuch as they are events, though they are ever-active inasmuch as they are the cause of men's salvation up to the end of time) can be assured only by the efficient action of Christ living in heaven, exercising itself on man by means of the sacraments. The problem of the sacraments' efficacy is thus intimately connected to that of the efficacy of Christ's humanity.

This brings us back to the classical schema concerning the production of grace. At the summit, God who is at once the First Cause (as for every kind of production) as well as the unique principal cause of this effect, namely, a participation in His nature, also renders

---

96. *ST* III, q. 64, a. 3.
97. Ibid., a. 4.
98. See §747 below.

the creature like unto Him in what is proper to Himself. Next, there is Christ's humanity, the conjoined instrument of His divinity. The Word, according to His divinity, indivisibly with the Father and the Holy Spirit, uses His humanity and makes it instrumentally produce in men the grace that He has merited, called for, and obtained for them by means of that humanity by His actions and passions. The Christ-man extends this saving action to each man through the sacraments which are, for the Word, the separated instruments that enable the conjoined instrument to efficaciously reach all the beneficiaries of redemption through time and space.

How are we to conceive of this instrumental causality exercised by Christ's humanity in any other way than what we proposed above for the sacraments, namely, by appealing to the power that is divinely communicated to His human *imperium*? This is indeed suggested by the Gospel, both in the order of miracles (when we see Him command the winds, sickness, or death) or in the very order of grace (when we see Him remit sins with authority, give the Holy Spirit, as well as realize and institute His real Eucharistic presence). This is what St. Thomas indicates when he characterizes His mastery over the sacraments through His power not only to institute them but also to go beyond them and produce their effect solely by willing it.

From this perspective, we must say that the omnipotent command of God, of Christ-God, elevates the human command of Christ and renders it efficacious. Christ, thus moved and super-elevated, moves and super-elevates the minister's command (and, through it, the sacramental rite by which it is realized and expressed) in such a way that, through the sacramental action, the Christ-man and the minister together instrumentally cause the grace of this sacrament.

By the same token, without needing recourse to the impossible notion of action at a distance, we find that another difficulty is thus resolved, namely, the significant difficulty that prevents so many good theologians from admitting the instrumental efficient causality of Christ's humanity in relation to grace (which also holds for the efficient causality of the sacraments in a number of cases): the lack of physical contact. Indeed, if the *imperium* is what is efficacious, being an act of the intellect and of the will together, the contact that it requires is intentional, not bodily. It is intentional but nonetheless real, for precisely speaking, it is a question of an efficacious idea. And given that only the concrete alone can be realized, it is obviously not any intentional presence whatsoever that can suffice in establishing the contact that this kind of efficacy requires. What is required is a "concrete knowledge" concerned with the singular in its ultimate, individual determination in the nexus of its existential circumstances. For man here-below, this is possible for the intellect only when it is prolonged by imagination and perception.

This is why it is impossible for one to exercise the sacramental action on something situated outside the limits of perception (e.g., were a priest to attempt to consecrate a host placed somewhere other than where he currently is). The *hoc* must designate something present. The "you" of the *Ego te absolve* must be present, as the person to whom one is speaking right now, presenting himself as a repentant sinner. By contrast, the matrimonial consent can be rendered present through a representative or a sign, as holds in natural contracts.* For Christ, whose intellect knows each being in its singularity and in its existential situation in the Beatific Vision (which is perfect experiential knowledge), the contact of His *imperium* with the sacramental minister is always assured, without any spatial or temporal limitation. The only thing needed is that both the minister and the beneficiary of the sacrament render themselves present to Christ, for Christ is continually present. Indeed, this role is played by the intention (both of the minister and of the believer) in the efficacy of the sacramental action.

The reversal of initiatives

{740} The fact that Christ has the power to cause sacramental grace without the sacraments is part of His "power of excellence," even though the sacraments are the means that He has chosen (ones that are perfectly conformed to human nature) for placing His present sanctifying action in continuity with the perfect, universal, perfectly sufficient, and unique saving action that He accomplished

---

* [Tr. note: Regarding the Byzantine East and this matter, see the translator's note at the start of this volume.]

on Calvary. Likewise, He does not sanctify men without the sacraments, at least without the desire for them. However, beyond this, the requirements of the sacramental order bring about a remarkable reversal of initiatives. Normally the initiative in a given action lies with the principal cause and in subordination to it. When an intermediary cause is involved (whether it be instrumental or not), the initiative for the action in question does not normally fall to it. Here, in the sacraments, the initiative lies with the ultimate instrumental cause, in whose service God's omnipotence and Christ's saving will seem to be placed. We can understand why this is so if we consider the fact that in this series of subordinated causes only the last one (i.e., the minister) belongs to the sacramental order, that is, to the order of that which is visible, signifying, and bearing that which is invisible. His initiative alone is manifest. If it were valid only following upon Christ's initiative, which can only be invisible and not manifest, the sacramental order would cease to be certain. It would cease to exist [precisely as sacramental].

All the possibilities of abuse in ministerial power arise from this autonomy of human initiative. If the sacramental action is a human act, it is submitted to the risk of all sorts of moral deviations. Nonetheless, the sanctifying will of God and of Christ are what are ever placed into action by it, for aside from this particular abuse, if one were to place into question the minister's sacramental efficacy, what would be compromised would be the salvation of all humanity such as it has been conceived of and willed by God.

This role played by human initiatives presupposes moral causality at the very foundation of the sacramental action. We must admit (and all do admit) that each time a competent minister correctly performs the sacramental rite (whatever might be his personal end or whatever might be the timeliness of his initiative), the Divine Omnipotence and the sanctifying will of Christ come into play, activating and super-elevating his instrumental power, making it arrive at the proper effect of this rite (unless there happens to be an obstacle on the part of the beneficiary, preventing this effect from being totally or partially produced). One can indeed say that this intervention is motivated by the moral dignity of the sacrament inasmuch as it represents the saving mysteries. However (and this is where the theory of moral causality is deficient), this divine intervention is exercised on the minster and on the rite in order to make them instrumentally produce grace and is not exercised immediately on the beneficiary.

THE ROLE OF THE SACRAMENTS IN THE CHURCH'S LIFE

Having studied the sacraments in themselves, we must now examine how they are the means used by the Church for extending Christ's presence and redemptive action throughout history up to the end of time.

The Active Presence of the Redemptive Mystery in and Through the Church by Means of the Sacramental Signs

The state of the question

{741} Through His passion, death, and resurrection, Christ saved men of all times and places. However, His passion, death, and resurrection are historical, situated, and dated events. Here, we are faced with an antinomy which, in fact, places the mystery of the Church into question and, through her, the mystery of redemption in its existential application to the men for whom Christ died. It is the antinomy between, on the one hand, the reality of the events of salvation, which implies historicity and therefore their inclusion in history, and on the other hand, their universal scope in time and space, which implies supra-historicity and the inclusion of all of history in them.

The solution to this antinomy is found in the sacraments. But how is this so? Will we simply say that the sacraments cause in the person who receives them the grace that Christ merited once upon a time for men? However, we have seen that they both signify the saving mysteries and cause what they signify, namely the beneficiary's actual participation in these mysteries, his encounter with Christ the Savior in the very act by which He saves. Nonetheless, how should we conceive of the idea that past events would exercise causality today?[99]

Solutions made by appealing to the identification of the sacraments and the saving mysteries

The so-called mysteric presence

{742} The primordial intuition that sustains this famous theory (which was proposed by Dom Odo Casel and, during the time separating the two World Wars, resulted in profound developments in sacramental theology) can be summarized as follows: the Christian life consists essentially in our participation, through liturgical worship, in the acts by which Christ saved us, namely in the passion, death, and resurrection which are the various phases of the same redemptive mystery.

This insight relies on Scripture, especially Romans 6:1–14, though also on the numerous Pauline texts where the believer's participation in the passion, crucifixion, death, and resurrection of Christ is affirmed. Casel also relied on the results of detailed Patristic investigations, whose results are generally contested today if not

---

99. See the following texts: Johannes Betz, *Die Eucharistie in der Zet in der griechischen Väter* (Freiburg: Herder, 1955). Humbert Bouëssé, *Le Sauveur du monde*, vol. 4 (*l'Économie sacramentaire*) (Chambéry-Leysse: Collège Théologique Dominicain, 1951), pts. 1 and 2. Bouyer, *Le rite et l'homme; La vie de la liturgie: une critique constructive du Mouvement liturgique* (Paris: Cerf, 1956); and "Le salut dans les religions à mystères," *Revue des Sciences Religieuses* 27 (1953), 1–6. Odo Casel, *Le mystère du culte dans le christianisme*, trans. Jean Hild (Paris: Cerf, 1946) [translation of *Das christliche Kultusmysterium* (Regensburg: Pustet, 1935)], and *Faites ceci en mémoire de moi*, trans. Jean-Charles Didier (Paris: Cerf, 1962) [translation of "Das Mysteriengedächtnis der Meßliturgie im Lichte der Tradition," *Jahrbuch für Liturgiewissenschaft*, 8:145–225]. Claire Champollion, "Où en-est la théologie des mystères?," *Dieu vivant* 25 (1953): 137–44, and "L'économie du salut et le cycle liturgique," *La Maison-dieu* 30 (1952). Jos. Cools, "La présence mystique du Christ dans le baptême," in *Mémorial Lagrange* (Paris: Gabalda, 1940), 295–305. Jean Daniélou, "Bulletin de théologie sacramentaire," *Recherches des sciences religieuses* 34 (1947): 369–84. Deluz, "Nécessité des sacrements." André Feuillet, "La recherché du Christ dans la Nouvelle Alliance d'après la christophanie de Jn 20, 11–18," *Mysterium Salutis. Dogmatique de l'histoire du salut* (Paris: Cerf, 1969), 1:93–112. Theodor Filthaut, *La théologie des mystères, exposé de la controverse* (Tournai: Desclée, 1954). Jean Gaillard, "Chronique de liturgie," *Revue thomiste* 57 (1957): 510–51. R. Masi, "La dottrina sacramentale del sacrificio della messa," *Euntes docete* 12 (1959): 141–81. Nicolas, "Réactualisation des mystères rédempteurs dans et par les sacrements," 20–54. Ignacio Onatibia, *La presencia de la obra redentora en el misterio del culto* (Vitoria: Editorial del seminario dio, 1954). Hugo Rahner, *Mythes grecs et mystères chrétiens*, trans. Henri Voirin (Paris: Payot, 1954). Roguet, *Les sacrements*, 414–30. O'Neill, *Meeting Christ in the Sacraments*, ch. 3, and *Sacramental Realism*.

in this primordial intuition, at least as regards the sacramental theory that Casel draws from it.

Indeed, for Casel, the consequence of this view was that cultic acts (and above all the sacraments) are the reactualization of the saving mysteries accomplished by Christ and that the believer, in performing these acts, participates in His mysteries. Thus, he defined the "mystery" (i.e., the sacramental action and more generally, liturgical action) as follows: "The mystery is a sacred ritual action in which a saving deed is made present through the rite; the congregation, by performing the rite, take part in the saving act, and thereby win salvation."[100]

Casel explained this presence of the past event by means of the power that is proper to symbols. [As is explained by Dom Eligius Dekkers]:

> The sacrament is not something that is brought about in us but instead is something in itself. It is the redemptive act of Christ in all of its reality and in all its fullness. However, having been dislocated on the moving stage of history, it is now condensed in the sacramental sign, which is, as it were, its liturgical face. Therefore, the sacrament is not a new hypostasis of the same reality. Instead, it is this very reality, although in a different form than how it was beheld by the more blessed eyes* of the apostles and contemporaries of Christ.[101]

This outlook expressly appeals to the Platonic notion of an image. According to this notion, the image is more than the mere representation of the thing. Instead, it is the thing itself:

> The image is not entirely devoid of reality. It has its proper existence outside of the awareness of the man who is aware of it. The image participates in the reality of the thing. At bottom, it is this very reality. Therefore, "eikon" in no way signifies a poorly constructed imitation. Rather, it is the epiphany of the very quintessence of the represented thing.[101b]

The notion here presented is that of "presence in mystery." It is complemented by that of "presence in substance." In cultic acts,

---

100. Casel, *Le mystère du culte dans le christianisme*, 102. [Tr. note: Taken from Odo Casel, *The Mystery of Christian Worship*, ed. Burkhard Neunheuser (New York: Crossroad, 1999), 54.]

* [Tr. note: Reading *plus* for *moins* in *les yeux moins heureux*.]

101. Eligius Dekkers, "La liturgie du mystère chrétien," *La Maison-Dieu* 14 (1948): 54.

101b. Ibid., 41.

we would have the presence of the events of salvation "according to their substance," not according to their historical contingency (somewhat like how Christ is present in the Eucharist *secundum substantiam*). However, how can one distinguish the substance of an event from its historical contingency?

Presence "in mystery," or "symbolic presence," is not a real presence. It procures a "sentiment of presence" that can be very lively but which depends on the acts of the subject, thus being subjective. Hence, the efficacy of the sacraments is reduced (whether or not one intends to do so) to their evocative power, and grace is given not in virtue of the sacrament, nor even in virtue of Christ's redemptive acts, but rather as the result of acts performed by the believer. For Dom Casel, it seems that the efficacy of the sacraments essentially consists in rendering really present the death and resurrection of Christ rather than in applying it efficaciously to us. Here, we are faced with a misunderstanding—one that is unintentional and even *contra intentionem*—concerning the absolute primacy of Christ's salvific action, not only in relation to humanity in general but also in relation to the person who believes and is effectively saved.

Principally for these two reasons, the identification that is affirmed between the salvific acts of Christ and cultic acts cannot be retained, or at least not without further clarification. The problem involving how these acts' salvific power is applied today through an act performed by Christ (and by the Church) is not truly resolved and seems to be insufficiently perceived by those holding this position. One cannot retain in an unchanged form the Caselian solution concerning the "mysteric presence" of the saving acts, this participation in the event of salvation procured by the sacraments.

Solution by means of the supra-temporality of the salvific acts

{743} Given that it is decidedly impossible to wrench a temporal event from the limits of time in order to make it exist at another time, it has been asked whether Christ's salvific acts might not be, by themselves, at least partially supra-temporal and, for this reason, able to coexist with the event of cultic activity performed at any given moment of time.

Some of Casel's followers thought that they could do this by appealing to Christ's Divine Personality. Christ's human acts are acts of the Divine Person who exists in eternity. Would they not be invested with a kind of eternal character? However, this solution would lead to the denial of Jesus' human activity, for if such human activity exists, it can only be measured by time, and the mystery of the Incarnation precisely consists in the fact that the eternal Word acts in history by becoming incarnate.

We are faced here with one of Thomism's customary ways of analyzing these facts. It consists in distinguishing in Christ's acts (especially in His salvific acts) that which passes away (the external element and interior element inasmuch as they are produced by human psychic activity) and a "permanent content," namely the act of vision and the act of charity measured by that vision. This act of beatific charity by which Christ willed and merited our salvation was the soul of the redemptive sacrifice and of all the other mysteries accomplished by the Savior in the flesh. Such is the permanent element that explains the contemporary relevance of the content of the liturgical mysteries:

> This same act of immobile oblation, which was signified in the historical acts of our salvation and is still now expressed in another form in the heavenly liturgy that Christ celebrates in glory, is also signified in the mysteries of the earthly liturgy of the Church. It is the *mysterion* of the saving acts. Whereas the historical act is represented in a symbolic image, we can truly have contact with its transcendent content, which is the act of Beatific Charity, since it is endowed with permanence.[102]

This is a very tempting solution, indeed, one that tempts Thomists of great renown. Nonetheless, it seems unacceptable to me, for it rests on an equivocation. In what sense is charity internal to the act that it enables one to perform and that it orders? It is not present internally in itself but, rather, is there in a participated manner. It is impossible that the internal element of a human act perdure when this act is past, for the internal element and external element are two dimensions of one and the same act. If someone gives alms through charity, his charity remains, but the act of giving alms entirely lies in

---

102. Gaillard, "Chronique de liturgie," 541.

the past, not only in its external element but also in its internal element, namely the intention to alleviate this misery here and now. Similarly, the martyr's charity does not pass away; however, the act of dying for Christ is an event that wholly lies in the past. Especially in what pertains to Christ's charity, we have seen that if His earthly acts were meritorious, this was not directly on account of His beatific charity, which is not meritorious, but, instead, was on account of the charity participated in by these acts, thus itself passing away with them.[103]

Finally, we must register the same objection as was expressed for the preceding solution. This removes the reality from Jesus' acts on earth and does not merely remove them from their temporal condition. The human person is not an atemporal being (the "soul") associated with a temporal being (the "body") but, rather, is a being that is wholly temporalized through its bodily dimension without, however, for all that and on account of its spiritual dimension, being completely submerged in time. (Indeed, this is true too, under pain of rendering the Incarnation unreal, in the case of the Incarnate Word precisely as incarnate, i.e., for the Word having become a human person [in the sense discussed in the previous volume]). So too, in a similar way, the earthly human act is entirely temporalized by its "external" dimension. The difference is that, for the human person, time is an extrinsic measure, so that, stripped of its bodily dimension through death, he continues to exist under another [durational] measure. On account of its external element, the human act as such is successive and temporal, thus purely and simply ceasing to exist when the succession in which it consists is brought to its conclusion. Its interior element cannot exist outside the external element in which it is incarnated and realized.

Solution by the supra-temporality of the efficacy of the salvific acts

{744} Here again, we encounter renowned Thomists, sometimes even the same ones as those holding the preceding solution, combining an additional element with it.

This solution can be reduced to saying that Christ's humanity is

---

103. See §406 in the previous volume.

the instrument of His divinity. As this position is articulated by Journet, one would say:

> (Christ's salvific act) was brought about through the power of the divinity that was conjoined to it. For the same reason, it was able to participate in the divine eternity and ubiquity, as an instrument participates in the dignity of the principal cause. The motion of the divinity conferred upon this transitory and localized act an instrumental influence reaching all later times and the whole extent of space.[104]

This explanation relies on a particular conception of instrumental causality, one that is quite widespread but which must be critiqued. Indeed, everyone admits that the instrumental cause must "do something." If it did nothing, it would serve no use, whereas it only has a meaning inasmuch as it "serves" the principal cause. Or, to put it another way, what is taken up by the principal cause is a cause. It is taken up into the action of causality. Its causal action is assumed. Therefore, its causality would need to be elevated in the very action to which it has been elevated, something that presupposes that this causality exists and indeed causes something. Thereupon, we see that it is not indispensable that it causes an effect that is distinct from the one that it produces along with the principal cause inasmuch as it is elevated by it. It can happen that it plays its own proper role in this common effect. In this case, one says that its proper causality is "dispositive." In other words, what it properly brings to bear in the causality plays the role of being a disposition in relation to the complete effect. Based on this image, it is imagined that the instrumental effect could have as its proper effect the "modification" of the action of the principal cause, making the latter be exercised in a particular manner (as breath, passing through a given musical instrument, produces a given particular sound).

However, this is illusory, for such causality would not be efficient but, instead, material. It would not be exercised on the effect but, instead, upon the principal cause. Now, the causality of an instrument *qua* instrument is an efficient causality that produces (along with the principal cause, and in subordination to it) the same effect that it does. On the other hand, the same objection that was registered

---

104. Journet, *L'Église du Verbe incarné*, 2:180.

above must be made when one applies this theory to the causality of salvific acts: even if the instrument's causality could be reduced to modifying the influence of the principal cause, it could exercise it only *inasmuch as it exists*. Thus, one does not at all explain how past salvific acts can act in the present by making appeal to the divine influence which is above time.

In this explanation, the relationship between the principal cause and the instrumental cause is curiously reversed. The latter acts only in virtue of the principal cause, under its action: *mediante eius virtute*. By contrast, this instrument is what is in contact with the patient on which the action is exercised, and the principal cause reaches this patient and can act upon it through the intermediacy of this instrument: the immediacy of contact is, in this instance, called "immediacy of the supposit." Suppress this immediacy of the supposit (the contact of the principal cause with its effect being assured by the instrumental cause) and the instrument finds itself excluded from every form of participation in the production of the effect. Must not the instrument serve the principal cause even if, moreover, the latter could do without it? Now, if its proper causality, in the very act of causing, does not precede the principal causality in some way, it does not serve the principal cause but, rather, on the contrary, is served by it (and it is not clear to what end, except to pretend to be of some kind of use). This is so because when the principal causality is performed, the effect is produced, leaving nothing more to be done. Because it obviously cannot precede it according to "power," it can have only priority over it according to supposit.[105] The difficulty is increased if the distance separating the instrumental cause from the patient is no longer only local but moreover is temporal, for efficient causality requires the coexistence of the cause and the being undergoing its action [*le patient*].

Thus, this attempt at explanation also leads to an impasse. Given that "action follows on being," one thought that, having ceased to exist in themselves, the redemptive acts of Christ could be rendered present anew through their action. However, the opposite was the case. If it is indeed true that "action follows on being," it necessarily

---

105. See *SCG* III, bk. 70. Cajetan, *In ST* I, q. 8, a. 1.

ceases with being, and it is illusory to seek to remedy the absence of being through action-presence.

Attempt at a solution by the conjunction of the sacraments' signification and efficacy

The efficient causality of Christ's salvific acts

{745} Men have been saved and are justified in virtue of Christ's salvific acts: His passion, death, and resurrection.

If one limits oneself solely to the meritorious, satisfactory, and impetratory power of these acts, there would be no difficulty in saying that, given that they are past, they are the cause of all the graces given in the world up to the end of time. Indeed, they are the motive for God's bestowal of these graces.

However, we have seen that this would be insufficient, for the grace of justification assimilates the Christian to Christ in the mysteries of His passion, death, and resurrection. Indeed, to explain this, we must think that He who produces such grace is Christ suffering, dying, and rising from the dead, for "the cause renders its effect like unto itself."[106]

The difficulty to be resolved is that of knowing how past acts can today cause the justification of men.

Christ, now living and glorious, is the one who acts in and through the sacraments for man's justification

{746} It is by means of sacramental acts that this efficacy of Christ's salvific acts is exercised:

> Because, as we have said, Christ's passion preceded as the universal cause of the remission of sins, it must be applied to each person for the obliteration of his particular sins. This is brought about through baptism, penance, and the other sacraments, which draw their efficacy for doing this from Christ's passion.[107]

However, who is the agent of these actions? It is the Church, immediately through her minister, though only in an instrumental

---

106. See *ST* III, q. 48, a. 1; q. 49, a. 1; q. 50, a. 6; q. 53, a. 3; q. 62, a. 5. Nicolas, "Réactualisation des mystères rédempteurs dans et par les sacrements," 20–54.
107. *ST* III, q. 49, a. 1, ad 4.

manner. It is Christ, as principal cause through His divinity and as the superior instrumental cause through His humanity. Now, the Christ who acts in and by the sacraments can be none other than the resurrected Christ, Christ currently living in His glory, for this is the manner in which He now exists.

However, as we said above (in §745), to conform the believer to Himself in His passion, death, and resurrection, it was necessary that Christ act on him on the basis of the redemptive mysteries that were accomplished by Him. Does this not imply a contradiction? The solution that we are now seeking must overcome this apparent contradiction.

The "relays" of the sacraments

{747} By sacrificially dying and rising from the dead, Jesus performed an act that, of itself, was powerful enough to justify and resurrect all men. This act rendered His passion and death satisfactory. This act rendered life and conferred glory on His body, for if the resurrection is an act of God, it is also, instrumentally, an act of His humanity:

> Thus, it is the case that the Word of God first conferred immortal life to the body that is naturally united to Him, and it is by means of this resurrected body that He (will) realize the resurrection in all others.[108]

Why is this efficacy of Christ's passion and resurrection not realized at the same instant? Obviously, because the prospective beneficiaries were not in a state of being submitted to the saving action, either because they did not yet exist (i.e., physical absence) or because they did not yet believe (i.e., spiritual absence). However, the agent, Christ, is ever-present, living, and able to act on each man as soon as the latter is disposed to receive His action.

This action, which He exercises through the Church's minister and by means of the sacrament, is the "renewal" and continuation of the action that He exercised on Calvary and at His resurrection (an action that, in itself, was wholly efficacious in itself). We have seen that the sacramental action (with its entire surrounding liturgical context) symbolizes the saving acts as well as the beneficiary's

---

108. ST III, q. 56, a. 1.

participation in these acts. It serves as a "relay" for the salvific action, which in itself is completed but did not exhaust all of its power on Calvary and will not exhaust its power until the end of time. On the basis of it and by means of it, the glorious Christ "takes up" for each person His saving action. The sacramental action is another action, but on account of its symbolic identification with the saving acts, the efficacy that it receives from the actual motion of the glorious Christ is the efficacy of the act of Christ suffering, dying, and rising again for men in the past on the cross and in the tomb.

Just as an agent renders its effect like unto itself according to the form by which it acts,* the glorious Christ, acting upon men in their earthly life through the sacraments (which are identical according to their form with the acts and states of His passion, death, and resurrection) assimilates the believer, not to His state of eschatological glory, but to His hidden state of death and resurrection.

Thus, the Caselian notion of "mysteric presence" and all the vivifying riches with which it is pregnant, are fully justified in theology if it is completed by the notion of Christ's contemporary activity in and through the sacraments. Left to itself, if such a mysteric presence is *a true presence*, it is not *a real presence*. Therefore, no more can it be an acting presence. Without it, there is no longer is a true presence of the saving mysteries (of the *mysterion* of Christ), even if their fruits are really produced. The motion exercised today by Christ in and by the sacraments gives reality to the presence and action of the mysteries. The sacraments represent these mysteries and configure man to them.

The sacramental efficacy of the mysteries of salvation
and the subject's disposition

{748} The proposed solution raises the problem concerning the dispositions required so that one may benefit from a sacramental action. Indeed, the relay of the sacraments was rendered necessary by something dispositionally lacking [*le défaut de disposition*] in those for whom Christ suffered, died, and rose again. However, this pre-

---

* [Tr. note: As was used earlier above, in a slightly modified form, this would be the scholastic metaphysical dictum *omne agens agit sibi simili*.]

supposes that the required dispositions are realized at the moment when the sacrament becomes the relay of the saving acts of Christ.

The necessity that the beneficiary of the sacrament have these personal dispositions ultimately comes from the fact that justification, while indeed being an act by God who justifies man through Christ, is also a human act that converts and returns the person to God through faith in Christ: "The Word (saves) not because it is pronounced but does so when it is believed."[109]

However, do we not say (and indeed, must we not say) that the sacraments act *ex opere operato*? This seems to preclude every form of participation by the person who benefits from the sacrament.

The formula *ex opere operato* The formula was introduced in the thirteenth century by Peter of Poitiers: "To baptize is the action of him who baptizes and is something different from the baptism itself, for it is a work to be done (*opus operis*), whereas the baptism is the work thus done (*opus operatum*)."[110]

He first applies this formula to Christ's passion in order to distinguish in it the *opus* (which is excellent) from the action of the executioners (which itself was a crime). Then he applies it to the minister who unworthily confers a sacrament. The sacrament is a good *opus*, whereas the *action* of the minister is wicked. Then, the future Pope Innocent III said: "Although the action itself (*opus operans*) could be impure, the work done (*opus operatum*) is pure."[111]

St. Bonaventure, and then St. Thomas, extended the application of the formula, using it to distinguish the sacraments of the Old Law, which justified "in virtue of the action (of the person coming to them)," *ex opere operantis*, from the sacraments of the New Law, which justify "by their own power," *ex opere operato*.

Finally, the expression has two complementary senses. First of all, the sacrament acts *ex opere operato* in the sense that the moral qualities of the minister do not influence its efficacy in any way. The minister is a mere instrument. The grace that he confers is not his own but, instead, is that of Christ, under whose motion he acts.

---

109. St. Augustine. [*sic*]
110. Albert Michel, "Opus operatum," *Dictionnaire de théologie catholique*, 11:1084–87.
111. Pope Innocent III, *De sanctissimo altaris mysterio*, PL 217:843.

Second, the sacrament likewise acts *ex opere operato* in the sense that its efficacity does not emanate from the acts of the beneficiary but, instead, solely from Christ's sanctifying action.

Does this mean that the beneficiary's dispositions play no role? We have seen that the opposite is the case.

The role played by the beneficiary's dispositions {749} With the exception of the particular case of the baptism of children, no justification is conceivable without a personal act performed by man: conversion (including the rejection of sin), movement toward God by faith, hope, and charity together, as well as one's commitment [*disposition*] to live in accord with Christ—"So you also must consider yourselves dead to sin and alive to God in Christ Jesus."[112]

This act (or, "these acts") are the dispositions without which the saving act cannot be exercised, because it consists precisely in making them be performed: the "righteousness" that they confer is operative. In other words, they are not a contribution purely effected by man but, rather, are the first effect of the grace of justification: man performs them, but he receives this performance as a gift.

How is he given this? *By the sacramental action itself.* Thus, we see why their presence and necessity do not undermine the principle of efficacy *ex opere operato*. The sacrament is not rendered efficacious by "man's dispositions." It is efficacious by itself and first causes these dispositions.

However, there is one thing that man can do by himself. He can shirk the action of grace and place himself in a state of counter-disposition. At this moment, the sacrament is rendered inefficacious (at least in what concerns justification itself). In reality, its own proper efficacy is not in question, no more than the efficacy of Christ's saving acts on Calvary are put into question by the fact that they were accomplished without having produced all of their effects in humanity. The subject is what has a defect here, not the cause.

---

112. Rom 6:11 (RSV).

"Mystical" spirituality and "mysterical" spirituality

{750} Casel opposed "mystical" spirituality, which he thought to be individualist and subjective, to "mysteric" spirituality, which would be, on the contrary, communitarian and objective. This opposition between what is subjective and what is objective in our religious life does not stand up to further analysis. It is too clear that the participation in the mysteries of Christ procured for the faithful through the liturgy cannot be anything but personal (and therefore cannot be anything but subjective, if one accepts the identification between the terms "subject" and "person"). Conversely, the union with God in Christ that the mystical life involves cannot be authentic if it is not objective and communal, for Christ is the one who unites us to the Father. Moreover, a closer union with Christ makes one belong more profoundly and completely to the Church, which is His body, making one participate more intensely in her activity.[113]

The "time of the Church"

{751} The term "the time of the Church" is used for speaking about the time between Christ's two comings. It refers to the "time" during which salvation is at once already accomplished and in the midst of being accomplished. It is the time of the sacraments, for the sacraments fill up this in-between, or rather, the Church fills it through her sacramental activity.[114]

The earthly Church is united to Christ and unites her members in Him to the degree that they have faith, by means of the sacraments, *in mysterio*. Indeed, she does so truly but secretly, by awaiting

---

113. See Louis Bouyer, *Introduction à la vie spirituelle* (Paris: Desclée de Brouwer, 1960), ch. 2. Léopold Malevez, "Connaisance discursive et connaisance mystique des mystères du salut," in *L'homme devant Dieu, Mélanges offerts au P. H. de Lubac*, vol. 3 (Paris: Aubier, 1963). Jacques Maritain, *Liturgie et contemplation* (Paris: Desclée de Brouwer, 1960). Jean-Hervé Nicolas, *Contemplation et vie contemplative en christianisme* (Fribourg / Paris: Éditions universitaires / Beauchesne, 1980), 303–6. Albert Plé, "Pour une mystique des mystères," *Vie Spiritualle, Supplément* (1952): 377–96.

114. Oscar Cullmann, *Christ et le temps* (Neuchâtel: Delachaux et Niestlé, 1966), and *Le salut dans l'histoire*. Henri de Lubac, *Histoire et Esprit* (Paris: Aubier, 1950), ch. 3, and *Catholicisme* (Paris: Cerf, 1952). Léopold Malevez, "La vision chrétienne de l'histoire," *Nouvelle revue théologique* 7 (1949): 113–34 and 244–65. Jean Mouroux, *Le mystère du temps* (Paris: Aubier, 1962), pt. 3. Max Seckler, *Le salut et l'histoire* (Paris: Cerf, 1967), 147.

the manifestation of Christ's glory and that of her own glory on the last day: *donec veniat.*

The Objective Consistency of the Earthly Church Assured by the Sacramental Signs

As visible signs of grace, which itself is invisible, the sacraments are closely connected to the Church's visibility, not only because they are one of the principal elements of this visibility but also because they assure it.

The double finality and double effect of the sacraments

The gift of eternal life and participation in the Church's earthly life

{752} Through the sacraments, Christ exercises His redemptive action on men to the degree that they present themselves to Him through faith and the sacramental action. This action was inaugurated and achieved in its essence upon the cross and at the resurrection. However, it must be incessantly "taken up again," as we have seen, in order to reach all of its beneficiaries who wish to accept it. Thus, through the sacraments, men first of all and principally receive the eternal life which is the life of the hereafter with the Trinity. From this perspective, the finality of the sacraments is supra-terrestrial.

However, this does not suffice for explaining their role and *raison d'être,* for in the economy of redemption, man does not immediately receive eternal life in its consummated state. He receives it hidden in faith so that he may first live in the conditions of his earthly life. Thus, the sacraments first of all designate salvation begun herebelow, man's entrance into the way of salvation.

The way of salvation is incorporation into Christ, the only Savior. All the members thus incorporated constitute the body of Christ. The sacraments also have a finality that is more immediate than that of eternal life in the hereafter. They are intended to signify and realize the redeemed person's belonging to the body of Christ, to the Church, a belonging that is the first stage required for salvation. In a manifest and public manner, they guarantee the redeemed person's belonging to the Church on earth.

Remission of sins and liberation from the bonds of sin

{753} Sin and its consequence (namely, exclusion from the kingdom) are the essential obstacles to this gift of life. Indeed, this gift of life itself is what removes them. Along with this new life, the sacraments bring the remission of sins, which is the effect of Christ's redemptive action.

Here again, one must bear in mind the earthly phase of redemption, which is its first phase for each person. Along with remission of all his sins, man receives freedom from every punishment to be undergone. We will see that one can say as much of all the sacraments, though noting a difference, namely, that the freedom from punishment that they bring depends on the subject's dispositions (because of the need to personally participate in satisfaction for sins committed after baptism). What remains is the inclination to sin, the "concupiscence" against which grace, supported by one's freedom, must fight in order to progressively triumph over it (though never completely doing so here-below).

Therefore, one of the sacraments' finalities is to aid man in triumphing over sin during his earthly life and thereby not being excluded from eternal life. In the eyes of medieval theologians (including St. Thomas during the first part of his career[115]), this finality seemed to be primary. Later in his career, he stated that this held a second rank in sacramental finality, although he thought that in the state of innocence the sacraments would have been useless.[116] Grace is what is necessary, and the state of sin in which humanity is placed is what makes the sacraments necessary as the means for receiving grace (or, at the very least, makes them the most adapted means for the reception of it). Thus, according to St. Thomas, were there no sin, the sacraments would be useless; however, it does not follow that their primary end would be the fact that they are a remedy for sin. Their end is to procure for man the benefits that he lost through his Fall, benefits which he can recover only if he is delivered from his sin (and which he can preserve only if he is gradually freed from his tendencies to sin).

---

115. See Aquinas, *Les sacrements*, ed. and trans. Roguet, 262–65.
116. *ST* III, q 61, a. 2.

This finality is nothing other than that which we spoke of earlier. The remission of sins is the negative face of the gift of life. (Life is what drives away death, and light dispels the darkness.) Similarly, the "remedy against the tendencies to sin" is no other finality than belonging to the earthly Church because, as we have seen, it is to the degree that a man is "holy" and freed from sin that he belongs to the Church.

Therefore, the sacraments have a twofold finality. One surpasses earthly realities, namely, the grace of the remission of sins and the gift of eternal life. The other, earthly one, is the redeemed person's manifest membership in the Church here-below, along with his participation in her holiness.

The earthly finality of the sacraments and the visibility of the Church

{754} If the sacraments' first and principal finality is above all "personal" (for the person is pardoned and lives the Trinitarian life with Christ and in Christ), their second finality is above all communal and ecclesial. By assuring that the Church's members manifestly belong to her, as well as the status of different members in the earthly ecclesial community (i.e., through various hierarchical bonds), the sacraments assure the consistency of the Church as well as her order inasmuch as she is a historical reality, a society. They assure her visibility.

However, how do they do this? This cannot be through the grace that they confer, for strictly speaking, the presence and action of grace in a given individual are an unverifiable datum. Indeed, the grace in question depends not only on the sacrament but also on the subject's dispositions, and it can be lost if these dispositions change. A Church that would have no other existence than the existence of grace in its members would be completely invisible. It would not be a reality belonging to this world. No more can the Church's visible existence be had solely from the sacramental rites, which are passing actions, therefore by themselves unable to assure the Church's stability and permanent consistency.

Therefore, we must make recourse to the notion of *res et sacramentum* that we have already encountered. One must hold that the state of "having received a sacrament" is a permanent state (at least if it is a question of the sacraments that by their direct effect make one part of the Church's essential order, either by making one enter the earthly Church or by making one occupy a determinate place in her). It is a state that *of itself* is independent of the personal situation of the beneficiary in relation to salvation (i.e., independent of the grace that he does or does not have).

This effect corresponds to the earthly finality of the sacraments.

However, is it visible? It is not visible by itself but, instead, is so through its strict connection with the sacramental rite performed. In other words, the (verifiable) certitude that a man has submitted himself to the sacramental rite begets certitude that he is actually (and permanently) "sacramentalized" in accord with this sacrament.

In this way (namely, as "fixing" the transitory sacramental rite as an "internal sacrament"), the *res et sacramentum* causes and assures the visibility of the Church, her consistency as a reality belonging to this world.

The relationship between these two finalities

{755} It is self-evident that these two finalities are subordinated to one another. To be incorporated into Christ and the Church has a meaning only in terms of eternal life, in which the body of Christ will come to its "fulfillment." The ultimate goal of redemption obviously is not to constitute the earthly Church but, rather, is to liberate man and bestow upon him an exaltation which extends beyond earthly life to eternal life. The Church here-below exists in a state of pilgrimage. She moves toward her rest. While the goal of the sacraments is the introduction of men into the Church, as well as enabling them to progress in this forward march, this goal is subordinated to the ultimate goal to which she leads them: eternal life.

Of these two finalities, which are thus subordinated, the inferior one is the finality on account of which the sacraments were instituted. It is their own proper finality, and it is by realizing it that they can attain their ultimate end, man's consummated salvation. If this salvation cannot be attained without them, this is because, in the economy of salvation established by God, sin cannot be remitted, nor the

Divine Life communicated, except by means of incorporation into Christ in the earthly Church. Likewise, this is so because the proximate finality that accounts for their institution and their necessity is the stage by which man's redemption necessarily begins. However, conversely, the sacraments can realize their own, proper finality only by subordinating it to their ultimate finality. Belonging to the earthly Church cannot be aimed at as though it were a self-sufficient end. It is itself ordered to something else, from which it cannot be separated without sterilizing it. Eternal life, sketched out here-below in faith, is truly the ultimate end of the sacraments, beyond and through the intermediary of their own proper ends. And this life, inasmuch as it is a participation by the creature in the very life of the Trinity, is the life of the eschatological Church, which is the "whole Christ," the Church in its integral state, she who finds her beginning in the communion of saints already brought about through Christ's grace: saints in their fullness in heaven; saints *in via* toward this fullness on earth.

The sacramental character and its equivalents

{756} Very early in the history of the development of the Church's sacramental doctrine, the need to recognize the existence of a permanent effect, independent of the personal situation of the beneficiary in relation to salvation, led to the discovery of this effect of certain sacraments, namely, what has come to be called the sacramental "character." By extension and because the production of this effect, which is needed for three of the sacraments in particular, corresponds to the general consideration of the sacraments, it was later on recognized that there is a more or less comparable equivalent for the other sacraments.

The Church's discovery of the "sacramental character"

This doctrine was gradually constituted on the occasion of the lengthy controversy concerning "rebaptism." This controversy began between St. Cyprian and the bishop of Rome. It was then continued by the Donatists who claimed that they were successors of St. Cyprian's thought and refused to recognize any value to the baptism and ordination conferred by the Catholic Church or conferred upon "traditors" (people who, during the persecutions, had handed over to the Roman authorities the books of the saints or at least those who were accused of having done this). The ultimate conclusion arrived at in the course of this controversy was recognized as dogmatic by the Council of Trent, which stated that the sacraments of baptism, confirmation, and holy orders impress an indelible character on the soul, a character that is not submitted to the fluctuations of free will (as is indeed the case for grace).[117] St. Cyprian said that baptism exists only in the Church and through the Church and that he who receives baptism (and holy orders) outside the Church (or who leaves her by apostasy, schism, or heresy) either receives nothing or loses what he once received. The Roman Church, on the basis of her traditions, responded that for the person who has received it, baptism is an inalienable reality and that if a baptized person comes to the Church or returns to her after having left her, he does not need to be baptized but, instead, only needs to be reconciled through the imposition of hands.

It was through reflection on this dogmatic fact and by seeking an explanation for it that St. Augustine was led to distinguish the truth (or, existence) of a sacrament from its fruitfulness. This led him to distinguish two effects brought about by the sacrament. First, there is the principal one, namely, the fruit of the sacrament, which is grace, an effect which can fail to be received or can be lost. Second, there is the other effect that is always caused as soon as baptism is conferred in accord with the rite, an effect which cannot be lost:

> Baptism is not given to the person who returns to the Church, for he did not lose it by leaving her. Just as wicked sons do not have in themselves the Holy Spirit whom the beloved sons have, likewise heretics have baptism even though they do not have the Church, which Catholics have. Therefore, just as there can be a baptism from which the Holy Spirit withdraws Himself, so too there can be a baptism where the Church is not found ... However, heretics have hands placed upon them after repenting on account of the communion in charity, which is the supreme gift of the Holy Spirit (and that without which all the other holy gifts that can be found in man have no worth for salvation).[118]

---

117. Council of Trent, session 7, in D.-*Sch.*, no. 1609.
118. St. Augustine, *De Baptismo*, PL 29 (1964), bk. 5, ch. 23, no. 33.

To these shepherds of the Catholic Church spread out throughout the entire world, who fortified the primitive custom later by the authority of a council, it seemed quite clear that even the lost sheep outside the Church who had received there the character of the Lord from those kidnappers received correction for his error, deliverance from his captivity, and healing of his wounds on the day when he comes to ask for salvation from the Christian communion. Far from frowning upon him, we recognized the character of the Lord in him.

Indeed, many wolves impress this character on wolves who certainly seem to be in the sheepfold but who (as is proven by their wicked conduct in which they persist up to the end) nonetheless do not belong to the one sheepfold (i.e., the Church) whose unity is not prevented by the multitude of her members.[119]

In what does the "sacramental character" consist?

{757} Based on this fundamental idea that the character is the sign and (formal) cause of belonging to the Church inasmuch as she is visible and earthly, we can then determine its nature and properties.

Membership in the Church on earth and participation in her worship If we ask what is the characteristic activity of the Church on earth, the proper work that is hers to accomplish, that work in which all of her members are called to concur, we will find that three options seem to offer possible answers. First, there is the preaching of the faith (i.e., the teaching of the faith, leading the children of God along the ways of the Gospel). Second, there is divine worship. Third, there is participation in the earthly work of men.

We find ourselves faced with a choice regarding this third point. Does the Church have as her specific role (indeed, the role that would suffice to justify her existence) her activity participating in the "development of the world"? Particularly on the basis of the constitution *Gaudium et Spes* and on a number of other indications given by the Second Vatican Council as well as during the years thereafter, great insistence has been voiced concerning the need for the Church to be present to the world. Certainly, if the Church exists, she exists *in the world and for the world*. However, it is nonetheless certain that there is no work that the Church has accomplished or

---

119. Ibid., bk. 6, ch. 1.

could accomplish in the domain of man's earthly activity (e.g., his technical activity, culture, charity, social or political activity, and so forth) that could not be performed by an institution fashioned by human hands. The organization and development of earthly life are entrusted by God to man, and it falls to man to provide for them by means of his intellect, heart, and labor. The Church was founded for the sake of something else: to assure the presence of Christ the Savior among men and to continue His redemptive work, which is itself elevated above earthly concerns, even though it is brought about on earth and in men living an earthly life. The part that can and must be taken up in man's properly secular activities cannot constitute her *raison d'être* and own, proper work.

The first point, by contrast, at first appears to be specific, and indeed it is. Nonetheless, we must not forget that the preaching of the Gospel is by its nature ordered to faith (in the full sense of the word), that is, to the reception of Christ by man. Now, our encounter with Christ occurs through the sacraments. It is through them that each man is personally engaged in the redemptive mystery, freed from his sins, saved, sanctified, and made a participant in the Divine Life, in life with God.

The redemptive action itself was the supreme act of the virtue of religion (inspired by charity, obviously). It is by His self-sacrifice that Jesus inaugurated the rite of Christian religion, offering Himself in sacrifice like a host to God, as St. Paul says.[120] On the cross, Jesus offered Himself and offered with Himself mankind contained in Him, as an expiatory victim for sins and simultaneously in adoration, thanksgiving, and supplication. By raising Him, the Father rendered life to Him for Himself and for all men. Worship consists in this ascending and descending mediation. The Church is associated with it through her liturgy, which can be considered as being her specific work (without diminishing her mission to announce the Gospel and make known the ways of salvation). This is the work to which she invites all those who hear the Word that she announces.[120b]

If the sacramental character is that by which someone belongs

---

120. See *ST* III, q. 62, a. 5 (St. Thomas cites Eph 5:2).
120b. See §983 below.

to the earthly Church, it is also that by which he is rendered capable of taking part in this work, namely, Christian worship: "For God is my witness, whom I serve with my spirit in the gospel of his Son…"[121] because of the grace given me by God to be a minister of Christ Jesus to the Gentiles in the priestly service of the gospel of God, so that the offering of the Gentiles may be acceptable, sanctified by the Holy Spirit."[121b] The *Traduction Oecuménique de la Bible* here notes: "The central idea of this verse is that the goal of Paul's apostolic ministry is to enable the pagans exist as an offering, a spiritual sacrifice to God. This is why he applies the sacrificial vocabulary of the Old Testament to his ministry."

Of course, the sacramental character also gives one, in the same way, a share in the Church's responsibility to announce the Gospel. However, this is included in the sacramental character's relation to the Church's worship.

Definition of character in terms of Christ's priesthood {758} St. Thomas defines the three characters (those of baptism, confirmation, and holy orders) as being participations in Christ's priesthood, deriving from Christ Himself.[122] This was a new and original conception in his era.[123] This definition would seem to be better* than when he defined it as: "assuring the conjunction between the external organization of the Church and her internal life of grace."[124] However, these two conceptions are thoroughly interconnected, at least if one understands that for St. Thomas, worship is the specific external activity performed by the Church. Indeed, Christ is the priest of Christian worship. This worship does not only stem from His sacrifice; it is the perpetual offering and application of His sacrifice. To participate in this Christian worship, one must participate in Christ's priesthood.

---

121. Rom 1:9 (RSV).
121b. Rom 15:16 (RSV).
122. See ST III, q. 63, a. 3.
123. See Jean Galot, *La nature du caractère sacramental. Étude de théologie médiévale* (Paris: Desclée de Brouwer, 1957).
* [Tr. note: Reading *plus heureux* for *moins heureux*, given the further context in the next two paragraphs.]
124. See Henri Barré, *Trinité que j'adore* (Paris: Lethielleux, 1965), 193n73.

When applied to the baptismal character, this conception of the sacramental character provides the best foundation for the priesthood of the Christian people, which we will discuss later on. Moreover, we will find the solution to the explanation of the distinction of the ministerial priesthood from the common priesthood of the faithful as well as their intimate connection by considering the character of holy orders as being a complement to the baptismal character.[124b]

Conceived in this way, the character is a "consecration" of the believing person, one analogous to the consecration of an object that is reserved for God. It is a consecration that cannot be brought about without the consent of the consecrated person (because this consecrated *res* is a person who, as such, is free). However, it is a consecration that can no longer be destroyed by the person once it has been given, though he could repudiate it.[125]

Sign-character and real spiritual power {759} This consecration is itself the sign of belonging to Christ and of belonging fully to the Church through grace and charity.

How is it a sign even though it is internal and hidden? We have said that this sign-character comes from the indefectible connection between the rite (*sacramentum tantum*) and this effect (*res et sacramentum*). The believer is dedicated by the sacramental rite to which he submits himself, and this consecration is a permanent internal state.

Must this consecration be an ontological modification in the believer, a new reality? Classical theology is confident in its affirmative answer. The modern mind is vigorously revolted by the idea. Is it not essentially a question of a moral reality, a bond linking the human person to the person of Christ? However, if this were so, how could we understand the fact that this consecration persists when the person, through his free choice, turns away from Christ and breaks his bond with Him? We forever must return to this foundation of the theology of the sacramental character.

124b. See §983 below.
125. See *In IV Sent.* d. 4, q. 1, a. 3, sol. 4.

Another reason requires us to admit that this reality exists. By his nature, man does not participate in the priesthood of Christ. In order to perform, with Christ, such priestly acts, he must receive a power that is not his own. This power is the sacramental character.

This is quite clear for the case of the ministerial priesthood, for in this case, it is a question of performing truly efficacious acts, sacramental actions. Certainly, this efficacy comes above all from Christ. However, as we have seen, it also comes from the minister (for Christ's action is invisible and must be manifested through the minister's visible action). On the other hand, the initiative in the sacramental action comes from the minister. This action must be efficacious each time that he decides to perform it, provided that he observes the essential rite. This presupposes that he be endowed with the power of performing these actions, a power for rendering them efficacious. And this power must be real, for it is a question of real efficacy.

This argument does not hold if one is content to hold that sacramental causality is solely moral, for it would thus suffice to say that if someone received the sacrament of holy orders, each time that he performs the sacramental actions for which he was ordained, Christ intervenes to invisibly cause what they signify. We have already discussed how this conception is insufficient.

St. Thomas extends this notion of "spiritual power" to the character of baptism, a "passive power," he says (*potestas passiva*).[126] This is not as clear of a case, for every human person is submitted to Christ's priestly action inasmuch as that person is a man, a member of mankind. One can only evade it through one's own "non-disposition." However, on reflection, we can see that this baptismal character is necessary. Indeed, we must admit that the person who has not received the sacrament of baptism cannot receive any other sacrament. This is a basic fact. It presupposes that participation in Christian worship, in which the *sancta*, the gifts of God, are communicated by the Church, also requires a "power" which is the first of the *sancta*.

This is understandable if we hold that all of God's gifts (and, first of all, the Holy Spirit, the primordial gift containing all the others

---

126. See *ST* III, q. 63, a. 2.

that flow forth from Him) are given by Christ to the Church. To put the matter more exactly, they are given to the Christ-man and extended from Him to His body, the Church. Therefore, the baptismal character, which makes someone a member of the Church, is also (and simultaneously) that which empowers that person to participate in this outpouring.

However, all of this is said without prejudice to the extension of this sanctifying action performed by Christ beyond the visible frontiers of the Church and without her direct (sacramental) action.[127]

To say that this character is a *potestas passiva* obviously does not mean that the Christian's participation in worship is purely passive. It is a pure passivity in relation to God's gifts because God alone saves and justifies. However, these gifts of God are principles of life and activities in the Christian person, especially of the acts by which he participates in the Church's worship.

Res et sacramentum in the sacraments that do not impress a character

{760} The same reasons for affirming the existence of a character for certain sacraments precludes the existence of a character in the cases of the other sacraments, for they can be repeated. First of all, there is the Eucharist, but the same can be said of all the others, except baptism, confirmation, and holy orders.

Reflection can justify this claim. Baptism and confirmation (which is a continuation of baptism) assure membership in the Church, and we have seen why they require a true (and therefore stable) "consecration." Similarly, such a consecration is needed in the case of holy orders, which establishes someone as the minister of the sacraments, who (as we have seen) takes part in the sacrament as an agent of the sacramental action. It is necessary that this also be designated to him in a verifiable way (and, therefore stably and definitively as well).

The Eucharist is the very essence of worship itself. It is the sacrament by whose celebration man participates in Christian worship. Therefore, it presupposes that the participant be capacitated and not himself confer such a capacitation. This also presupposes that the

---

127. See §690 above.

victim of the sacrifice, Jesus Christ, really be present there so as to be really offered by the Church, with Christ himself, and really eaten. Therefore, the sacrament of the Eucharist itself also includes a permanence, which makes it last beyond the very sacramental rite of consecration and makes it the sign and cause of the ultimate significate, the *res* that is the fruit of the sacrifice, one's entrance into the sanctuary (i.e., the Trinitarian life) through Jesus' blood.[128] Christ present sacramentally is the *res et sacramentum*.

Penance is the sacrament that repairs the broken bond between baptismal character and the *res* that it naturally signifies, namely union with Christ through grace and charity, as well as full membership in the Church. Therefore, it does not include a character. However, it does include an "ecclesial" effect, namely, visible reconciliation with the Church, as we will see in its own proper place. This is its *res et sacramentum*.

Something similar can be said for the anointing of the sick, while marriage's "ecclesial" effect is the sanctifying of the bond, of itself natural, between the spouses.

The stability of the sacramental order

The problem: A cause that is a sign of its effect

{761} Ordinarily, the effect is the sign of its cause. In the case of the sacraments, we have a manifest cause (the sacramental rite) that is the sign of its effect (the *res et sacramentum*). Then, there is the grace that is signified by the *res et sacramentum* and caused by it in the sense that the latter is the "prior disposition" in relation to the ultimate effect of the sacramental action (i.e., grace).

An important consequence flows from this. By applying the principle of causality, one can, with certitude, inductively reason from the effect to the cause. However, to so reason from the cause to the effect, the connection between the cause and the effect would need to be indefectible. We must be sure that once the cause is posited the effect infallibly follows. Thus, in order for the sacrament to be a certain sign and given that the effect is not itself verifiable, it is necessary that once the cause is posited (i.e., the sacramental action),

---

128. See Heb 10:19.

the effect infallibly flows from it. Given that it is a question of an instrumental cause and that the principal cause is God, who is omnipotent, this implies that the intervention of this omnipotent God is assured when the visible cause is posited.[129]

However, this also implies that if the visible cause is not posited, the invisible effect will not be produced. Certainly, the principal cause is omnipotent and could produce the effect, even if the instrumental cause were found to be wanting. However, this intervention by the principal cause would be unverifiable in this case and, therefore, so too would the effect thus produced. Now, the strict connection between the sacramental action and its effect is something held *de fide*. God's intervention in producing the effect of this action outside the sacramental action could be assured neither by faith nor by experience nor by reasoning. Not only would it be perfectly arbitrary to affirm it and imprudent to count on it, but this would moreover represent a misconception of the *raison d'être* of the sacraments, which is to make the secret action of God manifest. In the natural order, the effect compels one to affirm its cause. In the sacramental order, not only does the manifest cause (i.e., the sacrament) compel one to affirm the effect, but even the absence of the cause requires us to affirm the absence of the effect.

However, what effect are we speaking of? We have seen two things with regard to grace. On the one hand, it can be produced without the sacraments. On the other hand, it is possible for it not to be produced by the sacrament for want of the required dispositions in the subject, that is, for want of being personally received.[130] This indefectible connection between the visible cause (i.e., the sacrament) and the invisible effect that the sacramental order requires under pain of having no meaning and of no longer responding to the intention of God and of Christ, first of all pertains to the effect of the sacrament that we have called the *res et sacramentum* and, in particular, the "character." It is by it alone that the character can assure the objective and visible consistency without which the Church would have no reality.

---

129. See *ST* III, q. 62, a. 1, ad 1.
130. See §722 above.

Therefore, we must say with the full assurance of faith that each time the sacramental rite is correctly performed by the capacitated sacramental minister, and where a human person who is himself empowered to benefit from it submits himself to it, the *res et sacramentum* (of which this rite is the sign instituted by God) is produced (except in the exceptional case of the rejection of consent bearing on the sacramental action itself, either on the part of the minister or on the part of the beneficiary). Conversely, we can say that the *res et sacramentum* is *never* produced without the sacramental rite: "the character is never produced other than by the sacramental rite."[131]

Character (or its equivalents) and grace

Character with grace {762} From what we have said, it follows that the fixity of the sacramental order only assures, with certitude in the eyes of faith, the relation and connection between the sacramental sign and the character. However, when one considers Christ's intention in instituting the sacraments and the meaning immanent in the sacramental action, the latter signifies and produces the character (or its equivalent) only in view of grace. The character is the sign of this grace and is, at the same time, its "cause" in the sense that it is the prior disposition required for the production of the grace in question.

If, in a given case, this sign exists without a real significate (thus meaning that this disposition would be there without grace following upon it), this comes about because of the beneficiary's non-disposition and not because of a failure in the sacramental action. This does not make it be a deceptive sign. However, it is the case that it signifies grace only in a conditional manner.

We will see that "sacramental grace" is constituted by the grace-character complex (or, the equivalent to character [where one does not exist, strictly speaking]).

Character without grace Even when the recipient is not properly disposed (whether at the very moment of the sacramental action the beneficiary would have refused grace, or whether afterward he would

---

131. *ST* III, q. 64, a. 8, ad 2.

turn away from Christ) the character retains its twofold function as a sign and spiritual power. It is a sign of membership in the Church, which is real, though deficient.[132] Moreover, there is its power: an "active power" in the case of a priest, meaning that he can always perform the sacramental actions of which he sacramentally is the minister, efficaciously bestowing them; a "passive power" with regard to all the divine gifts which have their source in the Church for the baptized person, who can receive such gifts as soon as he eliminates the obstacle constituted by his non-disposition.

The first of these divine gifts is the grace corresponding to the sacrament which he received in this state of non-disposition, a grace which, for this reason, was "unfruitful" for him (according to the terminology of St. Augustine). Once the obstacle is removed, Christ will produce this grace in him by "taking up" the past sacramental action on the basis of the trace that it left, at least if this trace still remains. In the cases of a character-conferring sacrament, this trace is indelible, and the sacramental action can be taken up at any moment. In the cases of the other sacraments, this all depends on the persistence of the *res et sacramentum*. All of this ultimately pertains to the question concerning the "reviviscence of the sacraments."[133]

It is under the action of another sacrament (namely, penance) that reviviscence normally takes place, for what man has lost (or even never received) can be recovered only through Christ's action, which normally passes through the Church and the sacraments.

Grace without character We have seen that redemptive grace is offered to all and can be received by all, even apart from the sacramental action of the Church if the latter, in fact, is currently impossible for this or that particular person.[133b]

According to what we have said, we quite clearly must rule out the idea that the *res et sacramentum* (and, principally, the character) would be given in this way. Were it to lose its value as a sign (which it receives from the sacramental rite), the character would no longer have any meaning and would no longer be sacramental.

---

132. See §697 above.
133. See ST III, q. 69, a. 10.
133b. See §§686–703 above.

In particular, if the sacramental minister were constituted as such a minister by a completely hidden, non-sacramental action, the very sacrament that he confers would lose its visibility and, therefore, its value as a sacramental sign. The relationship between this manifest cause (i.e., the sacramental rite that he would perform) and its hidden effect would be uncertain, and the sacramental order would lose its fixity, without which it no longer has any meaning.

Sacramental Grace

{763} If[134] the sacraments have their *raison d'être* in signifying the grace conferred on their beneficiary and, at the same time, in being the instrument of this conferral, a grave difficulty arises. Indeed, there is only one grace, a participation in the infinitely simple Divine Nature conforming the believer to Christ. Hence, how can we explain the fact that there are seven distinct, non-interchangeable sacraments? Why are there seven sacraments if there is only one thing that is signified? Why are there seven different instruments if it is a question of producing only one effect?

If we say that the seven that differ among themselves correspond to these seven signs and seven causes, we will then need to distinguish these graces (which we will be led to call "sacramental") from grace in general, which makes men be children of God (which we call "the grace of the virtues and the gifts"). However, the latter is what Christ merited for us, the grace which justifies and sanctifies us. If this is not what the sacraments signify and cause, they serve no end, at least in anything essential.

Various ways of resolving the problem

We cannot here dwell at length on the history of this problem. A succinct presentation of it will need to suffice.[135]

Medieval theologians were oriented toward an explanation holding that "sacramental grace" is grace in general, though given through

---

134. See Robert Reginald Masterson, "Sacramental Graces: Modes of Sanctifying Grace," *The Thomist* 18 (1955): 311–72; Jean-Hervé Nicolas, "La grâce sacramentelle," *Revue thomiste* 61 (1961): 165–92 and 522–38; Charles A. Schleck, "St. Thomas on the Nature of Sacramental Grace," *The Thomist* 18 (1955): 1–30 and 242–78.

135. See Nicolas, "La grâce sacramentelle," 165–82.

the sacraments, thereby receiving a complement that varies according to the various sacraments, enabling a particular effect in the soul. In St. Thomas, this led to the idea that the sacraments produce their own, proper effects in man, effects emanating from sanctifying grace and unable to be produced without it, so that the sacraments produce it by producing their proper effect. This proper effect was defined, including by St. Thomas himself at the beginning of his career, as first of all bringing a remedy to the various weaknesses left by sin. Later on, St. Thomas emphasized the positive face of sacramental grace, namely that by which it assures incorporation into Christ from various perspectives. With Scotus, things return to the very first solution envisioned: sacramental grace is grace inasmuch as it is conferred by means of the sacraments. According to him, God disposed various sacraments not because there would be various graces to be produced but, instead, because grace corresponds to the various needs of man, according to his existential situation and because God decided to respond to these different needs by different means.

The commentators on St. Thomas sought to specify (which St. Thomas himself did not do) precisely what the particular nature of this "something more" is, this ordination to a special effect (as well as what special effect it is ordered to) that *the grace of the virtues and the gifts* receives from the sacrament. In this, they are divided into three great tendencies. *At one extreme*, following Capreolus, they thought that "sacramental graces" were different *habitus*, as the virtues are distinct *habitus* from grace, flowing from it so as to be the immediate principle of certain effects of holiness, of which [sanctifying] grace itself would be only the radical principle. This theory betrays its weakness when looking into the nature of these effects, for it is led to reduce them to the purification of venial faults and the liberation from temporal punishments due to sin. In other words, it comes back to attributing a wholly marginal role to the sacraments in sanctification. *At the other extreme*, Cajetan would like sacramental grace to be only an actual grace given by the sacrament at the same time as habitual grace, which would be the same for all, the same grace that is given without the sacraments. Thus, would the sacrament produce, as a proper effect of grace, only a passing and episodic aid? It would, unless you say, as do certain disciples of Cajetan, that once the sacrament has been received, and as long as the "interior sacrament" endures, one would have a permanent basis for receiving the actual graces needed for living the Christian life in the state in which one is placed by the sacrament. However, what need is there for a special basis for receiving from the divine mercy the actual grace needed for living as a Christian, as a child of God, in all the circumstances of one's existence?

John of St. Thomas seems to lead us in the right direction when he proposes that we see in sacramental grace an intrinsically modified form of grace in general, one that is modified in terms of a determinate effect to be produced. However, what is the effect? It would be conformity to Christ, in virtue of which grace would gradually become "connatural" to us, as it is connatural to Christ, also meaning that grace, which exists in Christ in its fullness, would develop its effects differently in His members, according to their particular situations. In this line of thought, though moreover seeking the modality proper to sacramental grace, Billot thought that the sacraments would gradually lead us to retrieve the habitual disposition by which, in the state of innocence, our inferior powers were perfectly ordered under the domination of reason. We would once again find it in the form of habitual dispositions that more or less reduce concupiscence in its manifold ramifications, in such a way that each sacrament would correspond to a specific chain to be broken. However, is not the task of triumphing over concupiscence something that belongs to grace as such? How could we hold that this would be a particular effect that grace would only have if it is given by means of the sacraments?

Sacramental grace is the single grace of Christ diversified
according to seven distinct modes

{764} Two principles command the solution to this question. First, it is not because there are seven distinct sacraments that there are seven distinct sacramental graces. Instead, conversely, there are seven sacraments because there are seven distinct sacramental graces to be produced. Second, considered in itself, grace is one. Therefore, the distinction between several graces can be taken only from a principle that is extrinsic to grace, namely, from the relation of grace to an element that is not grace, one that can vary.

On the basis of these principles, our reflection can proceed as follows. As we have seen,[136] the sacramental action is unified, and if it produces two effects, it is a question of two essentially subordinated effects. Obviously, the principal effect is what is specified, and this is indeed why one speaks of "sacramental grace." However, the first effect cannot, for all that, be neglected, given that it is an intermediary required by the very nature of this action. What does this mean if not that sacramental grace is grace inasmuch as it depends on the *res et sacramentum* and inasmuch as the latter depends on it?

We have seen that the grace that is caused by the sacrament is a grace of incorporation into the Church, the communion-society of the redeemed, the body and bride of Christ. Now, on the one hand, by itself, grace brings about divine filiation. On the other hand, incorporation into Christ in the Church is certainly an effect of grace. Are we not here faced with a contradiction? No. However, we must recognize that, in order to produce this effect, grace needs to be prolonged into a distinct principle that is not it, though it is nothing without it, a principle having the role of extending its action up to these particular effects.

Here we must quite simply use the analogy proposed to us by time-honored theologians, namely the analogy between sacramental grace and the grace of the virtues and the gifts. It helps to explain what we are considering, so long as we strive to understand it aright and to respect the differences that every analogy includes. Virtue is an operative *habitus* that renders a faculty capable of eliciting the act which has grace as its radical principle. The virtue is only a prolongation of grace. By it, grace is brought to its completion as a principle of activity [*operation*]. Thus, what should we call "the grace of the virtues and of the gifts"? Does this refer to the virtues and gifts considered in isolation, as opposed to sanctifying grace? This would be meaningless. It is clearly sanctifying grace, completed and fulfilled by the virtues and the gifts. It is unified because the radical principle

---

136. See §754 above.

of all the virtues and of all the gifts is one. It is the entitative *habitus* that makes the soul participate in the Divine Nature, the focal point of these activities in which the righteous person communicates through the infused virtues and gifts. Nonetheless, it is multiplied by these prolongations that extend it to the distinct virtues and gifts, which are principles of distinct activities. (In a similar way, the soul is one in its essence and nonetheless has a number of faculties, by which it acts.)

This is also the case for sacramental grace. Sanctifying grace is unified and, nonetheless, is multiplied according to the multiple effects of incorporation to Christ that it must produce in the redeemed righteous person. And just as the multiplicity of the grace of the virtues and the gifts is not only virtual (because the virtuous *habitus* are really distinct from each other and from sanctifying grace), so too the multiplicity of sacramental grace draws its reality from the real multiplicity of the principles that extend sanctifying grace to the sacramental effects, the *res et sacramentum* of the various sacraments. And, nonetheless, in both cases, it is not sanctifying grace itself that is divided. It is wholly and entirely present in each virtue and in each sacramental effect.

The principle of this multiplication is external to grace and does not affect it in itself. However, each virtue and each sacramental effect enables it to exercise a particular virtuality which existed in it (in the sense that one can speak of a virtual multiplicity), though which could be realized only through the prolongation of this virtue or this effect. Thus, one of the virtualities of grace is realized in a really distinct manner by a distinct virtue and by a distinct sacramental effect. Hence, the sacramental mode of grace is this virtuality thus actualized in exercise.

However, this makes clear the fact that there is a great difference between the terms of our analogy. Will it be said that virtue adds a "mode" to grace? Obviously not. The *grace of the virtues and the gifts* is sanctifying grace flowering forth into the virtues and gifts, and this flowering is necessary, not requiring any new action. There is another, subsequent difference. The virtues emanate from grace and receive everything from it, not adding anything to it, properly speaking. By contrast, grace is not sacramental of itself. It is not sufficient that grace be produced. What is also required is the production of the *res et sacramentum* that is distinct for each sacrament and that, far from flowing from grace, instead precedes it, either absolutely or inasmuch as it is a given sacramental grace. Therefore, the sacramental mode seems to be something added to grace, indeed externally. This difference from the case of the [infused] virtues is so evident that it turns the mind away from an analogy that seems more seductive than truly illuminating.

However, much to the contrary, this analogy is what will force us to determine more profoundly the relationship that exists between the *res et sacramentum* and the *res tantum* and, by this, to grasp what the "sacramental mode" of grace truly is. In contrast to the virtues, the *res et sacramentum* is added to grace externally and does not proceed from it. However, as we have seen, grace alone vivifies it and makes it play its own, proper role. It is related to grace as the body is related to the soul. It is wholly ordered to grace. By it and with it, grace deploys a virtuality that already existed in it. Thus, it adds no salvific value to grace but only offers it the supplementary support that it needs in order to effectively exercise one of its salvific values. It is, so to speak, akin to the restoration of the visual organ to someone born blind, an act that adds nothing to his soul as regards its vivifying principle but instead enables him to exercise the power of sight that virtually exists in the soul.

Thus, all the saving values of incorporation into Christ and membership in the Church are included in grace solely on account of the fact that the grace thus bestowed in the actual economy of salvation is the grace of Christ, redemptive grace. This is so because nobody can be justified without being incorporated into Christ and integrated into the Church, and all the distinct phases of this incorporation have only one principle, namely, the grace of Christ. This is clear for the sacraments that are directly ordered to the good of the person. However, this is also true for the two sacraments ordered directly to the good of the ecclesial community, namely, holy orders and marriage. Indeed, the sacrament of holy orders is an active participation in Christ's priesthood.

Now, if this participation is broken down into two gifts, namely sacerdotal power itself, which is assured by the character, and priestly grace, and if (alas!) they can come to be disconnected, this disjunction is profoundly abnormal. The priesthood of Christ is part of His grace and cannot be disconnected from it. It is a property of capital grace, and the intention of the sacrament of holy orders is to make a man participate in the priestly grace of Christ. Now, already, the grace received at baptism is Christ's grace, which is priestly. The character that the sacrament of holy orders impresses on him only enables this grace to be extended and to actualize the virtuality that it already had in itself. Consequently, we must say, concerning the sacrament of holy orders (as also for the cases of the other sacraments), that the character is the second effect of the sacrament and grace the principal one, although quite obviously this sacrament was instituted to transmit the priestly power. (In its normal dimensions, the priestly power is grace prolonged by the character and vivifying it.)

When it is found in a man without grace, it loses none of its efficacy precisely because this efficacy is instrumental and principally depends upon Christ's efficacy and, therefore, upon His grace. However, it absolutely loses its saving value for him who exercises it and who no longer is in Christ's hands except as the mere instrument of an action with which he does not personally associate himself. As regards marriage, it was instituted as a sacrament in order to integrate the couple as such (and by prolongation, their children) into the life of the Church.[137] The *res et sacramentum* is the contract that publicly binds together a Christian man and woman in the Church as the mysterious sign of the covenant that binds Christ to the Church and the Church to Christ. The *res tantum* is grace inasmuch as it elevates their union to this lofty height, namely, inasmuch as it penetrates their conjugal love (and then also their parental love) with supernatural charity. Here again, because charity obviously was already included in baptismal grace, it is clear that the conjugal union only opened up for baptismal grace the possibility of this sanctification of human love, which it had already possessed in its power [*vertu*].

---

137. Obviously, these overly rapid remarks on the sacraments of holy orders and of marriage will be the objects of particular studies below. See sections V and VI below.

Thus, in sum: each sacramental grace is grace (whether sanctifying or actual) extended by the *res et sacramentum* of a sacrament to an effect that it does not produce without this, although it had this efficacy already in its power [*pouvoir*].

Even though this solution is opposed to many of those that have been proposed by others, it only intends to be the result of a deepening of the majority of them. If the extension of sanctifying grace to the proper effects of the sacraments cannot be assured by *habitus* (as Capreolus wanted), we nonetheless must define sacramental grace by such an extension having the *res et sacramentum* as its means. Likewise, with Cajetan, we must recognize that sacramental grace includes all the actual graces required for fidelity to the sacrament received, though we must look for the insertion point for these graces neither in a moral title, nor solely in the power [*vertu*] that calls upon the divine assistance in order to be protected and put into action, but rather in the grace extended to the sacramental effects (in the way that was explained above). In short, the actual aids do not explain the sacramental mode of grace, but conversely, it is because grace is sacramental that it calls for such particular forms of assistance.

If we then come to John of St. Thomas, it is clear that our solution only intends to specify the nature of this "mode" that the sacrament adds to grace. John of St. Thomas's explanation, holding that this sacramental mode would consist in the fact that grace in the Christian would acquire something of the "naturality" that it had in Christ, hardly seems to need to be retained if one observes that this naturality in Christ comes from the Hypostatic Union. It is not clear how a Christian could participate in this, above all by the *res et sacramentum*, which would thus find itself, through an unsustainable paradox, above the *res tantum* in the order of saving values. However, it is true that sacramental grace is sanctifying grace inasmuch as it has the property of incorporating us into Christ (a property that it exercises gradually and through many supplementary sacramental effects) and therefore has the property of assuring that we receive the outpouring of capital grace, which originates in the Hypostatic Union. Grace is "connatural" to the Church, as it is connatural to Christ, because the Church is the body of Christ. And it is "connatural" to us inasmuch as we belong to the Church and inasmuch as the Church is realized in us. This is what grace accomplishes by means of the sacramental effects in which it is prolonged and through which it deploys its virtualities.

The universality of sacramental grace

The problem

{765} Having examined the problem concerning the inter-distinction of the various sacramental graces, must we now say that sacramental grace is also distinguished from common grace? In other words, is the grace produced by means of the sacraments a grace that differs from that which is produced in an extra-sacramental way (whether in those who, without any fault on their part, cannot be the subject of any sacramental activity whatsoever, as is the case for the "righteous on the outside," or even in those who, while belonging fully to the Church and receiving her sacraments, nonetheless likewise receive grace by other channels than that of the sacraments)? Or are these two graces in reality only one? Both of these positions raise grave difficulties.

Difficulty faced by the dualist position. If the grace caused by the sacraments is a different grace from that which is caused in the extra-sacramental way, will we need to conceive of two *habitus* of sanctifying grace that coexist with each other in the same person? Or will we need to say that, through the sacramental action, sacramental grace is substituted for the grace which was already received without the sacrament? And how are we then to distinguish two such kinds of sanctifying grace?

Difficulties faced by the position that identifies the two graces. How can one claim that grace is never given except by the sacraments? However, if it is said that the grace given by the extra-sacramental way is already sacramental grace, does this not contradict what we have said up to this point? Because sacramental grace is defined by the relation of grace to the *res et sacramentum* and because the latter can only be given through the corresponding sacrament, it cannot itself be given in an extra-sacramental way. However, as we have seen, it is also a form of sanctifying grace. Therefore, it must be distinct from the sanctifying grace given by another way than that of the sacraments.

Attempt at a solution

Sacramental grace is the grace of Christ inasmuch as it is ecclesial. It is not sanctifying grace *plus* the *res et sacramentum*. Rather, it is (habitual or actual) sanctifying grace *in relation to* the *res et sacramentum*. Now, this relation can exist before the *res et sacramentum* would have been effectively produced.

This is clear for the sacraments of baptism and penance. Nobody can receive the grace of the remission of sins without at least having the *votum sacramenti*, the intention to receive the sacrament.[138] This *votum* is a true anticipated presence of the sacrament which in this way is already the means used by God in order to give grace to this man: "If one says that the sacrament of baptism is absolutely necessary for salvation, this is so in the sense that man cannot be saved without this sacrament, at least in intention, which for God takes the place of the willed thing itself being realized."[139]

It is grace signified and caused not only by the external sacrament but simultaneously by the internal sacrament which God confers by Christ, though not through the sacramental action. He causes it in relation to the sacrament that has not been really received, though the person in question has indeed truly decided to receive it (granted, often in a very implicit manner). This in no way renders the sacrament useless. On the contrary, it renders it useful in advance, making this sacrament *to be received* into a means of grace *in the present* (even if, in fact, it never comes along for this man, though on the condition that this not be on account of his rejection thereof).

What is true concerning the first grace received by the "righteous on the outside" must be extended to the grace of reconciliation that they can receive if, after turning away from God, they return to him. Likewise, it must be extended to the case of the grace of reconciliation given to the baptized person when he sins after his baptism (a grace that he does not receive without the *votum* for the sacrament of penance). Why not extend this principle to all the graces that the

---

138. See Trent, session 19, *Decree on Justification*, January 13, 1547, ch. 4, in D.-*Sch.*, no. 1524, and ch. 14, in D.-*Sch.*, no. 1543.

139. *ST* III, q 68, a. 2, ad 3.

baptized person may receive outside the sacraments? All the actual graces received in daily life and every increase in sanctifying grace would thus formally be the sacramental grace of the Eucharist.

As regards the sacraments whose *res et sacramentum* consists in a particular mode of belonging to the Church (i.e., the sacraments of holy orders and of marriage), their sacramental grace is sanctifying grace considered in its relationship with the corresponding sacrament. One and the same sanctifying grace, considered in its relationship to the characters of baptism and confirmation, is the sacramental grace of these sacraments. Considered inasmuch as it is related to the Eucharist to be received (*votum sacramenti*), it is the grace of the Eucharist. There is nothing unsuitable in the fact that the same grace (i.e., the grace of the children of God) would be related to many sacraments by means of which it develops different effects in the subject in relation to the subject's incorporation into Christ in the Church here-below. The Eucharist, which has the role of being the vital source of the incorporation of the believer into Christ, does this for each person according to his situation in the body of Christ, the Church.

However, what then does the supervening sacrament add if the *res* that it signifies and causes is already given? What is lacking to grace that is received extra-sacramentally is not something that would make it be, of itself, less great or less rich. It can be a grace of authentic holiness and of lofty mysticism. It is to be enrooted in the subject. Indeed, it alone simultaneously bears with itself union with God (which is its proper effect) and, *by way of substitution* and imperfectly, membership in the Church, which is the dwelling place of grace. Now, grace, which in itself is perfectly stable (because it is an emanation in the soul coming from the love of God who is unwavering), *de facto* is unstable if one considers that its permanence depends on our free will, which is volatile. He who, not having the *res et sacramentum*, loses grace, loses his membership in the Church and all of its saving value, whereas he who has the *res et sacramentum* remains connected to the Church as to the source of grace.

If the sacramental grace of holy orders cannot be received in this way (i.e., without the *res et sacramentum*), this is because for this sacrament ecclesial finality takes precedence over the sacrament's personal finality, as we will see in due time in our further discussions concerning this particular sacrament. One is a priest for the Church, and we have seen that to be a priest in a hidden and unverifiable manner would be useless for the Church.

If this conception of sacramental grace is accurate, we must say that sacramental grace is the grace of Christ inasmuch as it is ecclesial. If every grace given in the economy of salvation by God is sacramental, this is because the Church is the universal mediatrix in this economy.[140]

CONCLUSION OF SECTION 1: THE SACRAMENTAL SEPTENARY AND THE CHURCH'S SACRAMENTALITY

{766} The Church's sacramentality extends far outside the celebration of the seven sacraments. It characterizes the profound nature of all her action and of her entire *raison d'être*. Through and in her, Christ, "having returned to the Father," and "exalted in the glory that He had with the Father before the world began," continues to be with His own and to act in the world so as to save it. It is an invisible action of which the Church's visible action is the bearer, signifying it, manifesting it, and extending it to men in all times and places. Through this action, the Son, "who is alongside the Father," sends the Holy Spirit, who brings the remission of sins, divinization, and the pledge of eternal life to those who receive Him.

This action by the Church is entirely sacramental because it has no meaning and existence except in function of being the invisible action which she signifies and makes use of. However, she is not reduced to the action that is properly sacramental (i.e., that which she exercises by means of the seven sacraments), for that action needs preparations to be undertaken, through the proclamation of the word and through all the activities that the latter requires, activities that condition it. It also needs to be accompanied by pastoral activity that is ordered toward constituting the living context of a conscientious community for which the celebration of the sacraments is (or

---

140. See Nicolas, *Les profondeurs de la grâce*, 320–30.

should be) the most intense moment of her existence, a pastoral activity also aiming to assure sacramental grace's penetration into the fabric of the temporal life of this community and of all those who are part of it.

Thus, properly sacramental action is not the entire activity of the Church. Far from it. However, every one of the Church's actions leads to it and derives from it. It is the culminating point of her activity and her ultimate *raison d'être,* for she exists, speaks, and acts only as the body and bride of Christ, sacramentally assuring that His presence to the world and His redemptive work remain continuous. It is not surprising that the closer that her own action comes to the redemptive action itself, to that degree does she disappear before the unique redeemer. Inasmuch she must prepare for Him pathways in the world and in minds, the men who make up the Church (and through whom she acts) bring to her their intelligence and resolution, with all the limitations and shortcomings that this involves. They act as second causes, and moreover, if their results bear the stamp of their personality, they also suffer from their personal narrowness and the deviations of their action. To the degree that this action draws closer to the very mystery of our salvation through Christ's blood, so too is it more greatly protected by the assistance of the Holy Spirit from the risk of deviation by those on whom she exercises the authentic ways of salvation.

But, when she passes over from such preparation for the redemptive action and places the latter in contact with those whom she has prepared, she can be nothing but an instrument, completely taken up by Christ the redeemer and integrated into the redemptive action, for this contact can be nothing but immediate. Thus, her only role here is to manifest and concretize this action, being the temporal means by which it is inserted into time, in each portion of time and of space where it must act so that it may reach each man who lets himself be saved. There, the Church (namely, the ministers through whom she acts) can only disappear completely in order to allow grace, the sanctifying action of Christ, pass through her. Certain theologians have thought that even this role of concurring instrumentally in the communication of grace was too much for the creature and that her cooperation in the saving action of Christ at the moment when she touches and transforms man could go no further than to ultimately dispose the person on whom she acts, leaving her action to remain on the hither side of the very communication of grace. Although, for a time, he himself held a position akin to this, St. Thomas believed that one could indeed say that the Church's sacramental action goes all the way to the end, up to the very transformation of the created spirit by the saving action, by the Holy Spirit, of whom she is the sign and, consequently, of whom she must also be the instrument so as to fully be the sacrament of Christ. However, it is clear that at this moment she neither adds nor removes anything from Christ's action. She can act only under His sway, without putting anything of herself into it except for the fact that she makes the secret work of salvation visible and manifest.

In this, she is given the task of truly cooperating in the salvation of mankind, by means of an agency that is founded upon the redemptive action itself, in which she cannot cooperate, given that she did not yet exist when it was performed and, indeed, given that she received her very being from it. However, by bearing this redemptive action to men in all times and places, she is truly sanctifying, as a sacrament of Christ.

Because her sanctifying action can be exercised only sacramentally, to the degree that she became aware of the diversity of the sanctifying powers that she received, she became aware of the diversity of sacramental means that Christ had prepared for her (or, in her). As we have seen, this was how the sacramental septenary gradually came to be formed.[141] It was not formed by way of creation but, instead, by recognition, through a successive discovery of the sacramental signs instituted by Christ, based on the two principal sacraments (baptism and the Eucharist) that she was manifestly aware of from the beginning.

We must now study these sacraments, considering each according to its particular and irreducible manner of being a sacrament.

---

141. See §731 above.

PART 2

BAPTISM AND CONFIRMATION

5

Introduction to the Theology of Baptism

From[1] the very beginning of the Church's existence, we find ourselves faced with the rite of baptism as it is connected to faith, conversion, and incorporation into the Church. In the books of the New Testament, we also find a veritable theology of baptism, which is the required point of departure and rule for every later reflection on this topic.

BAPTISM AT THE VERY BEGINNING OF THE CHURCH'S LIFE

The Practice of Baptism in the First Christian Community

{767} As we already see in the Acts of the Apostles and in the earliest Christian preaching, baptism presents the following characteristics:

---

1. See François-Marie Braun, *Jean le théologien* (Paris: Gabalda, 1972), 3:85–90. Lucien Cerfaux, *Le chrétien dans la theologie de saint Paul* (Paris: Cerf, 1962). Joseph Coppens, "Baptême," *Dictionnaire de la Bible*, 1:852–954. Oscar Cullmann, "Les sacrements dans l'évangile johannique," in *La foi et le culte dans l'Église primitive* (Neuchâtel: Delachaux et Niestlé, 1963), 131–210. Adalbert Hamman, *Baptême et confirmation* (Paris: Desclée, 1969). Joachim Jeremias, *Le baptême des enfants aux quatre premiers siècles*, trans. Bruno Hübsch and François Stoessel (Le Puy: Mappus, 1967). Ignace de La Potterie, "Naître de l'eau et naître de l'Espirit, le texte baptismal de Jn 3, 5," in *La vie selon l'Espirit, condition du chrétien* (Paris: Cerf, 1965), 31–64. Burkhard Neunheuser, "Meßopfertheorien," *Lexikon für Theologie und Kirche*, 2nd ed., ed. Josef Höfer und Karl Rahner (Freiburg im Breisgau: 1957), 7:350–52. Rudolf Schnackenburg, "Taufe," in *Bibeltheologisches Wörterbuch*, 1086–95. Alois Stenzel, *Il battesimo, genesi e evoluzione della liturgia battesimale*, trans. Mariano da Alatri (Alba: Edizioni Paoline, 1962).

1. It expresses perfect conversion and procures the remission of sins.² Conversion includes the complete renunciation of one's former life, at least one's sins,³ and the recognition that Jesus is the Messiah. Acceptance of the Christian message of salvation (i.e., acceptance of the *Word*) is presupposed for baptism.⁴ However, the remission of sins is what is the beginning of salvation, God's first eschatological act leading to eternal life.⁵

2. Baptism is administered in the name of Jesus Christ.⁶ He is the sole mediator.⁷

3. Baptism is the occasion, though also the cause and means, for the outpouring of the Spirit. Ordinarily, the gift of the Spirit is only bestowed on those who receive baptism. In the case of the centurion Cornelius, it precedes baptism. However, far from rendering baptism useless, it represents a pressing reason for it to be conferred.⁸

4. Finally, baptism signifies and brings about incorporation into the community of salvation, the Church, who visibly believes by means of this sacrament.⁹

Such are, from the start, all the data concerning the theology of baptism.¹⁰

The Theology of Baptism in the New Testament

In St. Paul

{768} The core of the Pauline theology of baptism is that through baptism the believer really participates, though in a mysterious way, in the mystery of Jesus' passion, death, burial, and resurrection.¹¹ This participation *in mysterio* raises many questions for the theologian. However, it cannot itself be placed into question.

This participation *in mysterio* has three consequences: Christ's

---

2. See Acts 2:18, 11:18, 22:16.
3. See Acts 3:17–19, 5:31, 17:30.
4. See Acts 2:41, 4:4, 8:4, 8:12, 10:43, 16:30–33, 18:8.
5. See Acts 11:18 and 13:40–48.
6. See Acts 2:38, 8:16, 10:48, 19:5.
7. See Acts 4:12.
8. See 10:44–48.
9. See Acts 2:41–47, 5:14, 11:24, 6:7, 9:31, 11:21.
10. See Schnackenburg, "Taufe," 1086–95.
11. See Rom 6:3–7, Gal 3:27, Col 2:12.

life in the believer, regeneration,[12] and the filial adoption that follows therefrom.[13]

The theme of adoption is closely tied to that of the gift of the Holy Spirit. St. Paul employs the formula "baptized in the Spirit"[14] in conjunction with "baptized in Christ."[15] The Holy Spirit is given at baptism, as a pledge and first fruit of salvation.

Finally, one must add that baptism is the principle and cause of the Church's unity on account of the Spirit given by means of it.

In St. Paul, we do not find even a trace of any supposed opposition between faith (salvation by faith) and baptism (salvation by baptism). One is saved through faith in Jesus Christ, not through works.[16] However, faith in Jesus Christ is expressed precisely through baptism.[17] Everything that St. Paul says about justification through faith (with what follows on it, namely, the remission of sins, filial adoption and a right to the [Father's] inheritance, the gift of the Spirit, and new life in Christ and in the Spirit) is presented as being inextricably the effect of both faith and of baptism. It is one and the same thing to believe in Jesus Christ and to be baptized.

In the Pauline dialectic of faith and works, baptism is situated on the side of faith, whereas circumcision is situated on the side of works. This is clear in his use of the prophetic theme concerning the "circumcision of the heart." For the prophets, it in no way excluded bodily circumcision but instead gives the latter its value before God.[18] For St. Paul, circumcision of the heart is what alone counts,[19] and it is brought about through baptism.[20]

In the First Letter of St. Peter

We share the view that this text presents an important testimony concerning the primitive baptismal liturgy and catechesis.[21] In it,

---

12. See Ti 3:5–7.
13. See Rom 8 and Gal 4.
14. See 1 Cor 12–13.
15. See Rom 6:3 and Gal 3:27.
16. See Rom 5:22–24 and 11:9.
17. See Rom 6:3 and Gal 3:26–27.
18. See Jer 4:4 and 9:25.
19. Rom 6:29 and Phil 3:2.
20. Col 2:11–12.
21. See Marie-Émile Boismard, "Une liturgie baptismale dans la Iª Petri," *Revue biblique* 63 (1956): 182–208; 64 (1957): 161–83.

we find figures of baptism that will become traditional: Jesus' descent into hell[22] and the ark with the eight people saved (representing all Christians), where the number eight represents the Paschal day. However, it seems that the whole letter (especially 1:3–2:10) partially reproduces a very ancient baptismal catechesis that St. Paul,[23] St. John,[24] and St. James would have known and used. The essential theme is concerned with the baptized person's divine rebirth, along with the promise of an incorruptible inheritance and of the manifestation of salvation in the last days.

In St. John

The idea of a divine rebirth is equally essential in St. John. We find it in the fourth Gospel's important passage concerning baptism (3:3–10) and in 1 John (2:29–3:9). Once again, we here find the term "rebirth." St. Paul uses it only in the letter to Timothy, and it is also found in the first letter of St. Peter. It seems that these three texts have a common source in the primitive catechesis mentioned above.

Conclusion

There is a remarkable coherence in this New Testament teaching concerning baptism. This coherence is explained by a common and wholly primitive source: the first baptismal catechesis. Baptism is the divine act by which this rebirth, this new birth, is brought about in the person who believes, in virtue of which the believer is a child of God right now and will be manifested as such on the last day by his entrance into his incorruptible inheritance. The Holy Spirit plays an essential role in this rebirth. On the one hand, He is the internal principle of this new life in the believer, the life of Christ. Therefore, He is given in and through the very act of baptism. On the other hand, He is at work in this act. The believer is baptized in the Spirit as much as into Christ. He is born of God. He is born of water and the Spirit. Finally, the unity of the Church is constituted by the Spirit and baptism together.

---

22. See Olivier Rousseau, "La descente aux enfers fondement du baptême chrétien," *Recherches des sciences religieuses* 40 (1952): 273–97.

23. See Ti 3:5–7 and Col 3:1–4.

24. See 1 Jn 2:29 and 3:9.

THE ORIGINS OF CHRISTIAN BAPTISM

{769} Today, all agree that we must seek out the origins of the Christian institutions in the Bible and Judaism, not the pagan mysteries. In particular, Christian baptism certainly comes from John's baptism, which is itself situated in the line of the Jewish practices of purification. (We must note that John's baptism, as reported by the three Synoptic Gospels and to which the fourth Gospel makes clear allusions,[25] made up part of the primitive catechesis[26] by being presented as being a prophetic proclamation of Christian baptism.)

John the Baptist

The ritual performed by John the Baptist was not itself lacking an antecedent. Rites of purification by ablution had existed in Judaism. There also was the baptism of proselytes (a baptism conferred on gentiles who came to Judaism and requested circumcision in order to be joined to Israel).*

In any case, John's baptism was remarkably original in comparison with its antecedents. In distinction from the purifying ablutions, it was given only once. It could be administered only by someone other than the person being baptized. It was proposed for all and not only for the impure and for "sinners." As regards the baptism of the proselytes, if it also was given only once and administered by another person, it was not proposed as something to be received by all but, instead, was only for non-Jews coming to Judaism. If John's baptism introduces one into the community of the People of God, which is eschatological in the sense that it tends toward the Messiah without having yet arrived at the messianic era, such a baptism is properly eschatological. It is given as an immediate preparation for the messianic era as a baptism of repentance.

---

25. See Jn 1:25.
26. See Acts 1:5–22.

* N.B. However, a dispute exists concerning the question of knowing whether the baptism of the proselytes existed already in Jesus' own time and during that of the apostolic Church. For arguments holding that it did exist then, see Jeremias, *Le baptême des enfants*, 30–38. In the negative, see Hamman, *Baptême et confirmation*, 13, and A. Hulsbosch, "Baptême," in *Dictionnaire encyclopédique de la Bible* (trans. from Dutch) (Paris: Brepols, 1960), col. 189.

Baptism Received by Jesus

The baptism that Jesus received is obviously not a "baptism of repentance." Nor is it an introduction to the messianic era. It is presented to us as being the public enthronement of the Messiah. In it, Jesus is recognized by John as the Messiah whose imminent coming he announced.[27]

Christian Baptism

Nonetheless, Christian baptism does not refer back to Jesus' baptism, as Christian baptism is concerned with being baptized into Christ's death and not with being baptized as Christ had been baptized. Christian baptism refers to John's baptism [more broadly].

Nonetheless, there is a fundamental difference between the two baptisms. John's baptism was prophetic. It announced another baptism "in the Spirit and fire."[28] From the beginning, the Church was aware of having been baptized in the Holy Spirit and fire (at Pentecost), and the baptism of water that she immediately began to administer was the means for making believers participate in this primordial baptism by which the Church as such was baptized. (This explains why it is nowhere said that the apostles were baptized by the new baptism, whereas St. Paul was, in fact, baptized.)

The Command to Baptize

However, Christian baptism cannot be explained as though it were created solely by the Church's own initiative, in imitation of John's baptism. On the contrary, it would, instead, be tempting to think that the baptism of the Spirit would render the baptism by water useless. Moreover, the doctrine of salvation through faith is not of itself in immediate harmony with the necessity of baptism by water. It is striking that universally and from the beginning there was something almost like self-evident agreement on this point. This can be explained only by an express command received from Jesus.

Indeed, the evangelists place this command on the lips of the

---

27. See Jn 1:33.
28. Mt 3:11–12.

risen Lord.²⁹ This is in conformity with a fundamental datum of the New Testament, namely, that the Holy Spirit was sent by Jesus only after His return to the Father. Moreover, the fourth Gospel mentions a baptism given during the lifetime of Jesus and under His authority, performed by His disciples in imitation of John's baptism (and, indeed, somewhat in competition with it). Doubtlessly, this was mentioned in order to mark out the continuity between the two baptisms. There was not to be a fundamental difference between this baptism and that of John.³⁰

Thus, obeying Jesus' command to baptize those who believe, the Church is placed in continuity with John the Baptist's activity, though, as the announced event is situated in the line of that which prophesied it.

Moreover, we cannot exclude the possibility that the Church would have drawn upon the baptism of the proselytes in some way, at least if the latter had already existed, given that she held that her baptism also was a sign and means of being joined to the community. However, the meaning of her baptism was quite different from baptism of the proselytes, as it was concerned with receiving salvation by Christ and with being incorporated into Christ.

The Trinitarian Formula

Even if the Matthean formula[31] is relatively late, it is attested to in the most ancient texts concerning baptism as an ecclesial practice. Its apparent opposition to the expression used in Acts (and by St. Paul), namely, "baptized in the name of Jesus," is no longer an issue today. There is general agreement that this does not bear witness to an opposition between the two formulas but, instead, baptism in the name of Jesus designates Christian baptism in what is particular and characteristic of it.[32]

---

29. See Mt 28:18–20 and Mk 16:16.
30. See Hulsbosch, "Baptême," col. 190. In contrast, however, see *ST* III, q. 66, a. 2.
31. See Mt 28:19.
32. See B. Van Iersel, "Quelques presupposes bibliques de la notion de sacrament," *Concilium* 31 (1968): 19.

6

The Effects of Baptism

As they are described in Scripture, the effects of baptism are *the remission of sins, regeneration, incorporation into the Church of Christ,* and *the gift of the Spirit,* which is the principle for the preceding effects and encompasses them. This is why we will examine it last, even though, in reality, it is the principal effect of baptism.

THE REMISSION OF SINS

The Divine Act of Remitting Sins and the Baptismal Rite

The remission of sins and justification

{770} God[1] grants pardon to him who repents. Every sincere repentance merits the pardoning of offenses.[2] Pardon is indisputably an act of God. However, once again, how should we conceive of this act?

We must exclude a juridical conception which would consider God's pardon as being a kind of amnesty. Indeed, in the relations between God and creatures, the entire reality of the relation is found on the side of the creature. On account of the reality proper to the creature, a wholly dependent reality, it is ordered to God. God is not, Himself, ordered to the creature. (However, because God is the real

---

1. See Nicolas, *Les profondeurs de la grâce,* 450–77.
2. Ceslas Spicq, *Théologie morale du Nouveau Testament* (Paris: Gabalda, 1965), 65. N.B. The term "merit" is used in an improper sense here. Pardon is a pure gift of mercy, which is in no way merited. We must say, "calls for the pardoning."

terminus of the creature's relation to Him, He is attained in His reality by this relative concept.)³ Thus, to say that God is "offended" or "angry" is to say that He is the real terminus of this relation to Him coming from the free creature that asserts itself against Him through sin. In like manner, I can conceive of God as being "appeased" only by considering Him as the terminus of a new relation to Him coming from the creature that not only ceases to offend Him but also laments the offense through a free act, thus being "converted" or "penitent."⁴

Thus, when God pardons, the creature changes, not Him. And for this reason, His pardon takes place in a way that, so to speak, runs in the opposite direction of what we experience in the case of a created authority.

However, does this not mean that it is not a divine act? This would be a denial of the fundamental biblical notion of the pardoning of sins. Indeed, it would be a form of Pelagianism. Thus, we must recall that God is the first efficient, formal (i.e., exemplar), and final principle of every change taking place in the creature (with the exception of the change that has its first principle in created freedom, namely, the failure of freedom, sin). This holds true doubly in the order of grace, where everything is God's gift, a communication by love. Therefore, one must say that the "conversion" of the free person, which founds this new relation to God, who has "become" appeased, has God's love as its First Cause. He is the one who, by His all-powerful grace, converts the heart of the creature and makes it "righteous" and "just," no longer deserving rejection and punishment: "Restore us to thyself, O LORD, that we may be restored!"⁵

Thus, if we consider the creature's conversion, his "penitence" (*metanoia*), as an act of free will, it is the condition of the divine pardon. However, if we consider it as being the effect of the merciful action of God upon the sinner—and it has both characters from two different perspectives, for God's mercy makes the sinner convert

---

3. See §308 above. Jean-Hervé Nicolas, "L'acte pur de saint Thomas d'Aquin et le Dieu vivant de l'évangile," *Angelicum* 51 (1974): 511–32.
4. See §489.
5. Lam 5:21 (RSV).

himself—it is this pardoning itself. By pardoning the unrighteous person, God makes him truly and really righteous.[6]

Baptism as a sign and realization of the divine pardon

{771} Baptism is the sign and instrument of this divine act of pardoning. It adds nothing to this act (as though it were a work performed by man, having God's pardon as its recompense). It is this very act, concretized in relation to this human person, thereby being rendered sensible and manifest. In general, the sign adds nothing to the signified. It manifests it. The instrument adds nothing to the principal cause. It is wholly dependent on it. It is that by which the principal cause applies its efficacy to a given point situated in time and in space. Here, it is a question of an action exercised by God on the human person. Baptism, considered as an action performed by God upon man, is an act of pure divine freedom, placing secondary causes into action according to an order instituted by Him.

From the perspective of the man who undergoes this action, baptism includes a personal and free process, conversion, which we discussed above. It is the sign of this process (inasmuch as it is an interior process) as well as the expression of it (for this process engages the whole man and must have an external, bodily dimension in order to be fully human). Here again, the act of receiving baptism does not add anything to the act of conversion. Both constitute one, single human undertaking, as the body and soul constitute the human person.

And God is the first cause of this undertaking. He does not wait for man at the baptismal font in order to bestow His pardon upon him. He leads him there, as He leads all those who contribute in bringing this person to baptism [*concourent au baptême*]. In short, baptism is simultaneously a sign of God's merciful love for this man whose sins He wills to pardon, as well as a sign of the conversion of the man who, under this love's action, asks to be pardoned.[7]

---

6. See *ST* I-II, q. 113, aa. 1–2.
7. Nicolas, *Les profondeurs de la grâce*, 473–74.

Baptism as a participation by the believer in the redemptive death of Christ and in His resurrection

{772} The universal cause of the remission of sins is Christ's sacrifice. This cause is also subordinated to God's love, for He wishes to pardon man and sent His Son precisely for this reason. However, Christ's sacrifice is the universal cause in the sense that the Incarnate Son is the universal mediator: "There is no other name under heaven given among men by which we must be saved."[8]

Baptism is the sign of Christ's passion, death, and resurrection. As we have seen in relation to the sacraments in general, it is a practical and dynamic sign. In other words, it is simultaneously the sign of the believer's personal participation in this event having a universal scope as well as the sign of the personal application to him of the redemption accomplished definitively for all men. It is the sign of God extending His love for His Christ (and for all humanity included in Him) to this person in his singularity.

It has been said that "all men have in principle received baptism long ago, namely on Golgotha, at Good Friday and Easter. There the essential act of baptism was carried out, entirely without our cooperation, and even without our faith."[9] We could contrast this with the views of contemporary Catholic theologians who, following Karl Rahner, would have every man belong to Christ merely on account of the redemptive act accomplished for all, so that a personal act (of refusal) in relation to Christ would be necessary in order for one to be excluded from personally participating in the redemption, not in order for one to be said to positively participate in it.[10]

In reality, if the redemption is absolutely universal in its scope and its sufficiency, properly speaking, it is concerned with human persons, who alone are saved (or are lost), and not with man's common nature. A person can be saved only by choosing, through a personal and free act, to participate in the redemptive act accomplished

---

8. Acts 4:12 (RSV).

9. Oscar Cullmann, *Le baptême des enfants et la doctrine biblique du baptême*, trans. Jean-Jacques von Allmen (Neuchâtel: Delachaux et Niestlé, 1948), 19, and ch. 2 [Tr. note: Oscar Cullmann, *Baptism in the New Testament*, trans. J. K. S. Reid (London: SCM Press, 1964), 23. The text cited by Fr. Nicolas is at the beginning of chapter 2.]

10. See §688 above.

for all men by Jesus Christ, thus placing himself in solidarity with the New Adam in grace and righteousness. By the same act, a person breaks his native solidarity with the Old Adam in sin. Man *is saved* by Jesus Christ. However, he simultaneously *saves himself* in Jesus Christ. In other words, he freely lets himself be saved. We will discuss the issue of infant baptism separately. As regards those who are saved without explicitly knowing Christ, we already covered this issue above.[11]

At least in ordinary cases, this undertaking is expressed through the acceptance of baptism. In comparison with Christ's redemptive act, this bodily undertaking, in relation to the spiritual process of conversion, plays the role that is played by Christ's external, bloody sacrifice in relation to His redemptive will.[12]

Thus, both as Christ's own action and as something undertaken by man, baptism does not add to the redemptive sacrifice. It is the application of the redemptive sacrifice to this person and the actualization of this person's virtual participation in this sacrifice, given from the start [of his life].[12b]

Liberation from sin and the continuous confrontation
of the baptized person with sin

{773} Nonetheless, there is a paradox at the heart of this theology of baptism, which is simultaneously exalting due to the promises that it contains and discouraging in that it leaves man in his native misery. While it is indeed true that man is totally freed from sin by Christ's passion and redemptive death, and while the power of the redemptive sacrifice is fully applied by baptism to the believer, it is also true that the baptized person is still submitted to sin: "Sin dwells in him."[13] After St. Paul, St. John warns us, "If we say we have no sin, we deceive ourselves, and the truth is not in us."[14]

The notion of forensic justification was intended to resolve this antinomy, which was so vigorously perceived by Luther. At once

---

11. See §§686–93 above.
12. See §493 in the second part of this course.
12b. See §§745–47.
13. See Rom 7:14–25.
14. 1 Jn 1:8 (RSV).

righteous and a sinner, the believer is righteous by Christ's righteousness, which is imputed to him, but this justice does not interiorly transform him. Thus, although he is justified, he remains what he was by himself, namely, a sinner. Without here entering into a discussion concerning this conception of justification (and above all, into a discussion concerning its Pauline authenticity), let us note, based on what we said earlier, that this would lead to the purely juridical conception of God's pardon that we critiqued earlier.

The formula *simul iustus et peccator* can be understood in a Catholic sense,[15] for it is true that the Christian is simultaneously righteous and a sinner in the sense that the grace that justifies him does not immunize him against the sins that he can commit later on and in the sense that such sins can fail to make him, properly speaking, an unrighteous person. His justice is real. It is a victory by grace over the sin that is man's native condition. However, it is a progressive victory that lasts throughout the whole of his earthly life. Therefore, it is a partial victory insofar as sin is not definitively vanquished from the start. Such is the Catholic solution to the paradox that was noted above:

If anyone denies that the guilt of original sin is remitted by the grace of our Lord Jesus Christ given in baptism or asserts that all that is sin in the true and proper sense is not taken away but only brushed over or not imputed, let him be anathema.

For, in those who are reborn God hates nothing, because "there is no condemnation" (Rom. 8:1) for those who were "buried with Christ by baptism in to death" (Rom. 6:4), "who do not walk according to the flesh" (Rom. 8:1), but who, putting off the old man and putting on the new man, created in accordance with God (cf. Eph. 4:22–24; Col. 3:9ff), innocent, unstained, pure, and guiltless, have become the beloved sons of God, "heirs of God and fellow heirs with Christ" (Rom. 8:17), so that nothing henceforth holds them back from entering into heaven.

The holy council, however, professes and thinks that concupiscence or the tinder of sin remains in the baptized. Since it is left for us to wrestle with, it cannot harm those who do not consent but manfully resist it by the grace of Jesus Christ. Rather, "one who strives lawfully will be crowned" (cf. 2 Tim. 2:5). Of this concupiscence, which the apostle

---

15. See Hans Küng, *La justification. La doctrine de K. Barth, réflexions catholiques*, trans. Henri Marie Rochais and Jean Evrard (Paris: Desclée de Brouwer, 1965).

occasionally calls "sin" (cf. Rom. 6:12–15, 7:7, 14–20), the holy council declares: The Catholic Church has never understood that it is called sin because it would be sin in the true and proper sense in those who have been reborn, but because it comes from sin and inclines to sin. If anyone thinks to the contrary, let him be anathema.[16]

To be understood aright, this solution must be situated within an eschatological perspective. Christ's complete victory over sin is assured for the believer at the end of his earthly existence and includes the extinction of all concupiscence and a complete inability to sin.

Thus, the baptized person is *simul iustus et peccator*, for while the person is entirely redeemed and belongs to Christ with regard to grace itself, he still partially evades redemption by his freely willed activity. This does not stem from some insufficiency in Christ's redemptive sacrifice, for complete liberation from sin will only come to this believer from that sacrifice, indeed from it alone. Rather, it stems from the fact that man must freely take part in this liberation, for such free activity is a condition for the application of the power of Christ's sacrifice to this person, thus being submitted to temporality (i.e., to progress), which comes with the risk of regression.

However, in a sense, this undertaking is absolute. It is my personal acceptance of what Christ did on the cross, leading all of humanity to the Father. Behold why baptism has as its effect the definitive remission of all the sins that had weighed down the baptized person. In another sense, it has a relative character, for the human person, who deploys himself only in time, can commit himself entirely (i.e., commit his destiny up to the end) only on the condition that he continually ratifies his present decision in those that follow. Now, he remains free during this future earthly duration of time. He can change. In the case occupying us now, given that it is a question of the fundamental commitment involved in baptism, a commitment that is required at once by God's will and by man's nature, if one repudiates it (whether totally or partially), one "fails" and comes up short of one's own freedom. However, such a failure occurs freely and is always possible, at least during one's earthly life.

Here we find the key to the paradox. Inasmuch as the baptized

---

16. Trent, *Decree on original sin*, ch. 5, in D.-Sch., no. 1515.

person remains in harmony with the conversion process that was his baptism, he is free from sin. He falls back under the slavery of sin when he betrays the intention that this process expressed.

Thus, it remains the case that the baptized person's life is a continuous battle against sin, with a sequence of small and great victories and defeats. Through the believer's victories, the complete victory won by Christ on Calvary is progressively established within himself. The baptized person's defeats come solely from himself, not from the incompleteness of Christ's victory but from the fact that the baptized person himself deviated from it.[17]

The Believer's Victory over Death through Baptism

Christ's resurrection and the Christian's resurrection

{774} "According to the unanimous testimony of the New Testament authors, baptism 'in Jesus' is an eschatological sacrament."[18] It makes the believer participate in Christ's resurrection. For this reason, it has a meaning only on the basis of Christ's resurrection. "If Christ has not been raised, then our preaching is in vain and your faith is in vain";[19] "if Christ has not been raised, your faith is futile and you are still in your sins."[20] Likewise, it has a meaning only on the basis of the believer's own resurrection: "You were buried with him in baptism, in which you were also raised with him through faith in the working of God, who raised him from the dead";[21] "God, who is rich in mercy, out of the great love with which he loved us, even when we were dead through our trespasses, made us alive together with Christ (by grace you have been saved), and raised us up with him, and made us sit with him in the heavenly places in Christ Jesus."[22]

However, remaining as one aspect of the Christian paradox, this participation in Christ's resurrection is spoken of as being at once present and future: "if Christ is in you, although your bodies are

---

17. See Ignace de La Potterie, "L'impeccabilité du chrétien d'après 1 Jn 3, 6–9," in *La vie selon l'Espirit, condition du chrétien* (Paris: Cerf, 1965), 197–216. Spicq, *Théologie morale du Nouveau Testament*, 175–98.
18. Jeremias, *Le baptême des enfants*, 57.
19. 1 Cor 15:14 (RSV).
20. 1 Cor 15:17 (RSV).
21. Col 2:12 (RSV).
22. Eph 2:4–6 (RSV).

dead because of sin, your spirits are alive because of righteousness. If the Spirit of him who raised Jesus from the dead dwells in you, he who raised Christ Jesus from the dead will give life to your mortal bodies also through his Spirit which dwells in you."[23]

Therefore, there is a present participation in Christ's resurrection, which must establish a particular manner of living: "If then you have been raised with Christ, seek the things that are above, where Christ is, seated at the right hand of God."[24] However, this present resurrection is a mystery hidden under the appearances of mortality and, in the end, of physical death. It is a future event, and the resurrection of the body will be the manifestation of this mystery: "For you have died, and your life is hid with Christ in God. When Christ who is our life appears, then you also will appear with him in glory";[25] "We ourselves, who have the first fruits of the Spirit, groan inwardly as we wait for adoption as sons, the redemption of our bodies."[26]

Baptism's character as something procuring eschatological goods in advance (and, precisely, the resurrection) is perhaps noted in a gripping manner in a quite enigmatic text in St. Paul: "Otherwise, (i.e., if Christ was not the first one resurrected, 'the first fruits of those who have died') what do people mean by being baptized on behalf of the dead?"[27] Indeed, according to Jeremias[28] (who relies on M. Raeder), this was not at all concerned with a form of substitutional baptism (*uper tôn necrôn*, on behalf of the dead) but with a baptism received in view of one day meeting a departed loved one in the resurrection (in view of the dead, that is, of dead Christians who themselves were baptized before dying). Note that this novel interpretation is absent from the main modern French translations of the New Testament.

In any case, this threefold signification of baptism—that is, to Christ's death and resurrection as an already accomplished event, to the baptized person's own resurrection as well as to that of all men,

---

23. Rom 8:10–11 (RSV).
24. Col 3:1 (RSV).
25. Col 3:3–4 (RSV).
26. Rom 8:23 (RSV).
27. 1 Cor 15:29 (RSV).
28. Jeremias, *Le baptême des enfants*, 47n89.

as to a future event, and to one's present participation in the life of the resurrected Christ—corresponds to the threefold signification that is constitutive for every sacrament.[29] More broadly, it is explained by eschatology, such as it must be understood on the basis of the New Testament. The event that is Jesus Christ (i.e., the Incarnation, Jesus' earthly life, passion, death, burial, and resurrection) constitutes the eschatological event *par excellence*, that toward which the whole of Old Testament eschatology tends. The history that follows (the entire "time of the Church") does not unroll from this event as from a point of departure. Instead, this history is enveloped by it. It makes successive generations, up to the end of time, enter into it and participate in it. Thus, although the resurrection of the dead must be a new event, it is already included in Christ's resurrection and is given with it.[30]

The fullness of the divine pardon and the persistence of sin's consequences

{775} This extra-temporal reference of the resurrection (i.e., to the end of time), along with its terrible consequence (namely, the persistence of all human sufferings of which death is the crown and also the symbol), nonetheless poses a grave problem from the perspective of the theology of baptism, namely, that of the reality of the divine pardon, as well as its absolute character. This is so because death has always been related to sin, a connection that is formally taught by St. Paul.[31] On the other hand, there can be no doubt that baptism brings God's complete pardon to the believer, given that Christ has fully made satisfaction for all of men's sins and, first of all, for the fundamental sin in which all are enveloped from their conception, what one calls "original sin."[32]

Thus, how are we to explain the fact that God's pardon does not deliver man from mortality and all its consequences?

We can find an extremely profound solution to this problem in

---

29. See §614 above.
30. See §544 in the previous volume. See Cullmann, *Christ et le temps*, 86–125, and *Le salut dans l'histoire*, 167–86.
31. See Rom 5:12–25.
32. See ST III, q. 68, a. 5; q. 62, a. 2.

St. Thomas's writings.[33] It is a solution that sets in order the entire *intellectus fidei* of the mystery of evil.

To understand this solution, we must bear in mind that the *poenalitates huius vitae* (the punishments inherent in the present earthly condition of humanity) are connected to human nature and cannot be considered as being "punishments" except in terms of God's merciful intention for man (an intention that is love, having persons as its direct object and concerned with [human] nature only inasmuch as it is realized in persons). On the other hand, sin first of all is concerned with persons. By way of privation and rupture, it is the interpersonal rupture between man and God. Thus (in a mysterious way that we cannot examine here), on account of the existential situation into which all human persons were placed at humanity's beginning through man's personal rupture with God, men have been handed over to their natural condition, which they have, moreover, aggravated through the proliferation of their sins.

Now, the divine pardon bestowed at baptism is directly concerned with persons. Therefore, it can be complete without, for all that, removing him (at least immediately, that is, during the earthly portion of his destiny) from the natural conditions of suffering and death into which he has been born. The three reasons that St. Thomas proposes for rendering account of this do not in any way claim to exclude the mystery of salvation's designs but, rather, simply make it stand forth in the light of faith and of theological reasoning (wisdom). Let us briefly comment on these three reasons.

First reason

By baptism, man is incorporated into Christ as a member of His body. Thus, it was fitting that as things are for the head, so too they would be for His members. Therefore, just as Christ during His earthly life was full of grace and truth as regards His spirit but submitted to suffering and death as regards his body (so that beyond His passion and death He may be raised and exalted to the life of glory), so too in baptism the Christian is made spiritually alive through grace whereas his body remains passible so that he would be able to suffer for Christ.

---

33. See *ST* III, q. 69, a. 3, co. and ad 3.

The Effects of Baptism

However, in the end, he must be resurrected and introduced to a life that is free from all suffering. What does it mean to say, "to suffer for Christ"? Can we not read in these words (at least implicitly) the Christian's earthly vocation, as well as that of the Church, to carry forward the redemptive suffering, up to the world's end, up to the conclusion of salvation history?

In any case, this reason is clearly inspired by a great Pauline theme: the Christian suffers, is crucified, and dies with Christ in order to be raised with Him. When we reflected on the mystery of the redemption in light of this theme, we were led to recognize that what Jesus Christ accomplished for sinful humanity (i.e., the painful return to the Father) must be taken up by each human person during his own life, in Him and with Him, so that the believer may personalize and come to own this undertaking in which he was implied without yet willing it and without yet knowing it at the time when it was fulfilled.[34] We personally cooperate with Jesus Christ through baptism. This very solidarity, in which both of our conditions are so tightly knotted together, requires baptism to leave him in his painful and mortal condition during the time of his earthly life, even though it makes him already participate in life with Christ in the Father's house.

Second reason

The second reason is drawn from the necessity of the spiritual struggle. This is the idea (one that is Pauline as well) that eternal life and our participation in Christ's kingdom must be a victory for man having glory as its crowning. This in no way contradicts St. Paul's words elsewhere, "The free gift of God is eternal life in Christ Jesus our Lord,"[35] for if man victoriously struggles here-below against hardships and temptations, he does so through the power of the Holy Spirit who, given by Christ, dwells in him and animates him. However, it is man who struggles, suffers, and dies, so that the victory of grace in him is also his victory. In an ancient [Eucharistic] preface, taken up today for the liturgy of the saints [in the Roman Rite], we read this

---

34. See §494 in the previous volume.
35. Rom 6:23 (RSV).

gripping formula, which translates in a powerful and condensed way a theme dear to St. Augustine: "In crowning their merits, you crown your own gifts."[36] Nonetheless, according to the divine design, even though eternal life is given to man by pure mercy, it also must be obtained by him through a great struggle, and this explains why man was given the chance to do battle, something given to him alongside the penalties inherent in humanity's earthly condition.

Third reason

Finally, the third reason emphasizes that the primary *raison d'être* for baptism is, as we explained above, to introduce man to eternal life from which he had turned himself away through sin. Would man not once more turn away from God (in the end, leaving the baptized person in the error of sin) by receiving baptism not for glory (i.e., the beatitude to which man has been called) but, rather, for the earthly happiness that would be assured to him through it (though only for a time, for the time of earthly life, by being exempted from this life's sorrows)? It is important that the baptized person's undertaking be ordered formally and without equivocation to that for which baptism was instituted, namely, his return to the Father's house by and with Christ. To this end, it is good for man not to expect any other good than this return. The relevance of this third reason is revealed by the grave deviations that have arisen on account of the temporal advantages that, as a result of historical circumstances, the reception of baptism has sometimes been able to procure.

Finally, all these reasons are ultimately reduced to the fact that man is personally freed from sin through baptism, receiving the gift of life with God and in God; however, he is in no way released from his solidarity with sinful men in bearing the consequences of sin. Baptism is not a form of disengagement but, on the contrary, is an engagement in imitation (and in the wake) of the Word's own engagement, by which, through the redemptive Incarnation, he partook in the pains of human history, leading it to the ultimate goal that gives it meaning.

---

36. Roman Missal, first preface of Saints. See St. Augustine, *Homélies sur l'évangile de S. Jean, tract. I-XVI*, OESA 71, 229, with the remarks of Berrouard at 860–61.

Nonetheless, God's pardon, which is bestowed upon the baptized person, is total. This is so because, for the person, mortality and all of its surroundings are no longer punishments but, rather, are the occasion and means for freely participating in his own redemption and in that of the world.[37]

Thus, we can quite clearly see the progressive character of redemption. It is progressive in relation to humanity's history as well as for each human person. This "progressivity" has its sole source in man, who is a developmental, "historical" being. Christ fulfilled it all at once. (However, this did not itself lack a kind of progressivity as well, namely, that of His human life, for given that the Word truly became a man and redeemed us inasmuch as He was a man, His redemptive action is also submitted to progressivity. Nonetheless, it found its definitive terminus in the resurrection and in His return to the Father.) Still, it is a progressivity whose point of departure is an absolute beginning, a purely gratuitous and first gift. As human life progresses and develops on the basis of the gift of human existence given at conception, so too the Christian life, the life divinized in grace, progresses and develops on the basis of the gift of Christian existence given at baptism or, likewise, returned by the sacrament of penance, for if death is an irreversible phenomenon in natural existence, God is He who resurrects the dead. When it is lost through sin, God has the power and merciful desire to restore this life which He gives at baptism.

REGENERATION, THE GRACE OF SONS

"The old being has passed away and a new one has come."[38] In order to perceive this *bipolarity* and, simultaneously, to note that the accent is placed on its positive aspect, we merely need to consider one time all of the expressions and images which the New Testament employs to interpret baptism or to speak about it.[39]

---

37. See Jean-Hervé Nicolas, "L'innocence originelle de la Nouvelle Eve," 15–35, and *L'amour de Deiu et la peine des hommes* (Paris: Beauchesne, 1969).

38. 2 Cor 5:17.

39. See Jeremias, *Le baptême des enfants*, 57. [Tr. note: See Joachim Jeremias, *Infant Baptism in the First Four Centuries*, trans. David Cairns (Eugene, Ore.: Wipf and Stock, 2004), 36. In the original French, Fr. Nicolas's language is close to that of Jeremias, but differs enough to

Here, the exegete, by his own proper methods, will discover St. Thomas's theological position, holding that the remission of sins (the "negative" face) is the effect of the infusion of grace by which man is introduced into a new existence, the participation in the Divine Life.[40] Therefore, like light chasing away the shadows, baptism in fact brings the remission of sins by communicating the Divine Life to the believer.

New Birth

{776} Through baptism, the believer becomes "a child of God." That is, he begins to partake in God's own life. This life is that of Christ and comes to him from Christ.

Participation in the Divine Life

The Divine Life consists in the interpersonal relations of the three Persons, relations of perfect knowledge and infinite friendship.

To participate in this life first and foremost means that one enters "into communion" with the Father and the Son[41] as well as with the Holy Spirit. In other words, it means that one recognizes and loves the Divine Persons, something that cannot happen without a super-elevation of one's spiritual faculties by grace.

This participation will be complete in the next life[42] when the created person will be fully absorbed by the Divine Life and completely concerned with God. Here-below, human life is not, cannot be, nor should be, a purely spiritual life. It not only has bodily "constraints" but also has temporal "objectives" through which its aspiration toward God, its hope and its charity, must normally pass (while also, however, outstripping these "objectives").

Thus, participation in the Divine Life on earth includes a considerable degree of "bodily" activity—though it is not solely bodily, so to put it a better way, let us say it has a bodily dimension—whereas

---

justify rendering it directly from the French. It seems that while directly relying on (and wishing to cite) the enumeration of texts offered by Jeremias, Fr. Nicholas has knowingly adapted to text to his own ends here.]

40. See *ST* I-II, q. 113, a. 2. [Tr. note: Fr. Nicolas does not cite the part of the *Summa* in the original.]

41. See 1 Cor 1:9; 1 Jn 1:3.

42. See 1 Jn 3:1–2.

God is pure spirit. However, this "bodily" activity must also be divinized. This continuity between life with God and life in this world is brought about by means of fraternal charity, through which one extends charity-love for God, by which men already participate in "eternal life," to this "worldly" domain where the life of the children of God necessarily unfolds.

Through Christ

This Divine Life is communicated by Christ to the believer through baptism. Above all, it is communicated in virtue of His redemption. However, if baptism is the individual application of the redemption brought about for all, it is clear that Christ Himself is the one who acts and saves in and through baptism. Must we speak of an instrumental causality exercised by Christ's humanity? We have seen how such a causality can be understood and admitted. It is certain that if we admit it, it emphasizes the realism of Christ's causal role in the sacraments in general and particularly in baptism. In order to deny it, one would need to show that it is impossible, and it is not impossible.[43]

In Christ

We have already seen that the love by which the Father loves men reaches them in Christ, in whom they are contained, as soon as they actualize this belonging and make it personal through their faith and love.[44] Now this love of God is what filial adoption realizes. Nonetheless, we must understand this in function of baptism's property of making the believer participate in Christ's redemptive action (and consequently in that which is the principle animator of this action, namely, the redemptive love, Jesus' charity in His earthly state of existence).

During his earthly life, the Christian is conformed to Christ as He lived on earth His human life as Son of God with peerless perfection. His charity, made in the image of Christ's, is a "penitential love." (In other words, without in any way taking part in men's sins, Christ

43. See §739 above.
44. See §436 in the previous volume as well as Nicolas, *Les profondeurs de la grâce*, 248–62.

experienced its shame, its pain, and the desire to make satisfaction for it.)[45] Such a love is one that tends toward suffering and death, not through a kind of machismo or a Manichean hatred of sensible joy but, instead, out of the same movement that drove Christ toward the cross while He was on earth. From the earliest days of the Church's life, this dimension of Christian grace has been expressed in the form of the desire for martyrdom.[46]

The Christian meaning of death comes from this. It is the ultimate earthly configuration to Christ the redeemer, a "physical" realization of the symbolic configuration brought about through baptism (though it is real as well, in its own order, namely, the sacramental order).

This is the "Christian paradox" presented anew. All at once, the believer participates in the transfigured life of the resurrected Christ, as well as in His crucified life. "Christian joy" is not done away with but rather is "contextualized" by the shadow of the cross. Full and entire, it is one of the two poles of the Christian's existential situation, the other pole being constituted by the sadness and agony of Christ in which the Christian simultaneously participates through his baptism.

This crucified situation of Christian grace is temporary, as was that of Christ. It must disappear in the hereafter, especially at the resurrection. Moreover, we have seen that the resurrection at the end of the time is itself also an effect of baptism. This means that even perfect communion with the Trinity, the ultimate fruit of baptism, will be a life "in Christ," a participation in the divinized life of the Christ-man.

Following in Christ's Footsteps

It is clear that this divinization of earthly human life, through which we must pass in order to arrive at the perfect communion to be found beyond this world, was realized in an absolute way in the earthly life of Jesus, the God-Man. To live in a Christian way means that we must practice the *sequela Christi*, attempting to live as Christ

---

45. See §492 in the previous volume.
46. See Louis Bouyer, *La spiritualité du Nouveau Testament et des Pères* (Paris: Aubier, 1960), 256–61.

lived. It is not a question of materially copying the way He lived, as His own earthly life was, in its factual details, conditioned by the givens of His age and environment. Instead, it is a question of living His life in its depths by judging, loving, and acting in accord with the mind of Christ or of the Gospel (which, in the end, are the same things) in the circumstances of one's own life.

Baptism makes the believer a disciple of Christ, indeed, all the more so to the degree that He has a broader and deeper sway over the baptized person's existence.

Divinization

{777} The term "divinization" was used by a number of the Greek Fathers[47] to designate the transformation brought about in the Christian by grace. It brings about a new birth, for grace does not bring a completely new being into existence but instead renews the man whom sin has damaged, infusing a new life into him, that which he had received from God at the dawn of his creation.

The term is not itself biblical. However, it is the equivalent to the biblical term "adoption." What it highlights is the character of the effect produced by baptism, a character that, of itself, is permanent. In short, the baptized person has become a living being who lives a divinized life.

As it is described by St. Paul, grace sometimes seems to be only a divine impulse, a continuous action exercised by God in the soul.[48] However, this does not exclude the possibility of a permanent gift, a habitual transformation of the person, something that is necessarily implied in the very idea of "life." Indeed, a living being is precisely the kind of being that has the principle of its action in itself. It is certainly the case that the Christian is moved by the Holy Spirit (indeed, in an increasingly continuous manner) so that he may participate in the acts of the Divine Life. However, this implies that

---

47. See Jules Gross, *La divinization du chrétien d'après les Pères grecs, contribution historique à la doctrine de la grâce* (Paris: Gabalda, 1938). Irénée-Henri Dalmais, "Divinisation," *Patristique grecque, Dictionnaire de spiritualité ascétique et mystique, doctrine et histoire*, ed. Marcel Viller (Paris: Beauchesne, 1937), 3:1376–89.

48. See Henri Bouillard, *Conversion et grâce chez S. Thomas d'Aquin* (Paris: Aubier, 1944).

he would have the source of these activities in himself in a habitual manner. Without this, they would not be his own and would not involve his freedom. They would not make him personally place himself in communion with the Divine Persons.

This source of the activities pertaining to man's participation in the Divine Life cannot be man's spirit by itself, for of itself it is not situated at this level of activity. Nonetheless, it must be man's spirit, for otherwise such activities would not be ones exercised by the human person. Therefore, it is man's spirit, really transformed, indeed, in a stable and permanent way by the Spirit of God. In other words, if God's grace is the Holy Spirit, the Holy Spirit cannot be given to the human person without the latter being transformed in his spiritual depths by a created gift, namely, sanctifying grace.[49]

Scholastic theology explained this gift by making use of a category having an Aristotelian origin (though, not without transforming it), namely the notion of an infused *habitus*. A *habitus* is a real and permanent modification of a spiritual faculty, empowering it to perform certain acts. However, in the domain of our experience, such a modification is gradually produced by the acts themselves, for it is ever a question of acts of which the faculty is capable by its very structure. They are within its range, and it only needs to be "habituated" in relation to them. Here, however, it is a question of activities that transcend the natural range of the soul and of its faculties. Therefore, *ex hypothesi*, the acts cannot precede this modification, this transformation of man's spirit. They are impossible without this modification. Thus, we must say that such *habitus* are produced in the soul through God's own direct action. (It is said that they are infused. However, this is a dangerous image! The *habitus* are not a reality that is independent of the soul, waiting to be introduced into them. They exist only as a modification of the soul and for this reason are not "infused" but, rather, are produced in it by the divine action.) It is an action that is exercised on the soul, enabling it to perform acts which it is not radically incapable of producing, though no more is it able to produce them by itself.

---

49. See §§219 and 233 in the first volume. Also, see Nicolas, *Les profondeurs de la grâce*, 126–49.

Baptism, acting by Christ's power, is the means of this divine action, as we saw above regarding the remission of sins. Indeed, it is the same action.

The spirit thus transformed becomes a living being that lives a divinized life. In other words, it is divine by participation, which consists in participating in the divine activities of knowledge and love, in knowing God in His mystery and loving Him in His intimate depths, and in entering into communion with the Divine Persons. It is a dynamic participation and a communion of life.[50] The spirit is this living being even when it does not bring forth the activities of the divinized life (either because it cannot or because it does not will to do so). Indeed, it is of man's nature that life could exist in him without being yet manifested by vital activities. A baby is a living being having an intellectual life, even before being able to elicit the least act of thought. We will see the importance of this point when we come to the question of infant baptism.

BEING GATHERED TOGETHER INTO THE CHURCH

Without a doubt, baptism is a rite of initiation. To receive baptism means that one enters into the Church and begins to be part of her.

However, the Church is not only a human society into which one would enter through a purely external undertaking, a society to which one would belong through solely juridical bonds. She is a supernatural reality, the body of Christ. One belongs to her through real, though mysterious, bonds. As a rite of initiation, baptism has the establishment of these bonds as its effect. However, certain questions remain to be answered. Is it not possible that he who freely has entered into the Church could freely leave her, and if so, can he suppress the bonds that baptism has established? Moreover, to what Church does it bind him—to the one Church of Jesus Christ or to the one that conferred baptism upon him?

---

50. See §207 in the first volume.

The Bonds That Baptism Establishes between the Baptized Person and the Church

{778} The Church is essentially a "communion" (with Christ and, in Him, with the Divine Persons, then also with other redeemed persons), and one belongs to this communion through grace and in charity. Baptism makes one enter into it by causing the effects considered up to this point. However, it is a communion rooted in a society to which one must normally belong in order to take part in that communion.

Hence, baptism not only causes grace, the source of life in communion with God (and with other men in Christ), but also is a sign of belonging to the Church as a society. It is a sign that, in itself, is invisible. It is made visible by its connection to the baptismal rite. It is the "internal sacrament," ever present there.

It is an indelible sign, for if membership in the Church depended on actual participation in the ecclesial communion (which is the effect of grace and of charity) it would be, strictly speaking, invisible and unverifiable (just as we cannot verify whether a given person actually does or does not have grace). The Church would thus be invisible.

It is a sign that is more than a sign. It includes the power to participate in the activity of the Church, that is, above all in her worship. Christian worship is the religious activity of Christ exercised by the Church with Him, by Him, and in Him. Nobody can take part in it (in a truly real way) except by being a member of the Church. Nobody can participate in the fruits of Christ's sacrifice, nor then offer it (while offering himself at the same time) if he is not incorporated into the Church. For this reason, baptism is "the gateway to the other sacraments."

This sign-power is what the [sacramental] character [of baptism] is. It must be conceived of as being a real modification of the person in his spirit and not a simple moral and intentional bond, even though it is perfectly invisible and even impossible to clearly conceive. Without this, its "indelibility" (which comes from the fact that it does not depend on the fluctuations of free choice) would be inconceivable, for it is quite clear that every purely moral bond depends on free choice.

Nonetheless, it must not be separated from grace. If Christ founded the Church, He did not do this so that there may be one more merely earthly society, though with a kind of increase added to it. Instead, He founded the Church so that believers may find, in her, communion with the Divine Persons and live with them. Membership in the earthly Church is the normal condition for this participation in that communion, and it loses its meaning if it is separated from that communion. Thus, the baptismal character, by its very nature and by Christ's intention, is ordered to grace and to charity.

Conversely, grace implies the character as its normal condition. Where it is given without the baptismal rite (and therefore without the [sacramental] character), it brings with it a kind of (tendential and precarious) membership in the Church as a society. It remains ordered to the character to be received (by the baptismal rite), not as though the character were its end and would be superior to it, but rather because the character remains necessary inasmuch as it is its normal existential condition.[51] (See the note below for a further remark on the consequences of the indelible character of baptism.)[52]

One Baptism, Many Churches?

{779} Since[53] the end of the second century, the Church has found herself confronted with the scandalous and troubling fact of divi-

---

51. See §762 above.

52. N.B. Another consequence—one that is quite contested today, though it remains certain—of the affirmation (which is *de fide*) of the production of an indelible character by the sacrament of baptism is that the person who has been baptized cannot cut off every bond with the Church, at least for as long as he lives on earth, no matter what may be the force and determination of his decision to break with her. *To have been baptized* is a datum that one cannot eliminate from one's present situation. He who, making use of his religious freedom, cuts himself off totally from the Church does not cease to depend on her. In our era, this does not have (nor can it have) any consequence for his individual and social life. No authority either can nor wishes to compel one to recognize the laws of the Church and be submitted to them. However, by contrast, this cannot fail to have consequences for one's relation to the sacraments. If such a person converts and returns to the Church, he will not be joined to her anew through baptism. If he marries outside the Church—and therefore in a non-sacramental manner—the Church will not be able to recognize his marriage as being valid (see §1010 below), even if she respects and honors the situation wherein the two spouses are placed in civil society. Thus, if the marriage is broken by the civil authority, the Church will not refuse such a person sacramental marriage with another partner.

53. See the following: Georges Bavaud, introduction to St. Augustine, *De Baptismo*, OESA 29, 9–46. Congar, "Introduction générale aux traités anti-donatistes de S. Augustin." Pierre-Yves Emery, "Le baptême: appurtenance fondamentale à l'Église," *Verbum Caro* 76 (1965): 59–68.

sion and the existence of many Christian confessions, all of which preserve baptism, claiming to be the sole source of true baptism.

There was a famous controversy between the Church of Africa (under the direction of St. Cyprian) and the Church of Rome which, on the basis of "tradition," affirmed that baptism that has been given according to the rite was valid even if it was given outside of the true Church and must not be repeated. St. Cyprian, on the contrary, thought that baptism belongs to the Church and that, when it is given outside of her and outside of the true faith, it was only a useless show. Before him, Tertullian (who had become a Montanist) also judged that only baptism performed in the true Church (for him, the Montanist sect) was valid.[54]

A first step forward toward a comprehensive solution was made by means of Optatus of Milevis's distinction between schism, which does not prevent baptism from being valid, and heresy, which suppresses such validity. Likewise, he expressed an energetic affirmation that Christ is the one who baptizes by means of the human minister. Following this first step, St. Augustine found the solution that henceforth became the Church's own: every baptism, performed according to the baptismal rite (and with the intention of baptizing "in the name of Jesus") is valid, *of itself* making one belong to the true Church of Christ, the sole Church.

However, the solution must be elaborated on the basis of the developments in the Church's doctrine concerning dissidents, above all the immense forms of progress realized by the Second Vatican Council which, for the first time, recognized that Christian confessions that are "dissidents" (in relation to her) have the title and character of being Churches [sic]* (though indeed not without specifying that the fullness of revealed truth and of the means of grace are found only in the Catholic Church).[55]

Jérôme Hamer, "Le baptême et l'Église," *Irenikon* 25 (1952): 142–64 and 263–75. Albert Houssiau, "Implications théologiques de la reconnaissance inter-ecclésiale du baptême," *Revue théologique de Louvain* (1970): 393–410.

54. See Hamer, "Le baptême et l'Église," 153.

* [Tr. note: Fr. Nicolas can at times seem a little loose with this language, though he notes clearly the qualitative difference existing between the Orthodox Churches and Protestant ecclesial bodies.]

55. See Vatican II, *Unitatis Redintegratio*, no. 3.

Certainly, baptism received in a given Church is a sign of belonging to this Church. However, baptism, instituted by Christ and by which Christ acts, bears a signification and an efficacy that is independent of the more or less clear and complete awareness that can be had about it not only by the minister administering it but also by the Church in whose name this minister acts. It incorporates its recipient into Christ and simultaneously into His body, which is the Church. To have discovered and proclaimed that the Church which is the body of Christ is also found, although only partially, in every Church that believes in Christ, enables the Catholic to provide a much richer solution to the problem of baptism by dissident Christian groups. The newly baptized person belongs to Christ's Church and is incorporated into her through the intermediary of his Church [sic]. However, that Church [sic] is part of the body of Christ only to the degree that, even without expressly knowing or willing it, it wholly tends toward the fullness that is found only in the Catholic Church.[56]

THE GIFT OF THE SPIRIT

The Gift That Includes All the Others

{780} In God, the Holy Spirit is personified love. Love is the first gift. This is so first of all because one gives through love, meaning that love

---

56. N.B. Here again, significant nuances must be provided regarding these matters. To the degree that the Church of Jesus Christ is made up of men, human values, institutions, and human behaviors, the Catholic Church includes many deficiencies [*manques*] and even deviations, from which this or that other Christian Church [sic] will have been able to better preserve itself. From this perspective, the latter would bring positive values in being united to the Catholic Church, which by this very fact would be modified in relation to that which exists in her in contrast with other Churches [sic]. However, we must maintain that these shortcomings [*manques*] and deviations have not been able to affect the essence of her message and of the apostolic tradition thanks to the promised assistance of the Holy Spirit who indefectibly maintains her. Thus, she has never ceased to be the Church founded by Jesus Christ, the One Church, while the others were also truly Churches [sic], although imperfectly and only by reference to her, at least in an implicit manner. This way of conceiving of union by means of the contribution of the positive Christian values of the other Churches to the Catholic Church by developing what is authentically Christian in them (and indeed thus enriching the Catholic Church herself) has become common and was ratified by the Second Vatican Council. Among the great sources of this approach, one must here name Fr. Congar. See Yves Congar, *Chrétiens désunis. Principes d'un oecuménisme catholique* (Paris: Cerf, 1937).

is the principle of every gift, endowing every gift with its meaning. Next, this is so because to the degree that one person loves another person (and to the degree that the person is loved for himself and on account of himself), that person gives himself to that other person.

God's primordial gift to the created person: To love Him

This, which is the foundational law of every form of love, is realized beyond every measure (and beyond everything that we can conceive) in God's love for the created person. The created person exists as a person both as loved and as being "loveable" (worthy of being loved by God) only through the love by which that creature is loved. Thus, this love is absolutely free. However, it is also absolutely real. That is, following on this divine initiative, the created person is loved for his own sake and on account of himself (and simultaneously on account of God, as he is made in the image of God through this very love, and also distinctly as a person, thus being rendered loveable by the very loveability of God, so that God continues to love Himself in this created person). Moreover, God gives himself personally to the beloved person, making him become His companion [*en société avec Lui*], which is the infinite companionship [*société*] and communion of the three Persons of the Trinity. More exactly, He offers Himself to him, for the gift can be blocked by a refusal on the part of created freedom. In this case, the person continues *to be loved from the perspective of election*[57] (i.e., as called by God and foundationally ordered to Him by this very appeal that makes him exist) and simultaneously is an enemy *in relation to the Gospel* (i.e., in relation to what such a person's vocation would be if it were accepted).[58]

The grace given at baptism (i.e., the grace of the remission of sins and the grace of divinization and adoption) is this love first of all. Next, it is the transformation of the created spirit which renders it capable of possessing the Divine Persons and of enjoying them. Finally, it is these very persons into whose companionship [*société*] the created person is introduced on account of this transformation. We

---

57. See Rom 11:28.
58. See ibid.

have seen how this very grace is the principle of full membership in the Church, which is a society and communion of all the children of God.

The reception of the Holy Spirit is what it means for the created person to be loved

{781} It is the three Persons together who love and are given. Why then is it said that the Holy Spirit is given at baptism?

The classic solution to this question consists in understanding this by "appropriation." That which is common to the three Persons is attributed to one Person in particular on account of the given gift's affinity with this Person's own, proper mode of existence. Let us briefly recall the nature of such appropriation.[59] We cannot have concepts expressing the *propria personarum* because all of our concepts are drawn from creatures and because the creative action (as well as the exemplarity founded upon it) are common to the three Persons. To attain these *propria* in some manner, we must pass through the *communia*, through what is common to the three Persons. (Moreover, to attain these *communia* we first needed to pass through our knowledge of creatures.) The procedure of appropriation consists in taking a notion that first of all expresses something common to the Persons and adapting it so that it may be applied to one Person in particular.

Many theologians today are very reluctant to accept this explanation, which seems to them incapable of doing justice to significant scriptural expressions concerning the gift of the Holy Spirit made to believers. Let us only note that Scripture says about the Father and about the Son what it also says about the Holy Spirit, namely, that He is given to us and that He dwells in us as in His temple. Let us also note that the Holy Spirit cannot be given separately, for the three Persons are inseparable. Likewise, let us note that, according to Scripture, He is the sign of the Father's and Son's love for believers as well as the sign of the gift that they make of themselves to us.[60]

The Holy Spirit is certainly given in His "distinct personal being,"

---

59. See §§191–98 in the first volume.
60. See Nicolas, *Les profondeurs de la grâce*, 110–25.

and this gift is the pledge of the love by which the believer is loved by the Father and the Son. He is not given separately. The three Persons are given distinctly, through a single gift. Appropriation consists in reserving this title, "Gift," for the Holy Spirit. Through this title, we attempt to express His "personal being," for given that He proceeds according to the manner of love, He is the gift of God *par excellence*.[61]

In What Sense Is the Gift of the Holy Spirit the Proper Effect of Baptism?

Through baptism, the Holy Spirit, who dwells in the Church and the soul, begins to dwell in the believer

{782} If the Holy Spirit is grace itself (given that created grace can be conceived of only as opening the created spirit up to reception of the Holy Spirit and of the two other Persons), every sacrament gives the Holy Spirit. However, each sacrament will have its own proper mode of giving Him, just as each has its own proper mode of giving grace.[62]

We have seen that even though this proper mode concerns grace itself, it can be conceived of only in terms of the particular way that each sacrament plays its unique role within the Church.

The Holy Spirit is forever He who gives charisms and ministries to the Church and who reincorporates them into ecclesial communion when they separate themselves from her through sin. What is proper to baptism is that it makes the believer participate in the gift of the Holy Spirit that was made to the entire Church at Pentecost, establishing the believer in a state of habitual communication with the Holy Spirit. Thus, every subsequent gift of the Spirit (whether or not it is the effect of a particular sacrament) will be a prolongation and ramification of the gift of the Spirit given at baptism.

The "measure" of the gift of the Spirit in baptism

Must we think (with St. Thomas[63]) that baptism of itself gives everyone the same grace and therefore gives the Holy Spirit to the same

---

61. See §151 in the first volume.
62. See §764 above.
63. See *ST* III, q. 69, a. 8.

degree, meaning that the only difference that could exist would be, in the case of adult baptism, based on the subject's greater or lesser disposition toward the reception of that grace?

This position is astounding. It also seems to clash with the general doctrine of grace held by St. Thomas himself.

Baptism has only an instrumental causality. The principal causality of baptism is that of the Holy Spirit (i.e., of the three Persons together). It is not clear what could enable one to say that the initial love by which a human person is loved (and which is his grace of conversion, his baptismal grace) has the same intensity for all. God's love is personal, and each person is loved to the degree that God alone can determine, as this love is absolutely gratuitous for all.

The Holy Spirit given before the existence of baptism

{783} A question thus emerges: how are we to conceive of the fact that before Christ and before His exaltation the Holy Spirit was not given to those who were in God's grace? Indeed, it is quite certain that grace was given before Christ.

St. Thomas proposes the following solution to this question. On the one hand, the sacraments of the Old Law did not have as their effect the giving of grace, of which Christ is the source. Instead, they were prophetic in relation to the means of grace that Christ would come to institute. On the other hand, although they were incapable of causing grace, they were a sign of faith in Christ who was to come, and grace was bestowed on account of this faith.[64] He extends this even to the regime of the "law of nature" (i.e., the state before and outside the Mosaic law).

To understand this response, it seems that, as regards "believers" before Christ, we must distinguish *their personal situation* from *the era of salvation [history]* in which they found themselves. A given era of salvation [history] is concerned with humanity taken as a whole in the stage of salvation history in which it finds itself. Given that Jesus is the Savior who saved man through His sacrifice and His resurrection, the eras of expectation and of prophecy (in which salvation is announced as something to come and therefore as something not

---

64. See *ST* I-II, q. 103, aa. 2–3; III, q. 70, a. 4.

yet accomplished) are obsolete as soon as the Savior comes and is at work. The gift of the Holy Spirit is at once the sign (the pledge) of salvation that has been accomplished and the realization of this salvation in humanity after Christ's exaltation. However, salvation is personal. It is the establishment (or, reestablishment) of interpersonal relations between man and God. Each human person is concerned with salvation and, nonetheless, the duration of his earthly existence is limited. Therefore, it is necessary that personal salvation was possible for people whose existence was situated in the phases of salvation history that preceded Christ's coming and His saving acts. Given that they belonged to an era in which salvation was still something to come, they were saved in the present in anticipation of the salvation that Christ would accomplish in His time, being saved through their faith in Christ who was to come (obviously an implicit faith, indeed one that was often very implicit).

To be saved means that one receives the grace of the remission of sins and of adoption. Does this not mean that one thus receives the Holy Spirit?

Here, we must bring a second distinction to bear, namely between *the invisible mission of the Spirit alone* and *the invisible mission manifested by the visible mission*. Nobody can receive grace without receiving the Spirit, for grace is the Holy Spirit. However, given that the visible mission is ordered to the invisible mission (without which the visible mission would be meaningless), it belongs to the era of salvation that has been accomplished. It was not bestowed to believers who found themselves in earlier eras. Given that it is not, precisely speaking, a question of two missions (as the visible mission is the manifestation of the invisible mission), the invisible mission is indeed modified when one passes from the era where it alone existed without [external] manifestations to the era when this invisible mission is supplemented and completed by the visible mission (and, likewise, when it is that to which believers are ordered by the visible mission).

In this sense, it is true to say, "As yet the Spirit had not been given,"[65] and that, on the contrary, baptism (in contrast to circum-

---

65. Jn 7:39 (RSV). See §238 in the first volume.

cision and every other sacrament of the Mosaic law or of the law of nature) has the giving of the Holy Spirit as its effect. This does not mean that this gift would necessarily need to be accompanied by new manifestations. Instead, it would mean that the Spirit is given in baptism by referring to the great (and, in a sense, unique) visible mission of the Holy Spirit at Pentecost. Through baptism, the believer personally participates in this gift of the Spirit which was given to the Church once and for all, for each existing believer and for those to come.

7

Baptism and Faith

As is the case for every sacrament, through baptism man encounters God in Christ; indeed, this is his first encounter. It includes God's action through Christ (and through the Church), one that we studied above, as well as an initiatve exercised by man, namely through faith in Christ. We must study this initiative in relation to baptism.

BAPTISM, SACRAMENT OF FAITH

Now,* it is said that baptism is the sacrament of faith on account of the fact that baptism includes a profession of faith and because through baptism one is joined to the community of believers.[1] To believe means nothing other than the fact that one has faith, and if one says that a small child believes, this is because it is understood that he has faith on account of the sacrament of faith.[2] [However, we must consider an essential issue that arises concerning the connection between faith and baptism.]

---

* See André Benoît, *Le Baptême chrétien au second siècle* (Paris: PUF, 1953), and *Saint Thomas d'Aquin. Somme théologique, Le baptême et la confirmation: 3a, Questions 66–72*, trans. Pierre-Thomas Camelot (Paris: Desclee & Cie, 1956), 371–74. Adalbert Hamman, *Le baptême d'après les Pères de l'Église (recueil detexts)* (Paris: Grasset, 1962). Villette, *Foi et sacrement*, vol. 1.

1. See *ST* III, q. 70, a. 1.
2. See St. Augustine, *Epistolae*, PL 33, ep. 98, no. 9 (co. 363).

The Problem

The faith caused by baptism: Baptism-illumination

{784} One of the traditional names given to baptism is "illumination." This term is found for the first time in St. Justin Martyr.[3] It is connected to Hebrews 6:4.[4] The expression regularly occurs in the Eastern Fathers in the fourth and fifth centuries.

On the one hand, the very rite of baptism introduces the neophyte into an understanding of the mysteries, especially that of the Trinity. On the other hand, the grace of illumination enables him to penetrate all the way to the intelligible significate beyond the sensible rite:

If you come forward in faith, men certainly will bring about something that their eyes can grasp. However, the Holy Spirit will give you that which does not fall under sight ... If you are worthy of grace, your soul will be illuminated, and you will be given a power that you did not have.[5]

Through the grace of baptism and the Spirit's illumination, one obtains full participation in the Incarnate Word, as well as perfect and true *gnosis* of God.[6]

We do not mean that the newly-baptized person would receive some sort of revelation. Instead, his mind is opened up so that he may receive teaching concerning the loftiest mysteries. According to an expression of St. Gregory of Nyssa: "After the soul separated itself from evil ... it was washed of the defilement of ignorance by water."[7]

Faith as a disposition to baptism

{785} However (and here is where the problem arises), faith is also the neophyte's own internal initiative, without which there is no baptism.

---

3. See St. Justin Martyr, *La philosophe passe au Christ: l'oeuvre de Justin: Apologie, I et II, Dialogue avec Tryphon*, trans. Adalbert Hamman, ed. Adalbert Hamman and François Garnier (Paris: Grasset, 1958), apol., 1.61.
4. See Ceslas Spicq, *L'epître aux Hébreux* (Paris: Gabalda, 1952), 2:150.
5. St. Cyril of Jerusalem, cat. 17, no. 37.
6. St. Cyril of Alexandria, *In Jn.*, PG 73–74:244.
7. See St. Gregory of Nyssa, *In Canticum*, PG 44:1001b.

This fact is already attested to in Acts, where baptism is proposed only at the end of a catechesis whose main lines have been preserved for us.[8]

This faith is above all a form of knowledge, and this is why baptism is proceeded by a lengthy instruction concerning the principal mysteries of faith: the Trinity, Christ, His saving action, and His teaching. Moreover, before being baptized, the neophyte professes faith.[9]

It is also a conversion and commitment to live in accord with Jesus' teachings: "If we desire to have a rooted faith, we must also have a pure rule of life, which holds fast to the Spirit. The power of faith undoubtedly depends on Him."[10]

The dilemma

If faith is the effect of baptism, how can it be a preliminary condition for it? However, if it precedes baptism, how can we think that baptism would still be necessary, except as a mere sign of a reality that is independent from it?

The Church found herself faced with an additional difficulty arising from the issue posed by baptism conferred by heretics. As they do not have the true faith, how can heretics baptize? In the end, as we have seen, the Roman tradition prevailed, and the Church recognized (and still recognizes) the validity of this kind of baptism.[11] (For the theory holding that faith would not precede the act of baptism but instead would follow upon it, see the paradoxical expressions found in the works of Oscar Cullmann concerning this matter.)[12]

The Search for a Theological Solution

In the Fathers

{786} The Fathers did not pose this problem so directly. However, they could not avoid encountering it.

---

8. See Acts 2:41; 8:12 and 33–37; 16:14–15 and 32–33; Heb 10:22. Also, see Spicq, *L'epître aux Hébreux*, 2:217.

9. See St. Basil of Caesarea, *Sur le Saint-Esprit*, trans. Benoît Pruche, SC 17bis (Paris: Cerf, 1968), chs. 10 and 12.

10. St. John Chrysostom, *De Verbis Apostoli*, PG 51:280 (2.1.9).

11. See §779 above.

12. See §772, no. 9 above.

They ordinarily presented the necessity of faith in the context of some form of exhortation. They addressed themselves to catechumens and insisted on the dispositions that they must bring and develop in themselves, the first of which is faith. Or they address themselves to Christians and exhort them to remain committed to the faith that they have professed. In this context, they emphasize that faith depends on them:

> One is not permitted to receive baptism many times (…). If you were poorly prepared, this matter is without remedy, for there is only one Lord, only one faith, and only one baptism (…). Therefore, have faith within you, as well as a firm hope. Prepare your heart to receive the doctrine so that you may participate in the holy mysteries.[12bis]
>
> We will speak about catechesis not so that you may merely hear what we say but so that you may ratify through faith what you hear (…). Therefore, purify the vessel of your soul so that you may receive a more abundant grace. Certainly, the remission of sins is given equally to all. However, participation in the Holy Spirit is conceded in proportion to faith. If you barely strive, you will not receive; however, if you strive vigorously, your recompense will be great.[13]

And Cyril of Jerusalem goes so far as to say: "Therefore, have that faith which comes from yourself and elevate yourself toward Christ so that you may receive from Him this other faith that acts beyond human powers."[14]

It would be anachronistic of us to interpret this as expressing a kind of anticipated form of "semi-Pelagianism." It is perfectly true and a purely biblical, as well as traditional, doctrine that faith (and conversion) are acts of free will on which the bestowal of grace depends: "If you believe (…) everything is possible for him who believes."[15] However, this very activity of faith is also a gift from God for which one must give thanks. The Fathers neither were unaware of this nor did they disregard it:

> Jesus says, "Do you wish to be healed?" O immense power of the Doctor who suspends His aid upon the will alone! Indeed, since salvation comes

---

12bis. St. Cyril of Jerusalem, *Procatecheses*, PG 33.4:345a and 361a.
13. St. Cyril of Jerusalem, *Catecheses*, cat. 1, no. 5 (PG 33:376a and 377a).
14. Ibid., cat. 2.
15. Mk 9:23.

from faith, he asks, "Do you wish for it?" He does this so that this will may bring forth its act (…). However, Jesus also gives this very willing. He approves of the faith and gratuitously bestows the gift.[16]

Likewise, St. John Chrysostom says that faith is the fruit of our merits and the gift of the Spirit.[17]

These two antinomic affirmations can be held in faith and taught in preaching without looking into how they are reconciled. Pelagianism begins when, on the pretense of reconciling them, one implies the exclusion of the second by the first.

However, even in the Fathers, we can find the beginning of a solution concerning the relations between faith and baptism. It consists in distinguishing two "faiths" or, rather, two states of faith. The first is imperfect and insufficient for salvation. It is the disposition required for baptism and depends on the human will. The other is perfect, opening out upon the contemplation of the mysteries and is an effect of baptism, the fruit of illumination:

> Therefore, prepare your soul so that you may become a child of God, an heir of God, and a coheir with Christ. If you prepare yourself thus, you will receive. If you come forward on the basis of faith, you will be rendered faithful, provided that you have freely stripped yourself of the old man.[18]

Faith and baptism, these two means of salvation, are both of the same nature and are indivisible. Faith receives its perfection from baptism, and baptism is founded on faith. Both receive their fullness from the Divine Names themselves. The profession of faith for salvation comes first. Baptism then comes in order to seal our assent.[19]

Proposed solution (following Aquinas)

Proposed solution for the general question concerning the relations between grace and freedom in conversion

{787} The theologian must seek to overcome a merely dialectic opposition of these two truths. Once the question concerning reconciliation has been raised, it no longer can be avoided.

Thus, we must say that there is a preparation for grace, consisting

---

16. St. Cyril of Jerusalem, *Hom. In Paralyticum*, PG 33:365c and 366c.
17. St. John Chrysostom, *De Verbis Apostoli*, PG 51:276 (1.9).
18. See Cyril of Jerusalem, *Hom. In Paralyticum*, PG:445a (3.15).
19. Basil of Caesarea, *Sur le Saint-Espirit* [*On the Holy Spirit*], ch. 12.

in a series of free acts, an approach toward Christ. However, these acts of freedom are themselves effects of grace. The Holy Spirit is the one who awakens the soul and gradually leads it to conversion through acts of freedom.[20]

If I consider these acts as coming from free choice and as depending upon it, discontinuity exists between them and the act of conversion itself, which is brought about under the action of the grace of the remission of sins and of divinization. From this perspective, the remission of sins is a pure grace.

If I consider these acts as proceeding from the Holy Spirit's action on man's freedom, the grace of the remission of sins is their crowning. It is what is already germinally and intentionally present in the first graces that arouse the sinner and lead him to conversion. Thus, the latter grace exists in continuity with the process of man's return to God.

Therefore, man can have dispositions to grace. However, these dispositions are themselves the work of grace itself in him.

This must be understood within the general perspectives of the Redemption. The true "first grace" for every man (which simultaneously is grace in its perfection) is redemptive grace, the grace of the man Jesus, having become (through His sacrificial death and resurrection) the grace of all men, offered to each person. All the graces bestowed upon a given person, from the very first one that rouses the sinner's spirit up to the final grace that definitively fixes in the love of God him who was led to the summits of holiness, are nothing more than a personalization of this grace given to humanity as a whole, though which is addressed to each person.

Proposed solution for the specific problem of the relations between faith and baptism

{788} *First*, the act of asking for baptism and of submitting oneself to it is an act of faith. It is a bodily action, though one that expresses and concretizes the interior action of faith by which man, by being converted, "comes to Christ." Therefore, it expresses the interior dispositions without which it would be inconceivable to say that

---

20. Nicolas, *Les profondeurs de la grâce*, 452–73.

salvation would be brought about. In this way, we eliminate Luther's violent objection against the sacrament's efficacy *ex opere operato*: "If the sacrament gives me grace because I receive it, I thus receive grace on account of my own work, not on account of faith. I do not perceive the promise in the sacrament but only perceive the sign instituted and prescribed by God."[21]

In reality, the sacrament indeed gives me grace through its own, proper power. However, it does so on the condition that I am open to grace, and this openness (i.e., my internal disposition) is expressed and concretized in the process undertaken by the person who comes to the sacrament. Yes, I am well aware that the sacrament is the sign of God's promise; however, this promise would be empty if I was not aware of it (whether because I do not accept it or because I rejected what it requires). My reception of the sacrament is a sign of the awareness that I have of the promise, as well as a sign of my acceptance of it.

Second, the grace of the remission of sins causes, in advance, the dispositions that are required in the subject (and, therefore, faith). It is baptismal grace itself. Thus, there is an anticipation of baptism's efficacy. On account of the foundational intention of the acts that lead one to conversion and that include a *votum baptismi* (even if it is very implicit), baptism in advance causes the grace of the remission of sins in an initial form consisting, first of all, in the graces that precede conversion and lead to it. Of course, this cannot be a question of an efficient causality exercised by baptism, which itself still lies in the future. Through Christ, God immediately causes these graces, though doing so in view of baptism whose causality in this case is of the moral order.

Here, we can make a distinction. There is the pure case (one that doubtlessly is very rare) when the catechumen comes to baptism without having yet received the grace of the remission of sins and of divinization. It is thus necessary that the acts of faith that led to baptism (in order to ask for it and to prepare oneself for it) were the effect of "elevating graces," making him perform them by means of intermittent acts of faith without conferring the "light of faith" upon

---

21. Cited by Villette, *Foi et sacrement*, 2:92.

him in a habitual manner. In this case, baptism completely fulfills its illuminative role. The doctrine which he "learned," but in which he truly "believed" only intermittently, then becomes his own. He "believes" and "knows." A transformation takes place in the depths of the spirit without him necessarily experiencing a corresponding psychological perception of this change. However, the most frequent case is that when, at any given moment of his progress, the catechumen received the grace of faith, though always in dependence on the baptism toward which he tends (e.g., the case of Cornelius in Acts).[22] Here, we have a case corresponding to the explanation provided by the Greek Fathers: baptism brings a "confirmation" of faith, a "deepening" of it, an enrooting of it, and a seal for it.

Third, this notion of anticipation is necessary in general for resolving the antinomy that is found in all the sacraments. Given that the sacramental action, inasmuch as it is an action of the Spirit of God, is exercised on man's spirit, it is necessarily instantaneous. Inasmuch as it is a bodily action exercised in time upon man, in accord with his bodily dimension, it is necessarily temporal and successive. However, it is only one action, ordered to the production of the divine effect. Therefore, one must admit that this effect is produced instantaneously at some given (divinely-chosen) moment of the performing of the sacramental action, though in such a way that it would be the effect toward which this action tends and which is produced by it. This requires that the effect would always be produced on account of the sacramental action, even when it happens before it comes to its completion. This is why this sacramental activity would not be interrupted upon the reception of such grace but, instead, would still be brought to completion, even after its effect would have thus been produced.

THE PROBLEM OF "FEIGNING"

"Someone is said to feign an action (here, in the reception of baptism) as soon as his will stands in contradiction either with baptism

---

22. See Acts 10:44–48.

itself or with its effect."²³ We have seen that the faith required for baptism was simultaneously "knowledge" of the true doctrine and "conversion" to Christ and the Gospel. Such feigning can take place either in the form of an interior opposition to the true faith or by an interior refusal to be truly converted. Moreover, there can be a manifest interior refusal of the sacrament (e.g., a baptism received as a kind of joke) or an interior refusal that is not manifest in this manner (e.g., constraint).

Feigning through an Absence of True Faith

A lack of true faith in someone who is only a catechumen

{789} Here,²⁴ we must make use of the Augustinian distinction between the sacrament's "truth" and its "fruitfulness." It is clear that he who does not in his heart accept the faith that he externally professes does not receive the sacrament in a fruitful manner. Inasmuch as baptism is also the sign and expression of the catechumen's faith, it here becomes, through the baptized person's fault, a deceptive sign. Moreover, given that man's conversion is the indispensable condition for the remission of sins and given that this conversion includes a movement of faith (because it is by faith that one goes forth toward Christ), refusal to believe presents an obstacle to grace.

Naturally, it is a question of "a refusal to believe," not of ignorance or of involuntary error. He who, at the moment of his baptism, sincerely professes the faith, beyond (and often despite) his own knowledge (which is always limited and perhaps erroneous), adheres to the Church's faith and makes it his own. By contrast, he who refuses to adhere to the faith of the Church even when he externally professes it, is a mere pretender. He does not interiorly draw closer to Christ, for he refuses to enter the Church, which is Christ's body.

Nonetheless, he receives the sacrament, which will not need to be repeated. As we have seen, the notion of "character" enables us to understand the Augustinian distinction. The sacramental rite

---

23. *ST* III, q. 63, a. 9.
24. See St. Augustine, *De baptismo*, PL 29, bk. 7; *ST* III, q. 68, a. 8. [Tr. note: Fr. Nicolas also cites "Bavaud, 1, 625–627," which correlates to the following entry in his bibliography: Georges Bavaud, introduction to St. Augustine, *De baptismo*, OESA 29, 9–46. It is not clear that any other entry would be appropriate.]

produces the *res et sacramentum* in him. That is, it produces the character, which is indelible. His internal resistance only prevents grace (to which the character is ordered, itself giving the character its meaning) from also being conferred to him. The reason for this is the necessary, objective consistency of the sacramental order.[25]

Note well, however, that this is not the case if such feigning pertains to the sacramental rite itself. This can happen through the refusal to really submit oneself to the rite, thus refusing to "receive baptism." Such a refusal can be made manifest by the context (e.g., in the case of a baptism that is given and received as a kind of joke or in the course of a stage play in which the actors in question are role-playing), or it can be completely concealed (though it can be afterward suspected or confessed, for example, in the case of a baptism received under constraint, under threat, or for material advantages accruing from it). In this case, what is refused is baptism itself. It is not clear how someone could be baptized against his will. This would make baptism into a magical ritual. Hence, we must say that in this case, the rite is only a charade. There is no baptism at all, and baptism would need to be conferred if he who acted in this way later came to the Church [through a true conversion].[26] This problem is connected to the question concerning the role played by one's intention, which we discussed above.[27] However, we must here note St. Augustine's hesitations, which show that it is not easy to specify the exact point where the "truth" [or, "validity"] of the sacrament ceases.[28]

Baptism by Churches that do not have the true faith

The controversy in the ancient Church concerning the reiteration of baptism

{790} The* Church's teaching on this point developed only at the cost of hesitations and reversals in the process of its articulation.

---

25. See §§761–62 above.
26. See *ST* III, q. 68, a. 7.
27. See §728 above.
28. See Augustine, loc. cit, ch. 43. [Tr. note: Here, Fr. Nicolas cites "Bavaud, 1, 625–627." See remarks above about this entry.]

* Concerning the controversy over the rebaptism of those converted from heresy in the third and fourth centuries, see Villette, *Foi et sacrement*, 1:105–58. Georges Bavaud, introduction to St. Augustine, *De baptismo*, OESA 29, 30–37. St. Cyprian, *De catholicae Ecclesiae*

In 256, against the African bishops, Pope Stephen affirmed the validity of baptism given even in a sect separated from union with the Church, threatening with excommunication those who continued to rebaptize those who received baptism in these conditions.[29] Nonetheless, the African bishops continued to rebaptize. Reconciliation was brought about at the Synod of Arles in 314. There, a more nuanced decree was issued, admitting the possibility of the existence of baptisms which do in fact need to be repudiated, though recognizing that the criterion of baptismal authenticity was solely the use of the Trinitarian formula: "If it is determined that he has been baptized in (the name of) the Father and the Son and the Holy Spirit, only hands should be imposed on him so that he may receive the Holy Spirit."[30] However, a little later on, the famous nineteenth canon of Nicaea was more restrictive. It requires true faith in the Trinity and for this reason ordered that the disciples of Paul of Samosata were to be rebaptized.[31]

Later, at the First Council of Constantinople, this practice was expanded. It accepted the notion that one can receive various heretics, including Arians, without rebaptizing them, though not without requiring them to recant their heresy, nor without the imposition of hands on them, and also not without anointing them with oil so as to confer the Holy Spirit upon them. The only ones who must be rebaptized are those who come from communities wherein the Trinity is expressly denied or wherein this denial is expressed in the rite of baptism (especially the Anomoeans, who performed only one immersion so as to affirm that only the Father was God).[32]

During the fourth century, the principal Fathers are much stricter and take up St. Cyprian's position while pushing it to its limits (in

---

unitate, trans. Pierre de Labriolle (Paris: Cerf, 1942), and *Epistolae* (*Correspondance*), trans. Louis Bayard (Paris: Société d'édition "Les Belles lettres" / Budé, 1925), letters 73 and 75 (letter of Firmilian to St. Cyprian). [Tr. note: Fr. Nicolas also includes a reference to a fourth entry not included in the bibliography. It refers to "435–461 (*Sententia*[e] *episcoporum* [the opinions of the bishops])".]

29. The letter itself is lost and is known by Firmilian's citations. See St. Cyprian, *Correspondance*, trans. Bayard (Budé, 1925), letter 75. Likewise, see *De rebaptismate* (CSEL 3/3, 69–92), where the position of the Church of Rome is laid out.

30. First Synod of Arles, c. 9, in D.-*Sch.*, no. 123.

31. See First Council of Nicaea, c. 19, in D.-*Sch.*, no. 128.

32. See First Council of Constantinople, c. 7.

particular Sts. Basil and Athanasius among the Eastern Fathers and St. Jerome among the Latin Fathers).³³ With Optatus of Milevis, we find ourselves on the way toward a more even-handed solution in Africa. This solution would come to be elaborated by St. Augustine by means of his liberating distinction between the "truth" (or, "existence") of baptism (which later on will be called its "validity") and its "fruitfulness" (*frui*) or "usefulness" (*uti*). (This distinction already was presupposed by Pope Stephen's thought in his controversy with St. Cyprian.) By making this distinction, St. Augustine will thus come to do full justice to St. Cyprian's central intuition (as well as the intuition of the Fathers of the fourth century), namely that because baptism is a sacrament of faith, it cannot fully be what Christ willed it to be if faith is lacking, namely the sacrament by means of which the sinful man is plunged into Christ's death and resurrection in order to receive from them the remission of sins and new life. However, this point was affirmed in this way without sacrificing another essential aspect of baptism, namely the fact that it makes him who receives it visibly belong to Christ. Thus, everywhere that baptism is conferred in accord with Jesus Christ's institution, he on whom it is conferred is really baptized, and baptism exists and persists. St. Augustine stated thus the principle that will become the rule admitted in the Catholic Church:

> (If one were to ask for my opinion in counsel), I would not at all hesitate to say that baptism is had by those who have received it as consecrated by the Gospel's formula, wherever they may be and from whosoever they may have received it, so long as they themselves did not feign their reception and received it with some degree of faith. Despite all this, without charity which alone can unite them to the Catholic Church, this would not serve them in their spiritual salvation ...³⁴

This traditional position was reaffirmed at the Second Vatican Council and provided the foundation for the official recognition of the baptism conferred in all Christian churches when it has been performed in accord with the traditional rite.³⁵

---

33. See Villette, *Foi et sacrement*, 1:137–55.
34. Augustine, *De baptismo*, 571.
35. See "Directory for the execution of what the 2nd Vatican Council promulgated concerning ecumenism," *AAS* 59 (1967): 578–81; *Documentation catholique* 64 (1967): 1077–80.

Theological explanation of the Church's position

{791} The fundamental reason for the Church's position, which was already highlighted by Pope Stephen, is that, through baptism, the minister communicates the Church's faith, not his own. This principle will command the resolution of the problem concerning unworthy ministers.

However, the problem we are faced with here is slightly different. The minister can be unworthy and can even not have faith. Still, he administers the sacrament in accord with the faith of His Church, and the latter is what the sacrament is the sign and expression of. However, what are we to say if the faith of the very Church that baptizes is not the true faith?

From within the ecumenical perspectives opened up by the Second Vatican Council, the resolution to this question can be reached more clearly than once upon a time. The Church that baptizes is still to a certain degree the Church, the one Church of Jesus Christ. To what degree is it such? To the degree that it preserves the true faith and institutions of salvation that come from Christ. Baptism is numbered among these institutions. This baptism is given in accord with this Church's faith, that is, in accord with what it preserves of the true faith and through which it partially remains united to the one Church [*reste une partie de l'unique Eglise*]. In other words, it baptizes in the faith of the Church, even if there are errors and lacunae mixed together with the true faith in its own profession of faith. Thus, there is only one baptism, one faith, and one Church.

The distinction that Optatus of Milevis made between schismatics and heretics with respect to baptism's validity corresponds to a just intuition (indeed, that of Nicaea). However, we must extend it to every confession that still keeps some portion of faith in Christ (which does not exist, in reality, without faith in the Trinity), without considering the personal situation of the founders and the leaders of this confession with regard to salvation. He who culpably rejects a single article of faith loses faith in what regards this particular matter. Moreover, he does not hold the other truths that he maintains "by faith" (i.e., on the authority of God who reveals) but instead holds them merely by a "personal choice." However, in themselves, these are truths of faith that pass into his confession, which are professed at baptism. Through them, such a person's confession remains connected to the true Church.[36]

Feigning through an Interior Refusal to Be Converted

Fruitless baptism

{792} When this refusal pertains to the internal adherence of faith or to the practical consequences of faith (e.g., conversion, new life), baptism is normally "valid" (in other words, "there is a baptism"), though it remains unfruitful, as we said above. The character is caused, not grace.

Reviviscence of baptismal grace

From the moment that one admits that there is a distinction between "true baptism" and "fruitful baptism" (and, consequently, from the moment when one refuses to repeat an unfruitful baptism), one is led to envision the possibility that an initially unfruitful baptism may be later rendered fruitful. In other words, we are here faced with the question of the reviviscence [of sacramental grace].

.Already, Pope Stephen spoke of an imposition of hands as a sign of penance. At the Synod of Arles, the point was expressed with greater specificity: an imposition of hands in order to receive the Holy Spirit. Unfruitful baptism is one in which the Holy Spirit is not received.

The reviviscence of the sacrament is theologically explained by the existence of the character and the fact that it is ordered to grace.

---

36. On the thought of Optatus, see Villette, *Foi et sacrement*, 1:155–58. [Tr. note: Here, Fr. Nicolas also cites "Bavaud, 1, 598–599." See remarks above about this entry.] N.B. It is important that one distinguish faith-lancunae in the Christian confession in which baptism is administered from those that may exist the minister who confers it. The minister acts as a representative of the Church [sic] (of his Church [sic]) and in its name. Were we to suppose that he does not have faith, this cannot in any way influence the validity of the baptism that he confers. The problem that we are discussing (and which was ruled on in a decisive manner by the recent declaration of the "Pontifical Council for Promoting Christian Unity," cited in note 00 above) is the problem concerning the faith professed by the community in whose name the baptism is given and into which baptism makes the neophyte enter. Even if this faith is incomplete, such a baptism is valid because by the mediation of this Christian confession, the Church of Jesus Christ, the one Church, is the one who baptizes.

This ordering, which is frustrated by an evil will, is fulfilled when the will comes to be converted.

From the perspective of the sacraments' efficacy, one cannot say that a baptism that was conferred in the past now becomes efficacious, except in the sense that the ultimate effect that it was ordered to produce is now produced. However, it is produced by Christ, immediately or by the intermediary of the sacrament of penance, though on the basis of the sacramental rite that was performed in the past.[37] We are here faced with the reverse case of the process of anticipatory efficacy which we spoke of earlier.

INFANT BAPTISM

The practice of baptism of infants born of Christian parents, a practice that is traditional in the Catholic Church and was fully accepted by the reformers,[38] raised lively controversies in Protestant Churches following Karl Barth's vigorous stance against this practice in 1943.[39]

There are three questions involved here: the traditional foundation of the practice, the theological interpretation of it, and pastoral considerations regarding it. The third question will be treated here only from the perspective of the principles that are involved.

The Traditional Foundation of This Practice

{793} Two great Protestant exegetes, Joachim Jeremias[40] and Oscar Cullmann,[41] have marshalled excellent arguments in defense of the

---

37. See *ST* III, q. 69, a. 10.
38. See Paul Althaus, "Martin Luther über die Kindertaufe," *Theologische Literaturzeitung* (1948): 705–14. Jean-Daniel Benoît, "Calvin et le baptême des enfants," *Revue d'Histoire et de Philosophie Religieuses* (1937): 457–73. Villette, *Foi et sacrement*, 2:83–203. Albrecht Wagner, "Reformatorum saeculi XVII de necessitate baptismi doctrina," *Divus Thomas* (Piacenza) (1942): 5–34.
39. See Karl Barth, "La doctrine ecclésiastique du baptême," *Foi et Vie* 47 (1949): 1–50. On the controversy itself, see André Benoît, "Le problème du pédobaptisme," *Revue d'Histoire et de Philosophie Religieuses* (1948–49): 132–41. M. Hurley, "Que peuvent apprendre les catholiques de la controverse sur le baptême des enfants?" *Concilium* 24 (1967): 21–28. James William McClendon, "Pourquoi les baptistes ne donnent-ils pas le baptême aux enfants," *Concilium* 24 (1967): 13–20. Jean-Nicolas Walty, "Controverses au sujet du baptême des enfants," *Revue des sciences philosophiques et théologiques* 34 (1952): 52–70.
40. See Jeremias, *Le baptême des enfants*.
41. See Cullmann, *Le baptême des enfants*.

Baptism and Faith 291

apostolic origins of infant baptism. For the opposed position, see the work of Franz Leenhardt.[42] On the traditional character of the practice of infant baptism, see the texts gathered in the note below.*

What is certain is that the practice is formally attested to from the beginning of the third century in Tertullian in the West[43] and in Origen in the East, whose testimony is of great weight because he presents this as being a universal practice coming from the apostles, having personally visited numerous churches, including the Church in Rome, and was born in Egypt and lived there, as well as in Caesarea (Palestine) when he wrote the works wherein he provides this testimony.

Theological Interpretation

How can baptism be given to a child who is capable neither of faith nor of forming an intention?

{794} After[44] first having appealed to the faith of one's parents to explain the baptism of children, St. Augustine was led to reduce the role of that faith to the public profession of faith (the latter being able to suffice, even in the absence of internal faith). He did this in order to highlight the role of the Church. According to him, children are baptized into the Church's faith.[45]

Comparing baptismal regeneration to natural birth, St. Thomas[46] explains the role of the Church as follows:

... Just as children that are still in their mother's womb cannot themselves take their nourishment but, instead, are fed by the nourishment that their

---

42. See Franz Leenhardt, *Le baptême chrétien, son origine, sa signification* (Neuchâtel: Delachaux et Niestlé, 1946).

* Jean-Charles Didier, *Faut-il baptiser les enfants? La réponse de la Tradition, Textes présentés par Jean-Charles Didier* (Paris: Cerf, 1967). St. Hippolytus of Rome, *La tradition apostolique*, ed. and trans. Bernard Botte, SC 11bis (Paris: Éditions du Cerf, 1968), ch. 21. Cyprian, *Epistolae (Correspondance)*, trans. Louis Bayard (Paris: Société d'édition "Les Belles lettres" / Budé, 1925), letter 64.

43. See Tertullian, *Traité du baptême*, ch. 18.

44. For the whole of section B, see Jean Jacques von Allmen, *Pastorale du baptême* (Fribourg: Éditions Universitaires, 1978). Maurice Corvez, "Le baptême des enfants," *Nova et Vetera* (1972): 138–40. Joseph Moingt, "L'initiation chrétienne des jeunes," *Études* 336 (1972): 437–54. Nicolas, *Les profondeurs de la grâce*, 486–90.

45. See Villette, *Foi et sacrement*, 1:312–21.

46. See *ST* III, q. 68, a. 9.

mother takes, so too children that do not yet have the use of reason, who are, as it were, placed in the maternal womb of the Church, receive salvation by means of acts that belong to the Church and not by their own, proper acts.[47]

"A metaphor is not a reason." How are we to explain the claim that the faith that is needed for baptism (indeed, the faith which is expressed through baptism) could be a faith "by proxy"?

In the end, we must once again make recourse to the initial inclusion of all men in Christ and in redemptive grace. On account of the redemption brought about by Christ, the human person, born into sin, is nonetheless fundamentally ordered to Christ, to whom he by rights belongs. This does not suffice for making one participate in redemption in a personal manner and therefore does not suffice for making one receive the remission of sins and the grace of adoption. However, it suffices so that, in relation to the sacramental action of baptism, he may exist in a state of voluntary acceptance (by the absence of a reluctant will), and this enables this action to be exercised upon him. In a first stage (according to an order of nature, not temporally), by this action he receives the character, which makes him a member of the Church and enables him to participate in the "Church's faith" and to make it his own.

To understand this better, one must consider how this case differs from that of a person who is capable of awareness and of willing. At this stage of his development, the person is indeed not oriented through his "fundamental willing," which no longer exists in a pure state but, instead, is oriented by the concrete form that he has deliberately given to this fundamental willing by his own acts of will. If this activity has oriented him toward Christ, he is personally in a state that is receptive to baptism. He participates in the Church's faith (and is already justified *in voto baptismi*).[48] However if, on the contrary, there is a refusal of Christ (even in a very implicit manner), he cannot participate in the Church's faith as one cannot believe without "willing to believe." In the two cases, he cannot truly receive baptism without willing to receive it and without accepting it

---

47. See ibid., ad 1.
48. See §§699 and 788 above.

freely. If he interiorly refused baptism, his "undertaking" would not be a human act, as we have seen.

However, how are we to resolve St. Augustine's hesitation: is the infant baptized into his parents' faith or into the Church's faith? If one says that the first is true, it seems that, in order to be fruitful, the child's baptism depends on the quality of the parents' faith (which can be "feigned" in the sense specified above).[49] However, does not the second risk justifying baptism given by the Church to a child without his parents' consent, in the name of her responsibility for the salvation of this child, whom she bears, according to St. Thomas's expression, *in utero suo*, in her womb?

We must respond by making a distinction. The act of presenting the child for baptism falls to the responsibility of the parents inasmuch as they are parents, for it is their duty to decide on behalf of the child, and the act of approaching baptism is a decision of a man who is not yet a member of the Church. It is an act performed in relation to the Church but in no way an act by the Church. However, in the baptismal rite itself, the parents (and with them, the community of whom they are part) testify to the Church's faith, in which they normally partake, though it is possible that they not partake in it. They act inasmuch as they are members of the Church, inasmuch as they represent this Church into which they request that the infant may be admitted (even if, in an extreme case, they are not themselves members of the Church, for in that case, it is in the name of the Church that they speak).

Why baptize infants?

{795} The practice of baptizing infants was not born of the doctrine of original sin. On the contrary, it greatly served in the further elaboration of this doctrine.

Before every attempt to interpret this difficult and disconcerting doctrine, and even before any further elaboration, Christian consciousness is faced with a fundamental certitude: a man who is "astray" (as regards his relations with God) is saved by Christ and only by Christ. On the other hand, from the beginning of the

---

49. See §789 above.

Church's history, baptism is presented as being the necessary means for receiving this salvation brought about by Jesus Christ.

Only gradually did there emerge a doctrine concerning the salvation of those who cannot ask for and receive baptism precisely because they have not heard the preaching of the Gospel, a situation that is not held against them as a fault. This development did not lead to a relativizing of the necessity for baptism but, rather, made one take into account the fact that baptism was able to act "by anticipation," doing so, certainly, by an act of God's mercy, though as conditioned by the *votum baptismi* on man's part. Therefore, it is performed through a voluntary and personal act.[50]

Does the act of baptizing an infant assure eternal salvation to him, meaning that he would not have had this if he were to die before being able to perform the personal act of conversion? We will see below that further thought must be given to this matter. However, in any case, this cannot be a decisive reason, nor the first, for baptism is given in view of life, not death. It is given in view of the divinized life accorded to us. Granted, this life will be fully lived only after our bodily death. However, it can and must be lived here-below, and just as parents do not educate their child by thinking about this end but instead do so by thinking about the child's future life (even though they know that this child will die one day), so too they have their child baptized so that he may receive the gift of God in his earthly existence.

That is the first and essential reason why Christian parents must have their child baptized. The gift of God (i.e., divinization) which we considered above, is immediately offered to each and every person, including to the infant, who is already able to receive it, even though he has not yet reached his earthly human perfection: "For God does not discriminate on the basis of age, any more than as regards the distinction of persons. Instead, in the distribution of heavenly grace, He is a father who equally parcels out His gifts to all persons."[51] It falls to (Christian) parents to procure this good for the child (of which the child is immediately capable) by having him baptized.

---

50. See §788 above.
51. See Cyprian, *Correspondance*, letter 64, at 2:215.

However, how can the Divine Life really be given to him and how can he be "a living being who lives by the Divine Life," even though he is not able to elicit any spiritual act, whereas this life is wholly spiritual?

We have seen that while this life, which is supernatural and is supernaturally given, like every form of life, essentially consists in the activities in relation to which it is defined, so too, like every form of life, it also includes in the living being a stable principle for these activities. For natural activities, this principle is the being's nature and faculties. For supernatural activities, this principle is the ensemble of "infused *habitus*" which are not merely superimposed upon nature and upon the faculties but, rather, penetrate them, modifying them in their depths, empowering them to produce these vital activities, which are supernatural from the perspective of the objects that they attain, while nonetheless coming forth from the depths of the nature that has been thus modified, enriched, enhanced, and supernaturalized. Sanctifying grace is the *habitus* that makes the person, constituted by his nature, into a living being that thus lives by this divinized life. The infused virtues are the *habitus* that place the faculties in a position to produce supernatural activities.[52]

In order to elicit these acts, the person needs the obstacles that he finds in himself, paralyzing or hindering the exercise of the infused virtues to be removed. During his infancy, these obstacles are the insufficient development of his sense and bodily faculties. Through the infused *habitus* [pl.] the child is a living being who lives by the divinized life before being able to perform the acts of this life. However, this is true also for natural spiritual acts (i.e., intellectual and volitional acts). The child is a human person lacking the ability to elicit any act of understanding, spiritual love, or freedom.

Let us add that, in what pertains to sin (and leaving aside for the moment the particular problem of children who have died without baptism), to have been baptized (and instructed in accord with one's baptism) is a favorable conditioning for distancing oneself from sin by adhering to Christ at the moment when the use of freedom will begin. If one once again admits—and to believe in Christ

---

52. See §777 above.

implies faith in this—that Christ is the only way of "salvation" for man (the only way for a true and authentic fulfillment of his human existence), one will not hold that this conditioning is a kind of limitation but, instead, a safeguard for the child's freedom.

Pastoral Considerations

Calling the generalized practice of childhood baptism into question

{796} Today, from various quarters (as much among Catholics as among Protestants), voices are raised to denounce the pastoral disadvantages that are born of an overly generalized practice of infant baptism and to submit this practice to a critical examination.[53] Jean Jacques von Allmen has examined this problem in a methodical and profound manner.[54] The arguments that he advances, generally advocating a significant restriction of the reception of baptism by infants, as well as the solutions that he recommends, meet the preoccupations of many priests and laymen in the Catholic Church. They are too serious not to be taken into consideration and also disputed (as well as at least partially received).

The legitimacy of infant baptism

Above all, by means of remarkably well chosen and presented arguments, he establishes the legitimacy of infant baptism, as well as its apostolic origin. However, in his opinion, this does not justify the generalized practice of infant baptism that was introduced into the Church from the fifth century onward, a practice which the reformers accepted.

Disadvantages of generalized infant baptism

He advances the following arguments against this kind of generalized baptismal practice:

1. Generalized infant baptism generalizes the exceptional case, which tends to distort the theology of baptism. First and foremost,

---

53. See Daniel Boureau, *L'avenir du baptême* (Lyon: Editions du Chalet, 1970). Pierre-André Liégé, "Le baptême des enfants," in "Débat pastoral et liturgique," *La Maison-Dieu* 107 (1971): 7–28. Note the bibliography in this latter text.

54. See von Allmen's *Pastorale du baptême* cited above.

baptism is addressed to adults and must be understood in function of adult baptism.

2. It attenuates the awareness that the Church ought to have of herself as an eschatological, messianic people. Given that most of her members are of the "world," the Church allows herself to be absorbed by the world. Thus, the radical conversion required by baptism comes to be practically neglected and forgotten.

3. It overwhelms ministers with crushing responsibilities which they cannot accommodate: to form a considerable number of people in the Christian faith in unfavorable and hostile sociological and religious conditions.

4. It perpetuates divisions, making one consider the multiplicity of Christian confessions as being an accepted fact.

5. It produces a devaluation of baptism and also a devaluation of the Church, which becomes an object mocked by the contradiction between the doctrine that she professes and the way most Christians live with her approval (at least her tacit approval).

6. It is bad for the baptized persons themselves. On the one hand, when they convert, they are deprived of the process prepared by God for this, namely, baptism. Even without conversion, he who was baptized without having expressly willed it and without being conscious of it is deprived of the possibility a freely engaged act—at least of that which is identified in the Bible. Moreover, he has taken on grave obligations without having willed them and without having been aware of them. (This is particularly stressed for the Catholic Church on account of the requirements of her morality, which require extremely onerous forms of conduct by the baptized person, for example, her rejection of contraception, as well as of abortion, and one could add to this list the complete indissolubility of marriage as well.)

7. Finally, this leads the Church to "look the other way," through a kind of "fraud," accepting the claim that parents will provide a Christian education to their children even though she knows quite well in a host of cases they are not capable of this and that they do not truly intend to fulfill their duty.

Solutions envisioned

He does not believe that baptism should be refused for a child whose parents ask for it if one has a reasonable assurance that they will furnish a Christian education for their children.

However, one should not push them to make this request (even in the case of the aforementioned parents). One should act prudently, aiming to return baptism to the age when the child will be able to ask for it himself.

One should impose this solution in all the cases wherein one cannot have the aforementioned assurance. (He even anticipates specific requirements.)

In these two cases, he proposes, in place of baptism, a right of solemn presentation of the Child to the Church, conceived along the lines of an inscription in the catechumenate. In this way, one would reestablish the normal order of Christian initiation: the proclamation of the Gospel, the acceptance of thereof, conversion, baptism, and the Eucharist.*

What must one think about this?

{797} At the foundation of this conception, there is the grave problem concerning the opposition between a "broad [*multitudinaire*] Church" and a "confessing Church." Let us note well that this problem cannot have a simple solution precisely because it is inscribed in the very nature of Christian preaching. On the one hand, the Gospel must be announced to all and, indeed, is for all. On the other hand, it requires a radical change of life on the part of those who receive it.

---

* N.B. von Allmen requires that if a child is baptized, this baptism would be a complete baptism, without restriction. (He takes this position against the idea holding that confirmation is the fulfillment of baptism when the latter is received in childhood, an idea that is widespread among Protestants and one that he wrongly thinks is the Catholic conception as well.) On this point, we must say that he is completely right. However, it is more questionable to say that the fact that this infant baptism is complete necessarily implies that the child must be admitted to the Eucharist. The expression that he employs to translate the practice of not admitting infants to the Eucharist, "excommunication on account of age" is bizarre and in no way is necessary. Similarly, to not allow the child to participate in the whole Eucharistic ceremony is not the same thing as excommunicating that child.

[Tr. note: See the translator's introduction regarding certain matters of concern regarding the Byzantine East.]

This change of life separates them and tends to make them into a "small flock."

Historically, during the first centuries of the Church's life, the "pragmatic" solution was the institution of the monastic life, which was then prolonged by multiple forms of religious life. However, here too, the multitude has played its role in weighing things down, bringing a lukewarm element to bear on the Christian life as well.

Biblically speaking, can we not draw a comparison with the relationship between the "people of Israel" and the "small remnant"? The "small remnant" is that which concentrates in itself the faith and hope of Israel. However, the people are not rejected. On the contrary, the people are pressed to follow the example of the "small remnant." Did the prophets have the illusion that the multitude would follow?

Despite its prestige, the solution of the "small flock" has grave drawbacks from the very perspective of the truth of the Gospel.

The Church is made up of sinful members, and a great number of them are quite distant from her, not only in practice but even in intending to enact the requirements of the Gospel. The Gospel speaks to us about the mixed state of the Church in this era—for example, in the images of good and bad fish and of darnel mixed with wheat. At the end of time, the bad fish will be cast aside, and the wicked grass will be burned up. However, it is in no way precluded that, through God's grace, the wicked grass may become good wheat. Indeed, this may happen by means of the Church's very own mediation, for she is the dwelling-place of grace. Those who are part of her, even in a merely *de facto manner* and not in heart, are close to the sources of grace. Another reflection that is immediately suggested by the parables in question is that men are not empowered to perform this discernment, nor above all to translate this discernment into an activity whereby they would determine who should be excluded.

"He who wishes to prove too much proves nothing." One will respond: therefore, do you want to give baptism to everyone? To all the children whose parents request it? Obviously not. One should accept the suggestions made by von Allmen for discerning the meaning of this request. Either the adult (or the parents on behalf of their children) must truly ask for baptism, with everything that it implies. However, how is one to judge concerning the sincerity of their request? Likewise, how is one to judge concerning their ability to keep their commitment?

The idea that, in a case of doubt, baptism should be replaced by a solemn inscription in the catechumenate is a very seductive hypothesis. However, it does not seem that it truly provides a remedy for the difficulties at hand. It would have the clearer benefit of not purely and simply turning away the parents who ask that their child be baptized. Otherwise, one of two things is possible. On the one hand, one would have good reasons for thinking that the parents will keep the promise to make the child follow the catechumenate. In this case, why should one refuse to give baptism, given that it is indeed legitimate to baptize a child? On the other hand, one would not have confidence in the child's parents, and in that case, the ceremony is once more meaningless, a "fraudulent" action.

It seems that an essential element is not sufficiently taken into account from von Allmen's perspective, namely, the grace of divinization that the child receives at baptism, as well as the grace of belonging to the Church. If the parents (even in a barely conscious manner) wish to give this to their child, it does not seem just to refuse it to them.

Is this to freight the child, in advance and without his consent, with obligations which will be an intolerable weight for him if he refuses them? In reality, this problem exists for all missionary activity. To believe in Christ is a fundamental obligation, and the obligations that are imposed by membership in Christ's Church are only an unfolding of this fundamental obligation. This primordial and universally encompassing obligation can concern only those who have been evangelized. Therefore, would one need to refrain from evangelizing them in order to leave them in their good faith? The obligation to believe in Jesus Christ and to follow Him is identical with the obligation that one has to let oneself be saved by God. To knowingly refuse this obligation, even if one has not voluntarily contracted it, is to be lost. The Church is responsible for the salvation of all men. She cannot conceal the saving truth from a great number of people out of fear that, being too heavy to bear, it would be refused or rejected by many. However, does this mean that she ought to give baptism, along with the commitments that it includes, to all the children who are presented to her?

Must all children of Christian parents be indiscriminately baptized?
{798} First of all, it is clear (and the Church's discipline on this point is firmly established) that one can baptize only those children whose parents (or those who stand in their place) present them to be baptized. The reason that St. Thomas gives for this is

> However, if they do not yet have the use of free will, in accord with the natural law, they are under the guardianship of their parents for as long as they cannot be responsible for themselves. Therefore, it would be contrary to natural justice if these children were baptized against the will of the parents just as much as would be the case for someone who would be baptized against his will when he had the use of reason.[55]

This explanation perfectly reflects, in different terms, the profound sentiment of all parents in this regard.

One must go even further than St. Thomas, who recognized that children have the right to request baptism as soon as they have the use of free will, as well as the Church's right to grant this to them, even "against their parents' will." We know better today that the dilemma, "They have or do not have the use of reason," is less clear-cut in reality. Free will, when it appears in the child, is still too conditioned for one to be able to think that they "have self-mastery" prior to a lengthy period of formation and development. If it is impossible for one to exactly determine the moment when the child sufficiently has self-mastery, it seems wise to respect the customs and laws that rule the autonomy of the child's civil life.

However, the pastoral problem is as follows. Many "Christian" parents present their child to be baptized for reasons that are quite different than concern to make that child partake in redemption and become a member of the Church, the body of Christ. Continuing the reasoning and analogy offered by St. Thomas, can one (indeed,

---

55. *ST* III, q. 68, a. 10.

ought not one) examine the reasons why baptism is requested for the child, just as one examines (and since the beginning this has been the case) the reasons why an adult desires baptism?

It seems that the touchstone needs to be the sincere resolution of the parents to educate the child when he later comes of age, for they are pledging that they will do so. Moreover, it is not precluded that other criteria might be involved.

Another question is that concerning baptisms given by missionaries to children in the danger of death. There was a time when this was considered an important missionary activity. Quite clearly, one must not make this concern for the salvation of particular individuals prevail over the goal of missionary activity, namely, the foundation of the Church [in that place]. However, no more is it the case that one should ban it, forgetting that, if one wishes to establish the Church where she does not yet exist and if one wishes to strengthen her and expand her numbers, this is indeed so that, through her, individuals may receive the revelation of Jesus Christ and be saved.

However, this particular question depends on what we must say concerning the fate of children who die without baptism.

8

The Necessity of Baptism

Is baptism necessary for salvation? On the one hand, we have Scripture's affirmations, as well as the universal practice of the Church from her beginning. On the other hand, is it not contrary to Christian freedom to connect man's salvation and righteousness to an external ritual? "For in Christ Jesus neither circumcision nor uncircumcision is of any avail, but faith working through love."[1]

Moreover, this necessity runs into obvious impossibilities for a host of adults and for the immense host of children who have died without baptism.

THE LAW OF BAPTISM

We have already noted that even though we may be tempted to contrast salvation by faith with salvation by baptism, such an opposition cannot be found in the texts of the New Testament, especially those of St. Paul.[2] We also noted that this connection established by the Church from her beginning and taught by her as being something self-evident cannot be sufficiently explained without there having been an express command coming from Jesus Himself (i.e., the command reported to us in Mt 28:20, Mk 16:16, and Jn 3:5).

---

1. See Gal 5:6 (RSV).
2. See §768.

The Command to Baptize and Its Meaning

The scriptural bases for the command to baptize

{799} The fact that, from her beginnings, the primitive Church practiced baptism as a self-evident aspect of her activity, holding that it is something required (although it could seem that the gift of the Spirit was not connected to baptism) can be understood only by holding that this came about in obedience to Jesus's command. If it is said that this command appears only on the lips of the risen Christ, one must respond that this is, on the contrary, a point of great importance, for the Spirit was "sent forth" (*entbunden*) only after the Ascension and had to fill, lead, and establish the orphaned community only after Jesus's departure.[3]

This command is reported to us by Matthew 28:18–20 and Mark 16:15–16. Even if the historical and literary authenticity of these texts is debated, they at least express, if not the very words pronounced by Jesus, at least

> the certitude given to the Church by the risen Christ that the practice of baptism was in conformity with God's redemptive plan, manifested and realized by Christ Jesus as well as actualized and applied by the Holy Spirit who is given to the believer ... The practice (of the primitive Church) as well as the words (reported by Matthew and Mark) have a common source and truth, the will of God revealed in Jesus Christ, understood and applied by the Church.[4]

Moreover, there is also John 3:5, which we examined earlier. If water is not mentioned as part of the primitive Johannine catechesis, it had to have been added by the final editor of the text, thus forming part of the fourth Gospel and not something added later on after this definitive redaction (indeed, all the manuscripts contain it).[5] (The problem here is the fact that it is unlikely that the very words of Jesus reported there would have contained, here at the beginning of His mission, such mention of the law of baptism, which had not yet been promulgated.)

---

3. Schnackenburg, "Taufe," cols. 1087–88.
4. Leenhardt, *Le baptême chrétien*, 43. See Villette, *Foi et sacrement*, 1:19–25.
5. See de La Potterie, "Naître de l'eau et naître de l'Espirit."

The meaning of the command to baptize

{800} The command to baptize is stated in the more general context of the institution of the sacraments, which itself can be understood in terms of the salvific will of the Father and of Christ, as well as in terms of salvation history such as it has been willed by God.

We do not need to repeat our discussion of the fact that God could have saved man in some other way than by Christ and through the bloody redemption offered by Him. Indeed, Christ is the sole and universal Savior, and He saved man by His death followed by His resurrection. There is no salvation for man in general, and for each man in particular, except by one's personal participation in the events of salvation.

Given that the Divine Will is infinitely wise and also immutable, even though this "order of things" completely depends on a free divine choice, it has the consistency, power, and necessity of a "natural order," that is, an order founded on being.*

The same must be said about the sacramental order. Certainly, it corresponds to one of human nature's needs, namely, the need to gain access to the spiritual order by means of symbols and signs, especially the need to concretize one's wholly interior spiritual undertaking in bodily actions. It corresponds to the Incarnation, the manifestation of God in the flesh. [It likewise corresponds to the human need for] society and communion. All of this gives the institution of the sacramental order its meaning, which theology must clarify. It is good and necessary for faith to have reason make clear the profound wisdom of the divine institution (to the degree that this can be expressed). Thus, it becomes clear that this free divine choice, on which salvation history depends, as well as the established order of the means of salvation, are not arbitrary. If they were, faith would be rendered difficult and nearly impossible. However, all these reasons would be insufficient for proving *a priori* the necessity of this order

---

* N.B. The word "order" is used in our context in two different senses that must not be confused. When I speak of the "command [*ordre*] to baptize," it is a question of a command. When I speak of the "order of things" or of the "sacramental order," etc., it is a question of an *ordo*, that is, of a number of termini connected to each other through fixed relations.

of things, and it remains the case that God could have acted in a different way.

Thus, the entire consistency and necessity of the sacramental order are founded on Christ's will, which is expressed in words and in writings, though above all as put into action and obeyed by the apostolic Church.

This is true as well for the order (the command) to baptize. It is what provides the foundation for the necessity of baptism for salvation and not vice-versa. However, one cannot hold that it is only a positive law that would be submitted to interpretations and dispensations, for the order (*ordo*) that it founds is a perfectly objective and stable order. Indeed, we have seen that the sacramental order could not exist in any other way than as being stable and infallibly guaranteed by the word of God. Without this "objective certitude," it would vanish.[6]

Salvation Prior to the Institution of Baptism

Nonetheless, it is true that baptism is a historical reality. The order that it founds is as objective and necessary as the natural order. However, it completely depends on a historically situated divine decision. Because of the divine immutability and because the current phase of salvation history is the last one (before the Parousia), we are assured that this decision is immutable.

Temporal variation in the means of salvation

{801} According[7] to St. Thomas, who in this follows St. Augustine, the objective fixed point of salvation history is Christ and His redemptive work, and its subjective fixed point is faith in Christ. The "sacraments" in general are signs of Christ's work and are *protestationes fidei* (i.e., public expressions of faith). Changes in the sacraments through the course of salvation history can be explained by man's different existential situations in relation to Christ the Savior in history. Thus, there are three great eras (and therefore three dif-

---

6. See §§761–62.
7. See Auguste Luneau, *L'histoire du salut chez les Pères de l'Eglise* (Paris: Beauchesne, 1964).

ferent situations). The first is the state of humanity before the Mosaic law. (Today, we are well aware that this extends over many hundreds of centuries.) It was traditionally called "the time of the law of nature." During this period, men were saved by faith in Christ (obviously a very implicit faith). St. Thomas thought this faith was expressed by humanly instituted rites, though not without some divine inspiration.[8] This notion introduces the very interesting idea of valuing so-called primitive religious rites.

The second era is the "time of the [Old] Law," during which Christ was believed in as someone still to come, and during this period one expressed one's faith by means of rites instituted by God. For this reason, they were obligatory and necessary for salvation.

Finally, with the coming of Christ and with His accomplishment of redemption, other rites have been instituted by God, for one expresses one's faith in Christ who has come and is active in a different way than how one expresses one's faith in Christ still to come, in promise.[9] This is the "time of the New Law."

However, what are we to say about men who belong to a given era of salvation at one and the same historical time, though without having any means for [consciously] situating themselves within this era? What are we to say for the case of all the peoples outside the Jewish people living during the time of the [Old] Law? Likewise, what about the Jews during the times after Christ and also about all the peoples who know neither Christ nor the [Old] Law today? With regard to the [Old] Law, St. Thomas recognized that it was not universal,[10] which suggests that for the peoples that it does not concern, the situation of the "law of nature" continued. With regard to the "Law of the Gospel," he distinguishes (in a somewhat juridical manner), following St. Augustine, the moment when this law begins (according to Him, at the death of Christ) from the moment when, the Gospel having been "announced" [*divulgué*] everywhere, the law becomes obligatory for all men and abrogates the "Mosaic law" (and, obviously, the "law of nature" as well).[11]

---

8. See *ST* I-II, q. 103, a. 1.
9. See *ST* I-II, q. 103, aa. 3–4; III, q. 61, aa. 3–4.
10. See *ST* III, q. 61, a. 2, ad 3.
11. See *ST III*, q. 103, a. 4, ad 1.

However, different conclusions can be drawn from this same principle, given that we now know that it is far from the case that the Gospel has really been "announced" everywhere. Where the "Law of the Gospel" is not "knowable" as the divine law, several possibilities present themselves. If it is a question of men who have received and recognize the "Mosaic law," the latter continues to be obligatory for them and is a source of salvation for them. If it is a question of men who are unaware of the "Mosaic law," all they can do is express their (implicit) faith in Christ through objectively inadequate means which nonetheless have a saving value for them. Here, the Second Vatican Council's remarks about the salvific value of non-Christian religions comes to mind:

> The Catholic Church rejects nothing that is true and holy in these religions. She regards with sincere reverence those ways of conduct and of life, those precepts and teachings which, though differing in many aspects from the ones she holds and sets forth, nonetheless often reflect a ray of that Truth which enlightens all men. Indeed, she proclaims, and ever must proclaim Christ "the way, the truth, and the life" (John 14:6), in whom men may find the fullness of religious life, in whom God has reconciled all things to Himself.[12]

Circumcision and baptism

By applying a principle of sacramental theology to baptism, St. Thomas thought that circumcision did not cause grace but, instead, was only a *protestatio fidei*. God then justified the circumcised person on account of this faith.[13]

At the same time, by circumcision, the believer was associated with the People of God. By means of it, he became a participant in the promises, thus becoming a participant in the anticipatory realization [of Christ's grace], namely in the holiness of the people and of individual members of that people, at least if they were faithful to the [Old] Law.

This in no way contradicts what St. Paul said about the powerlessness of the [Old] Law: "Now before faith came, we were confined

---

12. *Nostra Aetate*, no. 2.
13. See *ST* III, q. 70, a. 4.

under the law, kept under restraint until faith should be revealed."[14] On the contrary, it was not said that the [Old] Law (and, therefore, circumcision) caused salvation but, instead, that God caused salvation on account of the faith "which was to be revealed." Indeed, faith in Christ did not yet exist. However, it was enveloped in faith in the promise that established Israel as the People of God (a faith that was solemnly professed by circumcision).

Note that this conception of the saving value of the sacraments of the [Old] Law greatly resembles what the reformers believed to be the case for the saving value of the Christian sacraments. However, there is a difference, namely, that even before Christ's coming it is a question of a real justification and holiness accorded to the believer on account of his faith (and also on account of his belonging to the chosen people).

The same judgment must be rendered concerning those who were not able to know the [Old] Law. In whatever way their faith expressed itself, so long as it was an authentic faith, God justified them in advance on account of Christ, the (hidden) object of this faith.

SUBSTITUTES FOR BAPTISM

However, if one admits that the "law of baptism" is imposed only on those who belong effectively to the Christian era of salvation history (i.e., those who are in such a state that they may know and recognize Christ) are we not forced to renounce what we said earlier concerning the universality and necessity of baptism? On the basis of this fact, is it not the case that the rite of baptism is just one possible means of salvation alongside others?

The Necessity of Admitting That There Are Substitutes for Baptism

{802} As soon as the necessary saving activity includes a rite belonging to a visible and historically situated institution, it presupposes a number of conditions in order for it to be performed. Such

---

14. Gal 3:23 (RSV); see 3:24–29.

conditions depend on the situation of the individual in the world, on his familial, social, and cultural environment, on the formation that he has received, and so forth—conditions that, nonetheless, do not solely depend on his will.

Now, the divine intention that all be saved is universal. Nobody can be excluded from the salvation brought about by Christ except by voluntarily refusing it.

Therefore, the necessity of baptism cannot be understood as implying that anyone who has not effectively received baptism (even without any fault on his part) would be deprived of salvation and remain in his sins, thereby being rejected by God. There cannot fail to be means to substitute for baptism when it is, in fact, impossible.

The fact that such substitutes are not indicated in Scripture must not render them suspect. Scripture announces the "law of baptism" and can only announce it as being universally necessary, for it is. Baptism is the means of salvation instituted by Christ for all men, a means which must be proposed to each person, not as something that is optional but as something obligatory. Only gradually did the problem arise concerning what to do about those who, in fact, did not have baptism proposed to them or who had it proposed to them in such a way that they could not concretely receive it as something coming from God.

How One Should Understand These Substitutes

{803} These substitutes must not be understood as though they were equivalent means alongside baptism by water, at least for those who can receive such baptism. The latter ever remains necessary.

If a substitute exists, this is because the effect of baptism by water is produced without it, though by way of anticipation, in such a way that as soon as baptism by water becomes possible for the individual under consideration, it immediately becomes necessary for him.[15]

On the other hand, there is an effect that cannot be produced without baptism by water, namely, the character by which one is "incorporated" into Christ and into the Church and by which one visibly becomes a member of the Church, which herself is visible. The

---

15. See St. Augustine, *De baptismo*, bk. 3, ch. 22, and *ST* III, q. 66, a. 11.

character is nothing if it is not a sign. It can be a sign only if it is inseparable from the visible rite that confers it, for this character is, of itself, invisible.[16]

Thus, substitutes for baptism have worth only for the personal salvation of him who finds himself "historically" situated outside the community of believers (i.e., for him who is unable to know it as being such and also is unable to will to enter this community, without this being his fault). They cannot replace full and visible membership in this community, and for this reason they in no way render the water of baptism useless, which remains the sole means for the realization of full membership in the Church during man's earthly life. (Indeed, it is in function of baptism by water that such substitutes mysteriously operate.) The grace received by means of these substitutes can be very great and can very profoundly purify the person, uniting him to God quite intimately. (Indeed, it can do so in a much profounder manner and with a much greater intimacy than happens in other people by means of the grace received with baptism by water, but who are then guilty of negligence and personal infidelity.) What is missing is an "enrooting" in the subject. It is not in the soul as in a ground that has been prepared. This "preparation" consists in the fact that one is a member of the Church, which is the true dwelling-place of grace.[17]

Different Substitutes

Baptism of blood

{804} From[18] the earliest days of the Church's history, martyrdom was seen to be the consummation of the Christian perfection begun at baptism and also as taking the place of baptism for those who could not receive it.

The martyrdom that is here thought of (and it was, in fact, the

---

16. See §761 above.
17. See §765 above. Also, see Nicolas, "La grâce sacramentelle," 533–35.
18. See Hippolytus of Rome, *La tradition apostolique*, ch. 19. Bouyer, *La spiritualité du Nouveau Testament et des Pères*, 238–58. [Tr. note: Fr. Nicolas also cites the bibliographical entry for Karl Rahner's "Quelques remarques sur le traité dogmatique 'De Trinitate.'" It seems, however, that he likely is referring here to Rahner, "Essai sur le martyre," 3:171–203, originally "Martyrium," in *Lexikon für Theologie und Kirche*, 2nd ed., ed. Josef Höfer and Karl Rahner (Freiburg im Breisgau: Herder, 1957), 7:136–38.]

case that presented itself historically) was that of martyrdom suffered on behalf of Christ by confessing the faith. Therefore, it was a martyrdom that presupposed faith. This was above all the case for catechumens, or at least for candidates for baptism who were taken, judged, and executed before being able to receive baptism. However, we will see that very quickly the idea was extended to the case of children killed out of hatred for Christ.

St. Thomas is a faithful interpreter of the tradition when he explains the value of baptism by blood by explaining it in terms of physical conformity to Christ, an ultimate realization of the mystical conformity brought about by baptism by water.[19]

Of itself, this kind of substitute for baptism by water excludes the latter, which obviously has a value only in this life. However, there does exist the case of "confessors of the faith" who are imprisoned for Christ and are condemned to death, though avoiding it in the end. These "confessors" had an immense prestige and have played a role in the Church that poses problems: should a catechumen who has received "baptism by blood" without dying be baptized? Nothing enables us to doubt that he must be. Moreover, true martyrdom consists in a real death for Christ and not only "suffering for Christ."

In any case, the principle established above must be applied. Baptism by blood is the most perfect form of baptism, but it is not a sacrament. Thus, the necessity of receiving the sacrament remains in force when the obstacle that is opposed to it is removed.

Baptism of fire (i.e., of charity)

St. Augustine passed from the idea of *batismus sanguinis* to that of a supplement by faith and conversion of heart by invoking Jesus' words to the good thief: "Today you will be with me in paradise." He said that this is a proof that is not lacking in weight, and St. Cyprian admits it as well:

> Considering the matter over and over, I discover that not only death suffered for the sake of Christ can supply for baptism, but faith and conversion of heart can supply for it in the case wherein the circumstances are

---

19. See *ST* III, q. 66, a. 12.

such that they do not allow one to have recourse to the celebration of baptism.[20]

Moreover, the case had to be concretely posed as regards catechumens who died before having been admitted to baptism and in such conditions that there was not enough time for them to be baptized.

This development is self-evident if one thinks that martyrdom receives its value from the fact that it is the supreme manifestation of faith ("to confess Christ" to the point of death) and of charity ("there is no greater sign of love"). Martyrdom itself depends on other persons' wills and on the circumstances. However, the faith and charity that the martyr will eventually manifest depend only on the Holy Spirit and on man's freedom.

This connection appeared very early on. Every form of Christian asceticism, especially the monastic life, came to be connected to the idea of preparing for martyrdom. Indeed, it goes so far as to become a substitute for martyrdom, for if the preparation is fervent enough, it can be a true, nonbloody martyrdom.[21]

Moreover, as we have already seen, the catechumen is normally justified before in fact having received baptism.[22] However, we have also seen that this was *in voto baptismi*, which, far from rendering baptism by water useless, has a meaning only in function of one's willingness to receive it. This willingness implies real reception, and when external circumstances render such reception immediately possible (i.e., when "everything is ready" for baptism), it could be refused only by withdrawing one's intention to undergo real baptism, an intention which was included in the *baptismum flaminis* (baptism of desire). Of course, this later retraction does not annul the justification received as regards the remission of prior sins and of all the punishments corresponding to them ("the gifts of God are irrevocable"). Instead, it annuls it with regard to the grace of divinization and of becoming a coheir to the Kingdom. It also annuls the inchoate membership in the Church that depended on this grace.

---

20. See Augustine, *De baptismo*, bk. 4, ch. 22.
21. See Bouyer, *La spiritualité du Nouveau Testament et des Pères*, 255–61.
22. See §788 above.

The case of children who have died without baptism

{806} The[23] problem posed by the *de facto* disjunction that can exist between faith and baptism can be summarized in the following manner. On the one hand, the baptized infant has baptism without an act of faith, but faith is "implied" in the baptism (for he does not refuse the interior act of faith, which is signified by the external act of being baptized). On the other hand, the adult who is internally converted to Christ (above all if he confesses his faith through martyrdom) has faith without baptism, though baptism is implied in his act of faith, which includes the "desire to receive baptism." However, how do things stand for the unbaptized child? He has neither faith nor baptism. Thus, he seems to be excluded from the kingdom, into which one can enter only through faith and baptism. It is not clear how something could supplement for baptism in this particular case. However, how can we hold that these children would be excluded from the kingdom without them refusing it in any manner?

Principles involved in resolving the question

On the one hand,[24] there is the absolute principle concerning the necessity of baptism. As we have seen, this principle is not affected by the "supplements" for baptism. For what concerns children, this principle certainly holds as follows. If the child was not baptized, he will need to be baptized when he comes to the age of adulthood. If he is justified before this baptism, this will occur on account of one of the aforementioned reasons (i.e., in virtue of an interior conversion that is experienced, through God's grace, from the moment when he is capable of a human act). Up to that point, he is still a "sinner."

On the other hand, we have God's justice and love. His justice is irreproachable, absolutely precluding the possibility that a human person would be punished for a sin that he did not personally commit. His love is revealed as willing the salvation of all men and is

---

23. See Michel Labourdette, "Problèmes d'eschatologie," *Revue thomiste* 54 (1954): 658–75. William A. van Roo, "A Survey of Recent Literature and Determination of the State of Question," *Gregorianum* 35 (1954): 406–73.

24. See Nicolas, *Les profondeurs de la grâce*, 499–503.

concretized in Jesus' redemptive death for all. On account of this, nobody can be excluded from redemption if he has not personally rejected the redemptive love.

The classical solution

According to the classical solution to this issue, infants[25] who have died without baptism cannot approach the kingdom [of heaven]. However, no more is it the case that they can be punished. Under the pressure of this twofold certitude, theologians subsequent to St. Augustine gradually elaborated the notion of "Limbo," designating an intermediary state of perfect but natural happiness that would fall to such children. This idea, which was already commonly admitted and taught by medieval theologians, was presented by St. Thomas as though it were certain and was (and is still) commonly taught in the Church.[26]

Note, however, the following points. *First*, in reality, we can observe a shift in the modern explanation of Limbo in comparison with that offered in its older form, such as it appears not only in St. Thomas but also in the condemnation of the Jansenist council of Pistoia by Pius VI in 1794.[27] Here, Limbo is considered a "punishment," the "punishment of loss." In other words, if Limbo is a "fringe territory," it is the fringes of the kingdom of the damned. What one wishes to avoid is that this punishment, which reaches the person *ratione naturae* and not *ratione personae* (just like original sin) would be an affliction for the person. However, is it not a contradiction to speak of a non-afflictive pain? In the case of modern thinkers, one conceived of an intermediary state between divinization by participation in the Trinitarian life (i.e., supernatural consummation) and damnation (i.e., supernatural loss and rejection). In short, it would be the state of pure nature. However, is such a state conceivable for members of a humanity that was always called to the supernatural order?

Second, what is the dogmatic status of this notion of Limbo? The

---

25. See Charles Journet, *La volonté salvifique sur les petits enfants* (Paris: Desclée de Brouwer, 1958. Albert Michel, *Enfants mort sans baptême* (Paris: Tequi, 1961).
26. See, on the development of this idea, Bertrand Gaullier, *L'état des enfants morts sans baptême d'après S. Thomas d'Aquin* (Paris: Lethielleux, 1961).
27. See Pope Pius VI, Constitution *Auctorem Fidei*, no. 26 (D.-*Sch.*, no. 2626).

idea itself is obviously the fruit of theological elaboration. However, this elaboration was presented under the pressure of principles that are certainly taught by the Bible. It seems that one must consider it a theological hypothesis that is valid, necessary, and retained by the Church, as long as one cannot reconcile the principles in question in any other manner. The Jansenist pseudo-council of Pistoia (in 1786) had rejected this hypothesis. However, it did so in order to say that unbaptized infants were submitted to the punishment of fire. This is what Pius VI condemned by rejecting the condemnation expressed in this council's rejection of the idea of Limbo.[28]

Cajetan's solution

Cajetan proposed a famous solution,[29] holding that the children of Christian parents dying without baptism (thinking above all of miscarriages) could be saved by their parents' faith, whether or not it was manifested by an action or explicit prayer. The idea was extended to cases of parents who were not explicitly Christian who were nonetheless interiorly converted to Christ in the way indicated in our earlier discussion.[30] In any case, this solution is concerned with only a limited number of cases and therefore retains the hypothesis of Limbo for the other cases.

Criticism of the hypothesis of Limbo

On the one hand, this realization of the state of pure nature for a considerable number of human people hardly seems compatible with mankind's vocation to the supernatural order. On the other hand, this principled difficulty finds a particular application when one reflects on the state of these persons. Would they know about humanity's supernatural vocation? If yes, how could they not resent their exclusion from the kingdom as being a very painful privation? If not, how could one still say that this exclusion is a punishment for them?

---

28. See George Dyer, *The Denial of Limbo and the Jansenist Controversy* (Mundelein, Ill.: Saint Mary of the Lake Seminary, 1955).

29. See Cajetan, *In ST* III, q. 68, aa. 2 and 11.

30. See Vincent Héris, "Enfants (Salut des)," in *Catholicisme* 4:151–57, "Le salut des enfants morts sans baptême," *La Maison-Dieu* (1947): 86–105, and "Les limbes des enfants," *Vie Spirituelle* 108 (1963): 705–15.

Note that in the two texts where St. Thomas discusses the question of Limbo he manifests a hesitation on this subject. In the first,[31] he admits that the inhabitants of Limbo know that they are deprived of the Beatific Vision but that they do not suffer from this knowledge, wisely considering that this sublime good is not for them. In the second text,[32] he says, on the contrary, that they do not know it, but indulges in awkward explanations in order to show that it is still a privation. In the end, it remains very difficult (if not impossible) to reconcile this hypothesis with the principle of God's universal salvific will. It is not clear how an infant who dies without baptism may be regarded as someone who rejected the redemption that had been proposed to him.

Criticism of Cajetan's opinion

Besides the fact that this solution is concerned with only a restricted portion of the children who have died without baptism (and therefore entirely leaves the difficulty intact for others), it does not seem that this means of salvation by means of the faith of the child's parents would be compatible with the era of salvation after Christ. In Israel, the "faith of the child's parents," manifested through the circumcision of the child, was the normal means for the child's belonging to the messianic community, of which the child was part on account of his carnal birth. In the current economy of salvation, the community of grace and of salvation is no longer a people constituted through carnal generation. Instead, it is the Church, constituted precisely through the sacraments. For this reason, infants who receive baptism are supported by the Church's faith, not that of their parents.

The line of inquiry for a universal solution

We have seen that the most ancient tradition recognized martyrdom as an outstanding substitute for baptism. Now, very early on (from the fifth century onward and even before that),[33] the benefit of this

---

31. See *In II Sent.*, d. 33, q. 2, a. 2.
32. See *Quaestiones disputate de malo*, q. 5, a. 3.
33. See *Lexikon für Theologie und Kirche*, 2nd ed., ed. J. Höfer and K. Rahner (Freiburg im

supplement for baptism was extended to children killed out of hatred for Christ. However, it becomes immediately clear that this death is not a martyrdom in the traditional sense of the word, for it includes neither a profession of faith nor a sacrifice of love. What does it have in common with it? We have seen what it has in common: *imitatio operis* (an imitation of what Christ did, or better, of what He suffered). Through his death, man, redeemed by Christ, seeks to imitate Christ's death. Moreover, Christ "the universal man" is the one who continues to die in him. This is not "automatically" brought about by the person who is capable of an act of freedom. He must "take up his death" (i.e., must freely unite it to Christ's), for he is able to refuse to do so. However, can we not draw the same conclusion concerning the child who dies as we do for the child who is baptized? Because he is ordered to Christ by the deepest inclination of his will, which is not thwarted by an opposed free choice, he is disposed to being taken up by Christ, into His death.

Proposed solution

So long as the child lives, he remains in his native situation. On account of the sin of the nature into which he is born, he is separated from God. However, he is fundamentally ordered toward Christ the Savior in virtue of the creative act that made him in the image of God and on account of the redemption brought about by Christ, in which he is virtually implied. If the child happens to die without baptism, at the very moment when death overtakes the child and brings his earthly destiny to its close, it conforms him to Jesus in His redemptive death *secundum imitationem operis*, as baptism performed *secundum figuralem repraesentationem* would have done.

Confirmation

The First Letter of St. Peter, which probably provides us with fragments of a quite primitive baptismal catechesis,[34] speaks about the descent of Jesus to hell following upon His death, reflecting upon

---

Breisgau: Herder, 1965), 10:521. Prudentius, *Hymne XII en l'honneur des Saints Innocents, Livre d'Heures* (Paris: Belles-Lettres, 1943), 71–72.

34. See §768 above.

this in a context that is related to baptism. (Admittedly, it does so in a way that is not completely clear to the reader.) This theme played a significant role in the ancient theology of baptism.[35] St. Thomas took up this traditional theme, comparing this descent into hell for the souls of men who died in faith and charity before Christ with baptism for living men: "As the power of Christ's passion is applied to living beings by the sacraments, which configure us to Christ in His passion, so too it was applied to those who were already dead by Christ's descent into hell."[36] The comparison bears on the following two terms: on the one hand, there is Christ's action through baptism for living men (sometimes by way of anticipation); however, on the other hand, there is the immediate action of Christ on the child who dies, making his death into a participation in His passion.

Response to objections

{807} The great objection is that, in this case, justification is bestowed without baptism and therefore without the Church's mediation. However, precisely speaking, this child never belonged to the Church. Before the moment of his death, he is outside the Church. At the moment when he is justified (i.e., at the moment of his death) he is placed, by death itself, outside the earthly Church. Fr. Benoît says that according to St. Paul's teaching, baptism is absolutely necessary for one to be incorporated into the Church of heaven.[37] Following this reasoning, one would also need to exclude all the other substitutes for baptism. We are justified in thinking that the case of children who have died without baptism would not really be within the basic perspectives of a teaching destined to establish the necessity of receiving baptism, a teaching that presupposes the concrete possibility of being baptized.

It does not seem that there would be any disadvantage whatsoever in admitting this sole exception to the "law of baptism," given that it concerns only children who are obviously unable to abuse it.

---

35. See Rousseau, "La descente."
36. See ST III, q. 52, a. 1, ad 2.
37. See Pierre Benoît, "Le baptême des enfants et la doctrine biblique du baptême selon O. Cullmann," *Exégèse et Théologie* (Paris: Cerf, 1961), 2:212–23.

However, could not adults abuse it for them, neglecting to baptize them? Will not the practice of baptizing infants again be placed into question by such a theory? It is not clear that this consequence would follow. First of all, here again, we are speaking of a theological hypothesis, and nobody could have the right to voluntarily and deliberately compromise the eternal salvation of a child on the basis of a hypothesis. Moreover, the Church's mission is to make all men who are able (and, indeed, whom she is charged with making be able) to participate in redemption do so by the means which have been given to her. Just as missionary activity is justified and preserves all its urgency even when one believes that all men of good will can be saved, so too to believe that a child can be saved if he dies without baptism in no way removes the responsible adults' duty to have the child baptized if he is in a situation to receive baptism.

One can only say that this removes the dramatic character from the baptism of infants, but is this a wicked and dangerous thing?[38]

APPENDIX: THE RITE OF BAPTISM

{808} A theology of baptism aiming to be complete would need to include a study of the rite[s] of baptism, its historical development, and the theological and symbolic meaning of its various components. In the division of labor practiced in a faculty of theology, this question is left to a course in liturgy.

Here, it suffices to note the classic book by Alois Stenzel[39] and the book by von Allmen which we have already cited. The fourth chapter of the latter text contains an excellent exposition of the problems that are posed by the rites of baptism that exist in various Churches today. It discusses the modification of the Catholic

---

38. N.B. The Hungarian theologian Boros has proposed a completely different solution, which other theologians follow. He thinks that at the moment of the infant's death the child receives an illumination that places him in a state to be able to perform a free action in relation to Christ which would engage his eternal destiny. This is only an application of a general theory of death that we discussed earlier (see §581 in the previous volume). Let us only note here that if this hypothesis could be retained, it would have the effect of putting the destiny of baptized children into question. This is so because the power to say "yes" implies the power to say "no," and one could always doubt the way that the child, whether baptized or not, would choose.

39. See Stenzel, *Il battesimo*.

ritual[s], the various attempts in other Churches [sic], proposals for the Reformed Churches oriented toward a unification with other Churches [sic], and ecumenical aspects of the question.

From the ecumenical perspective, see the proposals of "Faith and Constitution" aiming at fixing the conditions that a baptism must fulfill when given in a Christian confession so that it may be recognized as valid by all the others:

> The celebration of baptism: the minister, the form, and the liturgy.
>
> The Churches are in agreement on the fact that the normal minister of baptism is an ordained minister, although there are cases when baptized believers can baptize.
>
> Baptism is performed with water, in the name of the Father, the Son, and the Holy Spirit.
>
> In a complete liturgy of baptism, the following acts are found before or after the baptismal action:
>
>> An affirmation of God's initiative in salvation, an affirmation of His continued fidelity, and an affirmation of our complete dependence upon His grace
>>
>> An invocation of the Holy Spirit
>>
>> A renunciation of everything that is opposed to Christ
>>
>> A profession of faith in Christ and an adherence to God the Father, Son, and Holy Spirit
>>
>> A declaration that the baptized person has become a child of God and a witness to the Gospel
>
> It is equally fitting that, in the case of baptism, one should give an explanation of its meaning in conformity with Scripture: participation in the death and resurrection of Christ, new birth in water and the Spirit, incorporation into the body of Christ, pardon of sins in communion with Christ and through Him.[40]

---

40. Foi et Constitution, *La reconciliation des Églises, baptême, eucharisti, ministère* (Taizé: Presses de Taizé, 1974), 17–18.

9

The Sacrament of Confirmation

Incorporated into the Church through baptism, the faithful are destined by the baptismal character for the worship of the Christian religion; reborn as sons of God they must confess before men the faith which they have received from God through the Church. They are more perfectly bound to the Church by the sacrament of Confirmation, and the Holy Spirit endows them with special strength so that they are more strictly obliged to spread and defend the faith, both by word and by deed, as true witnesses of Christ.[1]

This text expresses the doctrine that is commonly received in the Church today, leaving open a number of questions which we must examine.[2]

---

1. *Lumen Gentium*, no. 11.
2. See Jean-Jacques von Allmen, *Prophétisme sacramental* (Neuchâtel: Delachaux et Niestlé, 1964), 140–82. Boris Bobrinskoy, "Liturgie et eccleésiologie trinitaire de S. Basile," *Eucharistie d'Orient et d'Occident*, ed. B. Botte (Paris: Cerf, 1970), 197–240. Louis Bouyer, "La signification de la confirmation," *Vie Spirituelle, Supplément* 29 (1954): 162–79. Léonard-Alphonse Van Buchen, *L'homélie pseudo-eusébienne de Pentecôte. L'origine de la "confirmation" en Gaule méridionale et l'interprétation de ce rite par Fauste de Riez* (Nijmegen: Janssen, 1967). Saint Thomas d'Aquin. *Somme théologique, Le baptême et la confirmation: 3a, Questions 66–72*, trans. Pierre-Thomas Camelot (Paris: Desclee & Cie, 1956), 396–403. Jean Daniélou, *Théologie du Judéo-christianisme* (Paris: Desclée, 1958). Hamman, *Baptême et confirmation*. Joseph Lecuyer, "La confirmation chez les Pères," *La Maison-Dieu* 54 (1958): 29–52. Burkhard Neunheuser, *Baptême et confirmation* (Paris: Cerf, 1965). Panagiotis N. Trembelas, *Dogmatique de l'Église orthodoxe catholique*, vol. 3 (Paris: Desclée de Brouwer, 1967), 130–55.

THE THEOLOGICAL PROBLEM CONCERNING CONFIRMATION

{809} The Church's teaching of confirmation, defined at Florence and Trent, and reaffirmed at the Second Vatican Council, is that there is a specific, distinct sacrament, confirmation (called "Holy Chrismation" in the Eastern Church), which has the "giving of the Holy Spirit" as its proper effect. From the third century onward in the East, this sacrament has been conferred with a "signing" [*consignation*] made on the forehead with "chrism," an oil perfumed with myrrh and specially blessed by the bishop. In the West, its ordinary minister is the bishop, but he can delegate this liturgical action to a priest who is not a bishop. In the East, normally the same priest baptizes and confers Holy Chrismation in the course of the same ceremony, although the chrism must have been blessed by the bishop. In the West, the sacrament of confirmation is normally conferred in a different ceremony from that of baptism (in the case of infant baptism), one performed many years later (even after "first communion," though this certainly is a contestable custom, despite the fact that it is quite widespread).

Now, this poses problems both historically and doctrinally.

Problems in the Historical Order

First problem: The institution of confirmation

Can we say that confirmation was instituted by our Lord? In Scripture, we find very clear mention made of a rite of imposition of hands after baptism, whose effect is the pouring forth of the Holy Spirit.[3] However, is this our sacrament of confirmation? On the basis of the work of Coppens, Neunheuser thinks so,[4] as does Trembelas.[5] Others contest this.[6] For Daniélou, the *sphragis* mentioned in ancient documents refers to baptism.

Only gradually did the signing [*consignation*] by the bishop come to be separated from the rite of baptism, without it being clear

---

3. See Acts 8:4–20 and 19:1–7.
4. See Neunheuser, *Baptême et confirmation*, 49–52.
5. See Trembelas, *Dogmatique de l'Église orthodoxe catholique*, 3:132–35.
6. See Hamman, *Baptême et confirmation*, 194, and Daniélou, *Théologie du Judéo-christianisme*, 381.

whether this is a distinct rite or the final ceremony of baptism.[7] In the West, the connection between this rite and the bishop (a connection that was very strongly marked out from the beginning) was expressed by the reservation of its bestowal to the bishop. By the force of things, this led to the temporal separation of the two rites. In the East, by contrast, they remained connected in the same ceremony, to the detriment of the (equally primitive) character of the sacrament being something performed by the bishop. Nonetheless, in the two traditions, the "signing" [*consignation*] came to be held to be a distinct rite and a distinct sacrament.

Second problem: The development of the ritual

However early the intervention of the anointing with chrism appears in history, it is impossible to think that this rite would have been completely primitive. Scripture speaks only of the imposition of hands.

Therefore, even if the sacrament was instituted by Christ Himself (at least in the form of a "promise," as St. Thomas thought, leaving the apostles, inspired by the Spirit, to consciously establish a rite corresponding to the realization of this promise[8]), we must admit that there was a change in the rite by which it was conferred. Indeed, it seems to be a substantial change, as in both East and West the "signing" [*consignation*] with holy chrism is held to be essential for the sacrament. This difficulty brings us back to the problem of the institution of the sacraments by Christ.[9]

Doctrinal Difficulties

These difficulties are apparent from the first testimonies and are visible in all the theological explanations that have been proposed through the course of the ages. If the sacrament of confirmation gives the Spirit, are we forced to hold that baptism does not? Now, we have seen that the gift of the Holy Spirit is one of the effects of

---

7. See Hippolytus of Rome, *La tradition apostolique*, ch. 22. Tertullian, *Traité du baptême*, ch. 8. François Refoulé, "Introduction," in Tertullian, *"Traité du baptême" de Tertullien*, SC 35 (Paris: Cerf, 1952), 40–45. Trembelas, *Dogmatique de l'Église orthodoxe catholique*, 3:132–35.

8. See *ST* III, q. 71, a. 1, ad 1.

9. See §731 above.

baptism, indeed its global effect. However, if the Holy Spirit is already given by baptism, what does confirmation properly bring about? Generally speaking, everything that is said about the effects of the sacrament of confirmation seems to be a repetition of what is said about the effects of the sacrament of baptism. To attribute to baptism the negative effect of the remission of sins, while leaving the "signing" [*consignation*] to produce positive effects that are connected to the gifts of the Holy Spirit (as Tertullian seems to do) leads one to a twofold collision: on the one hand, with the Pauline and Johannine doctrine of baptism, as we have seen, and on the other, with the theological certainty that the remission of sin is the work of the Holy Spirit.

In short, it is not clear how we are to attribute a "significate" and "effect" to the sacrament of confirmation, one that would be proper to it, distinguishing it from baptism.

To speak of "fullness," as is often done, seems to be a kind of evasion, for strictly speaking, the fullness of the Holy Spirit would be consummated holiness, and nobody thinks that this sacrament gives consummated holiness. If it is only a question of an "opening" to the gift of the Holy Spirit, amenable to all the later outpourings to the degree that there is growth in the life of grace, it is not clear how or why the opening established in the believer by baptism would not suffice for these increases. The comparative terms "more perfectly" and "more strictly," which are prudently used by the conciliar definition, state the problem rather than provide a solution to it. [As it is put by Botte:]

Theories must be distinguished from facts. The latter seem incontestable to me. Christian baptism is a baptism in the Spirit and, on the other hand, from the time of the Apostolic age onward there existed a rite for conferring the gift of the Spirit. The fact that a theologian does not see how these two facts can be reconciled is a theological problem. However, the fact that these two data are historically established is a historical conclusion that is necessary and resists all theories.[10]

---

10. See Bernard Botte, "Compte-rendu du livre de G. Dix: The theology of confirmation in relation to baptism," *Bulletin de théologie ancienne et médiévale* V, no. 1279.

VARIOUS THEOLOGICAL EXPLANATIONS AND CRITICISM OF THEM

"On both heads, we seem to be enclosed within a dilemma: either the Holy Spirit intervenes in baptism or He does not. In the first case, confirmation is necessary. In the second case, it is useless."[11]

Tendency to Valorize Confirmation to the Detriment of Baptism

{810} This tendency, which could claim for itself the presentation made by Tertullian concerning the role of the "signing" [*consignatio*] in relation to baptism, is represented by Dom Gregory Dix.[12] His thesis can be summarized as follows. Baptism constitutes only one part of Christian initiation, indeed the preparatory portion which essentially consists in the remission of sins (i.e., the negative effect), though it also consists in incorporation into Christ and into His Mystical Body. The gift of the Spirit, the principal and decisive effect without which initiation remains incomplete (meaning that without it one is not yet a Christian, except in an inchoate manner) is the effect of confirmation which seals the Christian for eternity. He thus reproaches Western theology with having transferred the whole of the effects of initiation to the least important rite, which was only a preliminary, and also reproaches it with having thus devalued the sacrament of confirmation. It is clear that he himself valorizes it by devaluing baptism.

Historically, Dix's thesis, which does not take into account numerous testimonies from Scripture as well as from the most ancient tradition (both of which attribute the gift of the Spirit to baptism or present the Holy Spirit as the principal agent of baptism—e.g., baptism in and into the Spirit) cannot be retained. (Even though he inclines in Dix's direction, even Fr. Bouyer judges that Dix's claim

---

11. Ibid.

12. See Gregory Dix, *The Theology of Confirmation in Relation to Baptism* (Westminster: Dacre Press, 1946), and "The Seal in the Second Century," *Theology* 51 (1948): 7–12. It has been criticized in Botte, "Compte-rendu du livre de G. Dix," no. 1279. Also, for another critique, see Pierre-Thomas Camelot, "Compte-rendu du livre de G. Dix: 'The theology of confirmation in relation to baptism,'" *Revue des sciences philosophiques et théologiques* 38 (1954): 642–45.

that one would find in St. Paul mention of an anointing conferring the Holy Spirit prior to baptism by water is a "fanciful" [*fantastique*] claim.)[13] Theologically, the idea of a rite (baptism) which would confer the remission of sins and incorporation into Christ and into the Church without giving the Holy Spirit is unintelligible, for the remission of sins is the work of the Spirit. He is the one who dispels sin by His presence. He also is the one who incorporates one into the Church, and if a member of the Church can lose the Holy Spirit (through his sin) without ceasing to be incorporated into her and even if (in the case of "feigning") someone can be incorporated into the Church without receiving the Holy Spirit, this can be the case only through his own fault, through his voluntary refusal. It is inconceivable that a rite instituted by Christ, acting according to God's intention, would produce this abnormal situation.[14]

Fr. Bouyer himself openly leans in Dix's direction, reproaching classical theology (especially scholastic theology) with having misunderstood the sacrament of confirmation and, consequently, with having neglected what is given to us by it.[15] Nonetheless, he avoids the grave drawbacks noted above by employing the notion that I designated by the term "anticipation":[16]

> Baptism by itself does not give him the fullness of initiation. The Holy Spirit is already at work in baptism and in the non-confirmed baptized person. However, He is there because the baptized are destined and already committed through baptism by water to receive Him in His fullness in the chrismation that will give them Him who holds the place of Christ among us.[17]

The reader will note the scholarly balance of these formulas which, in the end, remain vague: the Holy Spirit is "at work," though because He must be received (in the future) in fullness, and the

---

13. See Bouyer, "La signification de la confirmation," 162n1.
14. N.B. According to Max Thurian, on account of Calvin's sentiment that the theology of confirmation (as it was presented at his time) implied the insufficiency of baptism, the reformer was pushed to reject the idea that confirmation is a sacrament and to interpret it as being only a public profession of the faith received at baptism after the necessary period of instruction. See Max Thurian, *La confirmation, consecration des laïcs* (Neuchâtel: Delachaux et Niestlé, 1957).
15. See Louis Bouyer, *Le sens de la vie monastique* (Turnhout: Brepols, 1950), 120–21.
16. See §788.
17. Bouyer, "La signification de la confirmation," 176.

anointing will give Him (though "in fullness" is no longer said). We have already noted the vagueness involved with this notion of "given in fullness" and with the implied comparison (i.e., though He was given in baptism, He was not given in fullness, but instead was given to a lesser degree). Here, this is emphasized by Dix's insistence on the fact that the Person of the Holy Spirit is what is given. How is one to understand a greater or lesser amount in the gift of a Person? Certainly, given that the Person of the Holy Spirit is infinite, He can never be received in His fullness by any created person. Obviously, there are degrees in the believer's reception of the Holy Spirit. However, where do these degrees come from? They come from the intensity of the created grace by means of which the Divine Person is received and which, in any case, must grow ceaselessly, even after the reception of the sacrament of confirmation. (We will see that this growth is the proper effect of the Eucharist.) What cannot vary is the gift itself, thus received in an unequal manner, for the person is given entirely from the beginning.

Above all, it is questionable that the notion of anticipation would be useful for our problem. Anticipation consists in the fact that God, whose action is not submitted to temporal succession (which, on the contrary, is the law of the sacramental action that He uses), produces the final effect at some given moment of the sacramental action (or even at some moment in the preparation that precedes it). This does not render the pursuit of the sacramental action useless, for the effect thus produced is the terminus to which this action is ordered by its nature, as that which is signified and normally produced by means of it so that what was produced by anticipation was produced in function of the sacramental action underway and on account of it. We have registered a specification, namely, that such anticipation can occur either in the course of the very sacramental action ordered to the production of the effect under consideration or can occur in the course of the preparation for this action (e.g., the catechumenate for baptism).

Now, it can happen that preparation for a sacrament would be brought about by an earlier sacrament. Thus, baptism is the required preparation for all the other sacraments, and penance is the required preparation for the Eucharist, at least for the person who has broken his bonds with Christ through sin. Hence, one can admit that the effect of a later sacrament could be produced in anticipation when one receives the preparatory sacrament. (Thus, we will see that the effect of the Eucharist is produced in anticipation already at baptism.) However, this preparatory sacrament must have a significate and an effect that would be proper to it. Without this, there would not be a sacrament but, rather, only a preliminary part of the sacrament for which it prepares. This is indeed what baptism is reduced to in Fr. Bouyer's explanation (which, for this reason, ultimately rejoins Dix's thesis, with all of its disadvantages). In the end, it would be the case that none of the effects attributed to baptism can be produced without the effect that is properly attributed to confirmation being produced, and for this reason, baptism no longer would be anything but a part of the single sacrament of initiation, namely, confirmation.

Finally, this tendency can be connected—though not without paradox!—to the theories that have said that confirmation makes the Christian into an apostle[18] or that have connected the priesthood of the believers to this sacrament.[19] Indeed, if the Christian participates in Christ's priesthood and if he participates in the apostolic responsibility of the Church, this is above all in virtue of his baptism.[20] To attribute this to confirmation is to strip baptism of its character as the sacrament that makes one be a Christian.

The Tendency to Minimize Confirmation

{811} When one pays heed to the fact that baptism gives the believer everything that he needs in order to be a Christian, one tends to hold that confirmation is a sacrament that adds nothing specific to baptism but that instead only augments what was given in the latter.

In this direction, one can present the theory of Geoffrey Lampe,[21] who took a position opposed to Dix, seeing the rite of chrismation

---

18. See the bibliography in Yves Congar, *Jalons pour une théologie du laïcat* (Paris: Cerf, 1954), 517 (no. 67).

19. See Damasus Winzen, *Die deutsche Thomas-Ausgabe. Die Sakramente, Taufe und Firmung* (Salzburg: Pustet, 1935).

20. See Congar, *Jalons pour une théologie du laïcat*, 488–530.

21. See Geoffrey William Hugo Lampe, *The Seal of the Spirit* (London: Longmans, Green, and Company, 1951).

and of the imposition of hands as being only a final development of baptism. He comes to this conclusion by implausibly interpreting Acts 19:6 as speaking of a kind of missionary ordination! In these conditions, it is no longer clear what remains specifically for confirmation to bring about. In other words, it is no longer clear how it is a distinct sacrament.

In the same line, though in a more nuanced and more theologically elaborated manner, Lionel Thornton[22] distinguishes two gifts of the Spirit for the Christian, corresponding to two interventions by the Spirit in Jesus' mission (first, at the annunciation for the Incarnation and, second, at His baptism, signifying His acceptance of the role as the suffering servant, therefore for the Redemption) and also to two stages in the Church's initiation (the first brought to completion on Easter and the other on Pentecost). Thus, for the Christian, the first stage of initiation is realized by baptism, whereby the Spirit enters the soul, and a second stage is realized at confirmation, whereby He becomes the source of living water. The first gift of the Spirit gives birth to the Christian life and incorporates the person into the Mystical Body. A second mission provides him with all the gifts need in order to live the life of this Body in fullness.

In this explanation, we see an obvious effort being made to distinguish a proper effect for confirmation. However, can one hold that this effort is successful? It is not clear in what way a second mission of the Spirit is needed for giving this fullness of life. In any case, it is not explained here in a satisfying manner.

The same thing must be said concerning Hamman's explanation,[23] although he himself wars against the minimization of confirmation for which scholasticism supposedly was responsible. To say that confirmation integrates the Christian into the Church which the Spirit established at Pentecost is not the same thing as giving it a specific effect, especially when one has shown quite well that baptism has the effect of incorporating the believer into the Church. There is no other Church than the one that the Spirit established at Pentecost! Likewise, to say that confirmation gives the divine

---

22. See Lionel Spencer Thornton, *Confirmation, Its Place in the Baptismal Mystery* (Westminster: Dacre, 1954).

23. See Adalbert Hamman, *Baptême et confirmation*, 215–18.

energy present at the heart of each Christian adds nothing real to the fact that baptism connects the Christian to the soteriological act of Christ. Indeed, the Christian draws the energy that exists in himself precisely from this act.

The Effort to Identify Confirmation's Proper Effect

St. Thomas's explanation

A key notion: *augmentum* in bodily life

{812} The[24] *augmentum* which St. Thomas has in mind when speaking about confirmation is not the simple maintenance of life or its continuous progress, which is brought about through nutrition. Instead, he is thinking of "growth," that is, the passage from the state of infancy to the state of manhood, the passage to adulthood. In the scholastics' "natural philosophy," this process of self-perfecting is attributed to a specific faculty of the vegetative soul.

In natural life, the soul suffices as the principle for the whole of its vital movement. However, the principle of the Christian's vital movement is Christ. If there is a specific "movement" in the Christian life, corresponding to this passage to adulthood, one must attribute it to a specific action by Christ (and therefore to a specific sacrament).

An annexed notion: Ordaining the Christian life to doing battle

St. Thomas was driven to this conclusion by his principal documentary source, the famous "Letter of Pope Miltiades," which came to him through the intermediary of Peter Lombard and the "false Decretals" of Gratian. In reality, this letter is only a Paschal homily, probably written by Faustus of Riez.[25]

Nonetheless, one must note that St. Thomas very skillfully connects this notion (at first glance quite unrelated to the first) to that of growth: the adult is capable of acting externally and taking up the tasks and battles of man. However, his fundamental idea, by which

---

24. See *ST* III, q. 72.
25. See Pierre-Thomas Camelot, "Sur la théologie de la confirmation," *Revue des sciences philosophiques et théologiques* 38 (1954): 642n18. Van Buchen, *L'homélie pseudo-eusébienne de Pentecôte*.

he finds himself united with what is best in the intuitions of modern thinkers (i.e., the fact that confirmation belongs to Christian initiation), is that the primary effect of confirmation is a perfection interior to man.[26] Thus, for him, the sacrament of confirmation retains all of its importance, even if occasions for externally doing battle are not present, as for example, for someone about to die.

On the other hand, it requires one to respect the conditions of analogical reasoning. The continuous succession and time that characterize the passage from childhood to adulthood in bodily life are a condition befalling the inferior analogate, one that is excluded by the transposition to the domain of spiritual life: "The soul can just as well be graced with spiritual birth at the time of old age as it can attain the fullness of maturity at the time of youth or even in one's childhood."

Criticisms registered against this explanation

{813} Even while recognizing that St. Thomas did everything he could and drew as much as could be possibly drawn from defective sources,[27] Fr. Bouyer rejects the idea of growth and strength to do battle as being a pure invention of the non-authoritative author of the "Letter of Miltiades," saying that all this was already given at baptism (especially "strength to do battle," given by the preparatory annointings in baptism): "We indeed speak about the Holy Spirit with regard to confirmation, but when we are pressed, we babble."[28]

Hamman[29] reports and makes his own criticisms that are just as lively. The formula "The Holy Spirit [given] for strength [to do battle]" would be foreign to all the Patristic and liturgical data and would be incompatible with the conception of confirmation as a complement to baptism. (A first response to the objection is found in what was said above concerning the way that St. Thomas interprets this "spiritual power" in terms of an internal development of the Christian existence received at baptism and not in function of external obstacles.) Likewise: "To make maturity consist in an event

---

26. See *ST* III, q. 72 a. 8, co. and ad 2; q. 73, a. 1, ad 1.
27. See Bouyer, "La signification de la confirmation," 165.
28. Ibid., 164.
29. See Hamman, *Baptême et confirmation*, 219.

is, in the end, to deny the analogy with which one started: growth is brought about on the basis of an initial living power."

No, this does respect the laws of analogical transposition, for in the case of a Christian life, if the initial power really does exist in this new living being that is the baptized person, it remains in immediate and continuous dependence upon Christ in whom this power resides, as properly belonging to Him. Therefore, if "growth" is the second stage of the formation of that living being, it is normal that it would be conferred by a new action coming from Christ, without preventing it from coming forth from the form given by the first action.

Modern theologians who make use of St. Thomas's views

Here, the work of Camelot can be cited.[30] Note that this author shows the traditional character of the idea that confirmation gives strength, something attested to in sources that are independent from the "Letter of Miltiades." He insists (too much, perhaps?) on the ordering of confirmation to action in witnessing to the faith. Along these same lines, see Aimé Georges Martimort's work as well.[31] These two authors do not sufficiently note that the effect of the sacrament is the personal perfection of the Christian, even though both powerfully note that confirmation "perfects" Christian initiation. Nonetheless, they are insufficiently attentive to the technical meaning (in natural philosophy) that the notion of *augmentum* had for St. Thomas. Along these lines, let us also cite Congar.[32]

INVESTIGATION INTO A SOLUTION

All the sources testify to the fact that confirmation would be ordered to giving the believer the Holy Spirit, indeed, to the point that this is what characterizes this sacrament. Also, there is abundant textu-

---

30. See Camelot, "Sur la théologie de la confirmation," 651–57. *Saint Thomas d'Aquin. Somme théologique, Le baptême et la confirmation: 3a, Questions 66–72*, trans. Thomas Camelot (Paris: Desclee & Cie, 1956), 403–7.

31. See Aimé Georges Martimort, "La confirmation," in *Communion solennelle et profession de foi* (Paris: Cerf, 1952), 159–201.

32. See Yves Congar, "Esprit Saint et confirmation," *Lumen Vitae* (1972).

al testimony for the idea that the Holy Spirit would be specially given *ad robur* [for strength].³³ Does this mean that the gift of the Holy Spirit to the believer is the proper effect of confirmation? This would ultimately come down to saying that it is the principal sacrament, to which all the others are ordered, indeed, the sole sacrament, for the gift of the Holy Spirit is what brings about the divinization to which the entire work of redemption is ordered. Does this also mean that confirmation would give the Holy Spirit only in the form of the gift of strength? However, the Holy Spirit Himself is the one who is the gift, and He brings all of His gifts with Him.

All the Sacraments Give the Holy Spirit

{814} To say that all the sacraments cause grace is the same as saying that they give the Holy Spirit, for even though grace is a created reality in the soul, it derives from the presence of the Holy Spirit.³⁴

If there are multiple sacraments that are distinct inasmuch as they are sacraments (and not only as various ceremonies of the same sacrament), each of them must have its own distinct significate-effect. Given that grace and the Holy Spirit are the significate-effect common to them all, each sacrament must cause grace and give the Holy Spirit under a specific modality. Here, we are faced with the distinction of seven different sacramental graces,³⁵ which involves the distinction of seven distinct modes of having the Holy Spirit, not the distinction of seven different gifts of the Holy Spirit. Let us recall that these modes are distinguished not according to the very grace that is given (and thus according to the Holy Spirit, who in each case is given as a person), but rather according to the second effect of incorporation into Christ and into the Church, which sanctifying grace (which itself is unique) produces by means of the *res et sacramentum* proper to each sacrament.

If this is how things stand, must we not revise the quite widespread manner of connecting the sacrament of confirmation to

---

33. See Camelot, "Sur la théologie de la confirmation," 653. Martimort, "La confirmation," 182–88. Against this, see Bouyer, "La signification de la confirmation," 169. Hamman, *Baptême et confirmation*, 218n66.

34. See Nicolas, *Les profondeurs de la grâce*, ch. 1.

35. See §764 above.

Pentecost (something that cannot be done without a kind of simplification)? On that day, the Holy Spirit was given to the Church once and for all, and by means of the Church, He is given to the members of the Church in accord with the degree proper to each and to their manner of being incorporated into her. Therefore, all seven sacraments (above all, the principal sacrament, the Eucharist) are connected to Pentecost, not only confirmation.

In What Specific Way Is the Holy Spirit Given and Received in Confirmation?

We have seen that St. Thomas sought out an explanation for the modality of confirmation's sacramental grace by making use of an analogy drawn from biological growth, based on the passage of a living being to adulthood. One can perhaps complete the analogy, as regards the particular living being that is the human person, by means of a social prolongation of this biological phenomenon, making use of the idea of one's initiation into adult life. This is the only direction open to our search, for neither the simple growth of grace (which would have nothing specific to it), nor, on the contrary, the idea that the gift of the Holy Spirit would be exclusively given in confirmation, can work, as we have seen.

The analogy of one's passage to adulthood

{815} St. Thomas (and the scholastics in general), following Aristotle, attributed the function of "growth" to a distinct faculty of the vegetative soul. Whatever one may think about this explanation, the phenomenon of "growth" is a fact, indeed one that is characteristic of life. The development of a living being tending toward the fulfillment of its being is fundamentally distinct from the development of the life that is in it. The first concerns its structure, and results in the perfection of the form which consists in fully being an individual of a given nature. Then it stops, whereas the living thing, thus "formed," continues to develop itself in the line of its own finality. The first kind of development is a prolongation of generation, as the terminus toward which it tends is the same as that to which generation tended, though the latter was not able to realize it itself: to make a complete being of the given nature.

In the human being, this passage is that of puberty, whose physiological and psychological importance is considerable, as is well known. In all (or nearly all) primitive religions, it is accompanied by rites of passage into adult life: physical and moral trials, a rupture with childhood, an initiation into the secrets of adult life, and so forth.[36]

This change is first of all a physical one. However, as a consequence of the moral, intellectual, and social changes that puberty brings with it, it is natural for man to transpose it into the religious domain. If we recall the fundamentally anthropological character of sacramental theology (i.e., that the sacraments are instituted for the sake of man, as responding to his natural need to have a firm basis upon the sensible order and upon the experiences of his life so that he may approach spiritual realities) one can understand and admit the idea that the divine pedagogy would have instituted a salvific sign corresponding to this universal experience in human life.

However, in order for this to be so, we must be able to discern, in the development of Christian experience, something that corresponds to this experience in man's earthly life.

The proper significate-effect brought about by confirmation

{816} If the divine action of sanctifying men through Christ is submitted to temporal succession, this is not on account of the conditions pertaining to the divine action itself. (God is above time and can instantaneously do what He wills.) Nor is it on account of the redemptive action, which was fully achieved on the cross and at the resurrection. Instead, it is on account of the developmental character of the human being. Man develops in time, either collectively through the passage of generations or individually. He physically develops from the basis of his first zygotic cell. Accordingly, he also develops sensibly, intellectually, and morally. The divine action could fully sanctify him in an instant. However, Divine Providence adapts its "project" to the natural condition of beings. Thus, sanctification has this progressive character, from one's birth into the life

---

36. See Mircea Eliade, *Naissances mystiques* (Paris: Gallimard, 1959), 21–125.

of grace (itself being preceded by a preparation) all the way to sanctity in its consummated form (in heaven) and to the resurrection.

This is what founds and justifies the analogy between the development of man's natural life and the development of the Christian life. On the basis of the former, one can understand and admit that Christian initiation, along the lines of the constitution of a human individual, is brought about in two stages (and, therefore, through two distinct actions), one corresponding to generation and the other to "formation."

Naturally, one must respect the conditions of analogical transposition. In other words, one must not transpose to the superior analogate the conditions that are proper only to the inferior one. Biological "formation" (and, consequently, intellectual formation, etc.) takes place over a relatively long period of time and therefore necessarily finds itself to be separated from birth. Spiritual progress, whose principal cause remains God acting through Christ, cannot necessarily be submitted to such a form of servitude. What can be retained as the analogy's *ratio analogata* is the notion that the Christian's formation is brought about in two moments and therefore by two different actions. What cannot be found in this *ratio analogata* is the notion of continuity, which conditions every bodily form of progress. Two "instants" are discontinuous and therefore do not require an interval of time for a determined duration.

Moreover, there is another difference deriving from the first. Whereas the principle of development is internal to the living being in the case of biological "growth," in "Christian growth," this principle is external to him (all the while remaining intimately present to him). This principle is Christ, and Christ acts by sending the Holy Spirit, (normally) making use of the Church and the sacraments to this end. However, if there are two "instants," there will also be two effects produced and, therefore, two distinct sacraments.

However, in what will this proper effect therefore consist? It can be thought of only by means of the analogy drawn from biological development. To become an adult is to arrive at the full stature of what it is to be a human, at the full stature and strength of being a man (though one individual can be much stronger than another).

On the other hand, it involves being able to play one's role in the human community, to which one had belonged from the time of one's birth, though without being able to assume the responsibilities falling to a fully constituted member. The analogy provides the following insights. Through baptism, one is already a member of the ecclesial community. However, he is an incompletely formed member who is incapable of assuming the responsibilities of a Christian, either in the Church or in relation to those who are "on the outside." As one is a member of the Church through faith, the fundamental Christian responsibility is witnessing to the faith (in the various forms that this can take). What is lacking in this member in order that he may be able to assume his responsibility (in the Church and in relation to the world) as a believer? He is lacking "strength," in the sense of complete growth. Therefore, he is not fully "formed" as a Christian. In other words, in traditional language, he is not fully initiated.

Just as the Holy Spirit gives being to the Christian, so too is the Holy Spirit the one who gives formation to the Christian being. Likewise, as it is a question of another moment in the constitution of the Christian, so too is there another manner of receiving and of having the Holy Spirit. However, this different manner can only be understood (as in general is the case for each form of sacramental grace) as sanctifying grace (and the fundamental gift of the Holy Spirit of which it is the effect and seal) in its relation to the *res et sacramentum* proper to confirmation, namely, the character by which the confirmed person is incorporated into the Church as a fully complete member.

However, if (as all too often happens) a baptized person never receives confirmation, will he never be a member of the Church "in full"? Will he spiritually be the equivalent to what a "dwarf" or "halfwit" is in the psychosomatic order? It is here that we must make use of the notion of anticipation. Just as a non-baptized person can have grace and, for this reason, can already be fully a member of the Church, so too an unconfirmed baptized person can be "formed" according to grace and thus already fully be a member of the Church. However, just as justification is caused in the first case by the baptism to be received, which already acts *propter votum baptismi*, so too here this effect of "formation" is produced by the confirmation whose intention (the *votum*) is already present, at least implicitly, in baptism. And just as this "anticipated" justification in no way does away with the necessity that one should receive baptism when this reception becomes concretely possible, so too this anticipated "formation" does not render confirmation useless. Thus, one must recognize, as a truth that is historically established and accepted today by a host of theologians, that confirmation completes Christian initiation and is the "seal" of this initiation. If it can be validly defined in reference to an external activity of witnessing (and therefore of the apostolate, which is essentially a "witnessing" to the faith), this is only true in an indirect way. He who has arrived at adulthood is able to accomplish the works of man. However, "adulthood" is first of all a perfection and a completion of the given person.[37]

The gift of the Holy Spirit bestowed at confirmation, all the while being a new and distinct gift, completes and fulfills the gift of the Holy Spirit which, as we have seen, "embraces" in itself all the effects of baptism. Thus, one can salvage a number of ancient texts in which the gift of the Holy Spirit is attributed to the "signing" [*signation*], with baptism seeming to be reduced solely to the remission of sins. The sacrament of confirmation gives the Holy Spirit to those who have already received baptism, fulfilling and completing this first gift in such a way that the baptized person already takes part in the kingdom and can therefore definitively enter into it if he dies without having received the sacrament of confirmation. For this reason, one indeed must recognize that, from the perspective of necessity, the sacrament of confirmation is less important than that of baptism. Nonetheless, it is the completion of it and for this reason is more elevated in the order of perfection. To state the matter more

---

37. N.B. This is why I do not think that one can retain Camelot's notion that the character of confirmation would be "active," in St. Thomas's sense (see *ST* III, q. 63, a. 2). The character of confirmation completes the character of baptism in its proper line, that of opening the person of the believer to the gifts of redemption. Therefore, it is marked by a fundamental passivity: "You were saved by grace." However, the grace thus received is a principle of activity, so that if the characters of baptism and confirmation can be called "passive powers" or "receptive powers," this in no way means that they doom those who receive them to a passivity in the order of salvation!

exactly: baptism that is completed by confirmation is more perfect than baptism by itself.

We still must ask why the characteristic of "giving the Holy Spirit" is attributed to confirmation with such insistence. Nonetheless, it is a sure, traditional datum: "The liturgy of confirmation, as we use it today, speaks only of one thing: the gift of the Holy Spirit. It refers to baptism from its first portion onward and beseeches that those who have been reborn in it, there receiving the remission of all their sins, may now receive the Holy Spirit."[38]

The other sacraments also give the Holy Spirit but do so only in relation to quite particular saving effects so that the consideration of this particularity prevails over that of the gift of the Holy Spirit which remains the source of said effect. (In penance, it is for the remission of sins committed after baptism. In the anointing of the sick it is for an ultimate purification enabling sickness and death to become the full realization of conformity to Christ's suffering and death, a conformation that had begun at baptism. In holy orders, it is for active cooperation in Christ's sanctifying action. Finally, in marriage, it is for the sanctifying and Christianizing of human love.) As regards the Eucharist, what obviously dominates in its case is union with Christ by means of the eating of His flesh. However, union with Christ is established through charity, which has the Holy Spirit as its source *par excellence*. Thus, what is primarily given consideration is the end toward which the Holy Spirit leads, namely, communion with the Divine Persons in Christ.

In the way that was specified above, confirmation is ordered purely to this: to the giving of the Holy Spirit. Indeed, it is for this reason that one attributes to it as its proper effect something which, in another sense, is the effect of all the sacraments.

Confirmation and the Eucharist

{817} If this is how things stand, baptism and confirmation themselves have, within the great Eucharistic unity, a wholly special relationship. In truth, they are only two successive, though inseparable, phases of one and

---

38. See Bouyer, "La signification de la confirmation," 169.

the same initiation. This is what wondrously emerges in the most venerable liturgical texts …[39]

We will say about them (i.e., about those who, though baptized, have not yet received confirmation) that there still remains something incomplete in their baptism and, therefore, incomplete in their participation in the Eucharist because the Church did not intend to achieve any of this without them (and, indeed, did not believe she could), prior to their free choice and prior to their conscious adherence.[40]

This outlook, which corresponds to the full rediscovery of confirmation as the "seal of baptism" and as the completion of Christian initiation, has some hints in St. Thomas:

> The sacrament that is related to divine worship in order to furnish it with "recipients" is baptism, for it gives man the power to receive the other sacraments of the Church. Thus, it is called the door to the other sacraments. In a particular manner, confirmation is also ordered to this, as we will see later on.[41]

Unfortunately, when he comes to show how the sacrament of confirmation is ordered to the Eucharist, St. Thomas surprisingly is content with noting: "Baptism has as its end the reception of the Eucharist, and confirmation perfects this in order that one may not draw back in fear from so great a sacrament."[42] This truly is very little!

However, how are we to understand the claim that confirmation completes the believer's ordering to the Eucharist, given that a person who is only baptized can participate in the Eucharist?* According to Fr. Bouyer, this is because confirmation is the second (in itself inseparable) phase of Christian initiation, so that it produces its effect in advance. This can be admitted, though with the reservations that we expressed above: baptism is a complete sacrament which produces its full effect by itself and, therefore, makes the believer a member of the People of God empowered to take part in Eucharistic worship. However, just as it includes beyond this (as we will see) a desire for the Eucharist (for its proper effect is itself ordered to

---

39. Ibid., 170.
40. Ibid., 178.
41. *ST* III, q. 63, a. 6.
42. *ST* III, q. 65, a. 3.

* [Tr. note: See the translator's introduction regarding certain matters of concern regarding the Byzantine East.]

something else), so too, beyond its signification and proper efficacy, it includes a desire for confirmation. Indeed, this is why the merely baptized person can already fully participate in the Eucharist.

Nonetheless, if one takes seriously the role played by the sacrament of confirmation in completing Christian initiation by "completing" baptism and if one really takes into consideration the traditional order of Christian initiation—baptism, signing [*sigillation*] (i.e., our confirmation), and the Eucharist—it seems that one should advocate for the bestowal of the sacrament of confirmation before the reception of the Eucharist. This was possible—and perhaps normal?—once upon a time when first communion was placed at the beginning of adolescence. However, since the reform of St. Pius X (which we obviously are not critiquing here, indeed, much to the contrary!), "first communion" [in the Roman Rite] has been placed at the point when one passes from their young childhood, though leaving confirmation for the beginning of adolescence before "solemn communion." (Sometimes it even comes after it, on account of practical contingencies such as the bishop's calendar!) Whatever may be the pastoral problems posed by "solemn communion," the idea was to connect confirmation to the renewal of promises made at baptism. This did imply a somewhat Protestant outlook, making it into the sacrament that completes the baptism received in infancy by incorporating into it a profession of one's personal faith as well as the conversion that was not possible at the time of baptism. Logically, this would make confirmation useless after a baptism that is received in adulthood.

This conception cannot be retained in any way. With von Allmen, we must forcefully hold that infant baptism either is or is not a complete baptism. If it needs to be "completed" by confirmation, this would not be because it is incomplete inasmuch as it is baptism, but rather because it is of baptism's nature to call for a completion that can be given only by another sacrament. Therefore, there is no need to connect the renewal of the baptismal promises to the sacrament of confirmation. It could be postponed to later, even much later, into conditions where it would signify a true personal engagement.

By contrast, confirmation given at the beginning of childhood, just before "first communion," would thus find its due placement.

One may ask, "Why not confer it at the very moment of baptism as is done in the Orthodox Church?" This custom is in no way to be condemned. However, it is not that of the Latin Church, and it seems that the latter's custom would be better.* Indeed, we have seen that there are disadvantages in conferring baptism at an age when the baptized person cannot be aware of what takes place, nor consent to it, nor consciously participate in it. We have also seen that in the case of baptism the advantage takes priority over the disadvantages, for it is the sacrament of entrance into the Church, the place of salvation and the temple of the Holy Spirit. It does not seem that the same is true for confirmation. For this sacrament, it is better to delay it to an age when the child could personally participate in it, which presupposes, obviously, fitting catechetical and spiritual preparation. However, it should not be postponed later than the time when the child will begin to participate in the Eucharist, for if he can participate in the Eucharist, he can just as well participate in confirmation. All the wonderful reasons that St. Pius X gave for justifying the admission of children to the holy table at the "age of reason" hold good just as much for confirmation.

The Character Bestowed by Confirmation

{818} To the degree (indeed, a very great degree) that confirmation was considered at the beginning of the Church's history as being the completion of baptism and its "seal," the non-repeatability of the one involved the non-repeatability of the other. Certainly, there is the problem of the imposition of hands recognized as being necessary for receiving back into the Church those who were baptized in a heretical or schismatic sect. However, it is questionable that this would have been our current sacrament of confirmation. In any case, once the latter is validly conferred, it is considered to have been given once and for all for the same reasons that hold for baptism.

This implies that the sacrament of confirmation indelibly impresses a character, namely, a participation in Christ's priesthood.

Between confirmation's character and sacramental grace (i.e., the

---

* [Tr. note: See the translator's introduction regarding certain matters of concern regarding the Byzantine East.]

gift of the Holy Spirit) we can find the relations that were specified above.[43] The character is wholly ordered to this grace. However, it continues to exist, with this ordering, even if the believer ceases, through his sin, to be in a state of grace—if he "grieve(s) the Holy Spirit of God."[44] Membership in the Church, which has the baptismal character (completed by the character of confirmation) as its formal principle, does not cease, even though the member thus connected to the Church does not participate in her life and is a dead member of her.

Consequently, to say that the confirmed person has received the perfection of Christian being is in no way to say that he has received Christian perfection. The first is perfection of the form, whereas the second is a perfection of the end. Given that the "end" by which Christian perfection is measured is the very perfection of God realized in man (i.e., the human perfection of Christ), it forever remains beyond the perfection that has been truly realized in a given human person. Indeed, on earth, one must ceaselessly tend toward this very perfection, which is only a participation in Christ's perfection. However, one can attain it only in the hereafter and, even ultimately, at the resurrection.

On the other hand, given that such perfection consists in charity, it cannot be truly possessed without the Holy Spirit. However, the opposite is the case for the perfection of the form. Even though this depends on the Holy Spirit in the sense that the Christian must be a living being who lives by the life of God, of which the Holy Spirit is the source, it can persist without one effectively possessing the Holy Spirit, like a structure that is ever capable of being animated or reanimated. To say that the sacrament of confirmation gives the Holy Spirit in His fullness is to speak of a permanent and structural opening of the person to the gift of the Spirit. It is a gift that normally is given at the moment when this structure is constituted, still imperfectly, at baptism. It is renewed on the basis of the completion that it receives by the sacrament of confirmation, a completion it receives precisely from this duplication of the gift. However, this does

---

43. See §762 above.
44. Eph 4:30. [Tr. note: Fr. Nicolas wrongly cites Eph 4:18.]

not prevent it from being the case that—on the contrary, it calls for it—the Holy Spirit will be sent to the believer ever more abundantly through the course of a faithful existence, especially by means of the Eucharist and also, on determinate occasions and for particular ends, by the other sacraments. Even if in a limit case the receptive structure for the Spirit were constituted without the Spirit in fact being received, this would not make it be the case that the sacrament of confirmation would be null and void, for with the character, the receptive structure remains ever open to the gift, which only waits to be accepted.

Therefore, the Holy Spirit must be given, and He is always given more abundantly so that the Christian "having arrived at adulthood," really lives by this divinized life for which he was "formed" and "initiated." Likewise, he needs the Holy Spirit, indeed to an ever-greater degree, so that he may realize the external works for which he has been rendered capable, works that ultimately amount to being a testimony to his faith.

Of course, as we saw above, it can happen that the Holy Spirit would be given and that such works would be accomplished before the "structure" has been prepared by the sacrament. Thus, a baptized person who is not yet confirmed can testify to his faith more vigorously than someone who is confirmed. This does not render the sacrament useless.

PART 3

THE SACRAMENT OF THE EUCHARIST

Turning now to the sacrament of the Eucharist, we find ourselves faced with not merely one sacrament set among the others but, rather, with that which is the very life of the Church, the sacrament that is the Christian mystery itself, confessed, celebrated, and lived by the Church on earth and by each believer in her and with her to the degree that he wills to do so.

MYSTERIUM FIDEI

The Eucharist is the *mysterium fidei* on two counts: it is *the very mystery of faith*; however, it is also *a particular mystery of faith*.

The Very Mystery of Faith

It is astonishing that the Eucharist was not mentioned in the Creedal statements of the faith. To account for this fact, St. Thomas proposes a somewhat underwhelming explanation. He says that, from the perspective of the act of faith, the Eucharist would not present a particular difficulty (!), given that it is included in the Holy Spirit's vivifying action ("I believe in the Holy Spirit, the giver of life") and in God's omnipotence ("I believe in One God, the Father Almighty").[1] Historically speaking, it seems that the Eucharist was not expressed in any Creedal statement simply because there had not yet been any controversies concerning it, meaning that the Church had not considered it necessary to mentioned it separately.

However, there is a more profound reason for this state of affairs (even if it is not a cause of it). Quite truly speaking, the Eucharist is not one part entering into the Creed. It is, itself, the Creed sacramentally expressed, not by formulas expressing the truth but rather by actions (obviously accompanied by formulas) which "do" the truth (in the sense in which St. John speaks of "doing the truth"). This is not the case for baptism, which is mentioned in the *Credo* as causing the remission of sins. It is a prerequisite act of faith for one to be able to enter the Church in which the mystery of faith is professed and proclaimed.

A Mystery of Faith

Nonetheless, it cannot be denied that, from another perspective, the Eucharist is one truth of the faith among the others. The Christian must believe that it is the "memorial" of the Savior's passion and resurrection. In it and through it the Church offers the sacrifice of the cross. The Christian must believe that in this celebration the bread and wine are really changed into the body and blood of Christ, which are offered there as nourishment in order to be, in it, a source of new life. Obviously, this involves particular difficulties and, indeed, is something that is difficult to believe.

Indeed, throughout the history of the Church, there was (and today still are) doctrinal controversies concerning the Eucharist as such. Such controversies are centered on the nature of the Eucharist, its role and value in the Church's life as well as in the personal life of the believer. These controversies led to interventions by the Magisterium, which fixed a "Eucharistic doctrine" in which the Church's faith is expressed as regards the Eucharist. Therefore, this doctrine indeed does constitute a particular mystery of faith.

---

1. See *ST* II-II, q. 1, a. 8, ad 6.

The Church's Faith in What Pertains to the Eucharist

Before the controversies

During her first centuries, the Church's faith was essentially expressed in liturgical texts.[2] Given that direct controversies pertaining to the Eucharist did not occur during this time, we do not find doctrinal determinations concerning it during these centuries.

What we do find in the Fathers (in addition to the catecheses that convey glosses on the liturgical texts) are references to faith in the Eucharist in relation to errors concerning other points. Thus, St. Ignatius of Antioch faults the Docetists with abstaining from the Eucharist because they do not believe in the reality of Christ's flesh.[3] St. Irenaeus presents the Eucharist as an argument in support of the resurrection of the flesh: "Therefore, how can they say that the flesh passes away in corruption and has no part in life, even though they are nourished by the Lord's body and blood? They must either repudiate the error that they commit by denying the resurrection of the body or must abstain from the Eucharist."[4]

Few explanations of the mystery are provided. However, we must note during this era that the term "to convert" (*metaballein*) was introduced, along with the idea of a physical transformation of the bread and wine, which is compared to the changing of the water into wine at the wedding feast of Cana.[5] This idea was taken up by St. Gregory of Nyssa, as well as all of the Alexandrian and Antiochian Fathers, with the notable exception of Theodoret.[6] As we will see, both the term and the idea were taken up by St. Ambrose and were introduced by him into Latin theology.

---

2. The principal texts are collected in Anton Hänggi and Irmgard Pahl, *Prex eucharistica. Textus e variis liturgiis antiquioribus selecti* (Fribourg: Éditions universitaires, 1968). Also, see Louis Bouyer, *Eucharistie. Théologie et de la prière eucharistique* (Paris: Desclée, 1966).
3. See Ignatius of Antioch, "Letter to the Smyrneans," 5–7.
4. St. Irenaeus of Lyon, *Contre les hérésies*, SC 100bis, 4.18.5 (611).
5. See St. Cyril of Jerusalem, *Catéchèses mystagogiques*, SC 126, trans. Auguste Piédagnel (Paris: Cerf, 1966), cat. 5 (154), and *Catéchèses baptismales et mystagogiques*, trans. Jean Bouvet (Namur: Éditions du Soleil Levant, 1962), cat. 22 (471).
6. See John Norman Davidson Kelly, *Initiation à la doctrine des Pères de l'Église*, trans. Ceslas Tunmer (Paris: Cerf, 1968), 454.

The controversies

The beginning of controversies concerning the Eucharist (and, first of all, concerning the "real presence") began in the ninth century in the West. We will speak about them in detail later on. They had the effect of leading the Church's Magisterium to define what the Church believes as regards the Eucharist. The first of these controversies were the retractions and confessions of faith imposed on Berengar of Tours in the eleventh century[7] and then the condemnation of Wycliffe at the Council of Constance in 1415.[8] Above all, there were the two great decrees of the Council of Trent, directed against the reformers: "On the Most Holy Eucharist" (in 1555) and "On the Most Holy Sacrifice of the Mass" (in 1562).

New developments in today's controversies

After the decrees of Trent, the Church's Eucharistic doctrine was peacefully held by all Catholics. The controversy with the Protestants aroused theological interpretations that were often contestable. Nonetheless, faith in the Eucharist was expressed—not without a notable displacement of the accent from what is essential to what is secondary—in the lavish ceremonies surrounding the real presence, sometimes tending to unfortunately defocus the Eucharistic celebration itself. In the twentieth century, there was a healthy reaction to this state of affairs. From the perspective of theological articulation, this reaction was expressed in the noteworthy rectifications by Billot and de la Taille. From the liturgical perspective, this reaction was found in a renewed attention concentrated on the assembly's participation in Mass.

After the war, there was a rather lively discounting, not of faith in the Eucharist, but of its traditional interpretation and even of its ordinary presentation. People sought out completely new explanations by availing themselves of phenomenology. (This will be studied below, and we will see both the positive contributions as well

---

7. See Pope Gregory VII, "Profession of Faith of Berengar of Tours," February 11, 1079, in D.-*Sch.*, no. 700.

8. See Council of Constance, Decree of Session 8, May 4, 1415 / February 22, 1418, nos. 1–5, in D.-*Sch.*, nos. 1151–55.

as the limitations of these explanations.) Here, let us only note that they led the Magisterium to precisely fix the inviolable content of the dogma of the Eucharist, hence fixing that which could not be undermined by these new investigations. The Dutch bishops wrote:

> We believe that we can allow theologians to freely investigate the way Christ is present in the Eucharist, so long as the changing of the bread and wine into the body and blood of the Lord (and thus, the reality of His presence in the Eucharistic *species*) are firmly maintained.[9]

This kind of investigation is what we will be undertaking in this treatise. We will be concerned with the various aspects of the Eucharistic mystery which must never be separated from each other, even if we find ourselves compelled to treat them separately.

THE THEOLOGY OF THE EUCHARIST AND THEOLOGIES OF THE EUCHARIST

{820} This distinction was proposed by Bouyer.[10] The "theology of the Eucharist" would be the theology implied in the ancient Eucharistic liturgies, elaborated in them as forms of praise and glorification of God. "Theologies of the Eucharist" would be a futile exercise of reason reflecting on problems it artificially posed, problems that would ultimately vanish were one to return to the theology of the Eucharist.

Nonetheless, one cannot deny that these problems arise, not for a rationalist [*raisonnante*] and intemperate reason, but rather, for believing reason. Likewise, one cannot deny that the Eucharistic celebrations arouse such problems without responding to them. To claim that the way that Christ is present under the *species*, the way the Eucharistic celebration is a sacrifice, and even the moment when the "conversion" is brought about are all false problems that turn us away from "the Eucharistic mystery" ultimately consigns one to an untenable paradox. Yes, such questions obviously must not be posed in the very course of the Eucharistic celebration itself. However, to

---

9. Dutch Episcopate, *Intervention du 9 mai 1965*, in *Documentation catholique* 62 (1965), col. 1178.
10. See Bouyer, *Eucharistie*, 7–20.

say that one could, indeed that the Church could, celebrate the Eucharist and affirm her faith in the liturgy while refusing to pose them or to acknowledge them as they arise, once again would ultimately lead to mere fideism, one depriving the "theology of the Eucharist" of all of its meaning and content. Indeed, the theology that is pregnant in the celebration itself must be made explicit, through the efforts of believing reason, which in itself has a methodology that is distinct from the direct liturgical action itself.

It is indeed true that faith is "lived" before being "explained" and that a theology that is not part of a lived faith, failing to constantly hold to it and to nourish itself upon it, greatly risks degenerating into a rational construction that would allow what is essential to evade notice. However, this contact with lived faith does not dispense one from having a reflective faith and from undertaking theological research. On the contrary, it pushes it onward. Indeed, such reflection is necessary, if not in the life of the individual believer as such, at least on the level of the Church's own life as a whole.

Therefore, we must refuse to accept this artificial distinction. The "theology of the Eucharist" includes, like theology in general, awareness of the mystery of faith (which, in this case, principally takes place in the liturgical celebration). However, it also includes the effort of explanation, the investigation into the *intellectus fidei* and into how one should respond to questions that are posed by the believing intellect in connection with the mystery (which it first of all accepts), as well as the critical examination of various responses that have been (or currently are) proposed. Not all of them are valid, and we must understand and explain why this is the case.

10

What the Church Believes Regarding the Eucharist

The theological study of a mystery of faith must begin by investigating what has been revealed to us about this mystery, for although faith is more than mere knowledge, it still is a form of knowledge. And theology is a reflection on this knowledge, not with the intention of adding something to it but with a view to obtaining an ever more profound assimilation of the revealed mystery by believing reason.

Given that we are here concerned with a sacred action (indeed, one that is at the heart of the Church's life, one which comes from Christ, from His intention as the founder of the Church, and from His continual vivifying influence) and not with a mere theoretical truth, the study of the revealed truths concerning the Eucharist is first of all a study of Christ's intention in instituting the Eucharist. However, given that revelation was made to the Church and that we receive it in her and through her, we cannot know Christ's will and what He has done without examining how the Church has understood (and still understands) the gift of the Eucharist that was given to her.*

---

* Bibliographical information is as follows: Johannes Alfrink, "Biblical Background to the Eucharist as a Sacrificial Meal," *Irish Theological Quarterly* 26 (1959): 290–302. Bernard Allo, *La première épître aux Corinthiens, traduction et commentaire* (Paris: Gabalda, 1956), 271–316. Jean-Paul Audet, *La Didachè. Instructions des apôtres* (Paris: Gabalda, 1958), 372–98, and "Esquisse

THE INSTITUTION OF THE EUCHARIST

The Last Supper

There can be no doubt that the Christian Eucharist originated at the final meal that Jesus had with His disciples prior to His death. However, this meal itself can only be understood within the general ritual framework of Jewish meals. Its unique character (though in continuity with them) becomes clear only by considering it within this context.

The Jewish antecedents to the Last Supper
{821} Here, we find ourselves faced with a classical difficulty: was the "Last Supper" the Passover meal? It seems that there may be an opposition between, on the one hand, the Synoptic Gospels, which

---

historique de la benediction juive et de l'eucharistie chrétienne," *Revue biblique* 65 (1958): 371–99. Pierre Battifol, *L'eucharistie, la presence réelle et la transubstantiation* (Paris: Gabalda, 1913). Pierre Benoît, "Le récit de la Cène dans Luc 22, 15–20," *Exégèse et Théologie* (Paris: Cerf, 1961), 1:163–203, and "Les récits de l'institution de l'eucharistie et leur portée," *Exégèse et Théologie* (Paris: Cerf, 1961), 1:210–39. Betz, *Die Eucharistie*. Marie-Émile Boismard, "L'eucharistie selon S. Paul," *Lumière et Vie* 31 (1957): 93–106. Bouyer, *Eucharistie*. François-Marie Braun, "In spiritu et veritate," *Revue thomiste* 52 (1952): 245–74 and 485–509. Joseph Coppens, "Eucharistie," *Dictionnaire de la Bible*, 2:1146–1215; "Miscellanea biblica, Mysterium fidei," *Ephemerides Theologicae Lovanienses* 33 (1957): 483–506; "Les origines de l'eucharistie, d'après les livres du Nouveau Testament," *Ephemerides Theologicae Lovanienses* 2 (1934): 30–60. Jacques Dupont, "Ceci est mon corps, ceci est mon sang," *Nouvelle revue théologique* 80 (1958): 1025–41. Feuillet, "Les thèmes bibliques." Werner Goossens, *Les origines de l'eucharistie sacrament et sacrifice* (Paris: Beauchesne, 1931). Adalbert Hamman, *La prière*, (Paris: Desclée, 1959 and 1963), 1:161–67. Joachim Jeremias, *La dernière Cène. Les paroles de Jésus* (Paris: Cerf, 1972). Marie-Joseph Lagrange, *Evangile selon Saint Jean* (Paris: Gabalda, 1936), 191–96 [Fr. Nicolas also cites pages 353–57 of a non-existent #4 in the bibliography listings for Fr. Lagrange]. Victorino Larranaga, "Las fuentes biblicas de la eucaristia en el N.T. Problemas de critica histórica suscitados dentro del protestantismo y racionalismo modern," *Estudios ecclesiasticos* 32 (1958): 71–92. Franz Leenhardt, *Ceci est mon corps. Explication de ces paroles de Jésus-Christ* (Neuchâtel: Delachaux et Niestlé, 1955). Xavier Léon-Dufour, "Le mystère du pain de vie," *Recherches des sciences religieuses* 46 (1958): 481–523 (481 contains an extended bibliography). Donatien Mollat, "Le chapitre VI de Saint Jean," *Lumen Vitae* 31 (1957): 107–19. J. A. Onate, "El discurso del 'Pan de Vida,'" *XXXV Congreso Eucarístico Internacional* (Barcelona, 1953), 2:402–12. Grégoire Rouiller and Marie-Christine Varone, "Saint Jean," *Les échos de Saint Maurice* 8 (1978): 181–91. Adrian Schenker, *Das Abendmahl Jesu als Brennpunkt des Alten Testaments* (Fribourg: Verlag Schweizerisches Katholisches Bibelwerk, 1977). Max Thurian, *L'eucharistie* (Neuchâtel: Delachaux et Niestlé, 1963). Trembelas, *Dogmatique de l'Église orthodoxe catholique*, 3:156–254. A. Vansteste, "Doctrina eucharistica, cap. VI ev. S. Joannis," *Coll. Burg. Et Gand.* 1 (1955): 215–24.

at least mention the Passover meal, and, on the other hand, St. John, who expressly places the beginning of the Passover on the evening of Jesus' death. Moreover, the Synoptic Gospels also provide details that preclude the possibility that the very day of Jesus' death would have been the Sabbath. Luke expressly says that it was the day of *preparation*.[1] Mark specifies that on the day of Jesus' crucifixion, Simon of Cyrene was coming back from the countryside, which would be unlikely on the Sabbath day.[2]

Joachim Jeremias holds that the meal was indeed a Passover meal and therefore that the Passover fell on a Thursday that year. St. John would have pre-dated the events by twenty-four hours.[3]

Benoît, for his part, thinks that, in any case, the supper took place "in a paschal atmosphere." By contrast, Bouyer thinks that:

> In fact, there can be no doubt that the Last Supper would have been this meal apart, whether alongside it or as a separate ritual [*à part ou un autre*]. Jesus connected the Eucharistic institution of the New Covenant to none of the details proper to the Passover meal. It is applied only to what the Passover meal had in common with all meals, that is, the rite of breaking bread at the beginning, and that of the great thanksgiving over the cup of [wine] mingled with water at the end.[4]

Ultimately, only a small nuance exists between these two positions, for the intentional reconciliation brought about between the immolation of the lambs and the death of Jesus is certain and admitted by all. Moreover, every Jewish ritual meal included Passover reminiscences.

In any case, the Last Supper is certainly situated within the framework of the Jewish "blessings" or "thanksgivings [*eucharisties*]." Jesus pronounced a "blessing" over the cup, and this blessing was without a doubt a recollection and a "memorial" of everything that God had done for Israel, though adding to it the work of salvation that was soon to be brought about through His death and resurrection.[5]

---

1. See Lk 23:24.
2. See Mk 15:21.
3. See Jeremias, *La dernière Cène*, ch. 1.
4. Bouyer, *Eucharistie*, 103.
5. See Audet, "Esquisse historique de la benediction juive et de l'eucharistie chrétienne," 371–99; Bouyer, *Eucharistie*, chs. 4 and 5.

What is absolutely new is the fact that all the "blessings" of the Old Testament are fulfilled in this ultimate and definitive "blessing" that Jesus pronounces and realizes. It is at once the fulfillment of the salvation brought about by God (through Jesus' death and resurrection) and man's perfect response to God's gift:

> Just as one can say that Jesus of Nazareth is the Word made flesh, one could also say that His humanity is man having come to pronounce the perfect "blessing," that wherein the whole of man gives himself over in a perfect response to God, who speaks. In Jesus's human life, the Divine Word finds its perfect creative and saving realization. The perfect blessing that Jesus comes to pronounce will be fulfilled in the supreme act of His existence, the Cross.[6]

The institution narratives

{822} We possess four accounts of the institution of the Eucharist: Mark 14:22–26 and Matthew 26:26–30 on the one hand (with the second depending on the first), and Luke 22:15–23 and 1 Corinthians 11:17–34, on the other hand (with Luke probably depending on Paul). They agree in what is essential, though only Paul (twice) and Luke (once) mention the command to repeat the action. However, Luke speaks of a cup at the beginning of the meal. Benoît thinks that, in reality, even in his account, there was only one cup. Bouyer, by contrast, explains this cup by the Jewish ritual meal which, in fact, included, a first cup at the beginning of the meal.[7]

The accounts that we possess already transmit liturgical traditions to us, retaining therein from Jesus' Last Supper only what had passed into the Eucharist celebrated by the first community.[8]

Several things follow from these accounts, which we will discuss under four headings.

---

6. Bouyer, *Eucharistie*, 95.
7. See Benoît, "Le récit de la Cène dans Luc 22, 15–20," 163–203, and Bouyer, *Eucharistie*, 83.
8. See Pierre Benoît, "Les récits de l'institution de l'eucharistie et leur portée," *Exégèse et Théologie* (Paris: Cerf, 1961), 1:231–32.
212–13, and Jeremias, *La dernière Cène*, ch. 3.

Jesus announced His death to His disciples as being something imminent and sacrificial
This is the proclamation that He will no longer drink the fruit of the vine with them. It is expressed in the words concerning "the body, given for you" (Luke) and above all, "the blood poured out for many" or "for you" (Luke).

The blood that will be poured out is the sign of the New Covenant
It seems that the very brief expression of Matthew and Mark, "blood of my covenant" (as Jeremias translates it), would have been the precise formula employed by Jesus.[9] In any case, this contains an obvious allusion to Exodus 24:8.

According to Ratzinger, the Pauline (and Lucan) formula, "the new covenant in my blood," would be connected to another current in the Old Testament tradition, namely, the prophetic current concerning the rejection of external worship on behalf of the interior offering of oneself, and he interprets Jesus' self-gift as being an act of martyrdom, in contrast to an act of worship.[10] However, is it exact to say that the prophetic current in question would have wished to reject every sort of worship? In reality, it tends only to emphasize that external worship can be approved by God only if it is the expression of a total self-gift.[11] On the basis of this insight, a prayer of self-offering is progressively introduced at the heart of the sacrifice, in the form of a *berekah* (blessing). As a substitution for the sacrifices during the Exile (when sacrifices were impossible), this blessing accompanied the morning and evening sacrifices before the reconstruction of the temple. Gradually,

> Jewish piety will extend the ramifications of these berakoth throughout the entire life of the pious Israelite ... From his awakening, to each of his actions of the day, up to his going to rest, they will consecrate all of his acts, and, simultaneously, will consecrate the world ... And by this, the whole of Israel will believe that she realizes the promise of the Book of Exodus,

---

9. See Bouyer, *Eucharistie*, 106.
10. See Joseph Ratzinger, "L'eucharistie est-elle un sacrifice?," *Concilium* 24 (1967): 73.
11. See Bouyer, *Eucharistie*, 40.

thus making it into an entirely priestly people, a kingdom of priests, who consecrate the whole universe to the Divine will, revealed in the Torah.[12]

This outlook certainly does represent a surpassing of the old ritual. However, Bouyer adds, far from implying the disappearance of every form of ritual, this transformation leads to a new ritual, which thus spontaneously emerges, the ritual meal:

> For the priests of Qumran or of Damascus, as for the Essenes or for the Therapeutae spoken of by Philo and Josephus, this meal comes to constitute not only a new equivalent to the old sacrifices, but even more, becomes the only remaining sacrifice, awaiting the new and eternal covenant. The great berakah pronounced over the new cup by the presider over the assembly and partaken in by all would invoke the imminent coming of the Messiah and would consecrate, in this expectation, the faithful "remnant" to the hoped-for kingdom. With this new sacrifice, we have arrived at what the Last Supper was, as well as the immediate prehistory of the Christian Eucharist.[13]

Thus, the covenant that Jesus announces is indeed the New Covenant announced by the prophets,[14] and it will also be that which is sealed by His blood: "(You have come to) the mediator of a new covenant, and to the sprinkled blood that speaks more graciously than the blood of Abel."[15] This requires us to nuance the idea that the new sacrifice would consist in the meal itself. The "blessing" pronounced by Jesus recalls the bloody immolation of Calvary.

We must also note the unique and unprecedented character (for the Jews) of what is offered so that one may participate in the sacrifice. In the Old Testament, the faithful are "sprinkled" with the blood. Here, they are invited to drink it.[16]

Finally, we must note the relationship expressly established between Christ's sacrificial death and the redemption from sins. This alone enables us to understand the fact that this complete self-

---

12. Ibid., 53.
13. Ibid., 54. See Otto Betz, "Le ministère cultuel dans la secte de Qumran et dans le christianisme primitive," in *La secte de Qumran et les origins du christianisme* (Paris: Desclée de Brouwer, 1959), 163–202.
14. See Jer 31:31–34.
15. Heb 12:24 (RSV). See Spicq, *L'epître aux Hébreux*, vol. 2, in loco.
16. See Jean-Dominique Barthélemy, *Dieu et son image* (Paris: Cerf, 1963), 220–28, and Léon-Dufour, "Le mystère du pain de vie," 515.

offering to God, which constitutes the essence of what a sacrifice is, would be the abandonment of His own life, a martyrdom and a bloody death. In this, we find a clear relationship between Christ and the person of the suffering servant in Isaiah.

Jesus gives Himself to His disciples as food and drink
The bread and wine are not only symbols that call to mind the passion (the body given, the blood outpoured). They themselves are realities. They are foods that one must truly eat.

Here, we are obviously faced with the traditional idea of participation by the faithful in the sacrifice by the eating of the victim[17] and not, therefore, with the conjunction between the life given in sacrifice (on the cross) and the life given as food, as Bouyer seems to hold.[18]

Must we think that these words express the idea that the bread and wine have really become the body and blood of Christ? We will examine this question later.

Jesus gives the command to repeat His actions
Mark and Matthew do not contain the command to repeat the actions performed at the meal. However, besides the fact that it is attested to by Luke and Paul, its authenticity is likewise clear in the fact that the first Christians immediately took up Jesus' action. The institution narratives themselves provide us with the most ancient liturgical formulas of the Eucharist. They do not claim to provide us with a detailed account of what took place, of the succession of the ceremonies of the meal such as it took place. They only preserve that part of the meal that precisely, on Jesus' command, must be repeated.

Oscar Cullmann connects the very first Eucharistic assemblies to the meal which the resurrected Christ had with his disciples.[19] [According to him,] through the influence of St. Paul, the Eucharistic meals would have come to be connected to the Last Supper shared

---

17. See Benoît, "Les récits de l'institution de l'eucharistie et leur portée," 220, and Dupont, "Ceci est mon corps, ceci est mon sang," 1025–41.
18. See Bouyer, *Eucharistie*, 105.
19. See Oscar Cullmann, "Le culte dans l'Église primitive," in *La foi et le culte dans l'Église primitive* (Neuchâtel: Delachaux et Niestlé, 1963), 112–14.

before the passion, and likewise, his influence would have led to the idea that the blood poured out by Christ is an integral part of the Eucharist. (However, Cullmann admits that even this first form of the Eucharistic meal indirectly goes back to the Last Supper because it is in remembrance of it that the disciples came together again after the Passover for the meal during which the resurrected One appeared to them.) However, Jeremias has shown the very great antiquity and "authenticity" of Mark's account, as well as its liturgical and cultural [sic] origin.[20]

Without precluding the idea that the first Christians' Eucharist would have been related to the meal had with the resurrected Jesus (and also to other meals had with Jesus during His mortal life), Benoît thinks:

> Nonetheless, there was a radically new element that transfigured these meals, making this presence of the Master concretely real in them. This new element was the repetition of the words and actions that changed the bread and wine into His body and blood. It is a new rite, though one that was grafted onto the fraternal meal easily enough, neglecting all the other details of the Passover ritual, which had become superfluous and obsolete. Thus, as we have seen, this provides an explanation for the liturgical narratives preserved for us by the gospels and St. Paul.[21]

In short, the command to repeat the actions in question essentially pertains to Jesus' words and actions expressed in the institution narratives. However, as we will see, we must ask whether it does not perhaps have a broader scope.

The Eucharistic doctrine of the fourth Gospel

{823} The fourth Gospel does not contain an institution narrative. However, besides the fact that the discourses that are gathered around the Last Supper contain certain allusions to the Eucharistic meal—perhaps even the episode of the washing of the feet is connected to a Jewish meal ceremony that immediately preceded the great blessing of the cup at the end of the meal[22]—a great discourse is placed on Je-

---

20. See Jeremias, *La dernière Cène*, ch. 2, and Pierre Benoît, "Notes sur une étude de J. Jeremias," *Exégèse et Théologie* (Paris: Cerf, 1961), 1:240–43.
21. Benoît, "Les récits de l'institution de l'eucharistie et leur portée," 223.
22. See Bouyer, *Eucharistie*, 84.

sus' own lips in the course of the Gospel, one containing a very precise and very rich Eucharistic doctrine.[23]

This "bread of life" discourse includes three distinct parts. The first presents Jesus as the bread of life who has come down from heaven (in contrast to the manna in the wilderness), one that must be approached by faith (6:22–48). The second speaks not only about believing in Christ but also about "eating his flesh" and "drinking his blood," using extremely realistic formulas (6:49–59). Finally, the third part, by way of conclusion, presents the reactions expressed by those hearing Him, as well as the final interpretation that Jesus Himself provides concerning His words: "It is the spirit that gives life, the flesh is of no avail; the words that I have spoken to you are spirit and life" (6:63, RSV; see 6:60–70).

A classical difficulty divides exegetes, namely: how are we to understand the idea that Jesus, during this first period of His ministry, could have given a teaching that could be understood only in light of the institution of the Christian Eucharist? For an exposition of the various positions concerning this question, see the works of Onate and Léon-Dufour.

According to Léon-Dufour, we would have only one discourse, really pronounced (at least substantially) during Jesus' earthly life, though being susceptible to two readings. From the perspective of His hearers, it is only a question of faith in Jesus, first in His Incarnation, then (and this would be, from this perspective, the meaning of the second part) faith in His sacrifice. To drink His blood (poured out in sacrifice) and to eat His flesh ("given for the salvation of the world") would simply be to find life through faith in the person of Jesus in His redemptive sacrifice.

André Feuillet also admits the literary unity of the discourse, but he thinks that the expressly Eucharistic intention of the second part resists Léon-Dufour's exegesis. Therefore, one would have a recomposition into which John would have placed explanations of these words really pronounced by Jesus on the occasion of this discourse as well as explanations drawn from the Church's own Eucharistic

---

23. See Jn 6:22–71. Feuillet, "Les thèmes bibliques." Léon-Dufour, "Le mystère du pain de vie," 481–523. Onate, "El discurso del 'Pan de Vida,'" 402–12.

practice. Moreover, these explanations may well have been given by Jesus Himself, at least at the time of the institution [of the Eucharist].[24] Therefore, founded on Jesus' own words, we would have an exposition of the first Christian community's Eucharistic doctrine. According to this doctrine, the body and blood of Christ are a real form of nourishment, not only a metaphorical one. Indeed, if the metaphor of nourishment is frequently found in the Bible for designating acceptance of the Word of God,[25] here it is a question of a real form of nourishment, which precludes a merely metaphorical meaning. There is another reason too, namely, the fact that in the Bible, to metaphorically eat someone's flesh and to drink one's blood means to persecute that person to the point of killing him.[26]

However, it is a spiritual nourishment (in contrast to the manna, which did not prevent the Israelites from dying). It descends from heaven. It is also expressly related to Jesus' glorification: "Then what if you were to see the Son of man ascending where he was before" (6:62, RSV). Therefore, it is not a question of being nourished on the body of Jesus materially, by making Him pass into one's own flesh. Instead, it is a question of receiving the life that will reanimate this flesh after the resurrection: "It is the spirit that gives life, the flesh is of no avail." The famous words that follow, "The words that I have spoken to you are spirit and life" (6:63, RSV), do not mean that everything preceding them must be understood allegorically. Many people, following St. Augustine, understand them as saying: the flesh that you will eat, my flesh, is a living and vivifying flesh, with a life that is the Spirit.[27] Others understand it as meaning that the spiritual man, not the carnal man, has understanding.[28] It seems that the first explanation would be in greater conformity with the context. In any case, what follows the account shows that the hearers were not satisfied by Jesus' response and continued to be scandalized, which means that they at least did not understand Him as only inviting them to take His words in a metaphorical sense.

---

24. Along similar lines, see Bouyer, *Eucharistie*, 104.
25. See Prv 9:4–6 and Dt 8:3 (a text cited by Jesus in Mt 4:4, Lk 4:4, Jn 4:32–34).
26. See Trembelas, *Dogmatique de l'Église orthodoxe catholique*, 3:189–90.
27. See François-Marie Braun, "In spiritu et veritate," 489. Cullmann, "Les sacrements," 190–92. Lagrange, *Evangile selon Saint Jean*, in loco.
28. See Feuillet, "Les thèmes bibliques."

On the other hand, this nourishment is placed in intimate relation, first, with the mystery of the Incarnation ("I am the bread which came down from heaven," 6:41, RSV), then with the sacrifice of the cross (as in the Synoptic Gospels, it is a question of eating the flesh that has been sacrificed and the blood that has been poured out).

Moreover, John situates the teaching of Jesus' discourse at the end of the meal offered to the multitude, something which cannot fail to be understood in relation to the Eucharist. It is what brings about the union of Christians with Christ, as well as their union with each other (symbolized by the image of the vine, which is the Johannine parallel to the Pauline metaphor of the body). Fraternal charity thus appears as being the fruit (and also as the condition) of the Eucharistic community.[29]

St. Paul's Eucharistic doctrine

{824} St. Paul speaks of the Eucharist not only in the text where he reports the institution narrative, indeed, as something that he himself received,[30] but also in relation to the sacred meals of the pagans, which he forbids Christians to participate in.[31]

The realism of his Eucharistic doctrine is striking. First of all, it is a realism identifying the bread with Christ's body. In [1 Cor 10:] 16–17 and what follows, the analogy with the sacrificial victims of the pagans would be meaningless if it were not a question of truly "eating" the victim of the sacrifice on Calvary. Likewise, the reproach registered against those Christians who fail to *discern the body* (of the Lord) can be understood only in a very realistic manner.[32]

As for the Eucharist's sacrificial character, it is placed in such high relief that some have advanced the idea that this referring of the Eucharist to the outpoured blood would be something that St. Paul created. (Such high relief is created by his comparison with the pagan sacrifices, as well as by the expression, "This blood is the New Covenant in my blood," which, according to Boismard, would

---

29. See ibid., 1060–62, and Cullmann, "Les sacrements dans l'évangile johannique," 196–97.
30. 1 Cor 11:23–32.
31. See 1 Cor 10:14–21.
32. See Benoit, "Corps, Tête et Plérôme dans les épîtres de la captivité," 2:107–53, and Boismard, "L'eucharistie selon S. Paul," 93–106.

be a literal citation of Jer 31:31, where we find a quite precise prophecy of a New Covenant destined to replace that of Sinai.) However, this takes into account neither St. Paul's own affirmation that he "received" the doctrine that he teaches there,[33] nor the fact that Mark in no way depends on Paul, despite the fact that he contains this same express reference to the blood of the Covenant.[34]

The "memorial" of the redemptive death

{825} "Do this in memory of me." These words of Jesus, which institute the Eucharist, also provide the key for understanding it.

The meaning of the command to repeat Jesus' actions

According to Bouyer (following Gregory Dix), the command does not pertain to the religious meal itself and to its ritual. (The repetition of such a meal would have been self-evident for the apostles, who were Jews.) Instead, it pertains to the fact that they are to re-perform, "in memory" of Jesus, that which He had done at the Last Supper.[35]

Nonetheless, we must specify that Jesus' words over the bread and the cup introduced a new ritual and that this is what was in fact repeated. Moreover, of the three "blessings'" that the Jewish meal ritual included, the third (which was an "anamnesis" of the marvels accomplished by God for His people) included variations either for the Sabbath day or for a feast day:

> On the particular thesis holding that the Last Supper would not have been the Passover meal, one can still ask whether Jesus would not have Himself improvised, in the third berakah, an explicit memorial of His blood poured out for the New Covenant.[36]

This is also Audet's opinion:

> What remains for us to suppose henceforth in the particular case of the Eucharist which Jesus left to His disciples on the evening of His last Passover with them? Simply the fact that the anamnesis of this Eucharist, following the laws of this genre and the very use made of it by Jesus such as we have already been able to discern it, would moreover have been a

---

33. See Allo, *La première épître aux Corinthiens, traduction et commentaire*, 307–10.
34. See Boismard, "L'eucharistie selon S. Paul," 133.
35. See Bouyer, *Eucharistie*, 107, and Jeremias, *Le dernière Cène, Les paroles de Jésus*, ch. 5.
36. See Bouyer, *Eucharistie*, 107.

properly evangelical anamnesis. That is, it would have been an ultimate and complete proclamation in admiration and joyous praise of the marvels that God had accomplished in Jesus the Messiah throughout the course of the Gospel and, more particularly, of the marvel *par excellence* that was very soon to crown it, namely, that of Jesus's death already having taken place by anticipation in hope and in the certitude of the glory of the resurrection. It is in this sense that on Jesus's lips (or in any case in His thought) an invitation to carry on such actions with bread and wine must necessarily be, at the same stroke, an invitation to do it in memory of Him.[37]

For his own part, Jeremias speaks of the Paschal meditation offered by Jesus, who doubtlessly prepared the apostles for the Eucharistic interpretation that He was going to give for the breaking of the bread and the distribution of the cup.[38]

However, what does "in memory of" mean? As Jeremias has shown (himself being followed by Bouyer and Thurian), it is a question of a fundamental notion of Jewish liturgy, namely, the memorial. The meaning of Jesus' words would be: "Do this as my memorial."[39]

The biblical notion of "memorial"

{826} In Jewish liturgical literature, the term "memorial" means much more than an evocation of the past, which is a subjective act (in the sense of "recalling," thus being a rite that would be executed in order to call to mind a past event). It is an objective reality that intends to render an event or person present, either for a faithful person or for God Himself. Max Thurian studied this biblical notion with much penetration.[40] With regard to the ritual of the unleavened bread [*azymes*] and of the dedication of the first-born, he observed:

> One could say that the liturgical act at once evokes and invokes. It is a sign and a memorial for man and for God together. Man is reminded of the promise of salvation as by the sign of the Cross on Cain (Gen. 4:15) and the faithful in Ezekiel's vision (Ez. 9:4). A mutual recollection of the deliverance corresponds to a reciprocal self-gift and belonging which exists between God and man. God says to His people, "I have saved you, and I save you." Israel responds to its God, "You have saved us, deliver us!" …

---

37. Audet, *La Didachè*, 389–90.
38. See Jeremias, *La dernière Cène*, 261ff.
39. See Bouyer, *Eucharistie*, 107.
40. See Thurian, *L'eucharistie*, 21–138.

The liturgical celebration of Passover and of the Unleavened Bread concretizes the mutual covenant between God and man. It recalls to God His promise of salvation and recalls to the believer the promise of his God. It is a testimony to God's fidelity before the world. The four characteristics of the Passover liturgy that will be found in the Eucharistic liturgy are thus defined: an affirmation of God's presence in His covenant, a communication of salvation as well as an efficacious intercession presented through the memorial itself, and finally, the proclamation of God's Word.[41]

Memorial and sacrifice

{827} The notion of sacrifice in the Bible is extremely complex.[42] This very general notion can be retained:

The sacrifice of the first-born is a particular case of the offering of plant or animal first-fruits. Through this very ancient custom, the religious man wishes to manifest that he is the absolute master of nothing. Refusing to take ownership of one's first fruits (which are the holiest portion, representing the whole of the harvest), he hands them over to the divinity by making them pass over to him through the offering or sacrifice.[43]

Every sacrifice is a memorial inasmuch as it has the function of reminding God about him who offers it or about a given event or promise. Even in the case of the "offering of jealousy,"[44] it is a question of reminding God about a fault so that He may not leave it unpunished. However, in a more precise manner, the memorial is one part of the sacrifice, the part that one makes rise like smoke before God *as a memorial,* the rest being consumed by the priests or the

---

41. Ibid., 49–51. Note, however: first of all, in order to understand what the Eucharist instituted by Christ is, one must admit as a necessary fact that this is how the rite would have been understood and lived in Israel and also in the Church at this privileged moment of salvation history when the Israel of God passed over into the Church (the passion and death of Jesus, the resurrection and the founding of the Church). However, one can ask oneself a question (indeed, a question that one cannot fail to pose): what is the meaning and value of this idea that one would recall to God His own promises, making a pledge to God in order to arouse Him to fulfill His promise? Everything is present to God. He has no need to remember things. On the other hand, a "sign" cannot directly pertain to God. Signs are for man. A full understanding of the Christian Eucharist also depends on the response that one will give to such a question.

42. See Charles Hauret, "Sacrifice," in *Vocabulaire de théologie biblique,* 1163–68. Gerhard von Rad, *Théologie de l'Ancien Testament,* trans. Étienne Peyer (Genève: Labor et Fides, 1967), 1:220–39. Roland de Vaux, *Les sacrifices de l'Ancien Testament* (Paris: Gabalda, 1964), 3.

43. See *Traduction œcuménique de la Bible* on Ex 13:12, note c.

44. Nm 5:15 (RSV).

faithful.[45] To the degree that the sacrifice is internalized, the memorial is the "blessing" that accompanies the sacrifice while expressing its meaning. It is a proclamation of God's name, a thanksgiving, and a self-offering.[46] It itself becomes the superior form of sacrifice, the sacrifice of thanksgiving or of praise, including, with the praise of God, the "fruit of our lips,"[47] the offering of a pure conscience and a right life,[48] and also charity, which has almsgiving as a sign.[49]

The notion of a "memorial" extends even further than that of sacrifice, for it can be applied to other ritual actions, to vestments, or to liturgical instruments, and thus to prayers, in which the person or people for whom one prays are "presented" before God.[50] However, all this is more or less connected to sacrifice, which remains the fundamental way for man to "present" himself to God.

The Eucharist's relation to Christ's sacrifice

{828} Even if every sacrifice does not necessarily include the immolation of a victim, there is no doubt that Christ's death is presented to us in the New Testament as being a sacrificial immolation, with an explicit reference to the suffering servant who is substituted for sinners. At the Last Supper, Jesus expressly referred His action to the imminent immolation that He was about to make of His own life for the remission of sins. The presentation of the separation of the body and blood had (and indeed could not have) any other meaning:

> Therefore, it is quite clear that Christ's celebration of the Last Supper [*sainte Cène*] with bread and wine, His body and blood, presented His disciples with the signs of a sacrifice: "*den bisri*—this is my body ... *den idemi*—this is my blood." The disciples had the signs of a sacrifice before them. As they took the paschal meal, they saw, in the bread and wine, Christ's body and blood, the new Paschal Lamb who would soon be sacrificed, Jesus Himself ... The tradition of the synoptic gospels will emphasize the relationship between the Eucharist and the meal in which the immolated lamb was eaten. For its part, the Johannine tradition will

---

45. See Lv 2:2–3.
46. See Bouyer, *Eucharistie*, 88–89.
47. Hos 14:2 (RSV). [Tr. note: Fr. Nicolas incorrectly cites Hos 14:3.]
48. Spicq, *L'epître aux Hébreux*, 429–30.
49. See Thurian, *L'eucharistie*, 154–55.
50. See ibid., 73–138.

emphasize the relationship between the death of the Crucified One and the immolation of the paschal lamb. In continuation of these two traditions, the Church will recognize in the Eucharist the sacrament of the sacrifice of the paschal lamb, Jesus Christ immolated on the Cross ..."[51]

Thus, the Eucharist emerges as being the "memorial" of a sacrifice, of the unique sacrifice which replaced all others, at once accomplishing that to which the others tended to no avail. By taking "memorial" in its fullest sense, one will be able to understand how the Church was able to see in this new rite much more than the simple commemoration of the sacrifice of Calvary. In it, she saw this very sacrifice actualized, re-presented (rendered present), not only for the community but also for God Himself. In short, she saw the sacrifice of the cross offered by her.

The eschatological meaning of the Eucharistic rite

{829} The institution narrative presented by St. Paul ends with an exhortation of extreme importance for understanding the meaning of the Christian Eucharist: "Indeed, each time that you eat this bread and that you drink this cup, you announce the Lord's death until He comes again" (1 Cor 11:26). Thurian, on the basis of how the word *katangellein* is used in many places in Acts and in St. Paul's writings, translates this as, "You proclaim," and holds that it has an expressly eschatological meaning. It would be a proclamation of the Lord's death, not as a past event but, rather, as currently founding the New Covenant and realizing the promise of salvation. (Indeed, we must note that the expression "the Lord's death" also encompasses the resurrection, for the Lord lives.) "Until you come": this is the proclamation of the definitive fulfillment of salvation with Christ's return.

This is corroborated and enriched by Jesus' mysterious words reported by the Synoptic Gospels: "From now on, I will no longer drink this fruit of the vine ..." A great number of commentators see a promise in this, namely, a promise to no longer drink of the vine until the kingdom comes. In this case, we would need to interpret, "Take and partake among yourselves," as meaning that Jesus

---

51. See ibid., 196.

What the Church Believes Regarding the Eucharist 369

Himself would not have drank at the supper, which seems absurd to Bouyer but is, by contrast, strongly supported by Jeremias.[52] However, Bouyer seems to admit the idea of a promise. Jeremias admits it and even translates the expression "do this in memory of me" as meaning, "So that God may remember me and establish the kingdom." This is contested by Benoît.[53]

After having established, through strong arguments, that we are here faced with a promise, Thurian shows the eschatological meaning that this gives to the Eucharist. Such a promise (the promise of the Nazirite, which was widely practiced at Jesus' time) has the meaning of being an insistent prayer, a kind of "challenge" offered to God. Through this promise, Jesus begins His engagement on the way of His passion and death, so that there will no longer be any meal for Him before the fulfillment of the kingdom. Thus, He already freely removes Himself from the world for this. He now only belongs to the kingdom. Finally and above all, He gives His disciples (and through them, the Church) the symbol of an insistent prayer for the coming of the kingdom at the same time that He leaves them the assurance that the promise will be fulfilled. Therefore, the Eucharistic liturgy opens up onto the kingdom to come, while at the same time being an interior and hidden participation in the kingdom that has already come (according to the dialectic of the "already and the not yet").[54]

St. Paul's words, "Until He comes," must be understood as meaning, "So that He may finally come":

> Through the proclamation of the Eucharist in words and deeds, the Church (like Christ at the first holy Meal [*premier sainte Cène*]), insistently prays and ardently makes supplication for the fulfillment of the Passover and for the coming of God's kingdom in glory, a prayer that is expressed from the beginning by the acclamation, "Maranatha—Come, O Lord!"

Therefore, the entire Eucharistic liturgy is eschatologically oriented toward the fulfillment of the Passover and toward the kingdom in which all the faithful will be resurrected. The New Covenant's worship, like that of the Old, is wholly directed toward this ultimate fullness in the kingdom,

---

52. See Bouyer, *Eucharistie*, 101, and Jeremias, *La dernière Cène*, 247–60. [Tr. note: I have added the closing parenthesis after this, as Fr. Nicolas only has an opening parenthesis for this remark.]
53. See Benoît, "Notes sur une étude de J. Jeremias," 242.
54. See Thurian, *L'eucharistie*, 212–22.

as St. Paul expressed to Agrippa: "And now I stand here on trial for hope in the promise made by God to our fathers, to which our twelve tribes hope to attain, as they earnestly worship night and day" (Acts 26:6–7, RSV).[55]

This eschatological intention is itself included in the idea of a "memorial," which is not only a re-presentation before God of something that He has already accomplished but, moreover, is the presentation of the pledge of the promise still to be realized, as well as a pressing invitation to finally realize it, as Jeremias has shown: "For Zion's sake I will not keep silent, and for Jerusalem's sake I will not rest, until her vindication goes forth as brightness, and her salvation as a burning torch."[56]

"You who put the LORD in remembrance, take no rest, and give him no rest until he establishes Jerusalem and makes it a praise in the earth."[57] The Eucharist is the *memorial* by which the Church continually, "without allowing God to rest," implores that the eschatological promise be realized, which in the context of the Last Supper, Luke relates thus: "You are those who have continued with me in my trials; and I assign to you, as my Father assigned to me, a kingdom, that you may eat and drink at my table in my kingdom, and sit on thrones judging the twelve tribes of Israel."[58]

Christ's presence in the Eucharistic meal

{830} From the first Eucharistic controversies up to our own days, great insistence has been made concerning Christ's "real presence" in the Eucharist at the expense of great biblical and liturgical perspectives on the Eucharist so that, by way of reaction, there has been a contemporary tendency, if not to minimize this real presence, at least to merge it into its general liturgical context. Moreover, obvious ecumenical preoccupations incline people in this direction, for if an agreement could be reached among the various Christian confessions concerning the Eucharist, it can obviously be reached on these liturgical grounds and on the religious and Christian meaning of the Eucharist, much more than on the recognition of the real

---

55. Ibid., 219–20.
56. Is 62:1 (RSV).
57. Is 62:6–7 (RSV).
58. Lk 22:28–30 (RSV).

presence (or at least on the meaning that one must give to "real" in the affirmation of this presence). A good testimony to this state of mind is furnished for us by this remark:

> Both Catholics and Lutherans are beginning to understand that we should not determine what is proper to the sacrament so much so in light of the notion of the *praesentia realis*. The Last Supper must be understood and explained on the basis of its organic situation in the ecclesiological context wherein the Lord of the Church is ceaselessly present in bringing about salvation in preaching and interpersonal relations.[59]

Doubtless, this is true, but we must *also* understand this sacrament in the light of the *praesentia realis*, for without this, it would be a simple evocation of Christ's eschatological presence, a "commemoration."

The Eucharist is a meal, a sacrificial meal. The meal is a classic eschatological symbol, one used by Jesus Himself to designate the definitive coming of the kingdom: a meal with the Messiah, with Christ. This is an idea reinforced in the apostles by the recollection of the meals they had with Jesus, above all with the resurrected Jesus. It is a sacrificial meal. In the most ancient biblical texts, it was a question of "eating and drinking in the presence of Yahweh":[60] "The participants knew Yahweh to be invisibly present as the guest of honour."[61] By understanding "memorial" in a strong sense (as we have seen is necessary), some have been led to hold that it seems sufficient to say that Christ is present in the Eucharistic meal as an invisible tablemate in whom one hopes and for whose coming in glory one implores.

Nonetheless, let us note that there is an element in the institution narrative that cannot be reduced to this outlook, namely, the fact that Jesus is presented in it as food and as drink, not as a tablemate. Neither God nor the Messiah are present as the tablemate* of the eschatological meal.

This is an irreducible element, not in the sense that the idea of

---

59. See Wilm Luurt Boelens, "La discussion sur la Sainte Cène dans l'Eglise évangélique," *Concilium* 24 (1967): 98.
60. See Ex 34:15, 1 Sm 9:12ff, 2 Kgs 10:19.
61. Von Rad, *Théologie de l'Ancien Testament*, 1:226. [Tr. note: Gerhard von Rad, *Old Testament Theology*, trans. D. M. G. Stalker (New York: Harper and Row, 1962), 1:257.]
* [Tr. note: Reading *comensal* where Fr. Nicolas has *nourriture*.]

being a tablemate would need to be excluded by it but, instead, in the sense that this element cannot be included directly in the idea of being nourishment but, rather, is added to it. In fact, the two ideas are not incompatible in the unique case presented by the Eucharistic meal. Indeed, we have seen that Jesus does not give His dead flesh and lifeless blood to be eaten and drunk but instead gives His living person, His resurrected flesh and His living blood. In this unfathomable mystery ("The words I have said to you are spirit and life"), the one who invites simultaneously can be (and is) nourishment as well as the tablemate of the meal: "Se nascens dedit socium, convescens in edulium" [By birth our fellowman was He, our food while seated at the board].[62]

If this is true, the words, "This is my body; this is my blood," cannot be sufficiently interpreted only by the notion of being a tablemate, nor by any other form of Christ's presence to His Church. It is a unique presence. What Christ gives His disciples to eat and drink at the Last Supper are His flesh and blood. This is what is given great emphasis by the strong expressions found in John 6.

In order to avoid understanding the words of institution in a realistic sense, one would need to be able to understand them allegorically. Benoît has shown that this was impossible. Indeed, it was not a question of leading the disciples' minds to a mysterious truth by means of an image that is closer to the senses and to the mind. (On the contrary, Jesus' flesh was in clear sight. They saw it with their eyes, whereas, from the first moment, the relationship of the bread and wine, which they saw before them, to this flesh and to the blood that animated it was mysterious.) It was a question of inviting them to a physical act (eating and drinking), and to this end, a nourishment and drink were proposed and given to them. Could they have anything other than a realistic understanding of what had been said to them concerning this nourishment (namely, that it was Jesus' flesh) and about this drink (namely, that it was His blood)?

The revealed mystery consists in this mysterious identification of the nourishment with Christ's flesh and of the drink with Christ's

---

62. St. Thomas, *Office for Corpus Christi*. [Tr. note: I have taken the translation of the terse Latin of the poetry of the *Verbum Supernum* from the classic translation of Neale et al.]

blood, realized at the same time. And, as we have seen, this mystery must be situated in the whole of the liturgical mystery. However, it cannot be diluted down into it. It has its own proper consistency.

[In the scriptural texts,] it is not said that the bread has become Christ's flesh and that the wine has become His blood. However, unless one were to reduce the revealed truth to an unintelligible (and therefore inadmissible) formula, to say, "This is my flesh," regarding something that was spoken about earlier by saying, "He took the bread," leads to the irresistible conclusion: the bread was changed into my flesh; it no longer is bread; it is my flesh.

In the "theories concerning the real presence" with which Max Thurian concludes the section of his book dedicated to the "real presence,"[63] he affirms the real, substantial, and bodily presence of Christ in the Eucharist very strongly and likewise affirms that the bread and wine truly, really, and substantially become His body and His blood according to the Gospel. However, he pushes back against every effort at explanation as being futile and careless. We will examine this position in due time. Here, it is important to note that Thurian bases himself on the data of the Gospel, having thoroughly studied them in light of what is taught in the Old Testament, establishing a foundation for his very firm affirmation of the real presence and of the real changing of the bread and wine into the body and blood of Christ.

The Celebration of the Eucharist by the Church

In a course on dogmatic theology, we cannot study how the primitive Church celebrated the Eucharist, nor the development of this celebration, for in order for such a study to be sufficiently detailed, it would go beyond the limits of such a course. The proper place for such a study is in a course on liturgy.*

---

63. See Thurian, *L'eucharistie*, 273–78.

* One will find a substantial exposition of this in Bouyer's *Eucharistie*, which we have cited many times. The principal ancient liturgical texts are gathered together in Hänggi and Pahl, *Prex eucharistica*. Also, see *Eucharistie d'Orient et d'Occident*, 2 vols., ed. Bernard Botte (Paris: Cerf, 1970).

THE EUCHARISTIC MYSTERY IN THE CHURCH'S TRADITION

Merely undertaking an exegesis of the scriptural texts concerned with the institution of the Eucharist cannot suffice for establishing the bases of our faith. Indeed, in the most conscientious and most learned of persons, this leads to divergent interpretations concerning what the Eucharist is and concerning what it must be for believers. If faith is founded on the Word of God such as it is recorded in Scripture, an understanding of Scripture is commanded already by faith and not only by exegetical and historical science. We receive from the Church the Word of God in which we believe. In the present case, it is important to know how the Church has received, understood, practiced, and taught the gift of the Eucharist.

Tradition

The Eucharistic oblation of the victim of Calvary

Before Nicaea

{831} The* most ancient post-apostolic texts related to the Church's faith in the Eucharist perhaps go back to the first century (if one follows Audet, who places the *Didache* between 50 and 70 A.D.).[64] In any case, they certainly go back to the beginning of the second century, in the letters of St. Ignatius of Antioch and then in the writings of St. Justin Martyr.

On account of their emphasis on the interior and spiritual character of Christian worship in contrast to the ancient sacrifices, these

---

* In this course, we cannot study all the testimonies of tradition in detail and chronologically. The reader may refer to the articles on the Eucharist and the Mass in the *Lexikon für Theologie und Kirche*, along with the rich bibliography that they contain. Also, see the articles "Eucharistie" and "Messe" in *Dictionnaire de théologie Catholique*, as well as the following texts: Battifol, *L'eucharistie*. Johannes Quasten, *Monumenta eucharistica et liturgica vetustissima, Florilegium patristicum*, Fasc. 7 (Bonnae: Hanstein, 1935). Jésus Solano, *Textus eucharisticos primitivos* (up to Gregory the Great) (Madrid: BAC, 1947 and 1954). Jean-François Noël de Watteville, *Le sacrifice dans les textes eucharistiques des quatre premiers siècles* (Neuchâtel: Delachaux et Niestlé, 1966). Josef Andreas Jüngmann, *Missarum solemnia* (Paris: Aubier, 1951). *Eucharistie d'Orient et d'Occident*, ed. Bernard Botte, 2 vols. (Paris: Cerf, 1970). Johannes Betz, "Sacrifice et action de grâces," *La Maison-Dieu* 87 (1966): 78–96.

64. Audet, *La Didachè. Instructions des apôtres*, 187–210.

texts at first glance seem to deliberately exclude the idea that the Eucharist would be a sacrifice. Such is the case in Athenagoras.[65] St. Justin, who holds that the only worship worthy of God consists in making use of His gifts for ourselves and for the poor "by giving Him thanks and by addressing our hymns of praise to Him for having created us, for having furnished us with all the proper means for our prosperity, for the variety of species and the cycle of seasons."[66] Clement of Alexandria writes: "The Church's sacrifice consists in the prayer that rises from holy souls like incense, containing in itself, along with the offering, an attitude of being a complete gift to God."[67]

However, all of this precludes the idea of bloody sacrifices, above all, a conception of sacrifice along the lines of a tribute offered to God, one that would be external to man himself, not engaging his person but, instead, aiming to put him on an even balance with God. By contrast and in line with the prophets, Christian authors insist on internal worship, which is the recognition of God as the Creator, thanksgiving for His benefits, and a complete self-offering. This connection to the teaching of the prophets is emphasized by these authors' references to the prophecy of Malachi,[68] which we can already find in the *Didache*,[69] and above all in Justin,[70] who expressly identifies the Eucharist with the sacrifice announced by Malachi, saying that the Eucharist is the sacrifice that Jesus Christ commanded to be offered.

Audet observes that there is no reason "to unduly freight this qualification of sacrifice (*thusia*) with the more or less conscious desire to include the *Didache* as being on the record for theological preoccupations that, in reality, came along quite later through the course of history."[71] By saying this, he only means that there is no "theory" of the Eucharist as a sacrifice in the *Didache*. However,

---

65. See Athenagoras, *Supplique au sujet des chrétiens*, SC 3, trans. Bernard Pouderon (Paris: Cerf, 1943), ch. 13, 98–100.
66. Justin Martyr, *La philosophe passe au Christ*, 1.13.
67. Clement of Alexandria, *Stromata*, PG 9, Strom. 7.7.
68. Mal 1:10–12.
69. See *Didache* 14.3.
70. Justin, *Dial.* 28.5, 41.2, 117.1.
71. Audet, *La Didachè*, 462–63.

there is something much more precious, namely, the expression of the way the first Christians lived the Eucharist as realizing the perfect sacrifice, the pure worship approved by God that had been announced by the prophets.

In the letters of St. Ignatius of Antioch, in which the Eucharist holds such an important place, it appears as a sacrifice through his mentioning of the flesh of Christ, who suffered for our sins,[72] as well as through his mentioning of the blood and the altar: "Therefore, take care only to participate in the one, singular Eucharist, for there is only one flesh of our Lord and Savior Jesus Christ and only one chalice for uniting us in His blood, as well as one altar and one bishop …".[73] As a sign that the idea of a self-offering in no way excluded the idea of a sacrifice, we must note here the sacrificial vocabulary used by Ignatius in speaking about his martyrdom. Now, this sacrificial vocabulary is also Eucharistic: "I am your expiatory victim, and I offer myself in sacrifice for your Church, Ephesians, which is renowned through the ages";[74] "Do not obtain anything for me beyond being poured out as a libation to God while the altar is still ready …";[75] "I am God's grain and am ground down by the teeth of beasts in order to become the pure bread of Christ … Implore Christ for me so that by means of the beasts I may become a victim offered to God."[76]

The Eucharistic character of this self-offering in martyrdom is quite noteworthy in the prayer of St. Polycarp reported in the account of his martyrdom.[77] [As Bouyer notes:]

The account of his martyrdom presents us with this bishop handing himself over to fire exactly as though he was going to celebrate the Eucharist for the last time. And in this ultimate celebration, where he is identified with the host that is Christ, one can think that his prayer traces the lines of the Eucharist that he himself had offered.[78]

---

72. See Ignatius of Antioch, "Letter to the Smyrnians," 7.1.
73. See his "Letter to the Philadelphians," 4.1.
74. See his "Letter to the Ephesians," 8.2.
75. See his "Letter to the Romans," 2.2.
76. See his "Letter to the Romans," 4.2–3.
77. See Justin, *Martyrdom of St. Polycarp*, 263.
78. Bouyer, *Eucharistie*, 117.

[Moreover, as observed by Martimort:] "In this brief thanksgiving, ... we can perceive, as it were, a vague echo of an episcopal Eucharist from this era, at once improvised and traditional."[79]

As a very ancient testimony to the sacrificial character of the Eucharistic liturgy at its origins, we must also cite a text which itself can only date from the beginning of the third century but which transmits to us a much more ancient tradition, namely the *Apostolic Tradition* of St. Hippolytus.[80] In the anaphora recorded in this text, we find a clear expression of the idea of a sacrifice connected to Christ's passion: "Therefore, remembering his death and resurrection, we offer you the bread and wine, giving thanks that you have judged us worthy of holding ourselves in your presence and with serving you" (a term that expresses liturgical service).[81]

In St. Irenaeus (born in approximately 140, becoming the bishop of Lyon around 180), we likewise find an obviously sacrificial conception of the Eucharist, though with an ambiguity. It seems that for him the sacrifice consists in the Church's offering of the goods of the earth (bread and wine) and, by means of them, the good deeds of the faithful. However, after saying that one offers oneself to God through the Word (and this is why, he says, the Jews do not offer it), he suddenly gives this reason why it is no longer the case that the assemblies of heretics offer it:

In addition, how will they be certain that the Eucharistic bread is the body of their Lord (and that the cup is His blood) if they do not say that He is the Son of the Author of the world (i.e., His Word) ... For us, our manner of thinking (about the resurrection of the body) is in accord with the Eucharist, and the Eucharist in turn confirms our way of thinking. Indeed, we offer Him that which is His own, for just as the bread that comes from the earth, after having received God's invocation, is no longer ordinary bread but instead is the Eucharist, constituted of two things (one earthly, the other heavenly) so too our bodies, which participate in the Eucharist, are no longer subject to corruption since they have the hope of the resurrection.[82]

---

79. Aimé Georges Martimort, *L'Église en prière, introduction à la liturgie* (Paris: Desclée, 1965), 272.

80. Bernard Botte, "Introduction," Hippolytus of Rome, *La tradition apostolique*, SC 11bis, 11–31, and Bouyer, *Eucharistie*, 158–68.

81. See St. Hippolytus of Rome, *The Apostolic Tradition*, ch. 4.

82. St. Irenaeus of Lyon, *Adversus Haereses, libri quinquie, Libri I-II*, ed. Ubaldo Mannucci,

Through an awkward formulation (and doubtlessly an awkward conception as well), it seems that we are here faced with the expression of an important dimension of the Eucharistic mystery. It includes the offering of oneself (i.e., of one's goods and one's good actions, above all one's acts of charity), as well as the assumption of these goods by Christ, who makes them His own, so that in the end, Christ is what is offered, and in virtue of the Eucharist, all the Christians in Him constitute His body.

This theological insight will find itself expressed in a much more acceptable manner by St. Cyprian in the next century (200–258), in his famous sixty-third letter, a veritable small treatise on the Eucharist, written against those who claimed to celebrate the Eucharist without wine. This is where we find the famous symbolic interpretation of the water mixed with the wine in the chalice, which signifies the Christian people offering itself with Christ:

> In consecrating the chalice of the Lord, the water alone cannot be offered, just as the wine alone cannot be offered, for if someone offers wine alone, the blood of Christ comes into being without the people. When they are mix together, being joined in a union in which they are mingled, then the spiritual and heavenly mystery (*sacramentum*) is brought about (*perficitur*).[83]

The entire letter affirms with impressive force that the Eucharist is a sacrifice. The argument constantly taken up against the Aquarians is that one does not have the right to do anything differing from what Christ did and told us to do:

> If one is not permitted to infringe the least of the Lord's commands, how much more will it be impious to transgress commands that are so great, so important, and so connected to the very mystery of the Lord's passion and that of our redemption or to change them into something other than what has been divinely instituted, doing so on account of a human tradition?[84]

We offer the same sacrifice as that of Calvary: "And because we make mention of the passion in all the sacrifices, indeed the passion of the

---

in *Bibliotheca sanctorum Patrum et scriptorium ecclesiasticorum* (Rome: Forzani, 1907), bk. 4, 18.4 (609–11).

83. See St. Cyprian in *Corpus scriptorium ecclesiasticorum latinorum* 3 (Vienna, 1868), 711–13.

84. Ibid., 713.

Lord is the sacrifice that we offer (*passio est enim Domini sacrificium quod offertimus*) ..."[85]

By looking backward in history, one can add that he whom St. Cyprian called his master (i.e., Tertullian) is also clear, though in a less developed manner, about the sacrificial character of the Eucharist. In him, we find expressed the distinction that will become classical later on, namely that between the Eucharist as nourishment (or, as will be said, as a sacrament) and the Eucharist as a sacrifice, a distinction used in relation to those who do not wish to attend the Eucharist so as not to break the fast! [For example, we find him stating:]

Therefore, does the Eucharist jeopardize our homage vowed to God? Will not your station (i.e., your fast) be more solemn if you present it on the altar to God? If you have received and preserved the body of the Lord, you assure two advantages for yourself: participation in the sacrifice (*participatio sacrificii*) and the fulfillment of your duty.[86]

We can conclude this rapid outline of ancient writers' thoughts concerning the sacrificial character of the Eucharist with a text that, even though it was composed at the end of the fourth century (around 380), can be considered the *terminus ad quem* of a very ancient development,[87] namely, the eighth book of the *Apostolic Constitutions*.[88] The anamnesis, after the very lengthy thanksgiving for creation and for Christ's redemptive action, and after the institution narrative, is clearly sacrificial: "We offer you, King and God, in accord with (Christ's) command, this bread and this cup, giving thanks to you through it for having rendered us worthy to stand before you and discharge this priesthood ..."[89]

After Nicaea

{832} During this era, the Eucharist is undeniably held to be the Christian sacrifice, that is, Christ's sacrifice, offered by the Church. As St. Cyril of Jerusalem expresses it: "A spiritual sacrifice, a non-

---

85. Ibid., 714.
86. Tertullian, *De oration*, CSEL 1, ch. 19, 192.
87. See Bouyer, *Eucharistie*, 10.
88. See Johannes Quasten, *Initiation aux Pères de l'Église*, trans. Jean Laporte (Paris: Cerf, 1956), 2:220–21, and Bouyer, *Eucharistie*, 245–61.
89. See Quasten, *Monumenta eucharistica et liturgica vetustissima, Florilegium patristicum*, 198, and Hänggi and Pahl, *Prex eucharistica*, 82ff.

bloody worship (performed) on this propitiatory victim."[90] St. John Chrysostom develops this doctrine broadly, explaining that our sacrifice is one, though offered many times:

> Just as there is only one body and not many bodies, even though it is offered in numerous places, so too the sacrifice is one and the same. Our High Priest is this same Christ who offered the sacrifice by which we are purified. The victim who was offered thus and who cannot be consumed is the same victim as the one that we offer now. [It is the sacrifice] that we now offer in memory of what was then done ... We do not offer another sacrifice but, instead, offer one that is ever the same. Or, rather, we celebrate the memory of it.[91]

The final trait mentioned will be noted, though it cannot suffice to annihilate the idea that in the Eucharist we offer Christ's sacrifice (an idea so clearly and strongly affirmed), though it recalls the fact that the Eucharist can be called a "sacrifice" only in a particular sense. The same idea is exposited at length, indeed interminably, in the two *Homilies on the Mass*.[92]

In Gregory Nazianzus, we can note a curious anticipation of what will later be called immolationist theories [of the Eucharistic sacrifice]: "Very reverend friend, do not cease to pray and intercede for me when you make the Word descend by His word, when by an unbloody division you divide the body and blood of the Lord using your voice in the guise of a lance."[93] For him, the Eucharist is the "external sacrifice, the figure [*antitype*] of the great mysteries," presupposing one's self-offering:

> Knowing this, as well as the fact that nobody is worthy of the grandeur of God, of the victim, and of the priest, if He did not previously offer Himself to God as a living and holy offering, if He did not present a reasonable and agreeable homage, if He did not immolate to God the victim of praise and a broken spirit, the only one that the Author of every gift demands to be offered, how could I dare offer the external sacrifice, that which is the figure of the great mysteries?[94]

---

90. St. Cyril of Jerusalem, *Catécèses mystagogiques*, cat. 5.

91. St. John Chrysostom, *Homélies sur l'épître aux Hébreux*, PG 63:161, hom. 17.3.

92. See Theodore of Mopsuestia, *Homélies catéchétiques*, ed. Raymond Tonneau and Robert Devresse (Vatican City: Biblioteca Apostolica Vaticana, 1949), 461–605.

93. See St. Gregory of Nazianzen, *Epistolae*, PG 37:280–81, letter 171.

94. See Gregory of Nazianzen, *Orationes*, orat. 2, §95, 497A.

The idea of a sacrifice connected to the Eucharist is also clearly expressed in the anamnesis that St. Ambrose cites, in a form that is very close to that of the Roman Canon: "We offer you this unblemished victim, this spiritual victim, this unbloody victim, this sacred bread and the chalice of eternal life, and we beseech you and pray that you would accept this offering by the hands of your angels upon your altar on high…"[95]

During the Patristic period, St. Augustine is the one who elaborated the most complete theology of the Eucharistic sacrifice (and, first of all, a theology of sacrifices in general).[96] He so insisted on the offering of the Mystical Body in the Eucharist that one could believe that, for him, Christ in Himself is not offered in it. However, it is quite clear that the Church offers herself in the Eucharist in union with the sacrifice really offered on Calvary:

> Thus, He is the priest. He Himself is the one who offers, and He Himself is the offering. And He willed that the Church's sacrifice would be the daily sacrifice of this reality, for given that she is the body having Him as her head, she learns that she offers herself in it.[97]
>
> This is so true that if there are four things to be considered in every sacrifice (he to whom one offers, he who offers it, that which is offered, and that for which one offers it), this sacrifice is at once the unique and true mediator Himself who, by reconciling us with God through the sacrifice of peace, remained one with Him who offers it, and made Himself one with those for whom He offered it—He who offered being one with what He offered.[98]

Conclusion

From the beginning and consistently, the Church has understood the Eucharist as being her sacrifice, the sacrifice of Christians. She

---

95. St. Ambrose, *De sacramentis*, SC 25bis, ed. and trans. Bernard Botte (Paris: Cerf, 1961), 4.6 (87).

96. See St. Augustine, *La Cité de Dieu*, OESA 33–37, bk. 10, ch. 6, §§5 and 7, and Joseph Lecuyer, "Le sacrifice selon S. Augustin," in *Augustinus Magister, Congrès international augustinien, Paris, 21–24 September 1954, Communications*. Études augustiniennes (Paris: Études Augustiniennes, 1954), 905–15.

97. See Augustine, *La Cité de Dieu*, bk. 10, ch. 6, §20.

98. See St. Augustine, *La Trinité*, Books I-VII, OESA 15, trans. Marcellin Mellet and Pierre-Thomas Camelot (Paris: Desclée de Brouwer, 1955), bk. 4, ch. 14 (389). See Bernard Quinot, "L'influence de l'épître aux Hébreux dans la notion augustinienne de vrai sacrifice," *Revue d'études augustiniennes* 8 (1962): 129–68.

has understood it as being the sacrifice in which she offers herself, in which she offers even the goods of the earth, though in which she above all offers man's good deeds, the works of charity. However, she has understood it as a sacrifice that is such only in reference to Christ's sacrifice on Calvary, the unique sacrifice into which her own sacrifice is assumed and which He has given her to offer.

Eucharistic conversion

The identity of the offerings and Christ's body and blood

{833} Expressions of this identity can be found in many forms from early on in the Church's history.[99] In St. Ignatius of Antioch[100] we find the first appearance of a theme that will be abundantly developed in subsequent years, namely the idea that the Eucharist is a *remedy for immortality, an antidote so that one may not die but, instead, may live in Jesus Christ* (see Jn 6:49–51).

One could cite Tertullian's very realistic texts, for example: "The flesh is nourished on the body and blood of Christ so that the soul may be filled with God."[101] Likewise, there is a text from Origen: "We eat the bread that, by the priest's power, has become [Christ's] body, a holy thing that sanctifies those who make use of it with a right intention."[102] Again, we could consider yet another one of his texts:

> You who regularly attend the divine mysteries know the kind of reverent precaution with which you guard the body of the Lord when it is given to you, out of fear that some crumb may fall from it and that part of the consecrated treasure may be lost. For you will be culpable—and you are right in this—if some part of it were lost on account of your negligence.[103]

Other authors from the third century could be consulted as well. However, we will see that an exact determination of these authors' thought is only possible if one clarifies the meaning of other expres-

---

99. See Ignatius of Antioch, "Letter to the Philippians," 4, "Letter to the Romans," 7.3, "Letter to the Smyrnaeans," 7.1. Justin, *Apology* 1.65–66. Battifol, *L'eucharistie*, 6–32. Irenaeus, *Contre les hérésies*, 4.18 (609–13).
100. See Ignatius of Antioch, "Letter to the Ephesians," 20.2.
101. Tertullian, *De resurrection carnis*, PL 2, ch. 8.
102. Origen, *Homélies sur l'Exode*, trans. P. Fortier, SC 16 (Paris: Cerf, 1947), 8.33.
103. Origen, *Contre Celse* [trans. Marcel Borret, SC 132 (Paris: Éditions du Cerf, 1967)], 13.3.

sions that they employ, expressions that at first glance suggest an identification of the offerings with the body and blood of Christ in a manner that is symbolic and not real.

In the fourth century in the East there the notion of a "conversion" begins to emerge, meaning a change in the elements (i.e., the bread and wine) which are changed in their nature by God's omnipotence. Most often, they are said to be changed by the Holy Spirit, though sometimes by the Word, becoming something they were not before, namely, the body and blood of Christ. In this vein, we must first of all cite Cyril of Jerusalem.[104]

Likewise, in a fragment of a sermon attributed to St. Athanasius, we read:

> As long as the prayers and invocation have not been performed, there is only bread and a cup. However, after the great and marvelous prayers have been said, the bread becomes the body and the cup becomes the blood of Our Lord, Jesus Christ ... When one lifts up the great prayers and holy supplications to God, the Word descends on the bread and the cup, and the bread becomes His body.[105]

In St. Gregory of Nyssa, we find an extraordinarily realistic explanation of this *conversion*:

> As Christ during His mortal life transformed bread into His flesh and wine into His blood (through digestion), so too now, as the Apostle says (1 Tim. 4:5), the bread is sanctified by the Word of God and by the prayer. Certainly, this does not mean that it passes into the body of the Word but, rather, that it is converted by the Word into His body, just as the Word Himself said: "This is my body ..." All this (man's divinization by the insertion of the body and blood of the Word into the very body of believers) is given by the nature of the visible things that have been changed into him.[106]

This ultra-realistic conception of Eucharistic communion as being physical contact between the believer's flesh and Christ's and as a penetration of Christ's body and blood into the organism was quite typical in this era, as much in the Antiochians as in the Alexandrians:

---

104. See St. Cyril of Jerusalem, *Catécèses mystagogiques*, SC 126, cat. 4, 66.1–2 (135–37).
105. See PG 26:1325.
106. St. Gregory of Nyssa, *Discours catéchétiques*, PG 45, ch. 37, c. 97 (cited in Trembelas, *Dogmatique de l'Église orthodoxe catholique*, 3:211–12).

"I form, as it were, one tissue with you," St. John Chrysostom said to Jesus.[107] Likewise, St. Cyril of Alexandria compares the communicant's contact with Christ's flesh to the contact of Jesus' hand that renders life to the child of the widow of Nain: "If that which is corrupted is enlivened by mere contact with the sacred flesh, how would we not receive more fruitfully the enlivening benediction, since we eat it? …"[108]

If equally strong expressions of this realism are found a little later on in someone like St. Hilary of Poitiers,[109] this Eucharistic realism, along with the notion of *conversion* (of the physical changing of the bread and wine into Christ's body and blood), passed into the Latin tradition, above all in St. Ambrose:

> You perhaps say, "This is my normal bread." However, this bread is bread before the sacramental words (*ante verba sacramentorum*). As soon as the consecration takes place, the bread is changed into Christ's body. Therefore, let us prove this. How can that which is bread be the body of Christ? Thus, by what words is the consecration brought about and from whom do these words come? From the Lord Jesus … What word of Christ? Indeed, it is that by which all things were made.

Then, he invokes creation:

> Therefore, if there is so great a power in the Lord Jesus's words that what did not exist begins to exist, how much more efficacious is it for making that which already existed exist and be changed into something else? (*Ut sint quae errant et in aliud commutentur*)

He thus recalls the virginal conception and the various miracles of the Bible, concluding:

> Does this not enable you to understand everything that was produced by this heavenly word? If it acted in an earthly fountain, as well as in other things, does it not act in the heavenly sacraments? Therefore, you know that the bread is changed into the body of Christ and that one places water and wine into the chalice, though that the consecration brought about by the heavenly word makes it into [His] blood.[110]

---

107. See Gross, *La divinization*, 258.
108. Ibid., 288.
109. See Mersch, *Le corps mystique du Christ*, 1:430–34.
110. St. Ambrose, *De sacramentis*, bk. 4, §§14–19.

Likewise, in the *De mysteriis*:

> Therefore, let us prove that it is not a question of what nature has produced but of what the blessing has consecrated. Indeed, the power of the blessing is greater than that of nature since the blessing changes nature itself (*quia benedictio etiam ipsa natura mutatur*).[111]

There can be no doubt that Ambrose is here speaking of a real and physical action exercised on the bread and wine in order to change them in a real way, that is, in order to make this thing that was bread no longer be bread so that it may become the body of Christ. If the term "transubstantiation" designates in a precise manner the change of the bread's substance into the substance of Christ's body and the change of the wine's substance into the blood's substance (with the appearances of bread and wine remaining), it is clear that such language belongs to a much more developed stage of theological reflection on the identity of the offerings and Christ's body.

However, the term *conversio* used by St. Ambrose (or other similar terms such as *commutare*, to transform) indeed signify, without otherwise explaining, this change in the fundamental reality of the offerings, leaving the appearances the same. Later on, the notion of "transubstantiation" will strive to explain this change. This distinction between what appears and what has, in reality, become something whose appearances have not changed (a distinction that the act of faith in the Eucharist makes from the start) is likewise expressed in this striking text drawn from Theodore of Mopsuestia:

> Therefore, the priest, in giving the offering, says, "The body of Christ," and he teaches you by this word not to look upon that which appears but, rather, to represent to yourself in your heart that which has come into being from that which had previously been present, indeed that which, through the coming of the Holy Spirit, is the body of Christ.[112]

However, the interpretation of all these texts raises a significant difficulty concerning the identification of the offerings with Christ's body and blood. Very often, they are mixed in with other texts that say that the bread and wine are the sign, likeness, or symbol (*tupos*

---

111. St. Ambrose, *De mysteriis*, §50.
112. Theodore of Mopsuestia, hom. 2, §28.

or *antitupos*) of Christ's body and blood. Does this not invite us to interpret all these texts as involving a purely symbolic identification?

The offerings as a "figure" of Christ's body and blood

{834} Wilmart[113] presents a series of characteristic texts along these lines.[114] (Other such texts can be found in Kelly.)[115]

Whatever thesis one adopts with regard to the prehistorical liturgy, it is a fact, indeed one that is repeated many times, that the words "figure of the body and blood" in the *De Sacramentis* (of St. Ambrose) find their Greek equivalent in an anamnesis of Serapian's *euchologion*,[116] which is a document contemporaneous to the *De sacramentis*. Hence, it is quite tempting to suppose that Tertullian, in arguing *ad hominem* against Marcion's Docetism and in speaking of the "figure of the body of Christ," was only taking up an expression that had already been consecrated by liturgical use.[117]

According to Wilmart:

If the meaning of the word *figura* is richer, our modern equivalent "figure" is more obscure, suggesting the idea of unreality, which is typically excluded from Latin use ... As regards the Eucharist, it is not wrong to read *figura* as indicating that it is a visible sign or a sacramental symbol. Consequently, *panis figura corporis* will mean that the Eucharistic bread is the sacrament of Christ's invisible body with a precise allusion to the external form of the bread which is configured to the immaterial body.[118]

In confirmation of this point, one can look at the specific texts in St. Augustine in which he expresses an equivalence between *figura* and *sacramentum*. Indeed, with regard to Judas, he notes that he was admitted[119] "to the feast during which He entrusted the figure of His body and blood and left it to them." Augustine expresses this elsewhere in other terms: "He did not leave his disciples unaware of the fact that such a great villain was among them, and nonetheless, He

---

113. See D. A. Wilmart, "Transfigurare," *Bulletin d'ancienne littérature et d'archéologie chrétiennes* (1911): 282–92.
114. See ibid., 286.
115. See Kelly, *Initiation à la doctrine des Pères de l'Église*, 450.
116. See Hänggi and Pahl, *Prex eucharistica*, 130–31, and Bouyer, *Eucharistie*, 203.
117. Wilmart, "Transfigurare," 288–89.
118. Ibid., 288.
119. See Augustine, *Enarrationes in Psalmos*, PL 36–37, in Ps. 3, §1.

gave to them all the sacrament of his body and blood for the first time."[120]

What forbids us from interpreting these expressions as though they indicated a purely symbolic identification is the fact that, at the same time in the Church's history, we can find such expressions being connected to realistic ones by one and the same author and, indeed, in one and the same text, thus absolutely precluding such a purely symbolic interpretation. Thus, St. Cyril of Jerusalem writes: "For in eating, you do not eat bread and wine but, instead, take the body and blood of Christ which they signify. (Literally: 'but, instead, the *antitypes* of the body and blood of Christ.')." This comes after the aforementioned text concerning the conversion of the bread and wine and just before a remarkable text on the reverence with which one must receive "the King," "the body of Christ":

> Indeed, tell me, if you had been given golden flakes, would you not hold them with the greatest of care, taking care not to lose any of them and not to allow them to suffer any damage? Therefore, will you not exercise much more care for an object that is more precious than gold and precious stones so that you may not lose a crumb of it?[121]

Likewise:

> We participate in a particular manner (*ôs*) in the body and blood of Christ. For, under the figure of bread you are given His body, and under the figure of wine, you are given His blood, so that you may become, by having taken part in Christ's body and blood, one body and one blood with Christ. Thus, we become bearers of Christ, His body and blood having spread out in our members. In this way, according to blessed Peter, we become partakers in the divine nature.

This final formula is already realistic, but behold the conclusion:

> You have received the teaching and are full of certitude. What appears as being bread is not bread, even though it seems to be so for your taste. No, it is the body of Christ. What appears to be wine is not wine, even though taste may so wish it to be such. No, it is the blood of Christ.[122]

---

120. See Couturier, "Sacramentum et mysterium dans l'oeuvre de S. Augustin," 161–332, and Gaston Lecordier, *La doctrine de l'eucharistie chez S. Augustin* (Paris: Gabalda, 1930).
121. St. Cyril of Jerusalem, *Catécèses mystagogiques*, SC 126, hom. 5.
122. Ibid., hom. 4.

In his two homilies on the Mass, Theodore of Mopsuestia says:

> Now, it is quite obvious[123] that, in giving the bread, He did not say, "This is the figure of my body," but instead, "This is my body." In the same way, He did not say, "This is the figure of my blood," but instead said, "This is my blood." For He wished that we would no longer look on the nature of these (the bread and the chalice) once they received the grace and coming of the Holy Spirit but, rather, should take them as being the body and blood of Our Lord.[124]

However, a few pages later, he writes: "Indeed, we will receive, in the sacramental figures by means of bread and wine, the immortality that we await, the promise of which has been given to us (in the Gospel's words, 'I am the bread of life')."[125]

Finally, St. Ambrose, whom we have already seen affirming his sacramental realism with such strength, in the same place speaks of the wine as being the symbol of [Christ's] blood.[126] Above all, referring to the liturgical words that precede the consecration, he cites this formula, which is certainly very ancient: "The prayer says, 'Grant us that this offering may be approved, spiritual, and acceptable, because it is the figure of the body and blood of Our Lord, Jesus Christ.'"[127] This prayer has passed over into our Roman Canon (which was constituted by the sixth century), though with this characteristic modification: "Deign to make this offering become for us the body and blood of Our Lord." This change does not indicate a modification in the idea. However, the term *figura*, which did not exclude the realistic sense for the ancients (a sense that the full context of St. Ambrose proclaims) inclined the mind toward a metaphorical sense and for this reason became inadequate for expressing the idea expressed in the older formulas.[128]

Indeed, if the idea of the identification of the offerings with the body and blood of Christ must be understood in a realistic sense (this identification being brought about by the power of the Holy

---

123. This is how Quasten translates the passage in Quasten, *Initiation aux Pères de l'Église*, 3:590.
124. Theodore of Mopsuestia, *Homélies catéchétiques*, 475.
125. Ibid., 479.
126. See Ambrose, *De sacramentis*, bk. 3, §20.
127. Ibid., §21.
128. See Wilmart, "Transfigurare," 288.

Spirit and of the prayer, in the very things and not merely, nor first of all, in the mind of the believer), it does not itself exclude a symbolic meaning. If the offering that the priest presents to the faithful is really the body of Christ, it preserves the appearances of bread. For the senses, it is bread. Therefore, the mind [*esprit*] is invited to pass from an object that is first attained (a sign, a "likeness," a "figure") to another object that is not directly attained but is attained by faith alone, on the basis of a perceived sign, namely, to the body of Christ. The act of faith in the real presence overcomes this dualism by affirming the identification of the sign and the signified, but it does not abolish it. This and this alone is what is expressed in the ancient formulas *figura corporis, antitypos,* or *typos*. This is what is equivalently expressed for us by the formula, "The sacrament of the body and blood of the Lord."

Spiritual nourishment

{835} Christ is in this sacrament because it is the body of Christ. Therefore, it provides spiritual, not bodily, nourishment. As the apostle says about its image [in the Old Testament]: "Our fathers ate a spiritual food and drank a spiritual drink." For the body of God is a spiritual body, and the body of Christ is the body of the Divine Spirit because Christ is Spirit, as we read, "The Lord Christ is Spirit placed before us."[129]

This text echoes a long tradition and played a considerable role in the formation of Eucharistic theology in the Middle Ages.[130] It emphasizes another dimension of the Eucharist which is constantly present to the Fathers' thought and in their expressions, namely, its "spiritual" character. Our question here is whether the affirmation of this spiritualism of the Eucharist contradicts and annuls the expressions of the realism of the identification of the Eucharist with Christ's body and blood, meaning that we would have two mutually incompatible traditions, or whether, on the contrary, they express two connected and interdependent aspects of one and the same mystery.

St. Augustine, who spoke so much about the Eucharist, is doubt-

---

129. Ambrose, *De mysteriis*, §58.
130. See de Lubac, *Corpus mystium*, 139–61.

lessly the doctor who had developed thought concerning this spiritual character of the Eucharistic mystery the most, to the point that his formulations at first glance incline one toward the most spiritualist interpretation of the "Eucharistic presence." One can take his thought as being the focal point for studying this problem.[131]

Following Van der Lof's schema, we can perceive a threefold tension in these texts by Augustine, giving rise to these contrasting formulas, which seem to dilute what later on will be called the "real presence."

A first tension exists between the Eucharist as the sacrament of the body and blood of Christ and as the sacrament of the Church as the body of Christ. The studies by de Lubac and Huftier highlight this back-and-forth (which can be surprising for us today) between these two different acceptations of the expression "body of Christ." Communion is at once an eating of the body and blood of Christ and the communion of the faithful, constituting the body of Christ.

However, we must note that this kind of back-and-forth is utterly classical. It was already indicated in the *Didache*'s metaphor (which had been taken up very often, even by St. Augustine himself[132]) between the bread made from a multitude of grains, the wine made from a multitude of grapes, and the Church made up of a multitude of men coming from all places. St. Paul himself invites such a comparison: "The bread which we break, is it not a participation in the body of Christ? Because there is one bread, we who are many are one body, for we all partake of the one bread."[133] This in no way signifies a minimization (ultimately to the point of extinction) of the Eucharist's identification with the real and physical body of Christ. Indeed, much to the contrary, this body is what gathers together and unifies the body that is the Church.[134] However, it means that the

---

131. See St. Augustine, *S. Aurelii Augustini textus eucharistici selecti, Florilegium patristicum*, fasc. 35 (Bonn: Hanstein, 1933). Pierre-Thomas Camelot, "Réalisme et symbolism dans la doctrine eucharistique de S. Augustin," *Revue des sciences philosophiques et théologiques* 31 (1947): 394–410. M. Huftier, "Corpus Christi. Amen," *Vie Spirituelle* 111 (1964): 477–501. De Lubac, *Corpus mystium*, chs. 1–2. L. J. Van der Lof, "Eucharistie et présence réelle selon Saint Augustin," *Revue d'études augustiniennes* 10 (1964): 295–304.
132. See Augustine, *S. Aurelii Augustini textus eucharistici selecti, Florilegium patristicum*, 20–22.
133. 1 Cor 10:16–17 (RSV).
134. See Benoît, "Corps, Tête et Plérôme dans les épîtres de la captivité," 107–53.

Eucharist's identification with the body of Christ is itself ordered to something else that is more important, something that gives its meaning, both for Christ and for us, namely the building up of the body of Christ: "What is seen has a bodily appearance. What the intellect attains produces a spiritual fruit."[135] This represents an essential aspect of the mystery of the Eucharist, a point of constant meditation for St. Augustine's thought. This conception is connected to the great and fruitful Augustinian distinction between sacramentally receiving the body of Christ and spiritually receiving it.[136] It is useless to eat the body and drink the blood *in sacramento* if one does not spiritually partake it.

The other tension (one that, in reality, is very close to the preceding one) exists between the two ways that Christ gives Himself as nourishment. In His word, He gives Himself in faith. In His sacrament, He gives Himself in the reception of the Eucharist, which itself has spiritual union, faith, as its fruit. This is connected to John 6 and to the twofold meaning of this great text's proclamation that Jesus is the bread of life. Already in the Alexandrians of the third century (Clement and Origen), we find this passage from the idea that in the Eucharist we eat Christ's body and drink His blood to the idea of nourishing our souls on Christ's teaching:

> This bread, which God the Word acknowledges as being His body, is the Word that nourishes the soul, the Word that proceeds from God the Word. It is the bread that proceeds from the heavenly bread ... This drink, which God the Word acknowledges as being His blood, is the Word who marvelously fills and intoxicates the heart of those who receive it ... The Word of God did not call His body the visible bread that He took between His hands but, rather, the word in sacrament (mystery) of which the bread was to be broken... Indeed, what can the body or blood of the Word be if not the word that nourishes and rejoices the heart?[137]

If this kind of text were not counterbalanced by other texts by the author expressly affirming the identification of the Eucharistic bread

---

135. See Augustine, *S. Aurelii Augustini textus eucharistici selecti, Florilegium patristicum*, loc. cit.

136. See Camelot, "Réalisme et symbolism dans la doctrine eucharistique de S. Augustin," 406–10.

137. Origen, cited and translated by Quasten, *Initiation aux Pères de l'Église*, 2:106.

with the body of Christ, we would need to interpret this text as denying it. However, Origen elsewhere acknowledges that the blood of Christ can be consumed in two ways, sacramentally and when we receive His vivifying words. And, as Quasten notes, he judges that the first manner is that of the unlearned, whereas the second is for the learned. In such an assertion, we find ourselves faced with a form of excessive spiritualism, which does not deny the sacraments in general (and, in particular the sacrament of the body and blood of Christ) but which tends to see this way of being united to Christ as being an inferior stage of the Christian life.

If the Fathers frequently interpret the words *panis noster quotidianus* as referring to the Eucharist,[138] in St. Augustine alone, who himself also proposes the aforementioned interpretation, it is also interpreted as referring to the word of God and to His commandments.[139] Here again, it is in no way a question of reducing the Eucharistic "heavenly bread" solely to the word of God. Rather, the concern here is to emphasize the primordial role of faith in "communion in the body of Christ."[140]

Finally, van der Lof notes yet another, third tension, one also having a biblical origin, namely, between Christ's presence to His Church and His absence from the time of the ascension onward. The Church awaits Christ who must return. The Eucharist thus would be completely stretched out toward the glorified Christ. He notes that St. Augustine, who in one text excludes the possibility of Christ being able to exist simultaneously on the cross and in other places, never had the thought of excluding the case of the Eucharistic presence.[141] Let us say that he does not pose the question in this manner (as is true of ecclesiastical authors up to his time). One will need to look much later to resolve this problem concerning the one body of Christ simultaneously present on a host of altars and in heaven. The hypothesis of "multilocation" is precluded of itself, without being considered apart [*seulement*]. No other hypothesis is proposed.

---

138. See Hélène Pétré, "Les leçcons du Panem nostrum quotidianum," *Recherches des sciences religieuses* 40 (1951–52): 63–79.
139. See ibid., 71ff.
140. See Villette, *Foi et sacrement*, 1:265–78.
141. See Van der Lof, "Eucharistie et présence réelle selon Saint Augustin," 304.

As we have seen, the tension between Christ who is present and Christ who has ascended to heaven and must return lies at the very heart of the Eucharistic mystery.¹⁴² Christ's Eucharistic presence is not a "historical" presence (after the manner of one person living among others). It is an "eschatological" presence, that of Christ "in His proper form" (*propria specie*), who has preceded His own people into the kingdom by promising that He would return, while remaining "mysteriously present" in their midst. We will see whether this implies that it is not the presence of the historical Christ. However, this way of posing the problem comes much later.

We cannot interpret the numerous spiritualist expressions used by St. Augustine as though they expressed a denial (or even a kind of forgetfulness) of the real identification of the Eucharist with Christ's true body and blood, for we can find a great number of very energetic affirmations of this identification in Augustine's own writings.¹⁴³

Spiritualism is in no way opposed to the real presence of Christ's body. Rather it is opposed to the bodily character of this presence, of the action that produces it, and of the effects which have it as their source.¹⁴⁴

The Development of Eucharistic Theology and the Determinations of the Magisterium

The continuity of the Patristic tradition in the Eastern Church

{836} Unlike the great dogmas of the Trinity and the Incarnation, which aroused impassioned controversies from the beginning of the Church's history, indeed ones that lasted for many centuries, the Church's Eucharistic dogma remained undebated for a long time. The doctrine of faith concerning it was principally expressed in liturgical practice and in the preaching preparing the faithful for it or that which accompanied it (above all in catechetical homilies).

Without major controversies, the Eastern Patristic tradition developed in the direction of an ever-firm, unambiguous affirmation,

---

142. See §829 above.
143. See Augustine, *S. Aurelii Augustini textus eucharistici selecti, Florilegium patristicum*, 18–19 and 21–23.
144. See de Lubac, *Corpus mysticum, L'Eucharistie et l'Église au Moyen Age*, 159.

both of the real presence and that Christ's unique sacrifice is offered at each celebration. In St. John Damascene, we must note the first affirmation of the consecratory efficacy of the epiclesis. This is the point of departure for a controversy that burst forth much later on between the Eastern Church and the Latin Church. We will study it later on in this volume.

In essence, the two Churches' faith in the Eucharist has remained identical, even at the most serious moments of controversies that resulted—alas!—in schism. The council of Ferrara-Florence, the last and ultimately-failed attempt at averting the worst outcome, witnesses to this agreement in a striking manner:

> The Church of Byzantium, even separated from Rome, remains a striking testimony to the faithful transmission of the Fathers' Eucharistic doctrine. She has not known the rich development that took place in the Latin West. However, in a way that is no less striking, she has kept and lived, in word and worship, the teaching that she had received concerning the Eucharist, a real commemoration of the Savior's action, as a sacrifice and a sacrificial meal. In a way, we can consider the Council of Ferrara-Florence as being a kind of endpoint. Granted, the decree of union dating July 6, 1439, *Laetentur coeli*, only makes mention of the Eucharistic controversy related to the unleavened bread, and in this regard, it approves each Church's custom. However, this absence of clarifications of itself witnesses to the identity of faith in the Eucharist expressed by both Churches. If the decree did not explicitly say anything more, this is precisely because the parties involved were aware that they were in agreement.[145]

The first Eucharistic controversies in the Latin Church

This[146] tranquil possession of faith, held and practiced in the liturgical celebration, will last in the West until the ninth century. It is at this time that controversies began. They aroused a vigorous effort of investigation, which led to precious theological elucidations, though also to divisions that are not easily repaired today.

---

145. Neunheuser, "Meßopfertheorien."
146. See Jean-Charles Didier, *Histoire de la presence réelle* (Paris: CLD, 1978). De Lubac, *Corpus mysticum*. Neunheuser, "Meßopfertheorien," 350–52.

The treatise of Paschasius Radbertus and the polemic aroused by it in the ninth century

{837} In 831, Paschasius Radbertus, the abbot of Corbie, wrote, under the title *De corpore et sanguine Domini*, a book that can be considered the first theological treatise dedicated to the Eucharist.[147]

His fundamental thesis holds that there is an identity between Christ's historical body and His Eucharistic body, without which the Eucharistic body would be only a shadow and an empty figure of the other. However, it does not have the same mode of being as the historical body. It is a question of a spiritual presence. The Eucharist is at once real [*vérité*] and a figure. It is real [*vérité*] because it really contains the body and blood of Christ. It is a figure because it recalls the immolation of the cross. It is a figure in everything that is externally perceived (*exterius sentitur*), whereas it is real [*verité*] in what is interiorly and correctly grasped by the mind or believed (*interius recte intelligitur aut creditur*). He barely pushes forward in explaining this spiritual mode of presence which leaves the appearances untouched.

This text, which was not polemical in any way, aroused a response, which itself was the point of departure for an ardent controversy. Another monk of the same abbey, Ratramnus, opposed him in a book having the same title. In that text, he denied the identification of the Eucharistic body of Christ with His historical body, insisting on the figure-aspect of the Eucharist, seeming to rule out that it could simultaneously be a figure and reality [*vérité*], as Paschasius said.

Are we here faced with a denial of the real presence or simply with an overly emphatic and insufficiently nuanced affirmation of the difference between the mode of being that the body of Christ had during His earthly, historical life and its sacramental mode of being? It is difficult to say. What is sure is that, one century later, Berengar of Tours (who read Ratramnus's text as being attributed to John Scotus Eriugena) placed his own theory of a purely symbolic

---

147. See Paschasius Radbertus, *De corpore et sanguine Domini*, ed. Beda Paulus (Turnhout: Brepols, 1969).

presence under its patronage. So too did the reformers of the sixteenth century. Among his contemporaries, his disciples (Florus of Lyon, Druthmar, and others), without formally denying the real presence, did not insist on it much, preferring to consider the sacrament in its figurative aspect and in its role in the spiritual life of the faithful.

Paschasius likewise had numerous disciples who strove to more fully develop his explanation of this identification of the Eucharistic body of Christ with His historical body. Haymon of Halberstadt was the most explicit of such disciples, using very intense expressions of the dogma of transubstantiation, merely failing to use the word itself.[148]

There can be no doubt that this abrupt affirmation of the identity of the Eucharistic body with Christ's historical body poses problems, at least terminologically. Likewise, we can be sure that Ratramnus's reaction, followed by the even more lively reaction of Rabanus Maurus, helped theology to advance by arousing the developments that came afterward.[149]

The Berengardian controversy

{838} If[150] hesitations can be registered with regard to Ratramnus, there can be no doubt that Berengar, the famous schoolmaster of Tours in the eleventh century, denied the real presence, reducing Christ's Eucharistic presence to a form of mere symbolism. Admitting in theology (as in every science) only purely rational knowledge ("dialectic"), he held that the position of his adversary, Lanfranc, was absurd. Lanfranc had said, in accord with the Catholic faith, that the bread disappears, even though some of its qualities remain. Berengar rejected the very principle of the distinction between substance and accidents, which someone like Paschasius did not yet know how to make (though it was the key to the explanation that he was seeking).

---

148. See Battifol, *L'eucharistie, la presence réelle et la transubstantiation*, 479.
149. See de Lubac, *Corpus mysticum*, ch. 3.
150. See Didier, *Histoire de la presence réelle*, 67–78. Jean de Montclos, *Lanfranc et Béranger: la controverse eucharistique du XIe siècle* (Louvain: Spicilegium Sacrum Lovaniense, 1971). Charles E. Sheedy, *The Eucharist Controversy of the 11th Century Against the Background of Pre-Scholastic Theology* (Washington, D.C.: The Catholic University of America Press, 1947).

For Berengar, the thing is identical with its sensible qualities. (In this, his very reason failed him. Theological rationalism sometimes betrays reason just as much as faith.) Likewise, he rejected any possibility that a body could not be localized, which would entail (according to Him) that one accept the idea of multilocation if one wished to maintain the real presence of Christ's body. Thus, he held that the Catholic position was intrinsically contradictory.

The great adversary of Berengar was Lanfranc, a monk of the abbey of Bec-Hellouin, who then became the abbot of Saint-Etienne of Caen and ultimately was the archbishop of Canterbury. His thought must be connected to that of Guitmond and Alger of Liège. If they were not yet ready use the distinction of substance and accidents (although the term "accident" is found in Guitmond) in opposition to Berengar, they affirmed against him—by relying on tradition and as a truth of faith that is anterior to any explanation—the substantial change of the bread into the body of Christ and of the wine in to His blood, holding that it is a fundamental change reaching the very reality of the bread. In this, they brought about notable theological progress in comparison to the simple affirmations of the Fathers, which we considered above, as well as in comparison to Paschasius Radbertus.

This progress paved the way for the development that would lead to the doctrine of the high scholastics. They affirmed that after the consecration the bread and wine are changed in an incomprehensible and ineffable manner into the substance of Christ's body and blood, the same body that was born of Mary and that had hung upon the cross. Moreover, against Berengar, who thought that the bread and wine remained unchanged, all the while becoming Christ's body in a symbolic manner, Lanfranc argued that the Fathers' affirmation (especially that of St. Ambrose) that the bread has become the body of Christ is incomprehensible if the bread has not ceased to be bread.

This led to a very beautiful and rich confession of faith by Lanfranc. In it, the abrupt formula of Paschasius Radbertus is very finely nuanced without being repudiated in the least. Moreover, the confession strongly emphasizes one aspect of the mystery, namely, the preservation of Christ's immutability in His eschatological existence in the Eucharistic mystery. We will see that this is a point of the greatest importance and also will discuss how it was overlooked in so-called Counter-Reformation theology. This was the profession of faith required of him:

> Therefore, we believe that the earthly substances which are divinely sanctified on the Lord's table by means of the priestly mystery are ineffably, incomprehensibly, and miraculously changed into the essence of the Lord's body through the activity of [His] awesome power, preserving the appearances of the same things and certain other qualities, in order to spare the horror that there would be were one to perceive naked and bloody flesh and also so that believers may obtain the recompenses connected to the faith. As regards the Lord's own body, it remains in the heavens at the right hand of the Father, immortal, inviolate, in its integrity, untouched, and unscathed, so that one could say that it is the same body drawn from the Virgin that one consumes and, likewise, that it is not the same body. It is the same, certainly, as regards the essence and what is proper to His true nature, as well as its saving power. However, it is not the same if one considers the external form of bread and wine and everything that was mentioned above.[151]

For his part, Guitmond sought to push a little further still his reflection on this change of the bread and wine. Berengar had distinguished three kinds of change: from a non-subject to a subject (i.e., generation), from a subject to a non-subject (i.e., corruption), and from a subject to a subject (*ut est motus*—it is not clear whether he is here thinking of local motion). Guitmond added a fourth kind of motion to this list, one that is unique and known only by faith, by which one existing subject is changed into another already existing subject (which therefore does not exist on account of this change). And, comparing the Eucharistic change, which is certainly difficult to believe in, to creation and annihilation, he thought that the former is less difficult to believe in than the latter. Consequently, he thought that if God can create and can annihilate, and if we are bound to believe this, we can also believe that He can bring about the Eucharistic conversion.

Another set of Berengar's objections remains. First, there are those that he registered against the simultaneous presence of Christ

---

151. Lanfranc, *Liber de corpore et sanguine Domini*, PL 150:430C.

on many altars, a fact that, according to him, would presuppose multilocation, which is impossible. Equally, there is his objection drawn from the error of the "Capharnaites" (i.e., those who heard Jesus at Capernaum), who imagined that a kind of cannibalism had been proposed to them and that Jesus refuted it by saying, "The words you have heard are spirit and life." Lanfranc insisted on the invisible and spiritual character of this presence, which nonetheless was real and substantial. The Eucharistic presence is perfectly compatible with Christ's presence in heaven *in propria specie* precisely because the Eucharistic presence is spiritual. He refused Berengar's dilemma: either the host is taken up to heaven or Christ descends to earth. However, he thought there was an inexplicable mystery in the fact that Christ could simultaneously exist on earth and in heaven—Berengar's objection is founded on human wisdom, not Divine Wisdom. We will see how awareness of these difficulties and the attempt to resolve them by appealing to a presence that is simultaneously spiritual and real prepared the way for the more developed explanations of high scholasticism, which were so rich and so well-balanced, especially those of St. Thomas.

Let us note Guitmond's effort in explaining how Christ can be really present in a number of hosts. He made use of a comparison to speech, noting how we can express our thought to a great number of people, while this thought nonetheless remains in our own mind. Each of our hearers receives the same word. Even if this rapprochement between the Eucharistic presence of the Word and His presence in the mind of the believer is here used with some clumsiness, it remains a very suggestive and traditional manner of approaching the mystery of the Eucharist.[152]

Finally, regarding the problem of Christ's complete presence in each of the sacramental species alongside the fact that there is a difference between the two consecrations (which are not simple repetitions of each other), we find in Alger of Liège a sketch of the solution that will be given later on. As we will see, it consists in making a distinction between the presence *vi sacramenti* (precisely in virtue

---

152. See Jacques Guillet, "Parole de Dieu," in *Dictionnaire de spiritualité ascétique et mystique, doctrine et histoire*, ed. Marcel Viller, SJ (Paris: Beauchesne, 1937ff), vol. 12, col. 241.

of the sacramental action) and *per concomitantiam* (on account of its conjunction with what is thus rendered present):

> The bread and the wine are formally (*per se*) consecrated into [His] body and blood, so that the (consecrated) bread is formally designated as being [His] body and the (consecrated) wine as being [His] blood, whereas, as we believe, we consume the entire Christ in His body and in His blood. Nonetheless, these are not two separate Christs; rather, each species is the unique Christ.[153]

As regards the permanence of the "appearances" ("qualities" and "form" in the terminology used by Lanfranc and Alger, "accidents" already in Guitmond), this is explained by recourse to the Divine Omnipotence which can hold these "forms" of substance in being and existence when the substance is no longer there. (Later on, one will say that the Divine Omnipotence can hold them in their subsistence in this state.)

Thus, the heretical denials of the presence of Christ's true body in the Eucharist (at least those found in Berengar) caused theologians to become aware of the problems that faith in the revealed mystery arouses for reason and to seek out solutions for these problems in order to approach an explanation enabling reason to assimilate the mystery and accept it by showing that it involves no contradiction (without, for all that, claiming to eliminate the mystery and its irreducible obscurity).

The appearance of the term "transubstantiation"

{839} From the time of high scholasticism and, above all, from the surety expressed by the Church's Magisterium at the Council of Trent, "transubstantiation" has become the means for expressing the realism of the Eucharistic presence. How must it be understood?

It entered into theology for the first time in 1140 under the quill of a theologian, Roland Bandinelli, who would go on to become pope under the name Alexander III (r. 1159–81). If the word is new, it expresses an idea that came to light during the controversy involving Berengar without yet coming to be expressed correctly, namely the

---

153. Alger of Liège, *De sacramentis corporis et sanguinis dominici*, PL 180:825D–826A.

idea of substantial conversion (*substantialiter transmutari*, substantial transmutation, as Guitmond said[154]). This term was not gradually adopted merely by way of authority, thereby entering into the terminology universally received and accepted from the second half of the twelfth century onward. Rather, it was adopted because it provided a very exact expression of what one wished to say when one opposed the substance of the bread, which was changed, to the form (i.e., its appearance) which remained the same. Thus, Peter of Poitiers wrote: "Indeed, no other term than 'to be transubstantiated' is proper here, for one substance passes over into another (substance), while the same properties remain."[155]

It is interesting to note that the novelty of the term, which thinkers were fully aware of, was justified by the Church's practice of introducing new words into dogmatic formulas for the sake of better defending the true faith (i.e., for the sake of expressing more clearly what the Church had always believed). As an example, the case of Nicaea's introduction of the term *homoousios* was cited.[156]

In truth, this term is loathed by many excellent theologians on account of the philosophical sophistication that the word "substance" would take on later in scholasticism. However, it did not mean anything different than the term *conversio*, which St. Ambrose employed, which itself translated the term *métabolé* from the Greek tradition. Therefore, it can be considered as being the most direct expression of the Church's faith.

The first dogmatic definitions

{840} The Church's Magisterium was not able to remain silent and neutral in the face of these controversies concerning that which is at the heart of the Church's life, the Eucharistic mystery. A first intervention in the course of the Berengarian controversy was not very felicitous. Having been called to Rome, Berengar had to endorse a formula composed by Cardinal Humbert. In order to unambigu-

---

154. See Guitmond of Aversa, *De corporis et sanguinis Christi veritate in Eucharistia*, PL 149:1143C.
155. Cited by Burkhard Neunheuser, *L'Eucharistie, II: au Moyen Age et à l'époque moderne*, trans. Althur Liefooghe (Paris: Cerf, 1966), 66.
156. See ibid., 66–67.

ously affirm the reality of Christ's presence in the Eucharist (and in this it was true, meaning that the Magisterium was protected from error), the formula proposed an interpretation of this presence which was awkward and clumsy, rather than erroneous, though it was not very conducive for making the interested party admit that he was in error:

> I hold that the bread and wine that are placed on the altar, after the consecration, are not only a sacrament [or, symbol] but also the true Body and Blood of our Lord Jesus Christ and that they are sensibly, not only in sacrament but in truth, touched and broken by the hands of priests and ground by the teeth of the faithful…[157]

It is not astonishing that Berengar later retracted it. However, later on (and doubtlessly following the elucidations brought to bear by his adversaries) another formula was imposed on him, one having perfect exactitude and balancing out the other one very well:

> I, Berengar, in my heart believe and with my lips confess that through the mystery of the sacred prayer and the words of our Redeemer the bread and wine that are placed on the altar are substantially changed into the true and proper and living flesh and blood of Jesus Christ, our Lord, and that after consecration it is the true body of Christ that was born of the Virgin and that, offered for the salvation of the world, was suspended on the Cross and that sits at the right hand of the Father, and the true blood of Christ, which was poured out from His side not only through the sign and power of the sacrament, but in its proper nature and in the truth of its substance.[158]

Even later on, in 1215, the term "transubstantiation," which had become current in theology, was introduced into a conciliar definition:

> His body and blood are truly contained in the sacrament of the altar under the appearances of bread and wine, the bread being transubstantiated into the body by the divine power and the wine into the blood, to the effect that we receive from what is His what He has received from what is ours in order that the mystery of unity may be accomplished…[159]

---

157. Pope Nicholas II, Synod of Rome, 1059, "Profession of Faith in the Eucharist Prescribed for Berengar of Tours," in D.-*Sch.*, no. 690.

158. Pope Gregory VII, Synod of Rome, February 11, 1079, "Profession of Faith of Berengar of Tours," in D.-*Sch.*, no. 700.

159. Fourth Lateran Council, "Definition Against the Albigensians and the Cathars," November 11–30, 1215, in D.-*Sch.*, no. 802.

As Raymonde Foreville notes:

> In this way, the symbol of [the Fourth] Lateran [Council] records the data acquired by theological research. Peter of Poitiers, Prevotin [of Cremona], Alain of Lille, and Steven Langton had conceptually articulated the notion of transubstantiation and used the term. The canonists Étienne of Tournai and Huguccio borrowed the expression from the theologians. As regards Innocent III, he had written (doubtlessly before his accession to the Papacy) a six-book treatise on the mystery of the altar in which he defined the mode and moment of transubstantiation.[160]

The way was thus open for the ultimate illuminations that would be offered by high scholasticism, which on this point as on so many others, found their culmination in St. Thomas. Given that his explanations will be the ones that we will propose when the time comes, it is not useful to continue to pursue this very rapid overview of the formation of Eucharistic theology in the Latin Church. Let us only note that at the Second Council of Lyon in 1274, the expression *transsubstantiatur* was simply taken up as expressing the Church's faith in the real presence. Moreover, let us recall[161] that at the Council of Florence there was a solemn proclamation of the communion in faith between the Eastern Church and the Western Church both as regards the reality of the changing of the substance of the bread and wine into Christ's body and blood, as well as Christ's complete presence under each of the two *species*,[162] and also in regard to that which concerns the sacrificial character of the Eucharist.[163]

The Eucharist in the reformers and in the decrees of Trent

The decline of Eucharistic theology in the fourteenth and fifteenth centuries

{841} From the fourteenth century onward, there begins to be a true decline in the theology of the Eucharist, especially following Ockham. The Eucharist is treated almost exclusively from the perspective of the real presence, this itself being studied like a philosophical and logical problem without any reference to the religious mean-

---

160. Foreville, *Latran*, 6:282.
161. See §826 above.
162. See Council of Florence, *Exsultate Deo*, November 22, 1439, in D.-*Sch.*, no. 1321.
163. See ibid., no. 1320.

ing of the Eucharist and to what it is in the life of the Church and of believers. Transubstantiation is admitted as a matter of faith. However, with the abandonment of the explanations offered by high scholasticism, it is no longer anything but the miraculous means by which Christ's body and blood are placed in the host and chalice, which are themselves visible and localized, as though the former were hidden by a veil. (This will be one the scandals experienced by Calvin, who will believe that this is the Catholic position.) Ockham never speaks of the Eucharist as a sacrifice. Rather, he renders the Church's faith in the sacrificial conception of the Eucharist unacceptable, for with his theory of the real presence (which is not a truly sacramental presence, *in signo*), it would be necessary to admit that a second immolation of Christ occurs in the Eucharist. In fact, it is not denied that the Eucharist would be a sacrifice. This is presupposed, excessively insisting (indeed, with an excessive character that will provoke the reformers' reaction) on its fruits and its efficacy, as though it dispensed one from personal religion.

A first reaction occurred in England with Wycliffe (starting in 1381). He rejected transubstantiation and maintained that the bread and wine remain unchanged in themselves but that, in virtue of the blessing, the body and blood of Christ are simultaneously present *sacramentaliter*. For its part, communion consists in being united to Christ *spiritualiter*. His theory remains vague enough, and we can ask ourselves whether it still is a question of a real presence. The theory was condemned in 1382 in Oxford and London and again at the Council of Constance in 1415. The same council condemned Jan Hus—alas, "physically"!—who said that there was an obligation to receive communion under the two *species* and that the Church had committed a crime by refusing to give the faithful the chalice. By solemnly affirming Christ's complete presence under each *species*, the Council legitimated this custom (of communion under one *species*), leaving the issue to the particular determinations of the Church.

The denial of the sacrificial character of the Eucharist by the reformers

{842} All the reformers agreed in rejecting the Catholic doctrine of the Eucharistic sacrifice. For them, the Eucharist is not a "work" by means of which man could make himself right with God. It is a sacrament that can be saving only for those who receive it.[164]

The essential point of Calvin's polemic[165] emphasizes the uniqueness of Christ's sacrifice, on account of which the idea of "repeating" this sacrifice at the Mass is violently rejected. However, he admits (in a concession made to the "ancients," i.e., to the Fathers of the Church, who openly spoke of the Eucharistic sacrifice):

(For our part, we do not deny) that Christ's oblation would be present to us in such a manner that we can contemplate him as though we were looking upon Him hanging on the Cross, for the Apostle says that Jesus Christ had been crucified among the Galatians when the preaching of His death had been declared to them.[166]

However, it is solely through communion that the Eucharist makes us partake in Christ's sacrifice, thus meaning that the "private Mass"—"I call masses 'private' every time that there is no participation by the faithful in our Lord's Last Supper"—is a profanation of the Holy Meal [*sainte Cène*], for it involves formal disobedience to Christ's own command to distribute the bread and wine among ourselves so that it may be eaten and drunk (without making any distinction between priests and the faithful). He only acknowledges thanksgiving sacrifices, which are all offices of charity, everything that we do to serve God and our own persons. By themselves, such sacrifices are in no way works that are able to obtain the remission of sins:

(This manner of sacrifice) intends only to magnify and glorify God, for it cannot be agreeable to Him if it does not emanate from those who,

---

164. See Hans Grass, "Luther et la liturgie eucharistique," in *Eucharistie d'Orient et d'Occident* (Paris: Cerf, 1970), 1:135–50. Maurius Lepin, *L'idée du sacrifice de la messe d'après le théologiens depuis l'origine jusqu'à nos jours* (Paris: Beauchesne, 1957), 241–52. Neunheuser, *L'Eucharistie, II: au Moyen Age et à l'époque moderne*, 113–15. Réginald Peuchmaurd, "La messe est-elle pour Luther une action de graces?," *Revue des sciences philosophiques et théologiques* 43 (1959): 632–42. Rivière, "Rédemption," *Dictionnaire de théologie Catholique*, vol. 13, cols. 1085–99. Th. Süss, "L'aspect sacrificiel de la Sainte Cène à la lumière de la tradition luthérienne," *Eucharistie d'Orient et d'Occident* (Paris: Cerf, 1970), 1:151–70. Vilmos Vatja, *La théologie du service religieux chez Martin Luther* (Göttingen: Vandenhoeck & Ruprecht, 1959). [Tr. note: The entry for Süss is cited as "Suess, 6." This appears to be the correct citation.]

165. See Calvin, *Institution chrétienne*, vol. 4, ch. 18. [Tr. note: No date provided by Fr. Nicolas.]

166. Ibid., 410.

having obtained the remission of sins, are already reconciled with Him and, moreover, justified.[167]

It is along these lines that he interprets the tradition of "spiritual offerings," the sacrifice announced by Malachi, and so forth.

Thus, the entire dispute centers on the notion of being *a repetition of Christ's sacrifice*. This problematic, a received theological datum in this era, leads the mind to see in the Eucharist another immolation of Christ, something that is quite certainly unacceptable. On the other hand, the notion of a "memorial," the only explanation remaining, was as completely misunderstood by the reformers as by the whole of Catholic theologians, so that in both parties' eyes, the idea of "a memorial of [His] sacrifice" seemed to preclude the possibility of the Eucharist being a sacrifice.

The reformers on the identification of the body and blood of Christ with the offerings

{843} As regards the question of the identification of Christ's body and blood with the offerings, grave divergences appeared in the reformers from the beginning.

Calvin sought a middle way between the radical denial of the real identification of them expressed by Zwingli, Oecolampadius, and Melanchthon, on the one hand, and Luther's own materializing conception of it, on the other. The first three held that there is only a pure symbol in the offerings and likewise that our eating of them was only a simple sign of our union with Christ, which can be brought about in many ways. For his part, Luther, basing himself on the words, "Hoc est corpus meum," to the end of his life affirmed a real identification, though without the bread and wine being changed (i.e., "consubstantiation" or "impanation"), admitting not only the presence of Christ's body but also a bodily presence with multilocation.[168]

---

167. Ibid., 143.
168. See ibid., vol. 4, ch. 17; vol. 2, 503–30. See Calvin, *Joannis Calvini opera selecta*, ed. Petrus Barth (Munich: Kaiser, 1926), 1:433–34. Jean Cadier, "La doctrine calviniste de la Sainte Cène," *Etudes théologiques et religieuses* (Montpellier, 1951), 1–160. Henry Chavannes, "La presence réelle chez S. Thomas et chez Calvin," *Verbum Caro* 13 (1959): 151–70. Thurian, *L'eucharistie*, 262–72.

- The universally recognized ambiguity of Calvin's thought concerning the "real presence" was based on an unresolved conflict in his thought. There is no doubt that he has a very lofty estimation of Eucharist by which we "commune" with Christ the Savior not only as regards the Spirit but also as regards His body and blood: "This is why, when we speak about the communion that the faithful have with Christ, we do not think any less about a communion in body and soul than one in spirit, thus meaning that they possess the whole Christ."[169]

Consequently, if the eating of Christ's flesh is brought about only through faith, it is different from the very act of believing and makes Christ's life truly pass into us:

> In this way, when the Lord called Himself the bread of life, He did not only wish to indicate that our salvation is not only found [*colloqué*] in [our] confidence in His death and resurrection, but that through the true communication that we have in Him His life is transferred into us and is made our own, just as bread, when it is taken as food, gives vigor to the body.[170]

On the other hand, his general doctrine on the sacraments (and, in general, his general doctrine of external means of salvation) is absolutely opposed to the idea of a change that would be produced in the bread and wine, being something other than solely a sign and attestation of what Christ brings about in us in virtue of His promise. For him, "the sacrament is, in sum, an external sign willed and instituted by God in order to provide for the weakness of our faith, which one must observe so that God may give us the promised grace, directly and from on high."[171]

The first perspective gives way to striking affirmations of the real identification of the body and blood of Christ with the offerings:

> Therefore, I say that at the Last Supper Jesus Christ truly gave us, under the signs of bread and wine, His body and blood, by which He accomplished all righteousness so as to acquire salvation for us.[172]

The bread is given to us so that it may be a figure of Jesus Christ for us, with the commandment to eat. And it is given to us by God, who is the

---

169. Calvin, *Joannis Calvini opera selecta*, 1:435.
170. Calvin, *Institution chrétienne*, vol. 4, ch. 17, §5 (353).
171. Congar, *Vraie et fausse réforme dans l'Église*, 391.
172. Calvin, *Institution chrétienne*, vol. 4 (359).

certain and immutable truth. If God can neither deceive nor lie, it follows that it accomplishes everything that it signifies. Therefore, it must be the case that we truly receive Jesus Christ's body and blood at the Holy Meal [*la Cène*] since the Lord represents for us communion in both of these. For, otherwise ... would he not have instituted this mystery under false signs?[173]

Whence, we have this affirmation in Max Thurian: "It remains the case that the Reformer believed very firmly in the real presence of Christ's body and blood."[174]

The second perspective gives way to the violent denial of transubstantiation, of consubstantiation, and of every form of change in the bread and wine.[175] We should add that the way transubstantiation was presented at that time justified his critique.[176] However, he equally refuses the much more ancient notion of "conversion." Rightly, he refuses the possibility of any change that Christ would undergo on account of transubstantiation. However, as we will see, the true notion of transubstantiation equally excludes such a change.

His solution is to appeal to the power of the Holy Spirit, who, not undergoing our limitations, can unite our body to Christ's body in heaven on the occasion of our eating of the Eucharistic bread:

> Although it seems unbelievable that Jesus Christ's body, which is separated from us by so great a distance, would come to us so that it may be food for us, let us think about how the secret power of the Holy Spirit surpasses in its loftiness all of our senses and what a folly it would be for us to understand the infinity of this power according to the measure of our own! Therefore, let faith receive what our understanding cannot conceive, namely, that the Spirit truly unites things that are spatially separated. Now, Jesus Christ attests and seals for us at the Last Supper this participation in His flesh and blood by which He makes His life flow into us, just as though He were entering into our bones and marrow. In it, He does not present us with an empty and frivolous sign. Rather, He deploys the power of His Spirit so that He may accomplish what He promises.[177]

---

173. Calvin, *Petit traité de la Sainte Cène*, in *Johannis Calvini opera selecta*, op. I, 503–30, at 509.
174. Thurian, *L'eucharistie*. [*sic*]
175. Calvin, *Institution chrétienne*, vol. 4, ch. 17, §§12ff.
176. See Chavannes, "La presence réelle chez S. Thomas et chez Calvin," 151–70.
177. Calvin, *Institution chrétienne*, loc. cit, §10, 357.

We must note that this explanation involves an impossibility, for two spatially separated bodies cannot, without contradiction, be joined in space while still remaining separated. The very reasons that Calvin gives against multilocation[178] hold true against his own solution. We will see that the bodily connection of the believer with Christ in communion can be explained only if Christ is present in a nonspatial, nonlocalized manner, something that can only take place by way of transubstantiation.

On the basis of his conception of these matters, Calvin draws forth a formal condemnation of the preservation of the holy sacrament, as well as a condemnation of adoration of it, even in the course of the Eucharistic liturgy. Just as the water of baptism is not in itself changed by the sacramental formula (even though "it begins to be that which it was not"),[179] so too the bread does not cease to be bread when, having been consecrated by the sacramental word, it becomes the body of Christ for us. Therefore, the bread and wine are the body and blood of Christ only in and for sacramental reception [*manducatio*]. Outside of this, they would be only bread and wine.*

The decrees of Trent

{844} It[180] is characteristic [of the proceedings of Trent] that the Eucharist would have given rise to two distinct sessions, leading to two decrees, separated by over a ten-year interval. First, the decree on the Eucharist in the thirteenth session (October 11, 1551) dedicated to the real presence; second, the decree on the sacrifice of the

---

178. Ibid., §17, 366, and §30, 380.
179. Ibid., §15, 363.
* N.B. As we will see, the difference consists in the fact that the water of baptism is only the instrument that God uses for purifying the believer's soul by means of bodily ablution. Therefore, it does not need to be holy in itself. The act of washing the body is what is holy. By contrast, in the Eucharist, the believer is the one who performs the holy action, which consists in "eating the body of Christ." This action is unintelligible if the body of Christ is not offered to be eaten. The act of eating is not what makes the bread to be the body of Christ. On the contrary, it presupposes that prior to this the bread would have become the body of Christ.
180. See Engelbert Gutwenger, "Substanz und Akzidens in der Eucharistielehre," *Zeitschrift für katholische Theologie* 83 (1961): 257–306. D. G. Guysens, "Présence réelle eucharistique et transsubstantiation dans les définitions de l'Église catholique," *Irenikon* 32 (1959): 420–35. Neunheuser, *L'Eucharistie, II: au Moyen Age et à l'époque moderne*, 120–30 (as well as a bibliography on 109). Piet Schoonenberg, "Dans quelle mesure la doctrine de la transsubstantiation a-t-elle été déterminée à Trente?," *Concilium* 24 (1967): 77–88.

Mass in the twenty-second session (September 17, 1562), to which we must add the decree promulgated at the twenty-first session (July 16, 1562) on communion under two kinds and communion of children.

These two decrees do not intend to express the entire Eucharistic doctrine of the Church. Rather, they aim to reaffirm those points of doctrine that were denied by the reformers. The sacrificial character of the Eucharist was affirmed very strongly, as well as its identity with the sacrifice of the cross *sola offerendi ratione diversa*. However, the Council did not seek to resolve the theological problem that was posed by this very identity-in-distinction. In general, it avoided settling controversies between theological schools.

The essential problem is that of knowing the degree to which the scholastic theology of the Eucharist was taken up by the Council and imposed upon faith. Certainly, for the majority of the Council Fathers, the formulas of the decrees were interpreted in scholastic categories. Nonetheless, one must note that the Fathers avoided the term "accidents," preferring, instead, to use the term *species*, which is broader and closer to the tradition, meaning nothing more than "appearances" or "external form." Consequently, the term "substance" in the conciliar texts is equally taken in the broad sense of common language and not in its philosophical sense. In this way, it wished to distance itself from a particular philosophy and from a theological explanation inspired by this philosophy. In what pertains to the real presence, it does not seem that the Council would have intended to affirm anything other than this: that which appeared (and was) bread and wine, while continuing to appear to be bread and wine, has become the body and blood of Christ through a change affecting the reality that these appearances manifest. Thus, it reaffirmed the traditional positions, though not without taking into account the precisions to which theological reflection had led.

One consequence of this is that the formulas of Trent did not in principle exclude an interpretation that would differ from that of the scholastics, even if the latter was, in fact, the interpretation held by the Fathers of Trent. However, in order for such a new interpretation to be acceptable, it will need to respect the essential affirmations of

What the Church Believes Regarding the Eucharist

the decree and give an account of them. Every interpretation that would be incompatible with these affirmations (and for this reason would contradict them) must be judged to be false.

The development of Eucharistic theology after Trent
Aberrant developments of scholastic explanations

So-called Counter-Reformation theology is characterized by a hardening of Catholic theology in the face of Protestant denials. Instead of returning to the profound, balanced explanations of the high scholastics, emphasis was instead placed upon the distorted positions against which the reformers had struggled (albeit with lamentable excess). In what concerns Christ's presence in the Eucharist, theologians came up with ingenious and absurd theories for responding to difficulties concerning Christ's "coming" under the *species* (e.g., multilocation, the invisibility of His body, His "squeezing" into the dimensions of the host, and so forth) instead of returning to the notion of presence *per modum substantiae*, which, as we will see, eliminates all of these false problems. The "Thomists" invented the distinction between the two effects of quantity, the second (consisting in the spreading out the parts of a body in space) being suspended for Christ's body in the Eucharist.[181] For others (Suarez, Soto, then, much later, Billuart*), transubstantiation is a "reproductive" action that produces Christ under a new mode of being, the mode of sacramental being. For others (e.g., Bellarmine) it is an "adductive" action that makes Christ come under the species. One must note that St. Thomas had been aware of an explanation of this kind and had denounced its impossibility.[182] For all, in order for Christ to be rendered present in the Eucharist, He would undergo a change.

These various theories were held to be classical and were generally taught up to the vigorous reaction of Billot and de La Taille, both of whom showed that one must exclude every form of change in Christ (doing justice to one of the criticisms registered by Calvin

---

181. John of St. Thomas, *Cursus theologicus*, vol. 9 (Paris: Vivès, 1886), and *In ST* III, disp. 28, a. 4 (492–500).

* [Tr. note: Reading "Billuart" for "Billuard."]

182. See *ST* III, q. 75, a. 2.

against the Catholic doctrine or at least what he believed it to be). Indeed, this was the true conception of the scholastics.[183]

As regards the Eucharistic sacrifice, the overly polemical concern with emphasizing its reality (against the denials of this registered by the reformers) led theologians to conceive of so-called immolationist theories, according to which Christ would be immolated anew in some (unbloody) manner in the Eucharist.[184] Nonetheless, one must note that during the same period, there developed in parallel theories that excluded any kind of new immolation of Christ in the Mass, the latter being the renewed offering of the unique sacrifice of Christ on Calvary. We will speak of them in relation to the theology of the sacrifice of the Mass.

Explanations of the Cartesian type

{846} Rejecting scholastic philosophy (indeed, above all, the distinction between substance and accidents, defining body by extension), Descartes was interpreted as being opposed to the dogma of the Eucharist, which would have been incompatible with his notion of body. In his letter to Fr. Mersenne on February 9, 1645,[185] he proposed an explanation within the framework of his dualistic and spiritualistic anthropology, according to which Christ's soul (which, for him, would have been the whole of His humanity) would inform the matter of the bread and wine. Many other "physicalist" explanations were proposed afterward, which all presuppose a bodily inclusion of Christ within the dimensions of the host. The adoption of this overall problematic doomed these attempts to failure, and they are not held by anyone today.

The return of Protestant theologians to Eucharistic realism

{847} Remarkably, in recent decades, a significant movement looking to return to a more realistic conception of the Eucharist has been

---

183. See Louis Billot, *De Ecclesiae Sacramentis* (Rome: Universitatis Gregorianae, 1924), q. 75, preamble. Maurice de la Taille, *Mysterium fidei. De augustissimo Corporis et Sanguinis Christi sacrificio atque sacramento* (Paris: Beauchesne, 1921), 619–34.

184. See Lepin, *L'idée du sacrifice*, 335.

185. See René Descartes, *Oeuvres et Lettres*, ed. André Bridoux (Paris: Gallimard, 1953), 1172–76.

What the Church Believes Regarding the Eucharist 413

sketched out in Protestant circles, both regarding Christ's Eucharistic presence and also regarding the re-actualization of the sacrifice of Calvary by the Eucharist.

Without being able to follow this movement in its various advances (and in its reservations as well), we can cite in the first place the studies of Francis Leenhardt and the sympathetic reception that his thought has received from a number of Catholic theologians.[186] Next, there was the work of Max Thurian, which we have cited many times, as well as his "theses on the real presence" which, while noting the ways it is distinct from the Catholic position, comes close enough to it that one could glimpse complete agreement on the essential points.[187] Numerous efforts at illumination, going in the direction of such a rapprochement, are also being undertaken in the Lutheran churches.[188]

This tendency is concretized in agreements between Catholic and non-Catholic theologians which are concrete steps toward unity, despite the difficulties encountered, the inevitable slowness of the process, and the imprecisions inevitably retained in the formulations. Let us simply cite the agreement of Dombes in 1972[189] and the "Declaration of agreement on Eucharistic doctrine" from the International Anglican-Roman Catholic commission, which must be read[190] alongside the elucidations that the same commission later on gave concerning it,[191] while also comparing it with the sympathetic but prudent reaction of the Sacred Congregation for Promoting Christian Unity [*S.C. pour l'unité de la foi*].[192]

---

186. See Franz Leenhardt, *Le sacrament de la Sainte Cène* (Neuchâtel: Delachaux et Niestlé, 1948), and *Ceci est mon corps. Explication de ces paroles de Jésus-Christ* (Neuchâtel: Delachaux et Niestlé, 1955). Pierre Benoît, "Sur deux études de F. J. Leenhardt," in *Exégèse et Théologie* (Paris: Cerf, 1961), 1:244–54. Marie-Joseph Le Guillou and A. M. Henry, "Un débat théologique sur l'eucharistie, à propos de l'ouvrage du Prof. Leenhardt *Ceci est mon corps*," *Istina* (1956): 210–40.

187. See Thurian, *L'eucharistie*, and Jean de la Croix Kaelin, "L'eucharistie selon Max Thurian," *Nova et Vetera* 35 (1960): 9–19.

188. Boelens, "La discussion sur la Sainte Cène." D. N. Egender, "Vers une doctrine eucharistique commune dans la théologie protestante d'Allemange," *Irenikon* 32 (1959). De Watteville, *Le sacrifice dans les textes eucharistiques*.

189. See D.C. 1972, 334–38.

190. See D.C. 1972, 80ff.

191. See D.C. 1979, 734–37.

192. See D.C. 1982, 508–9.

New interpretations of the Catholic doctrine

{848} We must first of all note Catholic theology's return to the sounder and more traditional conceptions of Eucharistic doctrine. From the perspective of the real presence, there has been the rediscovery of the true notion of transubstantiation, the great pioneer of which was Billot. From the point of view of the Eucharistic sacrifice, there has been the rejection of the "immolationist" theories and a return to the idea of an offering of Christ's unique sacrifice by the Church. With Casel and his school, there has been a revalorization of the notion of symbols and of its legitimate and necessary role in sacramental theology and in that of the Eucharist in particular. Beyond this, we must not forget the important return to the sources of the Eucharistic liturgy.

In what pertains to the real presence, however, a strong theological current has appeared which, being dissatisfied with the notion of transubstantiation (even when it is purified and restored), holds that this explanation depends on an outdated philosophy that is unacceptable for our contemporaries. This current of thought has sought to reinterpret the formulas of Eucharistic faith in light of modern philosophy. Indeed, if "substance" is the fundamental reality of things and if, on the other hand, the Eucharistic conversion can be understood only as being ordered to the believer's personal communion with Christ, must not new conceptions of being and of man lead us to rethink the theology of the Eucharist?

An originator of this tendency in Catholics is Yves De Montcheuil who (by expressly referring to an "Augustinian" conception of the world) held that the most fundamental reality of a thing (namely, its religious reality) is found in its signifying value, thus proposing the idea that the bread was substantially changed as soon as its fundamental signification was changed in the Eucharistic action and in virtue of its consecration:

> When, in virtue of the offering that is made of it according to a rite determined by Christ, they (i.e., the bread and wine) have become the efficacious symbol of Christ's sacrifice and, consequently, of His spiritual persistence, their religious being has changed. Through God's creative will, they have acquired a completely new being. Therefore, they have

undergone a transformation—indeed, the most profound of transformations, for they have been changed to the level of being that constitutes them in their true reality. This is what we can designate by transubstantiation.[193]

Joseph de Bacciochi's position is in this same line.[194] He develops at length this double theme that things are, fundamentally, what they are for Christ, and that Christ, in virtue of His "Lordship," can change them substantially without them being modified in their empirical properties, merely by the fact that He assigns a new role to them in salvation history, a role to which they were not naturally ordered:

> The object exists only as an element, this or that element in the universe. Therefore, what is the most determinative factor for its situation in the universe? Is it the ensemble of its empirical properties? No. It is its relation to Christ, the universal center of consistency and unity, the master of every vocation. It is true that the relation of things to Christ is modified by the changing of their function in relation to humanity, and this change arises as a rule from the changing of its empirical properties. Nonetheless, the sacramental order is at least an exception: it introduces fundamental functional changes connected to changes in signification while the empirical properties remain the same. Normally, this does not go so far as to change the substantial being of things, for they are significative and sacramental through an action, not in themselves (e.g., think of the baptismal water). The Eucharist is unique in the fact that in it Christ's act consists in giving (to God and to men) bread and wine not as bread and wine but, in all reality, as His body and His blood. This gift centers on the very being of the bread and wine. Brought about by the Lord, it makes this very bread and wine, *qua* given, into His body and blood. Thus is it a transubstantiative act.[195]

This insistence on Christ's act of giving of the Eucharist seems to be the fundamental point of this new explanation, principally along the lines that it has been developed by Dutch theologians.[196] It is an

---

193. N.B. Given that De Montcheuil's texts were never published because of his premature demise, we only possess extracts from them, cited by critics, generally without benevolence.
194. See Joseph de Baciocchi, "Le mystère eucharistique dans les perspectives de la Bible," *Nouvelle revue théologique* 77 (1955): 561–80; "Eucharistie," in *Catholicisme*, 4:130–57; and "Présence eucharistique et transsubstation," *Irenikon* 32 (1959): 139–64.
195. Bacciochi, "Présence eucharistique et transsubstation," 160.
196. See Edward Schillebeeckx, *Le presence du Christ dans l'eucharistie*, trans. Martin Benzerath (Paris: Cerf, 1970).

idea close to Calvin's (namely that the reality of the identity between Christ and the offerings is reduced to the reality of the believer's act of eating [*manducation*] Christ's flesh and blood, on account of this gift) though in a new philosophical context. By the mediation of the thing given, the "gift" consists in the offering that the giving person makes of himself, so that the acceptance of the gift produces (always by the mediation of the thing given and received) personal communion between the person who gives and him who receives. Therefore, there is a true "presence" of Christ in the Eucharist, with everything that the term and notion of "presence" connotes concerning a personal meaning without this requiring a change that would be situated in what the bread and wine are in themselves. The change is situated in what the bread and wine are for Christ who gives Himself and for the faithful who receive Him. Thus, the terms "transignification" and "transfinalization" have been adopted to designate this change. Here, let us merely note Durwell's efforts expended in attempting to overcome the opposition between these new theories and classical theories.[197]

Does this explanation truly account for the Church's faith in the Eucharistic mystery, as Scripture, tradition, and her liturgical practice from her beginnings have instructed her and as she herself has expressed it, even in her dogmatic formulas? We will need to examine this later on. Here, let us note that this explanation makes the justification of the permanence of the Eucharistic presence outside of liturgical action difficult. This permanence, expressly maintained by the majority of the theologians having this new tendency, is often denied, expressly or practically, in more popularized versions of their teaching.

New interventions by the Magisterium

{849} Indeed, without condemning what is positive and a real mark of progress in the new explanations, the Magisterium has very firmly recalled the traditional doctrine. Perhaps it can be rounded out by the new explanations. However, they cannot replace it without

---

197. See Francis-Xavier Durwell, *L'Eucharistie, présence du Christ*, 2nd ed. (Paris: Ed. Ouvrières, 1972).

thereby occluding the Eucharistic mystery precisely as the Church has always believed and taught it. To this end, the following texts can be consulted:

1. Pius XII's allocution to the participants in the First Congress on Pastoral Liturgy.[198]

2. Letter of the Dutch episcopate, May 9, 1965.[199]

3. Allocution of Paul VI to the Eucharistic Congress of Pisa, June 10, 1965.[200]

4. The Encyclical *Mysterium Fidei*, September 3, 1965.[201]

In all these documents, even though transignification and transfinalization are not at all rejected, they are declared to be insufficient for accounting for the mystery of the Eucharistic presence. Likewise, transubstantiation, meaning a change pertaining to the ontological reality of the bread and wine (a change presupposed for what the "Eucharistized" bread and wine may become for the believer, therefore an anterior and independent change), is affirmed.

It has been claimed that the recent liturgical reform, especially the new *ordo missae*, implies the abandonment of the sacrificial character of the Mass. To do justice to this criticism, one merely needs to read the new canons and the new prayers for the presentation of the gifts.

From these various perspectives (the re-presentation and re-actualization of the saving sacrifice, the real identity of the offerings with the body and blood of Christ, a real union of the believer with Christ by means of the bodily reception of "Eucharistized" bread and wine, participation in the redemptive sacrifice and in the redemption, and so forth), the Eucharistic mystery raises questions for believing reason, and it falls to theology to seek out a solution to them. Faith does not depend on this effort, nor above all on its results. However, it arouses this effort and judges what results from it.

---

198. See Pope Pius XII, "Allocution aux participants du premier congrès de pastorale liturgique," *AAS* 48 (1956): 711–25.

199. See Pope Benedict XV, *Maximum Illud*, November 30, 1919.

200. Dutch Episcopate, "Intervention du 9 mai 1965," *Documentation catholique* 62 (1965): 1175–79.

201. Pope Paul VI, *Mysterium Fidei*, in *AAS* 57 (1965): 753–74.

We can group these questions under four headings:

1. How is the Eucharist a sacrifice?

2. How are we to conceive of the real presence of Christ in the Eucharist?

3. How are we to conceive of the action by which the offerings "become" (*fiunt*) the body and blood of Christ?

4. Then, finally: how is Christ's continuous and active presence in His Church assured by the mystery of the Eucharist?

11

The Eucharistic Sacrifice

THE THEOLOGICAL PROBLEM

A Brief Analysis of the Notion of Sacrifice

{850} The[1] most general notion of "sacrifice," namely that which includes all the cultic acts that the Bible calls "sacrifices," is the notion of a gift made to God by man in homage to His sovereignty. As

---

1. See de Vaux, *Les sacrifices de l'Ancien Testament*, and "Sacrifice" in *Vocabulaire de théologie biblique*. For further reading related to this chapter, see Billot, *De Ecclesiae Sacramentis*, 1:580–659. Tomasso de Vio Cajetan, *De missae sacrificio, Opuscula Omnia*, vol. 3, opusc. 9 (Venice, 1594). Odo Casel, *Faites ceci en mémoire de moi*, trans. Jean-Charles Didier (Paris: Cerf, 1962.) [translation of "Das Mysteriengedächtnis der Meßliturgie im Lichte der Tradition," *Jahrbuch für Liturgiewissenschaft* 8:145–225]. Emmanuel Doronzo, *Tractatus dogmaticus de Eucharistia*, vol. 2 (Milwaukee, Wis.: Bruce, 1948). Pierre-Yves Émery, "Le baptême: appurtenance fondamentale à l'Église," *Verbum Caro* 76 (1965): 59–68. Jean Galot, *Eucharistie vivante* (Paris: Desclée de Brouwer, 1963). Auguste-Joseph Gaudel, "Le sacrifice de la messe dans l'Église latin du IVe siècle jusqu'à la veille de la Réforme," *Dictionnaire de théologie catholique*, 10:964–1085. Reginald Garrigou-Lagrange, *De Eucharistia* (Turin: Berruti, 1943), 264–313. Edgar Hocédez, *Histoire de la théologie au XIXe siècle* (Paris: Desclée de Brouwer, 1947), 288–301. Charles Journet, *La messe, préscence du sacrifice de la croix* (Paris: Desclée de Brouwer, 1957). Jüngmann, *Missarum solemnia*. Leenhardt, *Ceci est mon corps*, 41–49. Lepin, *L'idée du sacrifice de la messe*, 81–110. Eugène Masure, *Le sacrifice du corps mystique* (Paris: Desclée, 1950). Albert Michel, "La messe chez les théologiens postérieurs au concile de Trente. Essence et efficacité," *Dictionnaire de théologie catholique*, 10:1143–1316. Antonio Piolanti, *Il mistero eucaristico* (Florence, 1955). Colman E. O'Neill, *New Approaches to the Eucharist* (New York: Alba House, 1967). Jean Rivière, "La messe durant la période de la Réforme et du Concile de Trente," *Dictionnaire de théologie catholique*, 10:1085–99. Aimon-Marie Roguet (trans. and ed.), *Saint Thomas d'Aquin. Somme théologique / 3a, questions 79–83, L'eucharistie* (Paris: Cerf, 1967), 2:377–91. C. Ruch, "La messe d'après la Sainte Ecriture," in *Dictionnaire de théologie catholique*, 10:785–863. De La Taille, *Mysterium fidei*. Anscar Vonier, *La clef de la doctrine eucharistique*, trans. Aimon-Marie Roguet (Lyon: Éditions de l'Abeille, 1943).

God is not a visible being to whom one could give something and who would acquire it through a visible act, the act of sacrifice simultaneously includes two aspects of a gift. On the one hand, one hands over what one gives. On the other hand, it is acquired by the person to whom it is given. According to the brief definition provided by the translators of the Book of Exodus for the *Traduction oecoménique de la bible*: "(The religious man) refusing to receive the first fruits ... hands them over to the Godhead, making them pass over to him through an offering or a sacrifice."[2]

Among all the various acts of worship, the characteristic trait of sacrifice is the fact that it addresses God alone. By contrast, an offering (*simplex oblatio*) can be made to anyone who would be seen as representing God (e.g., a poor person, the minsters of worship). It is on this basis that St. Thomas says: "Every sacrifice is an offering but not vice-versa."[3] Here, we find the characteristic element of sacrifice, which St. Thomas describes in the following manner: "Properly speaking, there is a sacrifice when one acts on things offered to God." And he immediately specifies: "For we use the term 'sacrifice' to say that man does something sacred."[4] In short, we are here concerned with an action that takes the thing offered and removes it from use that would be made of it by men, thus making it pass over into the precincts of the sacred.

Ordinarily, this entails either the complete destruction of the thing offered (as in a holocaust) or its partial destruction, giving the undestroyed portion to the priests and participants. How should we explain this?

Fr. de Vaux refuses to accept the explanation offered by some who say that a sacrifice involves the "substitution" of the victim either for the offering person himself or for a good that is so precious that he would not be willing to destroy it (e.g., the offering of the first-born). However, the general goal of his argumentation is to show that human sacrifice never existed in Israel (at least officially), thus meaning that the immolation of an animal victim never was an

---

2. *Traduction oecoménique de la bible*, Ex 13:12, note c (155).
3. *ST* II-II, q. 85, a. 3, ad 3. [Tr. note: Fr. Nicholas does not include the article number.]
4. Ibid.

attenuation or humanization of a practice that was first in force and then later abandoned.

Now, the notion of "substitution," which seems essential to the notion of sacrifice, can be understood in a different way. Indeed, if sacrifice is understood as being an offering made to God (indeed, to God directly), we can first of all see that the exchange included in every offering (i.e., the surrender of the offering person's good, as well as the beneficiary's own reception and taking possession of this same good) cannot take place here: God remains invisible and transcendent. We cannot insert into the texture of the sacrificial action some action performed by God, through which He would take possession of the thing offered. Moreover, everything belongs to God. Everything is completely submitted to the divine sovereignty. Therefore, in worship, the action of God receiving the offering must be signified by a human action. ([In other words,] all worship takes place in the domain of signs.) Given that it is an offering made directly to God, this action cannot be that of an intermediary person receiving the offering in God's name. Therefore, the action of offering must itself at once signify the surrender of the good being offered and God's reception of it. Immolation responds to this necessity. Through the destruction of the good belonging to man (a destruction that is brought about ritually, in a liturgical context that emphasizes its meaning), it signifies man's solemnly performed act of "handing over" something that belongs to him, doing so in recognition of God's sovereign dominion over all His goods and over himself.

Here, external goods, which God does not need, can only play the role of being signs. They are a prolongation of the personality of the person who possesses them, being something of Himself. It would be meaningless if man were to recognize God's sovereignty over things without recognizing the sovereignty man has over himself. All earthly goods were created for man, and man himself is God's own thing [*la chose de Dieu*] (in the powerful expression of St. Thomas, man is *aliquid Dei*[5]).

Along these lines, human sacrifice would of itself be the most

---

5. See *ST* II-II, q. 85, a. 2, co.; a. 3, ad 2.

perfect form of sacrifice—the sacrifice of an enemy, of a member of a group, of a child, and finally of the very person who offers.

However, an insurmountable obstacle lies in the path of this unilateral development, namely, the fact that man's life is sacred, meaning that man does not have power over it. Certainly, this life is wholly relative to God. However, it is not relative to any other man. It is not a good that could be disposed of by man (including the very person who has received it). Indeed, the victim of a sacrifice must first of all be at the disposal of the person who offers. It must be a good that belongs to him, and he must be able to hand it over.

Hence, whether it be an animal or something else, the victim indeed has a substitutional function, though one that is *symbolic* and not juridical. What man offers to God in sacrifice is himself, by immolating to Him a victim that is something of himself, something that (in this process) is symbolically himself.

If such a ritual immolation also seems, in fact, destined to express repentance, this cannot be in the form of a penal substitution, which is both religiously and juridically inadmissible. (Such penal substitution would supposedly make the punishment that man deserves fall upon an animal.) It can be a question only of an act of voluntary reparation in which the repentant man offers himself, in order to eradicate and destroy the rejection he had expressed in his sin. The bloody appearance of the immolation is thus apt for symbolizing the bodily aspect of penance, which is first of all interior: *poenitet me hoc fecisse*, it is painful for me to have done this.[6]

Two attitudes and two antinomic lines of conduct are aroused by the recognition of God as the sovereign to whom all things belong (and to whom we ourselves belong, down to the deepest parts of our personality) and by our confession that He is the free and generous giver of all goods, including those that are the most personal and the most intimate. The first such attitude consists in receiving these goods from God's hands, praising Him by fully enjoying them. The second consists in radically depriving ourselves of them as a tribute to God.

In the truly religious man, each of these two attitudes should

---

6. See §493 in the previous volume.

balance the other, for each is true and authentic. Thus, one must not cancel out the other. In the Bible, it seems that the law of the offering of first fruits ("which are the holiest portion, representing the whole of the harvest"[7]) aims at assuring this equalization. More profoundly, the redemption of the first-born (prescribed by God Himself, an act which from its inception accompanied the offering of the first-born child, even though an animal was sacrificed) indicates what we could call "the dialectic of sacrifice": God gives, and man, aware that everything that he has comes from God, gives to God in homage that which he has received from Him, who in response, gives it back superabundantly. This dialectic finds its perfect form in Christ's sacrifice, which is consummated in the resurrection and in the bestowal of the "Name that is above every other name."

This leads to the two great Augustinian insights concerning true sacrifice.[8] Man ("all together and each one taken apart," *omnes et singuli*) is vowed to "God's service" (*Latreia*) because God has deigned to make man His temple. His own life is what he offers when he fights to the death for the truth. He offers his thanksgiving, his praise, his submission, and finally, his love: "There we find the worship of God. There we find the true religion. There alone is the service that we owe to Him (*debita servitus*)."

This *debita servitus* is translated in the form of ritual actions, the principal one being sacrifice (taken now in the sense of an external action, the giving of something to God), which can only be made to God. However, God has no need for our gifts: "We must not think that God has need of man's own justice, let alone of an animal or some other corruptible and earthly thing."

Man is the one who profits from worship in the sense that worship has as its end the uniting of man with God and the leading of his neighbor to God. What does this mean? "In relation to the invisible sacrifice, the visible sacrifice is a sacrament, that is, a sacred sign." In other words, visible sacrifices have their meaning in the fact that they represent one's self-gift to God ("a broken and contrite heart," as the Psalmist expresses it[9]) and to one's neighbor (i.e., through works of

---

7. *Traduction oecoménique de la bible,* loc. cit.
8. See St. Augustine, *La Cité de Dieu,* OESA 10.3–6.
9. Ps 51:17 (RSV). [Tr. note: Fr. Nicolas cites Ps 51:19.]

mercy): "Indeed, what one commonly calls sacrifice is, in fact, the sign of the true sacrifice. In the end, the true sacrifice is mercy."

Whence we have the well-known definition. Thus, we find a true sacrifice in every good work that is fulfilled for the purpose of uniting us to God in a holy society, that is, one which has as its goal the only good that could truly make us happy.

In the end, the true sacrifice is our complete self-gift to God, a gift of body[10] and soul,[11] meaning:

> Thus, assuredly, it follows that this city, which is entirely redeemed (i.e., the assembly and society of the saints), is offered to God as a universal sacrifice by the High Priest who, in the form of a slave went so far as to offer Himself for us in His passion in order to make us into the body of so great a head. Indeed, it was this form that He offered, and it is in her that He offers Himself because it is in her that He is the mediator, priest, and sacrifice.

This self-sacrifice which the Christian must perform constitutes the body of Christ. Whence we have the terse and somewhat peculiar formula: "Such is the sacrifice [offered by] Christians: many being one, single body in Christ." And the Church offers this sacrifice in the Eucharist: "This sacrifice is what the Church celebrates in the sacrament of the altar which is well known by the faithful, in which she is shown that she herself is offered in what she offers."

Thus, the "true sacrifice" is one's total self-gift to God, or more exactly, the re-giving of oneself: "an act of choosing or, rather, of choosing anew, for we had lost it through our negligence... we tend toward Him by love so that, when we come to the end, we may rest in Him." This sacrifice is expressed through the ritual and visible sacrifice, which has meaning and value only as a sign and figure of the former.

St. Thomas will specify that it is of man's nature to thus express this self-gift through a ritual action of giving: "And this is why natural reason enables man to know that he is to use sensible things, offering them to God as a sign of the submission and honor that he owes to Him, in imitation of those who offer gifts to their masters

---

10. See Rom 12:1.
11. See Rom 12:2.

in order to recognize their sovereignty."[12] What St. Augustine calls "the true sacrifice," St. Thomas calls "the internal, spiritual sacrifice" (even, "the principal" one).[13] However, for him, the first sense designated by the term "sacrifice" is the external sacrifice. Nonetheless, the other is the "true sacrifice" because it is what gives the external sacrifice its religious value and suitability [*acceptabilité*].

Thus, sacrifice properly so-called, the "external sacrifice," must be considered from two perspectives. *In itself*, it has its own, proper value, consisting in the fact that it is a ritual offering made immediately to God in order to manifest man's giving of the offered thing to God and its reception by God. (The latter take place in the form of a consecration making the offering a thing set apart, a sacred thing. It may take the form of a burnt offering, the "smoke of fat" or the perfume of incense that rises and disappears, symbolizing the passing of the thing into God's possession. It may also take the form of eating by the faithful in a sacred meal. Finally, it may sometimes take the form of mere destruction.) The external sacrifice can also be considered *in its own religious value*. In this case, it is the sign of the believer's and community's self-gift to God. It is a free ratification of the fact that he belongs to God, a fact arising first from creation and then from the covenant. We cannot neglect the first aspect to the benefit of the second on the pretext that the latter is the more important aspect of the sacrifice. Indeed, it is the sign of the personal gift precisely by being this ritual offering, and it is necessary that the personal gift be expressed in this manner.

The Identity of the Eucharistic Sacrifice with the Sacrifice of Calvary

{851} We need not insist on this point, which the entire tradition emphatically declares. Christ's sacrifice, which is perfect both as an external sacrifice and as an interior one, is absolutely sufficient for efficaciously realizing the goal of all worship, namely, the perfect union of all men (individually and collectively) with Christ. To offer God some other sacrifice is objectively a sacrilege, for such an

---

12. See *ST* II-II, q. 85, a. 1.
13. Ibid., a. 3, ad 2.

offering involves a lack of trust both as regards the reality or value of this unique sacrifice and as regards the Father's definitive acceptance of it (which He manifested through Jesus' resurrection and exaltation).

Man's offering of his earthly goods to God, which ancient authors (e.g., St. Irenaeus) emphasize, an offering which concretizes the offering of good deeds (especially the offering of works of mercy), cannot bestow upon the Eucharist a new meaning, making it into an offering to God of gifts differing from what Jesus offered on the cross by giving His own life. This is what St. Augustine expresses in the text cited above, and elsewhere, he says it with greater precision:

> Certainly, He is the only one who was a priest in such a way that He would, at the same time, be the sacrifice. And the sacrifice that He offered to God is nothing other than Himself. Indeed, he could not find outside of Himself the purest and self-aware victim, redeeming us by His blood, such a lamb without stain, incorporating us into Him, making us His members in such a way that we might, in Him, also be Christ.[14]

Christians (and their deeds in which they fulfill their freedom) give themselves to God in the Eucharist, not as distinct victims but, rather, as constituting the body of Christ (indeed, precisely on account of the faith and charity that aroused their deeds). They are one victim with Him.*

Given that the sacrifice of Calvary consisted in the immolation of Jesus Christ, the new and perfect Paschal lamb, we must therefore rule out the idea that there would be any new immolation involved in the Eucharistic sacrifice, whether it be a sacrifice of another "victim" or of the same one.

The Reality of the Eucharistic Sacrifice: The Church's Sacrifice

{852} However (and here the difficulty gets quite involved) the Eucharist is a sacrifice offered by the Church (i.e., by Christ with and

---

14. St. Augustine, *Enarrationes in Psalmos*, Ps. 26, ch. 260.

* N.B. Baptism's relationship with the Eucharist is founded on this fact: in order to offer the Eucharistic sacrifice and offer oneself in it, one must be a member of Christ. Such membership is the effect of baptism.

through His Church). The entire tradition indicates this fact, and the most ancient liturgical formulas express this idea.

How can the Eucharist at once be the same sacrifice as that of Calvary and also a distinct and infinitely multiplied sacrifice? This is the problem that the theologian cannot fail to raise for himself—even if it was not immediately raised by the faithful and even if many have been able (and ever are able to) truly and profoundly participate in the Eucharist without raising it for themselves or without seeing what its solution is (or even by giving different solutions for it). The theologian must strive to resolve it by doing justice to all its data. Moreover, given that the question has been raised for centuries now and has indeed been resolved by certain thinkers in a negative manner (i.e., by denying or overlooking the sacrificial aspect of the Eucharist), if we were to refuse to take it into consideration or to claim that it is a false problem, we would thereby effectively resolve it, indeed, in a negative manner.

INSUFFICIENT SOLUTIONS

Here, we do not intend to review the innumerable solutions that have been proposed for this problem. Nor do we intend to engage in empty polemics. The principal solutions can be found in historical order, along with criticism, in Lepin's text. They can be found systematically arranged in Journet.[15] Although the particular solutions vary in their details, they can be situated in a restricted number of lines of investigation whose value and prospects can be examine.

A Critical Analysis of the Idea of the Believer's
Participation in the Fruits of the Sacrifice of
Calvary Through the Eucharist

{853} It seems that Calvin reduced the Eucharist's relationship to the passion to a participation in the fruits of the sacrifice of Calvary. However, he does so precisely in order to deny its sacrificial character:

---

15. See Lepin, *L'idée du sacrifice de la messe*, 81–110, and Journet, *La messe, présence du sacrifice de la croix*, 333–55. Neunheuser, "Meßopfertheorien," 350–52.

For Jesus Christ did not once upon a time offer Himself on the condition that His sacrifice would be daily confirmed by new offerings. Rather, He offered Himself so that its fruit may be communicated to us through the preaching of the Gospel and the custom of the Supper [*la Cène*]. This is why St. Paul, after saying that Christ our paschal lamb has been sacrificed, commands us to eat him. Behold, therefore, the means by which the sacrifice of the Cross of our Lord Jesus is applied to us: namely, when it is communicated to us and when we receive it in true faith.[16]

As regards thanksgiving sacrifices or sacrifices of praise, which consist in doing everything in God's service and in His honor, they depend on the greater sacrifice by which we are body and soul consecrated and dedicated as holy temples to God. This is the sacrifice offered by Christ once and for all on the cross, the unique propitiatory sacrifice. From this comes Calvin's denial of Church's sacrificial power, as well as his denial of the priesthood.[17]

Catholic theologians who are tempted to look along these lines for an explanation of the Eucharist's character as a sacrifice offered by the Church to God in order to obtain from Him the remission of sins and all His benefits (something recognized by the most ancient tradition) must reflect on the fact that every sacrament (and principally baptism) is a means for participating in the fruits of the redemptive sacrifice, though none of them ever was a sacrifice, and none of them is celebrated as a sacrifice. Sacrifices are addressed to God to "bless" Him, to entreat Him, to obtain His grace, and by these means to cause His efficacy to extend over all those for whom it is offered. The sacrifice is efficacious only in relation to him who receives it in faith. This is how Calvin marked out his opposition to the Catholic doctrine of the Eucharistic sacrifice:

For the supper is a gift from God which must be taken and received with thanksgiving. Some claim that the sacrifice of the Mass is a payment offered to God and that He receives it from us in satisfaction. There is just as much difference between taking and giving as there is between the sacrament of the [last] supper and a sacrifice.

---

16. Calvin, *Institution chrétienne*, vol. 4, ch. 18 (406). [Tr. note: No date provided by Fr. Nicolas.]
17. Thurian, *L'eucharistie*, 226–57.

A Critical Analysis of the Notion of a Sacrifice-Meal

{854} According to Bouyer,[18] in Israel's earliest days, the Passover meal would only have been the sacrifice, and in Qumran community, this meal had come to take the place and meaning of the ancient sacrifices. Thus, many are tempted to see the Eucharist as being a memorial of the passion, inasmuch as it is a meal, gathering together the new Israel in memory of the Last Supper and in expectation of the eschatological feast.[19]

If we were to push this line of thought to its limits, similar to the Calvinist position above, it would hold that the Eucharist is efficacious only for those who effectively participate in the meal (i.e., those who receive communion).

On the other hand, it is not clear how we should understand the idea that the meal by itself would be a sacrifice. It can be only one part of a sacrifice, namely the participation in the already-accomplished sacrifice presupposed for such participation. Even if it is "a memorial of the sacrifice" in the strongest sense of the expression and even if it reactualizes the past sacrifice, "proclaiming" it to God so that he may recall it, it is not itself a sacrificial action, a "gift" given to God. As a meal, it can only be a gift received from God.

We must note that in the sacrament of the Eucharist, the sacramental act of giving the "Eucharistized" bread and wine and the act of receiving them (i.e., eating them) is necessarily preceded by the equally-sacramental action of "Eucharistizing" the bread and wine by the repetition of Christ's words. If the Eucharist is the "memorial of the passion," it is so first through the "re-presentation" of the blood outpoured. This re-presentation, which comes about in the form of bread and wine, is doubtlessly ordered to the meal, but it is presupposed by the meal. It cannot consist in the meal by itself, for it precedes the meal and makes it possible.

---

18. See Bouyer, *Eucharistie*, 82.
19. See ibid., 108.

A Critical Analysis of the Notion of a Reiteration of the Sacrifice of Calvary

{855} This notion, which was so violently attacked by Luther and, above all, by Calvin, is explained by Cajetan as follows:

> To the second objection, drawn from the idea of repetition, one must say that, in the New Testament, the sacrifice (or oblation) is not repeated. Rather, the unique sacrifice, offered only once, endures in the manner of an immolation (*immolatitio modo*). If repetition takes place, such repetition is not in the fact that it is offered but in the mode according to which the oblation endures. Indeed, the manner (the offering), which is repeated, does not contribute to the sacrifice taken in itself but rather commemorates the (bloody) oblation of the cross in an unbloody manner.[20]

Theologians today seem to avoid this expression, but it does come to the surface, for example, in someone like Fr. de La Taille. When he asks himself whether there is a new act of offering Christ at the Mass, he concludes negatively, admitting that the Church offers a new oblation of the unique sacrifice of Christ:

> Therefore, we should hold that the novelty of the sacrifice of the Mass in relation to the sacrifice of the Cross only comes from the Church, which makes her own the oblation that Christ offered once upon a time *and, nonetheless, renewing it* to the degree that the power and action of the sacrifice passes from the head to the body (emphasis added).[21]

Likewise, it comes to the surface in Lepin, when he writes:

> Not content with offering Himself, He wishes again to be offered by her. And this oblation of Christ by the Church, *which is complementary to Christ's own self-offering,* is no less essential to the sacrifice of the Mass in order for it to truly be a sacrifice (emphasis added).[22]

It is true that later on[23] the same author says that the Church's oblation is one with Christ's oblation. However, the entire context, even the immediate context, suggests that this does not mean the identification of the two offerings but rather a new offering, made under

---

20. Cajetan, *De missae sacrificio*, 218–20.
21. De La Taille, *Mysterium fidei.*
22. Lepin, *L'idée du sacrifice de la messe,* 752.
23. See ibid., 753.

the Eucharistic *species* by the Church's minister, one that includes a new oblation of Christ by Himself, completed by the oblation that the Church makes of the same Christ at the same time.

What should we think about this notion which seems to be necessarily implied by the datum of faith that tells us that the Mass is a true sacrifice, the sacrifice of the cross offered anew? Let us note the very lively criticism registered by Max Thurian.[24] In the history of Catholic theology, it is found in two forms that correspond to the two conceptions of sacrifice.

A repetition of Christ's immolation

{856} An[25] entire theological current, considering the fact that every sacrifice includes an immolation of its victim and wishing to establish that the Mass is a true sacrifice, sought to explain the sacrificial character of the Eucharist by holding that there is a new immolation of Christ in the Eucharist. Several paths are opened for such explanations. First, it could be presented a real immolation, consisting in the new conditions that Christ would receive (and would undergo by love) in the Eucharist. Second, it could be thought that it is a virtual immolation, consisting in the separation of the body and blood, a purely symbolic immolation on account of Christ's glorious state, though one that would be real otherwise [*sans cela*]. Finally, it could be thought that it is the destruction, not of Christ, but of the bread and wine on account of transubstantiation.

Clearly, when it is understood in this manner, the notion of repetition is unacceptable and contrary to the fundamental biblical datum that Christ's self-sacrifice on the cross is unique and was performed once and for all, indeed, that "Christ, now risen, dies no more."

A repetition of Christ's oblation

{857} Against this conception of sacrifice consisting in the immolation of the victim, another theological current was constituted from the eighteenth century onward. For those who have followed it, sac-

---

24. Thurian, *L'eucharistie*, 227.
25. See Lepin, *L'idée du sacrifice de la messe*, 2:721–26.

rifice essentially consists in the oblation of the victim by an internal act, which can either precede the immolation or follow it and be continued indefinitely: Christ the victim does not cease to offer Himself to the Father, as He began to offer Himself from the first moment of the Incarnation. Among the most striking modern theologians [expressing a position along these lines], let us note de La Taille, Lepin, Vonier, and Masure.

Thus, there would be no repetition of Christ's immolation, unless one means a "mystical" or "sacramental" immolation, namely that which the separation of the Eucharistic species symbolizes, thus rendering the immolation of Calvary present by rendering Christ present in His state as a victim on the altar. For these theologians, the term "sacrifice" is taken in the sense of "the immolated victim" (i.e., "the victim who has been immolated"). This victim is what is offered anew (virtually according de La Taille, formally according to most), with Christ, to the Father by the Church at each Mass. However, this novelty is not absolute. In reality, this is, rather, a continuation of Christ's oblation, though, nonetheless, in a new oblation, for Christ on the altar is offered in the Eucharistic liturgy under the Eucharistic species.

Certainly, the notion is more acceptable in this form, with the exception of the fact that it is debatable to say that we can distinguish between the notion of immolation and that of oblation involved in the notion of a sacrifice. However, if the sacrifice is said to consist in the oblation and not in the immolation, and if there is a new oblation of Christ at each Mass, how can we salvage the essential datum of faith holding that Christ's self-sacrifice on Calvary was unique? Even if we say that this oblation eternally endures in heaven, how will it not be another sacrifice, given that each celebration constitutes a new event (not only in relation to the sacrifice of Calvary but also in relation to its continuation in heaven) and given that this event is sacrificial?

A Critical Analysis of the Notion of a Heavenly Sacrifice

{858} This notion is very closely connected to that of a sacrifice-oblation. For an exposition of the debate, see de La Taille and Lepin.[26] Equally (without the expression), see Max Thurian.[27] On the biblical foundation of this idea, see Spicq,[28] based on the fact that "we have been sanctified through the offering of the body of Jesus Christ once for all."[29] (However, note a series of authors who reject this interpretation of the texts.)[30] For the opposite position, see Prat's criticism of the notion of a "heavenly sacrifice."[31]

The term "heavenly sacrifice" is used to designate the perpetual offering of the sacrifice on Calvary that Christ would [supposedly continue to] make to His Father. The perpetual intercession of Christ in heaven for His Church and all her members (*semper vivens ad interpellandum pro nobis*) would be founded on this offering (which certain thinkers see as being symbolized in the scars of the passion[32]).

There can be no doubt that Christ does not cease to intercede in heaven on behalf of men, founding His prayers on the merits of His sacrifice. Moreover, every grace which men receive derives from the sacrifice of the cross, by which and in Christ all men have been virtually reconciled with God and graced (i.e., sanctified and glorified).

However, to call this a sacrifice requires us to admit first of all that, in a sacrifice which consists in an immolation (as the sacrifice of Christ on Calvary most certainly was), the act of immolation (i.e., in the case of Christ's sacrifice, not the act of being put to death but Christ's act in handing Himself over to death and accepting it, personally assuming this death inflicted upon Him, making it His own[33]) is distinct from the act of oblation in which the sacrifice

---

26. See de La Taille, *Mysterium fidei*, 131–82 and 265–90, and Lepin, *L'idée du sacrifice de la messe*, 745–58.
27. See Thurian, *L'eucharistie*, 143–52.
28. See Spicq, *L'epître aux Hébreux*, 1:311–16.
29. Heb 10:10 (RSV). Equally, see 9:26–28 and 10:2.
30. See Spicq, *L'epître aux Hébreux*, 1:312n4.
31. See Prat, *Théologie de S. Paul*, pt. 1, bk. 4, §3.
32. See Thurian, *L'eucharistie*, 46–47.
33. See §§498–501 in the previous volume.

would essentially consist. Now, this distinction about which so great a case is made does not seem to be acceptable, for it is precisely through voluntary immolation that the victim is offered or offers himself to God.[34] However, even if we were to retain it, we would need to admit that the act of oblation eternally endures, whereas the act of immolation would be situated in time and in the past in relation to us. Many authors do say this and wish to explain the Church's offering of the sacrifice of Calvary at the Mass by these means.

However, how can we hold that the victim who totally and definitively handed himself over on Calvary and was totally and definitively accepted by the Father (an acceptance manifested by the resurrection) must still be offered, indeed, forever? "(Christ) entered once for all into the Holy Place ... thus securing an eternal redemption"[34b]—the goal of the sacrifice was attained. The task that remains is that of leading of all men to God, all men who still live according to an earthly existence, as well as all the generations that will follow until Christ's return. However, all of this, which is the work of the grace that was merited and obtained on Calvary by Jesus for all men and already bestowed on all in advance in Christ's own person at the resurrection, is already the fruit of the bloody sacrifice offered in love once and for all and accepted once and for all by the Father.

Why would we need to imagine a continuous sacrifice? As regards the idea of Christ's permanence as a victim in heaven, we must recall the theme (one that was classic in the Middle Ages[35] and was taken up favorably by the French School[36]) concerning the persistence of the scars of the passion in heaven, as a sign of the past immolation, which Christ does not cease to present to the Father. Thurian[37] applies the notion of a "memorial" to all these signs—a reminder to the Father Himself concerning the redemptive sacrifice. However, how can we speak of "signs" in heaven, where heaven is opposed to earthly life as the domain of "realities" is opposed to that of "signs"? How can we speak of "signs for God" without completely distorting the notion of sign and of symbol? And in what sense must

---

34. See §850 above.
34b. Heb 9:12 (RSV).
35. See *ST* III, q. 54, a. 4.
36. See Lepin, *L'idée du sacrifice de la messe*, 747.
37. See Thurian, *L'eucharistie*, 46–47.

we understand the idea that the memorial, in the earthly liturgy, would be a reminder given to God concerning His own promises?[38]

Now, we must ask how this notion of a "heavenly sacrifice" (which so poorly stands up in the face of criticism) can help us in understanding the Eucharistic sacrifice. It is said that "(the Mass) is the heavenly sacrifice rendered present on our altar,"[39] and this consists in the fact that Christ is rendered present on the altar such as He is in heaven, namely, as priest and victim. However, it is immediately noted that the Eucharistic sacrifice is connected in a proper way to the central sacrifice of the cross. In its classical form, this connection is brought about thanks to the two distinct *species* presenting us with the sign of His redemptive immolation. In this way, the heavenly sacrifice would be adapted to our earthly conditions and could become our own sacrifice.

By thus emphasizing the Eucharist's express and symbolic reference to the sacrifice of the cross, one thus recovers the most certain, most traditional, and most fundamental datum of the problem. However, at the same time, the recourse made to the "heavenly sacrifice" is thereby rendered ineffective and useless. Whether or not Jesus would perform a sacrifice in heaven, the Eucharistic sacrifice can only be understood and defined in relation to the past sacrifice accomplished on the cross and not in relation to such a heavenly sacrifice. This observation is confirmed by Lepin's curious expression used in speaking of "the oblation that constitutes the sacrifice of the Mass in parallel to the sacrifice of heaven."[40] Therefore, there would be two distinct ("parallel") sacrifices, each related to the same sacrifice of the cross, one by means of the scars preserved in heaven and the other by means of the presence under the two *species*. If this is the case, the second is not explained by the first.

Conclusion

{859} We must return to the only explanation that is well-founded, namely, that the Eucharist is the "sacrament of the passion." It is a sacrament in the sense of a "memorial," the passion being the sacri-

---

38. See §860 below.
39. Lepin, *L'idée du sacrifice de la messe*, 750.
40. Ibid., 749.

fice that Christ made of His own life on the cross through obedience and love. It indissolubly includes the bloody immolation (inasmuch as it is accepted, willed, and offered) and the "interior" sacrifice, that is, the gift of self (inasmuch as He is a man) and of mankind (contained in Him) made by Christ to the Father as the Creator and the ultimate end. It is a self-gift that, because of sin, is expressed by the bloody immolation and is consummated in the "definitive return to the Father" by Jesus inasmuch as He is a man, a self-gift that must be brought to its completion at the end of time by the definitive glorification of the Church. (Therefore, the "passion" includes Christ's resurrection and glorification.)

However, how should we understand the idea that the "sacrament of the sacrifice" would itself be a true sacrifice?

THE MEMORIAL OF THE PASSION

The Theological Meaning of the Notion of "Memorial"

{860} As we have seen, the traditional notion of a "memorial" included much more than man's simple evocation of past events charged with promises (a simple "calling to mind"). Beyond this, it is a question of recalling to God Himself the very promises that He has made so that He may fulfill them right now, for that part which is concerned with the present day, and in the future for what remains still to come: "In the Eucharistic liturgy, the Church ... does not cease to make the Lord recall His promise of the kingdom."[41] Now, what is the meaning of this?

In the Eucharist, matters stand just as they do for prayer in general, given that the Eucharist is the most urgent and totalizing form of prayer.[42] It is not a question of reminding God of our needs as though He did not know them, nor of His promises as though He had forgotten them, nor of presenting Him the "pledge" that He left us as though we could fear that He would be unfaithful. As St. Augustine said concerning sacrifices (and this holds for all the acts of the virtue of religion), they correspond to a human need and not to a need that

---

41. Thurian, *L'eucharistie*, 221.
42. See ibid., 212–21.

God would have. However, this does not at all mean that man would serve himself under the guise of serving God or that he would seek out his own interest under the pretext of glorifying God. Man's supreme interest lies his self-forgetful glorification of God, and he finds true freedom in really serving God by totally submitting himself to Him: "The very fact that we wish to unite ourselves to God in a spiritual society belongs to the reverence we owe Him."[43] Thus, the act of religion is really ordered to God and performed for Him. However, the entire reality of the relation to God established by it is found on the side of man. The corresponding relation in God is rationate [a *relatio rationis*].

This applies to the case of a "memorial." By presenting this "pledge" that has been left to him, man really recalls to God the benefits that He has given, as well as the promises that He has made. For man, this actualizes the past benefits and the promises made, placing himself, in relation to these promises, in God's eternal present. Through the Eucharist, the sacrifice of the cross, the resurrection, and Christ's glorification are rendered present for the Church and, especially, for the assembly that celebrates it, it enables the members of the Church to freely enter into them and participate in them with full confidence, involving themselves in their movement toward union with God to which this movement tends.

However, how can this be?

The Explanation Given by Odo Casel

{861} Dom Casel[44] rehabilitated the notion of "symbol" in sacramental theology. All of his thought in this domain is founded on the reality of presence *in mysterio* or *in symbol*. For the current problem, he thought that the Eucharist is the very mystery of the sacrifice of the cross, detached, in virtue of the sacramental mode of being, from its spatiotemporal limitations: "The end of the sacrament is precisely to maintain, in a living manner in the Church and as a still-active reality, the saving action which historically belongs to the past."[45] In response to the question facing us (i.e., "How can the

---

43. *ST* II-II, q. 85, a. 3, ad 1.
44. See Casel, *Faites ceci en mémoire de moi*. Also, see §751 above.
45. Ibid., 167.

sacrament of the sacrifice itself be a sacrifice?"), he holds: "Because the Passion was Christ's sacrifice, the sacramental representation of the Passion equally is the sacrifice of Christ, for the mystery contains in itself the reality of the thing signified."[46]

We cannot doubt that the principle of the solution would be found there. Nonetheless, there still are points in need of clarification, and it does not seem that Casel really explained how and under what conditions a symbolic presence can be a real presence, for it is most certainly the case that merely symbolic presences do exist as well. Time is part of the very texture of the event in question, meaning that the event cannot be separated from its own, proper temporal dimension, even miraculously. Thus,[47] it is difficult to understand the explanation he offers here, comparing the nonlocalized manner in which Christ's body is present in the Eucharist to the nontemporal manner by which the event of Christ's sacrificial death would be present in the Eucharistic action.[48]

An Attempt at Extending Casel's Explanation

The Church's Eucharistic action and Christ's sacrifice are identical

{862} We hold it as a datum of faith that the Eucharistic action performed today is the very sacrifice of Christ, accomplished once upon a time. Based on what we have already said, it is clear that in order to be able to meaningfully understand this datum, we must recognize that this sacrifice, in some way, envelops all time.

In what manner does it do this? We have rejected the idea of the

---

46. Ibid., 164.

47. See Nicolas, "Réactualisation des mystères rédempteurs dans et par les sacrements," and "Crainte et tremblement," *Vie Spirituelle* 99 (1958): 227–54.

48. N.B. Jacques Maritain (though seeking the solution to the problem of the Eucharistic sacrifice in a way that is totally different from Casel, and in a way that can be criticized for not doing sufficient justice to the requirements of sacramentality and symbolism) attempted to provide a philosophical explanation for this removal of an event from its temporal limitations by the Divine Omnipotence. He poses the problem in a much more rigorous manner by showing that it is a question of making two events situated at two different moments of temporal succession (i.e., the sacrifice of Calvary and the Eucharistic action performed today) coexist according to the measure of earthly time. It seems that merely posing the problem this way requires one to conclude that it is impossible, for it is a contradiction in terms to say that two successive moments would coincide according to the very measure of the duration in which they are successive. See Jacques Maritain, "Quelques réflexions sur le sacrifice de la messe," *Nova et Vetera* 43 (1968): 19–20.

perpetual permanence of the oblative action. It remains that Christ's oblative action on the cross, in which His sacrifice consisted, overflowed even the factual reality of the instant when it was accomplished. How was this possible if not in its redemptive efficacy?

However, in what does this redemptive efficacy consist? Through the sacrifice of His human life, the sign of His total self-gift to the Father in satisfaction for the offense of (mankind's) sin, Christ made the whole of humanity (whom He bore in Himself and who, through its sin, had turned away from God) "pass over to the Father." The redemptive efficacy of His death is the perfect acceptability of this sacrifice as well as its total acceptance by the Father. This acceptance was first manifested by Christ's resurrection and exaltation. Then it was manifested by the grace of the remission of sins, divinization, and ultimately the resurrection granted, in Christ, to all those who believe in Jesus and cling to Him (by baptism, by imitating Him, by the *sequela Christi*, and ultimately by death in Christ).

This grace, which is omnipotent in itself, has the power to save, sanctify, and vivify the whole of humanity, body and soul, for eternity. If its action is slow, progressive, and extended through time, this is because of the essentially progressive character of human nature, expressed in the progress of generations, as well as the progress in the destiny of each individual who must draw close to Christ, recognize Him, and imitate Him throughout the years of human life. This grace of God, given gradually, which slowly leads humanity, through many centuries, to the ultimate terminus of redemption (namely, the general resurrection at the end of time), is nothing other than the grace which Christ merited on Calvary and which the Father bestowed in a single stroke to all men by resurrecting His Christ and by exalting Him. This is why the mysteries of the passion and of Christ's sacrificial death, as well as of the life-giving resurrection, must be present and active in history for each generation and for each man.

This necessary permanence of the unique redemptive sacrifice through the course of history is assured through the Eucharist. How can this be?

The Eucharist is a sacramental action performed by the Church. In other words, it is the action of Christ sacramentally reproduced by the Church in such a way that this sacramental reproduction is not separate from the sacrifice of Christ just as, in general, the sign is not separate from what it signifies. Thus, we can conceive of things in the following manner.

The Church's action consists in the double consecration by which Christ Himself who offered Himself on Calvary is really made present and also by which the outpouring of blood in which His sacrifice consisted is symbolized. We will see that an important element of this explanation consists in the fact that these two parts of the consecratory action are not identical. By the first part, the immolated flesh (the body handed over for us) is rendered formally present (the blood and everything that constitutes Jesus' humanity being there "by concomitance"). By the second, the blood is rendered formally present. Thus, through Christ as really present, the Church's consecratory action aims at (and symbolically rejoins), outside the ages, the sacrificial separation of Christ's body and blood on Calvary.

Accordingly, a symbolic and sacramental identification is produced between this action by the Church (and by Christ as well, for Christ is the one who acts through His minister, who is also and simultaneously the minister and representative of the Church) and the salvific act of Christ on the cross (namely, the acceptance of suffering and death in homage to the Father). In virtue of this symbolic identification, this action (which, as an action performed by the Church and by Christ at this very temporal instant, is new, distinct, and separate in space and time) is clad with the sacrificial value of Christ's death. Thus, if it is another action and is performed by the Church, it is not another sacrifice. She offers Christ's sacrifice, accomplished once upon a time by Christ alone in a bloody manner, an ontological support in our time, in the community that celebrates the Eucharist and in the contemporary Church which is realized in it, in order that this sacrifice may be really present, active, and offered, no longer by Christ alone but by the Church with Him. (Now applied to the signal case of the sacrifice of the cross, this explanation is merely the application of what we proposed in general for the presence of the saving mysteries to the Church today by way of the sacraments.)

Here, we meet again with Cajetan's explanation:[49] "If repetition takes place, such repetition is not in the fact that it is offered but in the mode according to which the oblation endures."

If, in place of the words *res oblata* (the thing offered)—for sacrifice is an action, not a thing—we place "the sacrifice" and if the expression *perseverat immolatitio*[50] *modo* ("endures after the manner of an immolation") is understood as meaning that the act of Christ who is given in sacrifice on the cross in its very factual reality embraces all times up to Christ's return, we hold that the explanation that we have just proposed is a development of Cajetan's. The way the sacrifice endures is through the Church's Eucharistic action which through the ages does not multiply Christ's sacrifice, but rather, multiplies the ontological supports in which it is rendered present in as many times and places as the Church needs and wishes it to be present.

The Eucharist's sacrificial efficacy

{863} As[51] we saw above,[52] the reformers found this point of Catholic doctrine to be a stumbling block. They rejected the idea that the Eucharist had any other efficacy than that of sacramental reception accompanied by the Word. The Catholic Church professes that inasmuch as the Eucharist is a sacrifice, it is (or can be) of profit for those for whom this sacrifice is offered even if they do not communicate, even if they are not part of the community that celebrates the Eucharist and even if they have passed away from this life here-below and but still stand in need of the Church's prayers.

This consequence necessarily follows from the principle that the Eucharist is a sacrifice. Because the reformers rejected this point of doctrine, they did not come to coherently grant that the Eucharist has the sacrificial character which the most ancient tradition recognized to it (and, as we have seen, which they themselves did not wish to reject entirely). Indeed, the efficacy of a sacrifice consists in its acceptability and in its acceptance by God. On account of the sacrifice

---

49. See §855 above.
50. [Tr. note: Reading *immolatitio* for *immolatio*.]
51. See *ST* III, q. 79, aa. 5 and 7.
52. See §842 above.

offered and accepted, God gives His grace, gives of Himself, as the creature gives itself to Him. If the Eucharist is truly the renewed offering of the cross (in the sense specified above), it is, as such, perfectly acceptable and accepted, urging God to give His grace.

Protestants object that, in this case, grace would no longer be grace if man in any way possessed the means (through a work performed, namely, the Mass) for forcing God to give it. To this, we must respond that this work is the work of Christ and that it is itself a grace, the work that embraces every grace. Indeed, the Father sent His Son in order to offer His life as a propitiatory sacrifice and sent the Spirit (to Jesus inasmuch as He is a man) in order to arouse in His human soul the love and religion that rendered His sacrifice perfectly acceptable. Moreover, Jesus, through the Spirit and in perfect communion with the Father, instituted the Eucharist in order to leave a visible sacrifice for the Church, His beloved spouse.[53] By performing this work, the Church herself acts as the sacrament of Christ. That is, her proper efficacy does not add to Christ's efficacy but, instead, only perfectly realizes the self-efficacious work of Christ in this time and in this place.

Those who benefit from the Eucharist's sacrificial efficacy

However, can one speak here of an efficacy *ex opere operato*?[54]

This really is a twofold question. Is the Eucharistic sacrifice efficacious however it is celebrated (independent of the dispositions of the celebrant, of his own intentions, and of those of the present—or absent!—community)? Does the sacrifice produce its fruits in him for whom it is offered, whatever his dispositions may be, without any cooperation on his part? Let us begin by answering the second question.

Conditions for efficacy that are required on the part of
those for whom the sacrifice is offered

{864} According to St. Thomas, this sacrament (like Christ's passion, of which it is the memorial) has an effect only in those who are unit-

---

53. See Council of Trent, session 22, "Doctrine and Canons on the Sacrifice of the Mass," September 17, 1562, ch. 1, in D.-*Sch.*, no. 1740.

54. See §749 above.

ed to Him through faith and charity[55] and according to each person's devotion.[56]

This is a surprising response! Does he mean that, in order to benefit from Christ's sacrificial death, one must beforehand have faith, charity, and devotion? Obviously not! By himself, man is a sinner, alienated from God, and he becomes righteous and united to God (through faith, charity, and devotion) only by grace. Now, no grace is bestowed by God except in virtue of Christ's passion.[57] However, it is also the case that no work of grace is brought about in man without his free consent. Therefore, we must think in the following way about the problem at hand.

The grace obtained for man through the redemptive sacrifice arouses his freedom and gradually leads him, if he does not freely evade its action, to conversion, which at once is man's own freely performed action and the work of grace freely accepted. When it is a question of one's first conversion, the sacrament of baptism (and of confirmation) is the means for this work of grace. Through them, Christ's passion exercises its action on man in order to justify him, conforming him to Christ, divinizing him, and making him a member of the Church. When it is a question of one's "second conversion," the sacrament of penance is the means for such grace. By means of the sacrament of the Eucharist (as we will see below), Christ's sacrificial death is the cause of all the graces subsequently received by the "righteous man" so as to grow in righteousness and gradually heal the consequences of sin.

As regards the Eucharistic sacrifice, its effects are those of Christ's sacrificial death, which it sacramentally reactualizes. In other words, it obtains the grace of salvation (i.e., the remission of sins, the remission of the punishments that they deserved, adoption as sons, eternal life begun in faith and promised to find definitive fulfillment in glory) for the living persons for whom it is offered (and for the whole world). However, this grace is received only by the person who freely accepts it. It produces its fruits only in the person who does not resist it, indeed more or less, depending on how docile he

---

55. See *ST* III, q. 79, a. 7, ad 2.
56. See ibid., a. 5, co.
57. See *ST* III, q. 62, a. 5.

is to it. Its action is normally exercised by means of the sacraments, which require man's free consent so that they may produce grace as their effect. Thus, the sacraments are the means by which the sacrificial efficacy of the passion is exercised over men.

However, this free consent on man's part, a necessary condition for the application of the redemptive grace reactualized in the Eucharist, is itself caused by grace. It is a grace that is progressive in general, beginning with "illuminations" of the intellect and "excitations" of the will, continuing in motions toward acts that are preparatory for conversion, from the most remote ones to those that are most proximate. They are only sufficient graces (in the sense that they do not make one efficaciously produce the very act of conversion). However, they are graces that suffice, for each one calls for the following and contains it, as the flower contains the fruit, and this articulated series of preparatory graces is never interrupted except through human freedom's resistance.

If no proportion exists between this "preparation" of the human will and the very act of conversion, this is so from the perspective of human acts. Up to conversion, even though such a person begins to turn himself toward God, he remains attached to himself, enclosed in self-love, in the end preferring himself to all things and to God, even though he is increasingly becoming aware of the fact that God is preferable to all things and to himself. "Conversion" is a radical turning about, the beginning of a wholly new existence with a repudiation of one's past existence. However, to consider things from the perspective of God's grace (i.e., from the perspective of His love), there is a continuity, for from the beginning, grace (the most remote form of it, just as much as the most proximate) leads man to conversion. Indeed, it leads him to conversion and even to glory: "Those whom he called he also justified; and those whom he justified he also glorified."[58]

Here, the sacrificial efficacy appears under another aspect, both for Jesus' death as for the Eucharist. The grace that Christ obtained for the world through His sacrifice (and which the Church does not cease to obtain through the reactualization of this sacrifice) is the fullness of grace, including all the aforementioned preparatory graces. They are given to all, though all do not receive it, for some refuse it.

---

58. Rom 8:30 (RSV).

The Eucharistic Sacrifice

Therefore, one cannot say (as did Billot[59] and, to be fair, St. Thomas[60]) that the Eucharistic sacrifice only profits men if they are members of the Church, at least tendentially. It is offered for all men, but it is not efficacious for all, for certain men refuse the grace by which He draws them (unless one understands this "tendentially" as applying to the virtual belonging to the Church that pertains to every man so long as he is on earth).

As regards the application of the sacrifice of the Mass to the dead, it can be of worth only for those who are in a state of grace (because after this life, conversion is no longer possible) but who nonetheless do not yet exist in glory. In other words, it can be of worth only for those who are in purgatory. Here again, it is not a question of an automatic efficacy, for the sacrifice acts on God and appeals to His mercy, which is certain, but which is exercised only according to the divine freedom.[61]

With regard to the discussion concerning whether or not the sacrifice of the Mass has an infinite value, we must soberly respond as follows. If the Mass is no other sacrifice than that of the cross, it is clad with its sacrificial efficacy, which is infinite. However, this does not mean that it produces an infinite effect in those for whom it is offered (no more than Christ's passion produces an infinite effect in each person or even in the whole of mankind). The effect is limited in two ways, namely, on the one hand, by the divine freedom which gives His grace to whom God wills and as He wills, and on the other hand, by human freedom which is more or less (though never totally) receptive.

The efficacy of the Eucharistic sacrifice and the dispositions of those who offer it

{865} This[62] is a very delicate problem. On the one hand, the Eucharistic sacrifice has its objective value, as we have said, namely the very same value as the sacrifice of the cross. In this sense, it is infinite,

---

59. See Billot, *De Ecclesiae Sacramentis*, 1:638ff.
60. See *ST* III, q. 62, a. 7, ad 2.
61. See §§597–98 in the previous volume.
62. See Pope Pius XII, "Allocution aux participants." O'Neill, *New Approaches to the Eucharist*, 31–64. Karl Rahner, *Die vielen Messen und das eine Opfer*, Questiones disputatae 31 (Freiburg: Herder, 1966).

as is the cross's own value. On the other hand, it is an act performed by the Church, acting as a second cause, not instrumentally (except for the very act of consecration considered in its efficacy), for it is the Church's sacrifice, Christ's sacrifice offered by her, not without Christ but joined with Christ. We are not speaking of the act of consecration considered in its efficacy but, rather, are speaking about it considered in its intention (i.e., as an act that the Church freely posits in view of offering, with Christ, the unique redemptive sacrifice). From this perspective, it is a human and religious act, inspired by the Church's love and religion, which obviously are limited.

What does "an act performed by the Church" mean? Considered in this way, it is an act of the community who celebrates the sacrament with and through the ministerial priest. The Church is concretized in this community so that she may bring about this concrete, real human act.*

Therefore, returning to the subject at hand, let us recall that the exterior sacrifice draws all of its religious value from the interior sacrifice of which it is the sign and expression. The sacrifice that the Eucharistic community reactualizes is indivisibly Christ's interior and exterior sacrifice offered on Calvary. The infinite worth of this reactualization comes from this fact. However, because it is also the Church's own sacrifice, the Eucharistic celebration must also be the sign and expression of her own interior sacrifice.

Now, this sacrifice, constituted by acts of charity (with faith and hope) and of religion (i.e., adoration, thanksgiving, satisfaction, and supplication) is concretely realized in a given celebration, being thus concretized by the community's "devotion." Therefore, it is enclosed

---

* N.B. As regards the sacrament of holy orders, we will see that this power (and this duty) to offer the sacrifice of Calvary (in conjunction with Christ) constitutes what is essential in the Church's priesthood as such, that is, the priesthood of the People of God in which all the baptized participate through their baptism. The power of offering (and first of all, of efficaciously reactualizing) the sacrifice of Calvary belongs to her inasmuch as the priesthood proper to Christ is rendered visible in her and exercised by her. It is a power communicated by the sacrament of holy orders, a power that only ministerial priests exercise in the name of the Church. Thus, in the community that celebrates the Eucharist, the celebrating priest plays two roles. On the one hand, with the community and at its head, he represents the Church and exercises the priesthood proper to the Church. On the other hand, in virtue of the sacrament of holy orders, he sacramentally represents Christ the priest offering Himself for His Church.

within the limits of this devotion, limits that sometimes are very narrow.

Indeed, many contrary and sinful sentiments are mingled together with this devotion in the community. Will it be said that these sentiments not only limit but defile the Eucharistic sacrifice inasmuch as it is the Church's sacrifice? One must here return to the question of the Church's holiness. The celebrating community only realizes the Church *hic et nunc* to the degree that it participates in her holiness. To the degree that sinful sentiments, thoughts, and acts remain in it, they remain extraneous to the Church and thus cannot defile her sacrifice.

However, would this not be able to render it non-existent, at least in the edge case wherein the celebrating community would have no "devotion"? This seems possible only in the case of a Mass that is properly and formally an act of sacrilege, wherein the community would expressly repudiate the Church's "devotion" such as it is expressed by the formulas of prayer employed and by the entire liturgical context (and, as we will examine below, this would pose the problem of the validity of such a celebration).

We will also see that the liturgical community is not only the realization but [also] the sign of Christ's Church. On account of the symbolic identification, we must also say that to a certain degree (but to what degree?) the current devotion of the Church (in the heart of her members, spread out over all the earth) is actualized by devotion in this community's act and enriches it.

What are we to conclude from all this? Considered as an act performed by Christ, the Mass has an infinite objective value, independent of the fervor of those assisting and of the priest. Considered as an act performed by the Church, its value (i.e., what we have called its sacramental efficacy) is a function of the Church's holiness at the time when the given Eucharist is celebrated and, more still, of the fervor and "devotion" of the priest and liturgical community.

However, we must add that the Eucharist was not instituted for the sake of Christ, in order to bring His sacrifice to completion, for from Christ's perspective, this sacrifice is perfectly complete and had its complete efficacy from the moment it was offered. The Eucharist was instituted for the sake of the Church so that she may be able to make Christ's sacrifice her own and offer it with Him, making it possible that it be offered at every moment in time. Hence, it is very contestable to say that, given the infinite value of each Mass (for glorifying God and obtaining for men the grace that saves), the more that one celebrates the better, whatever may be the devotion with which these Masses are celebrated.

Because the sacrifice of the Mass has an infinite objective value, it calls for the most conscious, religious, and fervent participation possible on the part of the Church (and, therefore, on the part of the liturgical community in which the Church is concretized in a determinate celebration). To take refuge in this objective value so as to minimize the importance of this subjective fervor is to overlook the very meaning of the institution of the Eucharist, namely, the enabling of the Church to make Christ's sacrifice her own with all her soul.

It is pointless to ask what quantity of "devotion" is required in order for the Eucharistic celebration to still have a meaning. It suffices to say, once more, that it must not be limited by the fault of the community and of the celebrant.

The distinction between the Eucharist as a sacrament and the Eucharist as a sacrifice

{866} This distinction has been critiqued because it seems to suppose that the Eucharist would be a sacrifice in a non-sacramental manner.[63] This is a misunderstanding that needs to be clarified. As regards the Church, we have seen that the notion of sacramentality is broader than the notion that is applied to the sanctifying rites that we call "sacraments." When we speak of the "Eucharist as a sacrament," we look on it as one sanctifying rite among the seven—indeed, the most important of the seven, that to which the others are ordered. However, we also see that it is the rite which eminently realizes what characterizes the seven rites. In short, it is the believer's encounter with Christ, a twofold activity performed by Christ and the believer, the latter being necessary so that the prior may success-

---

63. See Salvatore Marsili, "Verso una nuova teologia eucaristica," *Via, Verità et Vità*, Roma 18 (1969): 13–28.

fully reach its end, for Christ saves only him who accepts the sacrifice that He brings. When we speak of the "Eucharist as a sacrifice," we do not at all intend to forget that this is a sacrifice only in a sacramental manner. However, it is thus considered as being addressed to God in order to glorify Him and obtain His grace and not as a sanctifying rite, exercising its action only on him who submits himself freely to it in faith.

Moreover, we will see that this sacrificial character is not something externally superadded to the sacrament of the Eucharist but that, on the contrary, it is an essential part of the first phase of this sacrament, that which precedes and prepares for its sanctifying action on the believer (i.e., the *res et sacramentum*, the "significate-sign"). This is so because Eucharistic communion is the believer's participation in the Eucharistic sacrifice, which is Christ's sacrifice in a sacramental manner.

CONCLUSION

{867} The theological problem whose solution we have been seeking is this: "How can the sacrament of the sacrifice of the cross itself be the sacrifice of the cross?"

The solution that we have proposed does not consist in saying that the Eucharist is the sacrifice of the cross only symbolically. However, more subtly and, I think, more profoundly, we have proposed that precisely because of the symbolic identification of the act by which the Church "Eucharistizes" the two species—that is, the bread and the wine, an act that reaches the body and blood of Christ in their very reality, though in two distinct ways—with Christ's act dying on the cross for the remission of sins, this act of the Church is really clad with the sacrificial value of the sacrifice of the cross. This act provides this sacrifice (which was accomplished once and for all, up to the end of time) an ontological insertion point into the present moment of salvation history, in the present moment of the Church. Thus, this unique sacrifice is what is currently offered by the Church *hic et nunc*. In other words, the very sacrifice that Christ offered on the cross is thus offered.

It seems that this explanation provides a sufficiently exact account of the Council of Trent's formula:

> For, the victim is one and the same: the same now offers himself on the cross; only the manner of offering is different. The fruits of this oblation (the bloody one, that is) are received in abundance through this unbloody <oblation>. By no means, then, does the latter detract from the former.[64]

---

64. Council of Trent, Session 22, in D.-*Sch.*, no. 1743.

12

The Eucharistic Presence of Christ
The Reality of This Presence

{868} However one explains it (provided that this way of explanation be one that is "valid," that is, in conformity with the data of faith) the Eucharistic sacrifice presupposes and requires the real identification of the offerings with Christ's flesh and blood. Without this, there would be no ecclesial act which could be clad with its sacrificial value through its sacramental relationship with that immolation. The victim of Calvary would not be present in a real manner so as to be offered by the Church, and what she would offer would be only bread and wine. In the Old Law, true sacrifices were offered, ones which, moreover, were prophetic signs of the sole sacrifice agreeable to God, namely, that which Jesus Christ would make of Himself on Calvary. However, now that this sacrifice has been accomplished "once and for all," it cannot be signified by a different sacrifice but, rather, must be signified by a rite that is a sacrifice only by signifying Christ's own sacrifice.

The same words of Christ simultaneously found our faith in the sacrificial value of the Eucharist and our faith in the identification of the offerings with Christ's body and blood: "Take and eat, this is my body, given for you ... Take and drink, this is my blood, which is poured out for you," along with the fourth Gospel's commentary, "My flesh is truly food and my blood is truly drink," and of St. Paul,

"Each time you eat this bread and drink this cup, you announce the Lord's death until He comes." To eat Christ's flesh and drink His blood is possible and conceivable only if the food and drink thus offered are truly Christ's body and blood.

The act of eating and drinking the body and blood cannot make what is eaten and drunk be His body and blood. Rather, the converse is the case. Likewise, the giving of the body and blood as food and drink cannot make what would be given be the body and blood. Indeed, in the two cases, the act (of giving and eating) presuppose the object constituted (i.e., the food given and eaten) and therefore cannot constitute it without implying a contradiction. This is different from the case of baptism, in which the water is sanctified only in and through the sanctifying action in which it is used because the water is only an instrument of sanctification, without the sanctifying action with which it is associated presupposing that this water would be holy *qua* water.

How should we conceive of this real identification? Today, two kinds of explanation are offered. On the one hand, there is the classical explanation by substantial conversion, holding that the bread and wine are really changed into the reality of Christ's body and blood. On the other hand, there are recent explanations by means of transignification and transfinalization. These latter have a kind of bias in their favor, first of all because they dispense with the idea of a miraculous and invisible transformation of the physical reality of the bread and wine, which the modern mind instinctively (and deliberately) rejects and then, second, because they appeal to a much richer and much more comprehensive notion of presence. We must examine them first and see whether, with all of their positive characteristics, they can truly dispense with the question for us without compromising faith itself.

CRITICAL STUDY OF THE EXPLANATION
OF THE EUCHARISTIC PRESENCE BY THE
NOTION OF TRANSIGNIFICATION AND
TRANSFINALIZATION

The Notion of Presence and Its
Application to the Eucharist

The relations involved in presence

{869} "Presence"[1] involves a network of interpersonal relations. A mere thing is not present, and a person is not present to a thing.

Purely objective knowledge, even of a person, does not suffice for bringing about a true form of presence. The person must be known not only as an object (for there is no knowledge of someone without this someone being an object of this knowledge), but beyond this, one must also be known as a subject, in his very subjectivity.[2] This knowledge of the subject in his subjectivity does not come about without love. Love unites the subjects as such, making one out of the two (at least partially) and enabling each one to experience the other by himself being experienced. At least, such knowledge does not occur without the beginning of love found in one's interest being concerned with the other person in his or her singularity, in what this other is for himself or herself.

He who speaks of love, speaks of reciprocity. The relation of presence cannot be unilateral. I cannot be present to the other without this other being present for me, even if the interpersonal relation of presence is more intense for one person than for the other.

For this reason, we can say that every true presence is spiritual, even though the two persons thus present to one another may not be purely spiritual and even though, for this reason, that which is present would also be bodily. More exactly stated, there is no true presence which would lack a spiritual component.

---

1. For the whole of section A, see Adolf Darlap, "Gegenwartsweisen," *Lexikon für Theologie und Kirche* (ed. Höfer and Rahner), 7:588–92. See also Nicolas, *Les profondeurs de la grâce*, 132–34 and 430–46.

2. See Jacques Maritain, "L'existant," in *Court traité de l'existence et de l'existant* (Paris: Hartmann, 1947), 103–39.

True and real presence: There-being

{870} From the moment that one speaks of persons who are (in part) bodily beings, one also evokes another sense of the word "presence" that, abstracting from their character as persons, considers them only as spatially and temporally situated beings. This "presence" is spatio-temporal coexistence: existence in the same place at the same time.

Moreover, this holds equally for purely spiritual beings who themselves likewise have a way of coexisting with another without thereby necessarily having interpersonal relations: thus, God exists at the heart of each being, at the source of its being.

To avoid expanding the notion of "presence" unduly, we could use the term "there-being" for this presence of mere coexistence. Correlatively, we can use the term "spiritual presence" for presence determined by the interpersonal relations we spoke of above.

Thus, the question can be posed in the following manner: "If *there-being* is not a true presence, does *spiritual presence* suffice for constituting a *real presence*?"

According to Yves de Montcheuil, "*spiritual presence*, above all when it is a question of a thought accompanied by love, is already superior to mere material proximity," and, "If one asks, 'What sort of presence?,' there is only one way to respond: 'The most real kind of presence there could be: *spiritual presence.*'"[3] Can this claim be sustained? Even if one were to conceive of the most intense form of *spiritual presence*, would this be capable of overcoming the absence of two beings who love each other, thus abolishing it? Can it abolish the separation of death? (Granted, in death, reciprocity, which is one of the elements of *spiritual presence*, disappears, at least from the field of consciousness of the person who remains.) Moreover, on the level of interpersonal relations, the absence of the beloved person can be experienced by the person who knew that this departed person loved him or her.

Two persons can be *really present* to one another only if their *spiritual presence* is founded on a *there-being*, and because, rightly so, these are persons having a bodily dimension, this there-being

---

3. Piolanti, *Il mistero eucaristico*, 7.

normally requires spatiotemporal coexistence. By itself, the latter form of coexistence is not a true presence. However, it is what confers reality to the true form of presence which, in fact, is spiritual.

The Eucharistic presence is spiritual and real

{871} By excessively insisting on the "reality" of Christ in the Eucharist, its "truth" has been neglected (more so in theological conceptualization than in lived piety). It is the presence of a someone to a someone, and this is what stands out in the entire tradition which presents us with the risen, ever-living Lord, master, and Savior currently present with His saving power in the Eucharist.

However, returning to the "truth" of said presence does not dispense one from explaining its "reality," which, as we have seen, is founded on offerings' real identification with Christ's body and blood. Christ is present there for the believers—however, He is indeed there. His presence is not that of a beloved and distant being, toward which our desires would tend, who would inhabit one's thought and heart without for all that abolishing the real separation thus experienced. He is indeed there so that He may dwell in one's thought and heart, though in such a manner that one's thought and heart may encounter Him in the real proximity into which He willed to place himself.

However intense it may be, *spiritual presence* does not suffice for creating this real proximity, which it in fact only makes one desire. Indeed, Christ is present to believers in the Church in a number of ways, and it is always a question of a spiritual presence. The Eucharistic presence does not make an exception to this. It is also a spiritual presence, meaning that it cannot be understood except as being situated among these other forms of presence. However, precisely speaking, it occupies a unique place among them and cannot be mistaken with any of them, for this spiritual presence is also a real presence. It is a real presence *par excellence*, as Pope Paul VI said.[4] In his terminology, the others are real in the sense of the "true presence" spoken of above. However, if we take the term "real" in its strict sense, meaning a presence assured by and in external things

---

4. See Pope Paul VI, *Mysterium Fidei*, in AAS 57 (1965): 762–64.

independent of every act of mind knowing or not knowing this thing, it alone is real.

Transignification and Transfinalization Presuppose the There-Being of Christ in the Eucharist without Explaining It

{872} By[5] insisting as they have on the personal implications of the notion of presence in general and on the ordering of the Eucharist to something other than itself (i.e., the believer's personal encounter with Jesus, which is an act of Christ giving Himself and of the believer uniting himself to Him by means of the Eucharist and through it) the theologians who are partisans of transignification have extracted an essential dimension of the sacrament and have placed it into clearer relief. However, in order for the Eucharist to be able to play this role, efficaciously "signifying" Christ's "presence" to the believer and vice-versa, does it suffice to say that the natural signification of the bread has changed? Or to make the point more clearly, can the bread really acquire this new signification without, for that reason, being changed in its reality as bread and in its substance?

To say that the profound reality of a given thing consists in its "signification" and in its "finalization," in what it is for man and for Christ, the "Lord of the universe" (see Bacciochi), one thus uses a formula that cannot itself be explanatory without first being explained in turn. "Signification" and "finalization" designate relations. The former can be rationate [i.e., a *relatio rationis*] (a thing, a gesture, a sound, etc., to which one conventionally and extrinsically attributes a significative function) or it can be real when this thing by its very nature takes the place of another thing in relation to man's awareness, mind, and heart; for example, a given free gesture, the sign of love or at least of interest or a given object which due to its likeness with another thing that played a role in the life of a given

---

5. See §848 above. Also, see Joseph Coppens, "Miscellanea biblica, Mysterium fidei," *Ephemerides Theologicae Lovanienses* 33 (1957): 483–506. Charles Journet, "La présence réelle du Christ sacrament," *Nova et Vetera* 40 (1965): 275–89, and "Transsubstantiation," *Nova et Vetera* 46 (1971): 161–72. Karl Rahner, "La presence du Christ dans le sacrament de l'eucharistie," *Ecrits théologiques* (Paris: Desclée de Brouwer, 1968), 9:116–17. Jean-Hervé Nicolas, "Présence réelle eucharistique et transsignification," *Revue thomiste* 72 (1972): 439–49.

person suddenly triggers off in a given person the phenomenon of "involuntary memory," described by Proust, leading him to rejoin his past, by the mediation of this object, not through a deliberative searching through our memory but in the form of a lived, or rather relived, experience.

As regards finalization, it also can be extrinsic (when one makes use of a being for one's own ends) or intrinsic (when it is a question of the end to which this thing, this being, is ordered on account of what it is). In any case, it is unthinkable and unintelligible to say that the thing would be constituted in being by its signification or its finality. This is self-evident if it is a question of a rationate signification or of an extrinsic finalization. However, this is also true when the thing by itself signifies and is finalized. Indeed, to say "by itself" is to say "in virtue of its constitutive principles and on account of what it is." (The reference made to "an Augustinian worldview" made by the partisans of such a position is too imprecise to have value as a proof or as an explanation.)[6]

Fr. de Lubac[7] has shown (in relation to another question, namely that of the supernatural) the strict relation that exists between a being's ontological structure and its own proper finality:

> Therefore, finality was considered only as being something rather extrinsic. It was not considered as being a destiny inscribed in the very structure of the being, orienting it from within, a destiny *which it cannot, ontologically, set aside*, but instead, was considered as being a simple destination received more or less externally and as an afterthought.[8]

Likewise, Jorge Laporta: "When speaking about natural end, this seems to be a pure tautology. Nothing can be more necessarily natural than the end of a being, that is, this very nature achieved."[9] Consequently, the intrinsic finality of a being (and we must say this just as much about its "natural signification," above all if one refers to a worldview holding that material things signify by their very nature)

---

6. See "Structure métaphysique de l'être créé d'après S. Augustin," *Recherches de Philosophie* 1 (1955): 57–84.
7. See Henri de Lubac, *Le mystère du surnaturel* (Paris: Aubier, 1965), 79–103.
8. Ibid., 97 (emphasis added).
9. Jorge Laporta, *La destinée de la nature humaine selon Thomas d'Aquin* (Paris: Vrin, 1965), 99.

cannot be changed without its ontological structure, its very being and substance, thereby being changed.

Some thinkers (e.g., Bacciochi) here appeal to "God's omnipotence." It is quite clear that the Eucharistic presence can only be explained by an intervention by God's omnipotence, and indeed, as we have seen, the Fathers in fact did make recourse to such an intervention.[10] However, we still must know and explain what effect the Divine Omnipotence produces in this precise case. God can certainly "change" the very reality of the being that He has created, as St. Ambrose already said. However, we are not looking for the cause of this change but, rather, are looking for what it consists in. Indeed, we must recognize that it cannot consist in the changing of the natural signification or of the intrinsic finalization, without there first of all being a change in the substantial reality that is expressed and unfolded in this signification and in this intrinsic finalization. Without this, we cannot in any way say that the reality has changed, that the bread is no longer bread, and that the offering has become the body of Christ. It would merely be a sign of a distant reality.

Using the terms "personal presence" and "spatial presence" for what I called "spiritual presence" and "there-being" above, the Dutch theologian Schoonenberg points out that the body is always the means of "personal presence." This position is summarized by Schillebeeckx as stating: "Personal presence is expressed by the bodily intermediary and is visibly realized in signs. It is an unveiling of oneself in freedom and a spiritual opening in bodiliness."[11] And he notes:

> Concerning this analysis offered by Schoonenberg, which we have recounted here in a brief and partial manner, we can say that it is generally accepted in contemporary existential thought ... Moreover, this new understanding of the world and of oneself constitutes, in a less-structured manner, the background of all the attempts undertaken to reinterpret the dogma of Trent, for example those of Ch. Davis and of L. Smith.[12]

As a way of demonstrating the mediating role of the body and of visible signs for assuring "personal presence," Smith proposed the parable of a hosted meal by means of which the master of the house

---

10. See §833 above.
11. See Schillebeeckx, *Le presence du Christ dans l'eucharistie*, 106–13.
12. See ibid., 111.

makes himself personally present to his guests, with his interest and his friendship:

> Thus, the material activities of human bodies or of human realities receive a new dimension. They become signs in the service of persons. Every manifestation or perception of knowledge becomes a sign of revelation and of faith, an efficacious sign of the human community, a manifestation and cause of personal presence.[13]

What should we think of this? It is quite true that the body, as well as bodily signs, are the necessary mediation for personal presence. However, in order for this personal presence to be real, the body as such still must be present (be there) in its own, proper manner (i.e., in a spatiotemporal manner). If the cup of tea, the gesture of offering it, and the smile accompanying the gesture are the means of a personal and real presence, this is first of all because the master of the house is present bodily.

This is not the case for the Eucharist, as Christ is present only in and by the very gift that He makes of Himself—in the Eucharistized bread and wine. Therefore, it is necessary that the given thing, as well as the act of giving, themselves assure not only the interpersonal relations of presence but also, and first of all, the "there-being" without which the personal presence would be unreal. If we can push the metaphor that has been proposed, we could note that if the master of the house were to prepare a meal for his guests and offer it to them without himself being present, no matter how great the love with which the dishes were prepared and presented, they would be insufficient for rendering him really present. Without involving ourselves in a manifest paradox, we cannot say only that they are a sign realizing his presence. They do not realize it. They presuppose it.[14]

One will respond to this (indeed, doing so in advance) that the Eucharistic presence has as its necessary preliminary Christ's presence in the community celebrating the Eucharist: "The Eucharist begins with a *praesentia realis* ... and its goal is to render this presence more real."[15]

---

13. Schoonenberg, cited by Schillebeeckx in *Le presence du Christ dans l'eucharistie*, 110.
14. See Nicolas, "Présence réelle eucharistique et transsignification," 439–49.
15. Schillebeeckx, *Le presence du Christ dans l'eucharistie*, 112.

However, this assertion contains a paralogism. Christ's presence to the community that celebrates is not itself a fully real presence, for it is in part constituted—in part only, for it is true, Christ by His loving glance, by His grace, is rendered present to the Church and to the believer—by the acts of the believer, by his faith and his love.

If, as is quite justly said,[16] we must distinguish, as it were, two degrees or two stages of real personal presence, namely, the "presence proposed" and the "presence received as a gift," the presence of grace in all its forms can be called real only if it is received as a gift and by the act of receiving it. For its part, the Eucharistic presence is real, independent of our reception of it. Its singularity lies in this fact. Of course, it will be a personal presence only if it is received. However, then, as a result of its own presence [*présentialité*], it will be a personal, fully real presence.

Therefore, the presence of grace is not what can confer reality upon the Eucharistic presence. The relation of the Eucharistic presence to Christ's other forms of presence to His Church (which we are in no way denying) is the reverse. The Eucharistic presence is what fulfills and seals all the others, providing the true foundation for their reality.

The notions of transignification and transfinalization are invaluable for explaining the sense and the *raison d'être* of Christ's presence in the Eucharist. However, they are radically incapable of explaining the reality of this presence. They cannot explain the reality of the gift of His flesh and blood as food and drink and, consequently, the reality of the reception [*manducation*] of the body and blood by the believer. By themselves, these notions would only explain an intentional union of the believer with Christ, a union for which the external presentation and reception [*manducation*] would be only an occasion for such union, which would solely be caused by the believer's acts of faith and charity. In other words, the only cause for such a union would be wholly subjective. Such a presence of Christ in the depths of the believer would not be of a different order than that which prayer can produce, whether solitary or communal prayer:

---

16. See ibid., 110.

"That Christ may dwell in your hearts through faith."[17] What is uniquely the case for the Eucharist would thus disappear. The traditional realism of the eating [*manducation*] of Christ's body would no longer be anything but verbal, and this would also be the case for the realism of the expressions that present the Eucharist as being the "memorial" of the passion and its "re-presentation," the Church's offering of the sacrifice of Calvary, performed at each celebration. It would no longer be anything but an evocative celebration which one would have no reason to privilege.

If Christ's "there-being" in the Eucharist, without which the Eucharistic presence cannot be real, is presupposed for the interpersonal relations of presence that the notions of transignification and of transfinalization are used to explain, it is therefore necessary that the very thing given and received be Christ Himself, prior to and before the emergence of these interpersonal relations, and consequently before every intervention of knowledge and of love by the person to whom it is offered. Here, we can take up Calvin's expression: "If God cannot deceive or lie, it follows that He brings about everything that He signifies. Therefore, we must truly receive the body and blood of Jesus Christ in the Last Supper [*Cène*] since the Lord there represents to us communion in both of them."[18] Thus, we must say that in order for the gift and reception of the body and blood to be true, it is necessary that what is given really be Christ's body and blood. It was bread and wine. Therefore, the bread and wine have been changed, "converted" into the reality of Christ's body and blood, and for this reason have lost their reality as bread and wine. Therefore, we are brought back to the notion of "substantial conversion," which the Church calls "transubstantiation."

IS IT POSSIBLE TO DISPENSE WITH THE NOTION OF TRANSUBSTANTIATION?

As we will see, in order to explain this "real presence" of Christ in the Eucharist, the theory of transubstantiation makes use of meta-

---

17. Eph 3:17 (RSV).
18. Calvin, *Petit traité de la Sainte Cène*, op. I, 509.

physical arguments that are not only extremely difficult and seem more to block our access to the mystery than to aid us in understanding it, but also appeal to a philosophy that is disagreeable to the contemporary mind. Indeed, this disagreement is not merely limited to those who must be presented with the mystery of the Eucharist. Beyond them, it is even disagreeable to the very theologians who are called on to present the mystery and, to this end, to reflect on it. I refer to the philosophy of being, which many today consider to be something passé.

Consequently, in modern theology (and especially in ecumenical theology) there is a very strong tendency to circumvent this difficulty and, to this end, to endeavor to arrive at the mystery in which we believe (i.e., "the real presence") by leaving transubstantiation aside as something that is too difficult for one to integrate into the *intellectus fidei* today.

Two forms of such a tendency can be discerned, and they are quite close to each other. [We will examine them sequentially.]

The Tendency to Merge the Mystery of the Eucharistic Presence into the Total Mystery of Christ's Presence to His Church

Exposition

{873} [We can see this tendency in statements like the following:]

As much from the Lutheran perspective as from the Catholic one, it is beginning to be understood that one may suitably determine what is proper to the sacrament in the light of something other than the notion of *praesentia realis*. The Last Supper must be seen and explained in function of its organic situation in the ecclesiological context wherein the Lord of the Church is ceaselessly present in bringing about salvation through the preaching and relations among men.[19]

And, likewise:

Communion with Christ in the Eucharist presupposes His true presence, efficaciously signified by the bread and wine which, in this mystery, become His body and blood. However, the real presence of Christ's body and blood can be understood only in the context of the redemptive work

---

19. Boelens, "La discussion sur la Sainte Cène," 98.

by which He gives Himself and by which, in Himself, he gives reconciliation, peace, and life to those who are His own ... Christ is present and active in many manners in the whole Eucharistic celebration. The same Lord who is present at the right hand of the Father (and therefore transcending the sacramental order) is He who in the Eucharistic signs thus offers to His Church the special gift of Himself.[20]

Thus, the Eucharistic presence is considered as being a privileged and intense form of Christ's presence. However, one either avoids asking how it is produced or rejects the very task of explaining it:

The glorified Christ sits at the right hand of the Father in His humanity and in His divinity. How He can make it be the case that He would also be present bodily in the Eucharist is a mystery, the work of the Holy Spirit, which the Church cannot ascertain ... Therefore, Christ, by the Holy Spirit, sovereignly takes hold of the elements of bread and wine and draws them to Himself, accepts them into the fullness of His humanity and His divinity so that they may truly, really, and substantially become His body and blood, in accord with what the Gospel says.[21]

In general, the various formulas of ecumenical agreement among theologians of different confessions affirm the real presence by avoiding pronunciations concerning the way it is realized, as though this were of secondary importance in relation to the affirmation of the mystery of the Eucharistic presence.

Critical remarks

{874} We must wholeheartedly recognize the dependent [*second*] character of the importance held by the theory of transubstantiation in relation to the mystery of the Eucharistic presence which is affirmed by faith, as well as the way that the Eucharistic mystery is included in the complete mystery of the Church. However, "dependent [*second*]" does not mean "secondary." That which is dependent [*second*] can be indispensable for this very thing in relation to which it is called dependent [*second*].

This is the case for the theory of transubstantiation in relation to the mystery of the Eucharistic presence. Quite rightly, one should

---

20. International Anglican-Roman Catholic Commission, "Declaration on the Eucharistic Doctrine," September 7, 1971, in *Documentation catholique* 69 (1972): 87.
21. See Thurian, *L'eucharistie*, 273–74.

situate the latter within the full mystery of Christ's relations with His Church. However, this must not have the consequence of turning our minds from what is unique to the Eucharistic presence, namely the fact that what is given to us to eat was bread and now really is Christ's body. To affirm the Eucharistic presence in its full extent (the presence of Christ's body to the believer by faith, the presence of Christ to His Church, and the unification of the body of Christ) cannot dispense with the theologian asking himself (under pain [of theology] becoming a purely verbal game): "What, therefore, has taken place so that what was once bread and wine now would be Christ's body and blood?" He cannot avoid considering the fact that there has been a "becoming" in the course of the liturgy and by means of it, and that something has taken place in these "elements," which were only bread and wine at the beginning of the liturgy, and which, (at least) at the moment of communion, are the body and blood of Christ.

To say, with Thurian, that this takes place through an action that is so mysterious that the Church cannot know it is an insufficient response. There can be no doubt that this becoming would be brought about by the Holy Spirit's action and that this action would be wholly mysterious. However, can the theologian avoid striving to come to an understanding of the result of this action? Certainly, one can admit not only that hosts of believers affirm the real presence and live by it without posing this question but also that through the centuries theologians themselves did not pose the question, at least in these terms. However, as we have seen, they came to increasingly affirm the real "conversion" in a realistic manner, and this affirmation could not avoid entailing the question: "How should we conceive of this change that is brought about?" The question was historically posed on the occasion of the controversy with Berengar of Tours. However, it would have been posed no matter what might have been the historical contingencies. Transubstantiation is one response to it. To declare that it is passé (at least in the ontic sense in which it was understood by those who gave it as a response to this question) requires the person who makes such a declaration to offer another meaning for it. Without this, the affirmation of the real presence risks turning into a mere verbalism. We have seen how the new theories of trans-finalization and of transignification have attempted to give a response that would provide such an explanatory replacement, and we have likewise seen that they have not succeeded in doing so.

The Tendency to Refer to the Ultra-Terrestrial and Ultra-Historical Conditions of Christ's Eschatological Existence

Exposition

{875} Durwell's[22] master intuition is that Christ, by His resurrection and glorification, left this world and hence can no longer be present in the world after the manner of a substance that belongs to this order here-below.[23] Consequently Christ's presence is eschatological and is a kind of anticipation, or even a beginning, of the realization of the Parousia. Now, in the Parousia, all things and all men will be transformed, not by an external intervention, but by a blossoming forth and exaltation of what is best in themselves, which indeed is their tendency toward Christ. Bread and wine are the signs and means for this Parousia which begins to be produced in and through the Eucharist. For this to be brought about, they do not need to be wrenched from their own proper nature (no more than men do not need to be wrenched from their own nature and personality in order to become the body of Christ). Instead, the bread becomes the body of Christ by "an overflowing of what it already is" by which "it finds itself in all of its reality [*vérité*]."[24] Indeed, in the passage cited, it is a question of creation in general, "the so-called first creation," but this is expressly said in order to explain the use of bread and wine, "so as to make from them the sacraments of His coming." Whence, we have the denial of a change in them:

The Eucharistic bread is not the body of Christ by way of addition. It itself is the presence and gift of this body. Total concentration on eschatology

---

22. See François-Xavier Durwell, *L'Eucharistie, presence du Christ*, 2nd ed. (Paris: Ed. Ouvrières, 1972); G. Martelet, *Résurrection, eucharistie et genèse de l'homme* (Paris: Desclée, 1972).
23. See Durwell, *L'Eucharistie, presence du Christ.*, 21.
24. Ibid., 44.

does not add a new reality to a preexisting one ... Therefore, Christ's Presence is not mediated by the bread. The latter does not screen off the encounter and the communion. It is the sacrament of them and realizes them.[25]

However, immediately afterward, the notion of change and conversion is—along such traditional lines!—retrieved:

Christ has so sovereign a sway over the natural elements that they may become the means of His integration into this world and the simple externalization of His vivifying presence, and this indeed constitutes a substantial change.[26]

Critical reflections

{876} It seems that at the end of all these considerations concerning eschatology, we would return in the end to the same point. We find ourselves left asking: "In what does Christ's sway over the elements of bread and wine consist? In what consists the fact that they are the sacraments of His presence (which they were not before this and which they will continue to be after the liturgy)?"[27]

Indeed, it is quite certain that the Christ who is present in and through the Eucharist is Christ who is the conqueror of death, in His eschatological existence. Classical theology was aware of this fact (using the expression, "Christ present in heaven") and every interpretation of transubstantiation that would claim "to register Christ's presence in the world after the manner of a substance that belongs to this order here-below" would need to be rejected. However, this would also be a false interpretation, indeed one contrary to that offered by the high scholastics, as we will see. Nonetheless, it is also certain that the Parousia is still "to come" and that when Christ returns, He will do so *in propria specie*, not by means of signs. The latter, the sacraments, belong precisely to the time of the Church, the time of expectation of Christ's return.

Hence, Christ's coming in the Eucharist is brought about by means of realities of this world, and all these considerations do not dispense us from asking, "How are we to understand the presence

25. Ibid., 58.
26. Ibid., 60.
27. See ibid., 65ff.

that is realized by the bread and wine?" As we have seen, if the "elements" remain bread and wine, the presence that they would signify would be only intentional, not real, by being a simple evocation in the believer's mind and imagination. And thus he who eats these elements neither truly eats Christ's body nor drinks His blood.

To say that when the bread becomes Christ's body it does not lose its own nature but rather "finds itself in all of its reality," is a pious, arbitrary, and meaningless affirmation. The profound reality of bread certainly is not to become the body of Christ.

To compare the transformation of the bread into Christ's body to the transformation of the believer and of the community into Christ's body is to limit oneself to an approximation that is detrimental to serious theological research. The transformation of a person and of the community of persons into "the body of Christ" is brought about from interpersonal relations of knowledge and love that leave the persons in their ontological distinction from each other and in relation to Christ. Given that the body and blood are obviously unable to form these interpersonal relations, they can become Christ's body and blood only by ontological identification or by a purely symbolic identification.

In the latter case, Christ is present only in the heart and mind of the person who is able to grasp the symbol and, in fact, does grasp it—and this is not a real presence. In the other case, it is contradictory to simultaneously say that the "elements" have become Christ's body and blood without ceasing to be bread and wine. The appeal made to St. Paul's expression, "Creation itself will be set free from its bondage to decay and obtain the glorious liberty of the children of God,"[28] cannot illuminate the Eucharistic mystery in any way, for in these mysterious words, it is not said that material creatures will be identical with Christ's body without ceasing to be themselves. Rather, it is only said that they "will obtain the glorious liberty of the children of God." It is not at all clear how this is realized for the Eucharistized bread and wine.

Thanks to this manner of explaining things, one believes that one can thus overcome all the oppositions between the ancient and

---

28. Rom 8:21 (RSV); see Rom 8:19–20.

modern explanations and even all the rational problems that these explanations seek to resolve, thus implying that they are false problems which are thereby rationally unresolvable. In the end, this kind of explanation is unacceptable because it expresses an outlook that is opposed to the very nature of sacramentality. Indeed, here, expositions based on earthly realities are rejected, holding that one would, instead, need to base one's argument on eschatological realities, which alone can furnish the principle of intelligibility for the Eucharistic mystery.[29] However, the sacraments were instituted precisely to make us pass from earthly realities to the eschatological realities of which they are signs. If we could grasp eschatological realities directly, we would have no need for sacramental signs. When Christ returns, they will be eliminated by His very presence. It is futile to claim that these problems do not emerge for believing reason at the level of the earthly realities from which Christ made the efficacious signs of His presence or that this very presence would bring us the solution to the question—and thus, precisely that this presence is known by us and given to us only in and through these signs. Moreover, the obvious embarrassment into which the author falls when[30] he ultimately finds that he must, like it or not, seek a solution to these problems shows well enough that his "principle of intelligibility" remains insufficient.

Introductory Conclusion for the Study of Transubstantiation

The ultimate dilemma remains. On the one hand, we have the Catholic Eucharist: Christ's immediate bodily presence among us. On the other hand, we have the Protestant Eucharist: the bread's immediate bodily presence, mediating Christ, who only exists in heaven.[31]

While wholly respecting the sincerity of one's intentions (for certain Protestant theologians would dispute Journet's judgment

---

29. See Durwell, *L'Eucharistie, presence du Christ*, 26.
30. See ibid., ch. 5.
31. [Tr. note: The entry here is "Journet, 19, 151." The pagination makes this problematic. The text in question is one of the following: Journet, *La messe, préscence du sacrifice de la crox*, or "Note sur un accord entre théologiens Anglicans et catholiques touchant la doctrine eucharistique," *Nova et Vetera* 46 (1971): 250–51.]

concerning the Protestant Eucharist), we must take heed of the fact that if we retain the reality of the bread and wine in the offerings after the Eucharistic prayer, this precludes their real identification with Christ's body and blood and, for this reason, means that they mediate Christ, who is no longer recognized as being really present (because "real presence" obviously means "immediate presence"). However, in this text, it is regrettable that Journet used the adjective "bodily," for it would be better to say "presence of the body." Indeed, as we will see, Cardinal Journet was well aware of this point and clearly expressed it, namely, that while Christ is present in the Eucharist with His body, He is not present in the manner in which a body is present to our experience (i.e., corporeally).

TRANSUBSTANTIATION

The Necessity of Admitting Transubstantiation

The problem

{877} Given that transubstantiation is the appointed explanation used by the Magisterium, classical theologians admit and teach it. However, a great number of people hold that it is not necessary for explaining Christ's "there-being" in the Eucharist (so that the true body of Christ would be in this sacrament, as St. Thomas states). By this they mean that it would be a question of a relative necessity, transubstantiation not being necessary so that Christ would be there (for God could do this in a different manner) but rather so that the sacramental words, which indicate to us what Christ in fact intended, may be verified.[32] Certain thinkers, following Scotus and Suarez, even think that it is not sufficient for explaining Christ's "there-being," which would require another action being exercised on Christ Himself so that he may become present (namely, an adductive action or reproductive action).

However, it is quite clear that transubstantiation itself is not directly taught by Scripture or the primitive tradition. What is formally declared in the sources of faith is the real identification of the

---

32. See Cajetan, *In ST* III, q. 75, a. 2, no. 9.

offerings with Christ's body and blood respectively. Moreover, it is formally declared that Christ who is present in the Eucharist is living and therefore that the body and blood are not really separated. The "conversion" of the bread into Christ's body and of the wine into His blood (which was called "transubstantiation" from the twelfth century onward) can be considered as being theologically certain to the degree that it appears that it is necessary for providing an intelligible meaning to the affirmation of faith that there is (from the moment when the bread and wine have been Eucharistized) an identification between the offerings and Christ's body and blood. For all the more reason, it could be introduced by the Magisterium into the formula that expresses this affirmation of faith only if this necessity is such that it would be impossible for one to deny the reality of the conversion without denying the identification of the offerings with Christ's body and blood. Therefore, it is futile to say that one believes in transubstantiation but that it is neither necessary nor even sufficient for explaining Christ's "there-being" in the Eucharist. If the latter point were true, transubstantiation would be only a theological hypothesis, indeed one that is unverifiable.

St. Thomas's position

{878} St. Thomas's position is incontestable: the identification of the offerings with Christ's body and blood after the sacramental action necessarily requires substantial conversion.[33]

The reasons that establish the necessity for substantial conversion

{879} Christ's "there-being" in the Eucharist follows on a "not being-there." Therefore, there has been a change. The change that makes a bodily being "be there" after not being there can be brought about in one of two ways. On the one hand, in the ordinary case, it can be brought about by a change that affects this being itself ([i.e.,] local movement). On the other hand, it can be brought about by a change that affects a bodily being that was already there and which, by this change, would become the being under consideration. (Thus, the

---

33. See *In IV Sent.*, d. 11, q. 1, a. 1, ad 1, quaestiuncula. *Quod.* V, q. 6, a. 1. *ST* III, q. 75, a. 2 and 3.

new living being is found in the maternal being by the transformation of the egg, on account of its union with the male gamete, into the first cell of the new living being.)

Obviously, one must exclude every kind of local movement that would affect Christ and make Him exist under the species. ("Under the *species*" is not a place into which a bodily being, however small or reduced in size it may be, would be lodged. If, on account of the Eucharistic there-being, Christ exists in a determined place, this can be only by means of the "species," in the place where the species are localized, as we will see below.)

Therefore, the bread and wine are what are changed into Christ's body and blood. However, it is clear that the "appearances" of bread and wine remain as before. (Indeed, what remains is not only that which is there for the naked eye, taste, and touch, but also that which one can know concerning the bread and wine by the procedures, methods, and analyses of experimental science.) Therefore, one must say that what has changed is the profound, substantial reality of the bread and wine (i.e., their "substance").*

This rules out the idea that there would be anything left of the substance of the bread and wine. The aforementioned example of the appearance of a new individual, a new being, in the maternal organism must itself also be analogically transposed. The new being in question did not exist before being there. Consequently, nothing prevents it from being the case that something of the previous being (the male and female gametes) would have passed into it (according to prime matter, as the Aristotelian cosmology will express the point). In the case of the Eucharist, the new being that is newly there is not a new being. This being exists independent of this

---

* N.B. Let us note that the notion of "substance" is taken, at this point of the investigation, in its most obvious sense, not yet having been philosophically analyzed. We understand it as meaning that which makes a thing be what it is (and sometimes different) in contrast to what one could think that it is according to its appearances (as though a thing which would have all the external appearances of bread were something other than bread). The difference is that, in this case, which falls within our experience, one would detect that it is not bread by experimental means, which shows that it did not have "all the appearances of bread." For this example to be of use, one must analogically transpose it, positing (on account of faith) a limit case wherein all the appearances are those of bread while, nonetheless, affirming (by an affirmation of faith) that it is not bread.

substantial change of the bread and wine. Therefore, we cannot say that some part of the being that was previously there would now again be found in the new being. The bread is totally changed into Christ's flesh "in such a manner that the substance of Christ's body replaces the bread's substance."[34]

In conclusion, transubstantiation shows itself to be the *sine qua non* condition of Christ's there-being, which itself founds the reality of His presence. Without it, everything that Scripture and tradition say about the reality of the gift that Christ makes of His body as food and of His blood as drink to the believer in the Eucharist could be understood only in a purely symbolic manner. There would be no real reception [*manducation*] of Christ's body and blood. We have seen that the texts do not suffer this interpretation, which the Church expressly rejects in the name of the faith. It remains for us to see how one can, henceforth, explain transubstantiation itself.

Transubstantiation Considered from the Perspective of the *terminus a quo*: The Change Undergone by the Bread and Wine

The subject of the change

Does transubstantiation involve a subject [of change]?

{880} Experience[35] discovers three kinds of change. The first is *local change*, a purely extrinsic change affecting the changed body only in its relations with other bodies. The second is *alteration*, a change that affects the changed body in itself, though only in its accidental determinations. The third kind is *generation*, which affects the very nature of the body that is changed, thus becoming another species.

In all of these cases, there is a subject that changes. In other words, the change leads that which was X to become Y. This is clear for the first two kinds of change mentioned above. For the first, the subject is the given bodily being, which has changed with regard to its situation in space and in relation to other bodies, while otherwise remaining the same. For the second, the subject is the given bodily

---

34. See *ST* III, q. 76, a. 5.
35. For section B, see *ST* III, q. 75, and Cajetan's commentary on these articles. See also Billot, *De Ecclesiae Sacramentis*. De La Taille, *Mysterium fidei*.

being that has intrinsically changed with regard to its quantity or its qualities, though without ceasing to be substantially the same. For the third kind of change, the need to explain the reality of this particular kind of movement, consisting in the "generation" of a new bodily being from a prior bodily being (not through a kind of mere substitution but through a "passage" from the one to the other), is what led Aristotle to distinguish two elements in bodily substances.

One was a universal substrate, deprived of every ontological qualification, though able to receive all of them and, for this reason, found identically in the ontological structure of all bodily beings. He called this element "prime matter." The other element is the qualifying element that makes the given bodily being be this or that, making it have a given nature. He called this second element "the substantial form." Given that matter is the same at the point of departure (in the being from which the new being is begotten) and at the point of arrival (in the newly begotten being), [prime] matter is what assures the continuity from the one to the other. Without such continuity, movement would be unintelligible. Indeed, without such continuity, the new being would not be produced from the preceding one but, instead, would be produced in place of it, which is meaningless and stands in contradiction to experience.

Now, creation, which we are led to affirm on the basis of the experience of the contingency holding for all the beings in our universe (and for the universe itself) and which cannot be experienced in any away, itself precludes every kind of [preexisting] subject. Creation is the complete production of a being, without any dependence or continuity in relation to a prior being. However, it also is not a change (even though the only way we can conceptualize it is by making use of our concept of change).

Now, for its part, transubstantiation is a change: this thing that was bread no longer is bread; it has become the body of Christ. However, as we have seen, it is a complete change, not leaving anything unchanged in the initial reality. If it is a change, there must be something common to the two termini of the change, something assuring continuity from one terminus to the other. If it is a complete change, this common thing cannot be a subject, properly so-called.

It must embrace the two termini in such a way that it would itself be changed without, however, entirely ceasing to be common to both of them.

St. Thomas proposed the most fully developed solution to this difficult problem.[36] After emphasizing that it was a question of supernatural change (appealing directly to God's own causality in what is proper to it) and not a natural change (i.e., a change that could be realized by a created agent), he says that the common element that assures the continuity of this unique movement is *communis natura entis*, the common nature of being.[37] For this reason, he sometimes says there is no subject [involved in this change].[38] At other times he says that the subject is the two substances together (the substance of the bread and the substance of the body of Christ).[39] Finally, on other occasions, he says that the accidents that remain are in some way similar to a subject.[40] In other words, it is not a subject in the proper sense but a "something" that plays the role of a subject; on the level of reality, it is the *communis natura entis*, and on the level of appearances, is the accidents of the bread and wine. We now must explain this conclusion.

The *natura communis entis*

{881}

1. The community of being in question obviously only pertains to creatures. It is *esse commune*, that which all beings have in common: existence [*être*].

2. However, *esse commune* is not a genus. It is only analogically common to different beings. In other words, the being by which two beings are alike is different in each one. Hence, what does it mean to say that such community in being can assure the continuity of the passage from one being to another?

---

36. See *ST* III, q. 75, a. 4, co., and also the responses to the objections.
37. See ibid., ad 3.
38. See ibid., ad 2.
39. See ibid., ad 1.
40. See ibid., a. 5, ad. 4.

3. In creation, such pseudo-movement takes place from nonbeing to being. Nothing is held in common between two contradictory termini, so that no passage from one terminus to the other is conceivable. In transubstantiation, however, the two termini have in common the fact that both are a realization of the common notion of being: "When the complete reality of the bread is changed into the body of Christ, what formally makes it be the case that a thing is a being remains. However, that which makes it be this being, bread, in its distinction, no longer does."[41]

4. Therefore, the problem is one of knowing whence comes the distinction of beings within their community in being. Of itself, being (i.e., the *perfectio essendi*) is one. If there happen to be a multiplicity of beings that are distinct from each other, this can come only from a limitation of the *perfectio essendi* in each of them. Now, given that pure multiplicity is unthinkable and impossible, whence comes the fact that this multiplicity of distinct beings preserves a kind of unity? They are all included in the idea of being, which is one. However, this unity would be deceptive if it were a something merely fashioned by the intellect, if the idea of being did not express some unity in the things themselves. This real unity arises from the fact that, at the principle and source of all beings, there is a perfect being in whom the *perfectio essendi* is realized without limitation and without admixture, pure and infinite: *ipsum esse subsistens*. Receiving being from Him, every being resembles Him (though in a deficient and imperfect manner, given that the *perfectio essendi* is necessarily limited where being is received). Diversity in the manners of limitation is the source of the diversity of beings (*entia*), whereas the unity of the transcendent exemplar which each being resembles in all that it is, through the *perfectio essendi* that is realized in it, maintains the real unity of all beings at the heart of their multiplicity.[42]

What explains the limitation of the *perfectio essendi* in a given being is the distinction between act (that which is received) and potency (that which receives). The act is *esse*; the potency is essence. This does not mean that *esse* would be pure act and essence would be a

---

41. Cajetan, *Commentaria in Summam theologicam Sancti Thomae*, in loco.
42. See Nicolas, *Dieu connue comme inconnu*, 94–99.

pure limitation. *Esse* itself is limited by the essence to which it is ordered as to its proper potency. The essence receives its richness from the *perfectio essendi* that is brought to it by this limited act to which it is ordered, its own *esse*. The being is the essence actuated by *esse*. In virtue of this actuation, the *perfectio essendi* is recognized in it in a limited and determinate manner (in a manner that is proper to it).

Therefore, the *communis natura entis* is not a univocal perfection found identically in all beings. It is the *perfectio essendi* proper to each one, its essence, though formally considered in its relation to the first Being, its transcendent exemplar and efficient cause. Can God, the sovereign cause of the *perfectio essendi* in each being in the limited conditions proper to it, through an act of His creative omnipotence (though which, in distinction from the creative action, is exercised on an existent being) lead a *perfectio essendi*, already given to a being, outside the ontological limits of this being in such a way as to rejoin the *perfectio essendi* proper to another being, to the point of merging [*se confondre*] with it? Indeed, it is the case that two *perfectiones essendi* are distinguished from each other only on account of the limitations of being that are realized in them.

We can conceive of transubstantiation as follows. By the divine action, the *perfectio essendi* realized in the substance of the bread is, as it were, wrenched from the limitations of this realization (and by the same fact, that in which it is realized is no longer bread) in order that it may be joined to the *perfectio essendi* realized in Christ's humanity and merged with it so that the being in which it is realized is now Christ's humanity.[43]

---

[43] N.B. If this explanation gives the impression of being too alien to modern preoccupations, the reader should note that, in reality, it does nothing other than analyze, in a rigorous manner (by determining their implications), what is said by contemporary authors who seek to avoid this explanation without replacing it. Thus, Fr. de Bacciochi appeals to the resurrected Christ's lordship, which gives Him power over all the beings of the universe. Fr. Martelet appeals to the "absolute mastery over the universe and over death" guaranteed to Christ in His resurrection (see Martelet, *Résurrection, eucharistie et genèse de l'homme*, 182). The explanation by transubstantiation also appeals to this lordship and mastery. However, it seeks to express a point that remains vague and indeterminate in the others, namely what Christ does when, in the Eucharistic liturgy, in virtue of His mastery over all beings, He changes the bread into His body and the wine into His blood.

The limitations of this explanation

1. {882} Above all, one must take into account the fact that this does not directly prove the possibility of transubstantiation. Indeed, one could object that God can create whatsoever being, giving it a *perfectio essendi* that is limited in accord with a given essence; however, once this *perfectio essendi* is enclosed within its ontological limits, it no longer can exist without them. One could not prove that such reasoning is false. However, no more is it the case that one can prove the falsity of the reasoning that seeks to establish the possibility of transubstantiation on the basis of the *communis natura entis*, for the two termini of the transmutation, considered in their common relation to God the Creator, are not contradictory. This is what faith affirms: that which was bread has become the body of Christ. This is what enables us to pass from such mere non-impossibility to the affirmation of possibility.

2. One must not get worked up about the excessive difficulty involved in this metaphysical explanation. If it itself depends on faith, faith does not depend on it. Someone can believe in transubstantiation without having any metaphysical explanation for the change. (Take, for example, St. Ambrose when he simply appeals to the omnipotence of God who created all things, who changed water into wine at Cana, and who made the virgin conceive.) Granted, this is much more difficult for the metaphysician whose metaphysics rejects the presuppositions of the explanation. Nonetheless, someone can believe in transubstantiation even while having a poor metaphysical explanation. However, can someone correctly believe in the Eucharist without admitting "this admirable and unique change of the whole substance of the bread into His body and of the whole substance of the wine into His blood, while the appearances of bread and wine remain, a change which the Catholic Church very appropriately calls 'transubstantiation'"?[44] As we have seen, this would be impossible.[45]

---

44. See Council of Trent, session 13, "Decree on the Sacrament of the Eucharist," October 11, 1551, c. 2.

45. N.B. Orthodox theology itself admits the notion and the term (*metousiôsis* and *metousiousthai*) transubstantiation as expressing the traditional faith in "the marvelous change

3. What is contradictory and must be resolutely ruled out is the idea that a new being could be produced by transubstantiation.[46] The complete production of a new being by definition is a creation, and it is a contradiction in terms to say that creation would be brought about on the basis of a preexisting terminus. Indeed, one merely bandies about words if one were to say, on the hypothesis of a "productive transubstantiation," that the new being is produced on the basis of the first. There would be no real relation from one to the other, as no element or part of the first would pass into the second, the latter being totally new (i.e., in itself and in all its parts).

Given that transubstantiation is a change, it can be brought about between two positive termini, two "beings," and its subject (or, that which stands in place of the subject) is *utraque substantia, sicut ordo et numerus* (both substances together, as the parts of an order or of an ensemble [of things] constitute a whole).[47] To put it another way, the Divine Omnipotence can change one existing being into another already existing being, but it cannot make a new being exist by changing an already existing being into it.

4. Is this even universally true? Can one think that a bodily being might be changed into a spiritual being (or vice-versa)? Cajetan again thought so,[48] all the while recognizing that this would be contrary to God's wisdom (and therefore *de facto* impossible). One must go further and say that this involves a contradiction. Indeed, matter is an element of a particular kind of ontological limitation, namely, that which not only distinguishes the ensemble of contingent beings from *ipsum esse*, but also one that divides into two metaphysical classes those beings that are enclosed within it from those that are free from it. It affects the very essence and, therefore, the *perfectio essendi* as such in its very relation to God. (This is the reason why ontological perfections that include this material limitation in their very definition cannot be transposed to God. They are "mixed perfections.")

---

produced in the two species of the divine Eucharist, surpassing human understanding but attested to by the words of institution." See Trembelas, *Dogmatique de l'Église orthodoxe catholique*, 3:208–14.

46. Against Cajetan, loc. cit, no. 15.

47. See *ST* III, q. 75, a. 4, ad 1.

48. See loc. cit., nos. 8 and 13.

Therefore, it is contradictory to say that a being affected by this limitation would be changed into a being that is free from it.

St. Thomas never envisioned this hypothesis. He sufficiently excluded it by presenting transubstantiation as "a change from the matter of one being into the matter of another, and from the form into the form of another."[49] More formally in the *Summa theologiae*, he writes: "The substantial form of bread is changed into the form of the body of Christ inasmuch as the latter gives being to the body." In this way, he excludes the idea that the substantial form of the bread would be changed into the spiritual soul as such.

5. One must also exclude the possibility that, in general, one personal being would be changed into another personal being. A person is not only a part of the universe, communicating in the *natura communis entis* with the others. He is, itself, in its relationship with God, a whole. It is made "in the image of God," and for this very reason is singular and unique.

6. Nonetheless, the bread is changed into a person, Christ. This is true. But, this is primarily in view of man's salvation, which quite obviously excludes any kind of "gratuitous" transubstantiation. However, equally, it is a question of a person, indeed, quite certainly one who is divine. However, it is a person who is reached inasmuch as He is incarnate, inasmuch as He has become a human person[50]—thus having, from this very fact, a bodily dimension, and also a bodily being, and it is precisely as such that the bread is changed into him. We will see that all the riches of the Incarnate Word's personality are also reached, for the person is indivisible, though they are reached by the mediation of this bodily dimension. Thus, a purely spiritual person could in no way be the *terminus ad quem* of transubstantiation. The bodily being which would stand at the point of departure could not be changed into a spiritual being, neither as regards its matter, nor with regard to its form, which is itself material in the sense that it can exist only in matter. (For all the more reason is it excluded that this spiritual person would be the *terminus a quo* of a

---

49. See *In* IV *Sent.*, d. 11, q. 1, a. 3, ad 1.
50. For the sense of this expression §314 in the previous volume of this work in English.

transubstantiation into a bodily being or even into another spiritual being for the aforementioned reason.)

7. These explanations enable us to justly, situate, and, in the end, to reject the reproach registered by Fr. Martelet against the scholastic theory of transubstantiation, saying that by providing a metaphysical interpretation of the mystery it substituted the vocabulary of substance for that of the body, which would lead to the fact that "given that the category of substance is unaware [*ignorant*] of these resources (of the category of 'body'), the reflection that is inspired by it will therefore not deny the conjugal union of Christ and the Church, but it will neglect it, almost without knowing it."[51] We will presently see whether the negligence thus denounced is inevitable in a theology that utilizes the conceptual register of substance. Here, let us only note that, for St. Thomas (and in truth), far from being opposed to the notion of personhood, the notion of substance serves in defining it. The person could have no ontological consistency (and therefore no reality) if all the spiritual, psychological, and moral riches that constitute it were not founded on the ontological reality of the substance without which it would not belong to the extramental universe (i.e., to the real world).[52]

On the other hand, it is certain that the body is a constitutive part of the human person, and one can even rightly say that the person is his body, for the human body is much more than an heap of cells, tissues, and organs. Indeed, it is all of this, though as unified, animated, and vivified by the soul, which is spiritual.[53] As we have seen, the Church is the "body" of Christ in this sense. That is, she is a person who has wholly passed over into Him through faith and love.[54] For its part, the Eucharistized bread is the "body" of Christ. That is, it is His entire person, present by His body (as each of us is present to the world by our body). In order to integrate these great traditional views, we do not need to renounce the "vocabulary of substance." We only need to use it correctly. Conversely, if the "vocabulary" of "body" is not supplemented and given precision by the

---

51. Martelet, *Résurrection, eucharistie et genèse de l'homme*, 146–50.
52. See §114 in the first volume.
53. See §568 in the previous volume.
54. See §640 above.

vocabulary of substance, it will indicate this only in a vague and indistinct manner, with a somewhat empty lyricism.

The non-annihilation of the *terminus a quo*

{883} Because the bread ceases to exist and because none of it is found again in the terminus of the change (i.e., the body of Christ), one is tempted to think that it is annihilated. A number of theologians have thought this (e.g., Scotus).

St. Thomas, who was aware of this position, refuted it.[55] His reason is always the same. The only conceivable way the body of Christ can be there is if the bread (which was there beforehand) would be changed into it. If the bread is annihilated, it is not changed, and the there-being of Christ remains unexplained and inexplicable.

However, he recognizes this grave objection: after the transubstantiation, the substance of the bread is not something (*aliquid*), and if it is not something, it is a non-thing (*nihil*). His response (one made in logical terms to an objection equally formulated in logical terms) is that the substance of the bread is not an *aliquid*, but that into which it has been changed is an *aliquid*. Anew, this is an appeal to the notion of a *total change* (a notion that is quite difficult to conceive), in other words, a change that leaves nothing unchanged in the being that undergoes it and which nonetheless is still a change. One must again have recourse to the idea that what distinguishes one being from another in being and in their *perfectio essendi* is their ontological limitation. This helps one to understand how the divine action, by suppressing that by which the bread is distinct (and which, at the same time, was what constituted it as *this* being, though not as a *being*), does not annihilate it, even though nothing remains of *this* being in its distinctive and unique character.

Transubstantiation Considered in its *terminus ad quem*: The Eucharistic Presence Excludes Every Change in Christ

{884} Obviously the changing of the bread and wine is of interest and meaningful only in relation to Christ's there-being in the Eucha-

---

55. See *ST* III, q. 75, a. 3.

rist. We have seen that it is the necessary condition for this presence. However, is it sufficient for assuring it? Indeed, in the end, it is an action that is exercised on the bread and the wine, and the outcome must be that Christ's body and blood are made present there.

If we follow the scholastics in calling Christ's "sacramental being" Christ's "there-being" under the species, must there not be a special action by God on Christ (in His humanity) so as to confer this new being upon Him?

As we have seen, for certain thinkers, this action is one that is distinct from transubstantiation. They refer to it as an adductive action. Likewise, we have shown, following St. Thomas, that this is an unacceptable notion. However, for other theologians, this would be the very converting action that was exercised not only on the bread and wine in order to produce the complete change which we have discussed but also on Christ so as to confer this new being upon Him. This position was not only held by thinkers like Francisco Suarez but also by important Thomists after the Council of Trent, including John of St. Thomas, who writes:

> There is a twofold change in the body of Christ. One is primordial and substantial. On account of it, this substance depends on God a second time, in such a way that if the generative action of the Virgin (*sic*!) ceased, it would still have had being in virtue of this conserving action. Indeed, this change is the foundation of a new dependence in Christ's body in relation to God. It makes it to be, for a second time, the terminus of His action and refers it in a new way to the *terminus a quo*, the bread.[56]

(The other, secondary change, which nonetheless is indispensable according to these authors, consists in the suspension of the second function of quantity, which would be the extension of bodily parts in space.)

In modern times, Billot and La Taille showed in a decisive manner that transubstantiation by its very nature excludes all change in the *terminus ad quem*.[57] Moreover, this was undoubtedly St. Thomas's position. It was the common position of his era.[58]

---

56. See John of St. Thomas, *Cursus theologicus*, vol. 9, diss. 28, a. 3, no. 5.
57. Billot, *De Ecclesiae Sacramentis*, vol. 1, q. 76, §4, and de La Taille, *Mysterium fidei*, 635–36.
58. *In IV Sent.*, d. 11, q. 1, a. 3, ad 1, q.c. and ad 3 (ed. Moos, nos. 76 and 79). *ST* III, q. 76, a. 6.

A reason drawn from the requirements of the Eucharist

{885} The idea that Christ, in His glory, could in some manner "undergo" the conserving action exercised by the Church here-below is strange and seems to have been rejected from the start.

Moreover, it does not stand up to serious examination. The Eucharist is a sacrament, a sign. It is a sign of the "Lord," of the resurrected Christ (of Christ who suffered, who is dead, but who has been resurrected and glorified). It is contrary to the Eucharist's sacramental nature that Christ would be modified by the very fact that He is signified.

Moreover (and here, we basically present the same argument), if Christ had a unique [*propre*] being in the Eucharist, one that is distinct from that which He has in His glory, the Eucharist would be a *res*, something absolute. Instead, because it is a sacrament, it can exist only as wholly referring to the reality that it signifies.

In short, the sacramental nature of the Eucharist requires that Christ, who is contained in it but is also signified by it (signified as contained), would be Christ as He is in His glory.

A reason drawn from the very nature of transubstantiation

{886} In every situation, action is exercised on some given being, namely, the being situated at the *terminus a quo* which is changed. When the *terminus ad quem* arrives, the change is terminated. Therefore, of itself, this being situated at the *terminus ad quem* is not changed by the change's own action.

If there is indeed a change, this is because the being situated at the *terminus a quo* is not totally changed. Some aspect of it (e.g., the subject of the change) passes over to the being that is at the *terminus ad quem* of the change, which finds itself changed. Thus, when digestion has been performed, the living being is modified by the nourishment that it has taken.

What characterizes transubstantiation is the fact that it is a total change, leaving nothing unchanged in the being which is the point of departure, therefore not introducing any part of that thing into that which is the endpoint of the change. We have seen that, on account of this fact, we were forced to exclude the idea that this change would lead to the production of a new being. For the same reason, it is precluded that the preexisting being which is at the *terminus ad quem* of this change would be modified in even the slightest way.

Christ's sacramental mode of being in the Eucharist

{887} How then is one to explain the fact that Christ's there-being would be obtained by an action that would produce nothing new in Him even though He is newly there?

The conserving action finds its termination in the fact that the bread has become the body of Christ: "Both the change and the action are terminated in the fact that the bread is the body of Christ. Indeed, this is what comes about and is new, happening precisely through the action that converts the bread into Christ's body."[59]

Thus, Christ, the terminus of this change, remains perfectly "immobile." The bread is what is changed into Him and which, for this reason, proves to be wholly tendential toward Him and relative to Him. However, what is the subject of this relation? It is no longer the bread itself, which has now passed over into the terminus of this relation. It can be only what remains of the bread, the appearances, the "sacrament." As regards Christ, because He remains completely unchanged, the correlation that orders Him to the species can only be a rationate relation [*relatio rationis*].

This double relation (the rationate relation corresponding to a real relation) is what constitutes Christ's sacramental being: "Christ's existence in Himself and His existence under the sacrament are not identical, for when we say that He is under the sacrament, this means that there is a particular relation from Christ to the sacrament."[60] It is quite obvious that the being by which Christ is found in the Eucharist is not (as some post-Tridentine theologians strangely imagined) a new *actus essendi*, for it is defined by a relation from Christ (who actually exists) to the "sacrament" (i.e., to the "sacramental sign," or again, to the "species"). Moreover, we will see that St. Thomas on many occasions says that it is a question of a rationate relation.

---

59. See Cajetan, *In ST* III, q. 75, a. 4, no. 6.
60. *ST* III, q. 76, a. 6.

However, what is an *esse* that is not an *actus essendi*? It is the *esse quod significat veritatem propositionis*, the being according to which the proposition is true:[61] Christ is present where the "species" are.

Thus we find ourselves faced with this question: How is this proposition verified on the basis of the transubstantiation of the bread and the wine, such as it has been analyzed?

The "there-being" of Christ Assured by Transubstantiation

{888} Transubstantiation involves, on the one hand, the complete change of the "substance" of the bread and wine, and on the other hand, a new relation of Christ to the "sacrament" resulting from this change. What is the "sacrament"? Up to now, we have maintained the dogmatic form in its intentional indetermination: the *species*, that is, the "external form," the appearances of bread and wine. We have seen that this obvious indetermination of the term "species" projected an analogous indetermination onto the correlative term, "substance." In the dogmatic formula, this term only means: the reality of the thing under consideration, that which makes it to be this or that, that on account of which I name it.[62]

Christ's relation to the sacrament

Distinction between substance and accidents

{889} The fact that the bread and wine would be really and completely changed into Christ's body and blood, without the appearances of bread and wine being modified in any way, necessarily implies (under pain of contradiction) that in this "thing" that is bread

---

61. See *ST* I, q. 3, a. 4, ad 2, and in a host of other places. [Tr. note: Although I have refrained from many editorial remarks in these volumes by Fr. Nicolas, on this seemingly cryptic point, deploying the notion of *ens ut verum*, may be somewhat illuminated by my remarks in Matthew Minerd, "Beyond Non-Being: Thomistic Metaphysics on Second Intentions, *Ens morale*, and *Ens artificale*," *American Catholic Philosophical Quarterly* 91, no. 3 (2017): 353–79. In particular, as regards the relevance for Thomistic sacramental theology, see the final footnote. Also, related to this matter, the reader will likely benefit from the lucid historical and systematic presentation found in Emmanuel Doronzo, "On the Essence of the Sacrifice of the Mass," *Proceedings of the Catholic Theological Society of America* (1952): 53–82. In particular, see Doronzo's own statement of his position, beginning on 70. Moreover, see both of his volumes *De eucharistia* (Milwaukee, Wis.: Bruce, 1947).]

62. See §844 above.

(and in every other bodily thing) the intrinsic principle that makes a thing be what it is is really distinct from the principle (or principles) that make it have this or that appearance.

This real distinction is posited and demonstrated by Aristotelian cosmology in its assertion that the substance is what constitutes the thing in its reality whereas the accidents are what make it have an appearance. It can be established either inductively or deductively. We inductively prove it on the basis of the experiential fact that a thing can be modified in its external appearances without ceasing to remain the same. We can prove it deductively on the basis of the intellectual perception of the specific unity of a multitude of individuals that are distinct from each other. The principle of their ontological similarity cannot simultaneously be the principle of their dissimilarity. They are alike according to their substance, a realization of the same "second substance" or nature in the conditions proper to each one. What makes for their difference are the ontological determinations proper to each individual, determinations that come from the "forms" by which the common nature is realized in this or that particular manner. These forms are the accidents. The common nature is realized in the individual substance, which is determined and individualized by the accidents.

Of itself, the substance is neither "perceivable" (*sensibilis*), nor extended, nor divisible, nor positioned in space. However, the material substance, as a condition of its existence, requires that it be quantified and qualified. It is not individualized of itself (because, of itself, it can be realized in a host of individuals). Rather, it can exist only as individualized. In other words, it requires, as a condition of its existence, that it be quantitatively determined and situated.

The accidents are what determine the substance, making it quantified, extended, positioned, visible, tangible, etc.

However, be quite careful not to think that this means that the accidents are what are quantified, extended, sensible, and so forth. The substance is quantified, extended, sensible, and so forth, by means of the accidents. In themselves, they are only forms, unable to exist on their own. They make the substance exist in a given manner. However, they are not identical to the substance and remain really distinct from it in the concrete material being. This is proven by the fact that they can be replaced by other accidents. The thing can change in its quality, in its position, in its sensible qualification, all without changing in itself, without ceasing to be the same thing, and without the substance being changed. However, because a given substance requires as a condition of its existence not only accidents [in general] but also this or that kind of accident, it can happen that the change would be of such a character that the new accidents would no longer be compatible with this substance. In this case, a substantial change is produced: corruption and generation.

Thus, the accidents manifest the substance in the sense that they make the substance apparent and perceptible to the senses. This appearance, produced by the accidents, is what enables one to detect the nature of the given substance after a variety of experiences. However, it can happen that various substances would have similar appearances. In contrast to what was said above about the various individuals of one and the same nature, they would resemble each other with regard to their accidents, all the while being dissimilar with regard to their substance. However, the substance can never be perceived except by means of its accidents. Their dissimilarity will come to light by differences in their accidents.[63]

---

63. N.B. The question of knowing whether there is a substantial or only an accidental difference between two given bodies cannot be resolved by a simply philosophical investigation. This would require a very intimate (and very rare) agreement between the viewpoint and competence proper to philosophy and those proper to the sciences. The philosopher can only exclude *a priori* that several bodies, each seeming to be a distinct individual (to common observation), would in reality constitute a single individual substance on account of the perpetual exchanges of particles from one to the other that scientific observation detects. Conversely, a body that appears to be an individual being can, in fact, only be an agglomeration of bodies. This is precisely the case for bread and wine. The (bodily) beings that the Lord makes use of for manifesting Himself and for giving Himself are not "simple bodies" in the scientific sense of the word, nor distinct "substances" in the philosophical sense of the word. They are realities of our experience whose unity arises from man and is defined in relation to man. (See Karl Rahner, "Sur la durée de la presence du Christ dans celui qui vient de communier," *Ecrits théologiques* [Paris: Desclée de Brouwer, 1968], 9:127–37.) What we call "the substance of the bread" is an agglomeration of substances which, being artificially conjoined by kneading and cooking, constitute a perfectly definite reality on the level of everyday human experience, a reality which we call "bread." What we have said about transubstantiation enables us to understand the fact that all these substances (without us needing to be able to distinguish them with precision and enumerate them) can be changed together into the unique body of Christ. The same must be said about the appearances. It is not important whether they arise from the accidents of a single substance or together from all the accidents of all the substances that

The relation of accidents to substance

The accidents render the substance present {890} The accidents render the substance present to man's awareness, for they make it perceptible and experiential, something knowable for man. They render it locally present, for by them the substance is quantified and therefore placed in relation with other bodies.

The accidents are entirely ordered to the substance that they determine An accident is not a being. It is a form of a being, of the substance. It exists only in and by it: *accidentis esse est inesse* (the existence of an accident is its inherence in the substance). In other words, it can be defined only in relation to the substance in which and for which it exists. Conversely, it normally cannot exist outside of this substance. That is, it cannot exist without the substance existing and making it exist.

It is not contradictory to say that the accidents would be maintained in existence when their proper substance has ceased to exist Because transubstantiation makes the substance of the bread disappear, whereas its appearances remain unchanged, one must admit that the accidents of bread continue to exist as before, though without the bread's substance, which no longer exists. However, they do not inhere in another substance. On the one hand, this other substance could only be the substance of Christ's body, which remains unchanged, as we have seen (which excludes the possibility of it being determined by other accidents than its own). On the other hand, it is contradictory to say that the accidents of one substance would continue to be accidents of another substance, as they are defined in relation to the substance that they are made to determine. Therefore, one must admit that they are maintained in being by the Divine Omnipotence, without the ontological support of a substance.

Is this conceivable? St. Thomas argues that it can be conceived

---

enter into this artificial whole. What they manifest is not each substance in its distinction but, rather, the whole that they compose, which we can call "substantial," given that it is made up of the conjunction of many substances. To explain the identification of Christ's body and blood with the offerings, we can therefore speak of the bread as a substance and of its appearances as arising from the accidents that determine this substance.

by saying that the First Cause can, by itself and immediately, do everything that second causes do, though not without the sovereign motion of the first cause.[64] How should we understand this argument?

We should first understand it as applying to the order of efficient causality, as it is a question of the preservation of the accidents in being. In what sense can we understand that the substance is the efficient cause of its accidents? In the straightforward sense that just as the being of the accidents follows upon that of the substance, the divine causality which makes the substance exist and preserves it in being (this ongoing causality in virtue of which every being is a creature of God, even if it was produced by second causes) extends up to the accidents and makes them exist by making the substance exist. The accidents ontologically depend on God *mediante substantia* (by the substance's mediation).

However, this makes the difficulty clear. The substance makes the accidents exist by being the ontological substrate of the accidents (i.e., their "material" cause). Quite clearly, God cannot make up for this, for He is not the first cause in that order.

This difficulty is sufficiently great that one could say, as we did above, that such an argument only proves the non-possibility of this. It does prove this; because God is the one who gives being to accidents *mediante substantia*, it is not contradictory to say that they continue to receive being from God even when the substance has disappeared, for God is the ultimate and sufficient explanation of the gift of being. One could object, in the case of accidents, that the mediation of substance is a necessary condition. However, as one cannot prove that God Himself (as the first cause of being) is bound by this condition (or, rather, that it is a question of an "intrinsic" condition that cannot be replaced [*insuppléable*]), one cannot prove that this is impossible.

By requiring us to admit transubstantiation, faith consequently invites reason to admit the fact of the accidents' continuance without a subject. This is the miraculous part of the Eucharistic mystery, whose explanation we neither can nor need to push to its ultimate

---

64. See *ST* III, q. 77, a. 1.

precisions. Above all, we need not attempt explanations of the scientific order concerning this. By definition, they cannot succeed, for scientific procedures and methods can only attain that which has not changed in the bread and wine. Therefore, they cannot account for the change itself, as much for what concerns the change in the accidents' existential status as for what concerns the disappearance of the substance.

(For the philosophical explanation of the continuance of the accidents in being—and, consequently, in their activity—refer above all to St. Thomas in the *Tertia pars*.[65] For modern attempts at a scientific interpretation, one can refer to the controversy between Selvaggi and Colombo.[66])

The relation of accidents to Christ after transubstantiation

{891} "The substance of Christ's body follows on the substance of the bread."[67] There is the "reason" for Christ's being-there. The substance to which the accidents themselves are wholly referred, the substance which they manifest and situate, has become the body of Christ. The latter is substituted for it, by the same fact, as the terminus of this relation. Thus, they now manifest and situate the body of Christ.

They manifest it, obviously for him who is aware of the change that is brought about. Therefore, they manifest it for the believer. However, this does not mean that his faith is what situates it there. His faith makes him recognize that it is there. However, this there-being arises from the relations of the accidents to the body of Christ, which is real and independent of faith.

They situate it. They do not do so in the same manner that they did for the substance of the bread, which was itself quantified and

---

65. See *ST* III, q. 77.

66. See Carlo Colombo, "Teologia, filosofia e fisica nella dottrin della transustanziazione," *La Scuola Cattolica* 83 (1955): 89–124; "Ancore sulla dottrina della transustanziazione e la fisica moderna," *La Scuola Cattolica* 84 (1956): 263–88; "Bilancio provisorio di una discussione eucaristica," *La Scuola Cattolica* 88 (1960): 23–55. Filippo Selvaggi, "Il concetto di sostanza nel dogma eucaristico in relazione alla fisica moderna," *Gregorianum* 30 (1949): 7–45; "Realità fisica e sostanza sensibile nella dottrina eucaristica," *Gregorianum* 37 (1956): 16–33; "Ancora intorno ai concetti di sostanza sensibile e realtà fisica," *Gregorianum* 38 (1957): 503–14. Masi, "La dottrina sacramentale."

67. *ST* III, q. 76, a. 5.

therefore subject to spatial relations. Nonetheless, they situate it in a real manner, for where the accidents are, there too is the substance to which they are intrinsically referred and that they render manifest.

In fact, it is not just any indiscriminate relation whatsoever of the "species" to Christ that would render him present. For example, in the case of the annihilation of the substance of the bread, the species could still symbolize Christ in His sacrifice. They would manifest it as being distant, precisely as not being there, as calling it back to one's awareness. However, we are here concerned with the relation that is constitutive of the accidents, that on account of which they are the accidents of the individual substance of this bread, which was substantially changed into the substance of Christ's body. On account of this relation, the substance of the bread was designated as being enveloped in the appearances, as being that which appeared. Having become the substance of Christ's body, the latter is designated in its place, really being signified as being enveloped in the appearances, "under the species."

However, if, as we have seen, Christ remains wholly unchanged, we must recognize the fact that, on His side, the relation to the species is a rationate relation (*relatio rationis*). Does this not undermine the reality of His "there-being"? This rather obvious objection is related to the more-general problem of the real value (or nonvalue) that a rationate relation can have. A rationate relation whose correlative is also a rationate relation obviously cannot be the principle of a real qualification. If I say, "*Lion* is a species of the genus animal," I do not designate anything real in the animal himself. However, a rationate relation that corresponds to a real relation can be the principle of a real qualification. Thus, God is really the Creator, even though in God it is a rationate relation.

Likewise, He is really in the depths of each created being on account of creation, even though, once again, this "there-being" is a rationate relation in Him. Why? Because the opposed relation, passive creation, is quite real indeed, engaging the entire being of the creature. God is the real terminus of this relation, and this is what confers reality on the description that is brought to Him by the opposed relation, even though the latter is a rationate relation. To this, one must add that the fact of this relation's rationate character arises from God's transcendence. The utterly real relation of total dependence with regard to being of itself would call for a real correlative. Something analogous must be said for the Eucharistic presence. Because the relation of the accidents to the substance of Christ's body is utterly real (on account of transubstantiation, which really has changed the bread's substance into that of Christ's body), the correlation that corresponds to it in the substance of Christ's body really qualifies Him as "being-there" (even though it would be constructed by our reason on account of the glorified Christ's transcendence in relation to the transubstantiating action).[68]

Consequently, if the *species* were to disappear (and when they disappear) through a corruption of the accidents, Christ's there-being ceases for the same reason. St. Thomas proposes three arguments from "fittingness" to explain the fact that Christ thus gives Himself as food *sub specie aliena*.[69] They are traditional reasons. Curiously, he seems to forget this necessary reason on which he founded the theory of transubstantiation:[70] if the substance of the bread were not changed into the substance of Christ's body in such a manner that its accidents (and therefore its appearances) would remain, Christ could not "be there" in any manner. Indeed, if the accidents were also changed with the substance of the bread, the bread would quite simply disappear, and Christ would remain unchanged, He would no more be there any more than He was before. The accidents of the bread are what make Christ be there after transubstantiation.

The twofold manner by which Christ "is there" in the Eucharist

The double consecration

{892} It[71] is only by conceiving of Christ's "there-being" as something determined by the double relation of the species to Christ and of Christ to the species that one can resolve the problem (which is unresolvable without this) that is posed by the double consecration (of bread and wine) in the realist conception of transubstantiation

---

68. Refer to §§305–9 in the previous volume.
69. See *ST* III, q. 75, a. 5.
70. See §838 above.
71. See *ST* III, q. 76, a. 1.

(which we have seen is necessary). Indeed, to speak of the "substance of Christ's body" is obviously an improper manner of speaking from a philosophical point of view. A human person is not composed of many substances but, rather, is one substance. One can break this substance apart into many "intelligible notions." However, in its reality, it remains undivided. The "body" or "bodily dimension" is one of these "notions."

The "blood" can be another if by the word "body" one understands "flesh" inasmuch as it is contrasted with the blood, in a perspective that is already religious and sacrificial. Such rationate distinctions can affect reality only by means of relation. Indeed, just as the real relation refers the subject in its indivisible totality, though only according to one of its aspects (i.e., the foundation of the relation), so too it has the correlative subject in its totality as its terminus, though only from the perspective of how it corresponds to the foundation. The substance of the bread is changed into the complete human substance of Christ. However, the relation that results from this and which, for want of the bread's substance, has disappeared as such, has as its subject the accidents that remain and for its terminus this substance of Christ inasmuch as it is "flesh." Likewise, the relation that results from the transubstantiation of the wine into Christ's blood has for its terminus the substance of [Christ]* inasmuch as it is "blood." The formulas of consecration, which quite precisely bring about what they signify, testify to this: "This is my body (my flesh); this is my blood." Flesh and blood are parts of one and the same indivisible whole, namely, the Person of the glorified, Incarnate Word. Also, along with His flesh and blood, this same whole really is there. Christ is wholly and entirely contained under each species, with His body, blood, soul, and divinity.[72]

Thus, it is said that by the transubstantiation of the bread, Christ's flesh is present *vi sacramenti*, that is, in virtue of the efficacious signification of the appearances of the bread and of the sacramental words joined to them. The other parts of this whole that is Christ are present *vi realis concomitantiae*, that is, as constituting the indivisible whole of which the body is only one part. Likewise, the

---

* [Tr. note: Reading "substance du Christ" for "substance du vin".]
72. See Trent, session 13, "Decree on the Sacrament of the Eucharist," chs. 1 and 3.

transubstantiation of the wine makes His blood be there *vi sacramenti* and makes the whole Christ be there *vi realis concomitantiae*.

The sacramental separation of Christ's body and blood

We have seen the essential role played by this separation in assuring the sacrificial character of the Eucharist.[73]

To play this role, it is in no way necessary that this separation would be real (and this is quite obviously impossible).

However, no more can it be purely symbolic, for the Eucharist is not only a "sacrament of the sacrifice of the cross." Rather, it is "the sacrifice (of the cross)" sacramentally "reactualized."

According to the solution that I have proposed, in order for this to be so, the action performed by the Church (represented by her minister)—an action that, because of its symbolism, is clad with the sacrificial value of Christ's act of offering His life on Calvary—must attain the body and blood distinctly or, better yet, attain the blood as poured out apart from the body. This is sufficiently realized by the double consecration, which does not separate the blood from the body (even virtually), though it separately attains the body and blood as *termini* of the relations that it founds in the two *species*.

The properties of Christ's "there-being" in the Eucharist

Presence *per modum substantiae*

{893} A substance is not normally present in a place by itself. Rather, it is there by means of its accidents, which qualify and situate it.

By contrast, in the case of transubstantiation, what is directly rendered present is Christ's substance. Therefore, it is there by itself, in virtue of transubstantiation, not by means of its proper accidents.

Quite obviously, its proper accidents are there with it. However, this is so *vi realis concomitantiae*. Instead of the substance being there by the mediation of its accidents, they are what is there by the mediation of the substance.

Consequently, the "there-being" of the whole Christ (with His dimensions, His bodily qualities, etc.) is there "after the manner of substance," as a substance by itself would be there, if one could

---

73. See §862 above.

conceive that such a substance could be attached to a determinate place.

Indivisible presence

The first result of this is that even though the Christ who is there would in Himself be divisible and "frangible," He Himself cannot be divided by any action that is exercised on the host—*signi tantum fit fractura* (the sign alone is broken). He is whole and entire in each part (as the soul is present whole and entire in each part of the body) and whole and entire in each fragment that is separated off.

Non-extensive presence

Without having recourse to the implausible hypothesis of the double function of quantity, with its function of extending parts out in space being suspended here, we must say, with St. Thomas,[74] that all the dimensions of Christ are really there, though not *per modum quantitatis*. They are there simply as part of the subject which terminates the relation of presence. However, it is not on account of them that Christ is there.

Therefore, we must absolutely rule out imagining that the consecrated host and the wine would constitute a kind of small receptacle into which we would somehow need to lodge Christ along with all of His dimensions.

A nonlocal presence

As a body is localized by the mediation of its proper accidents, we likewise must say that Christ is not localized in the Eucharist.

However, He is connected to the place where the species are found, as they enable Him to be there. Therefore, He is really moved when the species are moved, but He does not, for all that, undergo a local change, just as He does not undergo any other changes. That on account of which He is there is what undergoes the local movement (like the breaking discussed above).

A case of "delocalization" by a lack of accidents connected to quantity is furnished for us by the (ontological) situation of the soul

---

74. See *ST* III, q. 76, a. 1, ad 3 and 4.

after death. When death destroys the body—and thus it is the person who dies, as we saw in our discussions concerning eschatology[75]—the soul survives (and the person himself survives, being reduced to his soul). However, it is obviously stripped of all bodily accidents of which it was the subject, with the body and on account of it. Thus, it becomes totally absent from our material universe, to which it was present before this, not by itself but by the body. This is different from the case of Christ in the Eucharist because Christ is truly there on account of His relation to the subsisting accidents of the bread and wine. The resemblance bears on the fact that He is not there on account of His proper quantitative accidents, so that He is there without being localized. What are localized are the accidents of the bread and wine, the "species," the "sacrament." Christ is there where the "species" are.

Likewise, in this way, we rule out the pseudo-problem of multi-location. It is contradictory to say that a body would be localized in many places, as though one were to say that it could have simultaneously many different quantities all having the same dimensioning. However, Christ is in no way localized by His relation to the localized *species*, in which His there-being consists.

An invisible presence

For the same reason, even though Christ's body, which is present, would be visible, it is present in an invisible manner—as a substance that, by itself, is invisible.

St. Thomas gives the reason for this. While His argument seems outdated, only the form really is.[76] What must be retained from his reasoning is the fact that, in a general manner, Christ's body is there without being able to act physically in any manner whatsoever, for the substance, which is the foundational principle of the dynamism of being, can act only by the mediation of its accidents which render it locally present, placing it in contact with other bodies, etc. Consequently, Christ's body, which is present as though it were a pure substance, cannot exercise visible (as well as tangible and "tasteable")

---

75. See §574 in the previous volume.
76. See *ST* III, q. 76, a. 7.

action on the sense organs, and this action is absolutely required for perception.

One must note that, in the presence of Eucharistic miracles that he encountered in the schools, St. Thomas still refused to admit that one could see the glorious body of Christ Himself in the host.[77]

It is important to note that the *species* do not conceal Christ like a curtain.[78] On the contrary, they manifest His presence (to the eyes of faith), though it is a presence that is invisible by its nature. (And this is why signs are necessary. One sees the sign, which refers to the invisible significate, though one that "is there," not a distant significate.)

A spiritual presence

All of this enables us to understand how the adjective "spiritual" is justified. It is connected by the tradition to the Eucharistic presence[79] and has happily been taken up in the formulas for the presentation of the gifts in the new Eucharistic liturgy *ex quo nobis fiat potus spiritualis*. What is there is a bodily being, Christ. However, He is there not in a nonbodily and, in this sense, spiritual manner.

Another meaning of this expression, which we will encounter later on, is that He is there in order to be spiritually united to the believer.

77. See ibid., a. 8.
78. See ibid., a. 7, ad 1.
79. See §835 above.

13

The Sacramental Action by Which Transubstantiation Is Brought About

{894} We have studied the "becoming" by which that which was bread is changed into Christ's body and that which was wine into His blood. (In reality, it is a pseudo-becoming, as it does not involve an enduring subject which passes from being bread to being Christ's body. The bread itself is what becomes Christ's body, and the wine itself is what becomes Christ's blood.) We must now consider this "becoming" from the perspective of the action which brings it about. Clearly, it is an action that can only be performed by God, for only the First Cause has this power over being inasmuch as it is being. Nonetheless, it is not an action that is creative, properly speaking, for it is exercised on a preexisting being. The body of Christ is not produced *ex nihilo*. (As we have seen, it fully exists independent of this action.) It is produced not so that it may exist but, rather, so that it may exist where the substance of the bread was, in its place, on the basis of the bread (and the wine). Therefore, it can use a human instrument, and this instrument is, above all, Christ Himself in His humanity, as we see in the narrative of the Last Supper where the Eucharist was instituted. However, it also is the Church, through her minister (i.e., the ordained priest): "Do this in memory of me." The Church renders this action of Christ visible, doing so by exercising a

The Sacramental Action of Transubstantiation 499

visible action through which Christ Himself acts. In short, she does so through a sacramental action, an efficacious sign which simultaneously designates and actualizes Christ's action. In what does this sacramental action consist?

As we will see, a grave disagreement exists on this point between the Roman Catholic Church and the Greek Orthodox Church[es], namely the problem concerning the epiclesis.*

THE PROBLEM

The Sacramental Form of the Eucharist

{895} Smit, following Schillebeeckx, holds that the systematization of sacramental hylomorphism led to a narrowing of Latin (scholastic) theology on this point: "Whereas scholastic theology sees the sacrament as being an action accompanied by words, the Fathers see them as being a *materia consecrata*, a matter filled with the Spirit, a thing charged with the mystical *dunamis* of the Logos."[1]

This criticism does not hold against a sound interpretation of sacramental hylomorphism like what we doubtlessly can find in St. Thomas.[2] We have shown that, in general, a sacrament is an action, not a thing (an action that uses consecrated things),[3] and this was true also for the Fathers (e.g., baptism is not water, even if it ordinarily includes the use of previously-consecrated water.) However, the Eucharist presents a unique case, given that the "matter" in this sacrament is "consecrated," not only so that it may be a sign and

---

* See the following: Louis Bouyer, *Dictionnaire théologique* (Paris: Desclée, 1963), 115–20, and *Eucharistie*, 137–314. Doronzo, *Tractatus dogmaticus de Eucharistia*, 108–71 and 631–36. Johannes Petrus de Jong, "Epiklese," *Lexikon für Theologie und Kirche* (ed. Höfer and Rahner), 3:935–37. Jüngmann, *Missarum solemnia*. John Meyendorff, "Note sur l'interprétation orthodoxe de l'eucharistie," *Concilium* 24 (1967): 53–60. Aimon-Marie Roguet (ed. and trans.), *Saint Thomas d'Aquin, L'eucharistie*, 1:384–422. Sévérien Salaville, "Épiclèse eucharistique," *Dictionnaire de théologie catholique*, 5:194–300, and "Introduction," in Nicolas Cabasilas, *Explication de la divine liturgie*, trans. Sévérien Salaville, SC 4 (Paris: Cerf, 1943). Maurice de la Taille, *Mysterium fidei*, 435–75. Thurian, *L'eucharistie*, 221. Trembelas, *Dogmatique de l'Église orthodoxe catholique*, 3:172–79. G. C. Smit, "Épiclèse et théologie des sacrements," *Mélanges de science religieuse* 15 (1958): 95–136. *Eucharistie d'Orient et d'Occident*, ed. Bernard Botte, vol. 2 (Paris: Cerf, 1970).

1. See Smit, "Épiclèse et théologie des sacrements," 106.
2. See §725 above.
3. See §726 above.

means of sanctification, but first of all so that it may be the sign of Christ present in it and acting by it (i.e., the sacrificial efficacy [of the Eucharist]).[4] Consequently, in what concerns the Eucharist, it is just as true for the scholastics (at least for the high scholastics) as for the Fathers to say that it is a *materia consecrata*. It is consecrated in such a way that it has lost its proper substance in order that it may be identified, under its unchanged appearances, with the holy One.

The "form" is not the Spirit who penetrates the matter (and this holds for the Greek Fathers as much as for the scholastics). The form is the ensemble of words by which the Church (acting through the ordained priest who presides over the Eucharist) signifies and (instrumentally) causes this consecration. To understand the hylomorphic interpretation (i.e., the matter-form interpretation) of the sacrament here, one must recall what was said above,[5] a point that quite exactly rejoins what Schillebeeckx and Smit present as though it were a novelty (whereas it is only a question of rediscovering St. Thomas's authentic conception of the matter):

> The substance of the sacrament, that which makes it to be a sacrament, must be sought out in the *signification*, in that by which it is a sign. It is not a sign limited to itself but, rather, a sign whose signification is concretized in an action and an expression. Or again, from another perspective, we will say that the words and ritual actions are the constitutive factors of the sacrament where they are a *signum* and, therefore, in the line of signification.[6]

If "form" and "matter" are united in order to constitute a sign (and not a merely physical being), one can understand how this union (which is intentional) endures for as long as the matter persists, even though the words, obviously enough, pass away. This matter, over which the words have been pronounced, has been consecrated by the words. We adore the host because we know that these words have been pronounced over it. In the limit case when nobody would be aware of it (and where, consequently, it would not be adored), it would remain, in itself, a sign, containing its significate,

---

4. See *ST* III, q. 73, a. 1, ad 3.
5. See §725 above.
6. Smit, "Epiclèse et théologie des sacrements," 133.

though it would be a sign whose signification would not be perceptible (as though the key for perceiving it were thus lost).

The Latin Position

{896} The* Latin position is characterized by the assertion that the words, which are recognized as being the form of the Eucharist, are the very words of [Christ's] institution. This does not involve the absurd assertion that the entire remaining portion of the "Eucharistic prayer" and, in particular, the epiclesis, is worthless and useless. Rather, it is precisely understood as meaning that the uttering of these words of institution by the priest is the necessary and sufficient sacramental cause (i.e., the causal sign) for bringing about the Eucharistic consecration.

Can it be said that there is no dogmatic definition engaging our faith on this point?[7] Nonetheless, we must admit that the Catholic faith requires us to admit the consecratory efficacy of the words of institution.[8] Reticence on this point could hold only for the case involving a refusal to recognize that the epiclesis has any value as part of the "form of the Eucharist." We will see that the problem was not truly posed at the level of the Magisterium until the fourteenth century. At the Council of Florence, after a discussion between the Greeks and Latins, an agreement was reached regarding the recognition of the consecratory value of the words of institution (an agreement that was not then ratified by the Greek Church, though [*Cantate Domino*] explains that no definition had been expressed at the time of the decree [for the Armenians] itself). However, at the same Council, taking up one of St. Thomas's texts, the decree for the Armenians states: "The form of this sacrament is the words of the Savior with which he effected this sacrament."[9]

The Council of Trent did not wish to involve itself in a controversy with the Eastern Churches. However, it did declare that Christ is present *immediately after the consecration* and *in virtue of the words*,

---

* [Tr. note: Regarding these matters in relation to the Byzantine East, see the translator's note at the beginning of this volume.]

7. See ibid., 123.
8. See ibid., 124.
9. See Council of Florence, *Exsultate Deo*, November 22, 1439, in D.-Sch., no. 1321.

which doubtlessly means the words of consecration.[10] To this fact, we must add the custom, dating from the Middle Ages, of adoring the offerings immediately after the consecration. Here, we see an application of the adage, *Lex orandi, lex credendi*. Finally, we find a certain number of official decrees by the Holy See affirming,[11] against the Greeks, that the words of institution have complete efficacy for bringing about transubstantiation, independent of the epiclesis.[12]

The Position of the Eastern Churches

{897} In the various Eastern liturgies (not only in the liturgies of St. Basil and of St. John Chrysostom, which go back to the fourth century, but also in the very ancient liturgies on which they depend), an "invocation" to the Holy Spirit (i.e., the epiclesis) is found after the institution narrative. In this invocation, the Spirit is asked to intervene so as to bring about the change of the bread into Christ's body and of the wine into His blood.[13]

The specific problem concerning the epiclesis was not really posed until the fourteenth century. Up to that time, there was no real assertion that a contradiction existed between this request for the Holy Spirit to intervene and the words of institution which present the identification of the offerings with Christ's body and blood as something already brought about. A striking proof for this fact is found in St. John Chrysostom, whom we find affirming the power of the epiclesis in a very strongly worded text:

What are you doing, Christian? What! At the moment when the priest stands before the altar, holding his hands toward heaven, calling on the Holy Spirit so that He may come and touch the offerings, when you see

---

10. See Council of Trent, session 13, "Decree on the Sacrament of the Eucharist," October 11, 1551, ch. 3, in D.-*Sch.*, no. 1640.

11. See the texts gathered in Smit, "Epiclèse et théologie des sacrements," 123, and Roguet, *Somme théologique: L'eucharistie*, 2:387–90.

12. One must admit that the Church's declarations leave no doubt as regards the impossibility of holding the schismatic theory concerning the epiclesis (i.e., the theory holding that the words of institution would receive their consecratory power from the epiclesis, in themselves being deprived of it), "for their insistence on the consecratory value of the words of institution is diametrically opposed to the devaluation of them by the East." See Smit, "Epiclèse et théologie des sacrements," 124.

13. See the texts in Bouyer, *Eucharistie*, ch. 5. Also, see the texts gathered in Hänggi and Pahl, *Prex eucharistica*.

The Sacramental Action of Transubstantiation 503

the immolated and consumed Lamb, this is when you excite trouble tumult, quarrels, and injuries.

However, we likewise find him writing about the efficacy of the Lord's words in no less forceful a manner:

> Man is not the one who makes the offerings become Christ's body and blood. Rather, this is done by Christ Himself, crucified for us. The priest is there, representing Him and pronouncing the words, but the power and grace are from God. "This is my body," he says. This expression transforms the offerings.[14]

St. John Damascene was the first to affirm that the Eucharistic conversion was brought about by the epiclesis, not by the words of institution. He did so with regard to the liturgy of St. Basil by (wrongly) interpreting the formula that is situated between the words of consecration and the epiclesis, which reads, "... This is why O Holy Lord ... we offer you the *antitype* of the holy body and blood of your Christ and pray ... that your Holy Spirit may descent on us and on these gifts here present ..." He interpreted this as meaning that there is a *prototypa* (i.e., not the figures and sacrament of Christ's body but rather that which will become Christ's body, its image before the consecration), thus saying that at this moment it is still bread and wine, which become Christ's body and blood only at the end of the epiclesis. (Concerning the decisive role played by John Damascene in these matters, see the work of Salaville[15] and Smit.[16] For a very profound and nuanced interpretation of St. Basil's liturgy, see Boris Bobrinskoy.[17]) Damascene's interpretation of the word "antitype" was approved by the Second Council of Nicaea in the context of its condemnation of iconoclasm. (The iconoclasts claimed that the only images that merit our veneration were the Eucharistic body and blood. In response, it was said that, no, the Church, in St. Basil's liturgy, venerates the bread and wine which have not yet become Christ's body and blood.) Salaville remarks:

---

14. See Salaville, "Epiclèse eucharistique," cols. 236–40.
15. Ibid., cols. 243–54.
16. See Smit, "Epiclèse et théologie des sacrements," 114–15.
17. [Tr. note: Fr. Nicolas cites "Bobrinskoy, 2." However, there is no such entry in his bibliography. The only entry for Bobrinskoy is: Bobrinskoy, "Liturgie et eccleésiologie trinitaire de S. Basile."]

"The explanation of the word 'antitype' coming from St. John Damascene, and the affirmation that the consecration occurs by the epiclesis more or less explicitly alongside it, very quickly became classic in Byzantine theology."[18]

However, polemics between Latin and Eastern Christians did not yet exist on this point, even though Latin theology oriented itself with increasing clarity toward affirming that consecration took place by means of the words of institution. Moreover, the problem did not arise for the Latin liturgy which either did not include an epiclesis, properly speaking (i.e., in the express form of an invocation of the Holy Spirit), or if it did consider the Roman Canon's prayer *Quam oblationem* as being an epiclesis in a broad sense, it was placed before the words of institution. For St. Thomas, the "form" of the sacrament of the Eucharist is constituted by the words of institution.[19] When controversies did exist among Latin theologians, they were concerned with knowing what words are strictly required. Scotus, for example, thought that the complete institution narrative is necessary for validity, in order to give the full context for Christ's very words, which would lack their true meaning without this context.

Up to the beginning of the fourteenth century, the problem concerning the epiclesis did not exist, either in the East or in the West. For example, at the time of the temporary schism under Photius and at the beginning of the definitive separation under Cerularius, no grievance was expressed by either side concerning this subject. The question is not inscribed on the agenda of the Council of Lyon in 1274. The problem seems to have arisen from the objections of Latin missionaries when they discovered in the East a doctrine granting consecratory value to the epiclesis. Nicolas Cabasilas responded to these objections,[20] as thereafter did his disciple and successor, Simeon of Thessalonica.* At this time, the doctrine that will very quickly become common in the Orthodox Church becomes fixed. It holds that Christ is the one who personally consecrates at the

---

18. See Sévérin Salaville, "Introduction" in Nicolas Cabasilas, *Explication de la divine liturgie*, col. 250.

19. See *ST* III, q. 78, a. 1.

20. See Cabasilas, *Explication de la divine liturgie*, ch. 29.

* [Tr. note: As did others once upon a time, Fr. Nicolas apparently believed (wrongly) that Nicolas Cabasilas was the archbishop of Thessalonica.]

priest's petition. The words of institution are an integral part of the account and are narrative in nature. Nonetheless, they are indispensable, for this account and the entire liturgical context "signifies the Church's intention to execute here and now the Lord's Eucharistic testament and her capacity to infallibly solicit and obtain consecrating grace and Christ's intervention. Following the Church's prescriptions and assisted by the Holy Spirit, the minister simply reunites the conditions intended so that Christ may consecrate it. Her minister does not go any further than this."[21]

The Problem of the Efficacy of the "Form" of the Sacrament

{898} This controversy cannot be understood without considering the divergence of orientations which came to exist between Latin and Greek theology regarding the "form" of the sacraments in general, especially in the case of the Eucharist. Latin theology developed in the direction of discussing the efficacy of the sacraments (even if this "efficacy" is explained in different ways by different schools). Hence, the production of the sacrament's effect is attributed to the form, which brings about the sacrament in its sign-being. (Obviously, it is thus attributed in conjunction with the matter, though the matter receives its sacramental being and efficacy from the form.) In the case of the Eucharist, a twofold efficacy exists. On the one hand, there is that of the consecrated matter, which produces union with Christ in the person who receives it. On the other hand, there are the "words" that consecrate the matter. This position is well aware of the fact that the words' efficacy can only be instrumental and is received from Christ, Himself being the principal instrument in His humanity, the efficacy ultimately coming from the Divine Omnipotence.

We must also add that the efficacy does not belong to the words as such, like a kind of magical efficacy. Rather, it belongs to him who pronounces them and who must be qualified to do this by a "sacramental power," as we will see later on when we discuss the sacrament

---

21. See Jean Gouillard's introduction to *l'Explication de la divine liturgie de Nicolas Cabasilas*, 2nd ed., trans. Séverin Salaville, ed. René Bornert, Jean Gouillard, and Pierre Périchon, SC 4 bis (Paris: Cerf, 1963). For the current position of Eastern thinkers, see Trembelas's account in *Dogmatique de l'Église orthodoxe catholique*.

of holy orders.[22] Nonetheless, it is true that, in this line of development, the question naturally arises concerning which words bring about this sacramental efficacy, and this leads one to ask what would happen when only these words would be pronounced by the priest, ultimately coming to judge that they would still be efficacious in this limit case.[23] For St. Thomas, it was a question of a methodological abstraction. In order to know what the cause of a "phenomenon" is, we strive to know what would happen if we were to eliminate all the other factors that, in fact, are present when it is produced. After St. Thomas, this "abstraction" hardened in a nearly intolerable manner, attention being given to the efficacy of the words being retained, while the rest of the celebration in relation to them nearly seemed to be superfluous or at least of secondary importance. For the Greeks, by contrast, this efficacy of the words is what passed to the second rank, whereas the action of God was emphasized, especially the Holy Spirit's activity in transubstantiation, with the Church's role consisting in praying in order to produce this activity and to establish the liturgical conditions assuring the efficacy of this prayer.[24]

Can these two points of view be reconciled?

ELEMENTS OF A SOLUTION

The Epicletic Character of the Eucharist and of the Sacraments in General

{899} "We recognize the epicletic character of the whole of the Eucharistic prayer."[25]

The Eucharist is "epicletic" in an inextricably twofold sense. First, it is so because, quite obviously, only the Divine Power can bring about this marvelous and ineffable transformation of the offerings into the body and blood of Christ, meaning that the Eucharist necessarily includes prayer and invocation (*epiclesis*) in order to request the divine intervention. (Indeed, this is affirmed in all liturgies

---

22. See §729 above and §976 below. Also, see Jean-Hervé Nicolas, *L'amour de Dieu et la peine des hommes* (Paris: Beauchesne, 1969), 552ff.
23. See *ST* III, q. 78, a. 1, ad 4, and Roguet, "L'eucharistie," no. 101 (1:331).
24. See Meyendorff, "Note sur l'interprétation orthodoxe de l'eucharistie," 53–60.
25. See Groupe de Dombes, "Accord doctrinal sur l'eucharistie," *Documentation catholique* 69 (1972): 334–37 (no. 16).

and in all theological explanations.) Second, it is epicletic because this transformation has a meaning, in Christ's intention and that of the Church, only as realizing Christ's work, of which the Eucharist is the memorial, uniting all men to God in Christ and with each other: "Such is the sacrifice of Christians: a great number who are one body in Christ."[26] Now, this is the work of God by Christ. Only God can (and, in fact, does) do it.

Gradually, following the development of pneumatology, this invocation to God (which at first had a Trinitarian form) became more precisely an invocation to the Holy Spirit. (This was so from the fourth century onward.) Indeed, the Church became more aware both of the Holy Spirit's distinct personality and of His role in sanctification. The Holy Spirit is the one who arouses the gifts of faith and charity by which this union is established. Therefore, He too is the one who brings about transubstantiation, which is wholly ordered to bringing about this union and to making believers into the body of Christ.

There are two epicleses in the Eucharistic celebration. First, there is the consecratory epiclesis, calling the divine action upon the offerings in order to "Eucharisticize" them. Second, there is the epiclesis of communion, calling the Holy Spirit down upon the faithful in order to realize in them the end for which the Eucharist was instituted. It is impossible and pointless to oppose them (or even to separate them) as if one could exist without the other.

The Power of Christ's Words

{900} "The heart of the Eucharistic action (and by that, of the entire Mass) is, in all known liturgies, the institution narrative, containing the consecratory words."[27] The only exception is the (Nestorian) liturgy of the apostles Addai and Mari, which does not contain the words of institution in certain manuscripts. However, it seems that either they were suppressed during the Nestorian era only to be then reestablished thereafter[28] or were suppressed for some other reason.[29]

---

26. See St. Augustine, *La Cité de Dieu*, OESA 10.6.
27. Jüngmann, *Missarum solemnia*, 1:111.
28. Ibid., 1:111n.
29. See Douglas Webb, "La liturgie nestorienne des apôtres Addai et Mari," in *Eucharistie d'Orient et d'Occident* (Paris: Cerf, 1970), 2:25–49.

The universal use of the words of institution is also attested to by the very accounts of the institution in the Synoptic Gospels and in St. Paul, which already are liturgical texts. In St. Justin Martyr's description of the Christian Eucharist, after speaking merely about the prayer of thanksgiving and praise by which the bread and wine are Eucharisticized, he justifies Christians' faith in the following manner: "In their memorials, the apostles tell us that Jesus gave them a commandment. He took the bread and giving thanks, He said, 'Do this in memory of me. This is my body.' Likewise, he took the chalice, and having given thanks, He said to them, 'This is my blood.' And He gave it to them alone."[30]

On the other hand, from her beginnings, the Church has held that the very command to repeat this action involves the repetition of Christ's words, and our faith [in the Eucharist] is founded on the "truth" of these words, which, as we have seen, imply transubstantiation.

With Bouyer, we can conclude:

Is (the consecration) brought about solely in virtue of the *verba Christi* or by the epiclesis? The only response conformed to the whole of the tradition and mindful of its origins is that the consecration is brought about in virtue of the words of Christ instituting the Eucharist, formally recalled by the Church at the heart of the invocation where she hands herself over in virtue of the mystery that she commemorates.[31]

The Comprehensive Character of the Anaphora and the Instantaneousness of Transubstantiation

{901} Undoubtedly, the problem was not posed for centuries. The anaphora was considered as a whole, and one was content to note that the Eucharistic prayer produced the marvelous change so that the bread that was distributed to the faithful at the end of this prayer was no longer ordinary bread but, rather, was the body of Christ. The ancient account provided by St. Justin expresses this all-encompassing nature of the Eucharistic and Eucharisticizing prayer.

It is quite true that, considered existentially, the Eucharist is this

---

30. Justin Martyr, *La philosophe passe au Christ*, apol. 1, ch. 65.
31. Bouyer, *Dictionnaire théologique*, 120.

all-encompassing prayer. It is also true that an authentic theology of the Eucharist must be completed by this existential consideration, for it is a question of understanding the Eucharist as it exists in the Church, in the life of the believer, and is also a question of knowing it better so that, in the end, one may live the mystery more profoundly. However, this investigation into the *intellectus fidei* can only be brought about through the most refined analysis possible, leading to quite precise concepts and to rigorous chains of reasoning. Such analyses must not be arbitrarily interrupted on the pretext that they lead to abstractions, for it is by means of abstract concepts that our reason attains concrete reality in its existentiality.

Such an analysis has led us to conceive of the real Eucharistic presence as being the terminus of a radical ontological change of the bread and wine, namely, transubstantiation. By its very nature, such a change must be instantaneous, for progressive change would presuppose a subject that changes, and there is no such subject in this change. If it is instantaneous, there is a precise instant in the course of the anaphora when it is accomplished. Whether or not this instant can be determined is a different question.

The Instant of Transubstantiation

{902} Theological analysis can determine this instant. All of our faith in the real presence rests on the truth of Christ's words applied to these determinate offerings, which in the course of the liturgy are changed into Christ's body and blood. If transubstantiation were brought about only at the end of the epiclesis, itself placed after the words of institution repeated by priests *in persona Christi*, these words would be false.

It could be said that these words are pronounced in the form of a narrative (as [Nicholas] Cabasilas said and as the theologians Ambrosius Catharinus [*Catharin*], OP, and Christophe de Cheffontaines, OFM, will say in the sixteenth century in the spirit of reconciliation). However, this ultimately places us on a path that would lead us outside of the sacramental order. The sacrament is a visible action that signifies and assures the invisible action of the Holy Spirit. Besides the fact that the consecratory epiclesis is not found in Scripture, nor in the Roman Canon (whose great antiquity has been shown by Bouyer[32]) can give faith in the intervention of the Holy Spirit, but it does not signify it nor realize it. The idea that the words once pronounced by the Lord have an efficacy extending to all Eucharists when they are pronounced by the priest is very ancient and is testified to in a thousand ways both in the Latin tradition (e.g., St. Ambrose) and in the Greek tradition (e.g., St. John Chrysostom). This is what founds the Church's faith in the sacramental value of the words of institution pronounced in the name of Christ. These words make what they signify to be true. That is, they make it be the case that what the priest designates in pronouncing them are (or become) Christ's body.

THE WAY TOWARD A RECONCILIATION

The Requirements of Catholic Doctrine

{903} It does not seem that we can deny that the Church teaches as something to be held *de fide* that the words of institution produce transubstantiation when they are pronounced by an ordained priest.

Does this mean that they would produce it outside of every liturgical context whatsoever (e.g., as words pronounced simply over bread and wine) or even in an anti-liturgical context (e.g., expressly and manifestly sacrilegious Masses, such as "black Masses")? This is at least doubtful. In any case, one could not bring forth any Magisterial document in favor of this extreme thesis. Theologically speaking, it is certain that in order for a priest to exercise an authentic (and, therefore, valid) sacramental action, he must at the very least have an intention to do what the Church does. Now, there is no doubt that the liturgical context (i.e., essentially speaking, the anaphora) expresses this intention of the Church. To omit it in whole or in part through simple negligence, though in a semiotic context that would remain liturgical, would not put this authenticity (and therefore the validity of the celebration) into question. However, were one to completely omit liturigical contextualizaiton, would not that person thus expressly repudiate the intention of doing what the Church does?

Conversely, if the entire context were preserved (i.e., the anaphora

---

32. See Bouyer, *Eucharistie*, 212–34.

with the anamnesis and the epiclesis) but the words of institution were omitted, this would mean, according to the Catholic faith, that the sacramental action has not been performed and, hence, that the offering has not been consecrated. Moreover, let us note that, even according to Orthodox belief, there would not be a consecration if the epiclesis were pronounced without the words of institution being pronounced. The opposition between the two perspectives comes down to the following. For the Catholic Church, transubstantiation is realized as soon as the words of institution are pronounced, whether or not there was an epiclesis beforehand, thus meaning that however injurious the omission of the epiclesis would be for the Eucharistic prayer, this would not prevent transubstantiation from occurring. For the Orthodox Church, consecration is produced by the words of institution and the epiclesis conjointly, so that the offerings are transubstantiated only at the end of the epiclesis.

How Can the Two Doctrines Be Reconciled?

Various solutions have been proposed. An enumeration of them can be found in Smit.[33] Following Max Thurian's proposals,[34] can we return to the non-determination of the issue, as was the case in the first centuries of the Church's history, thus forgoing the attempt to fix the moment of transubstantiation? We explained above why it is impossible to return to the past state of affairs in this way.[35]

Following Schillebeeckx (as his theory is presented by Smit), will we say that the words of institution and the epiclesis constitute two "nuclei," two essential "moments" of the anaphora, the first bringing about the Eucharistic sacrifice and the second giving them their sacrificial value so that the Eucharist may produce its fruits in the faithful? However, besides the fact that this solution would not be accepted by Eastern Christians, who hold that the epiclesis has consecratory efficacy, moreover it does not seem to be acceptable in Catholic theology. Indeed, Christ present in and through the Eucharist is the one who has the power of sanctifying whosoever is united

---

33. See Smit, "Epiclèse et théologie des sacrements," 126–27.
34. See Thurian, *L'eucharistie*, 274–75.
35. See §901.

to the sacrifice and receives it sacramentally. It is hardly intelligible to say that a new effusion of the Holy Spirit would need to exist for this to occur. (Or, in other words, Christ is He who is present in the Eucharist which sanctifies those who eat His body and drink His blood in faith, by the Spirit whom He sends to them.) Certainly, nobody can deny the existence of a communion epiclesis. However, its end is not to bring the Eucharist to completion in itself, as though there were need of such a complement. Rather, its end is to obtain for the faithful the grace of being open to this sanctifying action.

Will it be said (as many do say) that in virtue of the Church's power over the sacraments, *their substance being preserved*, the Latin Church has attributed consecratory value to the words of institution, whereas the Greek Church reserved it to the epiclesis? (This is a solution rejected equally by Smit and by Roguet.)[36] This is hardly acceptable, for the Catholic Church attributes consecratory efficacy to the words of institution because they are the words of the Lord, which rules out the idea that she could modify the visible sacramental action which she has been commanded to repeat.

Therefore, the following solution is necessary. The meaning of the epiclesis (and also the meaning of the whole anaphora) is to emphasize not only that God alone brings about transubstantiation but also that He brings it about only for our sanctification, which is the work of the Holy Spirit. It is necessary that this meaning be made clear in an express prayer. However, this prayer finds its first realization by means of the very words of institution pronounced in Christ's name. The second realization is the Eucharistic communion by means of which the Holy Spirit makes the faithful into a single body in Christ. The chronological succession of the prayers is not important, for if the sacramental action must be instantaneous from the perspective of efficacy, it is natural that it be extended in such succession. Perhaps the foundation of the difficulty comes from the antinomy between the instantaneousness of the efficacy and the progressive character of its signification.

---

36. See Roguet, "L'eucharistie," 1:413.

14

Christ's Eucharistic Presence
Christ Present to the Church

{904} We have said that Christ's "there-being" by means of the identification of the body and blood with the offerings only has a meaning as an ontological support for the presence which, itself, consists in a host of interpersonal relations between Christ and believers. The Eucharist is an efficacious sign of these relations. However, in order to provide an acceptable interpretation concerning the real identification brought about between the offerings and Christ, we found it necessary to undertake lengthy, difficult explanations that, on the whole, are unsatisfying to the degree that the mystery ultimately evades our attempts to grasp it by means of our concepts and arguments. Indeed, these explanations must be considered as only being preparatory for the true "understanding of the mystery" that is here sought out by theology.

We have said that they are "interpersonal relations existing between Christ and believers." However, faith is communal. Obviously, we do not mean that it could not be considered as being a personal act, engaging the person who performs it. Instead, we mean that Christ, in whom a given person believes, is only found in the community and that the truths revealed by Him were revealed to the community. It is only in this community that they remain people who live [by faith]. By believing (and to the measure of one's faith), one becomes a member of the community of the redeemed, the Church. Through the Eucharist, Christ is made present to the community as Him in whom she believes. She believes His teachings and promises, and He is the "pioneer and perfecter of our faith."[1] In the community, He is made present to each of His members.[2]

THE EUCHARIST AS A SACRAMENT

{905} Eucharistic realism must not make us lose sight of the sacramental character of the Eucharist, as though Christ were there and acted directly, without the mediation of the sign.[3] Through undue reliance on the ultra-realist expressions of certain Fathers (e.g., St. Cyril of Jerusalem and St. John Chrysostom), writers sometimes speak of a kind of contact between Christ's flesh and the communicant's flesh.[4] However, we have seen that the most ancient tradition does not separate realism and symbolism in the Eucharist. Eucharistic realism does not make the Eucharist pass outside the domain of signs. (Indeed, were that the case, it would pass out of the sacramental order.) Rather, it consists in saying that the distance between the sign and the significate is abolished and that the significate is given in the sign not only in an intentional manner but, in fact, in a real manner. And this is so without it ceasing, for all that, to be "signified." In other words, it is reached only in and through the sign.[5]

The Three "Structures" of the Sacrament of the Eucharist

Like every sacrament, the Eucharist includes three moments or instants inasmuch as it includes an "order" of a sign to a significate.[6]

---

1. Heb 12:2 (RSV).

2. [Tr. note: It is not quite clear which text Fr. Nicolas is referring to here in his bibliography. He cites "Coll., 54, vol. 3," which is: Commission international anglicane-catholique romaine, "Déclaration sur la doctrine eucharistique," September 7, 1971, in *Documentation catholique* 69 (1972): 86–88.]

3. See Aimon-Marie Roguet, "Le à-peu-près de la prédication eucharistique," *La Maison-Dieu* 11:178–90.

4. See Benoît, "Les récits de l'institution de l'eucharistie et leur portée," 1:231–32.

5. See §834. Johannes Petrus de Jong, *L'eucharistie comme réalité symbolique*, trans. Antoine Freund (Paris: Cerf, 1972), and Didier, *Histoire de la presence réelle*.

6. See §834. De Jong, *L'eucharistie comme réalité symbolique*. Didier, *Histoire de la presence réelle*.

The first is the *sacramentum tantum*, which is the immediately perceptible sign. The second is the *res et sacramentum*, which is the first reality signified by the sign, the stable reality on which the objective consistency of the sacramental order rests,[7] itself a sign of the ultimate reality for which the sacrament was instituted and which gives it its meaning. This last and ultimate reality is the *res tantum*.

The sacramental sign in the Eucharist

Obviously, the sacramental sign is the enduring appearance of bread and wine.

The sacrament and the use of the Eucharist

{906} We have seen that, in general, sacraments are not things but, rather, actions. This claim seems to be disproven by the case of the Eucharist. St. Thomas notes this characteristic of the Eucharist among the sacraments: "The sacrament of the Eucharist is realized in the consecration of the matter. The other sacraments are realized by the application of matter to men so as to sanctify them."[8] Here, we find ourselves again faced with Calvin's fundamental opposition to the Catholic conception of the Eucharist. For him, this sacrament, like all others, consists essentially in the application of the matter to man's sanctification, that is, in Eucharistic reception [*manducation*]. This is the basis for his violent rejection of transubstantiation and his radical condemnation of the celebration of the Eucharist without those attending communing in the sacrament. (We find a contemporary echo of this condemnation in Thurian.)[9] To do justice to what is true and just in Calvin's conception here, must we accept his condemnation of the Catholic conception of the Eucharist?

If we look for this Catholic conception in St. Thomas, we see that the sacrament of the Eucharist is ordered *ad spiritualem refectionem*[10] (to man's spiritual renewal). The difference between the Eucharist and the other sacraments does not consist in the fact that the consecration of the matter would have its own self-contained worth,

---

7. See §730 above.
8. See *ST* III, q. 73, a. 1, ad 3.
9. See Thurian, *L'eucharistie*, 218 and 228.
10. See *ST* III, q. 73, a. 2.

as though it were a question of possessing and carefully conserving a sacred reality. (Some deviations in Eucharistic piety have gone in this direction.) Rather, it consists in the fact that even though, like all the other sacraments, the Eucharist is ordered to man's sanctification and therefore includes both an activity by Christ and by the Church as well as one by the beneficiary (i.e., an "application of the consecrated matter to man's sanctification"), it nonetheless is already constituted as a sacrament prior to this action. We have already explained the reason for this.[11] The action of giving and that of consuming a food can be "sacred" and "sacramentalized" only if this food is first made sacred and sacramentalized. However, it is clear that food calls for eating [*manducation*]. By nature, it is not something that one preserves, except in view of later consumption. By becoming food, Christ signifies that He wishes to be "eaten." Indeed, He says so expressly.

Thus, in the Eucharist, the sacrament-thing is only the preparatory phase for Christ's act (through the Church) of giving Himself as food and for the believer's act of sacramental reception [*manducation*]. In this way, the Eucharist already fits back into the common conditions of the sacraments. It also is principally an action.

It reenters these conditions in another way which is proper to the Eucharist. The consecrated species which are the sacrament-thing, in reality, are first the result of a sacramental action, the action of consecrating. We have seen how this action was sacrificial precisely thanks to its result, the symbolic and also real separation of the body and blood by which it rejoins Christ's sacrificial action on Calvary by being symbolically identified with it.

Therefore, the sacrament-thing is situated between two sacramental actions. It is the result of one of these sacramental actions which is sacrificial and is the sacrifice of Calvary offered by the Church with Christ. It is the matter and object of the other sacramental action, namely, the action of sacramentally eating His body and drinking His blood, an action corresponding to Christ's action of self-gift as food. The *sacramentum tantum* of the Eucharist is all of this together.

---

11. See §868 above.

The unity of the sacrament of the Eucharist

{907} Is[12] it not the case that all these sacred elements introduce a kind of multiplicity into the sacrament of the Eucharist?

First of all, there is the duality of the consecrated species, each of which assures a distinct "there-being" by Christ, as we have seen.[13] If we were forced to stop at the sacrament-thing, it is not clear how we could avoid saying that there are two sacraments. However, this duality is surmounted if we refer to the two actions in which the sacrament-thing is engaged. The two consecratory actions constitute a single sacrificial action. The two sacramental foods bring together in themselves one, a single *refectio* made up of eating and drinking.

However, the very duality of these actions remains. To understand how they can be reunified, one must appeal to this fundamental and traditional datum concerning the Eucharistic mystery: "The cup of blessing which we bless, is it not a participation in the blood of Christ? The bread which we break, is it not a participation in the body of Christ?"[14] The reception [*manducation*] of the Eucharist is the believer's sacramental participation in the sacramental sacrifice. Therefore, it is not a question of two completely separate actions but, rather, of two organically connected actions, with the second of these actions being the consummation of the first, its fulfillment.

Granting all of this, must we accept the condemnation of Eucharistic celebrations that do not include communion by those who assist in the sacrifice? To admit that the Eucharist includes the first action, which is sacrificial, is an admission that it has a saving value even for those who do not participate in the second action, including those who are absent. (Indeed, this includes even the dead, according to a very ancient line of tradition, which we have seen can be found already in Tertullian[15] and in even more ancient witnesses.[16]) However, we cannot conceive of a Eucharistic celebration without

---

12. See *ST* III, q. 73, aa. 2 and 4, and q. 80, a. 12.
13. See §892 above.
14. 1 Cor 10:16 (RSV). [Tr. note: Fr. Nicolas wrongly cites 1 Cor 11:16.]
15. See Tertullian, *De Corona*, CSEL 2, col. 1043, and *De exhortatione castitatis*, CSEL 2, col. 1031.
16. See Jüngmann, *Missarum solemnia*, 1:268, and Quasten, *Initiation aux Pères de l'Église*, 1:156.

at least the priest communicating.[17] This shows that the sacrificial action, of itself, must be brought to completion through sacramental reception [*manducation*]. However, the sacramental action is an act of the community, in which the latter is represented by the priest (or priests) who celebrate [the sacrament]. Moreover, this necessary fulfillment of the sacramental action by sacramental reception [*manducation*] is sufficiently assured even if the priest alone communicates. Therefore, *a fortiori*, it is fulfilled if a given number of the faithful present communicate with him. (The specific difficulty raised by this conception of the priest's role will be studied in relation to the sacrament of holy orders.)

However, should not sacramental reception [*manducation*] be performed under the two species, lest the *refectio sacramentalis* would be truncated? *From the perspective of "the sacrament,"* that is, from the perspective of the sacred signification, it is no doubt the case that communion under both species is preferable, without this being necessary, however, given that each species, *vi realis concomitantiae*, also signifies the content of the other. *From the perspective of efficacy*, the believer loses nothing by communicating under one species alone. Thus, sufficiently important reasons, drawn from the reverence owed to the sacrament and other practical considerations, can justify communion solely under the species of bread. However, this is so on the condition that the priest himself communicates under the two species so that the connection between the two sacramental actions may be safeguarded, as was said above, for the double consecration indeed is completely necessary in order for there to be a sacrifice.[18]

The "invisible sacrament" in the Eucharist

{908} The "invisible sacrament" (i.e., the *res et sacramentum*) of the Eucharist is Christ inasmuch as He is identical with the offerings and designated by the species as being there. This is what is designated by the expressions *panis vitae, potus spiritualis*.

It remains for as long as the accidents of the bread remain (i.e., as long as what we have before us on the level of appearances is still

---

17. See *ST* III, q. 82, a. 4.
18. See *ST* III, q. 80, a. 12.

bread and wine). Here, we are faced with an aspect of the Eucharistic mystery which the Church cannot renounce. It is connected to the earliest attestation to tradition, for already in Tertullian and Origen one can find very precise prescriptions and insistent recommendations concerning the honor that must surround the Eucharistic bread that the faithful have received. Moreover, it is also connected to the very nature of the sacrament. For as long as the species that have been Eucharisticized by the sacramental words last, they signify Christ's presence there, doing so on the basis of Christ's promise as well as the meaning of His words. This signification cannot be put into doubt without the sacrament immediately losing its value as a sign (in other words, without it losing its entire value).

If we were to say that we do not adore food, such an expression would not only be sacrilegious but, moreover, would be something irrational, in this case, for a believer. Indeed, it is not a question of any food whatsoever, that is, of "ordinary bread." No, it is a question of a sacred food, and if this was not a sacred food, there would no longer be a sacred eating [*manducation*], which such people say they believe in.

It is here that we find ourselves faced with the question concerning the respect that one must show for the particles that remain. Karl Rahner[19] greatly insists on the fact that bread is a human reality and that one therefore cannot decide on the basis of chemical analyses whether or not a particle that remains is bread. Rather, one must rely on the judgment of common sense: "This indeed is what I customarily eat, calling it 'bread.'"[20] He also relies on a judgment by St. Thomas who thinks that a drop of wine mixed with a great quantity of water ceases to be wine and also that when the particle of bread or the drop of wine is reduced to a very small quantity it ceases to have the dimension that is a required condition for the existence of the substance of bread or of wine and thus ceases to signify and realize Christ's "there-being."[21]

This can be admitted, though not without some reservations. In

---

19. See Karl Rahner, *L'eucharistie et les hommes d'aujourd'hui*, trans. Charles Muller (Paris: Mame, 1966), and "Sur la durée de la présence du Christ dans celui qui vient de communier," in *Ecrits théologiques* (Paris: Desclée de Brouwer, 1968), 9:127–37.
20. Rahner, *L'eucharistie et les hommes d'aujourd'hui*, 314.
21. See *ST* III, q. 77, a. 8.

reality, no matter who calls the little fragments of bread that remain on the table after a meal "crumbs of bread" and the droplets of wine that still cling to the sides of a glass a "drop of wine," this does not imply that one takes or gives this as being food. With regard to St. Thomas's judgment in this matter (which refers to a very different, though outdated, conception of the unity and reality of bread), it leaves open the question of knowing the point at which the particle becomes too small to still be bread.

We throw away the crumbs of bread that remain on our tables because they are bits of ordinary food. However, if one believes that the Eucharistic bread is a sacred food (indeed, the very body of Christ), one would thus treat the crumbs of this food with veneration, making sure that they would not be thrown away like a scrap item but, rather, taking care that they be gotten rid of in the manner foreseen by the very institution of the sacrament: by consuming them.

Allow two points to be noted here. It is quite true that in the Eucharist Christ cannot "suffer" any injury whatsoever, for the latter can only affect the species. However, to treat them with disrespect (either by commission or omission) is to commit an act of disrespect for Christ and to intentionally offend Him. If it is not a question of disrespect but, rather, of an involuntary accident, there is no offense subjectively speaking and therefore no longer one objectively, as Christ would in no way undergo any affront. Whence, Rahner does indeed make just observations concerning excessive and paralyzing scruples that make one place all of one's attention on Christ's "there-being" at the expense of spiritual union with Him (for which this there-being is the sign and means). However, once again, to believe in the reality of Christ's there-being requires immense respect in one's handling of the sacred species, even in relation to the particles that remain after the celebration of the liturgy.[22]

A second note. Here too, the theological problem concerning the adoration of the blessed sacrament equally arises.[23] As soon as one believes in the reality of Christ's "there-being" in the Eucharist,

---

22. See St. Cyril of Jerusalem, *Catéchèses mystagogiques*, SC 126, cat. 8, nos. 21–22.
23. See Jean-Marie-Roger Tillard, "Compte-rendu du livre d'Antonius Van Bruggen Réflexions sur l'adoration eucharistique," *La Maison-Dieu* 100 (1969): 196–98, and Antonius van

this practice is legitimate. (Indeed, we can say that, in principle, this practice is very ancient, for example as witnessed in the texts of St. Cyril of Jerusalem cited above.) The considerable developments that it underwent in the Latin Church from the Middle Ages onward should not be condemned in themselves, and it is impossible to overlook and underestimate the very strong current of Eucharistic piety that has formed around and in connection with the adoration of the host. However, we also can admit that there have been deviations and errors in sacramental conduct, leading the adoration of the host to be placed in the foreground and relegating the [liturgical] Eucharistic celebration itself into the background. The principle of rectification is found in a just estimation of the place of the sacrament-thing between the two actions that not only make it exist but also give it meaning. The adoration of the blessed sacrament is in some manner situated between these two actions. It is justified only as an extension of the People of God's attitude leading them to welcome the gift of the kingdom at the synaxis in the bread and the cup.[24] This naturally leads one to reduce the "bulk" of ceremonies related to adoration so that they may not crush the celebration of the Eucharist on account of their great quantity (and, consequently, through the meaning that is *perceived* on account of that great quantity). The celebration of the Eucharist must occupy, even externally and visibly, the principal place. However, this must not lead one to suppress them completely, nor above all, to scorn and condemn this religious practice in the communities in which it still holds a notable place (as in many religious congregations, even contemporary ones).

What is ultimately signified in the Eucharist

{909} Like every sacrament, the Eucharist signifies and actualizes Christ the Savior in the act of saving not only men in general but also these given men situated in time and space, here celebrating the sacrament. This includes a threefold, ordered signification:[25] the sacra-

---

Bruggen, *Réflexions sur l'adoration eucharistique* (Rome: Pontificia Universitas Gregoriana, 1968).

24. See Tillard, "Compte-rendu du livre d'Antonius Van Bruggen Réflexions sur l'adoration eucharistique," 198.

25. See §624 above.

ment signifies Christ's passion in the past, the current participation of the beneficiary by means of the sacrament in this matter [*à cette question*] and in its fruits, and the future triumph that will be brought about by Christ's return.

What is here specific to the Eucharist is that it does not only signify the saving sacrifice in the past, as the source of salvation currently offered to the beneficiary, but also reactualizes it itself in its value and its propitiatory, laudatory, and intercessory efficacy. Consequently, in the present, what it signifies and realizes is not only (nor primarily) the beneficiary's individual salvation, but also that of the Church, which has the sacrifice of Calvary (with its conclusion, the resurrection) as her principle of generation and growth, bearing in mind that the Church exists, grows, and is glorified through the purification, divinization, and glorification of the persons who become her members and grow in her in virtue of this sacrifice.

The Eucharist finds its ultimate meaning in its assurance of the permanent actuality and permanent efficacy of the redemptive sacrifice in the world through the Church.

The Eucharist and Faith

If[26] every sacrament is strictly related to faith, concretizing its progress, this fact is verified in a unique way in the case of the Eucharist.

Christ's presence to the believer by the Eucharist

{910} After having emphatically noted that Christ's "there-being" in the Eucharist in no way depends on the faith of those assisting [at Mass]—even if nobody recognizes or knows that He is there, He still is there in the consecrated host—we must note no less emphatically that this "there-being" becomes a [truly experienced] presence only for the person who believes. This obviously follows from the notion of presence that we discussed above.[27] The Eucharistic bread is the means of interpersonal communication between the redeemed person and Christ, a communication having faith as a fundamental component. It also is a communication that Christ's

---

26. See Bouyer, *Eucharistie*, ch. 3, and Karl Rahner, "Parole et Eucharistie," *Ecrits théologiques* (Paris: Desclée de Brouwer, 1968), 9:51–91.

27. See §§869–71.

"there-being" does not establish by itself but that, thanks to this presence, culminates in Christ really present, offered, and given.

This communication begins as soon as Christ, in the Eucharist, is offered to the believer's contemplation. It finds its culmination in sacramental reception [*manducation*], which must itself be spiritual if it is to reach its saving end.[28]

If every sacrament, inasmuch as it is an activity exercised by the beneficiary, is an act of faith concretized in a bodily act, this sacrament expresses the faith of the person who receives it—not only his belief in Christ's "there-being" in the offerings but also in the whole of His redemptive work, which is signified by the offerings, indeed, in His promise of salvation in relation to the beneficiary in particular and not only in relation to the entire world. Generally speaking, it is a question of faith concerning salvation as God willed and realized it by sending His son, by the Church that He instituted, and by the eschatological events that have been announced.

Christ present to the Church by the Eucharist

{911} This faith is the Church's faith, announced by her and lived in her. Well beyond the personal ideas of the believer, the Eucharist expresses the Church's faith, which the communicant openly professes by participating in the Eucharist. This participation is an ecclesial act in which each is invited to participate, obviously in a personal manner (indeed, it is an eminently personal act) though within the Church's communion, in and with the community, even when the community is reduced to a very small number, or even solely to the person of the communicant. In reality, as was said above,[29] the smallest* of communities itself renders the universal Church present.

The Eucharist and the Word [*Parole*]

{912} Calvin violently rose up against Eucharistic celebrations that would take place without the proclamation of the Word of God in

---

28. See *ST* III, q. 80, aa. 1–2.
29. See §865 above.
* [Tr. note: Reading *moins* for *plus* based on context.]

the Catholic Church.³⁰ He himself did not come to discern the proper role of the Eucharist in relation to the Word.³¹ Indeed, the current efforts at liturgical renewal in the Catholic Church have led to a revalorization of the role of the proclamation of the Word of God in the course of the celebration, as an integral part, in the form of readings of Scripture and preaching.

This is necessary, for in its very essence, the Eucharistic celebration is man's response to the Word of God, received by and in the Church.

Obviously, we would go too far were we to completely condemn every kind of Eucharistic celebration that would not include a Liturgy of the Word or at least a public proclamation (including, as Calvin did, communion taken to the sick, according to the Church's custom whose antiquity Calvin himself nonetheless recognized). Indeed, even then, the Eucharist preserves its meaning as a profession of the Church's faith and as an acceptance of God's Word. Nonetheless, we must say that the Liturgy of the Word is normally necessary so that one may deploy the full meaning of the Eucharistic mystery and also assure the Church's great responsibility to instruct in the faith not only those who come to her from without but also those who already are gathered within her.

THE MEANING THAT THE PROPERLY SACRIFICIAL CHARACTER OF THE EUCHARIST HAS FOR THE CHURCH

{913} Nonetheless, as His death was not meant to put an end to His priesthood, at the Last Supper, the night when He was handed over, He wished to leave the Church, His beloved spouse, a visible sacrifice (such as human nature calls for) whereby the bloody sacrifice that He was about to accomplish once and for all on the Cross might be represented and by which its remembrance may be perpetuated up to the end of the ages and by which the saving power would be applied to the redemption of the sins which we commit each day.³²

---

30. See Calvin, *Institution chrétienne*, bk. 4, ch. 17, §39. [Tr. note: No date provided by Fr. Nicolas.]

31. See Congar, *Vraie et fausse réforme dans l'Église*, 390–91.

32. See Council of Trent, session 22, "Doctrine and Canons on the Sacrifice of the Mass," September 17, 1562, ch. 1.

Here we have what the Eucharist's character as a sacrifice means for the Church's life. Sacrifice is the perfect cultic action, giving all the others their meaning, and Christ abolished all other sacrifices through His sacrifice on Calvary. Thus, if, as Calvin wished, the Church could take no part in the unique sacrificial action which would be approved by God, she could have only one diminished cultic activity, one stripped of all proper efficacy, reduced to receiving the fruits of the sacrifice of the cross and to giving thanks, without being able to approach God through an activity [*démarche*] that would be proper to her, thus giving herself to Him.

The Eucharistic sacrifice enables her to be a mediatrix along with Him, without in any way prejudicing Christ's unique mediation. It enables her to bless God with Him, to give herself to God with Him, to efficaciously make supplication for the world with Him. This is in line with God's desire to enable man to personally and freely participate in the process that snatches him from sin so as to make him draw close to God. It is something that Christ alone could accomplish, indeed, one that He did accomplish for all, though in such a fashion that each person can and must make it his own when he is touched by grace.

On the other hand, because the permanent efficacy of the sacrifice of the cross enables grace to be given to each person and to each generation by means of the sacraments, it was fitting that the Church would have the power to actualize this sacrifice in all times and places and make it her own. In this way, she is established as she whose specific role is to assure Christ's active presence over earth, *donec veniat*, until He comes again.[33]

THE SACRAMENT OF UNITY

{914} From St. Paul onward, the Eucharist has been presented as being the pledge and sign of Christians' unity: "Because there is one bread, we who are many are one body, for we all partake of the one bread."[34] Jesus' urgent exhortation to unity, which St. John relates

---

33. See §§661–65.
34. 1 Cor 10:17 (RSV). [Tr. note: Fr. Nicolas wrongly cites 1 Cor 11:17.]

in the discourse after the Last Supper, is incontestably connected to the institution of the Eucharist, even if St. John does not recount the latter. In St. Ignatius of Antioch, we find, from the first centuries of the post-apostolic Church, this theme which ever guided the Church's Eucharistic practice: the Eucharist is the sign and means of unity; to separate oneself from the "bishop's Eucharist" is to separate oneself from the Church. Conversely, he who separates himself from the Church can no longer participate in the Eucharist.

The idea that the Church's unity is the reality signified by the Eucharist is already clear in the *Didache* and in the most ancient liturgical texts. This theme was extensively developed by St. Augustine and thus became classic. St. Thomas refers to it as something that is self-evident.[35] However, it is surprising that he does not develop it in the article dedicated to the Eucharist's sacramental grace.[36] The place where he speaks most expressly about it is where he explains why the sinner cannot approach this sacrament.[37] There, he says that for the Eucharist "the reality that is signified and contained" is "Christ Himself," whereas the "reality that is signified and not contained" (i.e., the *res tantum*, the ultimate significate and reality) is "the mystical body, which is the communion [*société*] of the saints." The explanation that immediately follows is a bit "cramped." He says that he who communicates testifies by means of that communication that he is united and incorporated into Christ in such a manner that, if he is in reality separated from Christ by sin, "he incurs the reproach of falsifying this sacrament." We can find him making many other comments which invite us to think that he held that the Eucharist is related to the Church's unity in a very considerable and clear manner. (However, this would bring us to the difficult question concerning the place of ecclesiology in his synthesis, a point rendered difficult by the fact that the Church underlies his entire conception of Christianity without being treated for her own sake apart.)

In any case, we must develop this theme concerning the relations between the Eucharist and the Church more fully.

---

35. See *ST* III, q. 67, a. 2, co.; q. 73, a. 2, s.c.; q. 80, a. 5, ad 2; q. 82, a. 2, ad 3.
36. See *ST* III, q. 79, a. 1.
37. See *ST* III, q. 80, a. 4.

From the Individual Body of Christ to "His Body That Is the Church"

{915} Here, we must refer to the important theme of the Church as the body of Christ, which we developed above.[38] Certain exegetes hold that we should read the expression "body of Christ" in a literal sense when it is applied to the Church, which would thereby be understood as being the individual, physical body of Christ. In this case, the Eucharist would signify and form the Church by the physical contact of Christ's body with the body of the communicant. However, in addition to the fact that this physical gathering of believers into the individual body of Christ is hardly intelligible (and it is even less clear how they would preserve their distinct personality), we have seen that the idea of a "physical" contact between Christ's body and that of the communicant in Eucharistic reception [*manducation*] is not an acceptable idea. It is a question of a spiritual union, even if it is brought about between two persons each really having a bodily "dimension."

More wisely, Cerfaux, all the while interpreting the Pauline metaphor of the body in a very realistic manner,[39] speaks of an identification that is mystical, though one related to the real, individual body of Christ: "In the Eucharist (and in another manner by baptism), Christians are identified with this body in a very real manner, although one that also remains mystical. They are identified with this unique body. They are one with each other, all 'one' in relation to the very body of Christ."[40]

Thus, the Eucharist signifies this gathering together, this unification that constitutes the Church. It does so first through the symbolism connected to the bread and wine (grains gathered to make one bread, grapes merged into a single wine), a symbolism that has been proposed from the earliest days, in the *Didache*, and then becoming classic. Next (and principally), it does so because the body and blood of Christ, signified and contained under the species, are

---

38. See §§631–40.
39. See Cerfaux, *La théologie de l'Église*, 224–40.
40. See ibid., 234.

the unifying principle of the Church.[41] The Church is made up of all the members of the Church. She is the body of Christ. Through her, He is rendered visible and active in the world.

The Gathering Together of the Children of God Brought Together by the Eucharistic Sacrifice

{916} "[Ca'iaphas] did not say this of his own accord, but being high priest that year he prophesied that Jesus should die for the nation, and not for the nation only, but to gather into one the children of God who are scattered abroad."[42] Already through the Incarnation, men are mysteriously contained in Christ in a way that is not yet personal. They are in Him on account of the nature He has in common with all and because in this man Jesus, the Word incarnate, the aspiration to union with God which is found in each man on account of his nature's dynamism is realized in an absolute manner.[43] Through His sacrifice, Jesus obtained for all men the grace of the remission of sins and of divinization which enables each man, through an act of freedom, to personalize this first belonging to Christ by making it his own and to thus be united in Christ to all those who have themselves made this free adherence.

The Eucharistic sacrifice is the sacrifice of Calvary continued [through the ages], with the Church's participation currently realized on earth and especially in the community which celebrates it, in which the Church is concretized for this celebration. It tightens the bonds of those who are already united, being offered for the remission of sins, for sin is what separates. It is also offered for those who do not currently adhere to Christ, bringing about through its own proper propitiatory efficacy (though conditioned in a mysterious manner by man's free consent[44]) the approach to Christ by those who are still far off. Through their adherence to Christ, the Mystical Body grows.

Moreover, in the Eucharistic sacrifice, united to Christ's offering, there are the spiritual sacrifices of the faithful (i.e., their sacrifice of

---

41. See de La Taille, *Mysterium fidei*, 539–42. A. M. Roguet, *Saint Thomas d'Aquin, L'eucharistie*, 1:346–51.
42. Jn 11:51–52 (RSV).
43. See §435 in the previous volume.
44. See *ST* III, q. 79, a. 7, ad 2. Also see §864 above.

themselves and of themselves as a whole): "Such is the sacrifice of Christians: a great number who are only one body in Christ. And the Church does not cease to reproduce this sacrifice in the sacrament of the altar that is well known to the faithful, where she sees that she herself is offered in that which she offers."[45]

Thus, the Eucharist is the "sacrament of the unity of the Church" above all as a sacramental sacrifice. That is, she is realized by this sign. This indicates the great necessity, on the level of the signification deployed (for the liturgy's role is to highlight the fundamental signification of the sacrament and to render it sensible and manifest), that the Eucharistic liturgy arouse and make clear the active participation and unity of the community.

The Eucharistic Bread, Sign and Cause of the Unity of Christians

How it is such a sign and cause of unity

{917} Today, great insistence is expressed concerning the *refectio*, the meal, as being a sign of unity. In human experience, bread (i.e., the symbol of man's food) partaken in and eaten in common is a sign and producer [*facteur*] of union (e.g., the "common table"). The contemporary claim is that the institution of the Eucharist would have elevated this natural signification to the supernatural order. From this perspective, there can be a tendency to accentuate, in the evaluation of the Eucharist, the idea that it is a sacred meal taken in common, taken with Christ, as signifying and realizing the union of Christians in Christ.

However, we just saw that this signification, which indeed is essential to the Eucharist, as well as the communal dimension of the liturgy which results from it, belongs first of all to the Eucharist considered as a sacrifice. Therefore, it cannot lead one to relegate this first aspect of the Eucharist to a secondary status. Still less can it be used to say that the Eucharistic sacrifice would consist in the meal itself.

However, is it indeed the case that Eucharistic reception [*manducation*] signifies and truly causes the unity of the Church inasmuch

---

45. St. Augustine, *La Cité de Dieu*, OESA 10.6. See Mersch, *Le corps mystique du Christ*, 1:113–16.

as it is a meal in common? Against this, one can register the same critique as that made by de La Taille and Roguet against the often-expressed importance accorded to the signification of the Eucharistic species in relation to the Church's unity.[46] In a sacrament, the *sacramentum tantum* signifies the *res tantum* only by means of the *res et sacramentum*. The spiritual renewal does not truly signify the unity of the Church except by means of the spiritual food that is consumed in it, the "bread of life" and the "spiritual drink." As we said above, in Christ one is united to all those who eat the same bread and drink the same cup, for in eating this bread and drinking this wine, one is spiritually united to Jesus Christ, who by His very body is the principle of the Church's unity. Indeed, this is the organic connection with the sacramental sacrifice in which one participates through this reception [*manducation*], as we recalled above.

A fortiori, we must refuse to think that the "bodily" *agape* meals that could accompany this "spiritual" refection (along the lines of what seems to have sometimes occurred in the early Church) would have this signification, which can only belong to the sacrament itself.

However, a great problem emerges here, one of significant pastoral and ecumenical importance. If the Eucharist is the sign of the unity of the communicants' unity in Christ, it presupposes this unity. However, if it is the cause of this unity, the latter ought to result from it. For other sacraments, this dilemma is easily resolved by saying that the sacrament causes what it signifies. Now, here, we are concerned with a lengthy undertaking, which can be brought about only gradually and progressively. (Indeed, the Church's perfect unity will be realized only in the eschaton.) Hence, we can and must ask, "What unity is prerequisite for the common celebration of the Eucharist so that it may not be an empty and deceptive sign?"

What unity is prerequisite to the celebration of the Eucharist

The problem of intercommunion

As[*] a testimony to the community's faith in God's Word as well as to the community's unity, which is brought about through charity, the

---

46. See §916 above.

[*] Texts of the Catholic Magisterium: Vatican II, *Unitatis Redintegratio*, nos. 8 and 22.

Eucharist can be celebrated only by the ecclesial community composed of men and women professing the true faith (the faith of the Church) and united by charity, which is the bond of the *Catholica*. Therefore, heretics and schismatics are excluded from receiving the Eucharist.

During the first centuries of the Church, this rule was rigorously observed. There was the condemnation of dissident Eucharists (already found, for example, in St. Ignatius of Antioch), the refusal to celebrate the Eucharist together in the case of disagreement over matters of faith or schism, the removal of the name of the bishop of Rome from the "Diptychs" in Byzantium during periods of rupture, and so forth. However, precisely this last point makes clear the tragic difficulty posed by the disunion of Christian Churches, namely, that each Church thinks that it has true faith and authentic charity, believing for this reason that the others are "dissidents," at least in principle. Therefore, they look on each other not merely as being incapable of partaking in the Eucharist together but also as not having a right to the Eucharist (again: in principle).

Charles Journet very profoundly analyzed the concept "dissident Church" and emphatically noted that the concept of "heresy" and "schism" cannot be properly applied to Christians formed into a dissident Church (and consequently cannot be applied to the ensemble of Christians, including the leaders, in a given Church, even if the latter was, in fact, born of a formal schism or from a heresy).[47] Indeed, properly speaking, schism and heresy are sins. Schism is a sin against charity inasmuch as it is the bond of the Church. Heresy is a sin against faith inasmuch as it is the acceptance and profession of the Word of God addressed to the Church and proposed by her.[48] Consequently he who remains united to His Church by believing in good faith that it is the (or a?) true Church and who professes the

---

For the perspective of other Christian Churches [*sic*]: Boelens, "La discussion sur la Sainte Cène." Meyendorff, "Note sur l'interprétation orthodoxe de l'eucharistie." Max Thurian, *Le pain unique* (Taize: Les Presses de Taize, 1967). Other studies include Charles Journet, "L'eucharistie n'est pas malleable, elle est adorable," *Nova et Vetera* 44 (1969): 1–6. Joseph Moingt, "Problèmes d'inter-communion," *Études* 332, no. 1 (1970): 256–67. Jean-Hervé Nicolas, "Hospitalité eucharistique et oecuménisme," *Nova et Vetera* 50 (1975): 168–87.

47. See Journet, *L'Église du Verbe incarné*, 2:708–63.
48. See *ST* II-II, q. 39. Journet, *L'Église du Verbe incarné*, 2:818–41.

faith of this Church as being the true faith, cannot be called a heretic or a schismatic. Since the time of Journet's writing, the judgment expressed by Catholic theology and the Magisterium has developed significantly, as dissident Churches have been officially recognized as being "Christian Churches"—that is, as (partial and straying) realizations of the Church of Jesus Christ which is fully realized in all of its dimensions only in the Catholic Church. Therefore, one must understand that the Church of Christ is not made up of the assembly of Christian Churches, alongside which the Catholic Church would be numbered. Rather, it is the Catholic Church, and certain values that in reality are hers are authentically preserved and alive in the other Churches, producing their fruits of salvation and holiness in them.[49]

This could lead one to think that the Eucharist by which a Church expresses its faith in Christ and its fidelity could be recognized as being authentic by the other Churches. Each could therefore welcome the faithful of other Churches to its Eucharist (i.e., in "open communion") and also permit its own faithful to participate in other Eucharists (i.e., "reciprocal open communion"). Indeed, it could even be the case that members of different Churches could celebrate the Eucharist together (i.e., "intercommunion"). However, matters are not at all so simple.

Indeed, if we can say that all the professions of the Christian faith come together in what they contain as authentically taught by God (and indeed, by this, they tend to coalese into a common profession of faith), it nonetheless remains the case that each, in its specificity, excludes the others, at least on points of disagreement. Now, the Eucharist is a sign of agreement and of ecclesial unity. If it were to be celebrated together when there is disagreement on fundamental points of faith and on the fundamental requirements for unity in charity, the communities would give themselves over to a sham union, performing an act of sacrilege (at least objectively), for this is a question of a sacred sign.

However, what are the fundamental points of faith on which preliminary agreement is indispensable? First of all and obviously,

---

49. See §702 above. [Tr. note: Here again, Fr. Nicolas's somewhat ambiguous use of the single term "Church" in this context stands out in these comments.]

faith in the Eucharist itself is necessary. By recalling the positions of the reformers and also of contemporary Reformed theologians, we have seen that despite the obvious desire for a rapprochement, this agreement is far from being the case. Above all, there is one point where the opposition is intractable, namely, the case of how various churches understand the notion of a "minister." For the Catholic Church, only the duly ordained priest can really perform the sacrificial action and conversion in the Eucharistic liturgy. One can respect the Eucharist of dissident Churches, but they cannot be recognized as being the true Eucharist instituted by Christ:

[Though the ecclesial Communities which are separated from us lack the fullness of unity with us flowing from Baptism, and though we believe they have not retained the proper reality of the eucharistic mystery in its fullness,] especially because of the absence of the sacrament of Orders, nevertheless when they commemorate His death and resurrection in the Lord's Supper, they profess that it signifies life in communion with Christ and look forward to His coming in glory.[50]

Many times, private persons (both Catholics and people of other confessions of faith) have declared that after an in-depth study, they have discovered that nothing essential separates them concerning the mystery of the Eucharist. We must beware of such affirmations which can be read as saying, "We have discovered that we are separated only by what is inessential." Moreover, it does not fall to individual believers to say what is essential in their Church's faith.

Likewise, faith in the Eucharist implies faith in Jesus Christ the Savior, the Son of God, sent by the Father.

On the question of open, reciprocal communion, the Catholic Church makes an essential distinction between the Orthodox Christian Churches (which have the sacrament of holy orders and participate in her conviction concerning not only the necessity to receive this sacrament in order to validly preside over the Eucharist, but also participate in her conviction concerning the sacrament itself as a real presence and a sacrifice, as well as concerning Christ and salvation) and the other Christian Churches, whose Eucharist she cannot

---

50. Vatican II, *Unitatis Redintegratio*, no. 22. [Tr. note: The portion in brackets is given for full context, given that the official translation does not read as a independent block.]

recognize as being authentic. In a broad and open gesture, she permits her faithful to communicate in an Orthodox Eucharistic celebration when it would not be possible for them to do so in a Catholic community. However, the Orthodox church[es], more rigorously faithful to ancient tradition, refuses to allow her faithful the same possibility (except, of course, in the case of the danger of death).

On the question of intercommunion and, *a fortiori* of concelebration, the Church's position is firmly negative. The Eucharistic liturgy itself is an expression of the Church's faith, and so long as there is divergence between the two communities regarding matters of faith (at least in what concerns the articles of faith that are directly engaged in the Eucharistic celebration), they cannot celebrate the Eucharist in communion. To do so would only be possible if the Church were to relativize the faith (something that she can allow in no way).

Unity in the great problems and options facing temporally facing man

{919} In all ages, Christians have been violently opposed to each other on the temporal plane: wars, political or economic battles, conflicts of interests, and so forth. Indeed, this is even the case—alas!—within the Church and in her activities. Through this history, it did not seem that these divisions were of such a nature as to divide the ecclesiastical community as such to the point of preventing the common celebration of the Eucharist by the opposed groups. However, one cannot deny the painful fact that certain oppositions, above all in the social and political order, have led to large groups departing from the community that celebrates the Eucharist, the Church.

Today, when Christians are keenly aware of the necessity of temporal engagement (indeed, in the very name of their faith and charity), especially political engagement in the broadest and yet most proper sense of the term, the question begins to emerge: can we celebrate the Eucharist together without there being preliminary agreement concerning the fundamental temporal options, those choices that one makes in order to obey the requirements of his Christian faith (as we see them and experience them)? If one responds affirmatively on account of Christian unity, whose principle is faith and charity, and that the gravest temporal oppositions ought not to tear [Christians] apart, does one not risk making the Eucharist to be an empty and deceptive sign, so long as the participants do not succeed at really overcoming their oppositions?*

If one responds negatively, does one not repudiate Christian unity, charity, and, consequently, the Church herself? However, then the Eucharist will anew be an empty and deceptive sign, for she is the sign of this unity.

It has been proposed[51] that the celebration of the Eucharist should be more restricted and that it should be made more exceptional, prefacing it by a common meditation on the Word of God and common sharing. It is not clear how this would solve the problem, unless one awaits agreement concerning temporal options so that the Eucharist may be celebrated together. However, whether the Eucharistic celebration were frequent or not, this would ultimately lead to the dividing of the ecclesial community into many Eucharistic communities that are opposed to each other. Would this not be the very negation of the Eucharist?

It is here that we must recall that the Eucharist is not only the sign of ecclesial unity but also its cause. Moreover, we must recall that it is the sign and cause, directly at least, only of ecclesiastical unity. That is, it is the sign and cause of a unity that, of itself, neither resolves nor abolishes temporal divisions. It only must preclude hatred, division reaching men in the deepest parts of their personality, that is, in the point where they come back together inasmuch as they come from God and return to Him, inasmuch as they are made in God's image and redeemed by Christ, called by Him to all be gathered together in Him.

This unity is simultaneously a prerequisite for the Eucharistic celebration and is brought about by it. It is a *prerequisite* because nobody can (except through a sacrilegious deception) participate in the Eucharist without willing to be united with all men in Christ,

---

* N.B. Is this not the image that the closing of the parish Mass too often gives, when each person returns to his social class, to his family interests, and to his ideological group, which he in fact never had left, even when he Eucharistically communed with those of opposed groups?

51. See Patrick Jacquemont, "Du bon usage de l'eucharistie," *Informations catholiques internationales* 309 (July-August 1968): 6–7.

despite all divisions.* It is *brought about by it,* for the Eucharist that is celebrated with faith and love is already an act of overcoming temporal oppositions. One thus overcomes them on the level of signs, but in this way, through its own proper efficacy, this kind of semiotic overcoming of temporal oppositions leads one to overcome these oppositions internally as well as externally (through a renunciation of acts of hatred, vengeance, and so forth).

THE SACRAMENT OF CHARITY

In retrieving the communal-ecclesial dimension of the Eucharist, contemporary theology and pastoral practice risk neglecting its personal dimension. In reality, the first cannot be exaggerated because the Eucharist by its very nature is the sacrament of the Church's unity. However, it would be an error to oppose it to the second, whereas the community is one dimension of the person himself. It is by personally communicating in Christ through the Eucharist that the believer can communicate in Christ with all the other members of the Church.

The Sacramental Grace of the Eucharist

The believer's conformation to Christ

{920} Every sacrament causes grace, and with it, of course, charity. The sacraments give birth to the *habitus* that are infused into the soul if they are not there and bring an increase to them if they are. They also cause an actual grace that brings about the act by which the encounter with Christ in the sacrament is realized for the believer who celebrates and receives it, at least if the beneficiary has the required dispositions for this.

We have seen that the sacramental grace proper to a given sacra-

---

* N.B. One must be willing to be united to all men, not only to those with whom one currently partakes in the Eucharist, for the community that celebrates is itself a symbol of the entire Church. This is why the idea of grouping Christians together on account of their common holding of temporal options cannot be a fundamental solution to the problem, even though this could be, in certain cases, a pragmatic solution. (For it is psychologically easier to will to be united spiritually to political or social adversaries who are absent and to pardon them, than it is to find oneself next to them in one and the same celebration.)

ment is the (actual and habitual) grace intrinsically related to the *res et sacramentum* of this sacrament.[52] In the case of the Eucharist, the *res et sacramentum* is the body and blood of Christ made into food and drink.

Therefore, it is on the basis of this nutrition that we can determine what the sacramental grace of the Eucharist is. However, it is a question of spiritual nutrition. As we have seen, it is characterized by the fact that the food is not the dead remains of a person who has been destroyed but, rather, is the living person [of Jesus Christ]. The union produced by this "refection" is therefore a union of person to person. It is essentially spiritual, though by the mediation of a bodily sign. Therefore, following St. Thomas,[53] we can borrow from St. Augustine this beautiful expression of the mystery of the sacramental nourishment: "You will not change me into you, like your bodily food. Rather, you will be changed into me.[54] What the Eucharist brings about is the conformation of the believer to Christ, which is the end and consummation of the redemptive work.

It is clear that this conformity of the Christian to Christ is essentially established by charity and all the virtues, precisely inasmuch as they depend on charity. The Church is unified by this same charity inasmuch as it animates all Christians together, making them one in Christ. Thus, charity as personally uniting man to Christ (and in Him to the whole Trinity, inasmuch as He places that person into communion with the Divine Persons) is precisely what brings about the Church's unity. Therefore, it is not a question of two *res*, of two "graces."

Continuation up to the consummation of the redemptive work
{921} However, the Eucharist is ever renewed in the Church. Indeed, every Christian is invited to participate in it often, for if the redemptive work is realized in it, this occurs in a way that is still participative and progressive "until He comes again," *donec veniat*. In the Eucharist, one finds the most extreme point of tension of the "already" and

---

52. See §764.
53. See *ST* III, q. 73, a. 3, ad 2.
54. See St. Augustine, *Les Confessions*, OESA 10.16.

the "not yet" that is characteristic of Christian grace in the "time of the Church."[55] It is at once a terminus (though prophetically so, inasmuch as it is a sign of Christ's eschatological return and of the consummated holiness of the elect) and also a stage, a *viaticum* for the path that still must be traveled.[56]

By analyzing the effects of bodily nourishment, St. Thomas analogically describes the Eucharist's effects for personal perfection. One need only refer to this profound and beautiful text which needs no commentary.[57]

One can think that all the graces granted to a believer for the strengthening, defense, development, and full flowering of his personal Christian life participate in the sacramental grace of the Eucharist, even when they are given in an extra-sacramental manner[58] (for, in that case, they are not given without the *votum* or desire for the Eucharist which is inscribed at the heart of Christian grace here-below, as we will see).[59] One must note that, on the one hand, one's personal Christian life does not develop without an intensification of one's relation to the Church and to others in the Church. Furthermore, on the other hand, the Church internally develops, spreading out and deepening her unity, only through her members' progress in their personal adherence to Christ. Therefore, there is a perfect coherence, in sacramental grace, the *res* of the Eucharist, between the Church's unity on the one hand and the progress of the Christian in faith and charity on the other.

The Eucharist and Sin

{922} Traditionally, the Eucharist presupposes that he who participates in it be "worthy": "Whoever, therefore, eats the bread or drinks the cup of the Lord in an unworthy manner will be guilty of profan-

---

55. See Benoît, "Corps, Tête et Plérôme dans les épîtres de la captivité," 2:112–13.
56. See *ST* III, q. 73, a. 4.
57. See *ST* III, q. 73, a. 1. [Tr. note: Fr. Nicholas cites "q. 73, a. 1, 3.˙" It is not clear what the third thing referenced is. There are not three parts to the body of the article. The ad 3 of article is not directly related to the analogy with nourishment, which is, however, discussed in the body.]
58. See §765 above.
59. See §925 below.

ing the body and blood of the Lord."[60] As the context clearly invites us to read this passage, this "worthiness" has always been understood as a moral purity that excludes sin: "Gather on the Lord's Day, break the bread and give thanks after having first confessed your sins so that your sacrifice may be pure. He who has a dispute with his companion should not join with you before being reconciled for fear of profaning your sacrifice."[61] This is the most ancient text concerned with the necessity of penance for participation in the Eucharist. The most ancient liturgies precede the distribution of the Eucharist with the formula "holy things for the holy."[62] Also, the rule that forbids one to approach the holy table in a state of sin[63] is much more than a disciplinary measure. It is at the very foundation of the Eucharist.

However, this poses a theological problem. The Christ whom one receives in the Eucharist is the Savior, in His saving act. Therefore, the proper effect of this sacrament ought to be the remission of sins. One could add that sinners approached Jesus during His life and received the remission of sins from Him (e.g., Mary Magdalene, Zacchaeus, the paralytic, and others). Why would it not be the same for those who approach him when he is really present in the Eucharist?

The solution must be sought out in the notion of a sacramental sign.[64] The Eucharist is present to the believer's awareness as a food, and the sacramental action that the believer performs is his reception [*manducation*] of the sacrament. To eat and assimilate a food is an act of a living being. To spiritually eat Christ and allow oneself to be assimilated by Him is a spiritual act, which cannot be performed by the person who does not live spiritually. The comparison with the sinner's approach to Christ during His earthly life makes the sacramental character stand forth (i.e., the symbolic character of the Eucharist that we insisted on above). In the Eucharist, Christ is attained

---

60. See 1 Cor 11:27 (RSV).
61. Audet, *La Didachè*, ch. 14.
62. See St. Cyril of Jerusalem, *Catécèses mystagogiques*, SC 126, cat. 5, §19; Theodore of Mopsuestia, *Homélies catéchétiques*, 565.
63. See Council of Trent, session 13, "Decree on the Sacrament of the Eucharist," October 11, 1551, ch. 7 and c. 11 (D.-Sch., nos. 1647 and 1661).
64. See *ST* III, q. 76, aa. 1–6.

only by the mediation of sacramental signs and by the mediation of the sacramental action of the believer, namely, the believer's reception [*manducation*] in faith, indeed living faith.*

However, given that Christ is the one who acts and saves in the Eucharist (as in every other sacrament, though more than any other), we must say that sin paralyzes the sacrament's action, not directly but indirectly (i.e., by presenting an impediment, a counterdisposition in the subject), rendering impossible the sacramental act of the man which is the condition of Christ's saving action. However, no obstacle is present when a man on the one hand is not aware of his sinful state while, on the other, being disposed to let himself be conformed to Christ without opposing Him through a deliberate act of rejection. In such a case, the sacrament certainly brings about the remission of sins.

The question concerning the necessity of the sacrament of penance for passing out of the state of sin (which in fact is a different question), will be examined in relation to that sacrament. The rather complex problems aroused by this notion of "awareness of sin" fall to moral theology.

Of course, "venial sin" (i.e., in short, the sin that the righteous person commits without it making him "unrighteous") does not by itself constitute this kind of impediment to performing the spiritual act that is the necessary condition for the sacrament's efficacy. Therefore, we must purely and simply say that the Eucharist has the remission of venial sins as one of its effects, above all purifying the believer of them (though, as is always the case, to the degree that he repents of them).

---

* Hence, only he who lives a life that is foundationally animated by the Holy Spirit who is both sent by Christ and leads back to Him can perform the sacramental action of "spiritually eating" Christ the Lord under the appearances of bread and wine. Moreover (and by way of consequence), the act of approaching the holy table to receive Christ's body and blood while one is and remains in sin ultimately is a sign that has thus been rendered deceptive, for what it signifies is that one is united to Christ whereas one, in fact, is separated from Him by sin. In baptism, by contrast, the sacramental action required by the believer consists in one's voluntary submission to the action of the Church, who alone acts. The beneficiary of this action is purely (although deliberately) passive. Therefore, in order for him to benefit from the efficacy of this action, he does not need to already be one who lives a spiritual life. We will later see that matters are proportionally the same for the sacrament of penance.

Sacramental Reception and Spiritual Reception

{923} This distinction goes back to St. Augustine. St. Thomas explains it (and interprets his master well here) by specifying that what is placed in opposition are "merely sacramental communion" and "sacramental communion that is also spiritual." However, he also seems to speak of a spiritual communion that would not be sacramental,[65] but which for men here-below would not exist without the desire to receive this sacrament. Therefore, it is a question of a case of an anticipated action by the sacrament. In modern times, this was made into a notion of "spiritual communion" having a different sense than that which St. Augustine and St. Thomas gave to this expression.

This distinction is connected to what we said above. Reception [*manducation*] that is (solely) sacramental is that of the sinner who communicates without willing to be assimilated by Christ. This is a form of sacrilege, for it makes sacramental reception (and one's approach to the holy table) into a deceptive sign. However, this poses anew the problem of the "worthiness" required for the sacrament. After having severely denounced the sacrilege of those who communicate "without flicker of faith and without the affection of charity," Calvin turns back violently against the Catholic doctrine, which he accuses of demanding a false worthiness, a perfect innocence, one that is, moreover, obtained by means that he judges to be frivolous (i.e., confession and satisfaction).[66] Indeed, above all after the Reformation, there developed a spirituality of fear and trembling around the Eucharist, having its culminating point in Arnauld's *De la fréquente communion*.[67]

This problem recalls that of the prerequisite unity needed for the celebration of the Eucharist. To communicate, the recipient must be

---

65. See *ST* III, q. 80, a. 2.
66. See Calvin, *Institution chrétienne*, bk. 4, ch. 27, §§40 and 41.
67. Perhaps one would find in Christian antiquity antecedents to this state of mind, if it is true that a theory encouraging scarcity of communions existed in the fourth-century Greek Church, as Botte thinks there was, on the basis of a passage in St. Ambrose which is not entirely clear. See Ambrose, *De sacramentis* bk. 5, §25. Bernard Botte, introduction to Ambrose of Milan, *Des Sacraments et au Des mystères*, SC 25 (Paris: Cerf, 1949), 19. Hélène Pétré, "Les leçons du Panem nostrum quotidianum," *Recherches des sciences religieuses* 40 (1951–52): 63–79.

someone who lives a spiritual life and, therefore, must have charity. However, in fact, charity is compatible with, in the same person, a self-love that is still deviating while not being dominant. This is obviously an impurity, not only a moral one but above all a religious and theological one. However, it is an impurity that neither prevents one from receiving the sacrament nor from benefiting from its sanctifying action, as such a believer remains ordered to Christ crucified. The same must be said about the potential [*éventuel*] state of sin if it is not conscious, as we have seen. This directly responds to Calvin's attack: "If Our Lord in his defense does not receive someone for participation in the Supper if that person is not righteous and innocent, one would need no small assurance to be certain that he would have this justice which he hears that God requires." The true Catholic doctrine cannot intend to encourage paralyzing scruples, for it recognizes that the sacrament has the power to compensate for insufficient preparation—so long as there is a humble intention to be spiritually united to Christ and so long as there is not a rejection of some essential requirement for this union. Moreover, it does not intend to favor self-contentment and the sentiment of one's "worthiness," for even when the believer presumes that he is "in a state of grace," he knows not only that grace is a free gift but also that the state of grace does not eliminate all of his blemishes. He goes to Christ as the sinner goes to Him who alone can save him.

The Eucharist and the Other Sacraments

{924} Given that the *res* of the sacrament of the Eucharist is union with Christ and conformity to Him who is the principle and consummation of the Christian life, the alpha and omega, a question cannot be avoided: does it not suffice for assuring Christ's saving action over the believer, thus rendering all the other sacraments useless?

The unity of the sacramental order

Above all, we must bear in mind the unity of the sacramental order. It is a unity that is taken from the unique *res* that all the sacraments are ordered to signify and realize, namely salvation by Christ.[68] All

---

68. See §764 above.

the sacraments refer us, in the past, to Christ's sacrifice on Calvary. In him who receives them, they all bring about a participation in the fruits of this sacrifice and thus constitute the Church, making her live and develop herself at each moment of history until Christ's return. Finally, they all prophesy and draw closer to the end of time, in which they will be eliminated, for signs will then give way to realities.

Thus, what is the source of the distinction of the sacraments? It comes from the *res et sacramentum* proper to each one. In other words, as we have seen,[69] it comes from each one's contribution to the edification of the Church.

The specificity of the Eucharist

{925} This is the perspective that we must have in order to grasp the distinct character of the Eucharist. This is not difficult for the sacraments of holy orders and marriage. The first assures that the Church will have the exercise of her sacramental function, both by establishing the ministers by which she exercises it as well as by the subjects on whom she exercises it. Marriage constitutes the state of life that is a stable union of two children of God so that they may live together in Christ and may transmit life (and therefore, also, so that they may present the new generations of mankind to Christ's saving action by and in the Church). In these two cases, the sacrament in question is concerned with determining a particular situation in the Church (though in different manners). In the case of penance, this sacrament is concerned with bringing about a particular effect (corresponding to a particular necessity). The same can be said for anointing of the sick. The true difficulty is that of grasping the difference between baptism (and confirmation, which supplements baptism) and the Eucharist. Both constitute the Church in her universality, for both signify and actualize salvation in its universality for the beneficiary.

The distinction must be drawn from their sacramental significations, which are distinct. Baptism signifies birth into the Divine Life, to life in Christ (i.e., the remission of sins and regeneration).

---

69. See §765 above.

The Eucharist signifies the nourishing of this life, its development through spiritual nutrition.

On the basis of this, we can say that baptism bestows Christian being, whereas the Eucharist bestows Christian action up to its consummation in the grasping of the [ultimate] end [of the Christian life]. This shows how the two sacraments envelop each other, without one being able to replace the other.

Indeed, being and the good are at once identical and distinct. Every later development of being is still being, and in this sense, one can say that all the developments of the Christian life (in each person and in the Church) are the fructification of baptismal grace (as all the later developments of the plant are the unfolding of the seed's inner vitality). However, being develops itself through its own proper activity, which is given its finality by the good. Indeed, given that "every being is fundamentally ordered to its activity," the end is already given with being in the form of a fundamental tendency to that end and to the activities by which it will be able to be attained. In this sense, the Eucharist is already there from the time of baptism, acting for salvation and for the constituting of the Church.

This is explained in a technical manner by the "desire to receive this sacrament" which is implied in the baptismal process itself (and in the very first justifying activity of the person who cannot approach baptism as well). The "desire for baptism" implies "desire for the Eucharist" which therefore is implied in the act of baptism exercised on the infant who is incapable of a conscious act. One thus explains that the baptized child is already justified and ordered to eternal life, without there being a need to confer the sacrament to him before the age of reason.

Thus, baptism and the Eucharist are never separated. The one cannot act without the other. The non-baptized person could not "sacramentally eat" precisely because he does not belong to the ecclesial community that celebrates it. However, the baptized person could not live the life received at baptism without being fed by the Eucharist. Therefore, they cannot be separated, though they each have a distinct effect.

The excellence of the Eucharist in the sacramental order

{926} Given that the Eucharist is the sacrament of the "end" toward which the whole of salvation history is ordered, as is the whole earthly Church (herself being ordered only to the ultimate manifestation of Christ and of the Church), it is clear that the Eucharist is the unifying principle of the sacramental order. All the sacraments are ordered to it and, by it, to Christ the Savior, who is the principle and end of the sacraments and of the Church. The Eucharist is itself ordered only to itself, ever more consciously and profoundly celebrated and, beyond itself, to the reality that it signifies.

PART 4

PENANCE AND THE ANOINTING OF THE SICK

15

The Problem of the Sacrament of Penance

{927} The sacrament of penance poses [particular] problems for the theologian. Some of these issues come from the fact that this sacrament, as it has existed in both the Greek and Latin Churches since the High Middle Ages, is so different from the forms of penance practiced during the first centuries of the Church's existence that one wonders whether we find ourselves here faced with the same institution, likewise wondering whether the theology elaborated on the basis of our current practice (as well as through the application of a sacramental theology that was itself constituted rather later on in the Church's history) can hold for the ancient forms of penance. However, if this was not the case, this theology would founder for lack of a basis in tradition and Scripture. Other problems concern this theology itself. How are we to apply the general principles of sacramental theology to penance? To put the matter more precisely: how are we to admit that an external right would have efficacy and even signification in relation to a grace that seems to be the place where the divine act of merciful pardon meets a wholly interior human act of repentance and of one's return to God?*

---

* See the following texts: St. Ambrose, *La penitence*, ed. and trans. Roger Gryson, SC 179 (Paris: Cerf, 1971). Yves Congar, "Points d'appui doctrinaux pour une pastorale de la penitence," *La Maison-Dieu* 104 (1970): 73–87. Édouard Cothenet, "Sainteté de l'Eglise et péchés des chrétiens. Comment le Nouveau Testament envisages leur pardon," *Nouvelle revue théologique* 96 (1974): 449–70. Philippe Deschamps, *Théologie du péché* (Paris: Desclée de Brouwer, 1960), 49–124. André Feuillet, "La découverte du tombeau vide en Jn 20, 3–10 et la foi au Christ ressuscité," *Esprit et Vie* 19 (1977): 133–42, and "L'Exousia du Fils de l'homme

THE BROAD LINES OF THE HISTORICAL DEVELOPMENT OF THE SACRAMENT OF PENANCE

{928} The history of the sacrament of penance is too vast and complex for us to be able to treat it in this course.*

THE CHURCH'S GRADUAL AWARENESS OF HER POWER TO REMIT SINS

Here, we are primarily concerned with offering a "theological" reflection in order to enable us to extract the data of the theological problem concerning the sacrament of penance. First of all, we must ask how the Church has understood the meaning of this act of remitting sins, which she has performed from her beginnings by means of her penitential liturgy. Then, we will consider how we can hold that this liturgy has a sacramental nature.

For the first question, the history of the practice of "penance" shows us that the Church gradually discovered her power to remit sins by feeling her way through tensions which were felt and lived

---

(d'après Mc 2, 19–28 et par.)," *Recherches des sciences religieuses* 42 (1954): 161–92. F. Funk, "Panorama bibliographique sur la publication de ces dix dernières années touchant la confession," *Concilium* 61 (1971): 121–31. Pierre Grelot, "L'interprétation pénitentielle du lavement des pieds," in *L'homme devant Dieu, Mélanges offerts au P. H. de Lubac* (Paris: Aubier, 1963), 1:75–92. Hermas, *Le Pasteur*, 2nd ed., trans. Robert Joly (Paris: Éditions du Cerf, 1968). Stanislaus Lyonnet, "Péché," in *Vocabulaire de théologie biblique*, 936–46. Jerome Murphy O'Connor, "Péché et communauté dans le Nouveau Testament," *Revue biblique* 74 (1967): 161–93. Eugène Roche, "Pénitence et conversion dans l'évangile et la vie chrétienne," *Nouvelle revue théologique* 79 (1957): 113–34. Herbert Vorgrimmler, "Mathieu 16, 18s. et le sacrement de penitence," in *L'homme devant Dieu, Mélanges offerts au P. H. de Lubac* (Paris: Aubier, 1963), 1:51–61. See also the essays gathered in Bruno Schüller (ed.), *Péché, penitence et confession* (Paris: Mame, 1970); and Jean-Pierre Jossua, D. Duliscouët, B. D. Marliangeas, "Théologie, crise, et redécouverte du sacrement de penitence," *Revue des sciences philosophiques et théologiques* 52 (1968): 119–42.

* For the basic and indispensable points to be known concerning this matter, the reader can refer to the following works: Paul Galtier, *Aux origines du sacrament de penitence* (Rome: Apud Universitatis Gregorianae, 1951). Bernhard Poschmann, *Pénitence et onction des maladies* (Paris: Cerf, 1966). Henri Rondet, "Esquisse d'une histoire du sacrament de penitence," *Nouvelle revue théologique* 90 (1968): 561–84. Cyrille Vogel, *Le pécheur et la penitence au Moyen-Age. Textes traduits et présentés par Cyrille Vogel* (Paris: Cerf, 1969); "La discipline pénitentielle dans l'Église orthodoxe de Grèce," *Revue des Sciences Religieuses* 27 (1953): 374–99; and *La discipline pénitentielle en Gaule des origines à la fin du VII*[e] *siècle* (Paris: Letouzey and Ané, 1952). Louis Ligier, "Le sacrament de penitence selon la tradition orientale," *Nouvelle revue théologique* 89 (1967): 910–67.

through prior to being "formalized," tensions existing in the data furnished by the Gospel message, which at first sight seem to be mutually opposed to each other.

A First Tension: The Baptized Person Who Is "Dead to Sin" and Still Is a Sinner

{929} The apostolic Church already had the experience of this first tension. She forcefully preached that the baptized person receives the remission of all of his sins through Christ's death and resurrection, thus passing from death to life. However, she immediately observed that baptism did not continue to preserve its recipient from sin.[1]

It is clear that this intrusion of sin into the heart of the Church posed (and does not cease to pose) grave problems for her. The simplifying and reassuring schematic oppositions of light and darkness, the good and the wicked, and the elect and the rejected did not conform to reality, at least to the appearances of things. It was only through lengthy and difficult theological reflection (whose results, moreover, are not accepted by all) that we can discover, under all of these deceptive appearances, the reality presented by these schematic oppositions. In short, the Church, as such, is the light (the very light of Christ illuminating those who have received it and radiating forth from them), and the part of darkness that remains in each man is that by which he separates himself not only from Christ (an obvious assertion) but also and simultaneously from the Church (an assertion which would be equally obvious if we seriously reflect on the fact that she is the "body of Christ").[2] What was to be done, in the short term, regarding this situation? Was the sinner to be definitively rejected? It is clear that this was not the course of action taken by the apostles. Thus, from the start, the idea of a remission of sins committed after baptism imposed itself [on the Church's awareness].

(The well-known scriptural passages concerning unforgivable sins cannot be raised in objection here.[3] The common interpretation, at least for Catholics, is that this is not a question of God's refusal to pardon but, rather, an existential situation into which the

---

1. See §773 above.
2. See §683 above.
3. See Mt 12:31, 1 Jn 5:16, and Heb 6:4–8, 10:26, 12:16–17.

sinner places himself, namely, a state of soul in which he rejects the Holy Spirit, who is given through the pardoning of sins. For as long as such an existential situation remains in force, it makes it impossible that such a person can ask for pardon and receive it.[4])

Must baptism be repeated in such cases? We find no hint of this idea in the New Testament, and before the Church explicitly judged that baptism did not need to be repeated in any case, she held in practice that it places its recipient into a determinate situation in relation to Christ and salvation. Repetition of baptism (except in the case of invalidity) would not represent a mere development or complement to the doctrine of baptism but, rather, the complete abandonment thereof.

The solution to this issue emerged very early on. On the basis of what is said in the Gospel in Matthew 16:19 and 18:19, the Church affirmed that she is charged with reconciling the sinner with her, trusting that by this very fact she also reconciled him with God. (In *De pudicitia* 21.9, Tertullian was the first witness to the tradition of referring the power to remit sins to the power of the keys. In this work, he himself contested such a reference, given that he was personally opposed to the "Church of the bishops," against whom he was then struggling.)

However, even in light of this point, there was another aspect of the Gospel message that she did not (and, indeed, could not) abandon, namely, the fact that the Christian vocation and baptism, of itself, is definitive. If she had to recognize that Christians in fact have sinned, thus losing the life they received at baptism (and did so in an ever-increasing number to the extent that Christianity became a large-scale religion) and if she had to remedy this not only by means of her exhortations but also through an act of reconciliation, which made her become aware of the power she had received for remitting sins, she never accepted it. With a holy obstinacy, she always maintained that the situation of the sinful baptized person, however frequent and habitual it may be, was and remained profoundly abnormal and unacceptable.

---

4. See de La Potterie, "L'impeccabilité," 197–216. Poschmann, *Pénitence et onction des maladies*, 15–25. Spicq, *L'epître aux Hébreux*, 2:167–68.

It was here, through this profound sense of the non-repeatability of baptism, that the primitive penitential institution was led to an impasse, for it was understood in a juridical manner like a kind of ecclesiastical law having an immediately divine origin, thus meaning that the Church had no authority over it. *In its inspiration*, this law is profoundly evangelical. The Church's spontaneous reaction in the presence of the baptized person who separated himself from Christ through sin is twofold. On the one hand, she feels the desire to extend her hand in order to help him get out of this inextricable situation. On the other hand, she feels the need to warn him that he cannot begin again and therefore should not have to ask for pardon again. Thus, in the Gospel Jesus said, "Go and sin no more."

However, what will the Church do when, despite her admonitions and contrary to the promises that he made, the Christian falls back into sin? Here is where the hardening took place, for it is not clear why the situation of a penitent who returns to sin would be different from that of the baptized person who sins for the first time. The process undergone by the person seeking penance is irreversible, similar to that by which he asks for baptism. Indeed, it is a "conversion," and this conversion to God would not exist without definitively breaking with sin. However, after penance (just as after baptism), the Christian remains free to sin, and if he does, he finds himself in a situation that is analogous to that from which he emerged through penance. The rule of non-repetition expresses nothing other than the Church's recognition of the intention to sin no more, expressed by the sinner upon conversion (an intention which, of itself, is irrevocable). This rule is not meant to bar the route to a second return for the person who was unfaithful to this intention.

One obvious cause of this hardening is the fact that, conversely, the repetition of reconciliation, by masking the Church's acceptance of the sinner's intention by showing that she did not totally believe in it, risks completely diminishing this demand for irrevocability which is included in every authentic conversion. We are all too familiar with this reality today. What remains (and will always remain) is the obligation to turn back to God in a definitive manner so that one may receive the remission of one's sins.

Understood in this way (and even reduced to the intention to not place oneself anew into the state of needing to do penance and of needing to ask the Church for God's pardon), the rule of non-repetition was only concerned with "mortal" sins, which can be defined, in opposition to "venial" sins, as those by which the Christian cuts himself off from Christ, the Father, and the Holy Spirit, such that he can obtain the remission of sin only at the cost of an authentic "conversion." The idea of the "daily sins" that soil Christians without, for all that, placing him in the state of being cut off from God is certainly traditional. Thus, we read two assertions in sequence in the *Didache*: on the one hand, in its fourth chapter, we read: "In the assembly, you will confess your sins and will not go to prayer with a bad conscience";[5] then, by contrast, in its tenth chapter, we read: "If someone is holy, let him come; if he is not, let him do penance."[6] St. Ambrose wrote: "Certainly, every day, we must do penance for our sins. However, this daily penance is solely applied to sins of lesser gravity. The other kind of penance, namely public penance, is required for grave faults."[7]

This distinction is equally clear in this beautiful text from St. Augustine:

> Scripture presents us with three ways to envision penance. The first is that of catechumens desiring to receive baptism. I just spoke about it in accord with what the scriptural texts say about it.
>
> There is another, everyday kind of penance. Where do we find this kind of daily penance? There is no better Scriptural passage than that which tells us how to pray each day, where the Lord taught us to pray and say what is appropriate to the Father: "Forgive our debts as we forgive those who are indebted to us ..." (Mt 6:12).
>
> There remains a third kind of penance about which I will briefly speak so that I may achieve, with God's aid, the purpose that I have set for myself. It is a severe penance, one that is soaked with tears. It is the state of penitents in the Church, men and women who are forbidden to partake in the sacrament of the altar for fear that, by receiving it unworthily, they would eat and drink to their own condemnation. The wound is great. Perhaps it is adultery, murder, or some sacrilege. In any case, it is a

---

5. See Audet, *La Didachè*, ch. 4.
6. See ibid., ch. 10.
7. See Vogel, *Le pécheur et la pénitence dans l'Église ancienne*, 112.

grave matter and a dangerous and mortal wound, placing salvation in peril. However, the physician is all-powerful. After the temptation, delight, consent, and sinful act, the sinner gives off a foul odor like a corpse that has rotted for four days. However, the Lord does not abandon him. He calls, "Lazarus, come forth!" The weight of the tomb yields before the merciful voice, death recoils before life, and hell before heaven. Lazarus arises and comes forth from his tomb. Now, like sinners confessing their fault and doing penance, he was restricted by bonds. Already, they have been freed from death, for they would not profess to be penitents if they were not already freed from it. The very fact of doing penance shows that one has passed out from the night and the shadows. However, what does the Lord say to His Church? "Whatever you loose on earth shall be loosed in heaven" (Mt 18:18, RSV). Lazarus passes out of the tomb, for God has fulfilled His promise of mercy. We must lead the already putrid dead man to penance. The rest will be performed by the minister of the Church: "Unbind him, and let him go" (Jn 11:44, RSV).

Nonetheless, beloved brothers, nobody is disposed nor prepared to do this kind of penance, but if there is any reason to come, let nobody despair either. The traitor Judas died not so much on account of the crime that he committed but rather because he despaired of mercy. He was not deserving of mercy, and this is why the light did not illuminate his heart so that he may make haste to receive pardon from Him whom he had betrayed. Through despair, he committed suicide and strangled himself by hanging himself. What he did to his body also took place in his soul …

The pagans have a custom of insulting Christians on account of the penance that is carried out in the Church. The Catholic Church had to affirm the legitimacy of penance against the claims of certain heresies. Indeed, there were people who claimed that certain sins must be excluded from penance. These opponents were themselves excluded from the Church and became heretics. Holy Mother Church does not refuse her mercy for any sin. This was the source of insults expressed by certain pagans who did not know what they were talking about. They have not yet arrived at the Word of God, which gives eloquence to the tongues of children. They say, "You ensure that men will sin by promising pardon to them if they do penance. This is laxity and not education …"

As it is fitting to refute them, learn to do so, beloved brothers, for the Lord's mercy has disposed all things for the best in the Church. They say that we give permission to sin because we promise refuge in penance. Now, if the entrance of penance were closed, would not this or that sinner, on the contrary, heap up sin upon sin, and indeed do so all the more as he despairs of never being pardoned? Indeed, he would say to himself,

"I have sinned and committed a crime. There is no longer any pardon for me. Penance is powerless. Will I be damned? Why not live as is pleasing to me? Since I will find no mercy in the hereafter, here-below, I will indulge my desires. Why should I deprive myself of them? . . ."

So that we may not increase our sins through despair, the harbor of penance has been prepared for us. And, conversely, so that we may not increase the number of our sins through presumption, the day of our death remains uncertain.[8]

From the time when penance became private and secret, the Church gradually established the practice of also having recourse to penance for everyday faults. However, this in no way contradicts the ancient rule of non-repetition, as the two practices do not have the same object.

Thus, whereas the ecclesial institution from the time of the High Middle Ages onward requiring one to confess one's sins at regular intervals is literally opposed to the ancient rule of non-repetition for what pertains to mortal sins, this does not mean that the new form that was taken up for ecclesial penance with the introduction of private penance (and, ultimately, its universal substitution for public penance) would truly represent a break with what penance was in antiquity. It is a question of development, not abolition and replacement by something else.

A Second Tension: The Conflict between Mercy and Strictness

{930} This conflict is found in every society. Strictness assures that society prevails over the individual (in the case when the use of his freedom is opposed to it). On the other hand, mercy or "clemency" comes to the aid of the individual against the sometimes inhuman requirements of society (requirements that are often unjustly aggravated by the personal aggressiveness and egoism of those who exercise the authority of society in relation to a given guilty person). Clemency is justified by the fact that the person is never completely enclosed within the limits of an earthly society, whatever it may be. However, it is necessarily limited, not only by the requirements

---

8. St. Augustine, in Vogel, *Le pécheur et la pénitence dans l'Église ancienne*, 116–18.

of society's defense (which also are, at least implicitly, the requirements of the person, who cannot live without society), but also and more profoundly, by the requirements of the good. Were society not to punish the person who perpetrates evil would mean that society is not interested in this good and, therefore, in itself evil (at least when the evil in question is concerned with society itself, being set in opposition to and attacking the good in relation to which the society itself is defined and which is the justification of social authority).

In the society that is the Church, this conflict is increased by the fact that her constitutive good is transcendent. It is the very Good of God, shared with men in and by the Church. Consequently, the evil against which she must react does not concern only herself. Rather, it is an evil committed against God, sin. She cannot judge the sinner only in her own name and sovereignly. Rather, she must do so in God's name, by His authority, and in function of God's requirements.

What are these requirements? As regards sinful man, to whom Christ was sent, there is only mercy. The Church has the mission of announcing to all men the complete remission of sins in Christ and of being the instrument of this through baptism. The only requirement is faith. However, he who refuses to believe does not belong to the Church. Such a person's sins do not involve her. The same is not the case for the sins that are committed by those who are baptized, who are her own. Through their sins, such people cannot be opposed to Christ and to the Father without being opposed to her, and she cannot remain indifferent to their sins without being an accomplice in them. (If we can say that she is not herself sinful through the sins of her members, this is precisely because she rejects these sins, which she condemns.)

Here is where the conflict between mercy and strictness plays out. To fail to punish the sin would be to accept it, to participate in it, and to offend God along with the sinner. This would also lead one to demoralize the other members by relativizing the requirements of the Gospel by remaining indifferent to their fidelity to the Gospel and to baptism after having preached to them that this fidelity is the very condition for salvation. However, to punish it as is intrinsically merited by an offense committed against God would be to definitively reject the guilty person who, by sinning, has voluntarily separated himself from Christ and has rejected salvation.

At once aware of Christ's merciful designs for sinners (for which we can find numerous and certain scriptural testimonies) and of the power that she has received for remitting the sins committed by the baptized, the Church has always refused to follow the rigorist current which excluded the sinner from mercy when he fell after baptism. (Thus, she opposed people like Tertullian after he became a Montanist, as well as Novatian.) However, she has also refused to give herself over to unconditioned indulgence and for centuries maintained the requirements of the divine strictness in the form of long, hard, and humiliating penitential works. Given the juridical spirit mixed in with it, penance understood along these lines became impractical for most Christians. In principle, this led to the triumph of strictness. However, given that the Church could not excommunicate nearly the whole of her members, it in fact led to the lamentable situation that we find described in an ancient life of St. Columba (in relation to Gaul and Germany) concerning the arrival of the Irish missionaries at the end of the sixth century: "It is only with great difficulty that we can find the remedies of penance and love of mortification even in a few places."[9]

Then, there were the penitentials with their very high "fees," immediately mitigated by "redemptions."[10] In the end, this led to the situation that we still know: absolution accorded without any burdensome satisfaction (though not without requirements for conversion and changing one's life, which can themselves be very burdensome). Or, rather, we could say that confession of sins has itself become the principal satisfaction required. However, at this moment, a kind of imbalance appeared, and this confession followed by absolution, practically lacking any form of satisfaction, seemed to many people to be a purely formalistic and empty ritual.

---

9. See Jonas (of Bobbio), *S. Columbani vita*, PL 87:1011–46. [Tr. note: Fr. Nicolas cites this as cols. 1–17.]

10. See Vogel, *Le pécheur et la penitence au Moyen-Age*, cited above.

Nonetheless, we must not let the rigor of the penitential works required in ancient penance mask its merciful character, which in reality remained predominant. Indeed, these works were accompanied by prayers and supplications in which the entire Church participated. This means that they were not considered as being self-sufficient for obtaining divine pardon and reconciliation with the Church. Thus, the essential role of such works is not to compensate for satisfactions that he has been unduly accorded, bringing about such recompense through voluntary afflictions. Rather, their essential role is to express and concretize the penitent's own internal repentance. For this reason, they were radically relativized, and the development that has so radically modified the Church's penitential practice does not eliminate the coherence which exists between the current form (which is so different) and the ancient forms. However, we can ask whether or not it is a good thing to completely suppress such penitential works, for that which is relative is not, for all that, useless.

A Third Tension: The Antinomy between the External Character of Ecclesial Recollection and the Interior Character of the Divine Pardon

{931} This antinomy seems to be resolved by the expression: "Those whose sins you remit will have their sins remitted." Nonetheless, the difficulty remains in place if one thinks, on the one hand, that the divine pardon cannot be conceived as being an interior grace (and not a purely juridical act) and, on the other hand, that it has a free act (i.e., conversion, which itself is also completely interior) as a necessary condition. It is not clear how this is compatible with a juridical procedure like that which the Church must institute.

Moreover, this unease has been noticeable since the Church's beginning. Such great insistence was placed on the divine origin of pardon and on the necessity of undertaking penitential works that the role of the Church seemed to be reduced to praying to God with the penitent and indicating the ways of penance to him. Or else, then (a little later on, with St. Augustine), her role came to consist in externally unbinding the person whom God already internally pardoned, now integrating him into the ecclesiastical community:

We must examine the circumstances (that accompany sins) and then employ the power to bind or unbind. We must examine the fault and the penance that followed. We will absolve those to whom the all-powerful God has already given the grace of repentance. For absolution will be efficacious only if it follows the decision of an internal judge. The famed resurrection of Lazarus, who was dead for four days, stands in proof of what we say. Indeed, it demonstrates that the Lord first called Lazarus and granted life to his corpse, saying, "Lazarus, come forth" (Jn 11:43). Then only, when Lazarus had already had life rendered unto him, he was unbound by the disciples: "Unbind him, and let him go" (Jn 11:44, RSV).

Behold, therefore, the disciples who unbind him who was already alive and whom the Master first had raised from the dead. If the disciples had unbound Lazarus while he was still dead, they would have exposed his rotten state, which was beyond their power. The conclusion that we draw from this is that we must absolve by our pastoral authority those whom we know have already been vivified by grace. This rebirth is made manifest, prior to our absolution, by the confession of sins. Lazarus was not told, "Be reborn." Rather, he was told, "Come forth."

Every sinner, inasmuch as he hides his fault in his conscience, remains a prisoner, sunk into the shadows. The dead man comes into the light when the sinner spontaneously confesses his faults. Therefore, Lazarus is told, "Come forth." It is as though one said to the man who is entombed in his sin: "Why do you hide your crime inside yourself? Come forth into the light by confession, you who are closed up on account of your refusal to confess."

Therefore, let the sinner come forth. That is, let him confess his sin. The disciples will unbind him who comes forth from his tomb, just as the shepherds of the Church must remove the penalty that he who was not ashamed to confess merited. I will add indeed that the shepherds will carefully weigh out their decision to bind or unbind. However, whether the shepherd justly or unjustly binds, his decision must be respected by the flock of the faithful, otherwise the man who perhaps is bound unjustly may merit this injustice on account of another fault. Let the shepherd guard against binding and unbinding without discernment. The believer who is under the authority of a shepherd will dread being bound, even unjustly; let him not balk boldly against even an unjust sentence, otherwise, bound unjustly, his pride and haughty recriminations will be the cause of a fault which would otherwise not exist.[11]

---

11. See St. Gregory, in Vogel, *Le pécheur et la penitence au Moyen-Age*, 136.

Nonetheless, unless the Church had recourse (like Tertullian as a Montanist) to a special revelation,[12] how could she know with certitude that the "internal judge" decided to pardon this sinner? As a matter of fact, the act of reconciliation by the Church is the sign of this verdict of pardon, whence came the increasingly important place acknowledged for the Church's act. It is sacramental. That is, it is a sign and (instrumental) cause of the divine pardon. It is not because she knows that God pardoned the sinner that the Church then reconciles him. (Indeed, how could she know this?) It is by reconciling that she signifies God's own pardon and brings it to the penitent. From St. Leo's perspective, writing in the fifth century, it was a divine arrangement "that God's pardon could only be obtained through supplications and prayers" and that Christ entrusted the leaders of the Church with the power "to give those who confess their sin a penitential work to be performed and to admit to the sacraments, through the door of reconciliation, those who have been purified by a saving satisfaction."[13]

The juridical character of the Church's act came to be increasingly emphasized from the time that the penitentials were introduced. However, we will see that the central knot of the theological problem involved in ecclesial penance continues to be that of explaining the relationship that must be established between, on the one hand, this procedure and the judgment of reconciliation that terminates it, and on the other hand, the internal conversion of the penitent and the divine pardon.

THE SACRAMENTAL NATURE OF ECCLESIASTICAL PENANCE

{932} The sacramental septenary was enumerated for the first time by Peter Lombard,[14] and penance is listed therein. He then treats each individual sacrament, including penance, one by one.[14b] Moreover, this is presented as though it were a received doctrine, which

---

12. See Tertullian, *De pudicitia*, CSEL 2, col. 1326.
13. See St. Leo, *Epistolae*, PL 54:1011–12 (ep. 108.2).
14. See §714 above. Lombard, *Sententiae*, bk. 4, d. 2, ch. 1.
14b. See ibid., dd. 14–22.

then in fact immediately became classical. The Second Council of Lyon presents the sacramental septenary as being a doctrine to be held *de fide*, and from then it definitively entered into the Magisterium's teaching.

The relatively recent nature of "confession" in the form familiar to us, as the constitutive part of the rite of penance, poses a problem. If it is a sacrament, it must have been instituted by Christ. However, can we indeed say that it was instituted by Him? And if so, in what way was it so instituted?

Institution by Christ

{933} At the Council of Trent, in order to respond to the violent attacks expressed by the reformers against the obligatory character of confession in the Catholic Church, the Council Fathers strove to establish that the institution of the sacrament of penance goes back to Christ Himself.[15] They reasoned out this claim in the following manner. First of all, Christ gave the power of the keys to His apostles and to their successors. Now, this power (of binding and unbinding) cannot be exercised without the judge knowing the sins that he must absolve or retain. This recognition can only be reached through confession, at least as regards hidden faults. Therefore, confession was instituted by Christ Himself. From this, the conclusion was reached that it was of divine right.[16]

This reasoning has become classic. However, it is difficult to see how it accords with the fact that throughout the centuries ecclesial penance has been realized by other ways than by "confession" such as it is practiced today. On the other hand, we cannot say that it is a human invention—unless we wished to openly contradict the Council.

What we must do is reflect on the notion of how Christ can be said to institute a sacrament. The Church is the primordial sacrament. She is the sacrament of Christ's presence and redemptive action in history, from His ascension up to the end of time. She was

---

15. See Cavallera, "Le décret du concile de Trente," and "Le sacrament de penitence au concile de Trente," *Bulletin de littérature ecclésiastique* 24 (1923): 172–201.

16. See Trent, session 14, "Doctrinal Decree on the Sacrament of Penance," November 25, 1551, ch. 5.

founded as a sacrament, and her original sacramentality is what is communicated to the rites that we call sacraments.[17]

This does not mean that she would have the power to create such rites by herself. The "signifier" in the sacramental action is Christ. It falls to Him alone to confer a meaning upon an action, along with its corresponding efficacy in relation to the mysteries of salvation, which belong to Him. However, in order for this essential role as "signifier" to be His alone, we do not need to say that He Himself would have chosen in a determinate manner the rite that ultimately comes to signify, as he did for the Eucharist, in which He commanded the Church to perform anew what He Himself did. It suffices that He would have expressly given the Church a distinct sanctifying power so that the fundamental sacramentality of this power would tend, by Christ's institution, to be expressed and exercised in a distinct sacramental rite.

The Determination of the Rite by the Church and Its Variations

{934} In the present case, what is fundamental is what the Council of Trent says in the first two chapters [of this decree]. In its first chapter, it is said that Christ expressly gave His Church this sanctifying power which consists in the remission of sins committed after baptism. In the second chapter, it is said that this power is distinct. This suffices to establish that Christ Himself instituted the sacrament of penance, for in virtue of the Church's own essential sacramentality, she can exercise such a sanctifying power in no other way than sacramentally.

To render an account of what Trent says about the institution of confession by Christ, we must note well that the sacrament of penance could not exist without some form or rite. Even if the rite chosen by the Church is new in relation to the preceding rite, it always remains the sacrament instituted by Christ and is not a purely human invention.

Now, we must add that this rite can be chosen only in function of the proper requirements of the sanctifying power that it is a

---

17. See §732 above.

question of exercising, and the Church is continually assisted by the Holy Spirit in the determination of this rite. These requirements include a juridical form and, therefore, a role attributed to confession inasmuch as it expresses the sinner's repentance concerning the precise faults that he has committed. (Thus, we find the classical argument before us anew.) Ancient penance included such a confession. However, its role was, above all, introductory, such repentance being manifested moreover through the penitential works and the penitent's request for prayers.

Therefore, we cannot exclude the possibility of an external development of the rite of penance. However, in order for this development to be acceptable for (and accepted by) the Church, it will need to preserve what is essential in the exercise of this power of remitting sins. On the one hand, it will require the real repentance of the sinner, obviously including the renunciation of one's sins. (In other words, it must first of all include the renunciation of the very sins thus repented of. However, one must repent of all of one's sins, for if sins are multiple and varied, the state of sin is an [all-embracing] whole). On the other hand, it will require the external manifestation of this repentance and of this renunciation, as well as the reconciliation of the sinner brought about by the Church in the form of a definitive judgment.

This is what enables us to say that the exercise of the power of remitting sins belongs by divine right to the leaders of the Church. Moreover, the most ancient tradition requires that he who (even with the bishop's commission) exercises this power must be a priest. This fact again corresponds to the general notion of the Church's sacramentality. Through the Church, Christ is the one who remits sins, and the role of the priest is to represent Christ sacramentally.*

Therefore, it is childish to object that confession is not found in the Gospel, as though this were an argument against one's obligation to make use of the sacrament. It has always been the case that the sinful baptized person has been reconciled with the Church through

---

* N.B. On the problem that the privileged role of "confessors" poses here for the reconciliation of apostates, see Poschmann, *Pénitence et onction des maladies*, 70–73. For the question of confession to laymen in the Middle Ages, see Amédée Teetaert, *La confession aux laïcs dans l'Église latine depuis le VIIIe siècle jusqu'au XIVe siècle* (Paris: Gabalda, 1926).

one of her own actions. From the Middle Ages onward, the Church has performed such an act in the form of confession and solely in this form. For this reason, one is obligated to confess when one has ruptured one's relationship with Christ (and, consequently, with the Church)—just as it is obligatory for the Christian to return to Christ and to the Father when he has turned away through sin.

16

The Theology of the Sacrament of Penance

FORMATION OF THE THEOLOGY OF THE SACRAMENT OF PENANCE

Before St. Thomas

{935} The* elaboration of the theology of the sacrament of penance was the work of scholasticism. Fundamentally, we find that scholastic

---

* See the following texts: Paul Anciaux, *La théologie du sacrament de penitence au XIIe siècle* (Louvain: Nauwelaerts, 1949). Louis Braeckmans, *Confession et communion au Moyen Age et au concile de Trente* (Gembloux: Duculot, 1971). Ferdinand Cavallera, "Le sacrement de penitence au concile de Trente," *Bulletin de littérature ecclésiastique* 24 (1923): 172–201. Roy J. Deferrari, *Hugh of Saint Victor on the Sacraments of the Christian Faith (De sacramentis)* (Cambridge, Mass.: The Medieval Academy of America, 1951). Hyacinthe-François Dondaine, *L'attrition suffisante* (Paris: Vrin, 1943). Christian Duquoc, "Réconciliation réelle et réconciliation sacramentelle," *Concilium* 61 (1971): 25–34. Anton Eppacher, "Die 'Generalabsolution' bei den Scholastikern," *Zeitschrift für katholische Theologie* 90 (1968): 385–421. G. D'Ercola, "Notes sur les recherches concernant la collégialité épiscopale," *Concilium* 31 (1968): 125–37. John Fitzsimons, *Penance: Virtue and Sacrament* (London: Burns and Oates, 1969). Thomas Jude Jatosz, "Sacramental Penance in Alexander of Hales," *Franziskanische Studien* (Paderborn) 29 (1969): 302–46. Hubert Jedin, "La nécessité de la confession privée selon le concile de Trente," *La Maison-Dieu* 104 (1970): 88–115. José Luis Larrabe, "Permanencia y adaptacijón histórica en el Sacramento de la penitencia según Santo Tomás," *Miscellanea Comillas* 53 (1970): 127–62; "Estructuras y perspectivas en el sacramento de la penitencia," *Lumen* (Lisboa) 19 (1970): 353–58; and "La Penitencia," *Manresa* 43, no. 166 (1971): 47–58. J. McCue, "La penitence en tant que signe sacramental distinct," *Concilium* 61 (1971): 49–57. Harry McSorley, "La foi nécessaire pour le sacrement de penitence: la doctrine de Luther et celle du concile de Trente," *Concilium* 61 (1971): 91–100. Charles Meyer, *The Thomistic Concept of Justifying Contrition* (Mundelein, Ill.: Seminarium Sanctae Mariae ad Lacum, 1949). Hugh Patton, *The Efficacy of Putative Attrition in the Doctrine of the Theologians of the XVI and XVII Centuries* (Rome: Herder, 1966). Joseph Périnelle, *L'attrition d'après le concile de Trente et d'apreès Saint Thomas d'Aquin* (Kain: Revue des Sciences Philosophiques et Théologiques, 1927). Carl Peter, "Renewal of Penance

thinkers profoundly analyzed the notions of sin and the situation of the sinner before God and the Church.

Sin is essentially constituted by the sinner's *aversio*. By sinning, man turns away from God (*avertit se a Deo*). This leaves two traces. First, there is the *macula*, that is, the state of sin, the situation of man who has thus turned away from God (from His light, whence arises the stain of the *macula*). Then there is the *reatus*, which consists in the fact that the sinner, on account of his sin, deserves punishment. Moreover, by turning away from God, the sinner also turns away from the Church and deserves to be sanctioned by her even here-below.

Therefore, pardon cannot only involve the sin inasmuch as it is past. It also involves the sinner, freeing him from the sinful state in which he finds himself. However, given that he turns away by his will, becoming one who is *adversus*, meaning that this situation is essentially constituted by his free will, pardon cannot be thought of without a contrary movement of his will returning to God: the "conversion" that abolishes and redresses the *aversio*. Conversely, because the "conversion" abolishes the *aversio* in which sin consists, this sin is suppressed and, therefore, "pardoned" in this very act of conversion. And true penance, without which no pardon can exist, is inspired by charity:

Therefore, he who repents through fear is still a slave, for he dreads the rod. He is not yet a son who, because he loves his father, awaits the inheritance that comes from him . . This is why anyone whose repentance is marked by fear does not merit to be pardoned by this repentance. However, he who grants fear so as to inculcate, by means of fear, the need to repent, himself grants love with the repentance so that the penitent may be worthy of pardon. He was first warned through the beginning of wisdom so that he might then be appropriately thankful toward his benefactor. Therefore, why indeed does one say that fear is the beginning of wisdom if not because someone, having embraced the fear of the Lord and

and the Problem of God," *Theological Studies* 30 (1969): 489–97, and "L'intégrité de la confession et le concile de Trente," *Concilium* 61 (1971): 91–100. Alred Vanneste, "La théologie de la penitence chez quelques maîtres parisiens de la première moitié du XIIIe siècle," *Ephemerides Theologicae Lovanienses* 28 (1952): 24–28. George Hunston Williams, *Anselm: Communion and Atonement* (St. Louis, Mo.: Concordia, 1960). [Tr. note: Fr. Nicolas also includes a reference to "Donnelly" and "W. A. Newman" which have no correlatives in the bibliography.]

the duties that it entails, will be forearmed by the divine mercy before triumphing, through wisdom, over his sinful conduct? If one lacks penitential lamentations and the brightness of good works, how could such a person fail to be rejected as being insipid?[1]

Thus, the problem is enclosed in strict limits. The difficulty consists in determining the role of the sacrament in the event of God's pardon which is practically identical with conversion.

Abelard. For Abelard, who here shows himself still to be a profound theologian, God's pardon consists essentially in the fact that God inspires contrition in the sinner. However, this contrition, by itself, eradicates sin and all damnation:

> Therefore, as soon as there is true repentance—namely, repentance arising from love of God—even the slightest of scorn for God no longer remains ... and given that God no longer finds any sin in the penitent, he does not find in him any cause for damnation. With sin thus being eradicated, damnation—that is, the infliction of eternal punishment—disappears, and to say that the prior sin is pardoned by God is to say that God has lifted from him the eternal punishment that he had merited by this sin. However, although God no longer finds in the penitent something that he should punish by an endless punishment, one says that He remits the punishment merited by the prior sin when, by inspiring the groans of penance, He rendered him worthy of His pardon. In other words, He made it be the case that eternal punishment would no longer be owed to such a person, so that if he leaves this life in this state, only salvation is possible for him.[2]

However, what then is the use of confession? Abelard here proposes a solution which, despite its certainly unsatisfying character, opens up an interesting way that on the whole will be followed: it is necessary on account of how it humbles the penitent. Moreover, the priest's absolution is concerned with temporal punishment, that is, with the punishments that the Church has the office of inflicting. He reduced the "power of the keys" to this, even if he did not limit the beneficiaries of this power to the apostles alone, to the exclusion of their successors. This was one of the grave accusations made against him by St. Bernard at the Council of Sens.

Hugh of St. Victor. Substantially, the solution to the problem is

---

1. See Robert Pulleyn, *Sententiarum* VIII, PL 186:852–53.
2. Abelard, *In epistulam ad romanos*, PL 178:783–978.

the same for Hugh of St. Victor. God alone remits sins, doing so by inspiring true penance. The priest's absolution is only declarative. He more forcefully highlights the necessity of confession and of absolution (thereby making his doctrine more "orthodox"). However, he does this at the cost of a grave theological inconsistency. In short, he thinks that the remission of one's fault by God does not by itself suppress the damnation merited by the sin! Thus, the role of confession and of absolution is to "unbind" the penitent from this *reatus damnationis*.

In the line of Abelard. The general line of thought here sought to explain the role of confession and of absolution in a better way, for such an explanation was not provided by Abelard. Faithful to the Abelardian doctrine, Zachary of Besançon nonetheless introduced an important modification into it. He held that if the sinner presents himself for confession without contrition (and thus without yet being "converted"), he can receive the grace of conversion (and, therefore, the remission of sins) from the priest. This occurs either by the priest's exhortation and prayer or by the penance that he imposes. Therefore, it occurs through an action that is still situated in the psychological domain more than in the sacramental domain.[3]

Like most theologians of the age, Peter Lombard[4] affirmed the necessity of contrition, "which does not exist without charity," in order that one may receive the remission of sins. He also affirmed the sufficiency of contrition, rejecting the idea proposed by Hugh of St. Victor (i.e., that even if the penitent were contrite, he would be subject to damnation). He thus explains the power of the keys by reference to the satisfaction (the external penance) that the priest imposes (thus "binding") or by which he accords dispensation (thus "unbinding"). Moreover, by the mere fact of imposing satisfaction, he shows and signifies that the sinner was pardoned by God, and he imposes on him no satisfaction whose penance is judged to be insufficient. One will note this curious reversal of terms of the Gospel's promise: when the priest "binds" the penitent by imposing on him the obligation of a satisfactory work, he "unbinds in heaven"

---

3. See Anciaux, *La théologie du sacrament de penitence au XIIe siècle*, 216–17 and 318–21.
4. See Lombard, *Sententiae*, vol. 4, d. 18.

(or, rather, signifies that it has been unbound in heaven). Moreover, it seems that this depends on the priest's personal judgment, which remains susceptible to indecipherable self-deception. Hence, it is not clear how confession and absolution can constitute a "sacrament" (i.e., a sign given by God Himself and therefore certain by itself).

Thus, we find ourselves continuously faced by the same difficulty. Profoundly convinced that there cannot be a remission of sins without contrition, nor contrition without charity, they are led to ask whether one is enabled to approach the sacrament of penance precisely because one has returned to God through grace and charity. This makes it quite difficult for us to explain the necessity and sacramental efficacy of confession! Some thinkers sought to give a role to the priest so that we could say that the penitent obtains the grace of contrition by means of his prayer (e.g., William of Auvergne, then the great Franciscans, Alexander of Hales and St. Bonaventure). As regards the priest's power to bind and unbind exercised through absolution, the line of Abelard and Peter Lombard makes it hardly conceivable, except in reference to temporal punishments and to reconciliation with the Church. Likewise, St. Albert the Great will furnish St. Thomas with the idea that the acts of the penitent are the "matter" of the sacrament. However, for him, they are informed by the grace that inspires contrition, not by absolution. The sacrament of penance is thus defined as being a sorrow penetrated by grace and manifested by external signs.[5] The sole effect of absolution is the remission of temporal punishment. Hugh of Saint-Cher was the first one who attributed to "confession" (with absolution) the power to (instrumentally) cause the grace of contrition: "Indeed, through the power of confession and absolution, one is given either a growth in sorrow and detestation of sin or the grace by which attrition gives birth to contrition."[5b]

St. Thomas's Position

{936} The principal texts of St. Thomas concerning the sacrament of penance are found in *In IV Sent*, dd. 14–22 (esp. dd. 14 and 17),

---

5. See St. Albert the Great, *Opera Omnia*, ed. A. Borgnet (Paris: 1890–99), 29:740.
5b. See Poschmann, *Pénitence et onction des maladies*, 147.

the opusculum *De forma absolutionis poenitentiae sacramentalis* (composed in 1269–72) which is principally concerned with the efficacy of the sacraments and the conditions holding on the side of the subject for this efficacy to exist, and *ST* III, qq. 84–90, which is a treatise on the sacrament of penance which unfortunately was left incomplete.*

The following points can be taken as furnishing a kind of summary of St. Thomas's position concerning the relation of "confession" (understanding this term as including the admission of sins by the penitent and the imposition of satisfaction and absolution by the priest) to the remission of sins:

1. The acts of the penitent constitute the matter of the sacrament. The absolution of the priest is its form (*ST* III, q. 84, a. 5). This is not original.

2. The principal act among these (i.e., contrition, confession, and satisfaction) is contrition in that it is what gives the other two their saving value. However, in order for contrition to be part of the sacrament of penance, it is necessary that it be connected to the other two, at least by being ordered to them. Here we find a sketched-out form of the solution that St. Thomas will propose to the dilemma caught between the two assertions: without contrition, "confession" cannot remit sins; with contrition, it is useless, for sin would no longer exist. St. Thomas will respond that in order for contrition itself to be authentic, it must imply the *propositum* of confession (*Scriptum*, 17, 189; *De forma*, 686; *ST* III, q. 90, a. 2, ad 1).

3. Conversely, among these acts, confession (the admission of faults) is the act in which the penitential process is concretized. Penitence, in the sense whereby it designates the sacrament, principally consists in confession (*Scriptum*, 17, 508 [*sic*]). This does not imply a contradiction. Contrition is expressed by confession and is even realized by it, so that it does not exist without confession, at least the proposed idea of confession. The person who does not have the resolution to submit himself to the leaders of the Church is not held

---

* N.B. The *Scriptum* will be cited with two sets of numbers. The first is the number of the distinction and the second is the page number found in the edition edited by Moos (published by Lethielleux). For the *De forma*, refer to the numbering in the Marietti edition.

to be contrite. This is what is meant by having the sacrament *in voto* (*De forma*, 686).

4. If contrition cannot exist without confession (at least as something proposed), confession can exist without contrition. Then, it is *informis* (in the sense that one says that faith can be unformed)—see *Scriptum* 17, 473. Here is where the difficulty begins. "Unformed" confession is that which is performed without contrition. It is considered to be similar to the baptism which one comes to "fictus" and is treated in the same manner: "He who approached the sacrament in a fictive manner is not bound to receive it anew. He is only bound to confess the fiction." According to this, it seems that he who confesses without "contrition" cannot receive the effect of the sacrament. This seems to be contradicted by what follows.

5. Indeed, St. Thomas admits, on the one hand, that contrition (which does not exist without charity) immediately includes the remission of sins, so that he who approaches the sacrament already contrite receives an increase of grace, not the remission of sins (see *Scriptum*, 17, 508–10; *De forma*, 686). On the other hand, he admits that someone can approach the sacrament with "a sorrow caused by his sins, though one that does not suffice for contrition," and that in this case, if he does not put an obstacle in its way, he receives the remission of sins by virtue of absolution (see ibid.: "Therefore, it happens that certain people obtain justification in absolution itself, not having obtained it before that").

6. This disposition is imperfect, though it suffices so that the sacrament may act. (Therefore, it does not always and necessarily include a *fictio*, that is, a simulation that would render the sacrament ineffective.) St. Thomas gives this imperfect disposition the name, which was already classic, "attrition." Its principle is "servile fear" (*ST* III, q. 85, a. 5), by which "someone turns away from his sins through fear of punishments" (ibid.). On the other hand, charity is the principle of contrition, which is "penitence" properly speaking: "Through charity, sin is horrifying to someone on its own account and no longer on account of punishments [due to such sin]" (ibid.). Therefore, according to this opposition, one can say that attrition is remorse for having sinned, inspired by motives of personal interest

(which does not mean that attrition is "egoistical," for self-love is not always opposed to love of God[6]) whereas contrition is a detestation of sin inspired by love of God and concerned with sin as such (i.e., inasmuch as it is opposed to God). As Cajetan will say, "it is a horror of sin experienced as being supremely detestable"[7]—supremely so because it is even more detestable than is the greatly detestable reality of damnation.

7. In relation to conversion, attrition, without which we have no remission of sins (*ST* III, q. 86, a. 2), is part of the preparation for the grace of justification (*ST* III, q. 85, aa. 5–6; *Scriptum* 17, 130–40).

8. The efficacy of the sacrament of penance consists in producing in the attrite penitent the grace of conversion which is the very grace of justification. To resolve these apparent contradictions, only one solution is in fact possible. This grace of conversion, by which the soul decisively returns to God and, simultaneously, God returns to him by the gift of grace (i.e., by the remission of sins)—a conversion that includes an act of detestation of sin, which is nothing other than contrition[8]—is the effect of a grace from God, one given to the penitent through the ministration of the priest in confession, by absolution. This grace makes a "contrite person" out of the person who had heretofore only been an "attrite person." The formula that will become classic (one whose literal formulation goes back to William of Auvergne, although perhaps not in this precise sense) runs: "Under the action of the Church's sacramental power, the attrite penitent becomes contrite." St. Thomas did not employ it, but it alone can render account of the various elements involved in his solution.

9. Among the possible motives for attrition, in the *Scriptum* (14, 106, 114) St. Thomas speaks of a movement of love that precedes "penitence" (i.e., the virtue that has conversion as its act) and which, therefore, is not yet charity. This is given further specification (ibid., 17, 340). Note that this motive of love is not presented as something necessary which is always found in attrition.

---

6. See *ST* II-II, q. 17, a. 8, and q. 27, a. 3.
7. Tomasso de Vio Cajetan, *Quaestiones de Contritione* in Sancti Thomae Aquinatis, *Opera Omnia*, Leonine Edition (Rome: Ex Typographia Polyglotta, 1906), 12:342.
8. See *ST* I-II, q. 113, a. 5.

10. Finally, what is essential is that the sacrament of penance must cause the remission of sins only by the power of Christ's passion, which is applied to the penitent (*De forma*, 697; *ST* III, q. 85, a. 6, ad 3). This is what explains the fact that the sacrament of penance can be a cause of the remission of sins before even being conferred, for (as was already said in the second point, above) contrition produces the remission of sins only on account of the intention of confessing one's sins, an intention that contrition necessarily includes. It is not a question of saying that it would be an instrumental cause of the grace of conversion before that exists.[9] Rather, it is a question of saying that grace of conversion is bestowed upon the contrite penitent on account of this sacrament which he intends to receive. This holds in virtue of the principle that God considers that which is truly intended as being something in fact done. The comparison which frequently is made with the case of the grace of justification given before baptism lifts every doubt, for there too it is not a question of instrumental causality being exercised by an action that does not yet exist.

However, such a comparison goes even further still. Just as he who was justified without baptism really being received must nonetheless receive baptism when the occasion for its reception is presented to him, so too he who has received the divine pardon must submit himself to the power of the keys. This is so first of all because if the intention to confess one's sins is sincere, it must be realized when it becomes possible. Moreover, he must do so because the sacrament not only brings about reconciliation with God but also with the Church (*Scriptum*, 17, 3, 3, esp. 440–43; moreover, see 16, 79).

Conclusion. The considerable progress that St. Thomas brought to the theology of the sacrament of confession consists in the fact that his analysis views "contrition" as being brought about and signified by the sacrament. (Thus, he is one with all his contemporaries and predecessors in thinking that it is the necessary and sufficient condition for the remission of sins, something identical with the act of rejecting sin, which necessarily includes the act of conversion.)[10] The dilemma stated that the remission of sins is the fruit

---

9. In contrast to what is said in Poschmann, *Pénitence et onction des maladies*, 151.
10. See *ST* I-II, q. 113, a. 5.

either of contrition or of the sacrament. In the former case, it is not clear what purpose the sacrament would serve, and in the latter, it is not clear how a sinner can become just without contrition. Breaking this dilemma, St. Thomas discovered an objective order between contrition (or "penitence as a virtue") and the sacrament ("penitence as a sacrament"*). Nonetheless, obscurities remain here, standing in need of illumination. However, the solution to the problem and to all the questions connected to it must be sought out in this direction.

From St. Thomas to the Council of Trent

{937} Under the action of the Church's sacramental power, the penitent passes from being attrite to being contrite. This formula became classic. However, this remains ambiguous and can be interpreted in two ways. On the one hand, under the power of the sacrament, attrition becomes contrition, which would mean that the sinner's repentance (the *displicentia peccati*) would remain the same, meaning that his will would therefore remain unchanged. Confession (and absolution) would be the only source from which he would receive this surplus which was lacking as the sufficient condition for the remission of sins (i.e., so that he may be "contrite"). St. Thomas recognized this formulation and explicitly rejected it. On the other hand, one could interpret it as meaning that the penitent, under the power of the sacrament, would become contrite through a new act, namely, contrition. Thus, one means that the sacrament, by its own, proper efficacy, changes the penitent's will, making him perform an act which he had not hitherto come forward to perform. These are the two theological paths that are opened up in this matter, and each of them have a famous name attached to them: the way of Scotus and the way of Cajetan.

The way taken by Scotus

{938} With[11] Scotus, the ancient problematic that sought to situate the sacrament of penance in the line of the internal and personal

---

* [Tr. note: Throughout this chapter, I have at times chosen to translate French *pénitence* as "penance," even where, perhaps, "penitence" might have been justified.]

11. See Dondaine, *L'attrition suffisant*, 16–26, and Poschmann, *Pénitence et onction des malades*, 160–68.

movement of one's return to God is rejected. There are two ways or manners of returning to God when one has sinned: the way of internal conversion and that of the sacrament. The latter is proposed as being the surest and least onerous means. In virtue of a merciful divine disposition, "confession," as something undertaken by the penitent, takes the place of this interior return to God, of this detestation of sin, which is the condition for one to receive the remission of sins from God at the end of the internal process of returning to Him.

The first way of returning to God proceeds by means of what Scotus calls "sufficient attrition," which is the repentance for sins provoked by natural insights and sentiments (doubtlessly not without the aid of grace, though this is not specified). This disposition is called "sufficient" because God mercifully has decided to bestow pardon upon the person who thus repents to some extent:

> No disposition suffices more for this justification than this attrition that is perfectly determined as a moral act, so that, at the last moment (or at the moment that God fixed as that up to which attrition must last so as to merit justification *de congruo*), God infuses grace, and sin is immediately purely and simply effaced.[12]

Thus, without being changed in itself (i.e., in its motivation and its object), this imperfect act of repentance (i.e., attrition), becomes repentance properly speaking (i.e., contrition). Thus, Scotus rejoins, at least in appearance, the traditional idea that man returns to grace through contrition. In reality, what man contributes in this process is sufficient attrition, on account of which God pardons and gives grace, which means that this attrition is held as being contrition.

The second way of returning to God proceeds by the external process of confession and absolution. From the perspective of the sinner, all that is required is the simple sincerity of one's action. To confess one's sins means that one repents of having committed them and that, at least at the moment when one confesses them, one is detached from them. This suffices for confession to be sacramental and

---

12. See Scotus, *In IV Sent*, d. 14, q. 2 (18:74–76). [Tr. note: This citation of Scotus is evidence of some defect in the edition being consulted by Fr. Nicolas or one of his sources. There is no indication if this is from the *Lectura*, the *Ordinatio*, or perhaps (though less likely) one of the *Reportationes*.]

therefore for the absolution that follows it also to be sacramental and to produce its effect:

> Therefore, there is not only the penitent person who is attrite for a determined time (up to the moment that is fixed by God) who receives at this last moment the grace that effaces sin in virtue of a *de congruo* merit (i.e., a merit that is fitting). Beyond such a person, he who only wills to receive the sacrament from the Church, so long as he is free from the obstacle of a mortal sin currently being perpetrated or chosen, receives the effect of the sacrament (i.e., penitential grace) on account of a convention established by God, not on account of his merit. In this way, the person who is barely attrite, not even having sufficient attrition for meriting the remission of sins, while nonetheless willing to receive the sacrament of penance in the form that it is given in the Church and also free from the (current) obstacle of a mortal sin, receives the effect of the sacrament (i.e., penitential grace) at the final moment of the uttering of the words in which this sacrament is efficacious. He does not receive it because he merits it but rather does so in virtue of a convention established by God, who acts in this sacrament so as to produce the effect for which He instituted it. Without this, we could not easily see how the sacrament of penance is the second plank of salvation if this sacrament were never the means by which one could regain the grace that one had lost so long as one needed attrition as a preliminary condition and contrition as a completive disposition.[13]

Note that this mediocre attrition, which is even insufficient for meriting God's pardon in any manner, remains after receiving the sacrament as before. The grace and charity given by God with the remission of sins on account of the sacrament makes it into a form of "contrition" by a mere extrinsic denomination. However, in the sinner who is thus pardoned, there is no real repentance for his sin (or, at least, such a repentance is not required).

The Scotist school will come to accentuate this minimization of the dispositions required by the penitent, as well as this voluntarist character of the remission of sins brought about by the sacrament:

> Here a mere lack of indisposition suffices because the grace [in question] is conferred on account of a convention established by God, not by reason of merit—without any internal movement, only virtually willing to have displeasure in sin (i.e., only willing to perform one's confession correctly,

---

13. Op. cit, 158. See Dondaine, *L'attrition suffisant*, 19–21.

which constitutes a virtual repentance, since confession of itself is an act of repentance).

These formulas will bring about scandal and will be vigorously condemned by the reformers. Peter de Soto will write in 1550: "The heretics of these days are extremely shocked by this assertion: 'Sin is remitted for the adult without there being need for a good movement of heart …'" At Trent, it was written: "Falsely, therefore, do some accuse Catholic writers as if they maintained that the sacrament of penance confers grace without any good disposition on the part of those receiving it; this is something that the Church of God never taught or accepted."[14] Thus, the Council, by pushing back against this criticism, disassociated itself from these imprudent writers … who were all too self-consistent in their thought.

The way taken by Cajetan

{939} In the meantime, the contrary tendency also developed, one which accentuates the dispositions required by the penitent so that the sacrament may bear its fruits. This tendency found its resolute and coherent theorist in Cajetan.[15]

Without restriction, he takes up the position of the older theologians: there is no remission of sins (and therefore no effect by the sacrament of penance) without contrition, which itself is a remorse for sin inspired solely by the love of God above all.

The classical objection, which had been emphatically highlighted by Scotus, stated that if the sacrament of penance presupposes contrition, which itself suffices for the remission of sins, then the sacrament would serve no purpose. To this, Cajetan responded by proposing a distinction, one that was as new and as scarcely founded on the tradition as was that which Scotus offered by means of the distinction of two ways of returning to God. According to Cajetan, two kinds of contrition exist. One is "unformed" (in the same sense as when one speaks of "unformed faith," meaning faith that exists in a person who does not have charity), which is a repentance for sin which is inspired by love of God above all. Hence, it is a true form

---

14. Trent, "Doctrinal Decree on the Sacrament of Penance," ch. 4, in D.-*Sch.*, no. 1678.
15. See Cajetan, *Quaestiones de Contritione*, cited above.

of contrition. However, it is only natural in character, not meriting eternal life and therefore not bearing with it the remission of sins.

The other kind of contrition is "formed" (i.e., inspired by charity), meriting eternal life and, of itself, extinguishing sin. The first is an acquired kind of contrition. Thus, he finds himself led to rejoin the preoccupation that led Scotus to his notion of "sufficient attrition." It is a question of a disposition that man can acquire by his own effort (obviously not without the aid of grace, though, nonetheless, the motivations for this repentance remain "natural"). In order for this repentance to be a sufficient disposition for receiving the sacrament of penance fruitfully, the only thing that is required is that its principal motive would at minimum already be the love of God above all else. On the other hand, he does not admit that it would of itself be sufficient for obtaining the remission of sins. By infusing grace and charity, the sacrament of penance is what will make this contrition be "formed" by changing its motive, thus making such repentance be inspired no longer by natural love but also by charity. Only, he thinks (contrary to St. Thomas[16]) that just as faith itself remains while being transformed by charity which makes it into a *fides formata*, so too acquired contrition remains itself while being supernaturalized by charity, which comes about by the power of absolution.

He also thinks, oddly enough, that the penitent can acquire interior certitude of loving God above all things and of detesting sin on its own account and not for a self-interested motive. Meanwhile, the confessor, at least in principle, can discern the signs of such repentance and can give the sacrament only on the condition that these are present.

At the Council of Trent

{940} The Council treated the sacrament of penance at its fourteenth session. As in all the other theological questions disputed there, it refused to adjudicate the differences between the Catholic [theological] schools of that time and remained content with disavowing the extreme and unacceptable consequences of either tendency. We saw

---

16. See *In IV Sent.*, d. 17, q. 2, a. 1, ad 3 qu.

this above for the Scotist tendency. For the Cajetanian tendency, the Council affirmed that attrition suffices as a disposition for the sacrament and defined this attrition as being a repentance that commonly arises from the consideration of the repulsiveness of sin or from the fear of the penalties of hell,[17] without saying that its motive is the love of God above all things. Nonetheless, note that, in the decree *De Justificatione* describing the stages of the sinner's return to God, the Council speaks about an act by which, first shaken up by fear of the divine justice and then elevated by hope, the sinner begins "to love God as the source of all justice."[18] However, this beginning of love (which refers to the Augustinian tradition) is in no way related to Cajetan's notion of the natural love of God above all else.

Controversy between the Attritionists and Contritionists

{941} The Council was sufficiently "open" so that, after it, the (in fact, beneficial) conflict between the two tendencies continued. This conflict was arrayed between the attritionists (who tended to diminish the requirements for the penitent's repentance in the sacrament) and the contritionists (who, on the contrary, accentuated them).[19] Here, the Church was content with condemning the excessive consequences of either tendency. For the rigorist tendency, see the fifteenth condemned proposition of the Jansenists[20] and, most especially, the thirty-sixth condemned proposition of the pseudo-council of Pistoia.[21] For the minimizing tendency, see the fifty-seventh laxist proposition in the [Holy Office's] Decree from 1679.[22]

---

17. See Trent, "Doctrinal Decree on the Sacrament of Penance," ch. 4, in D.-*Sch.*, no. 1678.
18. See Trent, "Decree on Justification," ch. 6, in D.-*Sch.*, no. 1526.
19. See Périnelle, *L'attrition d'après le concile de Trente et d'apreès Saint Thomas d'Aquin*, cited above.
20. See Holy Office (Pope Alexander VIII), "Decree Concerning the Errors of the Jansenists," December 7, 1690, in D.-*Sch.*, no. 2315.
21. See Pope Pius VI, *Auctorem Fidei* (Condemnation of the Pseudo-Council of Pistoia), August 28, 1794, in D.-*Sch.*, no. 2636.
22. See Holy Office (Pope Innocent XI), "Condemned Propositions of the 'Laxists,'" March 2, 1679, no. 57, in Deninger, no. 2157.

THE GRACE OF CONVERSION AND THE SACRAMENT OF PENANCE

The question at hand is that of determining the real and necessary place occupied by the sacrament of penance in the process of justification.[23]

The Remission of Sins Committed after Baptism

God remits sins by reestablishing the sinner in grace

{942} We cannot think of the remission of sins as though it were a purely juridical act, solely being God's decision not to punish man. A "new" act of God, a change in God's attitude in relation to His creature, cannot be thought of without there being a change on the part of the creature caused by this act and specifying it. The will to punish is itself thought of only in function of the created person's relationship with God arising from the creature's own act of sin. The alteration of this willing into a benevolent will can be thought of only by considering a change in the sinner's own situation in relation to God. The source for this change can only be found in God, in an act of the divine freedom, for it obviously does not depend on man's freedom to have not sinned (and therefore to not provoke the Divine Will's punishment). Therefore, we must think of the "remission of sins" as being a free act by God in relation to man, an act that must produce a real change in man.

Obviously, this act by God is an act of love, for it is a question of willing a good to a person who not only does not merit it but even has demerited this good.

By loving, God communicates Himself to His free creature. Certainly, we could (abstractly) conceive of God's love being limited to the gift of created being and life. However, it is in fact the case that God created the world so that He may personally give Himself to His free creature. What the creature loses by sinning are not the gifts of created being and life. (It only risks privations in this domain

---

23. See Anciaux, *Le sacrament de la penitence*, cited above. Paul Galtier, *De poenitentia: tractatus dogmatico-historicus*, new ed. (Rome: Universitatis Gregorianae, 1957). Nicolas, *Les profondeurs de la grâce*, 503–19.

indirectly, by way of punishment.) Instead, it loses the gift that God made of Himself through love, a gift that can only be received in love (as it is in the gift of oneself that one person wishes to give to another).

Thus, the grace of the remission of sins is not merely the preliminary condition for the restoration of the gifts of grace. It consists in this very restoration. Or, rather, it is the free love by which God (newly) loves this man who made himself be a non-son through his sin ("I am not worthy to be called your son"), thus being unworthy of love ("the unfaithful and prostituted spouse"[24]) and "unrighteous." God's love makes him a son anew ("behold, my son was dead and now is alive") deserving of love ("For the LORD has called you … like a wife of youth when she is cast off"[25]) and righteous.

God cannot love an unrighteous man. By loving the sinner with this love that pardons, He makes him righteous, bestowing grace upon him, that is, the principle for his participation in the Divine Life wherein the true and unique righteousness are found, a participation in the very righteousness of God.[26]

The gift of grace presupposes and arouses conversion of heart

{943} Obviously, no creature has a participation in the Divine Life without charity. From the time of our life here-below, personal communion with God is realized through charity. Through charity, man, even on earth, tends toward the divine good, makes it his own, and orders all of his aspirations, deeds, and his whole self to it.

If sin represents a rupture from God and the interruption of the indwelling of God's Spirit in the sinner's spirit, this is not (at least immediately) on account of a "crime" that has been committed (as though God punished by withdrawing from him who disobeyed Him). It is first of all because, at the heart of every sin, there is a preference of self in place of God, a preference which is directly opposed to charity. To love and will the divine good as such (which is the proper Good of God) is to love God more than oneself and to love oneself only in God and for God. Conversely, to love oneself above

24. See Ezek 16.
25. Is 54:6 (RSV).
26. See *ST* I-II, q. 113, a. 2.

all else is to love and will one's own good apart from the divine good. This is so even if God is considered and desired as part of one's own good. In such a case, the sinner loves Him self-referentially and not for His own sake.

This rupture from God is an existential situation, one that indeed is determined by the act of sin but that lasts after it. By the orientation that the sinful person has given to himself, he remains dynamically stretched out toward a good that differs from the divine good, one that is separated from God, *aversa*. It is of little importance that the act of sin would be behind him and in the past and even that the sinner may no longer be interested in the particular good that led him to turn away from God. What remains in him is the reason for which he committed this sin in the past, the same reason that will perhaps lead him to commit a completely different and opposed sin today—namely, disordered love of self, self-love "to the point of scorning God."[27]

It is radically impossible for the gifts of grace, which are a communication of the Divine Life and necessarily include charity, to coexist in the person who is placed in this existential situation through this *aversio a Deo*. This would represent a contradiction in the order of activity, which is here just as unthinkable as contradiction is in the order of being. As the person is the principle of activity just as much as it is of being, this would represent a kind of rending of that personhood which of necessity must be unified in all of its activities by imposing the unity of a fundamental orientation upon them. Charity can exist in a person only as one's fundamental orientation toward God and therefore as triumphing over the contrary orientation toward one's self-oriented good, thus eliminating it.

However, the person is free, and this fundamental orientation toward God can be nothing other than an act of freedom, one that includes faith and hope, though it is essentially love and the gift of oneself to God.

This act by which the sinner leaves behind his sin represents his own, proper contribution. It is the ultimate disposition to grace without which the gift of grace (and therefore the remission of sins)

---

27. See Nicolas, *Contemplation et vie contemplative en christianisme*, ch. 3.

would be unintelligible. By this, the person brings about his return to God, which the Bible so often describes in terms of being a personal and free human act.[28]

Does this mean that it would be prior to the gift of grace and, therefore, prior to charity? We have seen that this was Cajetan's position. He imagined that by means of one's own intellect and will, without sanctifying grace and without charity (therefore, naturally, though obviously not without the aid of actual grace), the sinner could modify his will's fundamental orientation. In this way, he would bring an end to the situation of being *aversus a Deo*, in which his sinful state consists, thus orienting himself entirely toward God, namely by loving Him more than himself. However, this love would not yet be the love of charity (which is infused and springs up in the soul from the presence of the Holy Spirit). Rather, it would be a natural love of God above all things.

This position is completely untenable. First of all, it includes the impossible situation in which God would continue to hold that such a person is a sinner who is distant from Him (leading even to damnation if death were to come at this moment) even though this person loves Him more than all else and has ceased to love himself by the disordered love that had been the only obstacle to his reception of charity. Here, we must have recourse to St. Augustine's beautiful metaphor: God's love is like the sun which casts its rays over all created persons, and if His rays do not penetrate certain individuals, this is because they are closed in upon themselves, bringing about such self-enclosure by means of their self-love.

Moreover, in the background of this position there is a conception of the relation of the natural order to the supernatural order (a position that is very new, not only in relation to the Patristic tradition but also in relation to St. Thomas). According to this conception the natural order continues to exist next to the supernatural order, certainly in connection with it, though keeping its own, proper consistency. Thus, the person who has withdrawn from the supernatural order by sinning can remain or be reintegrated into the natural order. The idea that a sinner, by his natural powers, could retrieve

---

28. See "Pénitence" in *Vocabulaire de théologie biblique*.

the natural love of God above all things, by pushing this conception to its limits, in fact makes its unacceptability clear. (Note that St. Thomas expressly precludes the possibility of such a natural love [of God above all things] without charity.)[29]

Indeed, if this human goodness, perfect in its own order, were possible for man without charity, the latter would be an addition that could be integrated into man's destiny only with great difficulty. It would be like something added on externally. It could be imposed on him by an external law, one that differs from that which is inscribed in the depths of his being according to which he must find his fulfillment in accord with his human perfection. This superadded law would thus seem to be somewhat arbitrary. In reality, the supernatural [order] cannot be thought of except as the fulfillment of man's destiny, a fulfillment that could have not been given to him—and in this case man would have fulfilled himself, though imperfectly, in the natural order—but which, if it is given, becomes man's only fulfillment. We cannot turn aside from this fulfillment without turning away from our own human perfection. Concretely, this means that, for man such as he has been willed and realized by God, the love of God above all things, which is the universal principle of the fulfillment of all created beings, can be realized only by charity. There can be no middle term between loving God above all things through a love of charity and loving oneself more than all things.[30]

Thus, this free act of conversion that is man's necessary disposition for God's restitution of the gifts of grace cannot be prior to the gift of grace, as it must be made in charity and because charity is given with the Holy Spirit. Here, we are faced with the essential difficulty of the theological problem concerning justification. Briefly stated, let us recall St. Thomas's solution. Inasmuch as this act of conversion has God's merciful love—the Holy Spirit—as its first cause, it is the effect of grace. Inasmuch as it proceeds from man's freedom (inasmuch as the person freely goes to God through such freedom), it is the ultimate, indispensable disposition for receiving grace. In short,

---

29. See *ST* I-II, q. 109, a. 3.
30. See Nicolas, *Contemplation et vie contemplative en christianisme*, ch. 3.

grace is given (here: rendered [*rendue*]) only to the person who converts. However, it first makes him convert.[31]

Conversion of heart never comes about without repentance

{944} When we come to understand that sin is not only a past act (or an ensemble of such acts) but rather is the current situation of the sinner who has voluntarily and freely oriented himself in a direction that is not that of the divine good (and, thus, for that reason is turned away from God), it is quite clear that the sinner cannot reorient himself toward God (and thus "be converted") without turning away from his wicked way. This implies the repudiation of his sinful orientation. Given that the person engages himself through his free act in general and especially through the act by which he chooses his fundamental orientation, this repudiation involves a kind of self-condemnation inasmuch as he had previously expressed himself in the choice that now is repudiated. This self-condemnation is what repentance is: *Poenitet me hoc fecisse*, I repent for having done that. Repentance is not only an act of the virtue of penance. It is also (and first of all) a component of the love by which the sinner converts to God, abandoning his "wicked way." It is penitent love.

Contrition

Obviously, this repentance is above all an interior act. It is the act by which the person freely releases himself from the free choice by which he preferred himself to God. In the classical language of theology, which was taken up by Trent,[32] it is called "detestation" of sin or "horror" at sin. One must understand it as meaning "hatred of my sinful self."

Many motives can provoke this choice. One can detest sin on account of its evil consequences, whether they are currently real or feared in the future. One thus detests it out of an interest that is still personal. One can detest it because one is aware, in faith, that it prevents the full realization of oneself. This is still a kind of personal interest, though one that is superior.

---

31. See *ST* I-II, q. 113.
32. See Trent, "Decree on Justification," ch. 6, in D.-*Sch.*, no. 1526, and "Doctrinal Decree on the Sacrament of Penance," ch. 4, in D.-*Sch.*, no. 1676.

The detestation of sin implied by charity has a loftier motive. Sin is detested because of what it is, because of the evil that it is, independent of its consequences. That is, it is hated for God's own sake, for it is an evil precisely as something opposed to the divine good.[33] The "sinful self" is hated as being opposed to the personal God, to the three Persons, and especially, to the Holy Spirit: "do not grieve the Holy Spirit of God"[34] Every other motive is compatible with disordered self-love. Therefore, all such motives are, by themselves, insufficient for contrition, without which no true conversion exists. However, the fact that these motives would be insufficient by themselves does not imply that they would be evil and ought to be eliminated in order for contrition to exist.

Confession and satisfaction

{945} Contrition is an interior sentiment, but it must also be externalized so that it may be fully human. It suffices to recall a fundamental principle of Christian anthropology: the human person has two dimensions—one spiritual and the other bodily. Consequently, every personal act has these two dimensions. Repentance cannot be a purely spiritual act. It must be externalized and incarnated.

The sacraments were instituted precisely for the sake of externalizing the internal act of faith in Christ the Savior.[35] Their institution corresponds to a need on the part of man, though it is a need to which Christ alone can respond, for what saves man is the redemptive passion. Christ alone can give man the means for drawing close to this passion and for being united to it through an external act that would be really salvific.

We have seen that the Church had a degree of flexibility for determining how this act should look in the case of the sacrament of penance. Nonetheless, by its very institution, it includes two elements: the confession of sins and the works of penance. However, the value and relative place of these two elements has changed through the course of history. Even though there was a confession of sins during the first centuries, contrition was primarily externalized

---

33. See *ST* I, q. 48, a. 6.
34. Eph 4:30 (RSV).
35. See §722 above.

in works of penance. Later on (and still today), confession holds this place, and the Church's strict requirements are concerned with it, as we have seen. Nonetheless, satisfaction is not totally absent, and he who confesses manifests his resolution to fulfill the external penance that will be imposed on him.

Contrition, which includes the act of conversion, is not only one's internal repentance. It necessarily requires an external concretization which cannot be just any particular concretization. It must be that which the Church, commanded by Christ the Savior (of whom she is the sacrament), determines in His name and on His authority. Today (and, indeed, from the time of the establishment of "private penance") the sacramental action in which contrition must be externalized is the confession of sins to a priest who has been duly mandated by the bishop, along with the acceptance (which it implies) of the satisfaction that will be imposed. Continued development, leading to the modification of this external form, is not precluded *a priori*. However, the problem of the relations between contrition and confession still arises and will ever arise, for these two elements will ever need to be found in penance: an internal element (contrition) and an external expression (today, auricular confession). Therefore, we must look into these issues.

The Sacrament of Penance: Sign and Instrument of the Remission of Sins

{946} We have described the remission of sins as being a divine act of merciful love returning (i.e., converting) the heart, an act of human freedom converting under the action of grace, the infusion of the gifts of grace into the person of the sinner thus prepared to receive them, and finally, as being the pardon accorded to the penitent and purified sinner. Given these facts, this complex yet unified grace is the sacramental grace of penance. Such is St. Thomas's solution, the only one that gives the sacrament its full place without diminishing the internal and personal character both of penance and of the divine pardon.

The sacrament of penance is the sign and instrument of this grace. Turning our attention directly to the case of penance, let us study the three "moments" that are found in every sacrament.

The *sacramentum tantum*

At least as things stand right now, this is "confession," considered as a whole. However, "confession" includes two elements: the acts of the penitent who confesses his guilt to the priest, and the act of the priest who absolves him. Applying the schema of sacramental hylomorphism to the sacrament of penance, the former element is said to constitute the "matter" of the sacrament, whereas the latter constitutes its "form."

The "matter" of the sacrament of penance

Here, on the sacramental level (i.e., that of the sign, of that which appears), this matter-form distinction corresponds to the distinction that we have seen exists, in the case of justification, between the act of God that justifies and pardons and the act of human freedom that turns back to God.

The acts of the penitent: An integral part of the sacrament {947} However, a question immediately emerges. In this sacrament, why are the penitent's acts an integral part of the sacrament itself, whereas in baptism (which is a sacrament of justification as well, indeed the first) they are only a condition for the sacrament? St. Thomas gives a direct response to this question, though it is a bit deceiving.[36] However, he responds to it in a much more precise and convincing way in relation to the personal satisfaction required for this sacrament and not for baptism.

A first response can be formulated as follows. In baptism, the neophyte is taken up by Christ into His death. In this way, Christ's satisfaction becomes his own. In penance, he must appropriate this satisfaction himself through his own acts. For this reason, he participates in it in accord with the measure of his own acts.[37] This could seem like a *petitio principii*. However, it is completed and clarified elsewhere.[38] The sinful man cannot return to God by his own means. He cannot "make satisfaction." Christ has made satisfaction for him,

---

36. See *ST* III, q. 84, a. 1, ad 1.
37. See *ST* III, q. 86, a. 4, ad 3.
38. See *ST* III, q. 49, a. 3, ad 2.

and through a prolongation of this initiative, has extended this satisfaction to him by bringing him into His body through baptism. This is an absolute beginning, like physical birth.

However, because it is a question of a spiritual birth whose beneficiary exists as a free person before this new birth, this does not prevent him from needing to consent to it freely (if he is capable of exercising an act of freedom). This consent is a required condition for the sacrament to be able to reach the person. However, under the action of the sacrament, the person is wholly passive. The same is not true for the person who has separated himself from the body of Christ by a free act. He must return to it by means of a new act of his freedom exteriorized in a sacramental action. This is what he must do in order to return, in some way, to the influence flowing from his baptism, which he voluntarily interrupted by placing an obstacle in front of it. This is possible because his baptism always exists in him in the form of its character. If sin is a "spiritual death," it is (according to an analogy that, in reality, is defective) a death that the Christian can be healed of because he preserves in himself this connection with Christ the Savior, namely, the sacramental character of baptism.[39] However, it remains the case that the penitent's acts draw all of their saving value from Christ's satisfaction, which the penitent makes his own, though only in a partial manner, to the extent of these acts' intensity. (We will examine how this is the case below.)

Contrition—confession—satisfaction Contrition, confession, and satisfaction are traditionally held as being the three "acts of the penitent."[40] However, given that contrition is an internal act, it is not clear how it can be counted as constituting the matter of the sacrament next to confession and satisfaction.

Obviously, it plays this role only to the degree that it gives the other two elements their penitential and sacramental meaning. A confession can exist without repentance (a literary theme exploited, for example, in Camus's *The Fall* or in "Stavrogin's Confession" in Dostoyevsky's *The Possessed*). One's confession can be constrained (as in those made before a judge). Confession is sacramental only

---

39. See *In IV Sent.*, d. 22, q. 2, a. 1, ad 1 qu.
40. See *ST* III, q. 90.

when it is made spontaneously and with an intention to repent, in order to ask pardon for the sins that one has committed, and the context must render this observable. Thus, we can distinguish the brute act of confession (i.e., the simple admission of sins in accord with the Church's prescriptions) from this same act inasmuch as it expresses interior contrition by its spontaneity and its religious context. Satisfaction itself is sacramental only when made freely and is not externally imposed (even if it is fixed by the priest). Rather, it is a work that one imposes on oneself in a spirit of repentance.

Confession and the power of the keys The penitent comes to the Church, confessing to the priest, the bishop's representative. This is not only because she has received the exclusive right to render pardon. It is also and first of all because the sinner, in rupturing his ties with Christ, also separates himself from the Church to the same degree. Just as he is integrated into the Church by baptism at the same time and by the same movement by which he is integrated into Christ, so too he is reintegrated to Christ and the Church together by the sacrament of penance. Therefore, he must sacramentally manifest his repentance in relation to the Church (in relation to the ecclesial community), and this is what he does by confessing to the priest. From this perspective, the "penitential ceremonies" that some strive to organize today (though while seeking the [correct] formula for doing so) seem more apt for bringing this essential aspect of the sacrament to light.[41]

The form of the sacrament of penance

The formula of absolution {948} St. Thomas strongly insisted on the necessity of using an imperative formula, given that, for him, a supplicative [*déprécative*] formula would be devoid of sacramental value. Historically, this is not tenable. However, one must retain the reason that pushed St. Thomas to this intransigent position and recognize that absolution has a signification value and causality that are truly

---

41. On the ecclesial aspect of the sacrament of penance, see Karl Rahner, "Vérités oubliées sur le sacrament de pénitence," *Ecrits théologiques* (Paris: Desclée de Brouwer, 1969), 2:151–94. N.B. It is not proper to say that the matter of the sacrament of penance is either the acts of the penitent or [his] sins. The matter is the very person of the penitent, though as performing an act of penance, repenting of his sins, denouncing them by asking for pardon from the Church, Christ, and the Father.

sacramental. Indeed, given that the acts of the penitent take part in the sacrament itself and that the latter consists in the dialogue between the penitent and priest, it also has a therapeutic value in the moral and psychological order. Nonetheless, it is more than this. If it is an instrumentally salvific sacrament, it also must have a certain signification and, to this end, a kind of efficacy of itself independent from the psychological and moral efficacy of the penitent's acts, as well as one independent from such efficacy existing in the words of the confessor.

To assure this, St. Thomas thought that it was necessary that the formula retain its imperative form, and he went so far as to hold that this form had a real efficacy, as he did for the other sacraments.[42] We cannot reject supplication formulas as being non-sacramental. No, we absolutely must recognize that they have the same efficacy as that which St. Thomas accorded only to the imperative formula. For this, we must have recourse to the idea of an "infallibly answered prayer" (i.e., a prayer that, as soon as it is pronounced by the relevant person, in the required forms, is answered in virtue of a certain promise). Thus, the uttering of such a prayer has a value as a sign of the spiritual effect requested and certainly obtained.

It would not be impossible to say that such a prayer can have sacramental efficacy. In such a case, God would instrumentally use the act of a created will which is expressed in the prayer in order to realize this same prayer. However, we can ask ourselves whether this is indeed necessary. The notion of a sacrament (and therefore of sacramental causality) is not univocal. For this particular effect (i.e., the remission of sins), it seems that the normal role of the Church would be intercession. The notion of an infallibly answered prayer suffices for assuring the sacramental character [of the action] (i.e., the stable relation of the visible sign to the invisible significate and a relation of causality implying that the effect rigorously follows from the cause).

The minister of the sacrament According to the Church's doctrine, solemnly defined at Trent,[43] only priests endowed with the sacerdotal

---

42. See *ST* III, q. 84, a. 3, ad 3.
43. See Trent, "*Doctrinal Decree on the Sacrament of Penance*," chs. 6–7, cc. 10–11, in D.-*Sch.*, nos. 1684–88 and 1711–12.

character have the power to confer the sacrament of penance. However, the exercise of this power moreover requires that the priest has jurisdiction over the penitent. This means that the power of the keys belongs, by right, to the shepherds of the Church who are bishops. It can be delegated. However, this requires, moreover, the power of orders in the minister to whom it is delegated.

The justification of this determination must be sought out in tradition. The bishops (or councils) are quite clearly those who have the responsibility of admitting sinners to penance, even if there were a kind of overlap between "spiritual direction" (requiring only that the director have the personal qualities of holiness and wisdom) and "penance" properly speaking. We hold on faith that the privilege of confessors consisted in a right of recommendation, which certain thinkers have improperly wished to consider as being a right of reconciliation that, in fact, belonged to the bishop.[44]

The fact that the power of the keys belongs to the shepherds of the Church as such is obvious from the moment that one acknowledges the hierarchical structure of the Church, as it is a question of reintegrating into the Church someone who has broken off from communion with her (if only in a hidden way), thus belonging to the ecclesial society only in an imperfect and deficient manner.[45] Moreover, the fact that the power of holy orders would be required in the minister is connected to what we said above about the properly sacramental value of penance. Because we here have not only the acts of the penitent and their therapeutic value but also the real and truly effective act of the minister that signifies and causes the grace of the remission of sins, the minister himself must be sacramentally constituted.[46] Christ Himself is the one who remits the sins by the power of His passion. Through his sacramental character, the priest sacramentally represents Christ when he confers a sacrament, as we will specify later on with regard to the sacrament of holy orders.

The relation of absolution to confession This relation is presented as that of form to matter in the sacraments. This means that the sacra-

---

44. See Bernard Botte, introduction to Hippolytus of Rome, *La tradition apostolique*, SC 11bis, 27–28.
45. See §697 above.
46. See §729 above.

mental sign (a sign causing what it signifies) is constituted by absolution and confession together, with absolution "determining" the sacramental signification of confession, which, by itself, would remain "undetermined."[47]

Now, as is clear from St. Thomas's own visible hesitations, ascertaining this relationship of that which is determining to what is determined is difficult here.[48] Indeed, confession and absolution seem to be signs of two different things. One seems to be the sign of the sinner's contrition and repentance and the other of God's pardon. Moreover, "the sacraments bring about what they signify," and it is not clear that confession causes the contrition that it signifies. Much to the contrary, contrition is what should provoke confession.

On this last point, St. Thomas seems to concede that, in the sacrament of penance, the signification belongs to the confession (the matter) and the causality to the absolution (the form).[49] However, if signification principally belongs to confession in connection with absolution, it also has its own efficacy. Conversely, in the *Scriptum*, absolution is principally called efficacious, which seems to reserve for it some part in the signification as well.[50] In the *Summa theologiae*, he seems to insist more on the signifying value of absolution.[51]

To resolve this problem, we must observe that God's pardon, in the regime of mercy established by Christ's coming and redemptive death, is strictly connected to repentance and vice-versa. As we have seen, the first effect of the divine pardon consists in inspiring repentance. Consequently, confession receives its value as a sign from the absolution toward which it is ordered. Nonetheless, it is equally true that in order for absolution to exist, it needs a sinner who confesses. However, could we say that confession does not participate in the causality of the sacrament in any way? This would undermine the principle that the sacrament is a cause inasmuch as it is a sign.

Justification of the unrighteous person indivisibly includes, on the one hand, the act of free will by which one converts to God and

---

47. See §725 above.
48. See *In IV Sent.*, d. 22, q. 2, aa. 1–2.
49. See ibid., ad 1 qu.; 2um; ad 2 qu., co. [*sic*].
50. See ibid., ad 2 qu., co.
51. See *ST* III, q. 84, a. 3, ad 5.

is united to Him and, on the other hand, the act of God giving both the grace of this conversion and the grace of union with God. Confession causes this justification just as it signifies it. The acts of the penitent signify it and cause it from the perspective of the act of free choice, whereas absolution does so from the perspective of the divine act of pardon.

The *res tantum* of the sacrament of penance

{949} As was said above, the very remission of sins, with its twofold composition from grace and freedom, constitutes the sacramental grace of the sacrament of penance, its *res tantum*.

One can ask why this remission does not, like baptism, suppress every kind of "obligation for punishment" (*reatus poenae*). Does this represent some shortcoming of the sacrament? Is it a limitation of [God's] mercy?

The sacrament is the effect of a limitless mercy, the same one that is manifested by the sending of the Son and by His redemptive death, which is personally and decisively applied to each person through baptism in an intrinsically definitive way. It bears the power of Christ's passion. It is the means by which the repentant sinner comes into contact with this passion. Thus, at least inasmuch as Christ acts through it, the sacrament is able to abolish every sin and extinguish every debt. However, as we have seen, the acts of the penitent here enter into the very structure of the sacrament, introducing into it the limitations of the person under consideration. The effect of the sacrament is limited because the person is limited in his own penance.

What does not suffer from limitation is the first effect of the sacrament, namely, the remission of sins, for this is an absolute. Just as the *aversio a Deo* is an absolute that is found in every grave sin, so too the *conversio ad Deum* which abolishes it is, in every penance, an absolute, whose absence would render penance inefficacious and would render the sacrament purely and simply inefficacious. By contrast, there are degrees to the *conversio ad bonum commutabile* (i.e., the fixation in the passing good) included in every sin. These degrees are first expressed according to the greater or lesser degree that this good diverges from man's true good, though above all (and by way of consequence) according to the depth of the person's engagement with passing goods in general (i.e., in the end, according to the intensity of disordered self-love that is the reason for this engagement). Conversely, there are degrees in the *conversio ad Deum*, inasmuch as it is opposed no longer to the *aversio* but, rather, to the *conversio ad bonum commutabile* that entailed this *aversio*. They are taken from the satisfactory value of the penitential work by which the sinner, on account of his interior penance, strives to compensate for and annul the *conversio ad bonum commutabile* by which he turned away from God. However, these degrees are most especially taken from the intensity of the interior penance concretized in this penitential work.

Indeed, the human person is a complex being. By the best and deepest part of himself, he can convert to God, loving Him above all things, all the while preserving in himself many affective tendencies that belong to a self-love that is not yet perfectly ordered to God. The progress of charity consists in gradually integrating all these tendencies and assuming them [into the love of God above all else] so that self-love, in the end, may be completely included in charity.[52] Even though this complete integration may not be realized herebelow as a firm and habitual disposition, it can be realized in a transitory manner in a full and complete act of conversion. This is what, in contemporary religious language, one calls "perfect contrition." Such contrition makes the sacrament of penance (whether it is effectively received or only resolutely willed) attain its full effects, thus extinguishing every *reatus poenae*.

For the reason indicated above, such contrition does not exclude penitential works of satisfaction.[52b] On the contrary, it impels one to do them. However, in the case of "perfect contrition," these works are only the expression and concretization of interior penance. (The situation is a bit like how Christ's passion and death added nothing to His "penitent love" but, rather, furnished it with its necessary bodily dimension.)[53] On the contrary, in the case of a true but

---

52. See *ST* II-II, q. 2, a. 5. Nicolas, *Contemplation et vie contemplative en christianisme*, ch. 3.
52b. See §947 above.
53. See §493 in the second part of this course. Also, see Nicolas, *Les profondeurs de la grâce*, 267–68.

imperfect contrition (i.e., one inspired by a charity that has not yet completely assumed and integrated one's self-love), these works are also an exercise of charity, by means of which it increases its sway over the person, reducing his divergent affective tendencies. Simultaneously, they "satisfy" God's justice for past sins that have not yet been completely rejected.[54] For all this, with regard to what pertains to the degrees of contrition corresponding to the degrees of charity, see *ST* II-II, q. 24. With regard to what pertains to the *reatus poenae* left by the sacrament of penance, see *ST* III, q. 86, a. 4. However, note that in the latter text St. Thomas does not envision "perfect contrition." In the corresponding text in the *Scriptum*, he emphasizes that the *reatus poenae* is diminished in proportion to the intensity of contrition, and this correspondingly diminishes the penalty that the confessor must impose. In this way, the path is opened for the notion of "perfect contrition" by which the *reatus poenae* is completely abolished.

The *res et sacramentum* of the sacrament of penance

{950} In the case of the sacrament of penance, it is difficult to discover the intermediary effect (i.e., the *res et sacramentum*) existing between the rite (i.e., the *sacramentum tantum*) and the ultimate effect signified and produced by this rite, sacramental grace (the *res tantum*). However, we have seen that this intermediary is part of every sacrament's structure, corresponding to its ecclesial nature, assuring the new situation of the beneficiary in the Church. It is of the sacrament's nature to bring about this new situation.[55] The difficulty comes from the fact that, in the case of the sacrament of penance, the acts of the penitent belong to the very structure of the sacrament. Hence, if these acts are not as they should be, it seems that there will not be any sacrament at all. And if they are what they should be, it seems that the sacrament would immediately produce the *res* (i.e., the remission of sins). In the *Scriptum*, St. Thomas seems to exclude this intermediary effect: "In penance, the lack of disposition in the will prevents absolution from producing the least

---

54. See *ST* III, q. 86, a. 4, ad 1 and 2. *In* IV *Sent.*, d. 20, qu. un., a. 2.
55. See §754 above.

effect."[56] However, in the same work, he speaks of *confession informis*[57] (i.e., a confession that is not informed by charity). Such a notion presupposes that the sacrament causes an intermediate effect between the rite and the grace of the remission of sins, which never exists without charity. Indeed, if the sacrament has no other significate than grace, where grace is lacking, there really is no sign and therefore no sacrament, for the sacrament is a certain sign.

In the *Summa theologiae*, he expressly states that there is a *res et sacramentum* in the case of penitence. However, what he designates by it is the sinner's interior penance (i.e., his repentance).[58] As we have seen, this is hardly distinct from the *res* and does not correspond to the notion of a *res et sacramentum*, an intermediary effect produced in the beneficiary by the sacrament, independent of one's internal dispositions.

However, we can find something in the sacrament of penance corresponding to the *res et sacramentum*, namely reconciliation with the Church, the first effect and significate of the sacrament and, itself, a sign and cause of reconciliation with God.

The Church is a communion (of men with the Father, in the Son, through the Holy Spirit, and with each other) realized in a society. By breaking with this communion, the sinner distances himself from the Church-society even if he does not break with it (something that is the effect of only certain sins such as schism and heresy). Reintegration into the community by the remission of sins includes full reintegration into the ecclesial society. In this process of reintegration, visible reconciliation with the Church, signified and caused by confession followed by absolution, is the sign and cause, in turn, of reintegration into the Church's communion. Therefore, it is indeed the *res et sacramentum*, an intermediary between the *sacramentum tantum* (the sacramental rite) and the *res tantum* (the remission of sins). In the case of a confession without true repentance, the *res tantum* is not produced on account of the obstacle to charity that is posited by the person who has confessed. However, reconciliation with the Church remains on the level of the visible and sacramental order so

---

56. See *In IV Sent.*, d. 22, q. 2, a. 2, ad 3 qu.
57. See *In IV Sent.*, d. 17, q. 3, a. 4, qu. 1 (ed. Moos, 463–64 and 472–76).
58. See *ST* III, q. 84, a. 1, ad 3.

that, in order for the sacrament to produce its effect, it suffices that the obstacle be removed by interior contrition. A new confession will not be necessary, nor a new absolution.[59] Conversely, if someone has obtained God's pardon solely by interior contrition without the sacrament of penance, he will need to receive it when this becomes possible, for *non tamen adhuc Ecclesiae reconciliatus est*, he has not yet been reconciled with the Church.[60]

Perhaps this perspective allows one to bring to light the true meaning of the Gospel's words addressed to the apostles and on which, in the final analysis, the theology of the sacrament of penance is founded: "If you forgive the sins of any, they are forgiven; if you retain the sins of any, they are retained."[61] The shepherds of the Church directly reconcile the sinner with the ecclesial community. This reconciliation—which is visible, as is true for the first effect (in the genetic order) for every sacrament—is the *res et sacramentum*, an effect that in itself is hidden but is rendered visible by the rite, which, in virtue of Christ's promise, is the sacramental sign and (instrumental) cause of reconciliation with God and of the remission of sins. This can be prevented only by the interior obstacle of someone who would refuse (in an unmanifested way) to convert.

Moreover, this sheds new light on the problem encountered above concerning the efficacy of absolution.[62] Efficacy differs according to the genus of causality involved. If absolution has the reconciliation of the sinner with the Church as its first effect, its causality seems to belong to the moral order rather than to the order of efficient causality. The grace of reconciliation with God is really caused by means of it as soon as the Lord certainly supplies it, on account of His promise, to anyone who has been reconciled with the Church (unless that person places an obstacle to it). Moreover, nothing prevents this efficacy connected to the very formula of absolution (inasmuch as the sinner is reconciled with the Church by means of it) from having added to it the efficacy of the Church's prayer requesting that Christ's promise would be realized for this

---

59. See *In IV Sent.*, d. 17, q. 3, a. 4, ad 1, qu. c. (ed. Moos, 473).
60. See *In IV Sent.*, q. 3, a. 3, ad 1 qu. (ed. Moos, 442). [*sic*]
61. Jn 20:23 (RSV).
62. See §948 above.

penitent, leading him to be reconciled with God as she reconciles him with herself. In the same way, by praying the epiclesis in the Eucharistic celebration, she asks that the conversion of the offerings into the body and blood of Christ may be brought about, certain that her prayer will be answered. We have seen that this aspect of the efficacy of the sacrament of penance is best placed in relief by a deprecatory prayer formula.

However, we must note that this intermediary effect is, in this case, hardly something that is durable, for if a new sin is committed, it will need to be confessed. That is, in the case of the sacrament of penance, the *res et sacramentum* is so closely connected to the *res tantum* that it can scarcely be separated from it. The notion of a sacrament is not univocal, and one must not be astonished that it is applied to the various sacraments in different ways. Still, it remains important to recognize this intermediary effect, for it highlights the essential importance of reconciliation with the Church in the theology and practice of the sacrament of penance.[63]

THE DISPOSITION THAT IS REQUIRED IN THE SUBJECT SO THAT THE SACRAMENT OF PENANCE MAY PRODUCE ITS EFFECT

{951} Penance is a sacrament. Therefore, it is a certain sign and an infallible (instrumental) cause. The *res* of which it is the sign and cause is the remission of sins and the conversion of its recipient's heart. However, like every sacrament, it is a free act performed by the subject. It is an external act that is a sign of the interior act. If there is a disjunction between the two, if the internal process that is expressed by the external process is not really performed by the subject, this person, by refusing to perform this internal act, poses an obstacle that prevents the sacrament from producing its effect (and from truly signifying what it seems to signify, namely, the remission of sins). This is true for every sacrament, but a special difficulty is involved in the case of penance. In the other sacraments, this free act is prior

---

63. St. Thomas did not place this dimension of the sacrament of penance in high relief. He perhaps would have done so if he had been able to complete the treatise [on penance] in the *Summa theologiae*, for he does speak of it in the *Scriptum* (*In IV Sent.*, d. 17, q. 3, a. 3, ad 2 qu.).

to the sacrament, which can produce its effect as soon as man freely chooses to submit himself to its action. Here, what is this free act? It is a "conversion of heart." Now, as we have seen, a conversion of heart is inseparable from the remission of sins and is caused by the very grace of this remission. Therefore, it seems that it is not prior to the action of the sacrament but, on the contrary, follows upon it.

Here, in order to strive to resolve this issue in light of everything we have said, we encounter again the essential difficulty that has appeared at every step in the history of the development of the theology of the sacrament of penance: conversion of heart is the necessary and sufficient "disposition" for the grace of the remission of sins. By saying that conversion of heart is the internal act necessary for fruitfully receiving the sacrament of penance do we not thus say that in order to approach the sacrament one already must have received its effect, thus making it unintelligible for us to say that the sacrament would be necessary? St. Thomas's idea that the intention to confess is part of "conversion" does not seem to break free from this impasse, for it presupposes that "confession" (i.e., the sacrament of penance) can be defined by its relation, as a sign and cause, to the grace of the remission of sins.

Given that this grace itself is simultaneously the grace of the conversion of heart, this would mean that the same grace is simultaneously the significate-effect of the sacrament and its preliminary condition, which seems to imply a contradiction. Or, again, this would mean that if the subject were lacking the very *res* that the sacrament signifies and produces this would be an obstacle preventing the sacrament from producing and signifying this *res*. However, this is what St. Thomas seems to say: "Whence, it seems that the priest must not absolve him in whom he does not see a sign of contrition by which man is interiorly brought back to life, his sin having been remitted by God."[64] If we refuse to say this, are we not thereby forced to say that God, by the sacrament, remits the sins of someone who is insufficiently repentant and has not converted? Moreover, a further question emerges, namely, what is the minimum amount of repentance required, below which point, there could not be a sacrament,

---

64. See St. Thomas, *De forma absolutionis*, ch. 2, lines 98–102.

meaning that if the priest were to perceive this absence of disposition he must refuse absolution?

The Preparation of the Sinner for Grace

{952} If conversion itself is instantaneous, it is ordinarily preceded in the sinner by a free undertaking by which he begins to detach himself from sin and to draw closer to God. This is what is called "preparation for grace." It does not occur without actual grace, for God is always the one who starts this process, seeking out the sinner and placing him in motion. However, it precedes the infusion of sanctifying grace, meaning that the acts that constitute this preparation are supernaturally deficient acts (i.e., ones that are not informed by charity), performed by someone who still loves himself more than God and who, nonetheless, stretches out toward God, tends toward having a love of God above all else.[65] Like conversion itself, for which it prepares and toward which it tends, it includes two aspects: an approach toward God and a rejection of sin (or, repentance).

The approach of the sinner through faith and hope

The sinner of whom we speak, someone baptized and believing, through faith knows God's paternity, Christ, the Gospel ideal, and his own situation as a Christian. Through this faith, he can know that he is a sinner, turned away from God, having become, through his fault, "without God in this world."[66] Through hope, he can experience a nostalgia for all these goods received at baptism, which he has lost: peace with God even here-below, life with Christ, eternal life promised in the hereafter. Here, in these theological acts, he already attains God Himself, in His mystery, as well as Christ, even though he remains separated from Him because he does not have charity, which alone establishes communion. This knowledge and desire for God are, on the one hand, the very acts by which the sinner draws close to God and, on the other hand, the principle for other acts that he can perform in this direction, the first of which being the act of repentance.

---

65. See Nicolas, *Les profondeurs de la grâce*, 452–61.
66. Eph 2:12.

To repent, motivated by fear

This motive of fear was violently rejected by Luther because he believed that it made repentance hypocritical. It was recognized by the Council of Trent as being a valid motive on the condition that it makes us renounce sin.[67] However, it instinctively shocks us as well. Does one really repent and return to God by leaving sin behind solely out of fear of punishment? Still, it is undeniable that the threat of punishments is proposed in Scripture (in the Gospel and in St. Paul) as a motive for avoiding evil and remaining on the straight way.[68] Moreover, pastoral experience shows that this motive exists and leads to true conversions. ([Armand Jean le Bouthillier de] Rancé, returning after a brief absence, found his mistress dead; he was so shaken up by the sudden idea of death and of judgment that he began his conversion.)

To understand how and on what conditions fear of the divine punishments can be the motive for an authentic repentance ordered to conversion, one must reflect on a distinction provided by St. Thomas. On the one hand, there is purely servile fear (sometimes called *serviliter servilis*). On the other hand, there is servile fear that does not exclude charity, even when it does not in fact include it. To put it another way, on the one hand, there is servile fear as such and on the other hand there is fear that is called servile but that in fact is not inspired by a spirit of servitude.[69]

In the first case, punishment is what is principally feared. God is feared only on account of His punishment, thereby being feared as being He who will punish. Thus, the slave fears his master because his master is stronger than he is and because he cannot escape from this master. Far from including the least affective attachment, the smallest beginning of love, this fear begets hatred. As regards sin, it can indeed lead one to renounce a passing good, but this would be done on account of the very disordered self-love that had inspired the choice of this pursuit. In other words, the *aversio a Deo* in which

---

67. See Trent, "Decree on Justification," c. 8, in D.-*Sch.*, no. 1558.
68. See Ceslas Spicq, "La revelation de l'enfer dans la Sainte Écriture," in *La Théologie du renouveau*, ed. Guy-Marie Bertrand and Laurence K. Shook (Paris: Éditions du Cerf, 1968), 91–143.
69. See *ST* II-II, q. 19, aa. 2–8.

sin essentially consists remains (and therefore, too, his state of being a sinner). Man remains a sinner even if he ceases to sin. (Such fear is that "which only restrains one's hand," according to the expression of Quesnel taken up by the acts of Pistoia.)[70] Fear of punishments alone is evil because it does nothing more than "restrain the hand," without changing the heart. However, this is true of purely servile fear, not of every kind of fear of punishments.

In the second case, what is principally feared is God who punishes. He is feared not as the strongest person against whom no possible resistance can be made but, rather, as the justly-offended God whose anger has been merited—as Adam and Eve hid themselves from God.[71] A sense of having offended Him is implied in such a fear, a recognition of one's sin, which is a first step toward God.

It is a first step that would be brought to a standstill if hope did not come to make the forward progress continue. On the one hand, hope must make us recognize God as the ultimate good. On the other hand, and above all, it enables us, so to speak, to look behind the God who is offended and see the Father who is ready to pardon. Without it, the sinner would, like Cain, draw back from God out of desperation. By means of it, "he gets up and goes to the Father," like the prodigal son. However, fear of punishments can serve to awaken in the sinner's mind an awareness of his sinful situation.

It also serves as a counterbalance for the attractions of the earthly goods that were the cause of the *aversio a Deo*, thus freeing the desire for God included in hope.

Such fear, even if it is not yet inspired by charity (in the sinner) is susceptible to being so inspired. When it is so inspired (in the beginner), it is called the "fear of beginners." Therefore, it is itself open to charity.

To repent, motivated on account of the evils occasioned by sin

It is not a question of future consequences of sin (i.e., punishments) but of frustrations and damages that it currently causes for the sin-

---

70. See Pope Clement XI, *Unigenitus Dei Filius* (Against the Errors of Pasquier Quesnel), September 8, 1713, prop. 61, in D.-*Sch.*, no. 2461. Pope Pius VI, *Auctorem fidei* (Condemnation of the Pseudo-Council of Pistoia), August 28, 1794, no. 25, in D.-*Sch.*, no. 2625.

71. See Nicolas, *Les profondeurs de la grâce*, 458–61.

ner, symbolized by the situation of the prodigal son in the midst of the swine. Such a state can arise in the form of a troubled conscience, the disgust and deception that one finds in the goods that are preferred to God, the feeling of the loss of the goods that Christ brings, and perhaps too the temporal problems coming from sin: discord with one's familial or social environment, sicknesses, ruin, and solitude caused by sin.

What we said above concerning fear of future punishments applies here for these current frustrations. By themselves, they cannot inspire a legitimate form of repentance. However, they can help us become aware of our sinful state and turn back to God. This repentance is not yet inspired by charity, but it is open to it, at least if we do not return to God (and to the Church) solely or principally in order to recover the personal advantages that we have lost through our sin. The saving role played by this frustration is the fact that it furnishes an occasion for becoming aware that one has lost much more.

Virtual Love of God above All Things

{953} The repentance of which we are speaking *opens out upon* charity, but it is not yet *inspired by* charity. The sinner continues to love himself more than God, but his repentance is obviously not inspired by self-love as his final end, for it would thus be false and perverse. By what love, then, is it inspired (for love is always the principle of action)? There is only one possible response: it is inspired by the kind of self-love that can coexist with charity, self-love that, for this act of repentance (and for the act of faith and hope which is its positive face) remains in its natural ambivalence, being able to culminate in charity or, on the contrary, remain closed in on itself.[72]

This in no way involves a kind of purely natural love of God but, rather, involves the ordination to man's Last End (which, in fact, is the supernatural end) implied in the first movement of self-love, an ordination that does not turn away from God except by a sinner choosing to close in on himself. Given that man's natural orientation to God (an orientation that, on account of his supernatural vocation,

---

72. See Jean-Hervé Nicolas, "Amour de soi, amour de Dieu, amour des autres," *Revue thomiste* 56 (1956): 5–42, and *Contemplation et vie contemplative en christianisme*, 96–126.

orders one to personal communion with God offered in Christ) is prior to his closing in on himself, it is understandable that, in certain acts of freedom, the sinner follows this fundamental orientation without making it be subject to the deliberately chosen deviation that led him to choose himself as his ultimate end. Thus, he remains habitually *aversus a Deo* but, through such acts, he is not turned away from God and does not actualize his *aversio*. Through their fundamental orientation, such acts should culminate in love of God above all else. If they do not come to do so, this is because the sinner loves himself more than God. However, considered in themselves, these acts are performed so that they may be taken up by charity, without which they would not arrive at the ultimate goal of their movement. In short, they are the good acts that a sinner is able to perform.

Among these acts, we must count, for our purposes, acts of unformed faith and hope, which, as we have seen, initiate one's return to God. An act of unformed faith or hope is not necessarily open to charity. It can be performed with a deliberate refusal of charity and of its requirements in a sinner who is very conscious and impregnated with a great religious tradition, which he does not wish to repudiate all the while not wishing to accept the personal demands that it makes upon his life. However, it is a question of acts of faith and hope made without precluding charity, acts by which the sinner begins to draw closer to God.

One must also take into account repentance inspired by motives that could, certainly, come from love of self above all things but which are in no way incompatible with love of God above all. Such are the motives that we spoke of above: fear, disgust, and a longing for purity.

Even though these acts of faith, hope, and repentance cannot by themselves break the circle of self-love in which the sinner is enclosed, they stretch forth in an impotent but real way toward God as the center of life for the person who, habitually centered on himself, does not perform these acts for himself as for his final end.

To bring this explanation to its conclusion, we must appeal to the Church's own charity (for this sinner is a member of the Church) and to Christ's charity (from which the Church's own charity flows forth). It is at the root of these acts, moving the sinner externally because he does not personally participate in this charity.[73] The Holy Spirit is the one who inspires these acts. He does not do so from within the sinner, for He does not dwell within him. Rather, he does so from without, for He is the one who urges the sinner onward toward conversion.[74]

The disposition required for fruitfully receiving the sacrament of penance is the "opening to charity" that is found in this repentance—namely attrition, which is manifested by the very act of confession, as well as in the penitent's own attitude. It is not yet conversion, for it is not inspired by charity. However, it disposes one to it, for it is open to charity.*

Contrition: That Which Is Signified and Effected by the Sacrament of Penance

As we have seen, since the time of St. Thomas, the solution to the theological problem concerning the efficacy of the sacrament of penance has been expressed in the adage: "In virtue of the sacrament, the attrite penitent becomes contrite." What we have explained up to now enables us to see the meaning and value of this solution.

The efficacy of the priest's absolution

{954} We[75] have excluded the idea that the grace of the remission of sins could be granted without conversion of heart, which includes

---

73. See Journet, *L'Église du Verbe incarné*, 2:957.
74. See Trent, "Doctrinal Decree on the Sacrament of Penance," ch. 4, in D.-*Sch.*, no. 1678.
* N.B. Therefore, this problem is not correctly posed by contrasting two forms of attrition—the first being an attrition born of fear, which would be an insufficient disposition for receiving the sacrament, and the second being an attrition born of love, which would be required and sufficient (or not). A rejection of sin inspired by fear that excludes every form of love of God (i.e., a purely servile fear) would not be an authentic repentance of sin and therefore would not merit the name of attrition. Conversely, a repentance in which the motive of love of God would be fully explicit and, for this reason, would completely subordinate to itself the motive of fear (or every other self-interested motive), would no longer be attrition but, rather, would already be contrition. As we have seen, it is impossible and contradictory to demand contrition as the required disposition for fruitfully approaching the sacrament of penance.

75. N.B. Here, it is not a question of the particular problem treated above (See §§948 and 950 above) concerning the way that this efficacy is exercised (i.e., whether by way of a direct efficacy or by way of prayer). Rather, we are here concerned with the effect that it produces.

contrition. Therefore, how can attrition be a sufficient disposition for the sacrament of penance to produce its effect, namely, the remission of sins?

Obviously, this is possible because it enables absolution to produce the grace of conversion (and, therefore, contrition). This is understandable if one admits that charity is already virtually contained in attrition. Indeed, this means that the sinner's will is not in a state of resistance to God's love. It is not opposed to it by a counter-love but, on the contrary, is oriented in the direction of love of God above all things without, however, going all the way, without breaking the circle of love of self above all else in which the sinner is enclosed by his sin. The grace of conversion spans that distance, leading him to the conclusion toward which he had tended with an impotent act of will.

This grace, which is signified and produced (in one way or another) by absolution, is a conversion, a turning-about of the will which passes from its wicked ultimate end (the self, loved above all else) to the true ultimate end (God, loved above all else). However, at the same time—and this is what makes it possible on the side of the subject—it is the decisive maturation of charity, which was enveloped in the attrition, heretofore prevented from coming to birth because of an obstacle standing in its way. This obstacle was certainly something intrinsic to the person (for it was his fundamental attachment to himself). Nonetheless, it was extrinsic to these actions by which he returns to God, already engaging him in such actions, although imperfectly and inefficaciously.

By means of absolution, the mystery of mercy that is found in every "conversion" is brought about. God pardons only the person whose heart has "turned back." However, it is by His very pardoning that He turns back the heart.

It may be asked: "What role does freedom play in this activity?" We must respond that God's grace does not destroy freedom but, on the contrary, arouses it and restores it to itself. Such grace is a grace of liberation. In this act of conversion, we are faced with the profound conformity which exists between man's freedom and God's grace. This conformity highlights attrition's character as a free act of returning to God, something that is concretized and manifested through the external sacramental action [*démarche*], confession.

The efficacy of the penitent's acts

{955} The "matter" and "form" in a sacrament constitute a whole, namely, the unique sacramental sign, which is the cause of what it signifies. As we have seen, the penitent's confession and the priest's absolution are united in order to constitute the complete sign of the grace of the divine pardon. Simultaneously, together, they are the cause of it. Given that the sacrament causes grace by making the penitent pass from attrition to contrition, we must look into how the penitent's acts concur in producing contrition.

These acts (i.e., confession of sins and works of penance, perhaps already begun but, in any case, proposed) signify contrition. It is a contrition that is not yet formally present. However, as we have seen, it is virtually present as an objective aimed at and desired, even if not yet accessible. The acts that signify it at least psychologically contribute to the maturation we discussed above, thereby leading attrition to draw closer to contrition. Thus, at the decisive moment when this maturation arrives at its terminus, provoking conversion (which is a radical reversal of the person) the penitent is able to grasp hold of the grace of conversion on account of these acts, which by themselves were impotent for such a final act. Contrition is produced by them and by the absolution of the priest together (as, in general, the supernatural act is produced together by grace and freedom).

Therefore, the role of the penitent's acts in the production of the *res* of the sacrament is different from that played by the free act performed by the beneficiary in the other sacraments. Here, it is not only a question of disposing oneself so that the sacrament may act, but, rather, is a question of taking part in the action of the sacrament.*

---

* N.B. Naturally, as we have seen for baptism, it is in no way excluded (and, indeed, perhaps often happens) that the grace of the sacrament (here, contrition and the remission of sins) would be given before the sacramental rite (here, confession and absolution) would be performed. The Council of Trent foresaw this when it spoke of the sacrament of penance *in voto* (contained in advance in the resolution to ask for it), just as it spoke of baptism *in voto*. In both cases, the sacrament is not rendered useless by this intervention of grace which precedes it, for it is on account of the sacramental action and in view of it that such grace has intervened. Moreover, visible reconciliation with the Church, of which the penitential rite is the divinely

Some pastoral conclusions

{956} The importance of the penitent's acts in this sacrament today invites a renewal of the penitential liturgy, which has become less and less expressive of the interior sentiments that it is charged not only with expressing but also with arousing and, equally, is not overly expressive of the Church's pardon, which itself is a sign and cause of God's pardon.

A* question is posed today to (and by) theologians regarding "communal penitential liturgies." Currently, ecclesiastical authority requires individual confession of sins to a priest and individual absolution by this priest. Is this theologically necessary? Or could a "general absolution" be admitted without violating the substance of the sacrament?

To respond to this kind of question, one must distinguish the problem of confession (an act performed by the penitent) and that of absolution. For the first, it seems that the sacrament of penance could not be administered without one confessing one's own sins.

---

instituted means, is an integral part of the total effect of the sacrament (a part that of itself is preliminary, only accidentally and, of itself, provisionally prevented). If it is prevented by the grace of reconciliation with God, it still remains necessary, not in order to thereby add something to God's pardon but, rather, in order to give this pardon an ecclesial dimension that it itself includes and calls for.

* See the following: Z. Alzeghy, "Sara abolita la confessione?: riflessioni sopra una cronica," *Civiltà Cattolica* 2, no. 3 (1970): 252–60. A. M. Besnard, "Une pratique en mutation: la confession," *Recheres et Débats du Centre catholique des intellectuels français* 64 (1969): 45–64. M. Huftier, "Sur la penitence et la confession," *Esprit et Vie* 81 (1971): 617–25. F. Interdonnato, "Es dogmaticamente possible cambiar la doctrina y la practica de la confesión auricular et individual establecida en Trente?," in *Libro Annual, 1971* (Lima: Publicationes de la Faculdad de Theología Pontificia y Civil, 1971), 247–86. Claude Jean-Nesmy, "De quoi faut-il s'accuser," *Vie Spirituelle* 116 (1967), 293–308; "Pourquoi se confesser aujourd'hui?," in *La confession en contestation. Une enquête auprès de lecteurs de "Témoignance chrétien*," ed. Bruno; and Carra de Vaux (Paris: Témoignage chrétien, 1970). R.-L. Oechslin, "Dimension ecclésiale de la penitence," *Vie Spirituelle* 117 (1967), 553–65. José Ramos-Regidor, "La 'réconciliation' dans l'Église primitive. Suggestions pour la théologie et la pastorale actuelles," *Concilium* 61 (1971): 25–34. Peter J. Riga, "Penance: A New Orientation," *American Ecclesiastical Review* 163 (1970): 407–15. Aimon Marie Roguet, "Les célébrations communautaires de la penitence," *Vie Spirituelle* 116 (1967): 188–202. Henri Rondet, *Pourquoi se confesser. Le sacrement de penitence et le sacrement des maladies* (Paris: Beauchesne, 1971). Jean-Claude Sagne, *Tes péchés ont été pardonnés* (Paris: Chalet, 1977). Christoph Schönborn, "Evangélisation, celebration, et sacrement," *Communio* 3 (1978): 28–39. Sandro Spinsanti, "La visite de Dieu dans le pardon," *Communio* 4 (1971): 11–25, and "Les chrétiens parlent de la confession," *Vie Spirituelle* 119 (1968), no. 555. [Tr. note: Fr. Nicolas also refers to "Coulleau," which has no correlative entry in the bibliography.]

Therefore, individual confession is necessary. Recourse to ancient discipline cannot justify such "economization." First of all, ancient discipline foresaw a kind of confession of sins, even if it had neither the place nor the extent that the Council of Trent assigned to it. (The bishop or his representative knew why a given person was doing penance and what he was absolving him of.)

Second, this place was held by the external works of penance, which preceded reconciliation. To suppress both of them would be to suppress the penitent's external acts "against sin," and such acts are an integral and necessary part of the sacrament. Indeed, it is not clear how one could judge whether they were sufficiently replaced, or represented, by the collective acts by which repentance and one's return to God would be expressed in the penitential ceremonies. Indeed, the objects of the "penitent's acts" are not only the general situation of sin in which every man more or less finds himself. Beyond this, they are one's own sins, which have precisely placed this person in the situation of being a sinner wherein he currently finds himself.[76] These collective acts (preaching on penance, recitations of formulas of penance like the *Confiteor*, the *Miserere*, etc., hymns, and even collective works of penance such as alms, fasting, etc.) are an excellent preparation and stimulation for individual penance. However, they must be personalized for each person, here too in a given act that is performed, and this can only be something individual.

One must repent of one's own sins and do penance for them not only in an interior manner but also externally. Could this individual act of penance be anything but the act which the Church fixed through the course of the Middle Ages and solemnly promulgated at Trent (i.e., confession of one's own sins)? This seems impossible, for if this determination is undeniably the fruit of a lengthy development, this development was not arbitrary and does not seem to be reversible. Could it continue and arrive at another determination? This is not impossible *a priori*, but it is not clear in what other way the penitent could externalize his repentance and "submit himself to the keys of the Church" than through individual confession of his sins. (It seems entirely impossible that we could return to the ancient

---

76. See *ST* III, q. 84, a. 2.

penitential practices, as the Jansenists dreamed of doing, in particular Quesnel and then the participants at the pseudo-council of Pistoia.)

For the second problem (i.e., the possibility of an absolution given all together to all those who come to individually denounce their sins to a priest), our response can be more nuanced. It does not seem impossible for such a general absolution to be sufficiently individualized by the fact that it is addressed only to those who had individually taken part in the sacrament by confessing their sins. Given to all of them together, it would be simultaneously given to each one. However, one can legitimately ask whether the priest's act must not be individualized by the priest himself and not only by the penitent who would appropriate in some manner. Moreover, from the pastoral point of view, such a practice does not seem to recommend itself and should be avoided. Indeed, it favors a false conception of penance in the faithful, who would have trouble understanding that this absolution, which seems to be given to the entire community present, is applied to each one only to the degree that he has really confessed and to the degree that the sufficiency of his confession was accepted by the priest who received it. This minimization of the acts proper to the penitent directly contradicts the end pursued in this effort to renew the sacrament of penance. As for all the sacraments, such renewal involves developing and making more explicit the "sacred signification" by which it must introduce the penitent to the hidden reality that it signifies and produces: the remission of sins. Indeed, as we have seen, the external acts of the penitent are an integral part of the sacramental sign and therefore are at least partial bearers of its signification.

Of course, this holds only for "mortal sins," that is, sins properly so called, by which man ruptures his relationship with God. He can depart from this situation only by a "conversion." "Venial" sins, which leave the person oriented to God by charity (even if they themselves are acts wherein self-love prevails momentarily and accidentally over charity) do not require such a "conversion" and consequently do not require the sacrament of penance, which essentially is the sacrament of conversion. They only require a return to the demands of charity, with remorse for having ignored them. In other words, they still require "penitence," though in a diminished sense. Its principle is the charity that already exists in the heart of the person who has sinned. Penitential ceremonies bring great aid to this penance, and there is no difficulty in admitting that they are pardoned at this moment. (However, they are also pardoned by many other acts of religion, above all by Eucharistic communion.)[77]

Supplementary observations

{957} When we set the requirements of a true conversion of heart next to the existential situation of most Christians who confess (at least as it appears, even to the confessor), we can easily ask ourselves whether or not all of this is not a bit unreal. A demanding penitential practice would lead, today as in earlier times, to a situation that would gradually lead the Church to loosen her rigor. Thus, the great majority of the People of God would live on the margins of the Church, cut off from her sacraments, only asking her, through reconciliation *in extremis*, to abolish the consequences in the hereafter that follow on a life passed here-below heedless of the demands of the Christian ideal. However, does not an accommodating penitential practice ultimately relinquish conversion only to the serious and does it not, likewise, practically suppress the necessity (which, as we have seen, appears to be absolute) of the dispositions that one must bring to the sacrament of penance?

Paradoxically, if it seems unreal to require the "average" penitent to convert in the full sense of the term, it seems just as unreal to see in the "average" sinner this *aversio a Deo* which precisely motivates the *conversio ad Deum* that abolishes it. From this perspective, there arise adventuresome theories concern the extreme rarity and practical impossibility of "mortal" sin (i.e., sin in which the Christian's rupture with God is consummated). In short, the Christian is judged by many to be just as incapable of voluntarily turning away from God as he is of turning back toward Him.

Appearances seem to vindicate this skepticism. Nonetheless, such skepticism contradicts Scripture, which through and through

---

77. See *ST* III, q. 79, a. 4. [Tr. note: Fr. Nicolas also cites Jean-Hervé Nicolas, "Médiation mariale et maternité spirituelle," 67–88. It is not clear if this is correct or if he means some other text in his bibliography.]

is a call to conversion, and such conversion presupposes the aforementioned *aversio*. Also, this skepticism involves an underestimation of the human person, doubting his real capacity for freely engaging himself—and, all the while, we have never spoken so much about the freedom of the person and of the necessity of treating man as a "subject" and not as an "object." In salvation history, God treats man—indeed, each man—as a "subject." He proposes to man's freedom the gift that He has chosen to make of Himself, in the communion of three Persons.

Doubtlessly, one must pass beyond appearances. Man is not only a fluctuating individual, submitted to all the social and physical pressures that surround him and to the attraction of immediate goods. He is a person, and in the depths of his personality, he conceals the mysterious power of being able to orient himself, of being able to give a meaning to his destiny, *sese agere*, to act upon himself. This freedom must find its way through all the obscurities that blind it and all the pressures that are exercised on it from outside, so that it may realize itself in its external acts. It is easy to complain of all the conditions that paralyze it. However, it first of all takes place in man's own depths, and even the most conditioned of individuals still retains a real power for choosing God and for choosing Christ in the midst of the various objects that solicit his desires every day—or, on the contrary, the power to reject God by rejecting Christ. The mystery of the *aversio a Deo* and of the *conversio ad Deum* takes place within his depths.

Consequently, the signs of a true attrition are difficult to detect in the penitent. The clearest sign of it will be the sincere intention to change one's life in the particular matter that is contrary to the Gospel, even though it can happen that the penitent cannot see how this or that aspect of his life is contrary to the Gospel. It is better for the priest to incite the sinner to penance than to reject him on account of a lack of penitence, unless this lack is quite obvious.

Consequently, as well, this change and dislocation produced in the attrite sinner by confession and absolution together is not assuredly perceptible, neither for the penitent, nor for the confessor. It is situated in the depths of the person, where his encounter with Christ takes place.

17

The Anointing of the Sick

The relative space available for the sacrament of the anointing of the sick in a course in dogmatic theology is too restricted for it to be able to be treated adequately. A complete study would require a much longer treatment so that we would be able to pursue all the historical and dogmatic investigations that the matter calls for. For our part, we will only be able to provide indications and open up some avenues for further investigation.

INTRODUCTION

{958} The Church's doctrine with regard to this sacrament was fixed at the fourteenth session of the Council of Trent, which depended on the theological elaboration undertaken by scholastic theologians on the basis of liturgical usage as it had been fixed by the thirteenth century. This elaboration had been accepted and, as it were, codified, by the Council of Florence in the Decree for the Armenians.[1]

Faced with the attacks of the reformers, who held that the anointing of the sick was a purely ecclesiastical institution without any effect of grace, the Council of Trent affirmed that it is concerned with a true sacrament, instituted by Christ, with reference to a power of healing by means of anointing with oil, granted to the disciples

---

1. See Council of Florence, *Exsultate Deo*, November 22, 1439, in D.-*Sch.*, nos. 1324–25.

sent on mission by Christ,[2] as well as with reference to the prayer accompanied by the anointing with oil performed by the priests for a sick brother. It said that the effect of this sacrament was the production of

> a grace of the Holy Spirit, whose anointing cleanses one of sins if there are any remaining for expiation, as well as those things that follow upon sin. It alleviates and fortifies the sick person's soul by arousing in him great confidence in God's mercy. Thus alleviated, the sick person may more easily bear the sufferings and fatigues of the sickness and more easily resist the temptations of the devil.

However, it also left open the possibility of bodily healing as the effect, in accord with the text of St. James: "Sometimes, he recovers bodily health when this is used for the salvation of the soul." Finally, in a more inclusive manner than Florence (which allowed this sacrament to be administered only to someone "whose death is feared"), thus doing justice again to the obviously broader meaning of St. James's text ("If someone falls ill"[3]), it declared that "this anointing must be given to the sick, above all (*praesertim*) to those whose state is so perilous that they seem to have arrived at the end of their life, which led to it also being called the sacrament of the dying."

This *praesertim* then came to be restricted by the older [Code of] Canon Law into *nisi qui* ("to him alone who ..."[4]) but then, later on, was opened up much more broadly by the Second Vatican Council and by the new Code of Canon Law. In *Sacrosanctum Concilium*, it was written: "'Extreme unction,' which may also and more fittingly be called 'anointing of the sick,' is not a sacrament for those only who are at the point of death."[5] Finally, Trent pushed back against Luther's accusation, claiming that the Church's practice is opposed to the Letter of James: "By administering this anointing, the Roman Church, the mother and mistress of all the Churches, assuredly does nothing other for that which touches on the substance of this sacrament than what blessed James prescribed to be done."

This restriction ("for that which touches on the substance of this

---

2. See Mk 6:13.
3. Jas 5:14–15.
4. See c. 940 (1917 Code of Canon Law).
5. Vatican II, *Sacrosanctum Concilium*, no. 73.

sacrament"), as well as the problem of bodily healing attributed to this sacrament, highlights the great difficulties involved in the theology of the anointing of the sick. To be recognized as sacramental, two things must be addressed. On the one hand, this practice must have traditional and scriptural justifications, and these are difficult to establish. On the other hand, we must be able to discover a significate effect proper to this sacrament (i.e., a distinct sacramental grace). Here, we find ourselves confronted with the difficulty of unifying the two components of this grace, namely the remission of sins and bodily healing.

THE SEARCH FOR A SCRIPTURAL AND TRADITIONAL JUSTIFICATION OF THE SACRAMENTAL STATUS OF THE ANOINTING OF THE SICK

The Text of St. James

{959} In* this text, one must note the appeal that is made to the "presbyters." Without prejudging the delicate problem concerning the identification of these "presbyters" with the priests of the later ages of the Church, it is certain, in any case, that it is a question of people who are responsible for the ecclesial community. Therefore, it is also clear that the rite described therein is not an act of private devotion but, rather, has a "liturgical" character.

It is not a question of "preparation for death" but, rather, a true case of sickness. The rite includes an anointing with oil, a prayer by these presbyters, one that is official and liturgical. (A simple prayer would not require the presbyters to come.)

As regards the rite's effect, the expression *agerei auton o Kurios*

---

* See the following texts: Cavallera, "Le décret du concile de Trente sur l'extrême onction," *Bulletin de littérature ecclésiastique* 39 (1938): 3–29. Antoine Chavasse, *Étude sur l'onction des infirmes dans l'Église latine, du IIIe siècle à la Réforme carolingienne* (Lyon, 1942). Jean-Charles Didier, "Extême-onction," *Catholicisme* 4 (1954): 987–90. André Duval, "L'extrême-onction au concile de Trente," *La Maison-Dieu* 101 (1970): 127–72. *Saint Thomas d'Aquin. Somme théologique, L'extême-onction. Suppl. questions 29–33*, trans. Henri-Dominique Gardeil (Paris: Éditions du Cerf, 1967). B. Laurent, "Le magistère et le mot 'extrême-onction' depuis le concile de Trente," in *Problemi scelti di teologia contemporanea* (Rome: Pontificia Università Gregoriana, 1954), 219–32. Poschmann, *Pénitence et onction des maladies*, 203–24 (bibliography beginning on 203).

("the Lord will raise him up") indicates something that is indifferently related to a bodily healing or to a spiritual recovery. It is difficult to remove the idea of a healing from this text, and it indeed seems that it must be read in relation to Mark 6:13. On the contrary, it is impossible to reduce the entire scope of the text to the idea of a mere bodily healing, for the remission of sins is explicitly mentioned in the text. Moreover, we cannot retain the idea that, according to the Letter of James, the Church would have received the power to heal all sicknesses and to prevent the faithful from dying. The ambiguity of this sacrament, which is simultaneously ordered to bodily healing and to preparation for death (which presupposes that one assumes the possibility of not being healed), already stands out in this text. Perhaps it has its origin in the Gospel, where a mysterious connection appears between sickness, which leads to bodily death, and sin, which leads to the "second death," namely, that of the soul.[6]

Looking at this rite described and recommended by St. James, can we justly say that we see a sacrament, properly speaking, here? With regard to the sacraments in general (and in particular with regard to penance), we saw how this is an ambiguous question. The dogmatic notion of "sacrament" was elaborated quite late in the Church's history, and we can look for it neither in the expressions nor in the thought of the author of the letter or of its readers. However, this notion was not elaborated *a priori*, nor is it a purely mental construction. It intends to render account of the meaning and saving value of the rites which the Church practiced long before having a theory of them—rites that are bearers of grace, by which she exercises the sanctifying power that she was always aware of having received from the Lord. In this sense, we can say that the rite described by St. James presents the characteristics of what will be later on expressed (verbally and notionally) by the term "sacrament": an action performed by the Church on a believer, accompanied by prayer and ordered to the communication of a saving grace. The fact remains that this saving grace and, of course, the rite itself, are themselves still in a state of great indetermination [at the time of this text's composition].

---

6. See Mt 9:2, Mk 3:5, Lk 7:20.

The Anointing of the Sick

The Progress of Tradition

{960} Above all, we must note that we possess no testimony in relation to the anointing of the sick during the first two centuries of the Church's life. From the third century onward, documents appear, especially rituals that make mention of the anointing of the sick. What is remarkable is that these documents insist much more on the blessing of "the oil for the infirm" than on its application. This blessing is always reserved to the members of the hierarchy, whereas the application of the oil thus blessed seems to be left to each person.

Consequently, the most ancient rituals speak only of the blessing of the oil, which alone was submitted to precise liturgical rules. Among these rites, we must distinguish those that insist on bodily healing in the blessing formulas[7] and those that insist on the remission of sins (though without chronological succession).

The ritual forms related to the use of the oil (most often anointing, though also reception of it, *gustante*) during this first period (up to the ninth century) insist on the effects of bodily healing. Nonetheless, it is notable that, citing the text of James, they do not omit the part stating, "if he has committed sins, he will be forgiven" (RSV), which indicates that the spiritual effect is not, for all that, outside of their awareness. Indeed, they cite nearly the entire text of St. James and present the rite of anointing as applying to the sick the recommendation made in this text. It seems that during these six centuries, ecclesiastical authors became increasingly aware of the relation of this anointing to the remission of sins. From this very brief description of the rite, they retain two constant factors in the liturgy that is developing during this time (or that which they relate to us): oil and prayer.

The Elaboration of the Practice Current in the Middle Ages

{961} By contrast, from the ninth century onward, we have abundant witnesses to the sacrament of anointing. Here again, we find an important role played by the Carolingian reforms. The administration

---

7. For example, see Hippolytus of Rome, *La tradition apostolique*, SC 11 bis, ch. 5.

of the sacrament became strictly reserved to priests who were urged to carry blessed oil with them in their travels.

However, for many reasons, the sacrament was not administered very often. The faithful preferred to go to healers, holding that priests were negligent or greedy. On the other hand, if the sacrament healed the sick person, he was urged to take up heavy penitential obligations, for the anointing had been introduced into the penitential ritual. This explains how an anointing that was intended to help the sick recover their health came to be transformed into an anointing of the dying. Before long, Luther will be found mocking this deviation in comparison with St. James's text, showing the priest at the bedside of a dying person imploring his healing.[8]

On the basis of this, the high scholastics elaborated a theology of the sacrament in function of sacramental theology in general. This elaboration by Peter Lombard (and what follows it, making reference to the text of St. James as the proper place of the sacrament's institution) can be considered as being the foundational text for this elaboration: "Beyond those that we have discussed, there is another sacrament, the anointing of the sick, which is give in at the very end [of one's life] with oil that was consecrated by the bishop."[9]

The elements of this synthesis are found in St. Thomas's commentary on the *Sentences*.[10] It can be summarized as follows.

Extreme unction is a sacrament which was instituted by Christ and promulgated by the apostles. Its matter is olive oil consecrated by the bishop. Its form is made up of the prayer that accompanies the anointings. Its principal effect is the *dismissio peccatorum*, with regard to the "weakness" that sins have let in the sinner, also called *reliquiae peccati* (the things that follow upon sin). Moreover, it can happen that this sacrament may also cause the remission of sins purely and simply in the case when the beneficiary is found to be in a state of sin but does not present an obstacle to grace (i.e., a voluntary refusal of grace), as happens in the Eucharist and confirmation as well.

---

8. See Martin Luther, *Kommentar zu Galater* in *Martin Luthers Werke*, Weimarer Ausgabe, 40 (Weimar: H. Böhlau, 1883ff.), 568.

9. See Lombard, *Sententiae*, bk. 4, d. 23.

10. See *In IV Sent*, d. 23. Equally, see *SCG* IV, bk. 73.

As regards bodily healing, St. Thomas proposes a very refined and nuanced solution to the problem. Just as baptism is an action of bodily cleansing that is a sign and cause of "spiritual cleansing," so too extreme unction is an action of bodily medication that is a sign and cause of a spiritual medication. However, there is a difference between the two. Water washes the body by its own proper power so that the sacramental action in baptism action always produces its bodily effect. Here, on the contrary, the oil produces bodily healing only by the Divine Power, not by its own power, and "God does not act in an unreasonable manner" but, rather, does as He judges to be fit in relation to the sacramental effect itself, "that is, when this is useful for spiritual healing." The subject of this sacrament is the sick person who is about to die, and it must be given only to sick people whom men can judge to be approaching death. Here we see that the shifting of meaning noted above, as it were, theologically codified. Nonetheless, the sacrament can be repeated if the sick person recovers and then falls ill again. Finally, it cannot be administered by a layman.

The Anointing of the Sick, Considered at the Council of Trent

{962} It is clear that the thought of the Council Fathers of the Council of Trent on this issue depended greatly on how it was elaborated by scholastic thinkers. Moreover, they are not very occupied with the question, only dedicating a brief section of the fourteenth session (which itself was dedicated to the topic of penance) to it, as well as four canons following the fifteen dedicated to penance. The essential concern of the Council Fathers was to refute the attacks registered by the reformers and to maintain the legitimacy of the liturgical usage of extreme unction in relation to St. James's text. Also, they were concerned with maintaining its traditional qualifications as a sacrament.

As we have seen, the Second Vatican Council will rectify the deviation accepted by Trent (though not without a kind of opening to this rectification, in particular for those who are in such a danger of death that they seem to have arrived at the end of their life) by substituting the expression "anointing of the sick" for the expression "extreme unction" (which had become classical from the Middle Ages) without, however, suppressing every connection with "danger of death."

The Institution of the Sacrament of the Anointing of the Sick by Christ

{963} To resolve this difficult question, one can make use of the principle we recalled in relation to the sacrament of penance. If we are seeking a precise text in Scripture or in the tradition relating in a clear manner to the institution of a sacrament in its specificity, with the exception of baptism and the Eucharist, we will risk falling into an accommodating exegesis, interpreting ancient texts on the basis of practices and notions that came long after. However, if in these relatively recent practices we try to look for the exercise of a specific sanctifying power, we will perceive that she gradually became aware of this power that was given to her.

In the case of the anointing of the sick, it is a question of the Church's power for aiding believers in their sickness. It is clear in Scripture that sickness has a religious meaning and dimension, namely, that sickness would be a journey toward death and that death itself has a religious meaning. This is clear in all religions, especially those that expressly profess survival after death. For the Christian religion, it plays an essential role in the destiny of the person who has been called from his life here-below but whose vocation is not fully realized until after death (and also, in accord with the way that he lived here-below).

Very early on, the Church felt that she was responsible for Christians in their passage to death. In days when her penitential demands were most severe, this led to her desire to reconcile those who are dying and to give them *viaticum*. It is possible that her intervention by anointing and prayer did not at first appear to her clearly as being distinct from her intervention by means of reconciliation and by *viaticum*. However, the text of St. James played its role here, for it presented a rite properly pertaining to those who are sick (even though penance obviously was not something proper to the sick and even though it was first addressed those who had the time to do the penance). In the rite found in St. James's letter, the intention of bodily healing was closely connected to that of the remission of sins. It would be the work of theology to determine the particular way that the sacrament frees the sick person from his sins.

A SKETCH OF A THEOLOGY OF THE ANOINTING OF THE SICK

A[11] theological investigation into the sacrament of the anointing of the sick must first concern itself with the meaning of bodily sickness in relation to sin and to salvation. Then, by way of consequence, it must consider the relationship that we can grasp as existing between bodily healing and healing from sin. On the basis of this, it is then possible to specify what the *res* of this sacrament is (i.e., its proper significate-effect). Having done this, it becomes possible to ask whether or not it is the "sacrament of the dying," and if it is this, in what sense it can be called such.

Sickness and Sin

{964} There is a connection between sickness and sin, but what is it?

Certainly, it is not a connection of effect to cause, at least a direct connection of this sort. Whatever the causes of a sickness may be (even if it originates in sinful behaviors), they are not causes of sickness precisely inasmuch as the former are sinful. Cirrhosis of the liver caused by a person's abuse of alcohol is not medically different from cirrhosis arising from some other cause, entailing no responsibility on the part of the sick person.

There is an indirect connection, in the sense that a considerable portion of maladies arise in humanity on account of aberrant individual or collective behaviors whose origin is disobedience to God and irrationality. For all men and women, they arise, in a mysterious manner, from the aberrant behavior that faith tells us occurred at the beginning of human history, an aberration called "original sin."

Moreover, there is a connection as from a symbol to that which it

---

11. Roger Béraudy, "Le sacrement des maladies," *Nouvelle revue théologique* 106 (1974): 600–634, and Colman E. O'Neill, "Extreme-Unction: Suffering in Christ," *Doctrine and Life* 12 (1962): 501–9.

symbolizes. Sin reaches (and, indeed, diminishes) the person in his spiritual dimension, as sickness does in one's bodily dimension. Indeed, such symbolism expresses damnation by means of the notion of death: "the second death."[12] God is man's life. Loss of God is loss of one's life (though in such a way that the person who is thus deprived of Him who is his life subsists and bears this death within himself). Sin leads to (spiritual) death as sickness leads to (bodily) death.

Bodily Healing—Spiritual Healing

{965} Consequently, in the regime of grace where liberating grace is given by bodily means (i.e., sacred acts bearing grace), it is understandable that spiritual healing, a condition for the sinful person's liberation and union with God (a union that is his life), would be symbolized and brought about by means of bodily healing (i.e., by the application of a bodily remedy). Without a doubt, in the historical context of the Gospel and the Letter of James, anointing with oil was such a remedy.

Here, we can retain the profound explanation given by St. Thomas, which we discussed above. Water cleanses the body by the power proper to it. Therefore, the action of washing in a bodily manner bears the same meaning as merely saying that one washes. The washing of the body is part of the sacramental rite, like the water itself. By contrast, a remedy neither always acts, nor does so immediately—especially in this case when it is a question of a remedy prescribed by God and ordered to healing inasmuch as such healing is a work performed by God. Given that the sacramental sign is certain and produces what it signifies in virtue of the divine promise, if the anointing of the sick were the sacrament of bodily healing, it would be contrary to the sacramental order that the remedy would be applied and the sickness would not be instantaneously healed. However, it is the sacrament of a spiritual healing. That is, it is a bodily remedy ordered of itself to the production of bodily healing, though in such a manner that such healing is far from being certain (as is the case for every bodily remedy). By the intermediary of this uncertain bodily healing, this bodily remedy, which only

---

12. Rv 2:11 and 20:6–14.

has an intentional reality (i.e., as something included in the remedy as that toward which it naturally tends and that toward which it first of all orients one's thought), signifies and produces spiritual healing (though, with certitude as regards the latter).

This bodily healing is miraculous in character, for it is not a question of a remedy that is naturally apt to produce it, but rather of a remedy that can act only as an instrument of the Divine Power. Moreover, the remedy is not the "sacrament" (i.e., a certain sign and an indefectible cause). Hence, for these two reasons, beyond the application of the remedy, it makes an appeal to the "rational" will of God. If it is produced—and the possibility is not excluded that, in fact, in the apostolic Church the anointing of the sick played this role even in the exercise of the charism of healing[13]—it will also be an effect of the sacrament, though its secondary effect. Indeed, it is an effect of the sacrament because it is connected, in the divine intention, to spiritual healing, as sickness had been connected, in a mysterious manner, to spiritual lethargy. However, it is a secondary effect because it is ordered to the spiritual healing that is primarily aimed at and ordered by a free and unforeseeable choice by God.

The *res* (Sacramental Grace) of the Anointing of the Sick

{966} We still must determine the nature of the "spiritual lethargy" that is caused by sin and which the anointing of the sick brings healing to.

The difficulty here arises from the fact that the sacrament of penance is already ordered to delivering the Christian from his sins. Historically, it seems that the two sacraments only progressively came to be distinguished from each other. Even St. James's text could be considered as a source concerning the sacrament of penance, although even here this rite is differentiated from the simple rite of reconciliation on account of its use of oil and the fact that it is offered to the sick alone and is connected to bodily healing.

Given that this differentiation did not come about all at once, it is understandable that the anointing of the sick was not even

---

13. See 1 Cor 12:9 and Mk 6:13.

mentioned during the first centuries of the Church's life and that when it did appear it did not do so in a completely clear manner along with all the characteristics of what will later on be conceived as being a specific sanctifying power of the Church and explicitly called a sacrament. This does not mean that this sacrament was created by the Church. She discerned it gradually as being in the apostolic patrimony, in a way similar to what happened with regard to confirmation's relationship to the sacrament of baptism.

St. Thomas sought to explain this lethargy as being "those deficiencies by which man is spiritually wounded so that he does not have his full vigor for the acts of grace and glory. This deficiency is nothing other than a kind of weakness, an incapacity that is left in us by personal or original sin. Man is fortified against this weakness by this sacrament."[14] The allusion to original sin makes one here think of *concupiscentia*, a moral weakness that is left behind from original sin in the baptized person.[15] However, does St. Thomas mean that the suppression of *concupiscentia* is the effect of the anointing of the sick? If this must be the effect of some sacrament, it is not clear why it would not be the effect of baptism. "Debility" in the moral and spiritual order must be conquered, according to him, through spiritual combat, and if there is a sacrament ordered to assuring progressive victory in this combat, it is the Eucharist.[16] In truth, the solution proposed by St. Thomas in the *Scriptum* is rather imprecise and doubtlessly would have been given greater precision had he completed the *Summa theologiae*.

Thus, we see the path that I believe is needed for further investigations. Sickness and death are originally "a punishment for sin." By taking on humanity in its condition arising from sin and by taking suffering and death on Himself in this assumed humanity, the Word transformed humanity's dolorous condition. Through the punishment that He underwent, He offered satisfaction to God, who received it as a sacrifice. Taking up bodily death, which was the image of the second death and the gateway to it, He conformed it to

---

14. See *In IV Sent.*, d. 23, q. 1, a. 2, ad 3 qu.
15. See *ST* III, q. 69, a. 3.
16. See *ST* III, q. 79, a. 6.

His own victorious death over sin and made it into a gateway to the resurrection.

Thus, the anointing of the sick could be conceived as being a sacrament whose proper effect is giving the believer's sickness and death its "Christian" character as conforming to Christ's death in view of the resurrection.[17]

Sacrament of the Sick or Sacrament of Those Who Are Dying?

{967} Does this bring us back to the older conception holding that it is a "sacrament of the dying"?

Let us note that, for St. Thomas, a sacrament can act only on a Christian who is able to perform a human act.[18] According to him, it must not be given to the insane, nor to children. Therefore, it seems (although he does not say so explicitly) that one also must not, according to him, give it to a dying person without that person's knowledge. Moreover, he says that the *res et sacramentum* is a kind of internal devotion which is a spiritual anointing,[19] which obviously presupposes sufficient consciousness.

Historical circumstances led this sacrament to become the sacrament of the dying. However, one would be prey to an excessive reaction if every reference to death were excluded from discussions concerning this sacrament. It is addressed to a Christian who is truly sick, and sickness of itself leads to death. Inasmuch as it leads to death, sickness is a characteristic state of the Christian in the process of being redeemed. Undoubtedly (perhaps?), this can help us explain why the idea of sickness, in what pertains to this sacrament, was interpreted as meaning a sickness including a real danger of a fatal outcome and also why the Second Vatican Council extended this to old age, which is not, in itself, a sickness (though, inasmuch as it includes a real danger of death, it has a likeness to sickness). By claiming that there must be a freely willed participation by the sick person for this sacrament to produce its effect (somewhat as is the

---

17. See Karl Rahner, "Pour une théologie de la mort," *Écrits théologiques* (Paris: Desclée de Brouwer, 1963) 3:165.
18. *Scriptum* 1, ch. 2, 2, ad 3, qu. [*sic*]
19. Ibid., 1, 2, ad 3, qu. 3. [*sic*]

case for penance), St. Thomas justifies the idea that one should not wait until the last moments of life.

However, a question does still remain regarding this (something that likewise remains for penance as well). Is the dying person who cannot perform this freely chosen act (e.g., in a coma or in agony) capable of receiving these two sacraments? The Church's custom is to confer them in this case. Doubtlessly, one must here have recourse to an explanation that is analogous to that which is brought forth in justification of infant baptism. In this state of incapacity, the Christian does not perform an act contrary to the intention of the Church and of Christ which is expressed in the bestowing of the sacrament and thus does not pose an obstacle to it. Hence, we here see the saving character of Christ's coming fully expressed as being His work in man. However, the case of an adult is not the same as that of a child. If he has truly rejected Christ and has not withdrawn this rejection before losing the use of his reason and capacity to act freely, he is without a doubt in a state of resistance rendering the sacrament's action impossible.

Another difficult question remains. The Church does not allow this sacrament to be repeated during the same sickness. How is this to be explained theologically? The sacrament that has been administered lasts by means of its *res et sacramentum*. What is the *res et sacramentum* here? If it were *devotion*, as St. Thomas says, it is not clear how the sacrament could last beyond acts of "devotion." It would seem preferable, along the lines of the preceding explanation, to say that the *res et sacramentum* is the very state of the sick person consecrated by the sacrament, sacramentally identified with Christ's suffering and death and, for this reason, calling for the person who receives the sacrament to exercise the acts of "devotion" spoken of by St. Thomas, acts which seem, rather, to belong to the *res* of the sacrament. To say "sacramentally" also indicates "ecclesially," as the Christian is a member of Christ by being part of the "body of Christ which is the Church." Through his sickness (and through his death) thus consecrated, the Christian exists in a particular modality as a member of the Church. His sickness (as well as his death) is, as it were, taken up by the Church and presented to God by the Church, thus becoming a "saving" reality for him and for others. It is principally ordered to salvation, properly speaking, which always includes the remission of sins, divinization, and eternal life, while sometimes also including bodily healing (according to God's free disposition). One can thus speak of "sacramental reviviscence" in the case when, after having received anointing, this person would have fallen back into sin, only then to leave this sinful state once again through penance.

This "sacramentalization" of sickness (and of the sick person precisely as sick) obviously is not a character. However, it is connected with the baptismal character in some way insofar as it is a restoration of the full participation in Christ's death given at baptism, though more or less lost by personal sins. Thus, it would draw its stability from the baptismal character. However, it is also connected to the state of sickness and therefore itself ceases to exist when one no longer is ill after being healed.

PART 5

THE SACRAMENT OF HOLY ORDERS

INTRODUCTION

{968} The five sacraments spoken of up to this point are concerned with the personal sanctification of their recipients. Baptism, confirmation, and the Eucharist are directly concerned with this personal sanctification, for by means of them we are conformed to Christ, being adopted as sons by the Father and divinized by the Holy Spirit. Indirectly, penance and anointing of the sick sanctify their recipients by restoring this conformity to Christ if it has been lost by sin. Meanwhile, the two other sacraments of the "sacramental septenary."—holy orders* and marriage—obviously are concerned with individual persons. However, by their own particular character, they are not ordered, of themselves, to the personal sanctification of those who receive them, even though they are necessary for the Church herself (and therefore, for the sanctification of the People of God). The sacrament of holy orders above all is concerned with

---

* [Tr. Note: At the recommendation of the copy editor of this volume, I am generally translating "le sacrament de l'ordre" as "the sacrament of holy orders." It is not clear, at least to my eyes, whether Fr. Nicolas (who is opposed, in a nuanced fashion, to certain excesses found in the French school of priestly spirituality) wishes to convey "holy orders" or only "orders" in his terminology. However, "holy orders" is more standard in English and is therefore being used here. It is also a justified translation of the French.]

the Church as such, enabling her to assure the sacramental action by which Christ's saving action is rendered present and active in the world by some of her members.

As regards the sacrament of marriage, it is somewhat inappropriate to place it next to the sacrament of holy orders in contrast with the five others, presenting them as the two "social" sacraments in opposition to the "individual" sacraments. In reality, we will see that it is directly concerned with the sanctification of those who receive it. However, it is concerned with this sanctification inasmuch as it enables them to realize in the Church a form of the Christian vocation that is authentic, though not necessary [neither for all nor for the continuance of the sacramental order itself]. For this reason, we could say that it is situated between the five others and the sacrament of holy orders.

In this section, we will be occupied with the sacrament of holy orders, which is intended to make certain members of the Church "priests." This simple assertion runs into two grave difficulties which are, moreover, antinomic. On the one hand, in the regime of the New Covenant, there is only one priest, Jesus. On the other hand, Scripture tells us that all the faithful are priests. In any case, this consequently seems to exclude the idea of there being a sacrament which would make certain members of the People of God priests to the exclusion of others. Nonetheless, this is something the Church holds as *de fide* and has expressed in a host of documents. The principal documents expressing this point are: the Decree for the Armenians from the Council of Florence,[1] the Decree on the Sacrament of Orders from Trent,[2] Pius XII's encyclical, *Mediator Dei*,[3] the Apostolic Constitution *Sacramentum Ordinis* by Pius XII,[4] and the *Acts of Vatican II*.[5] To this, we must add a recent letter from the Congregation for the Doctrine of the Faith on the minister of the Eucharist, with the authorized commentary by Cardinal Ratzinger.[6] All these

---

1. See Council of Florence, *Exsultate Deo*, November 22, 1439, in D.-*Sch.*, no. 1326.
2. See Council of Trent, session 23, "Decree and Canons on the Sacrament of Orders," July 15, 1563, in D.-*Sch.*, nos. 1764–78.
3. Pope Pius XII, *Mediator Dei*, November 2, 1947, in *AAS* 39 (1947): 555, in D.-*Sch.*, no. 3852.
4. See Pope Pius XII, *Sacramentum ordinis*, November 30, 1947, in *AAS* 40 (1948): 5–7.
5. See Vatican II, *Lumen Gentium*, no. 10.
6. See *Documentation catholique* (1983): 885–88.

documents are relatively recent, for the sacrament of holy orders was placed into question in the Church only later on in her history. However, they are based on a tradition that was unanimously received from the first days of the her history.

Another difficulty comes from the twofold character of the priesthood as a "hierarchical" reality, simultaneously being a form of service and of power. Inasmuch as it is a form of service, it orders the priest to the service of the Church and therefore of the People of God—Christians and indeed all men, for all are called to be Christians. Inasmuch as it is a form of power, it includes authority and honor, even if these are only one of its aspects. In other words, it has the twofold character of being a function in the Church and a personal vocation for him who is ordained.

These two difficulties are encountered in nearly all the questions that are raised by the Church's faith concerning the sacrament of holy orders. Therefore, they will constantly be present in our discussions, and we will strive to resolve them each time that they present themselves.

18

The Priest in the Church

THE CHURCH'S PARTICIPATION IN CHRIST'S PRIESTHOOD

Christ: The Sole Priest of the New Covenant

{969} This* is a fundamental datum of the theology of salvation. The very idea of a "New Covenant" calls for that of a new priesthood, which, according to the Letter to the Hebrews, is that of Christ. It is characterized by the fact that it is perfect, efficacious of itself for reconciling sinful men with God, and perpetual. In distinction from the Levitical high priest, Jesus does not have a successor:

---

* It is neither possible nor necessary to provide a complete bibliography. Moreover, further information will be given in the course of our discussions in this chapter. Here, we will note only studies about the sacrament of holy orders in general. See the following texts: Michel Andrieux, "La carrière ecclésiastique des papes et les documents liturgiques du Moyen Age," *Recherches des sciences religieuses* (1947): 90–120. Gustave Bardy, "Les origins du sacerdoce chrétien," *Vie Spiritualle, Supplément* 47 (1936): 12–32 and 86–106. Humbert Bouëssé, *Le sacerdoce chrétien* (Paris: Desclée, 1957). Congar, *Sainte Église*, 240–73. Jean-Paul Deloupy, *Laïcs et prêtres, des idées pour demain* (Paris: Centurion, 1977). Clément Dillenschneider, *Le Christ, l'unique prêtre, et nous ses prêtres* (Paris: Cerf, 1967). André Feuillet, "Les chrétiens prêtres et rois d'après l'Apocalypse," *Revue thomiste* 75 (1975): 40–66. L. Marchal, "Evêques (origine divine des)," in *Dictionnaire de la Bible* 2:1297–1333. Jean-Hervé Nicolas, "Sacerdoce, célibat et sacrements," *Nova et Vetera* 53 (1978): 122–34. Julien Potel, *Les prêtres séculiers en France. Evolution de 1965 à 1975* (Paris: Centurion, 1977), and *D'autres prêtres? Leur place et leurs rôles* (Paris: Centurion, 1977). Also, see the collaborative works: *La Tradition sacerdotale* (Paris: Mappus, 1959), *Le ministère sacerdotal, Rapport de la Commission Théologique Internationale* (Paris: Cerf, 1971), "Études et recherches de Foi et Constitution," *Istina* 23 (1978): 5–55, and *L'épiscopat et l'Église universelle* (Paris: Cerf, 1962).

The former priests were many in number, because they were prevented by death from continuing in office; but he holds his priesthood permanently, because he continues for ever. Consequently, He is able for all time to save those who draw near to God through him, as he always lives to make intercession for them. For it was fitting that we should have such a high priest, holy, blameless, unstained, separated from sinners, exalted above the heavens.[1]

If everything that has salvific worth is found in Christ, it can be found in others only through conformity with Him, as being derived from Him, and as being actually dependent upon Him. This is particularly true for the priesthood. Christ is the unique priest because He is the unique mediator.[2] Therefore, the priesthood in the Church can be conceived only in function of Christ's priesthood.[3]

Let us recall what we said earlier concerning Christ's own priesthood, namely, that it must be defined as being ordered to the redemptive sacrifice by which, according to the expression of St. Thomas, "Christ opened the ritual order of the Christian religion by offering Himself to God as a sacrifice and victim."[4] The essential act of this priesthood, the unique act in which all the power of this perfect and perfectly efficacious priesthood is at once realized, was the sacrifice of the cross. By means of the Eucharist, this act continues throughout the time of the Church so that it may reach all generations and every man up to the end of time.

The Priesthood of the Church

{970} The Church's priesthood must be understood as being part of this temporal continuation of Christ's priestly action. Christ, who has returned to the Father, is present and active in the world through the Church for the salvation of the world.[5] Christ accomplishes this through the worship of the Christian religion, offering men to God and giving God to men.

The principal act of this priesthood is the Eucharistic sacrifice.

---

1. Heb 7:23–26 (RSV). See the remarks on this passage in Spicq, *L'epître aux Hébreux*, vol. 2, and Dillenschneider, *Le Christ, l'unique prêtre, et nous ses prêtres*, 37–55.
2. See 1 Tm 2:5.
3. See §518 in the previous volume.
4. See *ST* III, q. 6, a. 5.
5. See §§650ff. above.

As we have seen, it is Christ's sacrifice having become the Church's sacrifice, by which she ceaselessly offers the sacrifice of Calvary and by which she offers herself with Christ.[6] The entire liturgy wherein Christian worship unfolds is centered around the Eucharist and, above all, the sacraments, the essential liturgical celebrations which are wholly ordered to the Eucharist. The Church's preaching (including her missionary activity as well) is intimately connected with this properly sacramental action, as the word is connected to the sacraments.[7] Just as the Savior is the Word made flesh, so too the sacrament is the Word made a visible and efficacious sign so that the redemptive Incarnation may be extended up to our own time. The Word prepares for the sacrament, the sacrament bears the Word to the heart of its beneficiary, and its fruit is the full acceptance of the Word who saves.

The Church is a "priest" in the same way that she is a "mediatrix,"[8] namely, not only as depending on Christ but also as rendering Christ's mediating activity present and visible. Therefore, she is not a priest by placing herself between men who are to be saved and Christ the Savior. Rather, she is such by simultaneously and sacramentally being Christ the Savior in the act of saving as well as all saved men inasmuch as, and to the degree that, they are saved. In her, this union of men with God in Christ is realized, this union being the ultimate goal of Christ's mediation over men whose redemption was the reason for Christ's self-sacrifice. Therefore, the meaning of the Church's role as mediatrix first of all pertains to the exercise of Christ's mediation over men whose redemption was the reason for Christ's self-sacrifice. That is, she exercises Christ's mediation, on the one hand, over men whom redemption has not yet been reached through her missionary activity and, on the other, over baptized persons as regards that part of themselves that still is not under the sway of redemptive grace.[9] Second, she exercises her mediating activity in order to make thanksgiving (i.e., the self-offering that men make of themselves to God) rise up to God (through Christ). The consum-

---

6. See §862 above.
7. See §757 above.
8. See §537 in the previous volume.
9. See Jean-Hervé Nicolas, "Médiation mariale et maternité spirituelle," 68–76.

mation of this offering is Christ in all, the Church consummated, the whole Christ.

A Priestly People

{971} The universal priesthood of the faithful must be understood within the overall perspective of the Church's priesthood. This notion is principally founded on 1 Peter 2:1–10 and Revelation 1:6 and 20:6. However, these texts themselves explicitly refer to Exodus 19:6, a text to which numerous other texts in the Old Testament refer as well.[10] However, there are many more possible scriptural references, for the Christian community constitutes a "cultic community." The People of God is not a people merely wandering about. Rather, it proceeds toward a new sanctuary in order to offer the new worship there with the "high priest."[11] This cultic character of the Christian life is also expressed by the image of the temple and the prophets' notion of "spiritual worship," something itself taken up by St. Paul.[12]

This priestly character of the People of God (i.e., of all Christians inasmuch as they are part of the People of God) has given birth to a tendency to minimize or abolish the ministerial priesthood and, therefore, the sacrament of holy orders. In antiquity, we find an isolated witness to this tendency in Tertullian, claiming—in a writing taken from his period as a Montanist[13]—that the distinction between priests and laymen is something that has been created by the Church. In modern times, there was the position starkly asserted by Luther, holding that all Christians are priests,[14] then adopted by Calvin.[15] By a kind of reaction, their strong position on this matter led [Catholics] to mistrust the idea of the universal priesthood, even

---

10. For example, see 2 Mc 17–18. See also Feuillet, "Les chrétiens prêtres et rois d'après l'Apocalypse," 40–66.
11. See Heb 10:19–22. Spicq, *L'epître aux Hébreux*, 1:280–83 and 2:316–17. *Traduction oecuménique de la Bible*, 668–69.
12. See Rom 12:1 and Congar, *Le mystère du Temple*, 181–276.
13. See Tertullian, *De exhortation castitatis*, CSEL 2, 1024, and Pierre Grelot, *Église et ministère. Pour un dialogue critique avec Edward Schillebeeckx* (Paris: Cerf, 1983), 183–85.
14. See Martin Luther, *De captivitate Babylonica* in *Martin Luthers Werke*, Weimarer Ausgabe 40 (Weimar: H. Böhlau, 1883ff.), 568ff.
15. See Calvin, *Institution chrétienne*, vol. 4, ch. 18, §§2 and 17 et passim; ch. 19, §§22ff. [Tr. note: No date provided by Fr. Nicolas.]

though the idea is strongly attested to by ancient tradition.[16] Moreover, this minimization of the universal priesthood already appeared in the scholastics, and particularly in St. Thomas.[17] However, despite the very strong post-Tridentine tendency to valorize the ministerial priesthood as having a particular sanctifying value,[18] we can also recognize a return to the idea of the universal priesthood during this period.[19] This idea took on an increasingly larger place in modern theology and, finally, was placed in high relief by the Second Vatican Council.[20]

However, the central concern remained focused on the preservation of the specific character of the hierarchical priesthood, that which is constituted by the sacrament of holy orders and remains irreplaceable. This leads to a theological difficulty: if the hierarchical priesthood is defined by the power and responsibility of offering the Eucharistic sacrifice, what will be the priestly action of the baptized as such?

Many, following St. Thomas, looking for a parallel to what the Eucharistic sacrifice is in the case of the hierarchical priesthood, sought to place this activity in the offering of "spiritual sacrifices" and the sacrifice of one's life in the case of the universal priesthood.[21] Nonetheless, such a solution presents an insurmountable difficulty. In short, if the Eucharistic sacrifice is Christ's sacrifice, offered in time by the Church, that in which (as we have seen) she offers herself, what place can be admitted for the faithful's "spiritual sacrifices" next to Christ's unique sacrifice and the "Church's sacrifice"? Can St. Thomas's distinction between ecclesial activity and the private religious activity of believers be maintained? Doubtlessly, private

---

16. See Paul Dabin, *Le sacerdoce royal des fidèles dans la tradition ancienne et moderne* (Paris: L'Édition Universelle, 1950). Joseph Lecuyer, "Essai sur le sacerdoce des fidèles chez les Pères," *La Maison-Dieu* 27 (1951): 7–50. Dillenschneider, *Le Christ, l'unique prêtre, et nous ses prêtres*, 89–97.

17. See *In IV Sent.*, d. 13, q. 1, a. 1, sol. 1, ad 1; d. 24, q. 2, a. 2, ad 2. *ST* III, q. 82, a. 1.

18. See Michel Dupuy, *Bérulle et le sacerdoce* (Paris: Lethielleux, 1969).

19. See Anselme Robeyns, "L'idée du sacerdoce des fidèles dans la tradition, le concile de Trente et la théologie moderne," in *La participation active des fidèles au culte* (Louvain: Abbaye du Mont César, 1933).

20. See *Lumen Gentium*, no. 10.

21. See Congar, *Sainte Église*. Louis Charlier, "Le sacerdoce des fidèles," in *La participation active des fidèles au culte* (Louvain: Abbaye du Mont César, 1933). Dillenschneider, *Le Christ, l'unique prêtre, et nous ses prêtres*.

believers do indeed perform private religious activities. However, could it be approved by God if it were not ecclesial and Christic? In truth, it is not clear how believers' "spiritual sacrifices" could be distinct from the offering that the Church makes of herself in the Eucharist, except as the part is distinct from the whole.

On the other hand, the priesthood of believers is nothing other than the Church's priesthood, which is realized in each person only to the degree that he or she is a member of the Church and to the degree that the Church's own being is realized in him or her. Now, we have seen that the Eucharist is the central act of the Church's priesthood, taking up all the others. Therefore, through his participation in the Eucharist, the baptized person exercises the Church's priesthood for his own part.

What participation? As we have seen, in our discussions of the Eucharistic sacrifice, we must distinguish (for every sacrifice and, therefore, for this one as well) the "internal sacrifice" from the "external sacrifice" which is the sign of the former. In the Mass, the Church offers herself interiorly and spiritually with Christ, and the sacramental sacrifice is the sign and expression of this spiritual offering, as the real immolation of Christ on Calvary was the sign and expression of the gift that He made to the Father of the whole of Himself and of men in Him. If non-ordained believers cannot perform the sacramental action that constitutes the Eucharistic sacrifice, they can and must participate in it by offering themselves to the Father by offering Christ with the Church, doing so in accord with the way that the Eucharistic sacrifice expresses and realizes this offering. The "external sacrifice" would be nothing in God's eyes without the "spiritual sacrifice" by which the community offers herself in and with Christ.

Conversely, this spiritual sacrifice would be unreal if it were not concretized in the "external sacrifice," the only one that God accepted, that of His Son, ceaselessly offered sacramentally by the ecclesial community. Such is the nature of the essential priestly activity of the faithful. They perform it as a community because they are priests in a communal manner. And, in order to assure the reality of the priesthood of the believers, it is in no way necessary to discover and enumerate the "priestly" actions that each person would individually perform.²² Only two paths are possible in that direction of reflection: we would either be led to exclude the believer from the Church's own essential priestly activity (i.e., the Eucharistic sacrifice) or will find ourselves led to the inadmissible conclusion that the non-ordained believer has the power to perform the sacramental action of the Eucharist, the power to "preside over the Eucharist."

However, this is not a question of rejecting every form of participation by the faithful in the other acts by which the Church exercises her mediation, particularly in the proclamation of the Word. However, all these acts, including prayer and merit for others, are priestly only on account of their connection with the Eucharist.²³

Thus, the priesthood of the believers is the very priesthood of the Church, inasmuch as it is a participation in that of Christ, distinct from it, though totally dependent upon it.

THE MINISTERIAL AND HIERARCHICAL PRIESTHOOD

The Existence of the Ministerial Priesthood in the Church

{972} As* we have recalled, it is a *de fide* truth that there is "in the Catholic Church, a hierarchy instituted by a divine arrangement,

---

22. Despite what is said in Küng, *L'Église*, 115ff.
23. See §985 below.

* See the following texts: Bouyer, *L'Eglise de Dieu*, 373–448. Cerfaux, *La théologie de l'Église*, 351–400. Jean Colson, "Le ministère apostolique dans la littérature chétienne primitive," *L'épiscopat et l'Église universelle* (Paris: Cerf, 1962), 134–69. Congar, *L'Église une, sainte, catholique et apostolique*, 181–254. André Feuillet, *Le sacerdoce du Christ et de ses ministers* (Paris: Editions de Paris, 1972). Jean-Miguel Garrigues and Marie-Joseph Le Guillou, "Statut eschatologique et caractère ontologique de la succession apostolique," *Revue thomiste* 75 (1975): 395–417. Pierre Grelot, *Le ministère de la Nouvelle Alliance* (Paris: Cerf, 1967), and *Église et ministère. Pour un dialogue critique avec Edward Schillebeeckx* (Paris: Cerf, 1983). Antonio M. Javierre, "Le theme de la succession des apôtres dans la littérature chrétienne primitive," in *L'épiscopat et l'Église universelle* (Paris: Cerf, 1962), 171–226. Küng, *L'Église*, 503–656. Schnackenburg, *L'Église dans le Nouveau Testament*, 11–63 and 141–44. Carlos Josaphat Pinto de Oliveira, "Signification sacerdotal du ministère de l'évêque dans la Tradition apostolique d'Hippolyte de Rome," *Freiburger Zeitschrift für Philosophie und Theologie* 25 (1978): 398–427. [Tr. note: Reading the entry by Garrigues and Le Guillou as being the true referent for "Garrigues, 3," to which Fr. Nicholas in fact refers. No such entry explicitly exists in his bibliography.]

composed of bishops, priests, and ministers"[24] and that "those who have not been legitimately ordained nor sent by an ecclesiastical and canonical authority but, rather, come from elsewhere, are not legitimate ministers of the word and of the sacraments."[25] Now, the divine origin of this doctrine, which was strenuously contested by the reformers in the sixteenth century, is sometimes questioned today even within the Catholic Church, most particularly from an ecumenical perspective. Indeed, one of the great obstacles to the union of the Christian Churches is the question of ministers. With the exception of the Orthodox Church[es], whose ministerial connection to the apostolic succession nobody debates today, the received Catholic doctrine leads the Church to refuse to recognize the authenticity of the ministries that are exercised in other Christian Churches [*sic*]. (Obviously, this does not concern the Old Catholic Church, whose ordinations are doubtlessly valid, though a doubt perhaps[26] remains in the quite unique case of the Anglican Church.) The first and immediate consequence of this is that we believe "they have not retained the proper reality of the Eucharistic mystery in its fullness, especially because of the absence of the sacrament of Orders."[27] Hence, Catholics cannot be admitted to participation in their Eucharist. Thus, this question of ministry has been studied from every angle in order to see if a new approach might not enable us to envision the possibility of a "mutual recognition of ministries." For example, the agreement in Dombes on September 4–8, 1972, arose from this impetus.[28]

In this text, we can only provide a succinct treatment of this question. We must, however, note quite well from the start that we cannot reduce the authentic teaching of ministry in the Church to the teachings that are furnished by the New Testament, as though everything in the Church's doctrine that is not formally attested to in these texts were necessarily a later addition to the Church's apostolic

---

24. Trent, "Decree and Canons on the Sacrament of Orders," c. 6, in D.-*Sch.*, no. 1776.
25. See ibid., c. 7.
26. See A. F. von Gunten, "L'Église catholique pourrait-elle reconsidérer sa position sur les ordinations anglicanes?," *Nova et Vetera* 58 (1983): 252–67.
27. See Vatican II, *Unitatis Redintegratio*, no. 22.
28. See *Documentation Catholique* 70 (1973): 132–37.

structure and therefore could be non-necessary aspects which a given form of ministry could lack while nonetheless being held to be authentic (at least in certain conditions). After (and, indeed, before) the progressive and ultimate canonization of the texts that came to make up the New Testament *corpus*, the Church never admitted that the awareness that she had of herself and of her faith is reduced to what an independent exegesis could draw from them, however great the authority she grants to more or less directly apostolic texts. In our discussions of the sacraments in general (and of the sacrament of penance in particular), we saw that the Church lived in accord with the structures that were given to her from the beginning before elaborating a theory about these structures. Their existence and apostolic origin are also manifested by the way she lived and acted from the beginning. Thus, we must look upon many texts and facts found in the New Testament as being seeds for later developments, needing to be explained in light of them, instead of restricting the validity of these developments, allowing them only to be an exact reproduction of what these texts contain.[29]

Apostolic succession

{973} The fundamental fact is the designation of the Twelve by Christ Himself as persons who were charged with preaching His Gospel and with founding the Church. The close connection between the sending of the Son by the Father and the sending of the apostles by Christ is strongly emphasized in the Gospel, with the promise that He will be with them and will act by means of them. Thanks to the gift of the Spirit, this promise will be realized. They would accomplish His work by founding the Church.

Thus, they founded the Church of Christ, and the structures that they have given to her are the very structures that Christ willed, even if they were thought up by them and according to the circumstances facing them. The Church of today is the Church of Christ because she is the Church founded by the apostles: "Thus, we see that the initial and permanent dependence of the Church and the Spirit upon Christ was established upon the 'apostolate' and is affirmed

---

29. See Grelot, *Église et ministère*, 17–66.

upon it from age to age, in the strongest and most precise sense."[30]

The ministers established by the apostles in the Churches that they founded were closely dependent on the apostles' authority, as is quite clear in St. Paul's letters, for example (indeed, in a quite precise form) in the first Letter to the Corinthians.[31] This represented a unique situation which could no longer be repeated, and this forbids us from holding that a community from the apostolic era (e.g., the community of Corinth) could provide us with a model that could be reproduced later on. On the other hand, the Church's founding occurred in time and was brought to its completion only with the passing of the apostles. During this period, there certainly were practices that had only a provisional value and were *ipso facto* abolished to the degree that the essential structures of the Church were established. (For example, even if the Eucharist were presided over in this or that community by men who had not received the imposition of hands—something that is, however, far from an established fact—this would mean neither that such Eucharists were "inauthentic" nor, conversely, that a Eucharist celebrated in this manner today could be recognized as being authentic.)

If the Parousia had happened during the apostles' lifetime, the question of their succession would not have been raised. However, this was neither God's nor Christ's design. If the apostles had not chosen successors, sent by them as they were sent by Christ, the Church would be cut off from Christ. In fact, from the second century onward, almost everywhere and without dispute, we see bishops sitting at the heads of various communities, presiding over a college of priests, at once presenting themselves as "successors to the apostles" and being recognized as such. (Such testimonies come, for example, from Clement of Rome[32] and St. Irenaeus.)[33] With the passage of time, lists of this kind multiply in number. Even if these lists

---

30. See Bouyer, *L'Eglise de Dieu*, 382.

31. On the strict meaning and broad meaning of the term "apostle" in the apostolic Church, see Cerfaux, *La théologie de l'Église suivant saint Paul*, 353–64, and Grelot, *Église et ministère*, 21–27.

32. See St. Clement of Rome, *Épître aux Corinthiens*, trans. Annie Jaubert, SC 167 (Paris: Cerf, 1971), chs. 42–44.

33. See Irenaeus of Lyon, *Contre les hérésies*, bk. 3, ch. 3 [replaced by vols. 210 and 211 in SC], and Bardy, *La théologie de l'Eglise de S. Clément de Rome à S. Irénée*, ch. 4.

lose their historical value as these texts become increasingly separated in time from the apostles, they nonetheless are witnesses of the "unanimous conviction and importance that are attached to it. No bishop in the Church would be considered legitimate if his episcopacy did not lay in continuity with the apostolate in the strict sense, being linked thereto through the episcopacy of his predecessors."[34]

However, it is never a question of the bishops being new apostles! The apostles alone are the foundations of the Church. The bishops are their successors solely because they are charged with maintaining and continuing the Church that the apostles had founded:

> In contrast to the Apostles, bishops exist only in a Church that already exists, which is quite precisely that which the apostles established, such as they established it. Therefore, their function is not to establish another Church. Even less is it to modify her fundamental structure. On the contrary, their function is to preserve and "guard" it such as it has been established, and, certainly, to extend it, though always on this foundation and never on any other.[35]

For this reason, rather than saying that the bishops are the successors of the apostles, many theologians advocate (and not without reason) that we should say that, up to Christ's return, the apostles continue, through the bishops, their mission of "shepherding the flock of the Lord" (i.e. of governing the Church of God) which they received as their charge.[36] This perhaps provides a more profound response to the often-registered objection that this mission was entrusted to the apostles without reference being made to their successors. The apostles had to leave this world and history before Christ's return. However, through the collaborators who remained after them, and through those whom these successors would appoint and then leave after them, they continue to fulfill their mission beyond their death. This is the apostolic succession.

Just as we find at the beginning of the Church the group of the Twelve (plus Paul) together and integrally constituting the initial

---

34. See Bouyer, *L'Eglise de Dieu*, 391.

35. Ibid., 392.

36. See ibid., 390. Congar, *L'Église une, sainte, catholique et apostolique*, 194–95. Garrigues and Guillou, "Statut eschatologique et caractère ontologique de la succession apostolique," 395–417. Journet, *L'Église du Verbe incarné*, 1:463ff.

structure and "foundational" authority of the Church, so too from the beginning of the Church's life, apostolic succession is conceived not only as a given apostle transmitting to a given bishop the office of directing a particular church but, more broadly, as transmitting to the *episkopè* the responsibility of directing the Church founded by the apostles. This notion is found in a striking manner in the following text from Tertullian:

> In each city, the apostles founded the Churches from which, from this moment onward, the other Churches have borrowed the later graftings of the faith and the sowing of doctrine, and they borrowed it forever so that they may themselves become Churches. And by this very fact, they are considered to be apostolic, inasmuch as they are the offspring of apostolic Churches. Everything must be considered in relation to its origin. This is why, no matter how numerous and large these Churches may be, they are only this primitive apostolic Church from which they all proceed. They are all primitive and all apostolic, as they all are one.[37]

How the transmission of the mission conferred to the apostolic college by Christ Himself (and of the grace without which the fulfillment of this mission would be impossible) to the college of bishops came about is itself a historical problem. It is difficult to provide a clear solution to this question for lack of sufficient documentation. This situation leads to a number of difficulties and disputes, and they cannot be decided by irrefutable, scientific arguments:

> As has been said, in the first century, we unquestionably see apostles having established and establishing the Church. In the second century, we discover that the bishops occupy, without any objection or hesitation, the place that they left vacant there. However, between the two, there is, as it were, a tunnel, where we cannot follow the delicate details of a transmission and, more generally, of a transition, whose historical unfolding doubtlessly took on rather complex forms.[38]

This obscurity of beginnings is the law marking all cases of development, particularly of that which affects institutions. Doubtlessly, it is also the mark of the Holy Spirit who was the principal and hidden agent of the development about which we are speaking. Therefore, it

---

37. See Tertullian, *Traité de la prescription contre les hérétiques*, trans. François Refoulé and Pierre de Labriolle, SC 46 (Paris: Cerf, 1957), 20.5–8 (112).

38. Bouyer, *L'Eglise de Dieu*, 393 and 393n54.

would be completely false to say that the episcopacy, as the Church's essential structure, began in the midst of the second century, for this would be the very denial of the apostolic succession which, quite precisely, is affirmed as a constitutive element of the episcopacy from the time that it first appears. However, the roots which, from the very beginning, connect the episcopacy to the apostolic college from its beginning (and, through it, to the historical Christ), plunge down into such obscure depths that we cannot break through to them, although we can glimpse some aspects of it by reading the precious indications left to us by the pastoral epistles, or a text like the farewell of Paul to the presbyters of Ephesus in Miletus.[39]

The apostles' "priestly consecration"

{974} Can we establish that the apostles were priests (and bishops) in the sense that this term has in the Church's [contemporary] teaching? Without a doubt, this is indeed the way that the Church has thought of herself and her hierarchy for as far back as we can historically consider her understanding of the episcopacy. And she held that her bishops had received this quality from the apostles. Very early on, we find the "imposition of hands" as the means for transmitting the episcopal office of the apostles, including the priestly character.

Moreover, this is consistent with what we said above. If the apostles' essential role, which they transmitted to their successors, was to assure that the active presence of Christ the redeemer might exist amid the People of God for whom He died and was raised, and if the sacraments (principally the Eucharist) play the role of being the signs and means for bearing this active presence, which in itself is imperceptible, how could the apostles not have been empowered to celebrate the sacraments on account of their very function? Indeed, how could they not have first and foremost have been empowered to celebrate the Eucharist, the sacrament from which all the others derive and to which they all lead? [As Bouyer has noted:]

The transmission of the mystery, now entrusted to chosen men, the apostles of Christ, will necessarily present us with two aspects, something which was present from the beginning, as we have seen described in texts

---

39. See Acts 20:17–36.

in the Gospel. Once again, what the Apostles, through the special gift of the Holy Spirit which was given to them for us, must transmit to us first of all is the very presence of the Head and of His mystery, passing into us, acting in us, and extending to us. In other words, it exists in His Word and the sacramental signs of the permanent efficacy of the latter, for us and in us, we have something that totally exceeds these men who are only their pure instruments or, even simply passive transmitters of them.[40]

Can scriptural exegesis by itself establish the claim that the apostles expressly received a *priestly consecration* which would be the source and origin of the sacrament of holy orders? André Feuillet strove to articulate this conclusion in a close and rigorous exegesis of the fourth Gospel.[41] Let us merely note the reservations that Grelot registers regarding the results of this exegetic research, which he judges to be somewhat forced.[42] However, he himself very clearly admits that the ministry of the apostles was formally priestly in character and that what they transmitted to their collaborators was the capacity to fulfill this priestly function.[43] Whence do they themselves hold it? From Christ, obviously. Would it not be sufficient to say that Christ made them priests by commanding them to "do in memory of him" what He Himself did with the bread and wine, namely to offer Himself sacramentally in sacrifice and to distribute the fruits of the sacrifice of the Eucharist to the faithful?

The problem concerning the recognition of ministers

{975} If the apostolic function is priestly and if it was transmitted as such to the successors of the apostles—something that the Church holds to be *de fide*[44]—the problem concerning the recognition of ministries presents a difficulty, one that doubtlessly is insoluble from the perspective of Catholic doctrine. In short, if the "priestly character" of bishops and priests (in the form of a strictly ministerial priesthood, wholly and actually dependent on the priesthood of Jesus Christ) is that of the apostles transmitted to them by apostolic

---

40. See Bouyer, *L'Eglise de Dieu*, 387.
41. See Feuillet, *Le sacerdoce du Christ et de ses ministers*.
42. See Grelot, *Église et ministère*, 179n68.
43. See Grelot, *Le ministère de la Nouvelle Alliance*, 122–42, and *Église et ministère*, 173–81.
44. See Trent, "Decree and Canons on the Sacrament of Orders," ch. 1 and c. 2, in D.-*Sch*. nos. 1764 and 1772.

succession, it is not clear how the Church could recognize that such a character is had by someone who has not received it by means of this transmission. Indeed, from whom could it come to a man if not from Christ and from those to whom Christ first conferred it?

The traditional means of this transmission is the imposition of hands, a sacramental action. However, objections immediately arise: "Apostolic succession includes so much more! There is succession in fidelity to doctrine (the mission of announcing the Gospel) and in one's mode of life ('the following of Christ')." This is all doubtlessly true. Indeed, we will see that the meaning of the transmission of the priesthood is to assure that the People of God may still experience the presence and action of the apostles whom Christ Himself sent. However, here we are confronted anew with intrinsic requirements of the sacramental order, which is an order of signs. If ministerial priests are the means used by Christ for assuring His active presence among His people (an invisible presence and action, though visibly manifested), those by whom this action is exercised and in whom this presence is realized must be visibly designated in an incontestable manner.

We can be certain that the "priestly character" of the apostles was sacramentally transmitted to their successors in order to provide each generation of the People of God with men who thereby are successors to the apostles in doctrine and in the imitation of Christ. However, we can also be certain that these qualities of fidelity in doctrine and in the living imitation of Christ are not visible and cannot be objectively discerned with certitude. Therefore, they cannot by themselves assure the certitude of the sacramental order, that is, the certitude of Christ's active presence to His people. Sacramental transmission alone is visible and certain. Nothing can replace it. Moreover, given the objective indiscernibility of the presence or absence of intellectual, moral, and spiritual qualities befitting an authentic successor to the apostles in the person who is the object of this transmission, the constituting of a priest from among the People of God (and the designation of this person as incontestably being a priest) is sufficiently provided for by this visible transmission. Thus, he who was the beneficiary of it is a priest even if he does not show himself to be worthy of this status and role.

In short, it is utterly unclear how an agreement among the Churches—however generous its intention may be—could dispense a Christian from entering into the apostolic succession by means of the sacrament of holy orders in order to thus be an authentic "minister of the sacraments."

The Meaning of the Hierarchical Priesthood (and of the Sacrament of Holy Orders)

{976} By defining, as we have, the priesthood of the faithful as being the priesthood of the Church, do we not find ourselves travelling down a path that will end by making the hierarchical priesthood into a simple emanation from the priesthood of the believers? Abbé Long-Hasselmens had been engaged in investigations in this direction in a study that was published after his death by Fr. Congar along with critical notes:[45]

The priesthood of the entire body, wrote Long-Hasselmans, does not remain in the [Church-]society in a vague state. Rather, under the action of the Holy Spirit, who is its vital principle, it will externally produce the organs that it needs for its acts. These necessary organs are the leaders of the body of the Church because the society's own actions must be performed by leaders. Given that the body is entirely priestly, these organs will be priestly.[46]

Consequently (understanding, however, that this is Fr. Long-Hasselman's opinion, not our own), hierarchical priests are the delegates of the Christian community, their agents. Thus, he writes: "All Christians exercise their priesthood by delegating it to certain people, and ordination is an act of the Christian assembly's sovereignty."[47]

We must here note the kinship which exists between these views and those of the great German theologian of the nineteenth century, Johann Adam Möhler.[48] However, in Long-Hasselmans, they are

---

45. See Yves Congar, "Un essai de théologie sur le sacerdoce catholique," *Recherches des sciences religieuses* 25 (1971): 187–99 and 270–304.
46. See ibid., 174.
47. Ibid.
48. See Möhler, *L'unité dans l'Église*. Pierre Chaillet, "L'esprit du christianisme et du catholicisme," *Revue des sciences philosophiques et théologiques* 26 (1937): 483–98 and 713–26; 27 (1938): 161–83. Yves Congar, "Compte-rendu de la reedition du livre de Möhler: L'unité dans l'Église," *Revue des sciences philosophiques et théologiques* 27 (1938).

hardened into a kind of juridical "delegation," whereas for Möhler it was, instead, a question of a kind of vital development, thus better safeguarding the institution of the sacrament of holy orders by Christ.

We can also note, in what concerns the relationship between the two priesthoods, a curious rapprochement with Condren, who held that all believers are priests even though only ordained priests here-below exercise the priesthood.[49] Both cases represent minimizations of the sacrament of holy orders, which thereby loses its entire *raison d'être*. Indeed, it is not enough to say that there must be a "leader," for this could be a simple temporary function, exercised by believers on a rotating basis. One must recognize that, in order to play this role as the "leader" of worship, the baptized person must have received the sacrament of holy orders. Moreover, one must explain why this is necessary.

The only possible response is that which was already suggested when we spoke about the sacraments,[50] namely, that the sacrament is an action which implies a determinate agent. Inasmuch as he is the agent, he enters into the structure of the sacrament. Now, it is a question of an action performed by Christ. Christ is the unique priest, the unique cause of the sacramental actions by which His saving action is extended to all times and to all men. Because He is no longer visibly present and given that His saving action must be "rendered visible," it is necessary that He Himself be rendered visible inasmuch as He is the Savior saving this man and this community through this visible action (i.e., this sacramental action). This means that the agent of the sacramental action must be sacramentally designated and constituted, indeed, by a specific sacrament which, beyond the rite itself, endures in this man in the form of a character, the "interior sacrament."

Thus, the sacrament of holy orders makes its recipient into the visible representative, *in the sacramental action*, of Christ the priest, without whom the sacramental action would be a mere simulacrum.

---

49. See Dabin, *Le sacerdoce royal des fidèles dans la tradition ancienne et moderne*, 456, and Dupuy, *Bérulle et le sacerdoce*, 200.

50. See §729 above.

This is why the sacramental act as such does not depend on the personal holiness of the person who performs it (either in the sense that if the sacramentally constituted minister were a sinner he could not truly perform it or, in the opposite sense that a member of the People of God who is not sacramentally constituted as representing Christ the priest could perform it if he is holy). Above all, it depends on this sacramental designation which assures the Church and each of her members that when the person who has received this designation performs the sacramental action ritually, Christ the priest is the one who performs it through him and confers His saving power upon him.

The Hierarchical Priesthood and the Universal Priesthood

{977} Thus, the universal priesthood is that of the Church inasmuch as it is distinct from the priesthood of Christ—distinct and wholly dependent. It is the priesthood that the Church, in profound unity with Christ, exercises inasmuch as she is a distinct person. It belongs in a communal manner to the People of God and to all of its members, from the pope to the humble believer.

The ministerial priesthood is that of Christ, sacramentally represented. Of course, the Church must sacramentally represent Christ, and the "priest" in this office is at the service of the Church. However, she represents Him *as a distinct person*, though not *inasmuch as she is a distinct person*.[51] That is, in the sacramental actions, her person is a pure instrument of Christ (doubtlessly, an *instrumentum animatum anima rationali*, but an instrument nonetheless),[52] meaning that all the saving power attached to these actions solely comes from Christ.

It is pointless to ask which is superior. It is an immense dignity to be "a visible representative of Christ the priest," and it is a personal dignity because the person is the one who is endowed with it. However, it is a question of a purely sacramental representation which, of itself, does not designate a personal value of sanctity in

---

51. See §664 above.
52. See §399 in the previous volume.

its beneficiary. On the contrary, the universal priesthood is a treasure properly belonging to the Church, and it has a personal value for each person to the degree that he or she belongs to the Church.

In any case, these two priesthoods are distinct and, at the same time, are necessarily connected. Indeed, the priesthood of the Church can be exercised only in close dependence on Christ's priesthood (which has no meaning other than that of making the Church partake in His sacrifice). Thus, one can say that the "spiritual sacrifices" of believers are offered on the altar by the priest celebrating the Eucharist, which gives them their sacrificial value by uniting them to Christ's sacrifice by integrating them into it. This can be said so long as one understands that he does this through a purely instrumental activity. That is, Christ is the one who, in reality, does this invisibly through His visible minister. What the ordained priest personally brings to the Church's sacrifice—through his own association with it through faith, charity, and religion—are integrated into the spiritual sacrifice offered through the participation of the gathered community and of the universal Church whom this community represents. It is an activity of the universal priesthood in which the ordained priest obviously never ceases to participate.

The Mediation of the Ordained Priest and the Priestly People's Access to God

{978} A question raised by Hans Küng (and resolved by him in the direction of a rejection) is whether the priest (and even the Church) may play any role as mediator, given that each Christian, through his or her baptism, has immediate access to God in Christ.[53] In the opposite direction, the mediating role of the priest is accentuated to the extreme in someone like Bérulle and in the tradition [of the "French School"] arising from him, in the name of a [Pseudo-]Dionysian conception of the world and the Church:[54] "The dignity of the priesthood of Christ comes from the Hypostatic Union. Such is the dignity of our priesthood, coming from the special union that we have with Christ by the priestly state.—We are mediators be-

---

53. See Küng, *La justification*, 508–35.
54. See Dupuy, *Bérulle et le sacerdoce*, 145–61.

tween God and the people. O, what a perfection! O, what an edification of the people are owed to this state!"[55]

The mediation that is exercised by the ordained priest in the sacramental action—especially in the celebration of the Eucharist—is purely instrumental. It is the mediation of Christ rendered visible. This enables us to respond to Küng's objection to the idea of attributing a mediating role to the priest. The ordained priest is not placed in between Christ and the believer. He visibly represents Christ before believers by himself being totally effaced, though by rendering Christ's mediation visible through his person and the sacramental rite. At the same time, however, the mediation (through intercession and also through the Word) at the heart of Bérulle's thought is, in fact, the Church's mediation: the Church exercises it through him. However, she does so not only through him but also through all her members. Nonetheless, when it is a question of external acts of mediation (preaching and government), the priest and, above all, the bishop are the designated representatives of the Church to the degree that she entrusts these acts to them. In his execution of them, the bishop can normally appeal to the laity for collaboration.[56] If it is a question of intercession and substitution, it is clear that the priest participates in it like all the other members of the People of God to the degree of he has charity and fervor of heart.

Now, the Church's mediation is not interposed between Christ and the believer, for the Church is constituted of the believers to the degree that they are truly believers. However, she is the place wherein the sinful man has access to Christ (whether this sinful man is a person who is still outside of Christ or someone who no longer completely belongs to Him). She also is the one who, in the name of Christ, addresses the appeal of salvation to all men. Nonetheless, it is an appeal that, thus brought to the heart of each person, is realized through immediate union with Christ.

In this way, we can simultaneously understand and correct Bérulle (and the tradition of priestly spirituality that arose from him). What he says about the priest's mediation (which he, moreover,

---

55. Bérulle, cited by ibid., 279.
56. See Jean-Hervé Nicolas, "Les laïcs et l'annonce de la Parole de Dieu," *Nouvelle revue théologique* 93 (1971): 821–48.

extends to superiors as well) likewise holds true for all the faithful. It is nothing other than the theme of "the communion of saints," that is, of the role that each Christian can play in the salvation of his brothers by means of his prayers, sacrifices, and actions. However—and here we see the truth and the fecundity of the Berullian insights—this common mediating holiness must normally accompany the priest's instrumental mediation and, in this case, it is united to it so as to constitute a single mediating activity which we can call priestly, with all the nuanced elaborations that have been indicated, giving it a form that wholly differs from the *Celestial Hierarchies* of Dionysius.

THE THREE DEGREES OF THE SACRAMENT OF HOLY ORDERS

{979} According to the Church's teaching, the sacrament of holy orders not only sets apart among the People of God those who have received it, sacramentally constituting them as representatives of Christ and His instruments in cultic actions. Beyond this, it includes within itself several degrees that distinguish those who have received it in an unequal manner. These degrees are three in number: the episcopacy, the presbyterate, and the diaconate. Today, nobody recognizes the sacramentality of the so-called minor orders (including the sub-diaconate, which the Latin Church no longer considers to be a form of major orders). This point is beyond dispute.[57]

The Bishop: Symbol and Agent of the Church's Unity

The fullness of the priesthood

{980} If the bishop is a complete priest, having received the sacrament of holy orders in its fullness, everything that we said above about the priest's role in sacramentally representing Christ eminently holds true for the bishop.

This calls for a deepening and a supplementary point. We have

---

57. See Trent, "Decree and Canons on the Sacrament of Orders," c. 6, in D.-*Sch.*, no. 1776. Vatican II, *Lumen Gentium*, no. 3. Pope Paul VI, *Ministeria Quaedam*, August 15, 1972, *Documentation catholique* 69 (1972): 852–54.

spoken about the issue of representing Christ the priest. However, the bishop is also a shepherd. Therefore, he must sacramentally represent Christ the king and shepherd.

St. Thomas separates these two aspects, at least in the two texts expressly dedicated to the sacrament of holy orders, which date from early in his career. He holds that the sacrament only makes a Christian into a representative of Christ the priest. Beyond this, if the bishop represents Christ the king, this is by way of addition, through a consecration that does not belong to the sacrament.[58] Does this express some kind of inconsistency? In truth, it is not clear either how or why this real, spiritual, and sacramental power conferred by a rite would not be a sacrament, and it is even less clear how this sacrament could be something other than that of holy orders.

The Council of Trent treated the episcopacy as a degree of the sacrament of holy orders, and the Second Vatican Council, coming back to the traditional conception, explained it as being the "fullness of the sacrament of orders."[59]

To understand how the sacrament of holy orders, in its fullness, confers the sacramental representation of Christ the king and shepherd—whereas of itself it makes one participate in Christ's priesthood—we must see that Christ's priesthood and kingship coincide within Christ Himself. He is the priest-king.

On the one hand, His priesthood is at the service of His kingship, for He opens the way to the Father through His sacrifice, leading the faithful to Him as king and shepherd. On the other hand, His kingship finds its consummation in that which is the ultimate goal and fruit of His priesthood, namely, union with God, for He leads His people to the sanctuary.[60]

Thus, in virtue of his consecration, the bishop sacramentally represents Christ the priest inasmuch as He simultaneously is the king and the shepherd who leads His people.*

---

58. See *In IV Sent.*, d. 24, q. 3, a. 2, sol. 1, co., and ad 3; sol. 2; d. 24, q. 1, a. 2, ad 2.
59. See *Lumen Gentium*, no. 21.
60. See Heb 9:24–10:21.

* N.B. This is important in contemporary discussions in the Church. Whatever may be the way that the holders of authority are designated, they hold this authority as coming from Christ, not from the people. They participate in His authority and represent it in virtue of the sacrament received, not in virtue of the trust that the people place in them.

The collegiality of the pastoral power

{981} Thus, pastoral authority is also sacramental, conferred by the sacrament of holy orders with the (instrumental) power to perform, by Christ's power, sacramental actions and to confer grace by means of them. Authority in the Church does not come from the people, as in a democratic regime but, rather, comes from Christ who, through the sacrament of holy orders, at once designates and constitutes the holders of that power.

However, this obviously poses the problem concerning the governance of the universal Church. Historically, the various Christian communities ("the Churches") were founded on the basis of preexisting and localized human communities. The problem of unity was posed for each of them. This unity was realized through the monarchical episcopacy—an arrangement that was perhaps not found everywhere at the beginning, though it very quickly took hold. However, the unity of the ensemble of ecclesial communities needed to be assured. Thus, the idea of collegiality appeared (though, of course, it already existed at the very beginning of the Church, as is clear from the council that is sometimes called the "Council of Jerusalem"[61]). The unity of the Church will be assured by agreement among the various bishops. First of all, such agreement was expressed among neighboring bishops, and this was very quickly translated by a custom that St. Cyprian presents as coming from time immemorial, namely that of neighboring bishops gathering to provide for an empty see and to lay their hands on the newly chosen bishop. Very soon in the East, there also was the constitution of eparchies, that is, of great gatherings of local Churches under the authority of a principal bishop. Finally, the patriarchates were constituted.

However, the deepest roots of collegiality are found in Christ's own activity in establishing the Church. Certainly, Christ chose Peter as the head and foundation of His Church. However, He also chose the apostles to the announce of the Gospel, the bring the remission of sins, and found and govern the Church. As we have seen, the episcopal body followed upon the apostolic college. Like it, the

---

61. Acts 5:5–21.

episcopal body together receives the charge, power, and grace of preaching the Gospel and of governing the Church of God.[62]

To understand this collegiality, we must seek after its *raison d'être* in the very extent of the Church and in her catholicity. She exists for the whole of mankind and therefore must be established in the midst of the various nations, languages, and races. Therefore, it is connatural for her to be realized in a multitude of communities embracing the varying multitude of human societies. Consequently, we have the sure fact, one having verbal vestiges in Scripture, that the Church is composed of a multitude of Churches, each one standing in need of a principle of unity, the bishop who represents Christ and participates in His sanctifying, priestly, and royal powers.

However, just as Christ is one, and just as man is one in sin and grace, and likewise as men are called to one and the same vocation, this multitude of Churches must also be unified. This is possible only if a profound communion exists among the heads of this multitude of Churches. In other words, it is possible only if their multiplicity is reduced to unity. On the other hand, multiplicity cannot be reduced to unity without a principle of unity, that is, without there being a factor ordering the whole to itself (either as external to the multiplicity or within it). It is very clear that the Church has Christ as this factor. However, the Church is a communion realized in a visible society, even though this communion is, of itself, invisible. The unity of this visible society and, therefore, the principle that assures this unity, must be visible as well. This principle is the pope, designated by Christ in the person of Peter first and then in all of those who would come to follow, after him, in Peter's charge and by whom the latter continues to exercise his unifying ministry up to the end of time. The pope is at once the sign and necessary agent of the Church's visible unity, itself being the sacrament of her invisible unity, that is, the sacrament of Christ.[63]

Thus, one can historically discern, with Fr. Congar,[64] two lines of development in the Church's authority, depending on whether the

---

62. See Perler, "L'évêque représentant," 31–66.
63. See §§612–13.
64. See Congar, "De la communion des Églises," 227–60.

accent is placed either more on collegiality or on the principle of unity. However, one must note that in the line of collegiality, we will necessarily find ourselves at an impasse if we minimize the principle of unity, as unfortunately has been the case in the Orthodox Church. Already in the third century, St. Cyprian seems to have founded the unity of the Church on the communion of bishops to the exclusion of the primacy of one among them, having bitterly experienced dissatisfaction in the conflict that implacably set him in opposition to the Church of Rome on the subject of the date of Easter and, above all, on the subject of the rebaptism of heretics. It is pointless to hope that a multitude of men, even if they are equally aware of their duties and concerned with the same ideal, will always come to be in agreement, even on essential problems—indeed, above all on essential problems. One must also add, with regard to the Latin Church, that during the Middle Ages, political and social circumstances were of such a character that very grave abuses occurred on the level of particular Churches (arising from feudalism and the realities flowing from it), meaning that reform could only come from on high (e.g., in the Gregorian reform). This led to the growth of papal [*pontificale*] power and its direct intervention in the government of the Churches. The most ardent partisans of collegiality cannot contest that this was necessary and beneficial for the Church at this given time of her history.

However, this papal authority, which was defined at the First Vatican Council as an immediate, truly episcopal jurisdiction that is exercised over all the shepherds and all the faithful,[65] does not prevent each bishop from sacramentally receiving, by his consecration, authority over the People of God for leading them as representing Christ:

> Just as it is necessary that the authority of Peter should be perpetuated in the Roman Pontiff, so, by the fact that the bishops succeed the Apostles, they inherit their ordinary power, and thus the episcopal order necessarily belongs to the essential constitution of the Church. Although they do not receive plenary, or universal, or supreme authority, they are not to be looked as vicars of the Roman Pontiffs; because they exercise a power

---

[65]. See Vatican I, *Pastor Aeternus*, July 18, 1870, in D.-Sch., no. 3060.

really their own, and are most truly called the ordinary pastors of the peoples over whom they rule.⁶⁶

This statement drawn from Leo XIII expresses one of the essential data of the problem concerning authority in the Church. It belongs to her oldest tradition and has often been recognized by the ecclesiastical Magisterium. Theologians from the time of the great Gregorian reform onward have somewhat obscured this indispensable role played by the bishop in the Church's life, calling the pope the "universal bishop" and in practice thinking of the Church as though it were a single diocese of virtually unlimited extent with the pope being the sole source of its governance (*caput, fons et origo, fundamentum et basis, cardo*). Although they were imitated in the centuries following the Gregorian reforms, principally in the thirteenth century by St. Bonaventure and into the fourteenth century (e.g., by Matthew of Aquasparta who was one of Boniface VIII's advisors for the bull *Unam Sanctam*, as well as by Hervaeus Natalis and Peter of Palude⁶⁷), they were followed neither by the great post-Tridentine ecclesiologist St. Robert Bellarmine, nor by the First Vatican Council, nor by the modern popes.

Among the modern popes, we must cite the important documents of Pius XII, namely the encyclical *Mystici Corporis*, his discourse to the bishops given in 1954 (the year of the canonization of Pius X), and then in the encyclical *Fidei Donum*:

> But even though each bishop is the pastor of that portion only of the Lord's flock entrusted to him, nevertheless as lawful successor of the Apostles by God's institution and commandment he is also responsible, together with all the other bishops, for the Apostolic task of the Church.*

This idea had already been expressed by Pius XI in *Rerum Ecclesiae*⁶⁸ and Benedict XV in *Maximum Illud*,⁶⁹ indeed being first of all expressed by the First Vatican Council. In fact, the latter, after having defined papal primacy, adds:

---

66. Leo XIII, *Satis Cognitum*, June 29, 1896, no. 14 (D.-*Sch.*, no. 3308). [Tr. note: Taken from the official Vatican translation of the text.]

67. See Congar, "De la communion des Églises," 238–56.

* [Tr. note: Taken from no. 42 of the official Vatican translation of *Fidei Donum*.]

68. See Pope Pius XI, *Rerum Ecclesiae*, February 28, 1926.

69. Pope Benedict XV, *Maximum Illud*, November 30, 1919.

This power of the supreme pontiff, however, is far from standing in the way of the power of ordinary and immediate episcopal jurisdiction by which the bishops who, under appointment of the Holy See, succeed in the place of the apostles, feed and rule individually, as true shepherds, the particular flock assigned to them. Rather, this latter power is asserted, confirmed, and vindicated by this same supreme and universal shepherd, as in the words of St. Gregory the Great: "My honor is the honor of the whole Church. My honor is the firm strength of my brothers. I am truly honored when due honor is paid to each and everyone."[70]

Finally, the Second Vatican Council placed the proper and sacramental authority of the bishop in its full light.[71]

It is incontestable that, through his episcopal consecration, the bishop is Christ's representative in his diocese, the holder of the Church's authority, and that the pope's authority is not substituted for his own. We still must, however, consider how the proper authority of each bishop over his diocese is reconciled with the necessary communion of each bishop with all the others, without which the individual cannot be the representative of Christ, the sole shepherd, as well as how his authority is reconciled with his subordination to the bishop of Rome, which is the condition established by Christ Himself for assuring the unity of the episcopal body, the symbol and effect of his own, the cause of the Church's unity. In short, we here are faced with a problem that arouses great discussions today, namely, that of episcopal collegiality in relation to papal primacy.

The primacy of the pope and episcopal collegiality

Instead* of opposing papal primacy to collegiality (and, consequently, papal authority to episcopal authority), we must under-

---

70. Vatican I, *Pastor Aeternus*, no. 3, in D.-*Sch.*, no. 3061. See Olivier Rousseau, "La vraie valeur de l'épiscopat dans l'Église d'après d'importants documents de 1875," in *L'épiscopat et l'Église universelle* (Paris: Cerf, 1962), 709–38.

71. See Vatican II, *Lumen Gentium*, no. 2.

* For a first approach to the question concerning the theology of the episcopate, see the following works. *L'Eglise de Vatican II*, Unam Sanctam 51 a, b, c (Paris: Éditions du Cerf, 1966). Congar, *L'ecclésiologie du Haut Moyen-Age*, 131–248 and 324–84. D'Ercola, "Notes sur les recherches concernant la collégialité épiscopale." Joseph Lecuyer, "Communion épiscopale dans les conciles africains entre 400–425," in *Mélanges Charue* (Gembloux, 1969): 101–22. Henri de Lubac, *Catholicisme* (Paris: Cerf, 1952). Joseph Ratzinger, "Les implications pastorals de la doctrine de la collégialité," *Concilium* 7 (1965): 33–56. Thils, *Primauté pontificale et prérogative épiscopale*, and *L'Église et les Églises*, 47–74. Jean-Pierre, *La théologie de l'épiscopat au premier concile du Vatican* (Paris: Cerf, 1961).

stand that, as we said above, collegiality itself is not realized if unity is not assured, for it consists in the unification of that which is multiple. This unification requires that just as the bishop is the guarantor of his own community's unity, one member of the college of bishops, empowered to represent Christ in a perfectly objective and incontestable manner, is the guarantor of unity for the universal Church. This presupposes that this bishop would have a true authority over the others and that he could impose his will on them either in a matter of faith or in a matter of governance. (Of course, what is meant is that he can impose the will of the Holy Spirit on them, for this is not a question of a merely human community, but rather, of a community instituted and directed by Christ.) And this is what the First Vatican Council wished to affirm in speaking about the pope's immediate, ordinary, and episcopal jurisdiction. Indeed, it is clear that if the pope has authority over the bishop, he has authority through him and by him over his flock.

Moreover, a number of misperceptions have played a considerable role in this discussion, for many bishops understood the word "ordinary" as meaning that it would be normal for the pope to intervene in the affairs of their dioceses, which obviously would be quite poorly in line with the reality of their authority and with good governance. However, it has been decisively said and established that the word "ordinary" must be understood in its juridical sense. In other words, the pope holds this power by his very function and not because of particular circumstances. Likewise, the word "immediate" means that the laws and decrees issued by the pope by themselves obligate all Christians without needing to be ratified by an intermediary authority (as was asserted, for example, by the partisans of Gallicanism). However, this obviously does not prevent it from being the case that the bishop would be the natural intermediary between the pope and his faithful. Finally, the word "episcopal" does not mean that the pope is the universal bishop. Indeed, the expression "universal bishop" is an ambiguous term, given that, in reality, the pope is the bishop of the local Church of Rome and it is by rights of this that he is the principal member of the college of bishops. Rather, the word means that the authority that he exercises over all the members of his flock in the whole world is of the same nature as episcopal authority. Moreover, theologically and traditionally speaking, the term "episcopal" means nothing other than "pastoral." The fact that this episcopal body would be of divine right cannot in any way diminish the fact that the bishops are subordinate shepherds in relation to the first shepherd, the pope.

If we consider matters in this way, we thus can understand how it is that the pope is the natural head of the episcopal body. Even when he speaks and acts on his own, proper initiative, he speaks and acts in the name of the whole and entire episcopal body, somewhat like how St. Peter spoke in the name of the apostolic college.

To say that the episcopal body is part of the Church's divine constitution is to say that the pope could not govern the Church without the bishops. Or better yet, it is to say that there could not be a pope if bishops did not exist. This idea has been expressed by this quite just formula: the pope exercises his power over the Church (i.e., his primacy) but simultaneously and without there being an opposition, he exercises it in the Church (i.e., he is the head of the episcopal body[72] which is part of the Church). If no opposition exists between these two parts of the formula, this is because Christ is the one who, in reality, visibly exercises His invisible authority as supreme pastor by means of the pope and the bishops. However, simultaneously, the latter are personally submitted to the authority of Christ thus visibly manifested. Cardinal Journet expressed this admirably as follows: "Only (the sovereign pontiff) can proclaim a given truth that must be believed (e.g., the dogma of the Immaculate Conception or of the Assumption of the Virgin). However, he is greater when he believes it than he is when he proclaims it."[73]

A much-vexed but incontestable point was made above, namely that primacy would be impossible without the episcopacy, for nobody can be pope without being a bishop, and nobody can be a bishop without having been ordained by one or several bishops.[74] In

---

72. See Congar, "De la communion des Églises," 260.

73. Charles Journet, *La voie théologale. Dieu à la rencontre de l'homme* (Paris: Desclée de Brouwer, 1981), 44–45.

74. [Tr. note: Fr. Nicolas cites, "Lecuyer, 5, 790–791." However, the fifth Lecuyer entry is Lecuyer, "Communion épiscopale dans les conciles africains entre 400–425."]

short, in the Church as it has been instituted by Christ, the pope is first a bishop, the bishop of Rome, who moreover has authority over the whole of the church, for as bishop of Rome he succeeds Peter and inherits his prerogatives in relation to his brothers and his unifying function in the college of shepherds. And when the Church of Rome is deprived of her shepherd, it falls to her to give herself another shepherd, who in his capacity as bishop of Rome finds himself to be the head of the episcopal body and the leader of the universal Church. The prerogatives of the pope are first of all those of the Church of Rome.

Finally, we can ask: Does the bishop receive his power directly from Christ or from the pope? And when the bishops are united together in a Council, do they receive their power from the pope?

What was said about the connection of pastoral power to episcopal consecration would seem to force us to conclude that the bishop receives his power immediately from Christ. This theory is still held by certain theologians, but others hold that it was definitively eliminated as a possibility by Pius XII. Whatever may be the case on this point, it seems that the two assertions can be held together. First, it is quite clear that the bishop receives his jurisdictional authority over a determinate flock from the pope, so that the pastoral power that he has on account of his episcopal consecration cannot be exercised without the pope giving him a flock to govern. However, it is also the case that he is constituted as a shepherd through the sacramental ordination in which Christ is the one who acts invisibly through the visible action of the sacrament.

It seems that the solution to this problem ought to be sought along the following lines. The pastoral power that the bishop receives with his episcopal consecration is essentially a collegial power. He becomes a member of the episcopal body, which has pastoral power over the Church. However, the episcopal body has this power only in communion with the pope and under his authority. This is why a papal act is needed for determining the right to exercise pastoral authority by entrusting a particular Church to the bishop's governance.

In these conditions, one can admit that which is the most common and most authorized opinion today, namely, that the pastoral authority of the bishops, both over their particular flocks and over the Church, flows from the sovereign pontiff. This is the case not only because he is the one who designates them for the reception of episcopal consecration but also because pastoral authority in the Church can be exercised only under the authority of the bishop of Rome.

If we go back to the apostolic college, we can say that Christ gave Peter the fullness of His authority over the Church but also Himself gave it to the apostles. And now, in the Church, the successor of Peter has this fullness of power, but through him and by him, Christ confers it upon the episcopal body. The pope is entirely free to name this or that bishop and to give him this or that jurisdiction, or to withdraw all personal jurisdiction from him. However, he is not free to do away with the episcopal body, without which he would be nothing, as we have seen.

The holder of authority in the Church

There are not two holders of authority in the Church. The Church's authority is held by the episcopal body having the pope at its head. However, it is held in such a manner that it is found in its fullness in the pope and through him spreads forth over the bishops. And we have seen that it is already collegial when it is considered in the pope by himself, for it belongs to the pope inasmuch as he is the head of the episcopal body, just as it belonged to Peter inasmuch as he was the head of the apostolic college.

If we then go on to ask what councils add to the pope, I think we would need to respond along the following lines. It deploys the collegial character that is implied in the bishop of Rome's power, doing so first of all in a manifest manner, but also concretely by the contribution of the various bishops' judgments and experiences. Therefore, it adds nothing to this power in the sense that all authority in the Church finds itself to be concentrated in the pope. However, it develops it in a dimension that is essential and remains latent when it is exercised by the pope alone.

The Priest: Co-worker with the Bishop

The distinction between the priest and the bishop

According to the Church's teaching, the distinction between the priest and bishop does not consist only in the juridical situation holding between the two, the bishop having a superior authority and rank. Beyond this, it consists in the sacramental powers respectively conferred by priestly ordination and episcopal consecration. A simple priest has the power to *conficere eucharistiam* and therefore has the power to make real the Eucharistic sacrifice, as well as the power to remit sins. However, only a bishop has the power of conferring holy orders and the sacrament of confirmation (at least ordinarily; see below). By his consecration, he alone is sacramentally constituted as a shepherd, the visible representative of the one shepherd.

Historico-theological discussion concerning this question

{983} History reveals to us cases in which it seems that the sovereign pontiff would have granted simple priests the power of conferring holy orders.

Up to today, there are three known cases of these sorts of privileges being conceded by the Holy See. Perhaps there are others, at least if Vasquez is to be believed.[75] We will summarize these three cases of theological reflection in reverse chronological order.

Pope Innocent VIII's Bull *Exposcit* (April 9, 1489) In this bull, the pope granted the privilege of conferring the sub-diaconate and the diaconate to the abbot of Cîteaux for all the religious in his order, also granting this privilege to the abbots of the four mother abbeys [of the Cistercian Order] (La Ferté, Pontigny, Clairvaux, and Morimond).[76]

---

75. See Pius a Langonio, *De bulla innocentiana seu de potestate papae committendi simplici presbytero subdiaconatus et diaconatus collationem Disquisitio historico theoogica* (Rome, 1902), 18, and Colombon Bock, "La Bulle 'Gerentes ad vos' de Martin V," *Collectanea Cisterciensium Reformatorum* 13 (1951): 197n35.

76. See the texts in D.-*Sch.*, no. 1435, and Bock, "La Bulle," 198.

From the sixteenth century up to our own day, this bull has elicited three kinds of reactions among theologians:

- *Some* chose to reject the authenticity of the Bull (e.g., [Jean-Baptiste] Gonet, [Charles-René] Billuart,* the Salmanticenses, [Jean-Marie] Hervé, [Adolphe] Tanquerey, and [Albert] Michel).
- *Others*, while expressing doubts about its authenticity, admitted the possibility of the privilege (e.g., [Gabriel] Vasquez, [Leonard] Lessius, and [Joseph] Tixeront).
- *Finally*, others admitted both the authenticity of the text and the validity of the privilege (e.g., [Francisco] Suarez, [Gaetano] Sanseverino, [Jean] Morin, and [Franz] Diekamp).

Today, it does not seem that we can reasonably deny the authenticity of the bull.[77] Abbot Jean de Circey, who was its recipient, in fact published it in 1491 during the very life of Innocent VIII. On the other hand, and contrary to the affirmations registered by many of those who speak against it, it is certain that the abbots of Cîteaux commonly made use of their privilege all the way up to the Revolution, especially Jerome of Souchère, who assisted at the Council of Trent, even at its thirty-second session, and expressed no scruples about openly performing diaconal and sub-diaconal ordinations after the Council. (This stands in contradiction to those who say that the privilege would have been revoked after the Council.) Moreover, in the 1689 Cistercian ritual (and on the basis of that, in all the later editions), we find an *Ordo de ordinatione Subdiaconi* and a *de ordinatione Diaconi*. This privilege, which was in force up to the French Revolution, fell into disuse by the suppression of the abbey of Cîteaux and was not granted when, at the restoration of Cîteaux in 1898, Pope Leo XIII introduced the adverb *tantummodo* [only] before mentioning the privilege of conferring tonsure and the minor orders granted to Cistercian abbots. The revocation is explicit in the [1917] *Codex iuris canonici*, c. 964.

* [Tr. note: Reading "Billuart" for "Billuard."]

77. See Bock, "La Bulle," 199–202, and Yves Congar, "Faits, problèmes et réflexions à propos du pouvoir d'Order et des rapports entre le presbytérat et l'épiscopat," *La Maison-Dieu* 14 (1948): 111–12.

Martin V's Bull *Gerentes ad vos* (November 16, 1427) There was a concession granted for five years by Pope Martin V to the abbot and community of *Cella sanctae Mariae* (or, Altzella) in Saxony following a grave dispute that set it in opposition to the bishop of Meissen in the territory in which the monastery was found. According to this concession, the abbot for five years received the power to reconcile all the Churches and cemeteries falling under the monastery and, likewise, the power to confer all of the various holy orders upon all the monks of this abbey (as well as to the persons submitted to his abbatial jurisdiction) without requiring the permission of the diocesan bishop for this.[78]

According to Congar, this was a favor granted spontaneously. Expressing the opposite opinion, Bock notes that this bull came in response to the request made by the abbot to the Holy See complaining of the bishop's attempts to impinge on the enormous privileges that had been accorded to the abbey: "We easily give our agreement to your requests, above all to those that concern the injuries that you are suffering." Bock supposes, likely quite rightly, that among these attempts at impingement there could have been a kind of extortion for ordinations, "with the bishop making the ordination of subjects of the Abbey of Altzelle contingent upon the latter's payment of tithes or other benefits." Thus, the Holy See would have wished to settle such difficulties by granting this exorbitant privilege, which perhaps was not requested, though it responded to what had been asked of it.

Omnes etiam sacros ordines. According to the terminology of the time, in the pontifical acts, *ordines sacri* always means "holy orders," that is, the sub-diaconate, the diaconate, and the presbyterate, whereas the usual term for the episcopacy is *consecratio*.[79]

---

78. See Bock, "La Bulle," 197–205, and Congar, "Faits," 114–15. See also Karl August Fink, "Zur Spendung der höheren Weihen durch den Priester," *Zeitschrift der Saviny-Stiftung für Rechtsgeschichte*, Kan. Abt. 32 (1943): 506–8, and the text of the bull in D.-Sch., no. 1290. [Tr. note: Fr. Nicolas cites "p. 2" of Bock's article.]

79. See Fink, "Zur Spendung der höheren Weihen durch den Priester," 506–8.

According to Bock, the clause *diocesani licensia super hoc minime requisita* does not mean that one must reduce the privilege to a faculty allowing the religious [of the monastery] to be ordained by any given bishop without the authorization of the local ordinary. It is a question of a second privilege, for given that the Cistercians did not yet have the privilege of having ordinations performed by any given bishop, "the power to confer orders did not necessarily

Boniface IX's Bull *Sacra Religionis* (February 1, 1400) By this bull, published by Dom Fofi in 1924, the pope accorded to the abbot of St. Osith in Essex (a diocese under London) authorization to confer upon his subjects not only tonsure and minor orders but also the sub-diaconate and even the priesthood:

> Hence it is that, inclining in this matter to the requests of the abbot and community, We grant with apostolic authority by the tenor of these present [writings], to the same abbot and his successors and to their canons: that the same abbot and his successors in perpetuity, for the duration of their tenure as abbots of the same monastery, shall be able freely and licitly to confer at the times provided by law, all the minor [orders] and likewise the orders of the subdiaconate, diaconate, and presbyterate on all and singular, present and future, professed canons of the same monastery and that the said canons thus promoted by the said abbots shall be able to minister freely and licitly in the orders thus received.[80]

At the request of the bishop of London, this privilege was revoked three years later by the same pope. However, there was no question of it being invalid of itself. Rather, it was revoked solely because it was an infringement upon the bishop's prerogatives.

These facts can be interpreted in three different ways.

1. One could say that the privilege in question did not consist in the abbot himself conferring holy orders. Rather, the privilege would have allowed him to have the bishop of his choice confer them without the local bishop's authorization. This would have allowed the abbot to remove himself from the bishop's authority in this domain which was normally required either so that he himself might ordain the religious in question or in order to authorize another bishop to do so. Can the strong expressions of the bulls in fact be interpreted in this way? Moreover, this explanation does not hold for the privilege granted to the Cistercian abbots, as it is known that

---

imply the possibility of doing so licitly." Note, however, that as it stands, Bock's argumentation is nonetheless not absolutely convincing, for this could be the explanation of the privilege and not a second privilege (at least for those who would interpret this privilege as Bock critiques it).

80. Pope Boniface IX, *Sacra Religionis*, February 1, 1400, in D.-*Sch.*, no. 1145. See also Bock, "La Bulle," 197–205. Congar, "Faits," 107–28. Hocédez, *Histoire de la théologie au XIXe siècle*. Journet, *L'Église du Verbe incarné*, 1:112n2. Marie-Joseph Gerlaud, "Le minstre extraordinaire du sacrement de l'ordre," *Revue thomiste* (1931): 874–85.

they themselves performed ordinations. (Granted, however, in this case it was only a question of ordination to the diaconate.)

2. One could say that with his ordination the simple priest receives the radical power to ordain priests, though this power is bound and could be unbound by the pope's authorization. This solution is conceived as being analogous to the power of conferring confirmation accorded by the Pope to a simple priest which could not be validly exercised without this permission.[81] However, it is not easy to conceive of how the power of jurisdiction, which is "juridical" could thus interfere with the power of holy orders, which is real. In the text cited above, St. Thomas does not expressly say that confirmation conferred by a simple priest without the pope's authorization would be invalid, whatever may be said by the authority cited in the *sed contra* of that article. Moreover, we recognize the validity of confirmation conferred by a simple priest in the Orthodox Church[es], whereas it does not seem to be the case (except by recourse to subtleties that are not very convincing) that these priests would have the pope's authorization. Moreover, their Church[es] recognize that such simple priests have right to confer the "sacrament of Holy Chrismation" without any restriction, and therefore, do not need a special authorization from their bishop for this. Thus, one can seriously doubt that confirmation performed by a simple priest in the Latin Church without authorization—provided that he uses oil that was blessed by the bishop—would be invalid, all the more so because, for bishops, the sacramental power of conferring holy orders is not granted to them by a juridical act by the pope which could be revoked in the case of schism or excommunication but rather, is granted to them solely by their episcopal consecration. Therefore, there would be two disparate ways in which the power of ordaining priests would be unbound in a simple priest: either by a juridical act by the pope or by episcopal consecration. This is not very coherent.

3. One could admit that the popes who granted these privileges were poorly advised and mistaken. This is possible, for it is a question of particular, practical decisions, not the taking of a doctrinal position.

---

81. See *ST* III, q. 72, a. 11, ad 1.

Conclusion. However one interprets these cases, they are too rare, too isolated, and too contradicted by the most ancient and most universal tradition of the Church for us to be able to assert them against the Catholic position on this matter, namely, that only a validly ordained bishop has the sacramental power of conferring sacred orders to others. This is defined and must be held as being a truth of the faith.[82]

The meaning of the distinction between the episcopacy
and the presbyterate

{984} Defining the sacrament of holy orders by the power of "confecting the Eucharist" that it confers and situating the distinction between the priest and the bishop in the power that the ordained man has, secondarily, over the Mystical Body, St. Thomas was led to situate this distinction outside the sacrament of holy orders properly speaking.

Given that this position can no longer be retained,[83] one must place the distinction within the sacrament and say that the sacramental power (and therefore also the grace) that this sacrament confers are given only partially in priestly ordination and are completely given by episcopal consecration. This must hold true for the power of "confecting the Eucharist" (which remains, as we will see, the principal power [conferred by ordination]). In a text from the *Scriptum*, St. Thomas expresses the matter in a way that can only hold for

---

82. N.B. Today, to receive episcopal consecration, one must have received priestly ordination first. Without this, the consecration is considered to be invalid. Now, for a number of centuries, especially in Rome, episcopal consecration was conferred immediately upon deacons and even upon laymen. See Andrieux, "La carrière ecclésiastique." Does this weaken the distinction between the two powers, namely that of the priest and that of the bishop? Certainly not. If episcopal consecration conferred upon a layman or upon a deacon would be considered invalid today, this is because the Church formally forbids this and because her intention, when she consecrates a bishop, is to complete the sacrament of holy orders which he has received to an imperfect degree. Hence, if he who is consecrated has not at all received the sacrament of holy orders at the priestly degree, the consecration *such as it is conferred today* would not be valid. However, in the past, it was a question of directly making a deacon or laymen into a bishop. But, according to the conception that St. Thomas held concerning these matters, namely that episcopal consecration is not a sacrament (the very sacrament of holy orders), it would not be intelligible to say that one could confer consecration on someone who is not first a priest, for it could not make him into a priest.

83. See §980 above.

consecration considered from the perspective of efficient causality and therefore for the "realizing" of the Eucharistic sacrifice: "For that which is the primary act of the priesthood (i.e., the consecrating of the true body of Christ), the priest's act does not depend upon any superior power other than the divine power."[84]

However, if we no longer consider the Eucharistic mystery only in its sacramental reality but, moreover, consider the meaning that it has for the Church, understanding it as Christ's presence to her, His bride, and therefore as the visible expression of her unity at the same time as being its cause, it is then clear that the episcopacy (i.e., the visible representation of Christ the priest-king) is what is ordered to the Eucharist in the fullest and truest manner [*adéquatement*]. To celebrate the Eucharist as it should be celebrated, the priest must act in communion with his bishop and, through him, with the universal Church. Thus, one can clearly see the indecency of celebrations where, deliberately or arbitrarily, without any objective reason but, rather, for wholly personal considerations of the theological or historical order—indeed, most often for reasons that are very poorly founded—one violates the *ordo Ecclesiae*, sometimes on the gravest and most venerable of points. To do this is truly to celebrate the Eucharist outside [of communion with] the bishop and outside of the communion of the Church which the bishop represents and assures. (Indeed, this would be true even if a bishop took on responsibility for such celebrations—always being understanding that we are speaking of a case in which there would not be an objective reason judged to be sufficiently grave so that one need not follow the *ordo Ecclesiae* in this particular case and on a given precise point, for as we have seen, the bishop represents the Church only if he is and remains in communion with the other bishops and with the pope.)

The meaning of this diminished and incomplete bestowal of the sacrament of holy orders must be sought out in the earliest of liturgical traditions (already in the *Traditio apostolica* of St. Hippolytus), where priests are the bishop's collaborators, aiding him in the exercise of his pastoral function. The bishop has need of collaborators, and this need grows to the degree that the flock entrusted to him

---

84. See *In IV Sent.*, d. 24, q. 3, a. 2, ad 1.

grows in number and extends out in space. For many things, these collaborators can be laypersons. However, the need for multiplying Eucharistic celebrations and other cultic assemblies, as well as the need to place the sacraments in the reach of all, very early on required the bishop to confer on some of his collaborators the sacrament that made them sacramental representatives of Christ the priest in the acts of worship, namely the sacrament of holy orders.

However, a very grave reason, drawn from this very requirement for Christ's sacramental representation, led the Church to confer only that part of the sacrament that was necessary for assuring this cultic activity, reserving to the bishop the sacramental power to fully represent Christ the priest (i.e., the power to fully represent Him also as king and shepherd). Indeed, the multiplication of sacramental representatives of Christ the priest in cultic activities does not multiply (even merely on the level of the sign itself) the unique priesthood of Christ, for it is a question of a purely instrumental power, whose exercise refers immediately to the invisible priest who acts in all and in each—just as, *mutatis mutandis*, the multiplication of Eucharists does not multiply the unique sacrifice and the unique Savior. The same cannot be said for the various sacramental representations of Christ the king and shepherd, for their power is not purely instrumental. They render Christ the shepherd visible inasmuch as they are persons, exercising Christ's authority.

However, they exercise it as second causes, by means of acts in which their personalities are expressed in their own proper dimensions, with their natural or acquired qualities of intelligence, character, and morality, along with the gifts of grace which render them capable of acting in accord with the faith and in obedience to Christ, though with their limitations (and, ultimately, with their sins) as well.[85] For this reason, their multiplication in one and the same flock (i.e., in one and the same local Church) would be a counter-sign in relation to their significate, namely Christ the sole shepherd. Granted, there are a number of "flocks" within the one flock (i.e., local Churches within the one Church). However, in each local Church, the Church of Christ is what is realized (e.g., the Church which is

---

85. See §664 above.

at Ephesus, at Corinth, and so forth), and therefore it must be there with its essential properties, of which unity is the first, for that which is not one does not exist. Moreover, this multiplicity of local Churches is brought back to unity by collegiality and the primacy of the bishop of Rome together. Even if the bishop is assisted by other bishops, the bishop must be one within a given local Church so that he may signify and bring about the unity of the Church.

Therefore, the need for a unified government on the level of the Church as a visible and human society is not the most profound and most theological reason [for there to be only one bishop]. Were it viewed this way, it could be contested, corresponding to one form of government that is not the only one possible. Consequently, one could argue that it is not connected to what Christ has instituted but rather is connected to a human organization depending on a "political" conception that could be modified. The true reason is that all authority in the Church derives from Christ so that the need for a sacramental representation of the sole shepherd is the reason for the Church's "monarchical" government—as much for the local Church as for the universal Church.

Consequently, one can legitimately think that this "breaking up" of the sacrament of holy orders was brought about—in fact, very spontaneously and prior to any theoretical elaboration—by the Church herself, making use of the power that she received over the sacraments, *salva eorum substantia* [so long as their substance remained unharmed].*

This relationship of the priest to his bishop was beautifully highlighted at the Second Vatican Council.[86]

---

* N.B. One could raise an objection to this explanation by referring to the case of auxiliary bishops, who are collaborators with the bishop responsible for a Church. However, this has arisen on account of historical circumstances (e.g., the large geographical expanse of local Churches, the strict reservation of bestowal of the sacrament of confirmation to the bishop in the Latin Church, the concrete necessity of replacing a failing or absent bishop, and so forth). The fact that the bishop has a "presbyterium" primarily composed of simple priests enables one to situate these auxiliaries in relation to him as collaborators in a rank that is inferior to his even though they have the episcopal character. Hence, if they represent Christ the shepherd in this local Church, they do so in the same way that the simple priests do, namely, inasmuch as they represent the bishop and by his authority, and not on account of their episcopal consecration (which makes them represent Christ in the universal Church on account of their membership in the college of bishops).

86. See Vatican II, *Lumen Gentium*, no. 28.

The ministry of priests

Cultic function and pastoral function of the priest

Up* to recent times, the priesthood has been defined essentially in relation to cultic functions, especially in relation to the Eucharist and to the sacraments of baptism and penance. This goes back very far into the Church's tradition and, indeed, was already present in St. Cyprian.[87] It was systematized by the scholastics, especially by St. Thomas, and despite certain reactions,[88] passed into the common stream of theology. In recent times, however, there have been lively reactions to it. (Witnesses of this reaction can be found in the studies of Lécuyer, Denis, Audet, Colson, Le Guillou, Bouëssé, and Boismard.) According to Colson, this way of defining the priesthood by its cultic and Eucharistic function was the fruit of a "Judaizing of the ministerial priesthood" over the course of the ages.

The Second Vatican Council integrated pastoral and missionary functions into the priestly functions, though it did so while emphasizing the principal place held by its cultic role:

Priests, although they do not possess the highest degree of the priesthood, and although they are dependent on the bishops in the exercise of their power, nevertheless are united with the bishops in sacerdotal dignity. By the power of the sacrament of Orders, in the image of Christ the eternal high Priest (Heb. 5:1–10, 7:24, 9:11–28) they are consecrated to preach the Gospel and shepherd the faithful and to celebrate divine worship, so that they are true priests of the New Testament. Partakers of the function of Christ the sole Mediator (1 Tim. 2:5), on their level of ministry, they

---

* See the following texts: Jean-Paul Audet, *Mariage et célibat dans le service pastoral de l'Église* (Paris: Orante, 1967). Marie-Émile Boismard, "Compte rendu du livre de Bouëssé: Le sacerdoce chrétien," *Revue biblique* 65 (1958): 309–10. Colson, "Le ministère apostolique," 134–69; *Jésus-Christ, ou le sacerdoce de l'évangile* (Paris: Beauchesne, 1966); and *Prêtres et peuple sacerdotal* (Paris: Beauchesne, 1967). Albert-Marie Denis, "La function apostolique et la liturgie nouvelle en espirit," *Revue des sciences philosophiques et théologiques* 42 (1958): 401–36. André Duval, "L'Ordre au concile de Trente," in *Études sur le sacrement de l'ordre* (Paris: Cerf, 1957), 281–85. Jean Leclerc, "Le sacerdoce des moines," *Irenikon* 36 (1963): 5–40, and "Communication au congrès de l'érémitisme de la Mendola," in *Atti della seconda settimana international di studio* (Mendoza, 1962). Joseph Lecuyer, "Théologie du sacerdoce chrétien," in *La Tradition sacerdotale* (Paris: Mappus, 1959), 241–46. Marie-Joseph Le Guillou, *Le Christ et l'Église* (Paris: Centurion, 1963), 249–50. Nicolas, "Les laïcs et l'annonce de la Parole de Dieu."

87. See Audet, *Mariage et célibat dans le service pastoral de l'Église*, 125–26.
88. See Duval, "L'Ordre au concile de Trente," 281–85.

announce the divine word to all. They exercise their sacred function especially in the Eucharistic worship or the celebration of the Mass by which acting in the person of Christ and proclaiming His Mystery they unite the prayers of the faithful with the sacrifice of their Head and renew and apply in the sacrifice of the Mass until the coming of the Lord (cf. 1 Cor. 11:26) the only sacrifice of the New Testament namely that of Christ offering Himself once for all a spotless Victim to the Father (cf. Heb. 9:14–28).[89]

There is a contemporary thesis holding that "this ministry of the Word, which is immediately ordered to the sanctification of the faithful, should be an integral part of the ministerial priesthood."[90] This claim enters into conflict with another thesis, which is quite relevant today, holding that the ministry of the Word could also be bestowed on laymen and, consequently, that it is not necessarily connected to the sacrament of holy orders. By recalling (in contrast to Colson's remark cited above) that, in Judaism, what was the exclusive prerogative of priests was not the offering of victims but, rather, the communication of God's decrees to the people, Boismard cannot convince us that this should also be true for the Christian priesthood, as in that case, much to the contrary, it does not seem that the teaching and proclamation of the Word of God can be considered as the exclusive prerogative of ordained priests.[91]

Attempt at reconciliation

If the priest, precisely in virtue of the sacrament of holy orders, is constituted as being the bishop's collaborator, it is clear that, according to the words of the Second Vatican Council, he is also consecrated for the mission of evangelization and of shepherding. He is sacramentally designated to represent Christ the shepherd in subordination to the bishop and as sent by him.

We must grasp the intimate union existing between the cultic function and the evangelizing function [of the priesthood]. The latter has a goal, namely, the building up of the Church. Now, the primordial act of the Church, that in which she manifests her being and unity, is worship, which is centered on the Eucharist. On the other

---

89. *Lumen Gentium*, no. 28.
90. Boismard, "C.-R. du livre de Boüessé: Le sacerdoce chrétien," 309.
91. See Nicolas, "Les laïcs et l'annonce de la Parole de Dieu," 821–48.

hand, worship (and above all, the Eucharist) not only manifest but also realize the unity of the Church.[92] Thus, cultic activity is the terminus and the point of departure for missionary and pastoral activity. This latter activity sets forth from the Eucharist, in which the unity of mankind in Christ (i.e., the Church) is expressed and begins to be realized, so as to perfect this unity that is still very imperfect (on account of the mass of men who are not yet part of her and of all those who are incompletely part of her), and it leads all back to it because the Eucharist is man's response to the Word received and accepted.[93] Thus, the priest's function in announcing the Word and, thereby, in nourishing the flock of Christ entrusted to the bishop, adds nothing beyond his function in celebrating the Eucharist but, rather, is intimately part of it, although in a secondary manner.

This does not prevent it from being the case that this function could also be entrusted to laypersons. In them too, it will set forth from the Eucharist and lead back to it, for they also take part in the Eucharistic function of the priest, in virtue of their universal priesthood, as we have seen. However, given that the priest, by his ordination, is permanently constituted as the sacramental representative of Christ in acts of worship, he is also constituted in a permanent and total manner as a collaborator with the bishop for the fulfillment of the latter's pastoral mission. This is the basis of the requirements of total self-gift attached by the Church to the bestowal of the sacrament of holy orders.

Moreover, the layperson can totally consecrate himself to this pastoral and missionary collaboration, and his status in the Church can be utterly akin to that of the priest from this perspective. However, it remains the case that the cultic activities are part of the bishop's pastoral mission and that, for this, only ordained priests can represent the bishop. Because of this, they are more completely united with him *in partem sollicitudinis*.

In short, the full ensemble of priestly functions (i.e., the actions that the ordained priest is charged with performing among the People of God, as well as the results to be obtained by these

---

92. See §914 above.
93. See Bouyer, *Eucharistie*, 35–54.

actions) constitute a whole, which can be called "the proclamation of the Gospel," so long as one understands this as meaning not only preaching but also the sacraments by which the Gospel, accepted by faith, exercises its saving and divinizing efficacy on each believer and builds up the Church as the community of the saved. The Eucharistic sacrifice is the nucleus and center of this whole, for it is the central and essential act of the Church's life of on earth. All of her other acts lead to it and find their fulfillment therein. At the same time, it is the act from which all of the others flow forth (in virtue of the dialectic of the "already" and the "not yet"). In the order of the "already," the Eucharistic sacrifice and the Eucharistic communion in which it is brought to completion is a "consummation." In the order of the "not yet," it is the inspiring principle of the proclamation of the Gospel in all of the externally various forms that it can take. Only the ordained priest can perform the action of offering the Eucharistic sacrifice, in the sense of performing the sacrificial action in communion with the Eucharistic community and with the whole Church that is concretized therein. Conversely, a layperson can also perform any of the other actions (apart from the bestowal of the other sacraments, which in some manner take part in the Eucharist). However, by the very fact that he is ordained so as to offer the Eucharistic sacrifice, the priest is specially (although not exclusively) designated to perform the other actions, which comprehensively constitute the proclamation of the Gospel.

Thus, one can and must, in our opinion, maintain that the sacrament of holy orders is defined in relation to "presiding over the Eucharist" (i.e., in relation to the performing of the sacrificial action of the Eucharist), though, on the condition that one recognizes that this action includes the comprehensive totality of actions constituting the proclamation of the Gospel, understood in the way specified above. This can furnish the solution to the twofold objection that we have encountered. On the one hand, the actions that constitute the proclamation of the Gospel can be performed by a (baptized) layperson and, nonetheless, as an ensemble (and not each in particular), they are part of the functions for which the priest is "ordained." On the other hand, given that each priest is obviously not charged with all and each of the functions that constitute the proclamation of the Gospel, it can happen that a priest would be dispensed from exercising the functions of announcing the Gospel for personal reasons, the most typical of which is the monastic vocation, recognized by the Church and sanctioned by religious profession. Still in this case, one cannot say that the priest purely and simply is not ordained for these functions by the sacrament that he has received. He remains ordained to them by the mediation of the Eucharistic sacrifice for which he has been sacramentally capacitated. He is only dispensed from exercising them on account of personal circumstances. For these priests as well, the Eucharist that they celebrate is the Eucharist of the whole Church and is inserted into the whole of the Church's missionary activities. Still, when reduced solely to the celebration of worship and even in a community in which their cultic ministry would not be necessary, their collaboration with the bishop remains, even though it is in fact reduced to a purely spiritual and mystical activity.

The "desacralization" of the priesthood

By contrast, what is unthinkable is the idea of "desacralizing" the priesthood as well as the idea of desacralizing the worship that is connected to it. Any of the non-sacred activities of the priest could quite perfectly be performed by a non-priest and even, moreover, by someone who is not baptized. Accordingly, it is meaningless to wish to define the priest by secular tasks, of whatever order they may be.

This does not preclude that a priest could give himself over to secular activities—either because quite simply he does not, in fact, consecrate his whole life and activity to his priestly functions, or because he would need to perform secular tasks for the sake of accomplishing his priestly functions. However, in the latter case, such secular tasks belong to the order of the sacred through their intention. This precludes one from saying that he was ordained a priest for these tasks and, consequently, that he could renounce all sacred activity, even when a profane activity can be elevated to the order of the sacred by its willed ordination to the work of evangelization. To do so would, by this very fact, betray the intention that the Church had in making him a priest. For this reason, St. Thomas thought that a priest could not completely stop celebrating Mass without thereby being guilty of a grave sin.[94]

This explains why the members of a religious community who are priests normally participate in the common Eucharist inasmuch as they are priests (i.e., by "concelebrating"). Certainly, this adds nothing to the value of this Eucharist. However, constituted as collaborators with the bishop on account of their ordination, not only in preaching the Gospel and shepherding but also for cultic acts (most especially the Eucharist), it is on this head that they take part in worship in this community.

---

94. See *ST* III, q. 82, a. 10.

19

The Character Imprinted by the Sacrament of Holy Orders

THE NOTION OF THE PRIESTLY "CHARACTER"

The Existence of a "Character" Impressed by the Sacrament of Holy Orders

{986} The Council of Trent defined, as being something that Catholics hold *de fide*, that "the three sacraments of baptism, confirmation, and orders impress a character in the soul, that is, a particular spiritual and indelible mark, which does not permit them to be given multiple times,"[1] and likewise, "ordination impresses a character, and he who was at one time ordained a priest cannot become a layman again."[2] By providing a more clearly defined form, the Council took up what already had been expressed in the Council of Florence's "Decree for the Armenians."[3] It took a position against Luther's denials, especially as expressed in the *De captivitate babylonica*. Luther denied not only the priestly character (claiming that the priest returned to being a layman if he ceased preaching) but

---

1. Council of Trent, session 7, "Decree on the Sacraments in General," March 3, 1547, c. 9, in D.-*Sch.*, no. 1609. [Tr. note: The canon is expressed in negative language so as to be condemned. Fr. Nicolas has rendered it in a positive manner, as he has also done for the next citation as well. I have followed his French.]

2. Council of Trent, session 22, "Doctrine and Canons on the Sacrifice of the Mass," September 17, 1562, c. 4, in D.-*Sch.*, no. 1774.

3. Holy Office (Pope Alexander VIII), "Decree Concerning the Errors of the Jansenists," no. 23, in D.-*Sch.*, no. 1313.

even the very sacrament of holy orders, as well as the existence of a ministerial priesthood which would establish a distinction between those are invested with it and other believers.

For the doctrine of character in general and its sources in tradition, recall that the Church became aware of the sacramental "character" in response to questions raised concerning the non-repetition of both baptism and holy orders. It was not considered first of all as a determinate reality having a given nature and given properties but, rather, as a real and definitive change produced by the sacrament in the person who received it. Consequently, it was considered as being something independent of the movements of its recipient's free will.[4] He who has received the sacrament of baptism or that of holy orders no longer is what he once was. Something has taken place in him, and for this reason, he is no longer the same as what he was among the People of God. It is an interior "sacrament," a sacred sign, a "mark" that distinguishes him from others (who have not received the sacrament).

The Council of Trent did not wish to take a position concerning the nature of the sacramental character. That is a theological question that the Magisterium as such is not empowered to resolve. In the soberest manner possible, it affirmed [the Church's] faith concerning this matter. This affirmation is what must rule the theologian's investigation into this matter and must be found again in the response that is given to the question.

The *raison d'être* of the Sacerdotal Character

{987} We are here faced with the question of assuring the reality of the ministerial priesthood. The "priest" is not a member of the cultic assembly receiving from the assembly (or even from the head of the assembly) a temporary delegation to preside over the Eucharist and to confer the other sacraments. He is "sacramentally designated," distinguished from others as a person who will sacramentally represent Christ the priest in the cultic celebration. This wholly interior "mark" is not visible. However, it was produced in him by the visible sacramental rite so that there is in him, as well as for the oth-

---

4. See §747 above.

er members of the People of God, a "fixing" and permanency of this rite, which in itself is something that took place in the past. The People of God know that he who received the sacrament at a given moment of his existence is thus marked and designated.

For this to be true, one must admit—and this is part of the very affirmation of faith concerning this matter—that this mark is inalienable. Without this, there would be a breakdown concerning the certitude of sacramental orders, for the only thing that can be known here with certitude is that this man received the sacrament. If he could "lose the sacrament"—that is, if the effect of the sacrament could disappear from him for some reason—one could not know whether or not he still is the sacramental representative of Christ the priest. The entire signifying value of the sacramental rite would vanish if he who was formerly "designated" as a priest could no longer be "designated" as one today, unless a certain "sign" could assure us that he still is a priest or no longer is one. Just as the bread is the body of Christ once it has been ritually consecrated, and just as the Christian is a member of Christ once he has been baptized (even if he has severed himself from Him), so too the priest is the certain agent of the sacramental action once he has been invested by the Holy Spirit and by priestly ordination.

FROM THE NOTION OF CHARACTER TO THE NOTION OF POWER

The Power to Perform Sacramental Actions

The existence of this power

{988} If the sacraments produced grace only through a form of moral causality, the agent obviously would not need to have a power in the ontological sense of the word (i.e., a *potentia activa*) so that he may perform the sacramental actions. Indeed, [if sacramental causality were only moral in nature], he would only need to perform the rite (which, obviously, any man can perform by his natural powers) and, on account of this rite, God would immediately produce the effects of grace that are attached to this rite. Thus, the "character" would be a mere sign that would assure believers that

God would always intervene to produce these effects when the sacramental action is ritually performed by the Christian who has thus been designated.

If we must, as I believe we must,[5] admit that the sacraments involve efficient causality, this means that this efficient causality is exercised by the priest. Now, he is not capable of exercising such causality in relation to the effects of grace by means of his natural powers.

However, the following objection could be raised against this argument. In any case, this efficient causality exercised by the priest can only be (and indeed is only) instrumental. That is, Christ is the one who acts by him in each case and exercises his saving activity through him. Hence, must there be a habitual power in the priest? Would it not suffice that each time he performs the rite Christ would act in him and make him participate *per modum actus* in his sanctifying activity?

An objection of this kind brings out the relativity of theological reasoning each time that it is exercised in a domain wherein everything depends on the will of God and on Christ's free disposition. On the hypothesis that the character would not be a real power in the priest, everything that the Church believes could be assured, on the condition of admitting that Christ always acts and always produces the effects of grace connected to a sacramental action when it is performed by the sacramentally designated minister. However, we could indeed say that this would not correspond to the general principles of the divine action in the world and, especially in the order of salvation, such as they can be known on the basis of revelation and the experience of faith.

Indeed, God does not only give His creatures that which is good. He gives them the power to communicate to other creatures the good that exists in them, and for this, He gives them, along with their being, the power to act upon one another. However, one will note that, at least according to St. Thomas,[6] the gifts of prophecy and of performing miracles are not permanent powers but rather are

---

5. See §724 above.
6. See *ST* II-II, q. 171, a. 2, and q. 178, a. 1.

actual (charismatic) graces given on each occasion. The reason given for this is difficult to interpret and makes no allusion to the sacramental power. We must see the difference in the very nature of the sacramental action and in the nature of its efficacy. Its effect is invisible and therefore its efficacy indiscernible. Hence, as we have noted, it is necessary that the agent who is capable of this efficacy should be designated in a certain manner as having the corresponding power.

Therefore, it is necessary that this power exist in him in a habitual manner. By contrast, prophecy and miracles are perceptible effects which are the sign that he who prophesies or performs the miracle is (or, rather, was) a prophet or wonder-worker in this act. Therefore, it is not necessary that he have the power of prophesying or of performing miracles in a habitual manner. On the other hand, the end of prophecy and of miracles is quite precisely to render an extraordinary, unforeseeable divine intervention sensible. Conversely, the end of the sacramental action is to assure in an ordinary and certain manner the continuity and application of Christ's salvific action to each person. This is why, although both gifts are first of all and principally "for others" and not "for him who receives it," there is this difference, namely that the good of the others in the first case requires that it be accorded in an intermittent fashion, whereas the second requires that it be given in a habitual fashion.[7]

The paradox of this power

{989} Normally, the principal cause has the initiative in the action as well as the use of the instrument. Here, the instrument (i.e., the person who is the instrument) has the initiative. The reason is always the same: the very decision to actualize the sanctifying action of Christ for this community or for this person must also belong to the order of signs. Thus, it must come from the minister, who therefore must make the decision to produce the sacramental action. For this reason, we cannot exclude the possibility that this decision would be sinful, being performed when it should not have been performed, in a way that it should not be performed, and for an un-

---

7. See Marie-Joseph Nicolas, "La nature ontologique du caractère sacerdotal dans la pensée de Saint Thomas," in *Atti del congresso internazionale Tommaso d'Aquino nel suo settimo centenario* (Naples: Edizioni Domenicane Italiane, 1976), 4:486–92.

acceptable end. While the sacramental action as such is an action performed by Christ, nonetheless, inasmuch as it is a human action engaging the person of the ministerial priest, it is a free action by this person and therefore can be meritorious or not.[8]

Therefore, we must admit that God and Christ in His humanity intervene each time that this act is performed by the minister. For this reason, it is impossible to entirely exclude from sacramental theology that which scholastic thinkers [*anciens*] expressed by the notion of a *pactio divina* (before or at the time of St. Thomas, Alexander of Hales, St. Bonaventure, and St. Albert, as well as Scotus and many others after him). This indefectible connection between God's sovereign intervention (and Christ's as a man) and the sacramental action performed by the minister has been conceived (and is still conceived by some) in the form of a contract which would be a kind of everlasting obligation for God. This notion can be criticized on account of its arbitrary and extrinsic character. However, if it is replaced by the biblical notion of a coventant [*promesse*], the explanation that it proposed retrieves all of its value: by instituting the sacrament, Christ promised this intervention by the Divine Power, and His promise is indefectible. This promise is what assures the stability of the sacramental order which we discussed above.[9]

However, this is not a surreptitious return to the theory of the moral causality of the sacraments, (which we critiqued in its proper place).[10] Indeed, God's action through Christ that is the object of this promise is exercised by means of the sacrament as an instrumental cause, not immediately.

It remains the case that the manifold divine interventions required by sacramental causality do not multiply God's unique action and causality any more than do the multiplicity of God's interventions as the first cause required by natural causality. One cannot speak in either case of a "divine contract." Rather, one must see that all these divine interventions only realize successively in time the gift of God made once and for all, with the creation of natures on one hand and the institution of the sacraments on the other.

8. See §740 above.
9. See §734 above.
10. For all of this section, see §752 above.

Power of the Mystical Body

{990} Here, we have a delicate passage from ontological power to moral power which is exercised over free wills. The first is the real power to do something. Certainly, this means that it is a power to do something in the order of grace, but if the order of grace consists essentially in interpersonal relations between man and God, in order for these relations to be real, they must be founded on real, ontological modifications. They can be modifications of man, as is the case in the transformation of man by grace. They can also be modifications of things, as happens in the changing of bread and wine into Jesus' body and blood. Moral power is the power to direct people through orders or counsels. Such people can indeed transgress such a power. Nonetheless, they obligate, so that through such transgressions, such people are guilty of doing evil. Such moral power is authority.

Juridical power and ontological power

Of itself, authority would not call for an ontological modification, a character, in the person who is invested with it if the case of ecclesial authority did not involve the mysterious connection between the visible shepherd and Christ. Such a connection is neither purely juridical nor physical. As we have seen, it is sacramental. To say that it is sacramental is to say that it is "real," for the sacraments realize what they signify. The ministerial priest really represents Christ, not in an intermittent manner but in virtue of the sacrament of holy orders that he has received.

This "reality" is assured by the character, to which the assistance of the Holy Spirit is connected, meaning that it is a permanent charism,[11] that is, one that is indefectibly assured by the promise that we spoke about above.[12] It is the *charisma veritatis* spoken of by St. Irenaeus.[13]

However, this sacramental "authority" cannot be exercised out-

---

11. See Grelot, *Le ministère de la Nouvelle Alliance*.
12. See §978 above.
13. See Louis Ligier, "Le 'charisma veritatis certum' des évêques; ses attaches liturgiques, patristiques, et bibliques," *L'homme devant Dieu, Mélanges offerts au P. H. de Lubac* (Paris: Aubier, 1963), 1:247–68.

side of manifest ecclesial communion, in distinction from the power of performing sacramental actions. As we have seen, the reason for this is that the true subject of pastoral authority is the college [of bishops]. (If the head of the college is also, himself alone, the subject of this authority, this is because the college is included in him.)[14] By his consecration, the bishop is constituted as a member of the college and, by this fact, a personal participant in the Church's pastoral authority. If he separates himself from the college through schism or heresy, this personal participation ceases of itself. By contrast, the power to perform sacramental actions and produce by them the effect of grace that is proper to them is connected to the person who was consecrated for this. He can exercise it legitimately only in the Church's communion because this exercise itself comes from pastoral authority. However, if he exercises it outside of this communion, he does not, for all of that, cease to be, in the sacramental action, the sacramental sign and instrument of Christ the priest. Indeed, in order for the certitude of the sacramental sign to remain inviolable for the good of the People of God, Christ does not cease acting by means of the sacramental action, even when this is deserving of condemnation for the person who performs it and for those who consciously separate themselves from communion with the Church in this very action. Thus, the bishop separated from communion preserves not only the power of *conficere eucharistiam* but also that of ordaining priests.

Here, we must, however, note that one cannot pass in silence over the observations by Grelot on the topic of the "absolute" ordinations declared invalid by the Council of Chalcedon.[15] This author, "inclined to reason like an Eastern Christian [*en oriental*]," suggests the idea of connecting these kinds of ordinations to the ordinations performed at Ecône by a "bishop of no Church." Here, there something deserving reflection, for this judgment is based on both ancient tradition and the consideration of the very finality of ministry, which is a service to the Church.

However, despite this fact, I cannot concur with this suggestion,

---

14. See §971 above.
15. See Grelot, *Église et ministère*, 127n2.

all the while submitting my own reflection (as does Fr. Grelot himself) to the competent authorities and to the decisions that they may pronounce. From the dogmatic perspective, to my eyes, this seems to compromise the stability of the sacramental order, for how can one judge with incontestable objective certitude that the recipient is not or will not be assigned to any service in the Church, as soon as one extends—with the Council of Chalcedon—this notion to assignment "to a particular church, an official sanctuary, or a monastery"? (Indeed, would a hermit need to be excluded?) With regard to the minister who proceeds to ordination, what is necessary so that he may be considered—always with objective certitude—"a bishop of a Church"? Would this not put into question, for example, the Old Catholic bishops and their power to ordain priests? Would this not require the pope to solemnly declare that a given bishop no longer has this power which he received at his ordination? And could he do so without placing into question the inadmissibility of claiming that the sacrament of holy orders could be reiterated? From the pastoral perspective, however offensive these "illegal" [*sauvage*] ordinations may be for the People of God, it seems that such a declaration, being directed to a bishop designated by name, has no precedent in the Church's history and would only add to the confusion, for it would be rejected by those who have received these ordinations and by those who approve of them.

Certainly, there can be no doubt that "the very finality of ministry"—and therefore of the sacrament that confers it—is gravely deflected when this sacrament is conferred and received through disobedience bearing precisely on the very act of conferring it and on the act of receiving it. However, as we have seen, the intention that is strictly required for the sacrament to exist (i.e., for it to be valid) pertains to the very act of conferring the sacrament, not on the finalities that the Church pursues in conferring it.[16]

The authority of bishops and the authority of simple priests
{991} As we have seen, what characterizes the bishop is the fact that he is sacramentally constituted as representing Christ the shepherd.

---

16. See §728.

That is, he is invested with His authority over the flock. This confers upon him responsibility for the flock, a collegial responsibility over the whole flock, and personal responsibility for the part of the flock that makes up the Church that has been entrusted to him. Without a doubt, this responsibility is what is evoked in the Gospel by the image of the good shepherd, who gives his life for his flock, and is extended to the apostles as they are also themselves shepherds.

St. Thomas thought that the bishop had been dedicated [*voué*] by his state, consecrated to the salvation of souls—dedicated by his personal engagement, simply consisting in his acceptance of the episcopacy, and consecrated by the solemn episcopal consecration: "the solemnity of consecration, moreover, accompanies the aforementioned profession."[17] Thus, he established an intimate connection between the episcopacy and responsibility for the flock, itself implying a personal obligation to everything required by perfection. Given that we more frankly consider episcopal consecration a sacrament than did St. Thomas, namely the sacrament of holy orders in its fullness, and therefore conceiving of the episcopacy as being a character and a power, we can prolong his reflection and see this character as involving a sacramental consecration to the pastorate and therefore to the flock. Likewise, we can see in this power a sacramental participation in Christ's pastoral function and in the authority that is connected with it. Thus, one can understand how the power to perform sacred actions (a power over Christ's Eucharistic body, according to St. Thomas) is intrinsically connected, in the bishop, to his pastoral authority, given that it is at once a participation in Christ inasmuch as He is priest and shepherd. Thus, the act of confirming and the act of conferring holy orders are at once acts of pastoral authority and of the sacramental power proper to the bishop.

The simple priest is a collaborator with the bishop. On the one hand, this means that he is empowered by his very ordination to participate in the pastoral responsibility and authority of the bishop. On the other hand, it means that he does not receive this responsibility directly in his ordination. This is what makes possible the case of a simple priest without pastoral responsibility. St. Thomas

---

17. *ST* II-II, q. 184, a. 5. One should read the whole of q. 185 as well.

concluded from this (in a passage that is difficult to interpret [*d'une interprétation difficile*]) that by his ordination the simple priest was not specifically obligated to perfection.[18] This can be understood only in the sociological context of the medieval Church, where the presbyterate was a social position. Today, it does not seem that the Church has or could have any other intention in ordaining a priest than to make him a collaborator with the bishops in their pastoral activity, even if this were in the wholly spiritual and mystical manner that we spoke about above for the priest vowed to the contemplative life.[19] Only the first of the two reasons that St. Thomas advances as justifications for discharging a priest from all *cura animarum* (i.e., his entrance into religious life) can be retained. (Obviously, we must add to them physical or psychological impotence arising from sickness or old age.) Consequently, St. Thomas's idea that a priest is not vowed to Christian perfection solely because of his ordination should be adjusted.[20] Naturally, we must also extend this notion of "collaborators as shepherds." Today, there are many completely new ways of being engaged for the good of the flock in collaboration with the bishop who is its shepherd.

FROM THE NOTION OF POWER TO THE NOTION OF SERVICE

{992} Fr. Congar has shown that the terms signifying the ideas of authority and power are very rarely applied in the New Testament to persons in charge of the Church.[21] He does not draw from this fact the radical conclusions which Küng drew, holding that the very idea of sovereignty would be excluded by the notion of *diaconia*, which is more regularly used to designate the role played by the leaders of the Church.[22] On the contrary, Congar notes first that "the idea of authority is included as a reality in the institution of the apostolate by Christ." Then, he notes that St. Paul in fact appeals on

---

18. See *ST* II-II, q. 184, a. 6.
19. See §974.
20. See §995 below. [Tr. note: Reading "995" for "985."]
21. See Congar, *La Tradition et les traditions*, 31ff.
22. See Küng, *La justification*, 538.

many occasions to his authority as an apostle.[23] On the other hand, it is quite clear that Titus and Timothy's charge, as specified to them by St. Paul, is an authoritative function. However, Congar notes quite correctly that Paul, in fact, does not prefer to take advantage of his authority. He appeals to Jesus' authority and to the requirements of *agápē*. This is rooted in the very foundational teachings of the Gospel.

Jesus: Master and Servant

One must first of all refer to the Christological hymn in the Letter to the Philippians which presents the Incarnation as being a renunciation of lordly prerogatives in order to take on the conditions of a slave.[24] Then, there is the commendation of taking the last place,[25] proposing Jesus as an example: "For the Son of man has not come to be served but to serve." Finally, this is the great lesson of the washing of the feet: "Do you know what I have done to you? You call me Teacher and Lord; and you are right, for so I am. If I then, your Lord and Teacher, have washed your feet, you also ought to wash one another's feet."[26]

Note well that Jesus, in these very instances, proclaims Himself to be master and Lord, does not exclude the idea that particular people would be "great" in the Church (i.e., in the context, that particular people would be leaders). What He proposes is a particular way of exercising the commandment in a way that is opposed to that of kings of the nations and of those who prevail over them.[27] He proposes the complete effacement and abasement of the person who exercises authority.

The fundamental truth is that God alone is the master upon whom all are equally and humbly dependent. All are to become like children. This is a humility that must be found again in the relationships established by the person who exercises authority over others, who are and remain his brothers.

---

23. See 1 Cor 7:10, 12, 17, and 2 Cor 10:8.
24. See Phil 2:6–7.
25. See Mk 10:42–45 and Mt 20:25–28.
26. Jn 13:12–13 (RSV).
27. See Lk 22:25.

However, the authority of the Word of God and of the Gospel remains. The visible shepherds are the bearers of this authority, the sacramental representatives of Christ, assisted by the Holy Spirit. Through them, the Gospel is announced to mankind. Theirs is the task of defining the meaning of the truths contained therein. They recall its requirements. Through them, those who have received the Gospel are led in accord with the Gospel. And this is the exercise of a true authority, though of an authority that is not ultimately possessed by him who exercises it, an authority that is not his own. It is Christ's authority.

Fr. Congar has suggested[28] that, in the popes of the Gregorian reform, the expression *vicarius Christi* (and equally, *vicarius Petri*) slid from its mystical meaning (the pope sacramentally representing Christ) to a juridical meaning (the pope, the delegate of Christ, vested by him with an authority for acting in His place). The two meanings are precise, for the bishop is the person by whom Christ visibly acts (mystical meaning), but he also is a person who is distinct from Christ, who acts on his own accord as a second cause, inasmuch as he is Christ's delegate. However, it is clear that, in the second meaning, there is a natural tendency to appropriate authority to oneself and distinguish oneself from the flock that the bishop leads and rules.[29] However, the second meaning, which, by contrast, calls for the effacement of the person of the shepherd before that of Christ whom he represents, cannot be an effacement of the authority itself. This would not be an effacement before Christ but, rather, would be the effacement of Christ.

Pastoral Power at the Service of Christ

This follows from what we have said. As St. Paul said of himself, the shepherd is "a servant of Jesus Christ."[30] He does not lead the flock in his own name. The flock belongs to Christ who paid for the flock with His own blood, and he was placed at the head of this flock by Christ: "Take heed to yourselves and to all the flock, in which the

---

28. See Congar, *La Tradition et les traditions*, 55, and *L'ecclésiologie du Haut Moyen-Age*, 296–307.
29. Congar, *La Tradition et les traditions*, 97–128.
30. Rom 1:1.

Holy Spirit has made you overseers, to care for the church of God which he obtained with the blood of his own Son."[31]

Pastoral Power at the Service of the People of God

Christ Himself placed Himself at the service of mankind—first through His Incarnation, then through His life and death. This service primarily consisted in his giving of His life. The same must be true for the visible shepherd.

However, it also consists in acting on man so that he may accept the obedience of faith in order that he may submit to the requirements of faith. Without this, Christ's death and resurrection are of no use. The necessary authority of the Church in Christ's service and at the service of the Word comes from this fact.

Yes, it is in the service of the People of God. However, we must understand and admit that this pastoral service consists in directing and, therefore, in making prescriptions (indeed, prescribing not only what one must do but also what one must believe, that which the Word of God imposes upon us for belief), as well as in forbidding. It even potentially involves excluding people from the flock.[32]

Sovereignty and Abasement

The Church is a communion. The relationships existing within this communion are relations of charity, not of precedence. The order of charity alone will remain in the eschatological Church.

This communion on earth is realized in a society. There, we find a true hierarchy, that is, an order of precedence (not only of honor but of authority) founded on visible values—sacramental values, the priestly and episcopal characters. Therefore, they are holy, inasmuch as they are a participation in Christ's holiness. However, they are independent from the personal holiness of the person who is thus valorized.

Moreover—and this belongs to the contingent, historical order—the Church as a society is inserted into "political" societies and plays

---

31. Acts 20:28 (RSV). See Jacques Dupont, *Le discours de Milet* (Paris: Cerf, 1962). Pierre Benoît, "Les origins de l'épiscopat dans le Nouveau Testament," *Exégèse et Théologie* (Paris: Cerf, 1961), 2:232–46.

32. See Ti 3:9.

a role there. This means that her "hierarchy" is more or less recognized, honored, protected, and by this very fact hampered by political society. Purely ecclesial precedence, which would be found even in the catacombs, finds itself to be simultaneously reinforced and weighed down by honors and powers that it does not require of itself, which often distort it, and which are not essential to it. Therefore, she can benefit from ridding herself of them if historical circumstances change.

A tension exists between the effacement of the person, which is called for by good exercise of authority in the Church, and the affirmation of the person which every authority naturally includes, one that will never be able to be definitively resolved and, therefore, will never disappear. The parable of the last place and the symbolic gesture of washing feet indicate a direction and inspiration for how to negotiate this tension. However, they do not provide a kind of ready-made solution that would be immediately applied without requiring the need to discover the way this demeanor is to be applied in each given situation.

THE PRIESTLY VOCATION

{993} Up to this point, our focus has been on those who receive the sacrament of holy orders and thereby are distinguished within the People of God, being modified in their Christian being through a singular, new, and permanent participation in Christ's priesthood, being placed for this reason above others in the Church by means of their roles as authorities. However, a question remains to be answered, namely, how and by what means is this choice made concerning the members of the People of God who are called to receive this sacrament and to exercise the corresponding functions?

Only He Who Is Called

"And one does not take the honor upon himself, but he is called by God, just as Aaron was."[33]

Quite precisely because authority in the Church is first of all a

---

33. Heb 5:4 (RSV). Also, see the *Traduction œcuménique de la Bible* for this text.

form of service to Christ, the one priest and shepherd, nobody can decide by himself to become an ordained priest, this singular representative of Christ the priest and shepherd. Every man is called to be part of Christ's flock, indeed, called by Christ. Every member of Christ's flock is called to realize, in his or her own manner and in accord with his or her particular grace, everything that the Christian vocation includes: holiness here-below and participation in the Church's evangelizing mission; glory in the hereafter.[34]

This calling can be replaced neither by one's willingness to consecrate oneself entirely to Christ and to the kingdom, nor by one's personal holiness, nor by all the human gifts that are related to the Word of God or to governance.

God's Call and Personal Desire

Clearly, this principle in no way excludes the role of personal desire in this matter. At least ordinarily, the Holy spirit enables one to know Christ's calling by inspiring desires and one's inclination.

Quite obviously, the decision to request the sacrament of holy orders can only be made after long deliberation. This explains the time that is left for each person to question oneself, weighing out the *pros* and *cons*, before taking the decisive step.

---

34. It is in this sense that, for St. Thomas, the "vocation to the religious life" is not a vocation that is distinct from the Christian vocation (See *ST* II-II, q. 189; "Contra retrahentes," chs. 6 and 7). Obviously, this calls for many qualifications and distinctions. It must not be understood as though the Christian vocation implied a particular form of Christian life, such as the religious life in fact is. (Moreover, St. Thomas himself distinguishes the decision "to enter into religion" in general from the particular way one "enters into religion," along with the choice of the form of religious life into which one enters. Now, it is clear that today there are many more and different manners for realizing what St. Thomas meant by "to enter into religion" than only entering into a determinate religious order.) What remains the case is that the "religious vocation" is not a new vocation in relation to the Christian vocation but, rather, is a radicalization of it, so that the decision to "enter into religion" is a decision that one can make by oneself, for it is nothing other than a prolongation of the decision to follow Christ which is at the basis of the Christian life. By contrast, the "priestly vocation" is a new vocation in relation to the Christian vocation in that the former is in no way [essentially] included in the latter, even though it must be integrated into the Christian vocation by the person to whom it is addressed and who has received it. It is a particular task that is proposed to him for his earthly life, a task whose faithful fulfillment must lead him to holiness, which is one amid its diversity, though invested with a unique modality in each person. The decision to consecrate oneself to the fulfillment of this task (and therefore, to tend to holiness under the corresponding modality) presupposes this particular vocation and therefore can be taken only as a response to a calling that is not included in the Christian vocation [precisely as such].

However, the object of this deliberation is to know whether one is called. In a profound sense, this deliberation is completely different from that which leads one to the choice of a profession, a kind of life, or marriage to a particular person. In such cases, such discernment is concerned with self-questioning concerning what is befitting for oneself. In the case of the priesthood, one's discernment involves questioning the Holy Spirit, even if He manifests Himself through what is befitting for the person discerning, something which nonetheless is only held to be a sign of His will.

The difference is particularly clear today in religious orders whose members are indifferently priests or non-priests, notably in monasteries, where a tendency is emerging leading to the distinction between the decision to "seek God"[35] through the monastic life and the vocation to the priesthood, a distinction that was made in the first centuries [of monastic life in the early Church].

Personal Desire and Acceptance by the Church

Between the two wars, there was a great controversy concerning the subject of vocations, though the controversy is now quite forgotten. Certain thinkers held that the priestly vocation is purely and simply merged with the Church's calling. According to them, it was the Church's responsibility to choose from among her members the shepherds that she had need of and that this choice was the very calling of God. (Such people were obviously thinking of the shepherds of the Church, though one could extend the matter to the Christian community in general.)

As it stands, this thesis is untenable. It is clear that the priestly functions, of themselves, include particular and heavy obligations. The Church can impose on Christians only the obligations that flow from the Christian vocation alone.

It remains the case that the Church has an important role to play in the question of one's vocation. Above all, she plays the role of rendering a judgment concerning it. While one's inclinations and desires for it are signs of the will of the Spirit of God, they are not certain signs, even for the person who experiences them. It falls to the

---

35. As the Rule of St. Benedict says: "if he truly seeks God."

Church to render a judgment concerning the authenticity of a vocation. How? By leaving it to develop itself and undergo the trial of doubt and of difficulties; by examining the motivations for it; and also by examining the subject's capacities for fulfilling the priestly functions (i.e., intellectual capacities but also those of character and of moral conduct).

She also has the right and duty to set conditions for the realization of the vocation. Among such conditions are those of moral and intellectual formation, for one is a priest for the People of God and must be able to respond to its expectations, taking into account the many ways in which priestly service can be realized for the benefit of the People of God. Moreover, there are also conditions of the commitment undertaken. This commitment is personal and can be nothing but definitive, for the sacrament of holy orders confers an indelible consecration. However, it is also a commitment to exercise the priestly functions in the service of Christ and the People of God, the Church. Now, it falls to the shepherds responsible for the flock to establish the conditions for such service. Obviously, they must not do so arbitrarily! Rather, they must do so, on the one hand, in reference to the Gospel ideal and, on the other, in reference to the requirements of the priestly service as she perceives them. And it falls to her to judge and decide, with the assistance of the Holy Spirit, whether these requirements truly refer to the authentic nature of the Gospel and the priesthood.

Among these conditions, there is one in particular that raises protestations today, namely the requirement of celibacy. Is it good and legitimate to concretize the commitment to the priestly service in the very particular form of a commitment to celibacy?*

In this difficult question, which we cannot fully treat here, one must above all pose the problem correctly. Two questions must be distinguished. On the one hand, is the Church correct in considering celibacy as the concrete form of the priest's commitment, which the priestly vocation of itself includes? On the other hand, in considering this, does the Church have the right to impose celibacy upon her priests?[36]

---

* [Tr. note: As regards certain matters touching on the Eastern Catholic Churches, see the translator's introduction.]

36. See Audet, *Mariage et célibat dans le service pastoral de l'Église*. Grelot, *Église et*

For the first question, a discussion is possible, obviously within the framework of faith. One cannot place into question the Christian value of consecrated celibacy, of celibacy devoted to God, both for the Christian vocation in general and for the priestly vocation in particular. However, as this recognized value suppresses neither the legitimacy of marriage nor its Christian value, one can ask whether and why it is fitting to require it of priests. Such a discussion, which cannot be pursued here, cannot be undertaken without paying great attention to the very ancient practice of the Church, not only in the West but also in the East. (In the latter, married men can be ordained. However, ordained Christians cannot be married and married priests cannot accede to the highest functions. This undeniably implies that there is a close bond between the priesthood and consecrated celibacy, even if this bond is less strict than in the Western Church.) This practice testifies to a Christian experience that cannot be ignored, even if some think that it could be reconsidered today either on account of the particular revalorization of marriage as a manner of realizing one's Christian vocation or on account of modifications to the priestly lifestyle that have been brought about by historical circumstances. (In fact, faced with particular sensational and certainly precipitous declarations, the Holy See has been led to take a position and has forcefully and determinately reaffirmed the untouchable character of the law of priestly celibacy in her opinion.[37] The theologians and shepherds who study this problem in compliance with these positions suggest that one should separately treat the problem concerning the ordination of married men, as is done in the discipline of the Eastern Churches.[38] This certainly merits a thorough examination.)

The second question can only be discussed on account of an underlying prejudice, which is not acceptable. This prejudice is that every Christian who has the desire to be a priest and who has or can acquire the necessary capacities for fulfilling priestly functions *has a*

---

ministère, 145–72 and 248–50. Jean-Hervé Nicolas, *Liberté chrétienne et sexualité* (Fribourg: Editions S. Paul, 1972).

37. See "Le concile pastoral de Hollande et ses suites," *Documentation catholique* 67 (1970): 162–87.

38. See Grelot, *Église et ministère*, 229–34.

right to receive the sacrament of holy orders. Hence, the Church would not have the right to impose on him obligations that would extend beyond those imposed on every Christian precisely on account of his Christian vocation. If one has understood that the priestly vocation is not necessarily included in the Christian vocation and that the Church has the responsibility for organizing the concrete realization of this vocation in function of the mission that she has received, one will admit that she has the right to impose the obligation of celibacy as a condition of this realization. This is not a dogmatic decision. However, it is not a purely disciplinary decision as well. It is a practical decision which falls under her prudence and the Holy Spirit's assistance.

However, one may object: if one's vocation comes from the Holy Spirit, does not the person who has such a vocation have the right to be permitted to realize it, even if he refuses to be committed to celibacy because the connection between celibacy and the priesthood is not a dogmatic truth? We must simply respond to such a question by saying that the Holy Spirit who inclines a Christian to wish to be a priest is the same Spirit who assists the Church in the determination of the conditions for realizing the priestly vocation. In the current state of things, so long as the Church maintains her requirement, we must admit that an authentic vocation to the priesthood includes a vocation to consecrated celibacy. Although some today readily oppose the priestly vocation to the purpose of consecrated celibacy, the latter being a charism and for this reason falling only to the conscience of the individual, this opposition does not, in fact, hold true. The priestly vocation is also a charism, one that, in the current state of things, implies the other—the Holy Spirit is not divided against Himself! To those who contest the very principle of this explanation, which the Church maintains not as something expressly established by the Lord but as something established by her in the Spirit of the Lord, she could say with St. Paul: "What! Did the word of God originate with you, or are you the only ones it has reached?"[39]

---

39. 1 Cor 14:36 (RSV).

The Problem Concerning the Exclusion of Women from the Ministerial Priesthood

The question of fact

{994} Priestly* functions have never been granted to women. From the beginning of the Church's history, the sacrament of holy orders has been strictly reserved to men.

The Church holds that this bears on the validity of the sacrament and not merely on a matter of discipline (as though it were only a question of an ecclesiastical decision forbidding the ordination of women): "A baptized male alone receives sacred ordination validly."[40] Up to recent days, classical theology considered this fact to be unalterable and connected this exclusion to the very institution of the sacrament by Christ (i.e., to the very "nature" of the sacrament).

Today, this fact has been publicly (and vociferously) placed into question.[41] However, it has been firmly reaffirmed, in a very strongly and well-argued manner, by the Congregation for the Doctrine of the Faith.[42]

---

* See the following texts: Congregation for the Doctrine of Faith, "Declaration on the Question of the Admission of Women to Ministerial Priesthood," October 15, 1976, *Documentation catholique* 74 (1977): 158–74. Jean-Jacques von Allmen, "Est-il légitime de consacrer des femmes au ministère pastoral?," *Verbum Caro* 65 (1963): 5–28. J. J. Begley and C. J. Armbruster, "Woman and Office in the Church," *American Ecclesiastical Review* 165 (1971): 145–57. Paul Brand, "Notes sur le problème de l'accès de la femme au minitère pastoral," *Verbum Caro* 78 (1966): 47–66. Paul-Laurent Carle, "La femme et les ministères pastoraux selon l'Ecriture," *Nova et Vetera* 47 (1972): 161–87; "La femme et les ministères pastoraux d'après la Tradition," *Nova et Vetera* 47 (1972): 263–90; and "La femme et les ministères pastoraux. Étude théologique," *Nova et Vetera* 48 (1973): 17–36. Mary Daly, *Le deuxième sexe conteste*, trans. Suzanne Valles (Paris: Mame, 1969) (translation of Mary Daly, *The Church and the Second Sex* [New York: Harper & Row, 1968]). Philippe Delhaye, "Rétrospective et prospective des ministères féminins dans l'Église," *Ephemerides Theologicae Lovanienses* 3 (1972): 55–75. Grelot, *Le ministère de la Nouvelle Alliance*, 143–67, and *Église et ministère*, 223. Charles Journet, "L'Église et la femme," *Nova et Vetera* 4 (1957): 299–313. Bernard Lambert, "L'Église catholique peut-elle admettre des femmes à l'ordination sacerdotale?," *Documentation catholique* 73 (1976): 773–80. Philips, "La femme dans l'Église." Haye van der Meer, *Sacerdotio della donna? Saggio di storia della teologia*, trans. Rosa Paini (Brescia: Morcelliana, 1971). Marie-Thérèse van Lunen-Chenu, "Féminisme chrétien: jusque et y compris le sacerdoce," *Revue Nouv. Belg.* 51 (1970): 366–72.

40. 1983 Code of Canon Law, c. 1024. [Tr. note: Taken from the official translation.]

41. See Daly, *Le deuxième sexe conteste*, and M. T. van Lunen-Chenu, "Féminisme chrétien: jusque et y compris le sacerdoce," *Revue Nouv. Belg.* 51 (1970): 366–72.

42. Congregation for the Faith, "Declaration on the Question of the Admission of Women to Ministerial Priesthood," October 15, 1976, *Documentation catholique* 74 (1977): 158–74.

It is not *a priori* impossible that the invalidity in question would not emerge from the "nature" of the sacrament but, rather, from the existential conditions that the Church, in virtue of her power over the sacraments *salva eorum substantia*, has given to it up to now, thus meaning that this situation could be changed. One could think, by analogy, of Pius XII's decision modifying the conditions for the validity of the sacrament of holy orders.[43]

Every serious study of the question must begin by a historical investigation into the meaning that the exclusion of women from the priesthood has in fact had from the beginning of the Church and in the years following. Did it depend simply on socioeconomic conditions as is quite peremptorily claimed by those who offer no proof of it, namely those men and women who fight for the admission of women to the priesthood? Or, on the contrary, did it correspond to a properly theological intention? With Grelot, we must note that Jesus had no fear of distancing himself from the traditions and practices of Judaism of His era.[44] And as for St. Paul, he proclaimed the equality of all in Christ. Therefore, one cannot claim, without thoroughly studying the topic, that the sole reason that he did not admit women to ministerial functions was his conformity to the ideas of his age.

The question of the theological meaning of this exclusion

One must resolutely rule out a supposed and unjustifiable incapacity of women for fulfilling the functions of the priesthood, *as though this were an argument against the accession of women to the priesthood*. Likewise, one must resolutely rule out the promotion of women in contemporary society *as though this were an argument for it*. The reason to maintain or abolish the exclusion of women from the priesthood can only be theological.

The theological meaning for this exclusion could be sought along the following lines. Christ is a man, fully man, having come for all the members of mankind, men and women alike. However, He Himself is of the male sex. It is not at all a question of seeing in this fact some kind of superiority of one sex over the other from the

---

43. See Pope Pius XII, *Sacramentum Ordinis*, in *AAS* 40 (1948): 5–7.
44. See Grelot, *Le ministère de la Nouvelle Alliance*, 143–67.

perspective of salvation history (a superiority expressly denied by St. Paul). Rather, it is a question of seeing here a differentiation in the order of symbolism, men symbolizing Christ who saves, women symbolizing humanity who has been saved, while noting that man saving and humanity saved are precisely one in Christ. Hence, we can understand the idea that men are more apt than are women for being chosen to sacramentally represent Christ the priest, Christ in the act of saving. Here, we see something comparable to the natural likeness of things like water, bread, and oil to the effect of grace conferred in the sacrament, thus predisposing such elements for being chosen to be the matter for a given sacrament.[45]

Of course, quite clearly, through such arguments, we neither can nor wish to demonstrate *a priori* that the sacrament of holy orders is not for women. It is only a question of explaining *a posteriori* why this is so. Of itself, this leaves open the question of knowing if it is necessarily so [*ce qui de soi laisse ouverte la question de savoir si vraiment il en est nécessairement ainsi*].

The consequences of this exclusion for the situation of women in the Church

One cannot deny that this exclusion entails a kind of effacement of women in the Church, as the sacrament of holy orders establishes a hierarchy in the Church, a hierarchy to which women do not have access.

Moreover, it has in fact led to a situation of inferiority, not only in relation to the hierarchy but also in relation to laymen (under the influence of a variety of factors of the sociocultural and historical orders, and not necessarily of the theological order).

It can be said that the first kind of marginalization [*minorisation*] consists in not being able to accede to functions of authority. The second involves women being submitted to ecclesiastical authorities in a different way than men are, indeed more so than they are.

---

45. See §711 above. See also Congregation for the Faith, "Declaration on the Question of the Admission of Women to Ministerial Priesthood," *Documentation catholique* 74 (1977): 162. Grelot, *Le ministère de la Nouvelle Alliance*, 143–67. René Laurentin, *Marie, L'Église et le sacerdoce*, vol. 2 (Paris: Lethielleux, 1953), chs. 2 and 3. Semmelroth, *L'Église*.

The second kind of inferiority is in no way necessary and should change alongside the progress that has taken place for the situation of women in political society, up to the point of reaching equal conditions. Let us note that this progress has already begun.

On the other hand, the first kind of inferiority is the necessary consequence of the exclusion of women from the priesthood and cannot disappear for as long as this exclusion is not abolished (an abolition that remains, as things stand, very problematic). How does it not contradict the equality of all in Christ as it was proclaimed by St. Paul?[46]

To understand and admit it, one must come back to the fundamental principle of the vocation to the priesthood. It is not implied by the Christian vocation and depends on Christ's sovereignly free choice. The equality spoken of by St. Paul is to be understood in relation to the Christian vocation, which is our principal vocation, that which spiritually valorizes the person, for it is the vocation to divinization.

Far from arousing in men a sentiment of pride or of vanity, the exclusion of women from the priesthood ought to make him aware of the entirely gratuitous and, of itself, non-valorizing character of the vocation to the priesthood. Jesus calls whom He wills and does so for the service of the People of God. He does not necessarily call the best, and this call does not make them better than the others. True Christian greatness is greatness in holiness, not hierarchical greatness.[47]

---

46. See Gal 10:28.

47. See Journet, *L'Église du Verbe incarné*, 1:118–21. Therefore, it is not a question of inviting women to humility all the while leaving the field open for priestly pride to be exercised by men. Rather, on the contrary, it is a question of inviting men to humility in the very fact that he is apt to be called to the priesthood to the exclusion of women. Indeed, this prerogative is not the sign of superiority over women which he would have in the People of God through his nature or through grace. Among the children of God, there is no other superiority than that which comes from a love that is greater. Christ is the one who is the perfect priest, and if He exercises His saving priesthood only by means of male members of His redeemed people, this is for the service of all these redeemed members, be they men or women. He does so in order to invest them, through His grace, with the only dignity having a value before God, namely, that of being children in the kingdom.

THE SACRAMENTAL CHARACTER AND GRACE OF HOLY ORDERS

In the desert of Sin, the power of striking the rock would not have quenched Moses's thirst. Rather, what quenched it was the very water that flowed forth abundantly, which he was able to drink just like all the people. Similarly, the power of orders cannot by itself sanctify those who are in the hierarchy. Rather, what sanctifies them is the grace that flows from this power, a grace that they can receive on the same terms as all Christian people.[48]

Must we say that the sacrament of holy orders does not confer grace on the person who receives it and that the call to the priesthood is not a grace? However, if it is a grace, what is its relationship with the grace that all Christians have?

Is There a Sacramental Grace of Holy Orders?

Arguments for and against

Arguments against

{995} From what we have said, it follows that the sacrament of holy orders was not instituted for the sanctification of the person who receives it but, rather, for the service of other members of the People of God and therefore of Jesus Christ, He who is primarily the Savior. If the priest participates in the gifts of grace, this is on account of his Christian vocation, through his self-submission to the Church's own sanctifying power, not on account of his priestly vocation and in virtue of its own proper sanctifying power.

This is confirmed by the fact that this sanctifying power instrumentally exercised by the priest is exercised just as efficaciously when he is a sinner as when he is a saint.

Finally, holiness is given to (and required of) all Christians. The sacrament of holy orders is conferred only on certain people. Therefore, we must hold that the priestly life is one way, alongside many others, of realizing the Christian vocation without it enjoying, by itself, some kind of superiority.

---

48. Journet, *Théologie de l'Église*, 136.

Arguments for

Holy orders is a sacrament, and the first effect of every sacrament is grace.[49]

Moreover, it is a principle of God's action in salvation history that He never makes use of a person for His work of grace without that person somehow participating in this grace of which he is the means. For this reason, it is impossible to think that a special grace would not be involved in being chosen to serve Christ and the Church.

In fact, in the most ancient texts of the liturgy of ordinations we can find a request for grace to be given to the recipients of holy orders.[50] Moreover, the action of laying one's hands on another person, an action already found in Scripture for the consecration of deacons and of presbyters, sacramentally signifies the gift of the Holy Spirit.[51]

There certainly is a sacramental grace of holy orders

We have seen that the sacrament of holy orders "consecrates" a Christian for sacramental actions.

The holiness thus conferred is first and foremost of the sacred order (i.e., it is a form of "ontological holiness," for Christ is the one who acts by means of His minister in the sacramental action). However, the minister is a person, and in the sacramental action, he acts as a person (if not precisely inasmuch as he is a person). For the minister who performs the sacramental action, such an act is a human act which can be either holy or wicked. If this human act is morally wicked, the sacramental action remains holy, without the person performing it partaking in this holiness. However, this represents an abnormal situation. Of itself, a holy action demands that the person performing it should do so by being intentionally united to the superior person who makes him do it, thereby using the human person as an instrument.

Thus, even though the sacralization of the person produced by the sacrament of holy orders (thus producing the sacramental

---

49. See §744 and *ST* III, q. 62.
50. See Hippolytus of Rome, *La tradition apostolique*, SC 11 bis, ch. 4, §§8–9.
51. Vatican II, P., ch. 3 [*sic*].

"character" of such orders) could be found in a sinner, of itself it calls for the sanctification of this same person. To put it another way, if Christ makes a person holy for the needs pertaining to His sacramental representation on earth, He sanctifies such a person by the same token, at least so long as that person does not voluntarily place an obstacle in His way.

The Relationship between Character and Grace in the Sacrament of Holy Orders

{996} What is primary in the sacrament of baptism (in the intention of Christ and that of the Church) is grace, by means of which the baptized person participates in the redemption and in its fruits, namely, divinization. The character is second, assuring that the child of God belongs to the Church, the place of grace. Is the same true for the sacrament of holy orders?

The primacy of the character from the perspective of service to the Church

The Church, the original sacrament, is the one who is charged with sacramentally representing Christ the priest just as she at the same time participates in this priesthood so as to be united to the saving sacrifice and receive its fruits.

However, the Church exists only in her members. In all of her members, she gives reality and existence to her own priesthood by means of the sacraments of baptism and confirmation. She gives reality, existence, and efficacy to the sacramental representation of Christ's priesthood by means of the sacrament of holy orders.

As regards the first point, we have seen that the Christian exercises the universal priesthood only in communion with Christ and the other members of the Church—a communion of grace and charity. Moreover, it is precisely by conferring grace that baptism and confirmation that the Church's priesthood has this reality. By contrast, the ordained priest exercises his power to sacramentally represent Christ primarily through the sacramental character of holy orders.

Consequently, from the perspective of Christ's intention in instituting the sacrament, as well as from the perspective of the Church's intention when she confers this sacrament, the first end aimed at by the conferral of orders is to make ministers in whom and through whom the Church can assure this sacramental representation of Christ without which the sacramental order would disappear and cease to exist.

Always from this perspective, which is that of the common good of the earthly Church, the grace of personal sanctification that the sacrament of holy orders confers is secondary. Certainly, it would be better if the sacramental actions were performed in a holy manner. However, what is of paramount importance is that they be performed.

The primacy of grace from the perspective of the ordained priest's personal destiny

What is second in relation to the common good of the earthly Church is first if one considers the personal destiny of the person who receives the sacrament. The Church continues to exist and to be holy, the place and source of holiness for the world even if one of her members, through his sin, separates himself from communion with her. However, for this person, such a separation from communion with the Church involves the loss of all that one has and even of oneself. To have the power to sacramentally represent Christ is of no use to such a person. However, if the priesthood had no saving value for the person who receives it, there would be no worth in desiring, requesting, or receiving it.

To say that the priestly vocation is not included in the Christian vocation does not mean that it is situated outside of it. It is only to say that it is not implied by it and that it is another vocation. All those who are the object of the former are not the object of the latter. However, it is clear that, for the person who is the object of this vocation, it is inscribed within his Christian vocation as a consecration and personalization of that vocation.

To say that the priesthood is defined by the state of service is to say that it was not primarily instituted for the sanctification of the Christian who has received it. The Christian has everything that is necessary for his personal sanctification in the five sacraments ordered to it. However, this does not mean that it is useless for the sanctification of the ordained priest, for it is a grace of serving Christ and the People of God. It represents a unique way of participating in Christ's holiness inasmuch as He became the servant of all.

One is not consecrated to the service of Christ and of the People of God for one's own personal interest—even one's spiritual and eschatological interest. However, to the degree that this consecration exists and remains freely willed, it, in fact, does represent a lofty valorization of the person in the order of salvation and of holiness.

From this perspective, the comparison with the staff of Moses is not a very good metaphor. Through the sacrament of holy orders, Christ does not only wish to give the Christian the staff that will make His grace pour forth in the midst of men. He makes grace pour forth at the heart of this Christian first, at least if he does not place an obstacle in its way.

Attempt at a synthesis

If the personal good of an individual Christian and the common good of the Church were separate, these two perspectives could not be reconciled. However, the good of each person is included in the common good of the Church. If, in conferring the sacrament of holy orders, she wishes to communicate her sanctifying power to particular members in her, she does so in order to sanctify all men by means of this power, including these same members. If the priest does not wound the Church's holiness by separating himself from ecclesial communion, he nonetheless diminishes it when he does so, for it is made up of the holiness of all of its members and of all men, who are potentially members of this communion.

Therefore, in conferring this sacrament, the Church (and Christ) intends not only to provide for the perpetuation of the ministerial priesthood and for its better exercise by likewise conferring the grace that will enable her sacred ministers to exercise their power in a worthy manner, but also intends for this to sanctify these members whom she places in her service (while, however, herself remaining at their service).

The Sacramental Grace of Holy Orders and the Common Grace of Christians

Let us recall that sacramental grace is not a grace that differs from common grace. It is common grace in connection with the character in question.[52] Here, in the case of the sacrament of holy orders, it is sanctifying grace in connection with the sacralizing character.

The sacralization of the priest is instrumental and diaconal. Because of this connection to the character of orders, the common grace that the consecrated priest receives, not only through his ordination, but moreover through all the various means of grace, will be the grace of an instrument and a grace of service.

Grace of an instrument

{997} In the sacramental action, the ministerial priest is sacramentally identified with Christ. In order to consecrate the bread and wine in the Eucharist, he pronounces the very words that Christ pronounced at the Last Supper. In the other sacraments, he speaks in Christ's name and on account of His mandate. The man lends Christ his own humanity so that Christ may represent His own humanity and make manifest His sovereign action which, in itself, is secret and invisible. This puts into action all the virtues of self-effacement that are included in Christian grace.

Such an effacement paradoxically includes a strong self-affirmation, for Christ must be affirmed by His representative. However, Christ is the one who must be affirmed in His minister, not the minister for his own account and, especially, not as though he were appropriating Christ's authority to himself.

The first condition of this effacement in such self-affirmation is "collegiality" in the broad sense, that is, the interpersonal union of the shepherds who represent Christ the shepherd only as an ensemble. This collegiality is expressed in the communion of priests with their bishop and, through him, with the other bishops and the pope. Priestly grace as such is this grace of communion in the utterly personal exercise of the sacramental power and of pastoral authority

---

52. See §755 above.

with the *presbyterium* gathered around the bishop and, through him, with all the bishops gathered around the bishop of Rome.

It would not be false to say that it is a grace of obedience, so long as we understand this word in its broadest and most profound sense. Far beyond the mere acceptance of a discipline, such obedience must be understood as meaning an intimately accepted, willed, and loved subordination to the "priestly order," that is, to the hierarchical whole of the shepherds and, through it, to the supreme shepherd, the sole true shepherd: Jesus Christ. All the other shepherds are only expressive figures of Him, and through them He manifests His continuous presence and His indefectible saving activity. Therefore, such obedience must not only be loving but first and foremost must be a form of charity penetrated by obedience, an obedient love.

Certainly, the shepherds are instruments of Christ in the strict sense only in sacramental actions. In other pastoral activities, they act as second causes.[53] However, if, as we have striven to show, all these pastoral activities lead to the Eucharist and find their consummation therein,[54] likewise deriving therefrom, then all the shepherd's powers derive from his sacramental power and participate in its instrumentality. However personal his activity may be and however great his own responsibility may be in this activity, the shepherd must act only in Christ's name. We do not mean that he must act as Christ would have acted in the same circumstances, for such a proposal is barely intelligible. Rather, he must always act in accord with the will and spirit of Christ, as a good and faithful servant. In other words, in faith and love, he must seek out perfect dependence upon Christ. This is what the strict instrumentality of the sacrament consists in, and when the priest is aware of it and conforms his will to it, he makes a free and loving submission to it in the sacramental action itself.

A grace of service
{998} The priest must bear in mind the fact that he has been ordained for others—for the other members of the flock and for those who are not yet members thereof.

53. See §611 above.
54. See §974 above.

We have said that, in the case of a priest vowed to solitude and contemplation, this service could exist only in a wholly mystical and spiritual order. It is impossible to truly live in accord with priestly grace without such responsibility for others.

As is manifested by all of holy priests whom the Lord raises up in His Church in each generation, this grace of service is most especially characterized by missionary zeal. Such zeal can be concerned with distant missions or with home missions. Indeed, it can be concerned with the mission that the Church tirelessly pursues among the sheep who have remained faithful but who all in some part of themselves still must be brought back into the fold, thus provoking the compassionate and anxious solicitude of Christ the supreme pastor and of His servants. The grace of the sacrament of holy orders arouses this ardent solicitude in the priest's soul. It is ever reflected in prayer for the salvation of men and, ordinarily, in activity in the service of Christ the Savior and of the men whom He desires to save. This action takes on many forms. Its principle and source are found in priestly grace, which makes the priest participate in Jesus Christ's redemptive charity.

It is true that this is not the office of priests alone. Through baptism and confirmation, every Christian is united to Jesus Christ and thus participates in His zeal for the salvation of the world. The very history of the Church presents us with a host of laypersons—in monasteries and in the world—whose life is or was occupied with zeal for the salvation of the world, indeed sometimes to the point of unbounded dedication. We cannot doubt this fact in any way. Therefore, it is not a question of attributing such a zeal to priestly grace exclusively. In reality, it is part of so-called common grace, for it is offered to all and bestowed upon whoever receives it. Nonetheless, it also characterizes the proper grace of the sacrament of holy orders.

In what sense is this the case? In the sense that this grace is constituted by the grace-character complex which establishes the priest in his priestly function, giving him the power to fulfill it, and specially calls for grace inasmuch as it includes this zeal among its virtualities. Conversely, this zeal, which can develop in a wholly normal manner in the person who has not been endowed with this character, finds in this character a place in which it can enroot itself. This does not necessarily render it more intense—that is an affair of the freedom of the Spirit, who gives grace to each according to the degree that He wills and of the freedom of man who more or less generously welcomes the grace that is given to him or who, on the contrary, places an obstacle before it. Instead, this situation renders it more stable and more habitual. The mediocre priest who has not lost grace through his sin will be zealous in a mediocre way. However, he will not be lacking in zeal. And if he loses grace, the process of his return to God will perhaps (indeed, often does) begin for him by means of the reawakening of this zeal, arising from his awareness of his priesthood, which is present in him through the sacramental character.

This zeal, as well as all the virtues required for faithful ministry, which are detailed in the two letters to Timothy, are a charism—not in the sense that they would properly belong to those who have received the charism of ministry but, rather, in the sense that the charism received at ordination, which has placed its roots down into the priest's spirit by means of the sacramental character, includes these virtues and calls for them.

A priestly spirituality

{999} Hence, can we speak of a priestly spirituality? To furnish an appropriate response to this question, we must first of all specify what is meant by this term, "a spirituality." A sufficient treatment of this would lead us too far afield here.

First of all, let us say that if spirituality were identified with morality, then, given the unity of Christian morality, there could be only one Christian spirituality, which would be defined by the primacy of charity (the love of God and of neighbor) through the sway of charity over the whole of human life through the moral virtues and the welcoming of both grace and the means of grace (Christ, the Church, the sacraments, and docility to the Holy Spirit who is present in the believer and acts in him by means of grace). However, such morality leads to many very different ways of life under the action of the Spirit, as well as through the exercise of human freedom.

Thus, if we use the term "spirituality" to designate an art of living in conformity with Christian morality (i.e., in accord with grace acting on and through freedom and placing it under the sway of charity), we can thus speak of multiple spiritualities. Why not of a priestly spirituality?

Obviously, such a spirituality would be inspired by charity, like every Christian spirituality, though having the particular modality of participating in the redemptive charity and virtues of the good shepherd. This would be a particular way of life proper to priests. Through such a way of life, they live in accord with the grace of baptism shared in common by all, practicing the virtues that are required by the priestly function, though they are also required of all Christians according to different modalities.

Nonetheless, we must not forget that priests, like other baptized persons, themselves belong to different spiritual families. We cannot speak of a spirituality proper to diocesan priests that would be common to all priests, as though religious profession and the rule to which it obligates those who live under would obscure the priestly vocation and the ideal that it prescribes, making it pass into the background. Likewise, we cannot even speak of such a spirituality as though all diocesan priests were to constitute a spiritual family welded together by this single priestly ideal. The idea of a spirituality that would be distinct from all others because of its exclusively priestly character is a utopian ideal, for there are many ways to follow one's Christian vocation in accord with the grace of the priesthood, and each is necessarily particular. It seems that this utopia might have led astray someone like Bérulle and his disciples, however great and fruitful their activity on behalf of the spiritual formation of the clergy may otherwise have been. However, does every authentic priest recognize himself necessarily in the spirituality of Bérulle and the Oratory? In reality, the constant factors in so-called priestly spirituality are, in fact, found in the spirituality of all priests, though intimately united in all of them to other elements belonging to particular spiritualities, with mutual repercussions on both the constant factors and the latter, particular elements. There is a Carthusian way to be a priest, as well as a Benedictine way, a Dominican way, a Jesuit way, a Pradosian way, and so forth. However, the priesthood introduces its own characteristics into all of these various spiritualities.

Moreover, do we not find this indetermination in every form of spirituality, so that it may be gradually filled out by determinations coming from elsewhere? Definitively, each person's spirituality is unique in its ultimate determination.

The grace of being a priest

{1000} Therefore, like every sacrament, the sacrament of holy orders is the sign and means of a particular grace given to the person who receives it. It is first of all granted in view of the Church's own common good (i.e., the good of the People of God) and, in this sense, has something of the appearance of a so-called charismatic grace. However, it is granted in a definitive manner, and if, like every grace, it can be lost by the fault of the person who has received it, it nonetheless retains a root (i.e., the character) from which it can always flower again through the Father's mercy and the sanctifying power of the Spirit, conforming the priest anew to the Son. By this, it stands on the side of sanctifying grace.

We have sought after a solution to this apparent antinomy by distinguishing two perspectives in priestly grace, namely that according to which it is in the service of the Church and that according to which it can be integrated into the personal destiny of its beneficiary. This distinction is valid for every charismatic grace, for if it is said that a charism is given to someone in view of its common usefulness, this does not preclude the idea that it would also be given for the good of the charismatic himself. If God loves His people, he personally loves all those who are part of His people to the degree that they are part of it—virtually and sometimes very distantly, actually but incompletely, and, too often, very little, while, in others, in a very motivated and very engaged manner, and in some, through their whole being.

God's love extends to each person in the Whole that constitutes sinful and redeemed mankind. Could we think that He would place a person in the service of His love for others in such a way that this person would himself be excluded from this love? Every grace is the effect of God's love, its concrete realization. Grace given to someone for the sake of others is given to him for himself as well (or at least is offered to him). If he closes himself off to it, he will not benefit from it personally, though this will be his own fault. Thus, charismatic grace cannot sanctify the person who receives it, nor lead him to salvation (and for this reason, it is not a sufficient sign of his holiness). However, if it is welcomed by him, it saves him and sanctifies him as well. When the process of canonization has led to a judgment concerning the heroic character of someone's virtues, founded on witnesses and the other indications left behind in the examples and works concerning the person being investigated, then the process takes into consideration the charismatic actions that he possibly performed, seeing therein a sign of the sanctifying presence of the Holy Spirit in him.

Thus, it is a personal grace to be a priest: one may say [*si l'on veut*], a grace offered, one which can produce the fruits of holiness only in the person who, in accord with St. Paul's exhortation to Timothy, "does not neglect the gift he has, which was given him by prophetic utterance when the council of elders laid their hands upon him."[55]

It is a grace to be a priest, and it is good and just to give thanks for it, as is done by the priest or priests who recite the second Eucharistic prayer, drawn from the *Apostolic Tradition* of St. Hippolytus: "And we give thanks to you, for you have chosen us to (liturgically) 'serve' in your presence."

If one ought to give thanks when one receives it, it is also legitimate and very good to desire it, at least if the Holy Spirit is the one who arouses this desire. Granted, there can be self-interested motivations of a more or less base character for this desire, and we can indeed admit that such motivations are always mixed in with the first manifestations of the desire to be a priest. Absolute disinterest in the service of God, true "pure love," is rare and found only at the end of a long process of purification. However, this desire must be considered to be a sign of a vocation when, after serious examination and demanding testing, it is clear, not that it is totally pure, but that its dominating motivation is the grace of being a priest.

55. See 1 Tm 4:14 (RSV).

Therefore, we cannot hold that a given, precise need felt by the People of God is the only criterion for the presence of a priestly vocation. Although it is not instituted for the personal sanctification of the Christian, the sacrament of holy orders can and must be the means of personal sanctification for the person who is called to it. It can be desired for this, though it is subject to the Church's own role in regulating vocations.[56]

---

56. In an article that we noted above—"A propos de l'École Française," *Revue thomiste* 71 (1971): 463–79—Jacques Maritain profoundly developed the functional idea of the priesthood (though not without neglecting certain aspects of the problem nor without overvaluing other aspects of it). Our discussions above sufficiently show where I am in agreement with him and what separates me from this study which, in any case, helps the reader ponder the danger that gave birth to a valorization of the priestly grace which was not unreasonable [*excessive*], certainly, but was indiscriminate, as though the priest were (or ought to be) a super-Christian on account of his priesthood. Like every baptized person, the priest must tend to the perfection of charity by means that are offered in the Church to all. However, his priestly grace is a new sign for him and for others, a form of this perfection that is proper to him.

PART 6

THE SACRAMENT OF MARRIAGE

INTRODUCTORY REMARKS

{1001} The sacramental septenary includes a seventh sacrament: marriage. We cannot here study this sacrament in all of its dimensions. As a multi-faceted reality, it also falls to moral theology, pastoral theology, and canon law. Here, we are only concerned with examining, rather briefly, how marriage realizes the notion of a sacrament.

Given that every sacrament includes three aspects, we must consider marriage from each of these three constitutive perspectives: the sacramental rite (*sacramentum tantum*), the ecclesial effect signified and produced by the rite, itself in some way a sign and cause of the effect of grace (*res et sacramentum*), and its sacramental grace (*res tantum*).[1]

---

1. See §621 above. See the following sources: Pierre Adnès, *Le Mariage* (Paris: Desclée, 1963), which includes a bibliography, and *Le mariage engagement pour la vie* (Paris: Desclée de Brouwer, 1971). Henri Crouzel, *L'Église primitive face au divorce* (Paris: Beauchesne, 1971). Pierre Grelot, *Le couple humain dans l'Écriture* (Paris: Cerf, 1969). Pierre-Marie Gy, "Le rite sacramental du mariage et la tradition liturgique," *Revue des sciences philosophiques et théologiques* 38 (1954): 258–69. Labourdette, "Problèmes du mariage." Gabriel Le Bras, "La doctrine du mariage chez les théologiens et les canonistes depuis l'an mille," in "Mariage," in *Dictionnaire de théologie catholique*, 9:2123–2317. Nicolas, *Liberté chrétienne et sexualité*, and *Homme et femme il les créa. L'idée chrétienne du mariage* (Paris: Téqui, 1977). Korbinian Ritzer, *Le mariage dans les Églises chrétiennes* (Paris: Cerf, 1970). Henri Rondet, *Introduction à l'étude de la théologie du mariage* (Paris: Lethielleux, 1960). Olivier Rousseau, "Divorce et remarriage."

Orient et Occident," *Concilium* 24 (1967): 107–25. Edward Schillebeeckx, *Le mariage, réalité terrestre et mystère de salut* (Paris: Cerf, 1966), and *Le mariage est un sacrament* (Bruxelles: La Pensée Catholique, 1961). [Tr. note: Fr. Nicolas also refers to "Textes, 47." No such entry exists in the bibliography, which only has 17 such Magisterial texts. Entry 7 is an intervention by the Dutch Episcopate on May 9, 1965, found in *Documentation catholique* 62 (1965): 1175–79; entry 17 is Pope Pius XII's *Mediator Dei*.]

20

What Is the Sacrament of Marriage?

Here, we find ourselves faced with the great difficulty of seeing whether marriage is a sacrament and, if so, how it is one. Indeed, in contrast with the other sacraments, marriage exists outside the Church. It is a this-worldly reality, one that is concerned with "natural" human life, whether or not it is lived in accord with faith.

MARRIAGE IS A SACRAMENT

Let us recall that a sacrament is an efficacious sign instituted by Christ by which the grace of salvation and of sanctification is conferred upon a human person in virtue of the redemption of mankind brought about by Christ on the cross, inasmuch as this grace implies and determines a particular form of belonging to the Church.[1]

The Sacred Character of Marriage

{1002} It is a fact that marriage is invested with a "sacred" character in all societies, at least those that have not reached the point of "desacralization." Even in these latter kinds of societies, marriage is an institution ruled by law—not only as regards its civil effects (e.g., of the economic order, concerning parental rights, etc.), but also as regards the commitment of spouses toward one another. Certain societies have

---

1. See §§707–15 above.

attempted to make marriage into a purely private affair. However, this has led to results that are contrary to nature and has not continued to be pursued. Even in the civil order, marriage is invested with a ceremonial and sacred aspect.

If one reflects on the reasons for this, one will discover that marriage is created by God and involves the spouses' collaboration with God in the transmission of life.

Marriage is something created by God

Calvin wrote: "Marriage is a good and holy institution of God, just like the trades of the plowman, the mason, the shoemaker, and the barber, all of which, nonetheless, are not sacraments."[2] As offering us a kind of contrast, this paradoxical comparison brings to the foreground the sacred character of marriage. The professions and other human institutions are works of man, depending on him. If they are part of God's creation, this is because man can only act within this creation, for his very life is created. However, marriage is not a work created by man. God is the one who created man (*homo*) as male (*vir*) and woman, creating them so that they may be united. The human being, created by God, is man and woman. Such is the meaning of the priestly creation account.[3]

This is the text on which Jesus relies in legislating concerning marriage. He expressly refers to God's creative will so as to withdraw the laws of marriage from man's powers to freely arrange realities.[4]

Creation as such is sacred in the sense that it is a sign of God and a form of His presence. However, material creation as a whole, including the animals, was not given to man so that he may misuse or abuse it but, rather, so that he may make use of it so as to fulfill his earthly destiny. This is why, despite its obvious exaggeration, there is something true in the religious sentiment of certain civilizations that consider all life "sacred" and untouchable. Man can make use of inferior living beings for his own use, up to the point of taking their lives. By contrast, the woman was given to man, and man to the woman,

---

2. See Calvin, *Institution chrétienne*, bk. 4, ch. 19, §35. [Tr. note: No date provided by Fr. Nicolas.]
3. Gn 1:27–28.
4. Mk 10:2–12 and Mt 19:3–12.

so that she may be his companion and he hers, so that they may mutually cling to one another.[5]

Man and woman are something sacred in their shared nature, by which they are made in the image of God—each as a distinct person and together as a couple. Also, for this reason, their union has a sacred character, being the realization of the creative plan according to which the human creature, all the while making up an integral part of the universe, is set apart from all the other material creatures, who exist for man, whereas man exists immediately for God. Each human person is free to contract marriage or to not do so, to be united in marriage to this or that given person. However, he cannot freely arrange the nature of marriage, which God Himself arranged in creating man.

The collaboration of the spouses with God in the transmission of life

All creatures share in the activity of transmitting life. What is proper to man is that the new living being, in the best part of himself, is immediately created by God, in the image of God, and immediately ordered to God.

It would be false to say that in the transmission of life man and woman are collaborators with God in the act of creating being. The act of creation excludes every form of creaturely collaboration. However, the new living being is not a soul but, rather, is a person, constituted from the soul created by God and the body prepared by the parents. The soul created by God is what makes this body a human body, meaning that no matter how similar in appearance this bodily being may be to the animals, it nonetheless immeasurably transcends them and merits being called a person, for this is indeed what it is. However, this person is not himself created but, rather, is begotten and receives human life from his progenitors. Thus, this life has an origin that is at once transcendent and immanent.

Here, one must reflect on the entire biblical teaching concerning God's paternal Providence for man: each person is a son or daughter, treated as such or (personally) called to become one. Hence, it is clear that the act by which human life is transmitted to a new person is an act that transcends the biological order as well as the psychological

---

5. See Gn 1:18–24 and Mt 19:3–12.

order, thus approaching the spiritual order and, beyond that, the sacred order, as soon as it aims at producing a being that is foundationally ordered to God. Whence, we see that there is something sacred about the sexual union of man and woman, by which they together are made the principle of this act. Likewise, there is something sacred about marriage as well, which unites a man and a woman so that they may give the whole of their lives to each other.

Marriage and God's Covenant with His People

God's Covenant with Israel

{1003} It is quite remarkable that throughout the whole Bible, God's Covenant with the people of Israel is presented as being a marriage and, conversely, that Israel's apostasies are presented as being forms of adultery.

Thus, even though marriage was not contracted within a religious ceremony in Israel, it was a religious act, bringing about something sacred. For example, consider the way that God Himself designates a spouse for Isaac[6] or for Tobias.[7]

Likewise and consequently, adultery is presented as being a sacrilege.[8] It is true that the sacrilege was viewed unequally for man and woman. For the woman, it involved her being unfaithful to her spouse, whereas for the man, it involved him taking another person's wife.[9] Jesus will come to say that this inequality is not in conformity with God's creative intention, and Christianity will eliminate it.

The union of Christ and the Church

The New Testament is in continuity with the Old in presenting the New Covenant as a kind of conjugal union. However, the New Testament teaching contains something extraordinarily new. On the one hand, the spouse is now Christ. On the other hand, the People of God is now the Church, who has the vocation of gathering all the nations and not only one particular nation.[10]

---

6. See Gn 24.
7. See Tb 8.
8. See Prv 2:17.
9. See Dt 22:22–39.
10. Eph 5:21–33. See §635 above.

Thus, just as was the case for the covenant with Israel, the union between man and woman serves in helping us to understand something about the mystery of the Church. However, conversely, the mystery of Christ and the Church serves as a paradigm for the conjugal union of man and woman. In Ephesians 5, St. Paul is precisely concerned with illuminating the morality of conjugal life in light of the relationship between Christ and the Church.

The Institution of the Sacrament of Marriage

{1004} All of this sufficiently explains the fact that, from her beginnings, the Church would have been aware of the fact that marriage was an affair that was of concern for her, for it was concerned with a way of living as a Christian and with the salvation of her members.

It is difficult to say at what moment a specific religious ceremony was introduced and what its form would have been. Moreover, we will see that, on account of this sacrament's singular character as existing in human life before being a sacrament, it did not absolutely need a particular rite in order to exist, even as a sacrament.

Consequently, in this case, the institution of the sacrament does not include the determination of a rite but only the assumption of the preexisting institution of marriage into the Church's life, into the ecclesial situation of a baptized person.

THE MATTER OF THE SACRAMENT OF MARRIAGE

Given that the sacrament of marriage is the sacramentalized union of man and woman, taken up into the Church's life, this union is the matter of the sacrament. Obviously, it is not the sexual union itself. Rather, it is the spiritual, moral, and juridical bond between the persons. The sexual union is simultaneously the focal point and expression of this bond. The sacrament of marriage makes an ecclesial reality out of this spiritual, moral, and juridical bond, giving it a sanctifying and saving worth.

The Commitment of Man and Woman to Each Other

{1005} Sexuality is inherently a reality of the biological order. However, without ceasing to be a reality of the biological order (being related to the transmission of life, a characteristic activity living beings), even in animals it enters into the psychological domain, including in itself movements of the passions. Doubtlessly, these movements are essentially ego-centric. Nonetheless, in an indistinct manner, their object is the other: the partner and, in an even more indistinct manner, their future offspring.

In man, this reality does not cease to be biological and does not lose its retinue of emotions and desires. Nonetheless, it reaches the domain of the personal. From the perspective of love, what characterizes the person is the power to love the other as other, for his or her own sake. Hence, the orientation toward the other that characterizes sexuality on the biological level, the initial altruism that this orientation receives when it arrives at the psychological level, becomes (or tends toward becoming) an oblative form of love, the offering of one's person to the other, a mutual gift.

In the hierarchy of being and of the good, a superior degree is at once discontinuous with the inferior degree (for it introduces an absolutely new element—here, in the ensouled order first of all and then, and above all, in the spiritual order) and yet in continuity with it, for the superior level takes up all the ontological riches that were found in the inferior levels. In the present case, we must say that human sexuality is of a wholly different order than animal sexuality on account of its "personalization" (i.e., on account of this love for the other) and nonetheless lies in continuity with it. Indeed, animal sexuality is what is thus "personalized." Being penetrated with spirituality, it remains a biological and sensible reality.

In animals, where sexuality alone exists, it is what is the animating principle of the sexual encounter, by means of which nature realizes its fundamental intention for the perpetuation of the species. Because sensible emotions are, of themselves, fleeting and connected to circumstances, the joining of individual animals at this level is as fleeting as is sexual union itself. In man, the principle of life is (or, ought to be) spiritual, even as regards the principle of bodily and sense life. For this reason, sexual attraction in man and woman calls out to be penetrated and elevated by love for the other in the highest form, oblative love. This latter is part of human sexuality inasmuch as it is human. It should be its dominating and regulative element.

It is love in the form of self-gift. Indeed, it is a total self-gift, for this mutual love finds its expression—its symbol and realization—in sexual union, which is ordered to the transmission of human life (i.e., to creating interpersonal relations between the person of the child to be born and the two persons of the parents, taken together and therefore united). On the other hand, there is the education of the children, which is the natural prolongation of generation, calling for the stability of the household. Obviously, this topic requires further elaboration in order to provide the full force and scope needed for this consideration. Let us only say that God is the one who willed to unite man and woman on the level of individuals in as strict of a manner (in the form of a permanent and monogamous union) as He did on the level of the species, where the two sexes constitute the two complementary, inseparable, correlative parts of the human being. However, it is first of all a question of a spiritual union whose principle is interpersonal love, whose fulfillment and expression, as well as whose means, is bodily union (as, in general, the body expresses the soul and serves it).

Thus, it is a requirement of sexuality itself—though of sexuality taken up to the personal level and spiritualized, without ceasing to be physical and sensible—that establishes as the principle of the union of the sexes, in man, a mutual, oblative, and total love by which each person definitively gives of himself or herself to the other, simultaneously receiving the gift that he or she makes of himself or herself. Let us note that this reciprocity and totality of the gift are what prevent the possession of one person by the other from being a form of alienation. On the contrary, alienation exists—above all for the woman—when such self-giving becomes a fleeting affair wherein each person is used by the other for the other person's ends.

The Two Dimensions of This Commitment

The transmission of life

{1006} In this question, no matter how "personalized" the union of persons may be in marriage, we must not separate this union from sexual union. The latter is not only a mere occasion for interpersonal union—and much less the pretext for it. It is constitutive of it, even if, considered as a partial element of this union, it holds an inferior place in relation to the other, loftier forms of exchange that the union of persons include. Moreover, it is not only a partial element. From another perspective, it concerns the full extent of this union. On the one hand, it is its expression and means. On the other hand and more profoundly, it is the very foundation for the very existence of this union.

Two persons can be profoundly united, communing in the loftiest of values, without giving themselves to each other in the singular manner that brings forth in the married couple the unity of mankind which is, at first, divided by the distinction of the sexes. Indeed, in such cases, friendship does indeed exist, perhaps with mutual commitment. However, there is not a mutual possession. The more or less powerful character of commitment comes solely from the decision of the persons, not from the nature of this commitment. In this way, friendship can exist between persons of the same sex as much as it can between those of different sexes. Indeed, it can be a friendship that gathers more than two persons together.

Man's commitment to woman and woman's commitment to man, which is brought about by God's creative will, constituting marriage as a unique form of friendship, a form of union which is distinct from every other kind of union, is characterized by its ordination to sexual union. It is a union that, in the divine intention and in conformity with man's true nature is not a merely bodily union but, rather, is a total union of two persons through the mediation of their bodies.[11]

Moreover, one cannot deny that, by its very nature, sexual union

---

11. See Jean-Hervé Nicolas, *La virginité de Marie. Étude théologique* (Fribourg: Éditions universitaires, 1962), 30–38, and *Homme et femme il les créa*, 11–28.

is ordered to the transmission of life. Here, we do not intend to deal with the difficult ethical problems involved in this. What we must say is that, however different human sexuality may be from animal and biological sexuality, when it rises to the level of interpersonal relations, sexuality does not lose its proper structure, by which it is ordered to the perpetuation of the species. In particular, the permissibility of homosexuality cannot be recognized in any manner, for it is a violation of this very structure. The personalization of sexuality elevates it to the level of personal beings; it does not strip it of its fundamental nature.

Mutual love

Elevated to the level of interpersonal relations, sexuality includes oblative love, the love of persons, not as its crown but, rather, as the principle that takes it up and elevates it to the fully human level. In relation to this love, sexual union plays an essential role. It has a proper and irreplaceable value, both as an expression of this love and a means for it. From this perspective, we must emphasize the insufficient nature of the older theological analysis holding that marriage was essentially a "remedy for concupiscence."

There is no opposition, at least *de iure*, between mutual love, which is at the basis of the union of the sexes (because it is first of all a joining of persons) and the parental love that is at the basis of the transmission of life. What is proper to parental love, its beauty, is that it flows forth from the mutual love of the parents, is nourished upon it, and realizes the profound intention of love, which communicates not only the good but also love itself. Of course, it is all too well known that there can be conflict in a given situation. The examination of such conflicts falls to moral theology.

Another conflict which reaches the very notion of marriage, when it is defined on the basis of the mutual love of the persons, appears in the case of commitment without love, either in the case wherein there never was true love or that wherein such love has disappeared. Thus, the conflict is between the intrinsic requirements of the commitment of the persons to each other and their personal dispositions, which can stand in contradiction to this commitment.

It is impossible to make commitment depend on love to such a degree that the loss of love would lead to an abolition of one's commitment. Indeed, according to God's plan, the love which forms the human couple, joining the man and woman together as *one flesh*, is, by nature, a love that definitively engages them. What one must say is that this love is simultaneously implied and signified by the commitment. Hence, it belongs to persons to place their heart in agreement with this commitment. However, conjugal union cannot be defined by the current, personal love that the spouses have for one another.

The Notion of a Matrimonial Contract

{1007} From the time of the High Middle Ages onward, Latin theology has appealed to the notion of a contract for defining marriage.[12] Obviously, this notion is insufficient. On the one hand, it finds itself poorly applied to this case, for we are not here faced with a question concerning rights over "goods" but, rather, with a bond between persons. On the other hand, it seems incompatible with the very nature of this bond, which is a bond of love before being a bond of obligation.

Nonetheless, we must recall that the use of this notion was primarily introduced so as to highlight an essential aspect of the conjugal commitment, namely, that it is a free decision on the part of the people involved and not the result of a decision made by others. Indeed, if it is a contract, the object of this contract is the persons who give themselves to each other. Only persons, who are free and freed by Christ, can give themselves in this way.

This notion can be retained precisely in order to preserve the consistency of the commitment taken, preserving it from the fluctuations of the human heart. One commits oneself through love (or, at least, the commitment taken signified this and implied this), and one is committed to loving. If love remains and develops, everything concerning obligations included in the notion of a contract finds itself realized on a superior level—the level where the relations between the spouses ought to be established. The obligation remains

---

12. See Ritzer, *Le mariage dans les Églises chrétiennes*.

even if the love fades or even disappears, and the notion of a contract can be used to express this.

The notion of rights over the other person's body (*ius ad corpus*) is also juridical in nature. As soon as one introduces the notion of a contract, one must define its content. However, it is clear that the *ius ad corpus* designates a minimum and does not claim to be restrictive. Of all the interactions that conjugal relations include, this is the one that can be the most clearly delimited and, moreover, it includes all the others, given that it is their expression. Nonetheless, one must recognize that this notion can only have a partial value in the elaboration of a theology of marriage.

THE FORM OF THE SACRAMENT OF MARRIAGE

{1008} In the Latin Church, the form of the sacrament is constituted by the exchange of consent by two baptized persons being united in ecclesial communion. For the Orthodox Church[es], this exchange of consent is only a preliminary affair, the sign of the spouses' intention to be united. The form is the blessing, of which the priest is the only competent minister.[13]

The Latin Church's position is more in conformity with the historical data. Indeed, it does not seem that there was a specific marriage ritual at the beginning of the Church, and it especially does not seem that couples who came to be baptized were given a nuptial blessing.[14] Moreover, throughout the centuries, the validity of clandestine marriages has been admitted, at least in the Latin Church. These sorts of marriages were prohibited at Trent only because of the abuses that arose from the complete absence of solemnizing of the bond.[15] Even today, when one finds it impossible to find a priest in a timely manner, marriage can be contracted in the Church without a priest's blessing.

This is also more in conformity with the nature of the sacrament, for what is sacralized by the sacrament is the very union of man and

---

13. See Trembelas, *Dogmatique de l'Église orthodoxe catholique*, 3:364–66. [Tr. note: On this topic in relation to the Byzantine Catholic Churches, see the translator's introduction.]
14. See Ritzer, *Le mariage dans les Églises chrétiennes*, 81–126.
15. See ibid., 373.

woman. Now, as such, it is a salvific reality when it is contracted in the Church by two baptized people. It is not clear why this sacralization must be super-added, as though there could be a non-sacramental conjugal union for two Christians.

Retaining and developing a suggestion made by Schillebeeckx, one could say that the baptism of the spouses gives their mutual commitment its sacramental character.[16] It is as though marriage extends to the couple as such the baptism that each spouse had individually received.

Thus, will it be said that, despite the decision of the Council of Trent and of Canon Law,[17] a marriage will be valid and sacramental as soon as there is a mutual consent, even if the prescribed canonical and liturgical forms are not observed? Certainly not! Given that this consent is not a solely private decision but, rather, creates an ecclesial situation for each of the spouses and for the couple, the Church certainly has the right to make mandatory prescriptions regarding the forms that it must take. Indeed, for Catholics, "mutual consent" necessarily includes consent to the sacrament and therefore the acceptance of the forms prescribed by the Church. She is fully justified in refusing to recognize it if it does not follow these forms. Such a refusal means that it does not exist as an ecclesial reality (i.e., as a sacrament): "The holy council now renders incapable of marriage any who may attempt to contract marriage otherwise than in the presence of the parish priest or another priest, with the permission of the parish priest or the Ordinary, and two or three witnesses; and it decrees that such contracts are null and invalid and renders them so by this decree."[18] In doing this, she does not determine a new "form" of the sacrament of marriage (in the sense of sacramental hylomorphism). Rather, she determines the "forms" (in the juridical sense) that the consent must take so that they may be valid—as civil society can and indeed does for all contracts that have public effects, which it must recognize and protected (e.g., the form of a will, of testimony before the courts, and so forth).

Thus, we find that it is wholly impossible to hold the notion and

---

16. See Schillebeeckx, *Le mariage*, 34–37.
17. See 1983 Code of Canon Law, c. 1108.
18. Council of Trent, session 24, "Decree *Tametsi*," in D.-*Sch*., no. 1816.

practice (which is not only expanding [socially] but claims to have a theological justification) holding that fiancés could consider themselves as being married solely on account of their mutual consent, before submitting themselves to the liturgical rite of marriage.

Some theologians go even further and tend toward claiming that the liturgical blessing plays the role of being the "form" of the sacrament of marriage, holding that the priest is the minster of this sacrament.[19] Their arguments are far from being worthless, but they must explain two things in this case. First, they must explain the fact that the Church recognizes in specified cases the validity of a marriage contracted in a Church but without the presence of a priest (presuming that this presence has been rendered impossible by a grave obstacle). Above all, they must explain how two spouses, wed through a valid natural marriage, thereafter are considered to be sacramentally married without any liturgical ceremony if both of them come to be baptized.

19. Eugenio Corecco, "Il sacerdote ministro del matrimonio," *Sc Catt* 98 (1970): 343–427.

21

The Effects of the Sacrament of Marriage

THE ECCLESIAL EFFECT (*RES ET SACRAMENTUM*) OF THE SACRAMENT OF MARRIAGE

{1009} In speaking as we have about mutual commitment, we have somewhat gone beyond a mere consideration of the *sacramentum tantum*. This latter aspect can consist only in the signs of this commitment, that is, the exchange of consent in a context wherein the spouses' intention to really commit themselves to one another is clear, accepting this bond as sacramental and thus taking up the requirements of conjugal commitment.

The *res et sacramentum* will be the result of this commitment for the spouses' ecclesial situation. That is, it will be the interpersonal bond that it establishes between two baptized people, making them something new in their relation to the Church, no longer only two baptized people but now also a baptized couple:[1] "The perceivable, external rites are the *sacramenta tantum* (constituting the sacramental rite). However, the *res et sacramentum* is the obligation of each spouse toward the other, which proceeds from these acts."[2]

---

1. See *In IV Sent.*, d. 26, q. 2, a. 1, ad 5.
2. N.B. Obviously, the external acts by which the spouses manifest their mutual consent have a value only as signs of this consent, which is interior. Thus, if one can later on prove that there was not an interior consent, one must recognize that the sacrament of marriage did not exist. Here, we are once again faced with the notion of *fictio* which is found throughout the whole of sacramental theology, though here it is translated in practice by declarations of marital nullity declaring that the *sacramentum tantum* was not true and valid. Therefore, it declares

The Conjugal Bond

{1010} How does the conjugal bond constitute a sacramental reality? The answer to this question follows from what we have already said. It places two baptized people into a new relationship with one another in relation to the Church, both of them together in their commitment to one another. This new situation is concerned with their manner of being Christians and of living as Christians.

As is true for all the sacraments, marriage's *res et sacramentum* is an ecclesial reality.[3] If we retain the idea that the sacrament of marriage extends baptism (which is received individually by the parties) to the couple as such, we can see how marriage modifies the spouses' belonging to the Church in line with their baptism. In this way, we likewise can see that, just as the individual becomes a member of the Church through his or her baptism, so too does the couple and, then, the familial society that is constituted around the couple, constitute an ecclesial unit.

Thus, there is an ecclesial mission in the spouses' mutual activity in fulfillment of their educative task. Likewise, we can thereby see that the role to be played by all the baptized in the Church's mission and in her priesthood is henceforth an affair of the couple and of the familial society and no longer of the individuals alone.

The Church's Power Over the Conjugal Bond

Quite naturally, if the conjugal bond is an ecclesial reality, it is submitted to the Church's authority, given that this bond is, as we have seen, also a juridical reality, a contract. However, it is also a natural reality and a divine institution that preexists the Church herself. To this extent, it has its own laws. It is here that we find ourselves faced with a particular difficulty.

---

that the two Christians involved were never bound to each other by the conjugal bond. For the other sacraments, such a declaration does not exist. This difference comes from the juridical character that marriage retains, even as a sacrament. (See *In IV Sent.*, d. 27, q. 1, a. 2, sol. 4.)

3. See §§747ff. above.

The Church's power to set conditions for the establishment of the conjugal bond

{1011} The question posed here is not concerned with the external forms that the Church imposes on the exchange of consents. The problems raised by this were treated above.[4] Here, we are concerned with the canonical impediments determined by the Church, making it impossible for two Christians to commit themselves to one another in the bond of conjugal union in a given case, even if they wish to do so. On the history of this problem, one can consult the works of Le Bras and Rondet.[5]

The Church has always thought that she has the right to legislate in this matter. This right is founded on the fact discussed above, namely that the conjugal bond is an ecclesial reality.

Nonetheless, it is clear that this right cannot be exercised in an arbitrary way. Against all the rigorist tendencies that periodically surfaced in the Church's history, she has always recognized the fundamental right of every man and woman to contract marriage. In establishing impediments, she has only wished to juridically determine the natural and supernatural impediments to marriage. To say that she has wished to juridically determine these impediments does not mean that she has only intended to *declare* them, as though the impediment existed in any event. Rather it means that she has intended, through a law that obligates on account of her own authority, to fix the prescriptions of the natural or supernatural law that are, of themselves, indeterminate. (Thus, the precept to attend Mass on Sunday is a positive law that obligates in virtue of the Church's authority. However, it only fixes the obligations flowing from the divine law requiring one to participate in the Eucharist in order to be saved. Likewise, the law forbidding marriage between cousins of a given degree of separation is a positive law. However, it is based on the natural law that forbids consanguineous marriages. It only fixes the degree of consanguinity to which this law is applied.)

This is precisely where the question of mixed marriages is

---

4. See §999 above.
5. See Le Bras, "La doctrine du mariage," and Rondet, *Introduction à l'étude de la théologie du mariage*.

situated. Here, it is not a question of the natural law but rather, of supernatural law. It is absolutely impossible to accept the complaint registered by Hans Küng: "Whence have the leaders of the Church arrogated to themselves the right to render decisions concerning the validity and invalidity of marriages in this manner?"[6] Here, we are even faced with a grave contradiction, for if the leaders of the Church did not have this right, no more would they have the right to determine the forms of marriage, which, in the end, would in no way be sacramental. Thus, we would need to say that marriage is a matter falling only to civil society—and, ultimately, not even to it, for we are reminded that marriage is a natural right, and "if it is to be presumed that no bishop or pope could prevent two human beings from making use of this right," the same thing is to be presumed for every head of state or civil legislator. But, such opinions would, of themselves, lead to the idea of marriage being a free union! We are not here concerned with discussing the merit of the existing rules. Let us only say that the Church has the right and duty to promulgate rules. Equally, she can change them, for although they may be inspired by the supernatural law, which obligates every baptized person in the Catholic Church to be faithful to his baptism, they are contingent legislative dispositions. Granted, they do partly depend on historical circumstances, and their disadvantages, which were unnoticed or poorly noticed in a given era, were able to manifest themselves through the course of later societal developments.[7]

Religious marriage and civil marriage

{1012} However, this right held by the Church poses grave problems for every civil society where the Church's right is not recognized as being normative—in other words, for every modern society. At least this must be the case for every modern society, for religious and philosophical pluralism is the real situation of modern man living in society.

Indeed, the Church does not recognize the validity—and therefore the existence—of a marriage contracted by a Catholic in

6. *Le Monde* (June 7–8, 1980), 19.
7. See Georges Duby, *Le chevalier, la femme et le prêtre. Le mariage dans la France féodale* (Paris: Hachette, 1981).

opposition to her law. However, such a marriage exists from the perspective of civil law or that of the religious law of another Church (in the case of a mixed marriage). On the history of this progressive separation of civil law from religious law in the West as regards marital legislation, see the works of Rondet and Le Bras.[8]

Before the *de facto* situation created, on the one hand, by the constitution of civil marital legislation and, on the other, by the constitution of Christian Churches not recognizing the Catholic Church's canonical legislation, some theologians (like [Melchior] Cano) proposed that two things can be distinguished in marriage: the contract, which would fall wholly under civil legislations, and the sacrament, which would fall under canonical legislation. According to this conception of the matter, the "contract" or mutual commitment of the spouses would be the matter of the sacrament, whose form would be the blessing of the priest. Thus, one was led back to the position of the Greek Orthodox Church (which is still held today), holding (like the Orthodox even today), that there can be a true marriage between baptized Christians that would not be sacramental. The problem was thus resolved by saying that marriage contracted in opposition to the Church's legislation would be a true marriage but would not be a sacrament.

The Catholic Church did not accept this solution.[9] She judged that there can only be a sacramental marriage between two Christians.

Does this mean that one must hold that Catholics in this situation are living in "concubinage"? The expression has been employed in some texts, even official ones. It is no longer used today, and with good reason. Even if the distinction between a contract and a sacrament remains theologically contestable, it has become a factual reality, along with the distinction between civil marriage and religious marriage, each ruled by its own legislation and each establishing the conjugal bond respectively in the Church and in civil society. This distinction is made by the majority of civil laws and it is possible to think that it is established as the only one consistent with the actual situation of the Christian in the world.

---

8. See the works of Rondet and Le Bras cited above.
9. See Rondet, *Introduction à l'étude de la théologie du mariage*, 112.

From the Church's perspective, we must not say that civil marriage is a true marriage that would only be lacking sacralization by the sacrament. However, it is impossible to say that it is a form of concubinage, even from the Church's perspective.

How is one to resolve this antinomy? Without distinguishing two marriages—one civil and one religious—one can and must distinguish two aspects in marriage, even in that of a Christian. On the one hand, there is the aspect by which it is an ecclesial reality, thus having a value in the order of sanctity. On the other hand, there is the aspect by which it is a reality belonging to this world, thus having a moral value in relation to the earthly finalities of man. The conjugal bond that is contracted by the Christian who is married outside of the Church is not a true marriage. This is why, at least in the name of the proper requirements for belonging in the Church, the Church will not impose on it the obligations that result from marriage—and, first of all, indissolubility. However, it remains a reality belonging to this world and has a moral value which the Church respects, just as she respects other values belonging to this world. The fault committed by this Christian is a fault expressly contrary to his membership in the Church, against his baptism inasmuch as this made him a member of the Church. Certainly, such a fault is not compatible with grace, but it is compatible with the relative moral value that belongs to conformity of one's life to the requirements of the earthly human good.*

---

* N.B. If the Catholic Church does not recognize a marriage entered into by two baptized Catholics in opposition to her law (or simply outside of her law), she cannot consider the civil authority's dissolution of this conjugal bond as being a divorce, for in her eyes this bond never existed. She does not refuse a sacramental marriage to the man or woman who asks for it following on such a marriage and its rupture. This is sometimes shocking for people, indeed, all the more so as in many cases the rupture of the bond formerly contracted was unjust on the part of one of the two partners and therefore constituted a moral fault. There are other duties of mutual fidelity between a man and a woman than those which come from the conjugal bond. However, the Church cannot see the depths of hearts. Moreover, she does not refuse a religious marriage to a divorced person as though she were punishing a fault (whatever this fault may be), though many feel that this is why she thus refuses it. Rather, she does this because the conjugal bond already established renders those who are thus bound before God, indeed definitively, disempowered to contract marriage for as long as the first partner lives. However, the conjugal bond may not have been established. On the one hand, this can occur because the marriage took place outside of the Church, which is the case that we are examining here. On the other hand, it may not exist because after a serious examination the Church judges that true consent was lacking or that the partners did not have it in their power

Here, in this domain, we must apply the principle of religious liberty recognized and affirmed at the Second Vatican Council. Membership in the Church is a personal and absolutely free decision on which no pressure (and, *a fortiori*, no constraint) can be exercised. The same is true for the various decisions in which fidelity to the Church is concretized, as is, in a given case, the decision to be religiously married or the decision to renounce a union that is opposed to the Church's law. This does not mean that this decision does not gravely involve the person's moral responsibility, as though he were free in relation to God Himself. No more does it mean that the Church, in what concerns her, should not draw out the consequences of such a decision each time that it is externalized, just as she has the right to exclude from membership in her those who, through a public act, disregard the requirements of their belonging to her. However, this means that she respects the decision made and continues to treat with honor (like every other man or woman who is not rendered unworthy of being honored as a human person) the man or woman whom she can no longer recognize completely as her own.

The Church's power over the conjugal bond itself

"For the good of the spouses and their off-spring as well as of society, the existence of the sacred bond no longer depends on human decisions alone (*non ex humano aribtrio pendet*)."[10] Is it also the case that it does not depend on the free decision of the Church? The two great properties of the conjugal bond are indissolubility and fidelity, which includes monogamy.

---

to commit themselves to one another at the moment of their marriage. In both kinds of cases where the bond has not been established, she then holds that such people are free, only appearing to be bound when, in fact, they are not. However, God sees the depths of hearts, and if a fault was at the foundation of this freedom [to remarry], the man or woman who acted in a sinful way is culpable before Him. Moreover, as we have seen, such a person is also culpable before the Church, and if such a person makes his or her fault known to her and repents of it, he or she will receive pardon. Once again, such a person will not be required to renounce the sacramental marriage that he or she has asked for, for the refusal of marriage is never a sanction. Such a sanction would be contrary to every man and woman's fundamental right to contract marriage.

10. Vatican II, *Gaudium et Spes*, no. 48. [Tr. note: Fr. Nicolas wrongly cites *Lumen Gentium*.]

The Church does not have power over the principle of fidelity

{1013} Monogamy is a property of marriage, recognized by the majority of modern societies. It is closely connected to the very nature of conjugal commitment and, in particular, to the dignity of the woman. From her earliest days, the Church recognized and enforced it. The polygamy that was recognized and accepted in the law of Moses was judged, by Jesus Himself, as being a concession that the New Law abolished.

In virtue of this principle, she neither authorizes nor recognizes marriage of divorced people. By contrast, despite tendencies in the contrary direction, she has always admitted that second marriages are legitimate [after the death of a spouse]. Moreover, this was expressly recognized by St. Paul. Of itself, the conjugal bond is unbound upon the death of one of the spouses.

Does the Church have power over the principle of indissolubility?

{1014} It is well known that the Roman Church does not recognize this right. The Eastern Church[es] think that [they] can use the principle of *oikonomia*, or of mercy, with regard to the divine law of indissolubility.[11]

From the theological perspective, the Catholic Church's position is based on Jesus' words.[12] The Church holds that these words mean that she herself does not have the right to offer a dispensation in this matter.

However, does the prohibition, "Let man not separate what God has united," hold for the Church (i.e., for those who have received the office of being shepherds in the Church)? The pope and the bishops "bind and unbind" by means of Christ's authority. If they were to make a decision to dissolve a marriage, would it be imputable to man as the Gospel texts understands it to be? It is true that the Church, deciding humanly but by Christ's authority as a kind of middle term between God and man, is totally absent from the text, which must

---

11. See Crouzel, *L'Église primitive face au divorce*. Pierre L'Huillier, "Un point de vue orthodox à propos du divorce," in *Divorce et indissolubilité du mariage* (Paris: Cerf-Desclée, 1971), 121–24. Rousseau, "Divorce et remarriage."

12. See Mt 19:1–9, Mk 10:1–2, Lk 16:18.

be interpreted in accord with the way that the Church herself has understood it and put it into practice through the course of the ages. On this point, certain historical facts feed a controversy that we cannot enter into here. However, there is a certain fact that has ever existed: the Church has recognized (and still recognizes) that she has the right to dissolve a marriage that is valid but not consummated.[13]

Now, it is certain and recognized by all that marriage exists completely from the moment of the spouses' consent, exchanged according to the proper ritual forms. Does not such a case involve "separating what God has already united"? Hence, could not this power that the Church recognizes as hers be extended to the dissolution of an already consummated marriage? Could it perhaps be extended to the dissolution of a marriage that has already lasted for a number of years? The theologian cannot respond with assurance to such a question, for the Church is the definitive judge of what she can or cannot do. In any case, it is certain that if she can do this—and she has never thought that she could—she alone can do it and nobody could substitute himself for her, expressing himself through her highest jurisdictions [*s'exprimant par ses plus hautes instances*], in order to do so, by accepting in her name an exchange of consent in a case where one of the spouses is already sacramentally bound to someone else. Even if such an exchange were made before a priest and with all the appearances of the sacramental rite, it nonetheless would be null and void.

From the pastoral perspective, one must recognize that this would make it practically impossible to avoid a limitless extension of the possibility of divorce. No limitations that theologians and canonists strive to elaborate today could resist the perception of arbitrariness and the rebellion that would be inevitably provoked by a refusal, even one that would be founded on the most convincing reasons without, however, ever being able to marshal evidence for them, above all recognized and accepted evidence. The Catholic Church is certainly as open to compassion for the all-too-numerous victims of matrimonial failure as as [are] the Church[es]. However, the desire to maintain the irreplaceable value of sacramental marriage forbids

---

13. See 1983 Code of Canon Law, c. 1142.

her to open up a process that would inevitably lead, beyond the particular good of the divided couples, to the great evil of a loss of the very value of sacramental marriage.[14]

As we have said, the conjugal bond is submitted to the conditions of canon law. Likewise, it is dependent on an act of consent that is externally signified but must also be interior and free. These facts make the matter quite delicate, and the Church naturally holds that she has the right to judge whether a true marriage does not exist in a given case and, thus, whether there is no conjugal bond. Such decisions, which take place at the end of a long and secret process, resemble a sentence of divorce too much for this not to pose a problem. On the other hand, the Church acts in justice when she agrees to recognize the freedom of the spouses if marriage had, in fact, not taken place. Moreover, it would be false and unjust to deny it to them.

Many of these separations followed by a religious marriage have been critiqued. Perhaps in certain cases the question could be raised: even if the conjugal bond is not real, when the spouses lived in good faith during their marriage, is it morally just for one of them to abandon the other one who would like to continue the common life and has not deserved to be thus abandoned? Perhaps, in contrast to such illegitimate divorces, there likewise are cases of people who are in a canonically correct ecclesial situation but who entered into marriage in an unjust and sinful manner. In this case, they respected their baptism externally in the fact that baptism makes them members of the Church as a society. However, they have been unfaithful to its requirements inasmuch as it made them enter into the Church's communion. But, once such a fault has been committed, how could the Church refuse to pardon it in virtue of the keys if the man or woman who committed it sincerely repents? And how could she punish [*sanctionner*] it by refusing a subsequent marriage? These are situations in which the Church cannot avoid being judged negatively by those who only look upon her from outside ... and sometimes by her own members.

---

14. See Nicolas, *Homme et femme il les créa*, 114–23.

THE SACRAMENTAL GRACE (*RES TANTUM*) OF THE SACRAMENT OF MARRIAGE

{1015} Here we are speaking of grace and, therefore, of sanctification, for sacramental grace is not, first of all, a charismatic grace but, rather, a form of sanctifying grace, here considered in connection with the *res et sacramentum* of marriage (i.e., the conjugal bond).[15] Now, we have seen that this bond essentially consists in mutual love, at least inasmuch as it is virtually contained in the mutual commitment of the spouses. Therefore, it is sanctifying grace inasmuch as it is connected to the mutual love of the spouses and also to the parental love that flows from it.

The Natural Love of the Spouses and Charity

Conjugal love is not charity

{1016} Fraternal charity, according to which each spouse is the other's neighbor to be loved in Christ, and conjugal love, according to which each gives himself or herself to the other so as to be one flesh with that other person, cannot be identified with each other, for they have incompatible [*antinomique*] properties. The first is universal, extending to every man and woman, whereas the second is exclusive by its very nature, requiring exclusivity from the partner. The first is founded on the common Christian vocation and on sharing in eternal life. The second is founded on sharing in an earthly life. It is a form of life that is open to eternal life but has proper goods that are not substantially modified by this opening.

One can and must love all men and women out of charity. One can very specifically love a given person or people in this way without, for all that, being able to—or without intending to—espouse the person loved in this way.

Conversely, a man and a woman who do not have charity can love one another with an authentic, strong, profound, and total love.

---

15. See §755 above.

The conjugal love of two children of God must be penetrated by charity

This love, which comes from God the Creator and for this reason is possible and natural even for those who do not recognize Him as their Father, is blessed by God the Father. It must be lived by the children of God in the Church and, therefore, must be lived in charity.

These two children of God are united more profoundly in Christ by charity than by their mutual love. From the moment that they love one another and are committed to loving one another with a conjugal love, these two ways of loving each other (i.e., naturally and supernaturally) cannot fail to be coordinated so as to constitute a single love (without, however, wholly merging them into one).

If they were to love each other only out of charity, they would not partake in their earthly good up to the point of bodily union. If they were to love each other only by a natural love, they would not be concerned with partaking in eternal life here-below and for eternity.

They share their entire destiny through this complex love, made up of natural love and charity—with charity taking up and integrating into itself the natural love between the man and woman without making it lose its specificity. It is an earthly destiny that of itself is natural and temporal, though supernaturalized and open to eternity, a supernatural and eternal destiny.

Conjugal love strengthened by charity

Mutual love has its own, proper power, which comes from nature. Charity has its own, which comes from grace and from the love of God.

Because it is much closer to the human heart and to man's awareness, the mutual love of spouses seems much stronger than the love of charity, which seems a bit distant and abstract. However, experience shows how fragile and endangered mutual love is. The human heart is mutable. Mutual transparency between persons is quite limited and, indeed, it is frequently quite opaque. This is the source of misunderstandings and conflicts. Men and women, greedy for freedom and independence, accept being limited and constrained by a commitment only with effort, even when this effort is made with great freedom and joy. The power of charity is great, being weak only in appearance. It is the very power of God communicated to man's heart. Certainly, man can be unfaithful and shirk it. Still, the child of God retains the desire to be faithful to God, the feeling that one's spouse is more than a man or a woman, that he or she is a child of God, as he himself or she herself is, whom God himself has entrusted to his or her solicitude and love so that they may achieve their salvation together. All of this is the source of a secret power which, in Christian spouses, helps human love to develop and increase through the whole of life by overcoming external and internal obstacles.

Indeed, human love is often imperiled. Sometimes, it is threatened by precise dangers such as loss of affection or infidelity. Left to themselves, men and women are weak, easily abandoned to their momentary desire. A preservative is provided by the spouses' concern not to offend God by betraying a commitment made before Him, and moreover by the concern not to offend one's spouse, who is a neighbor with a kind of doubly intense proximity. If someone sees one's brother in need and closes himself off to all compassion, how could God's love remain in him? Is not the husband and the wife's fundamental need, each toward the other, to be loved? And is not infidelity essentially the rejection of this love?

So too must parental love be supported by charity

The same thing can be said concerning parents' love for their children. It is natural. However, while parents are not responsible for their whole destiny as children of God (for each one, to the degree that he becomes more of a person, is responsible for himself), he or she has the feeling of being responsible at least for the primary orientation of this destiny, thus rendering this love more vigilant and more protected against being deceived.

And, to the degree that the parents have succeeded in creating a climate of charity in their home, which is particularly contributed to by the way they love each other and their children, these children also learn to love their parents with a love that is penetrated by charity.

The Sacrament of Marriage and the Charity of Spouses and Parents

{1017} This charity, considered in particular in relation to the spouses' mutual love and with parental love, is the grace of the sacrament of marriage. For "God's love has been poured into our hearts through the Holy Spirit which has been given to us."[16]

It is a permanent and growing grace, for if the sacrament of marriage is itself a passing rite (i.e., one is married on a given day and in a given place), its lasting effect is the state of marriage, the permanent bond of the familial society. This effect is the source of a grace that is constantly offered and renewed.

This means that the whole grace that is given to the spouses by ordinary ways (i.e., through the Eucharist, penance, prayer, etc.) not only brings them their personal growth in Christ but also in particular orders their charity, thus super-elevating, sustaining, and protecting their mutual love, as we have said.

Now, in order for charity's inspiration to be realized, it needs many virtues: all the virtues required by good harmony, so that they may face daily duties, sacrifices, and so forth. Inasmuch as charity places all of these virtues in the service of conjugal love and of mutual love, they are also a constantly renewed effect of the sacrament of marriage.

And the same obviously holds for the actual graces required for fulfilling these acts of charity and of the other virtues.

Charity at the Aid of Conjugal Love

{1018} When one considers the reality on the ground, all of these points seem terribly idealistic.

However, they must be understood in a humble and sober manner. Like every grace in general, the grace of the sacrament of marriage does not have dramatic and dazzling effects. It gently permeates into the framework of everyday life, into all of life's inevitable disputes and little quarrels. Its self-manifestation is subdued, taking place in actions that are so simple that those who perform them may

---

16. Rom 5:5 (RSV).

not think to attribute them to grace, above all to exceptional grace (e.g., in a reconciliation after a quarrel).

Now, there can be no doubt that loveless marriages do indeed exist. They might well have been entered into without love (e.g., once upon a time, and still in certain societies, because they were arranged by parents out of self-interested motives; today, because they are entered into carelessly by youths who confuse love with the feelings of the heart when the latter are not just merely sensual feelings). And then, there are—alas!—many marriages that began with a true love but have lost it in the midst of life, for love is difficult and demands true asceticism, an exercise of self-forgetfulness, which is often quite demanding, given the difficulties of human existence. If one can gradually lose charity, even after having been joyfully committed to the service of God, and either leave Christ and the Church or continue to live in her and in religious life without love or fervor, it is not impossible that spouses who were truly in love with each other could cease to love one another and live their conjugal life without fervor.

Will it be said that in this case the conjugal state of itself is dissolved (as it consists in an interpersonal bond, a bond that quite precisely is love)? Some do indeed say this, and it seems quite obvious to them. However, we must beware of simplistic claims that seem obvious. Beyond the personal drama of the spouses and beyond even the precious and indispensable value of conjugal union for the Church and for man, what is at play here is the sacrament, which is the overriding value in which the preceding is included and in relation to which, from the perspective of faith and of salvation, it must be judged. We have been led to carefully distinguish between two significate effects in every sacrament.

On the one hand, there is that which is directly concerned with the person and his immediate relation to God (i.e., grace). On the other hand, there is that which is concerned with the situation of the person in the People of God, the Church. And we have seen that these two significate effects are closely ordered and subordinated to one another in the intention inscribed by Christ (and following upon Him, by the Church) in the very movement of the sacramental action. Nonetheless, as we have seen as well, personal infidelity can separate them, breaking up this order. The sacramental rite, which is a pure sign, is intrinsically ordered to signify and cause this sacrament's grace, though through the intermediary of the ecclesial effect that it signifies and produces first. In this movement's continuous unfolding, grace is typically produced and develops. The sacramental action is prevented from arriving at its terminus through the refusal of grace or through its later rejection by the person who has received the sacrament. However, the ecclesial effect remains and is the bearer of grace, wholly tending toward it. And as we have also seen, grace itself, when it is present, is modified and given a unique quality inasmuch as it is the grace of this sacrament on account of this connection with the ecclesial effect. It exists in it virtually.

In the case that now occupies us, the grace of the sacrament of marriage is charity inasmuch as it penetrates conjugal love (which, of itself, is a natural love), rectifying it as needed, assuming it and integrating it to itself. To say that the disappearance of love—if it is indeed possible to verify this with certitude—extinguishes the sacrament is to forget that love, which has disappeared from one or both of their hearts, virtually remains present in the bond that unites these two baptized people in the Church (or, possibly, this or that baptized man or woman with this or that unbaptized woman or man). We have seen that without this, the sacramental order would lose the purpose for which it was instituted, its power to manifest the effect of grace (which is invisible) in a visible and perfectly objective way.

This is true even if the two spouses never loved one another, for their consent was the public acceptance of the obligation to love one another, made in the Church. All the other obligations derive from that. Moreover, who will say with certitude that they never loved each other? The failure of their union is certainly not a sufficient sign of this, for one can—in human love as in love of God—cease loving after having authentically loved. And the spouses themselves, in the throes of a crisis, are poor witnesses to their earlier sentiments. Who has not experienced the natural tendency to interpret the past in function of one's present situation?

We have seen that charity, the fruit of the sacrament, rightly must prevent this disappearance of love. However, it does not always succeed at doing so, and love does not depend on one person alone.

In the case where love no longer exists, at least presumably, charity must supply for it in the case of the children of God. One must do out of charity what normally ought to be done out of mutual love. In this way, the grace of the sacrament of marriage does not cease, at least in the spouse or spouses who still have charity.

And then, it is difficult to say whether mutual love has totally disappeared. It is difficult, indeed humanly impossible, for charity to resurrect it if it is dead. Nonetheless, it can reignite the flame from the ember buried under the ashes and from the wick that still is smoking. And this is not wholly unheard of.

Still, there remains the case in which conjugal life has truly become impossible. In such an event, without admitting that the conjugal bond ceases before the death of one of the spouses, the Church allows for separation. Charity thus continues, and if the separated spouse is a child of God and wishes to remain one, he or she must not cease loving his or her spouse with a unique love. Whatever the wrongs may be, the idea of vengeance is wholly precluded.

In particular, in the utterly agonizing question of the rights of the married couple over the children, one must silence all resentments. One must not destroy the child's love for the absent spouse.

All of this too is part of the grace of the sacrament of marriage.

General Conclusion
From the Trinity to the Trinity

We have striven to impress the Trinitarian rhythm of the Creedal statements of the faith onto our modest attempt to present a dogmatic synthesis. In the humble sphere of the notions belonging to the believer and, first, the prophet who brought the Word of God to him, these statements express the teaching on which their faith is nourished, striving to translate the transcendent reality of the Father, the Son, and the Holy Spirit, in whom we believe and to whom we are united by faith, penetrated and elevated by love.

Indeed, the absolute immobility of the Godhead is not an inert, dead, pure privation of movement. It is the very movement of the Divine Life, a movement having an infinite amplitude, at its terminal fullness, where it is immobilized from the very first instant, the unique and infinitely comprehensive instant of eternity. It is a rest that is not inferior to action but rather triumphs over the frustration and absence that exist at the beginning of every movement and which movement by its very nature strives to fill, itself coming to its own end when, reaching its goal, it attains the plenitude toward which it stretched forth. For God, this plenitude is present from the start, deploying a dynamism that did not need to develop itself through movement, which indeed would have been useless and, moreover, impossible, a kind of infinite vibration. An unmoved movement, a throbbing immobility—such are the divine processions that revelation makes known to us, the eternal outpouring of the Son and of the Holy Spirit within the Father's bosom.

The principle of these processions in God is the Father, who holds the divinity from no other person, communicating it first to the Son and then, with the Son, to the Holy Spirit, perfectly identical in this divinity, uniting the three Persons, who are distinguished by the processions, in the unity of the Divine Nature, which from the fourth century the Church has called consubstantiality. The Holy Spirit, who proceeds from the Father and the Son inasmuch as they are One through love, returns to the Father by the Son, as love returns to him who loves by bringing the beloved to him. This is the Trinitarian circle, dazzling but hidden in the light, in which the eternally immutable and supremely active Divine Life, eternal life, exalts in itself.

The three Persons together created, just as together they are the one God. That is, in this common action, the Father is the principle, certainly with the two others, but they hold from Him the fact that they are agents of this action with Him, just as they hold from Him the fact that they are God with Him. In this sense, man proceeds from the free love of the Father, partaken in by the other two Persons, but as holding it from Him. He was created in the image of the Father, though also of the Son precisely in the sense that the Son is, by what is hypostatically proper to Him, the perfect image of the Father, as well as in the image of the Holy Spirit in the sense that, given that He is the personified mutual love of the Father and the Son, what is hypostatically proper to Him is the activity of rendering those who receive Him like unto the Father and the Son. Thus, in his depths, man bears the mark of the three distinct and consubstantial Persons, being called to enter into the infinite friendship in which the Trinitarian existence consists.

However, he has shirked this vocation. Such is the drama and mystery of man's Fall. From the beginning of his existence, he is engaged in the way of dissimilitude, which for him is also the way of disgrace and misery, just as the way of similitude, open before his steps by grace, from the time of his creation, was the way of glory and beatitude. God has not abandoned His loving design, which has thus been frustrated by a rejection that rendered its realization impossible. He has taken it up, not through the mere renewal of His promise but, rather, through a new promise and the gift of a new good, one that is incomparably greater and more fulfilling than the goods that man had refused. These goods have been included in this new good and exalted by it: "God so loved the world that He gave His only Son."[1] He gave Him so that He may restore the image of the Trinity in man, His creature. He gave Him in order to restore it in a much more perfect way than it could have been in its first realization—more perfect through all that distance which elevates above Adam, who was a mere creature, the man whom the Son became through the Incarnation, without failing to remain the eternal Son. He gave Him to man in order to bring him back to the way of similitude, to free him from the bonds of his sin, and to save him, giving him the dignity of being a child of God.

Many theologians (and not the least among them) have been indignant and have refused to admit that man would have become greater and that the universe, with him and for him, would have been magnified on account of the sin committed and of man's original infidelity. According to them, the Incarnation of the Word and the Redemption would only have bestowed upon man what he had miserably lost, that which God had chosen to give Him from the beginning. Indeed, how can one admit that sin would have been the source of any advantage whatsoever—above all the source of this supreme good, the gift of the Son? Even what man has through the Incarnation, cross, and resurrection of Christ, he would have had all of this in any case because he receives it from the free love of the Father, and one must not think that the Father's love needed sin in order for it to express its full bounty.

Thus, making use of a theme that is indeed ancient, many say that the Incarnation was included among the goods which God had chosen to bestow upon man and the angels from the beginning. We examined this hypothesis in its proper place. However, does it avoid recognizing the fact that man's sin has earned him an increase of love and of gifts? If the Father gave the Son, He did not do so only through the Incarnation. Indeed, He did so by "delivering" Him to death for sinners and by raising Him for their salvation. How could

---

1. Jn 3:16 (RSV).

one doubt that the Son's sacrificial gift of His human life to the Father for the Redemption of the world, as well as the restoration of this very life—though, glorious and exalted—would bring to man a new and more acute witness of love, a redoubling of the initial gift, even if the Incarnation were included in it?

This is why others, more logically but more rashly as well, go so far as to say that the Incarnation itself brought nothing to man that he would have had without it. It was God's means for giving His Son anew to man after man would have scorned the gift and for making him accept it, but in any case (and just as much without the Incarnation), the Son had been given and even had been "destined before the foundation of the world"[2] (in a way that is, in truth, difficult to understand). The Incarnation would only be a detour that love had to impose in order to circumvent the obstacle of sin and to realize its initial destiny, which would have been the same.

Thus, theology engages itself in a wager, gambling against the faith, when it minimizes and underestimates God's marvelous gift, the Incarnation, in itself and regardless of its motivations, as well as all the gifts that it brings with it: the Mother of God, the Church, man's victory over Satan (the prince of this world), and the great host of saints who, by following Christ bearing His cross, letting themselves be crucified with Him and conforming themselves to Him, have borne human grandeur to the summits that would have been inaccessible without Christ. Indeed, it is a wager, moreover, against the theologian's own faith, which is better than his theology, most especially in this case, giving Christ a central place in the restored universe, acknowledging the irreplaceable role that He plays as holding the first rank in the order of grace, not only as the Word but as the Word incarnate, as well as His role as the loftiest realization of God's love and grace: "He is the beginning, the first-born from the dead, that in everything He might be pre-eminent. For in Him all the fullness of God was pleased to dwell, and through Him to reconcile to Himself all things, whether on earth or in heaven, making peace by the blood of His cross."[3]

---

2. 1 Pt 1:20 (RSV).
3. Col 1:18–20 (RSV).

Now, this wager is lost in advance, and it comes from a misunderstanding. It is quite clear that the redemptive Incarnation in no way is the fruit of sin, which is nothing other than the destruction of the good, a kind of counter-love. The Father's love for man, His creature, here exercises all of its inventiveness. Instead of wishing to consider the offense perpetrated by man in his rebellion against Him, an offense that could only provoke His severity, the Father wished instead to consider only the misery into which man had hurled himself, a misery that has drawn His mercy. Mercy is what prevailed and responded to the counter-love by a redoubling of love, responding to the offense with overflowing generosity. Man's sin is a challenge hurled at God's love, a challenge that love takes up by way of an even greater élan of love. Salvation history is scattered with such challenges, which God then takes up in this way. There is Mary Magdalene, the sinful woman to whom He gave a stronger and more faithful love than that of the apostles. There is St. Augustine, the son of Monica's tears, who through all the follies of the spirit and the flesh was mercifully led to become a beacon for faith-filled intelligence in the Church. There is the good thief, who was led to the cross by his crimes, where he found, against all odds, the pardon of his sin and a purity much loftier than that which had been soiled by his faults: glory and beatitude. This is hardly surprising if God's entire salvific work consists in taking up, through a superabundant grace, the challenge hurled at His love by man's sin: "where sin increased, grace abounded all the more."[4]

God's love is freely given. This means that all of His gifts arise from His mercy and His freedom. Everything that He makes—creation first, as well as the [supernatural] vocation implied in it—is a pure gift. The fact that God could forever give more abundantly does not diminish the value of what He gives and does not attenuate the power of the witness expressed by His love, which is the gift that he has chosen to give. Hence, however great and marvelous the gift may be, His love forever has reserves from which He can draw so as to take up the challenge that has been hurled at Him by the ingratitude of His beloved creature.[5]

---

4. Rom 5:20 (RSV).
5. See Jean-Hervé Nicolas, "La supreme logique de l'amour et la théologie," *Revue Thomiste* 83 (1983): 639–59.

The Word became flesh without ceasing to be what He was, the Son of God, God with the Father, by the same and unique divinity. He became a man, consubstantial with us according to His humanity, just as, in His divinity, He is consubstantial to the Father. He is a true man, and one could say, paraphrasing St. Paul, "born of a true woman."[6] This is the staggering mystery of the Incarnation, to which a lengthy portion of our dogmatic synthesis was dedicated. In it, reason, illuminated by faith, exerted itself in search of as profound of an understanding as is possible concerning the reality of the divinity and humanity of this unique Person, Jesus Christ, having come into this world from the Father.

However, if the Word became incarnate and lived among men, if He suffered at their hands and died, He did so in order to save man and to lead him back to the Father by sacrificing this human life that He made his own so that He may give it in this way. The Redemption, which began with and was substantially accomplished by Christ's first coming, His entrance into human history, must find its consummation in the second coming at the end of time. It is inseparable from the Incarnation such as it was in fact realized—whatever may be the case regarding the hypothesis of the Incarnation taking place independent of man sinning, a redemption that would therefore be non-redemptive. Hence, Christ is the way, the only way, for sinful and redeemed humanity to return to God: "There is salvation in no one else, for there is no other name under heaven given among men by which we must be saved."[7]

Therefore, to study man's return to God through Jesus Christ is, in fact, a continuation of theological reflection on Christ—Himself the perfect testimony rendered to the Father and to His love. This reflection thus encounters the third Person, the Holy Spirit, as well as the permanent and universal means of His manifestation, the Church.

Through the Holy Spirit, whom the resurrected and exalted Christ sent from the Father to the tiny band of disciples, the Church of God at Pentecost came into existence, from the open side of

---

6. Gal 4:4.
7. Acts 4:12 (RSV).

Christ on the cross, from which blood and water had symbolically flowed—the water of baptism and the blood of the Eucharistic sacrifice. These are the super-sacraments that continually nourish the sacramentality of the Church deriving from them, connecting her by an intimate bond to the sacramentality of Christ, by which the Father's mercy has brought about the salvation of man in the power of the Spirit. This is what enables one to say (and understand) that the Church as such was baptized with the baptism of the Spirit, announced by John the Baptist and promised by the Lord. This baptism gave her existence and brought her all the gifts of the Spirit, making her the place and means for the indefectible, intra-worldly presence of the Savior, who has ascended to heaven and nonetheless is present, in her and by her. Thus, He makes her, at once, the visible sign and instrument of the invisible action by which He ceaselessly exercises His priesthood in the world for the salvation of man.

Through the ministry of the Word, she proclaims to the world the salvation prepared by the Father from all eternity in His Incarnate Son, brought about by the Incarnate Son on the cross and bestowed at the resurrection and brought to all men and women up to the end of time through the power of the Spirit. Through the seven sacraments, she bestows this salvation unto those who believe, gathering them together into her, by making them to be, in her, the members of Christ, whose body she is. Through her governance, she leads them, following (and enabling them to follow) the obscure and austere paths of earthly life to eternal life, in which the salvation begun here-below through faith and the sacraments must be brought to their consummation. She herself grows, like a living being, through the sacraments. By the multitude of saints whom she begets to eternal life, the heavenly Jerusalem is progressively formed in the hereafter. There is where the earthly Church sees her fulfilled form, and her destiny is to be entirely engulfed into that reality at the end of time.

Through the dazzling and exhilarating images that are given to us in the Book of Revelation, she is presented in all the life, glory, and beatitude of this heavenly Jerusalem. She is aware that she bears in herself, in faith, the first fruits of this reality, which is nothing other than eternal communion with the Divine Persons in light and joy.

These first fruits are "the Holy Spirit, which is the guarantee of our inheritance."[8]

Thus, the Spirit, sent from the Father by Christ to the Church, manifested by her, and communicated by her to those who believe, leads to the Father all those who do not close themselves off to His coming and who welcome Him, "so that God may be all in all."[9]

---

8. Eph 1:14 (RSV).
9. 1 Cor 15:28.

Works Cited

Abelard. *Commenaria in epistulam ad Romanos*. Edited by Eligius Buytaert. Turnhout: Brepols, 1969.
Adnès, Pierre. *Le Mariage*. Paris: Desclée, 1963.
Albert the Great. *Opera Omnia*. Edited by August Borgnet. Paris, 1890–99.
Alfrink, Johannes. "Biblical Background to the Eucharist as a Sacrificial Meal." *Irish Theological Quarterly* 26 (1959): 290–302.
Alger of Liège. *De sacramentis corporis et sanguinis dominici*. PL 180.
Allmen, Jean Jacques von. "Est-il légitime de consacrer des femmes au ministère pastoral?" *Verbum Caro* 65 (1963): 5–28.
———. *Prophétisme sacramental*. Neuchâtel: Delachaux et Niestlé, 1964.
———. *Une réforme dans l'Église, possiblités, critères, acteurs, étapes*. Gembloux: Duculot, 1971.
———. *La primauté de l'Église de Pierre et de Paul*. Fribourg: Éditions universitaires, 1977.
———. *Pastorale du baptême*. Fribourg: Éditions Universitaires, 1978.
Allo, Bernard. *La première épître aux Corinthiens, traduction et commentaire*. Paris: Gabalda, 1956.
Althaus, Paul. "Martin Luther über die Kindertaufe." *Theologische Literaturzeitung* (1948): 705–14.
Alzeghy, Z. "Sara abolita la confessione?: riflessioni sopra una cronica." *Civiltà Cattolica* 2, no. 3 (1970): 252–60.
Ambrose of Milan. *Des mystères*. Edited and translated by Bernad Botte. SC 25bis. Paris: Éditions du Cerf, 1961.
———. *La penitence*. Edited and translated by Roger Gryson. SC 179. Paris: Éditions du Cerf, 1971.
Anciaux, Paul. *La théologie du sacrament de penitence au XIIe siècle*. Louvain: Nauwelaerts, 1949.
Andriessen, Paul. "La nouvelle Eve, corps du nouvel Adam." In *Aux origins de l'Église*, 87–109. Paris: Desclée de Brouwer, 1965.
Andrieux, Michel. "La carrière ecclésiastique des papes et les documents liturgiques du Moyen Age." *Recherches des sciences religieuses* (1947): 90–120.

Athenagoras. *Supplique au sujet des chrétiens.* Translated by Bernard Pouderon. SC 3. Paris: Éditions du Cerf, 1943.

Audet, Jean-Paul. *La Didachè: Instructions des apôtres.* Paris: Gabalda, 1958.

———. "Esquisse historique de la benediction juive et de l'eucharistie chrétienne." *Revue biblique* 65 (1958): 371–99.

———. *Mariage et célibat dans le service pastoral de l'Église.* Paris: Orante, 1967.

Augustine of Hippo. *S. Aurelii Augustini textus eucharistici selecti, Florilegium patristicum.* Fasc. 35. Bonn: Hanstein, 1933.

———. *De Baptismo.* PL 29.

———. *La Cité de Dieu.* OESA 33–37. Paris: Desclée de Brouwer, 1959–60.

———. *La doctrine chrétienne.* OESA 11.2. [Paris: Desclée de Brouwer, 1997.]

———. *Enarrationes in Psalmos.* PL 36–37.

———. *Epistolae.* PL 33.

———. *La foi chrétienne (De vera religione. De utilitate credendi. De fide rerum quae non videntur. De fide et operibus).* OESA 8. [Paris: Desclée de Brouwer, 1982.]

———. *Homélies sur l'évangile de S. Jean, tract. I–XVI.* OESA 71. Translated by Marie-François Berrouard. [Paris: Descleé De Brouwer, 1969.]

———. *Homilies on the Gospel of St. John.* PL 35.

———. *Retractions (Les Révisions).* OESA 12. Turnhout: Brepols, 1964.

———. *Sermones.* PL 38.

———. *La Trinité. Livres I–VII.* OESA 15. Translated by Marcellin Mellet et Pierre-Thomas Camelot. Paris: Desclée de Brouwer, 1955.

———. *De virginitate.* PL 40.

Baciocchi, Joseph de. "Eucharistie." *Catholicisme* 4:130–57.

———. "Le mystère eucharistique dans les perspectives de la Bible." *Nouvelle revue théologique* 77 (1955): 561–80.

———. "Présence eucharistique et transsubstantion." *Irenikon* 32 (1959): 139–64.

Balthasar, Hans Urs von. *Sponsa Verbi.* Einsiedeln: Johannes Verlag, 1960.

———. *Cordula ou l'épreuve decisive.* Translated by Bernard Fraigneau-Julien. Paris: Beauchesne, 1969.

Bardy, Gustave. "Les origins du sacerdoce chrétien." *Vie Spiritualle, Supplément* 47 (1936): 12–32 and 86–106.

———. *La théologie de l'Eglise de S. Clément de Rome à S. Irénée.* Paris: Éditions du Cerf, 1945.

———. *La théologie de l'Eglise de S. Irénée au concile de Nicée.* Paris: Éditions du Cerf, 1947.

Barré, Henri. *Trinité que j'adore.* Paris: Lethielleux, 1965.

Barth, Karl. "La doctrine ecclésiastique du baptême." *Foi et Vie* 47 (1949): 1–50.

Barthélemy, Jean-Dominique. *Dieu et son image.* Paris: Éditions du Cerf, 1963.

Battifol, Pierre. *L'eucharistie, la presence réelle et la transubstantiation.* Paris: Gabalda, 1913.

Basil of Caesarea. *Sur le Saint-Esprit.* Translated by Benoît Pruche. SC 17bis. Paris: Éditions du Cerf, 1968.

Baum, Gregory. *Les Juifs et l'Evangile.* Translated by Jacques Mignon. Paris: Éditions du Cerf, 1965.

———. "Notes sur les relations d'Israël et de l'Eglise." In *Le diacre dans l'Église et le monde d'aujourd'hui*. Paris: Éditions du Cerf, 1966.
Bavaud, Georges. "Le pécheur n'appartient pas à l'Eglise. Réflexions sur un thème augustinien." In *Oikumene*, 47–53. Catania: Centro di studi sull'antico cristianesimo, Università di Catania, 1964.
———. "Le mystère de la sainteté de l'Eglise. S. Augustin, arbiter des controversies actuelles." *Recherches augustiniennes* 3 (1965): 161–66.
Begley, J. J., and C. J. Armbruster. "Woman and Office in the Church." *American Ecclesiastical Review* 165 (1971): 145–57.
Bellarmine, Robert. *De Conciliis* in *Roberti Bellarmini opera omnia*, vol. 2. Naples: Apud Josephum Giuliano, 1857.
Benedict XV, Pope. *Maximum Illud*. Apostolic Letter. November 30, 1919.
Benoît, André. "Le problème du pédobaptisme." *Revue d'Histoire et de Philosophie Religieuses* (1948–49): 132–41.
Benoît, Pierre. *Le Baptême chrétien au second siècle*. Paris: PUF, 1953.
———. "Le baptême des enfants et la doctrine biblique du baptême selon O. Cullmann." In *Exégèse et Théologie*, 2:212–23. Paris: Éditions du Cerf, 1961.
———. "Corps, Tête et Plérôme dans les épîtres de la captivité." In *Exégèse et Théologie*, 2:107–53. Paris: Éditions du Cerf, 1961.
———. "Notes sur une étude de J. Jeremias." In *Exégèse et Théologie*, 1:240–43. Paris: Éditions du Cerf, 1961.
———. "Les origins de l'épiscopat dans le Nouveau Testament." *Exégèse et Théologie*, 2:232–46. Paris: Éditions du Cerf, 1961.
———. "Le récit de la Cène dans Luc 22, 15–20." In *Exégèse et Théologie*, 1:163–203. Paris: Éditions du Cerf, 1961.
———. "Les récits de l'institution de l'eucharistie et leur portée." In *Exégèse et Théologie*, 1:210–39. Paris: Éditions du Cerf, 1961.
———. "Sur deux études de F. J. Leenhardt." In *Exégèse et Théologie*, 1:244–54. Paris: Éditions du Cerf, 1961.
———. "Compte-rendu du livre de Gr. Baum, 'Les Juifs et l'Evangile.'" In *Exégèse et Théologie*, 3:397–99. Paris: Éditions du Cerf, 1968.
———. "L'unité de l'Église selon l'épitre aux Ephésiens." In *Exégèse et Théologie*, 3:335–57. Paris: Éditions du Cerf, 1968.
Benoît, Jean-Daniel. "Calvin et le baptême des enfants." *Revue d'Histoire et de Philosophie Religieuses* (1937): 457–73.
Béraudy, Roger. "Le sacrement des maladies." *Nouvelle revue théologique* 106 (1974): 600–634.
Besnard, A. M. "Une pratique en mutation: la confession." *Recheres et Débats du Centre catholique des intellectuels français* 64 (1969): 45–64.
Betz, Johannes. *Die Eucharistie in der Zeit der griechischen Väter*. Freiburg: Herder, 1955.
———. "Sacrifice et action de grâces." *La Maison-Dieu* 87 (1966): 78–96.
Betz, Otto. "Le ministère cultuel dans la secte de Qumran et dans le christianisme primitive." In *La secte de Qumran et les origins du christianisme*, 163–202. Paris: Desclée de Brouwer, 1959.

Billot, Louis. *De Ecclesiae Sacramentis*, vol. 1. Rome: Universitatis Gregorianae, 1924.
Bobrinskoy, Boris. "Liturgie et ecclésiologie trinitaire de S. Basile." In *Eucharistie d'Orient et d'Occident*, edited by Bernard Botte, 197–240. Paris: Éditions du Cerf, 1970.
Bock, Colomban. "La Bulle 'Gerentes ad vos' de Martin V." *Collectanea Cisterciensium Reformatorum* 13 (1951): 1–7 and 197–205.
Boelens, Wilm Luurt. "La discussion sur la Sainte Cène dans l'Eglise évangélique." *Concilium* 24 (1967): 91–106.
Boismard, Marie-Émile. "L'eucharistie selon S. Paul." *Lumière et Vie* 31 (1957): 93–106.
———. "Une liturgie baptismale dans la Iª Petri." *Revue biblique* 63 (1956): 182–208; 64 (1957): 161–83.
———. "Compte rendu du livre de Bouüessé: Le sacerdoce chrétien." *Revue biblique* 65 (1958): 309–10.
Boniface IX, Pope. *Sacra Religionis*. Papal bull. February 1, 1400.
Botte, Bernard. "Compte-rendu du livre de G. Dix: The Theology of Confirmation in Relation to Baptism." *Bulletin de théologie ancienne et médiévale* 5, no. 1279.
———. *Le Sauveur du monde*, vol. 4 (*l'Économie sacramentaire*). Chambéry-Leysse: Collège Théologique Dominicain, 1951.
———. *Eucharistie d'Orient et d'Occident*. 2 vols. Paris: Éditions du Cerf, 1970.
Bouëssé, Humbert. *Le sacerdoce chrétien*. Paris: Desclée, 1957.
Bouillard, Henri. *Conversion et grâce chez S. Thomas d'Aquin*. Paris: Aubier, 1944.
Bouyer, Louis. "Mystique, essai sur l'histoire d'un mot." *Vie Spiritualle, Supplément* 9 (1949): 5–23.
———. *Le sens de la vie monastique*. Turnhout: Brepols, 1950.
———. "Le salut dans les religions à mystères." *Revue des Sciences Religieuses* 27 (1953): 1–6.
———. "La signification de la confirmation." *Vie Spiritualle, Supplément* 29 (1954): 162–79.
———. *Le culte de la Mère de Dieu*. Chevetogne: Éditions de Chevetogne, 1955.
———. *La vie de la liturgie: Une critique constructive du Mouvement liturgique*. Paris: Éditions du Cerf, 1956.
———. *Introduction à la vie spirituelle*. Paris: Desclée de Brouwer, 1960.
———. *La spiritualité du Nouveau Testament et des Pères*. Paris: Aubier, 1960.
———. *Le rite et l'homme*. Paris: Éditions du Cerf, 1962.
———. *Dictionnaire théologique*. Paris: Desclée, 1963.
———. *Eucharistie. Théologie et de la prière eucharistique*. Paris: Desclée, 1966.
———. "L'Église de Hans Küng.'" *Civitas* (Luzern) 23 (1968): 933–40.
———. *L'Église de Dieu*. Paris: Éditions du Cerf, 1970.
Braeckmans, Louis. *Confession et communion au Moyen Age et au concile de Trente*. Gembloux: Duculot, 1971.
Brand, Paul. "Notes sur le problème de l'accès de la femme au minitère pastoral." *Verbum Caro* 78 (1966): 47–66.

Braun, François-Marie. "In spiritu et veritate." *Revue thomiste* 52 (1952): 245–74 and 485–509.

———. *Jean le théologien*, vols. 1–3. Paris: Gabalda, 1959–72.

Bruggen, Antonius van. *Réflexions sur l'adoration eucharistique*. Rome: Pontificia Universitas Gregoriana, 1968.

Buchen, Alphonse van. *L'homélie pseudo-eusébienne de Pentecôte. L'origine de la "confirmation' en Gaule méridionale et l'interprétation de ce rite par Fauste de Riez*. Nijmegen: Janssen, 1967.

Cabasilas, Nicolas. *Explication de la divine liturgie*. Translated by Sévérien Salaville. SC 4. Paris: Éditions du Cerf, 1943.

———. *L'Explication de la divine liturgie*. Second edition. Translated by Séverin Salaville. Edited by René Bornert, Jean Gouillard, and Pierre Périchon. SC 4bis. Paris: Éditions du Cerf, 1963.

Cadier, Jean. "La doctrine calviniste de la Sainte Cène." *Etudes théologiques et religieuses* (1951): 1–160.

Calvin, John. *Institution chrétienne*. Genève: Labor et Fideles, 1967.

———. *Joannis Calvini opera selecta*, vol. 1. Edited by Petrus Barth. Munich: Kaiser, 1926.

———. *Petit traité de la Sainte Cène, Johannis Calvini opera selecta*. Edited by Petrus Barth. Munich: Kaiser, 1926.

Camelot, Pierre-Thomas. "Réalisme et symbolism dans la doctrine eucharistique de S. Augustin." *Revue des sciences philosophiques et théologiques* 31 (1947): 394–410.

———. "Compte-rendu du livre de G. Dix: 'The theology of confirmation in relation to baptism.'" *Revue des sciences philosophiques et théologiques* 38 (1954): 642–45.

———. "Sur la théologie de la confirmation." *Revue des sciences philosophiques et théologiques* 38 (1954): 637–57.

Caperan, Louis. *Le problème du salut des infidels, Essai historique*. Toulouse: Grand séminaire de Toulouse, 1934.

———. *L'appel des non-chrétiens au salut*. Paris: Éditions du Centurion, 1961.

Carle, Paul-Laurent. "La femme et les ministères pastoraux d'après la Tradition." *Nova et Vetera* 47 (1972): 263–90.

———. "La femme et les ministères pastoraux selon l'Ecriture." *Nova et Vetera* 47 (1972): 161–87.

———. "La femme et les ministères pastoraux. Étude théologique." *Nova et Vetera* 48 (1973): 17–36.

Carra de Vaux, Bruno, ed. *La confession en contestation. Une enquête auprès de lectures de "Témoignance chrétien."* Paris: Témoignage chrétien, 1970.

Carreteros, Manuel Useros. "'Statuta Ecclesiae' y 'sacramenta Ecclesiae'" en la eclesiología de St. Tomás de Aquino: reflexión tomista sobre el derecho de la Iglesia en paralelismo a la actual temática eclesiológico-canónica*. Rome: Pontificia Universitas Gregoriana, 1962.

Casel, Odo. *Das christliche Kultusmysterium*. Regensburg: Pustet, 1935.

———. *Le mystère du culte dans le christianisme.* Translated by Jean Hild. Paris: Éditions du Cerf, 1946.

———. *Faites ceci en mémoire de moi.* Translated by Jean-Charles Didier. Paris: Éditions du Cerf, 1962.

———. "Das Mysteriengedächtnis der Meßliturgie im Lichte der Tradition." *Jahrbuch für Liturgiewissenschaft,* 8:145–225.

Cavallera, Ferdinand. "Le décret du concile de Trente sur les sacrements en general." *Bulletin de littérature ecclésiastique* (1918): 170–75.

———. "Le sacrament de penitence au concile de Trente." *Bulletin de littérature ecclésiastique* 24 (1923): 172–201.

———. "Le décret du concile de Trente sur la pénitence et l'extrême onction." *Bulletin de littérature ecclésiastique* 33 (1932): 73–95, 114–40, and 224–38.

Cerfaux, Lucien. *Le chrétien dans la theologie de saint Paul.* Paris: Éditions du Cerf, 1962.

Chaillet, Pierre. "L'esprit du christianisme et du catholicisme." *Revue des sciences philosophiques et théologiques* 26 (1937): 483–98 and 713–26; 27 (1938): 161–83.

Champollion, Claire. "Où en-est la théologie des mystères?" *Dieu vivant* 25 (1953): 137–41.

Charue, André Marie. "L'enseignement de S.S. Pie XII et de S.S. Jean XXIII sur l'épiscopate." In *L'épiscopat et l'Église universelle,* edited by Yves Congar, 7–16. Paris: Éditions du Cerf, 1962.

Chavannes, Henry. "La presence réelle chez S. Thomas et chez Calvin." *Verbum Caro* 13 (1959): 151–70.

Chavasse, Antoine. *Étude sur l'onction des infirmes dans l'Église latine, du IIIe siècle à la Réforme carolingienne.* Lyon: Librairie du Sacré-Cœur, 1942.

Cerfaux, Lucien. *La théologie de l'Église suivant saint Paul.* Paris: Éditions du Cerf, 1965.

Chaillet, Pierre. "Introduction." In Johann Adam Möhler, *L'unité dans l'Eglise,* translated by André de Lilienfeld. Paris: Éditions du Cerf, 1938.

———. "La Tradition vivante. Hommage à J.-A. Möhler." *Revue des sciences philosophiques et théologiques* (1938): 161–212.

Chardin, Teilhard de. *Oeuvres.* Paris: Seuil, 1955–76.

"Les chrétiens parlent de la confession." *Vie Spirituelle* 119, no. 555 (1968).

Clement XI, Pope. *Unigenitus Dei Filius* (Against the Errors of Pasquier Quesnel). Papal Bull. September 8, 1713.

Clement of Alexandria. *Stromata.* PG 9.

Clement of Rome. *Épître aux Corinthiens.* Translated by Annie Jaubert. SC 167. Paris: Éditions du Cerf, 1971.

Coathalem, Hervé. *Le parallélisme entre la Vierge et l'Église dans la tradition latine jusqu'à la fin du XIIe siècle.* Rome: Apud aedes Universitatis Gregorianae, 1954.

Codex Iuris Canonici. January 25, 1983.

Colombo, Carlo. "Teologia, filosofia e fisica nella dottrin della transustanziazione." *La Scuola Cattolica* 83 (1955): 89–124.

———. "Ancore sulla dottrina della transustanziazione e la fisica moderna." *La Scuola Cattolica* 84 (1956): 263–88.
———. "Bilancio provisorio di una discussione eucaristica." *La Scuola Cattolica* 88 (1960): 23–55.
Colson, Jean. "Le ministère apostolique dans la littérature chétienne primitive." In *L'épiscopat et l'Église universelle*, 134–69. Paris: Éditions du Cerf, 1962.
———. *Jésus-Christ, ou le sacerdoce de l'évangile*. Paris: Beauchesne, 1966.
———. *Prêtres et peuple sacerdotal*. Paris: Beauchesne, 1967.
"Le concile pastoral de Hollande et ses suites." *Documentation catholique* 67 (1970): 162–87.
Congar, Yves. *Chrétiens désunis. Principes d'un oecuménisme catholique*. Paris: Éditions du Cerf, 1937.
———. "Compte-rendu de la réédition du livre de Möhler: L'unité dans l'Église." *Revue des sciences philosophiques et théologiques* 27 (1938).
———. "La croix de Jésus, du P. Chardon." *Vie Spiritualle, Supplément* 51 (1937): 42–57.
———. *Esquisses du mystère de l'Église*. Paris: Éditions du Cerf, 1941.
———. "Faits, problèmes et réflexions à propos du pouvoir d'Order et des rapports entre le presbytérat et l'épiscopat." *La Maison-Dieu* 14 (1948): 107–28.
———. "Ecclesia ab Abel." In *Ahandlungen über Theologie und Kirche. Festschrift für Karl Adam*, 79–108. Düsseldorf: Schwann, 1952.
———. *Jalons pour une théologie du laïcat*. Paris: Éditions du Cerf, 1954.
———. "De la communion des Églises à une ecclésiologie de l'Église universelle." In *L'épiscopat et l'Église universelle*, 227–60. Paris: Éditions du Cerf, 1962.
———. "Introduction générale aux traités anti-donatistes de S. Augustin." In OESA 28. Paris: Desclée de Brouwer, 1963.
———. *Sainte Église*. Paris: Éditions du Cerf, 1963.
———. *La Tradition et les traditions*. Paris: Fayard, 1963.
———. "L'Église comme peuple de Dieu." *Concilium* 1 (1965): 15–32.
———. *l'Ecclésiologie du Haut Moyen Age*. Paris: Éditions du Cerf, 1968.
———. "Bulletin d'ecclésiologie (i): 'l'Église' de Hans Küng." *Revue des Sciences philosophiques et théologiques* 53 (1969): 693–706.
———. *Vraie et fausse réforme dans l'Église*. Paris: Éditions du Cerf, 1969.
———. *l'Église de saint Augustin à l'époque modern*. Paris: Éditions du Cerf, 1970.
———. *L'Église une, sainte, catholique et apostolique*. Paris: Éditions du Cerf, 1970.
———. "Un essai de théologie sur le sacerdoce catholique." *Recherches des sciences religieuses* 25 (1971): 187–99 and 270–304.
———. "La Personne-Eglise." *Revue thomiste* 71 (1971): 613–40.
———. "Points d'appui doctrinaux pour une pastorale de la penitence." *La Maison-Dieu* 104 (1970): 73–87.
———. "Esprit Saint et confirmation." *Lumen Vitae* (1972).
Congregation for the Doctrine of the Faith. "Declaration on the Question of the Admission of Women to Ministerial Priesthood." October 15, 1976. *Documentation catholique* 74 (1977): 158–74.

Cools, Jos. "La présence mystique du Christ dans le baptême." In *Mémorial Lagrange*, 295–305. Paris: Gabalda, 1940.

Coppens, Joseph. "Baptême." *Dictionnaire de la Bible*, 1:852–954.

———. "Eucharistie." *Dictionnaire de la Bible*, 2:1146–1215.

———. "Les origines de l'eucharistie, d'après les livres du Nouveau Testament." *Ephemerides Theologicae Lovanienses* 2 (1934): 30–60.

———. "Miscellanea biblica, Mysterium fidei." *Ephemerides Theologicae Lovanienses* 33 (1957): 483–506.

———. "L'Église dans l'optique de Hans Küng." *Ephemerides Theologicae Lovanienses* 46 (1970): 121–30.

Corecco, Eugenio. "Il sacerdote ministro del matrimonio." *Sc Catt* 98 (1970): 343–427.

Corvez, Maurice. "Le baptême des enfants." *Nova et Vetera* (1972): 138–40.

Cothenet, Édouard. "Sainteté de l'Eglise et péchés des chrétiens. Comment le Nouveau Testament envisages leur pardon." *Nouvelle revue théologique* 96 (1974): 449–70.

Council of Constance. Decree of Session 8. May 4, 1415 / February 22, 1418.

Council of Florence. *Exsultate Deo*. November 22, 1439.

Council of Trent. *Decree on Communion Under Both Kinds and by Infants*. July 16, 1562.

———. *Decree on Justification*. January 13, 1547.

———. *Decree on Original Sin*. June 17, 1546.

———. *Decree on the Sacrament of the Eucharist*. October 11, 1551.

———. *Decree on the Sacraments in General*. March 3, 1547.

———. *Decree on the Sacrifice of the Mass*. September 17, 1562.

———. *Decree on the Sacrament of Orders*. July 15, 1563.

———. *Decree on the Sacrament of Penance*. November 25, 1551.

———. *Decree Tametsi* (On Clandestine Marriages). November 11, 1563.

Couturier, Charles. "*Sacramentum* et *mysterium* dans l'oeuvre de S. Augustin." In *Études augustiniennes*, 161–332. Paris: Aubier, 1953.

———. "Structure métaphysique de l'être créé d'après S. Augustin." *Recherches de Philosophie* 1 (1955): 57–84.

Crouzel, Henri. *L'Église primitive face au divorce*. Paris: Beauchesne, 1971.

Cullmann, Oscar. *Le baptême des enfants et la doctrine biblique du baptême*. Translated by Jean-Jacques von Allmen. Neuchâtel: Delachaux et Niestlé, 1948.

———. *Saint Pierre, disciple, apôtre, martyr*. Neuchâtel: Delachaux et Niestlé, 1952.

———. *La foi et le culte dans l'Église primitive*. Neuchâtel: Delachaux et Niestlé, 1963.

———. *Christ et le temps*. Neuchâtel: Delachaux et Niestlé, 1966.

———. *Le salut dans l'histoire. L'existence chrétienne selon le Nouveau Testament*. Translated by Marc Kohler. Neuchâtel: Delachaux et Niestlé, 1966.

Cyprian. *De catholicae Ecclesiae unitate*. Translated by Pierre de Labriolle. Paris: Éditions du Cerf, 1942.

Cyril of Alexandria. *Commentary on John*. PG 73–74.

Cyril of Jerusalem. *Catéchèses baptismales et mystagogiques*. Translated by Jean Bouvet. Namur: Éditions du Soleil Levant, 1962.

———. *Catéchèses mystagogiques*. Translated by Auguste Piédagnel. SC 126. Paris: Éditions du Cerf, 1966.

———. *Epistolae (Correspondance)*. Translated by Louis Bayard. Paris: Société d'édition "Les Belles lettres" / Budé, 1925.

———. *Procatecheses* and *Catecheses*. PG 33.

Dabin, Paul. *Le sacerdoce royal des fidèles dans la tradition ancienne et moderne*. Paris: L'Édition Universelle, 1950.

Dalmais, Irénée-Henri. "Divinisation." In *Patristique grecque, Dictionnaire de spiritualité ascétique et mystique, doctrine et histoire*, edited by Marcel Viller, 3:1376–89. Paris: Beauchesne, 1937.

Daly, Mary. *Le deuxième sexe conteste*. Translated by Suzanne Valles. Paris: Mame, 1969.

Daniélou, Jean. "Bulletin de théologie sacramentaire." *Recherches des sciences religieuses* 34 (1947): 369–84.

———. *Théologie du Judéo-christianisme*. Paris: Desclée, 1958.

Darlap, Adolf. "Gegenwartsweisen." *Lexikon für Theologie und Kirche*, vol. 4, edited by Josef Höfer and Karl Rahner, 588–92. Freiburg im Breisgau: Herder, 1957.

Deferrari, Roy J. *Hugh of Saint Victor on the Sacraments of the Christian Faith (De sacramentis)*. Cambridge, Mass.: The Medieval Academy of America, 1951.

Dejaifve, Gustave. "Primauté et collégialité au premier concile du Vatican." In *L'épiscopat et l'Église universelle*, 639–60. Paris: Éditions du Cerf, 1962.

———. "À propos d'un livre recent." *Nouvelle revue théologique* 89 (1967): 1085–95.

Dekkers, Éloi. "La liturgie du mystère chrétien." *La Maison-Dieu* 14 (1948): 30–65.

Delhaye, Philippe. "Rétrospective et prospective des ministères féminins dans l'Église." *Ephemerides Theologicae Lovanienses* 3 (1972): 55–75.

Deloupy, Jean-Paul. *Laïcs et prêtres, des idées pour demain*. Paris: Centurion, 1977.

Deluz, Gaston. "Nécessité des sacrements." In *La Saint Cène, Cahiers théologiques de l'actualité protestante*. Neuchâtel: Delachaux et Niestlé, 1945.

Denis, Albert-Marie. "La function apostolique et la liturgie nouvelle en espirit." *Revue des sciences philosophiques et théologiques* 42 (1958): 401–36.

Denis, Henri. *Des sacrements et des hommes: dix ans après Vatican II*. Lyon: Chalet, 1976.

Descartes, René. *Oeuvres et Lettres*. Edited by André Bridoux. Paris: Gallimard, 1953.

Deschamps, Philippe. *Théologie du péché*. Paris: Desclée de Brouwer, 1960.

Didier, Jean-Charles. "Extême-onction." *Catholicisme* 4 (1954): 987–90.

———. *Faut-il baptiser les enfants? La réponse de la Tradition, Textes présentés par Jean-Charles Didier*. Paris: Éditions du Cerf, 1967.

———. *Histoire de la presence réelle*. Paris: CLD, 1978.

Dillenschneider, Clément. *Le Christ, l'unique prêtre, et nous ses prêtres*. Paris: Éditions du Cerf, 1967.

"Directory for the execution of what the Second Vatican Council promulgated concerning ecumenism." *Acta Apostolicae Sedis* 59 (1967): 578–81.

Dix, Gregory. *The Theology of Confirmation in Relation to Baptism.* London: Dacre Press, 1946.

———. "The Seal in the Second Century." *Theology* 51 (1948): 7–12.

Dondaine, Hyacinthe François. *L'attrition suffisante.* Paris: Vrin, 1943.

———. "La définition des sacrements dans la Somme théologique." *Revue des sciences philosophiques et théologiques* 31 (1947): 213–28.

Doronzo, Emmanuel. *Tractatus dogmaticus de Eucharistia*, vol. 2. Milwaukee, Wis.: Bruce, 1948.

Dubarle, André-Marie. "L'origine dans l'Ancien Testament de la notion paulinienne de l'Église 'Corps du Christ.'" In *Studiorum Paulinorum Congressus Internationalis Catholicus 1961*, 231–40. Rome: Pontifical Biblical Institute Press, 1963.

Duby, Georges. *Le chevalier, la femme et le prêtre. Le mariage dans la France féodale.* Paris: Hachette, 1981.

Dumont, Christophe-Jean. *Les voies de l'unité chrétienne.* Paris: Éditions du Cerf, 1954.

Dupont, Jacques. "Ceci est mon corps, ceci est mon sang." *Nouvelle revue théologique* 80 (1958): 1025–41.

———. *Le discours de Milet.* Paris: Éditions du Cerf, 1962.

Dupuy, Michel. *Bérulle et le sacerdoce.* Paris: Lethielleux, 1969.

Duquoc, Christian. "Réconciliation réelle et réconciliation sacramentelle." *Concilium* 61 (1971): 25–34.

Durwell, Francis-Xavier. *L'Eucharistie, présence du Christ.* Second edition. Paris: Ed. Ouvrières, 1972.

Dutch Episcopate. "Intervention du 9 mai 1965." *Documentation catholique* 62 (1965): 1175–79.

Duval, André. "L'Ordre au concile de Trente." In *Études sur le sacrement de l'ordre*, 281–85. Paris: Éditions du Cerf, 1957.

———. "L'extrême-onction au concile de Trente." *La Maison-Dieu* 101 (1970): 127–72.

Dyer, George. *The Denial of Limbo and the Jansenist Controversy.* Mundelein, Ill.: Saint Mary of the Lake Seminary, 1955.

"L'économie du salut et le cycle liturgique." *La Maison-dieu* 30 (1952).

Egender, D. N. "Vers une doctrine eucharistique commune dans la théologie protestante d'Allemange." *Irenikon* 32 (1959).

L'Eglise de Vatican II coll. Unam Sanctam 51 a, b, c. Paris: Éditions du Cerf, 1966.

Eliade, Mircea. *Naissances mystiques.* Paris: Gallimard, 1959.

Emery, Pierre-Yves. "Le baptême: appurtenance fondamentale à l'Église." *Verbum Caro* 76 (1965): 59–68.

L'épiscopat et l'Église universelle. Paris: Éditions du Cerf, 1962.

Eppacher, Anton. "Die 'Generalabsolution' bei den Scholastikern." *Zeitschrift für katholische Theologie* 90 (1968): 385–421.

D'Ercola, G. "Notes sur les recherches concernant la collégialité épiscopale." *Concilium* 31 (1968): 125–37.

"Études et recherches de Foi et Constitution." *Istina* 23 (1978): 5–55.

"Eucharistie" (multiple articles and authors). In *Dictionnaire de théologie catholique*, edited by Alfred Vacant et al., 5.1–2:980–1368. Paris: Letouzey et Ané, 1913 and 1924.

Eynde, Damien van den. *Les définitions des sacrements pendant la première période de la théologie scolastique (1050–1240)*. Rome / Louvain: Antonianum / Nauwelaerts, 1950.

Feuillet, André. "L'Exousia du Fils de l'homme (d'après Mc 2, 19–28 et par.)." *Recherches des sciences religieuses* 42 (1954): 161–92.

———. "Les thèmes bibliques majeurs du discours sur le pain de vie (Jn 6)." *Nouvelle revue théologique* 82 (1960): 803–22, 918–39, and 1040–52.

———. "L'hymne christologique de l'êpitre aux Ephéiens." *Revue biblique* 72 (1965): 481–506.

———. *Le prologue du IVe évangile*. Paris: Desclée de Brouwer, 1968.

———. "La recherché du Christ dans la Nouvelle Alliance d'après la christophanie de Jn 20, 11–18." *Mysterium Salutis. Dogmatique de l'histoire du salut*, 1:93–112. Paris: Éditions du Cerf, 1969.

———. *Le mystère de l'amour divin dans la théologie johannique*. Paris: Gabalda, 1972.

———. *Le sacerdoce du Christ et de ses ministers*. Paris: Edions de Paris, 1972.

———. *Christologie paulinienne et tradition biblique*. Paris: Desclée de Brouwer, 1973.

———. "Les chrétiens prêtres et rois d'après l'Apocalypse." *Revue thomiste* 75 (1975): 40–66.

———. "La découverte du tombeau vide en Jn 20, 3–10 et la foi au Christ ressuscité." *Esprit et Vie* 19 (1977): 133–42.

Filthaut, Theodor. *La théologie des mystères, exposé de la controverse*. Tournai: Desclée, 1954.

Fink, Karl August. "Zur Spendung der höheren Weihen durch den Priester." *Zeitschrift der Saviny-Stiftung für Rechtsgeschicte*, Kan. Abt. 32 (1943): 506–8.

First Council of Constantinople. *Canons*. 381 A.D.

First Council of Nicaea. *Canons*. June 19, 325.

First Synod of Arles. *Decrees*. (Started) August 1, 314.

Fitzsimons, John. *Penance: Virtue and Sacrament*. London: Burns and Oates, 1969.

Florand, François. "Introduction." In Louis Chardon, *La croix de Jésus*. Paris: Éditions du Cerf, 1937.

———. "Études et recherches de Foi et Constitution." *Istina* 23 (1978): 5–55.

Foi et Constitution. *La reconciliation des Églises, baptême, eucharisti, ministère*. Taizé: Presses de Taizé, 1974.

Foreville, Raymond. *Latran I, II, II, and Latran IV, HCO*, vol. 6. Paris: Éditions de l'Orante, 1965.

Fourth Lateran Council. *Definition Against the Albigensians and the Cathars*. November 11–30, 1215.

Funk, F. "Panorama bibliographique sur la publication de ces dix dernières années touchant la confession." *Concilium* 61 (1971): 121–31.

Gaillard, Jean. "Chronique de liturgie." *Revue thomiste* 57 (1957): 510–51.

Galot, Jean. *La nature du caractère sacramental. Étude de théologie médiévale*. Paris: Desclée de Brouwer, 1957.

———. *Eucharistie vivante*. Paris: Desclée de Brouwer, 1963.

Galtier, Paul. *Aux origines du sacrament de penitence*. Rome: Apud Universitatis Gregorianae, 1951.

———. *De poenitentia: tractatus dogmatico-historicus*. New edition. Rome: Universitatis Gregorianae, 1957.

Garrigou-Lagrange, Reginald. *De Eucharistia*. Turin: Berruti, 1943.

Garrigues, Jean-Miguel, and Marie-Joseph Le Guillou. "Statut eschatologique et caractère ontologique de la succession apostolique." *Revue thomiste* 75 (1975): 395–417.

Gaudel, Auguste-Joseph. "Le sacrifice de la messe dans l'Église latin du IVe siècle jusqu'à la veille de la Réforme." In *Dictionnaire de théologie catholique*, 10:964–1085. Paris: Letouzey et Ané, 1927.

Gaullier, Bertrand. *L'état des enfants morts sans baptême d'après S. Thomas d'Aquin*. Paris: Lethielleux, 1961.

Geremia, Francesco. *I primi due capitoli dell "Lumen Gentium." Genesi ed elaborazione del testo concilaro*. Rome: Ed. Marianum, 1971.

Gerlaud, Marie-Joseph. "Le minstre extraordinaire du sacrement de l'ordre." *Revue thomiste* (1931): 874–85.

Ghellinck, Joseph de. *Pour l'histoire du mot Sacramentum*. Louvain / Paris: Spicilegium sacrum Lovaniense / Librairie Ancienne Honoré Édouard Champion, 1924.

———. "Un chapitre dans l'histoire de la définition des sacrements au XIIIe siècle." In *Mélanges Mandonnet*, 79–96. Paris: Vrin, 1953.

Goossens, Werner. *Les origines de l'eucharistie sacrament et sacrifice*. Paris: Beauchesne, 1931.

Grass, Hans. "Luther et la liturgie eucharistique." *Eucharistie d'Orient et d'Occident*, 1:135–50. Paris: Éditions du Cerf, 1970.

Gregory VII, Pope (Synod of Rome). *Profession of Faith of Berengar of Tours*. February 11, 1079.

Gregory of Nazianzus. *Epistolae*. PG 37.

Gregory of Nyssa. *Catechetical Discourses*. PG 45.

———. *Homilies on the Song of Songs*. PG 44.

Grelot, Pierre. "Peuple." In *Vocabulaire de théologie biblique*, edited by Xavier Léon-Doufour et al. Paris: Éditions du Cerf, 1962.

———. "L'interprétation pénitentielle du lavement des pieds." *L'homme devant Dieu, Mélanges offerts au P. H. de Lubac*, 1:75–92. Paris: Aubier, 1963.

———. *Le ministère de la Nouvelle Alliance*. Paris: Éditions du Cerf, 1967.

———. *Le couple humain dans l'Écriture*. Paris: Éditions du Cerf, 1969.

———. *Église et ministère. Pour un dialogue critique avec Edward Schillebeeckx*. Paris: Éditions du Cerf, 1983.

Gross, Jules. *La divinization du chrétien d'après les Pères grecs, contribution historique à la doctrine de la grâce*. Paris: Gabalda, 1938.

Groupe de Dombes. "Accord doctrinal sur l'eucharistie." *Documentation catholique* 69 (1972): 334–37.
Guillet, Jacques. "Parole de Dieu." In *Dictionnaire de spiritualité ascétique et mystique, doctrine et histoire*, vol. 12, edited by Marcel Viller. Paris: Beauchesne, 1937.
Guillou, Marie-Joseph Le. *Le Christ et l'Église*. Paris: Centurion, 1963.
Guitmond of Aversa. *De corporis et sanguinis Christi veritate in Eucharistia*. PL 149.
Gunten, A. F. von. "L'Église catholique pourrait-elle reconsidérer sa position sur les ordinations anglicanes?" *Nova et Vetera* 58 (1983): 252–67.
Gutwenger, Engelbert. "Substanz und Akzidens in der Eucharistielehre." *Zeitschrift für katholische Theologie* 83 (1961): 257–306.
Guysens, D. G. "Présence réelle eucharistique et transsubstantiation dans les definitions de l'Église catholique." *Irenikon* 32 (1959): 420–35.
Gy, Pierre-Marie. "Le rite sacramental du mariage et la tradition liturgique." *Revue des sciences philosophiques et théologiques* 38 (1954): 258–69.
Hajjar, Joseph. "La collégialité dans la tradition orientale." In *L'Eglise de Vatican II*, 847–70. Paris: Éditions du Cerf, 1966.
Hamer, Jérôme. "Le baptême et l'Église." *Irenikon* 25 (1952): 142–64 and 263–75.
———. *La prière*, vol. 1. Paris: Desclée, 1959 and 1963.
———. *Le baptême d'après les Pères de l'Église (recueil detexts)*. Paris: Grasset, 1962.
———. *L'Église est une communion*. Paris: Éditions du Cerf, 1962.
Hamman, Adalbert. *Baptême et confirmation*. Paris: Desclée, 1969.
Hänggi, Anton, and Irmgard Pahl. *Prex eucharistica. Textus e variis liturgiis antiquioribus selecti*. Fribourg: Éditions universitaires, 1968.
Häring, Hermann, and Josef Nolte, eds. *Diskussion um H. Küng "Die Kirche."* Freiburg: Herder, 1971.
Hauret, Charles. "Sacrifice." In *Vocabulaire de théologie biblique*, edited by Xavier Léon-Doufour, 1163–68.
Héris, Vincent. "Enfants (Salut des)." *Catholicisme* 4:151–57.
———. "Le salut des enfants morts sans baptême." *La Maison-Dieu* (1947): 86–105.
———. "Les limbes des enfants." *Vie Spirituelle* 108 (1963): 705–15.
Hermas. *Le Pasteur*. Second edition. Translated by Robert Joly. Paris: Éditions du Cerf, 1968.
Hippolytus of Rome. *La tradition apostolique*. Translated by Bernard Botte. SC 11bis. Paris: Éditions du Cerf, 1968.
Hocédez, Edgar. *Histoire de la théologie au XIXe siècle*. Paris: Desclée de Brouwer, 1947.
Holy Office (Pope Alexander VIII). *Decree Concerning the Errors of the Jansenists*. December 7, 1690.
Holy Office (Pope Innocent XI). *Condemned Propositions of the "Laxists."* March 2, 1679.
Houssiau, Albert. "Implications théologiques de la reconnaissance inter-ecclésiale du baptême." *Revue théologique de Louvain* (1970): 393–410.
Huftier, M. "Corpus Christi. Amen." *Vie Spirituelle* 111 (1964): 477–501.

---. "Sur la penitence et la confession." *Esprit et Vie* 81 (1971): 617–25.
L'Huillier, Pierre. "Un point de vue orthodox à propos du divorce." In *Divorce et indissolubilité du mariage*. Paris: Éditions du Cerf, 1971.
Hulsbosch, A. "Baptême." In *Dictionnaire encyclopédique de la Bible* (translated from Dutch). Paris: Brepols, 1960.
Hurley, M. "Que peuvent apprendre les catholiques de la controverse sur le baptême des enfants?" *Concilium* 24 (1967): 21–28.
Ignatius of Antioch. *Lettres*. Translated by Pierre-Thomas Camelot. Paris: Éditions du Cerf, 1945.
Innocent III, Pope. *De sanctissimo altaris mysterio*. PL 217.
Innocent VIII, Pope. *Exposcit*. April 9, 1489.
Interdonnato, F. "Es dogmaticamente possible cambiar la doctrina y la practica de la confesión auricular et individual establecida en Trente?" In *Libro Annual, 1971*, 247–86. Lima: Publicationes de la Faculdad de Theología Pontificia y Civil, 1971.
International Anglican-Roman Catholic Commission. "Declaration on the Eucharistic Doctrine." September 7, 1971. *Documentation catholique* 69 (1972): 86–88.
Irenaeus of Lyon. *Adversus Haereses, libri quinquie, Libri I-II*. Edited by Ubaldo Mannucci. Rome: Forzani, 1907.
---. *Contre les hérésies*. Book 3. Translated by François Sagnard. SC 34. Paris: Éditions du Cerf, 1952. [New edition. Translated by Adelin Rousseau and Louis Doutreleau. SC 210–11. Paris: Éditions du Cerf, 1974 / 2002.]
---. *Contre les hérésies*. Book 4. Translated by Adelin Rousseau, Louis Doutreleau, Charles Mercier, and Bertrand Hemmerdinger. SC 100 and 100bis. Paris: Éditions du Cerf, 1965.
---. *Contre les hérésies*. Book 5. Translated by Adelin Rousseau, Louis Doutreleau, and Charles Mercier. SC 152–53. Paris: Éditions du Cerf, 1969.
Jacquemont, Patrick. "Du bon usage de l'eucharistie." *Informations catholiques internationales* 309 (July–August 1968): 6–7.
Jaki, Stanley. *Les tendances nouvelles de l'ecclésiologie*. Rome: Herder, 1957.
Jatosz, Thomas Jude. "Sacramental Penance in Alexander of Hales." *Franziskanische Studien* (Paderborn) 29 (1969): 302–46.
Javierre, Antonio M. "Le theme de la succession des apôtres dans la littérature chrétienne primitive," in *L'épiscopat et l'Église universelle*, 171–226. Paris: Éditions du Cerf, 1962.
---. "Pourquoi se confesser aujourd'hui?" In *La confession en contestation. Une enquête auprès de lecteurs de "Témoignage chrétien,"* edited by Bruno Carra de Vaux. Paris: Témoignage chrétien, 1970.
Jean-Nesmy, Claude. "De quoi faut-il s'accuser." *Vie Spirituelle* 116 (1967): 293–308.
Jedin, Hubert. "La nécessité de la confession privée selon le concile de Trente." *La Maison-Dieu* 104 (1970): 88–115.
Jeremias, Joachim. *Le baptême des enfants aux quatre premiers siècles*. Translated by Bruno Hübsch et François Stoessel. Le Puy: Mappus, 1967.
---. *La dernière Cène. Les paroles de Jésus*. Paris: Éditions du Cerf, 1972.

John Chrysostom. *Homilies on the Letter to the Hebrews*. PG 63.
John of St. Thomas. *Cursus philosophicus*, vol. 1. Edited by Beatus Reiser. Turin: Marietti, 1930.
———. *Cursus theologicus*, vol. 9. Paris: Vivès, 1886.
Jonas (of Bobbio). *S. Columbani vita*. PL 87.
Jong, Johannes Petrus de. "Epiklese." In *Lexikon für Theologie und Kirche*, vol. 3, edited by Josef Höfer and Karl Rahner, 935–37. Second edition. Freiburg im Breisgau, 1957.
———. *L'eucharistie comme réalité symbolique*. Translated by Antoine Freund. Paris: Éditions du Cerf, 1972.
Jossua, Jean-Pierre, D. Duliscouët, and B. D. Marliangeas. "Théologie, crise, et redécouverte du sacrement de penitence." *Revue des sciences philosophiques et théologiques* 52 (1968): 119–42.
Journet, Charles. *L'Église du Verbe Incarné*. Paris: Desclée de Brouwer, 1951–69.
———. "L'Église et la femme." *Nova et Vetera* 4 (1957): 299–313.
———. *La messe, préscence du sacrifice de la croix*. Paris: Desclée de Brouwer, 1957.
———. *Théologie de l'Église*. Paris: Desclée de Brouwer, 1958.
———. *La volonté salvifique sur les petits enfants*. Paris: Desclée de Brouwer, 1958.
———. "Qui est member de l'Église?" *Nova et Vetera* 36 (1961): 193–203.
———. "Controverse avec Congar." *Nova et Vetera* 38 (1963): 308.
———. "La présence réelle du Christ sacrament." *Nova et Vetera* 40 (1965): 275–89.
———. "L'eucharistie n'est pas malleable, elle est adorable." *Nova et Vetera* 44 (1969): 1–6.
———. "L'Église de dieu, le livre du Père Bouyer." *Nova et vetera* 46 (1971): 129–47.
———. "Note sur un accord entre théologiens Anglicans et catholiques touchant la doctrine eucharistique." *Nova et Vetera* 46 (1971): 250–51.
———. "La sainteté de l'Église: le livre de Jacques Maritain." *Nova et Vetera* 46 (1971): 1–33.
———. "Transsubstantiation." *Nova et Vetera* 46 (1971): 161–72.
———. "Le mystère de la sacramentalité. Le Christ, l'Église et les sept sacrements." *Nova et Vetera* 49 (1974): 161–214.
———. *La voie théologale. Dieu à la rencontre de l'homme*. Paris: Desclée de Brouwer, 1981.
Jüngmann, Josef Andreas. *Missarum solemnia*. Paris: Aubier, 1951.
Justin Martyr. *La philosophe passe au Christ: l'oeuvre de Justin: Apologie, I et II, Dialogue avec Tryphon*. Translated by Adalbert Hamman. Edited by Adalbert Hamman and François Garnier. Paris: Grasset, 1958.
Kaelin, Jean de la Croix. "L'eucharistie selon Max Thurian." *Nova et Vetera* 35 (1960): 9–19.
Kelly, John Norman Davidson. *Initiation à la doctrine des Pères de l'Église*. Translated by Ceslas Tunmer. Paris: Éditions du Cerf, 1968.
King, Ronald F. "The Origin and Evolution of a Sacramental Formula: *sacramentum tantum, res et sacramentum, res tantum*." *The Thomist* 31 (1967): 21–82.
Korn, Ernest. "Compte-rendu du livre de D. Olivier, Le procès de Luther." *Nova et Vetera* 46 (1971): 312–14.

Koster, Mannes Dominikus. *Ekklesiologie im Werden*. Paderborn: Verlag der Bonifacius-Druckerei, 1940.
Küng, Hans. *Structures de l'Église*. Translated by Henri Marie Rochais and Jean Evrard. Paris: Desclée de Brouwer, 1963.
———. *La justification. La doctrine de K. Barth, réflexions catholiques*. Translated by Henri Marie Rochais and Jean Evrard. Paris: Desclée de Brouwer, 1965.
———. *L'Église*. Translated by Henri Marie Rochais and Jean Evrard. Paris: Desclée de Brouwer, 1968.
———. *Infaillible? Un interpretation*. Translated by Henri Rochais. Paris: Desclée de Brouwer, 1971.
Labourdette, Michel. "Problèmes d'eschatologie." *Revue thomiste* 54 (1954): 658–75.
———. "Problèmes du mariage." *Revue thomiste* 68 (1968): 125–48.
Lagrange, Marie-Joseph. *Evangile selon Saint Jean*. Paris: Gabalda, 1936.
Lambert, Bernard. "L'Église catholique peut-elle admettre des femmes à l'ordination sacerdotale?" *Documentation catholique* 73 (1976): 773–80.
Lampe, Geoffrey William Hugo. *The Seal of the Spirit*. London: Longmans, Green, and Company, 1951.
Lanfranc. *Liber de corpore et sanguine Domini*. PL 150.
Laporta, Jorge. *La destinée de la nature humaine selon Thomas d'Aquin*. Paris: Vrin, 1965.
Larrabe, José Luis. "Estructuras y perspectivas en el sacramento de la penitencia." *Lumen* (Lisboa) 19 (1970): 353–58.
———. "Permanencia y adaptación histórica en el Sacramento de la penitencia según Santo Tomás." *Comillas* 53 (1970): 127–62.
———. "La Penitencia." *Manresa* 43, no. 166 (1971): 47–58.
Larranaga, Victoriano. "Las fuentes biblicas de la eucaristia en el N.T. Problemas de critica histórica suscitados dentro del protestantismo y racionalismo modern." *Estudios ecclesiasticos* 32 (1958): 71–92.
Laurent, B. "Le magistère et le mot 'extrême-onction' depuis le concile de Trente." In *Problemi scelti di teologia contemporanea*, 219–32. Rome: Pontificia Università Gregoriana, 1954.
Laurentin, René. *Marie, L'Église et le sacerdoce*, vol. 2. Paris: Lethielleux, 1953.
———. *La question mariale*. Paris: Seuil, 1963.
———. *Court traité sur la Vierge Marie*. Paris: Lethielleux, 1967.
Le Bras, Gabriel. "La doctrine du mariage chez les théologiens et les canonistes depuis l'an mille." In *Dictionnaire de théologie catholique*, ed. Alfred Vacant et al., 9:2123–2317. Paris: Letouzey et Ané, 1927.
Le Guillou, Marie-Joseph, and A. M. Henry. "Un débat théologique sur l'eucharistie, à propos de l'ouvrage du Prof. Leenhardt Ceci est mon corps." *Istina* (1956): 210–40.
Leclerc, Jean. "Le sacerdoce des moines." *Irenikon* 36 (1963): 5–40.
Lecordier, Gaston. *La doctrine de l'eucharistie chez S. Augustin*. Paris: Gabalda, 1930.
Lecuyer, Joseph. "Essai sur le sacerdoce des fidèles chez les Pères." *La Maison-Dieu* 27 (1951): 7–50.

———. "Le sacrifice selon S. Augustin." In *Augustinus Magister, Congrès international augustinien, Paris, 21–24 September 1954, Communications. Études augustiniennes*, 905–15. Paris: Études Augustiniennes, 1954.

———. "La confirmation chez les Pères." *La Maison-Dieu* 54 (1958): 29–52.

———. "Théologie du sacerdoce chrétien." In *La Tradition sacerdotale*, 241–246. Paris: Mappus, 1959.

———. "Communion épiscopale dans les conciles africains entre 400–425." In *Au service de la parole de Dieu: mélanges offerts à Monseigneur André-Marie Charue, évêque de Namur*. Gembloux: Duculot, 1969.

Leeming, Bernard. *Principles of Sacramental Theology*. London: Longmans, 1960.

Leenhardt, Franz. *Le baptême chrétien, son origine, sa signification*. Neuchâtel: Delachaux et Niestlé, 1946.

———. *Le sacrament de la Sainte Cène*. Neuchâtel: Delachaux et Niestlé, 1948.

———. *Ceci est mon corps. Explication de ces paroles de Jésus-Christ*. Neuchâtel: Delachaux et Niestlé, 1955.

Leo the Great. *Epistolae*. PL 54.

Leo XIII. Pope. *Satis Cognitum*. Encyclical Letter. June 29, 1896.

Léon-Dufour, Xavier. "Le mystère du pain de vie." *Recherches des sciences religieuses* 46 (1958): 481–523.

Lepin, Maurius. *L'idée du sacrifice de la messe d'après le théologiens depuis l'origine jusqu'à nos jours*, 241–52. Paris: Beauchesne, 1957.

Leroy, Marie-Vincent. "L'Église de H. Küng." *Revue thomiste* (1970): 293–310.

Liégé, Pierre-André. "Le baptême des enfants," in "Débat pastoral et liturgique." *La Maison-Dieu* 107 (1971): 7–28.

Ligier, Louis. "Le 'charisma veritatis certum' des évêques; ses attaches liturgiques, patristiques, et bibliques." In *L'homme devant Dieu, Mélanges offerts au P. H. de Lubac*, 1:247–68. Paris: Aubier, 1963.

———. "Le sacrament de penitence selon la tradition orientale." *Nouvelle revue théologique* 89 (1967): 910–67.

Lof, L. J. van der. "Eucharistie et présence réelle selon Saint Augustin." *Revue d'études augustiniennes* 10 (1964): 295–304.

Lombardi, Riccardo. *The Salvation of the Unbeliever*. Translated by Dorothy M. White. London: Burns & Oates, 1956.

Lossky, Vladimir. "Panhagia." In *À l'image et à la resemblance de Dieu*. Paris: Aubier, 1967.

Lubac, Henri de. *Corpus mystium, L'Eucharistie et l'Église au Moyen Age*. Paris: Aubier, 1949.

———. *Histoire et Esprit*. Paris: Aubier, 1950.

———. *Catholicisme*. Paris: Éditions du Cerf, 1952.

———. *Le mystère du surnaturel*. Paris: Aubier, 1965.

———. *Les Églises particulières dans l'Église universelle*. Paris: Aubier, 1971.

Luneau, Auguste. *L'histoire du salut chez les Pères de l'Eglise*. Paris: Beauchesne, 1964.

Luneau, Auguste, and Marius Bobichon. *Église ou troupeau? Du troupeau fidèle au people de Dieu*. Paris: Editions Ouvrières, 1972.

Lunen-Chenu, Marie-Thérèse van. "Féminisme chrétien: jusque et y compris le sacerdoce." *Revue Nouv. Belg.* 51 (1970): 366–72.
Luther, Martin. *De captivitate Babylonica* in *Martin Luthers Werke*. Weimarer Ausgabe 40. Weimar: H. Böhlau, 1883.
———. *Kommentar zu Galater*. In *Martin Luthers Werke*. Weimarer Ausgabe 40. Weimar: H. Böhlau, 1883.
Lyonnet, Stanislaus. "Péché." In *Vocabulaire de théologie biblique*, edited by Xavier Léon-Doufour, 936–46.
Malevez, Léopold. "La vision chrétienne de l'histoire." *Nouvelle revue théologique* 7 (1949): 113–34 and 244–65.
———. "Connaisance discursive et connaisance mystique des mystères du salut." In *L'homme devant Dieu, Mélanges offerts au P. H. de Lubac*, 3:167–84. Paris: Aubier, 1963.
Marchal, L. "Evêques (origine divine des)." *Dictionnaire de la Bible* 2:1297–1333.
Mansi, Giovanni Domenico. *Sacrorum Conciliorum nova et amplissima Collectio*. Florence, 1758; Venice, 1799; Paris, 1901–27.
Le mariage: engagement pour la vie. Paris: Desclée de Brouwer, 1971.
"Marie et l'Église." *Etudes Mariales*. Paris: Lethielleux, 1951–53.
Maritain, Jacques. "Signe et symbole." In *Quatre essais sur l'esprit dans sa condition charnelle*, 63–127. Paris: Desclée de Brouwer, 1939.
———. *Court traité de l'existence et de l'existant*. Paris: Hartmann, 1947.
———. *Liturgie et contemplation*. Paris: Desclée de Brouwer, 1960.
———. "Quelques réflexions sur le sacrifice de la messe." *Nova et Vetera* 43 (1968): 1–35.
———. *De l'Église du Christe, la Personne de l'Église et son personnel*. Paris: Desclée de Brouwer, 1970.
———. "A propos de l'École Française." *Revue thomiste* 71 (1971): 463–79.
Marsili, Salvatore. "Verso una nuova teologia eucaristica." *Via, Verità et Vità* (Rome) 18 (1969): 13–28.
Martimort, Aimé Georges. "La confirmation." In *Communion solennelle et profession de foi*. Paris: Éditions du Cerf, 1952.
———. *L'Église en prière, introduction à la liturgie*. Paris: Desclée, 1965.
Martin V, Pope. *Gerentes ad Vos*. Papal Bull. November 16, 1427.
Masi, R. "La dottrina sacramentale del sacrificio della messa." *Euntes docete* 12 (1959): 141–81.
Masterson, Robert Reginald. "Sacramental graces: modes of sanctifying grace." *The Thomist* 18 (1955): 311–72.
Masure, Eugène. *Le sacrifice du corps mystique*. Paris: Desclée, 1950.
———. *Le Signe: le Passage du visible a l'invisible; Psychologie, Histoire, Mystère; le geste, l'outil, le langage, le rite, le miracle*. Paris: Bloud et Gay, 1954.
McClendon, James William. "Pourquoi les baptistes ne donnent-ils pas le baptême aux enfants." *Concilium* 24 (1967): 13–20.
McCue, J. "La penitence en tant que signe sacramental distinct." *Concilium* 61 (1971): 49–57.

Works Cited

McSorley, Harry. "La foi nécessaire pour le sacrement de penitence: la doctrine de Luther et celle du concile de Trente." *Concilium* 61 (1971): 91–100.
Meer, Haye van der. *Sacerdotio della donna? Saggio di storia della teologia*. Translated by Rosa Paini. Brescia: Morcelliana, 1971.
Mersch, Émil. *La théologie du corps mystique*. Louvain: Desclée de Brouwer, 1943.
———. *Le corps mystique du Christ. Études de théologie historique*, vols. 1–2. Paris: Desclée de Brouwer, 1951.
"La messe" (multiple articles and authors). In *Dictionnaire de théologie catholique*, edited by Alfred Vacant et al., vol. 10.1–2:795–1403. Paris: Letouzey et Ané, 1928–29.
Meyendorff, John. "Note sur l'interprétation orthodoxe de l'eucharistie." *Concilium* 24 (1967): 53–60.
Meyer, Charles. *The Thomistic Concept of Justifying Contrition*. Mundelein: Seminarium Sanctae Mariae ad Lacum, 1949.
Michel, Albert. "La messe chez les théologiens postérieurs au concile de Trente. Essence et efficacité." In *Dictionnaire de théologie catholique*, edited by Alfred Vacant et al., vol. 10.1:1143–1316. Paris: Letouzey et Ané, 1928.
———. "Opus operatum." In *Dictionnaire de théologie catholique*, ed. Alfred Vacant et al., 11.1:1084–87. Paris: Letouzey et Ané, 1931.
———. "Sacrements." In *Dictionnaire de Théologie Catholique*, ed. Alfred Vacant et al., 14:485–644. Paris: Letouzey et Ané, 1939.
———. *Enfants mort sans baptême*. Paris: Tequi, 1961.
Mohrmann, Christine. "Sacramentum dans les plus anciens textes chrétiens." *Harvard Theological Review* 47 (1954): 141–53.
Moingt, Joseph. "Problèmes d'inter-communion." *Études* 332, no. 1 (1970): 256–67.
———. "L'initiation chrétienne des jeunes." *Études* 336 (1972): 437–54.
Mollat, Donatien. "Le chapitre VI de Saint Jean." *Lumen Vitae* 31 (1957): 107–19.
Möller, Johann Adam. *L'unité dans l'église ou le principe du catholicisme, avec introduction du Pierre Chaillet*. Translated by André de Lilienfeld. Paris: Éditions du Cerf, 1938.
Montclos, Jean de. *Lanfranc et Béranger: la controverse eucharistique du XIe siècle*. Louvain: Spicilegium Sacrum Lovaniense, 1971.
Mouroux, Jean. *Le mystère du temps*. Paris: Aubier, 1962.
Mühlen, Heribert. *L'Éspirit dans l'Église*. Translated by Arthur Liefooghe, Marthe Massart, and René Virrion. Paris: Éditions du Cerf, 1969.
Müller, Alois. *Ecclesia-Maria. Die Einheit Marias und der Kierche*. Fribourg: Editions universitaires, 1955.
Neunheuser, Burkhard. "Meßopfertheorien." In *Lexikon für Theologie und Kirche*, edited by Josef Höfer and Karl Rahner, 7:350–52. Second edition. Freiburg im Breisgau: Herder, 1957.
———. *Baptême et confirmation*. Paris: Éditions du Cerf, 1965.
———. *L'Eucharistie, II: au Moyen Age et à l'époque moderne*. Translated by Althur Liefooghe. Paris: Éditions du Cerf, 1966.
Nicholas II, Pope (Synod of Rome). *Profession of Faith in the Eucharist Prescribed for Berengar of Tours*. 1059 A.D.

Nicolas, Jean-Hervé. "Théologie de l'Église, Études critiques." *Revue thomiste* 46 (1946): 383–89.

———. "Amour de soi, amour de Dieu, amour des autres." *Revue thomiste* 56 (1956): 5–42.

———. "Crainte et tremblement." *Vie Spirituelle* 99 (1958): 227–54.

———. "L'innocence originelle de la Nouvelle Eve." In *Etudes Mariales*, 15–35. Paris: Lethielleux, 1958.

———. "Réactualisation des mystères rédempteurs dans et par les sacrements." *Revue thomiste* 58 (1958): 20–54.

———. "La grâce sacramentelle." *Revue thomiste* 61 (1961): 165–92 and 522–38.

———. "La maternité spirituelle de Marie." *Etudes Mariales* 3. Paris: Lethielleux, 1961.

———. "La causalité des sacrements." *Revue thomiste* 62 (1962): 547–52.

———. "Médiation mariale et maternité spirituelle." In *La maternité spirituelle de Marie, Actes du VIIIe congrès marial national, Lisieux 5–9 July 1961*, 67–88. Paris: Lethielleux, 1962.

———. *La virginité de Marie. Étude théologique*. Fribourg: Éditions universitaires, 1962.

———. *Theotokos, le mystère de Marie*. Paris: Desclée de Brouwer, 1965.

———. *Dieu connue comme inconnu*. Paris: Desclée de Brouwer, 1966.

———. "Le sens et la valeur en ecclésiologie du parallélisme de structure entre le Christ et l'Église." *Angelicum* 43 (1966): 353–58.

———. *L'amour de Dieu et la peine des hommes*. Paris: Beauchesne, 1969.

———. *Les profondeurs de la grâce*. Paris: Beauchesne, 1969.

———. "Les laïcs et l'annonce de la Parole de Dieu." *Nouvelle revue théologique* 93 (1971): 821–48.

———. *Le ministère sacerdotal, Rapport de la Commission Théologique Internationale*. Paris: Éditions du Cerf, 1971.

———. *Liberté chrétienne et sexualité*. Fribourg: Editions S. Paul, 1972.

———. "Présence réelle eucharistique et transsignification." *Revue thomiste* 72 (1972): 439–49.

———. "L'acte pur de saint Thomas d'Aquin et le Dieu vivant de l'évangile." *Angelicum* 51 (1974): 511–32.

———. "Liberté du théologien et authorité du magistère." *Freiburger Zeitschrift für Philosophie und Theologie* 21 (1974): 439–58.

———. "Hospitalité eucharistique et oecuménisme." *Nova et Vetera* 50 (1975): 168–87.

———. "La nature ontologique du caractère sacerdotal dans la pensée de Saint Thomas." In *Atti del congresso internazionale Tommaso d'Aquino nel suo settimo centenario*, 4:486–92. Naples: Edizioni Domenicane Italiane, 1976.

———. "Universalité de la mediation du Christ et salut de ceux qui ne connaissent pas le Christ." In *Acta del Congresso internazionale Tommaso d'Aquino nel suo settimo centenario*, 4:261–73. Naples: Edizioni domenicane italiane, 1976.

———. *Homme et femme il les créa. L'idée chrétienne du mariage*. Paris: Téqui, 1977.

———. "Sacerdoce, célibat et sacrements." *Nova et Vetera* 53 (1978): 122–34.

———. *Contemplation et vie contemplative en christianisme*. Fribourg / Paris: Éditions universitaires / Beauchesne, 1980.

———. "L'appartenance à l'Église selon la théologie catholique." In *Austritt aus der Kirche*, edited by Louis Carlen, 131–45. Fribourg: Universitätsverlag, 1982.

———. "Grâce et divinization." In *La Teologia morale nella storia e nella problematica attuale: miscellanea P. Louis Bertrand Gillon*. [Milan]: Massimo, 1982.

———. "Le Saint-Esprit principe de l'unité de l'Église." In *Credo in Spiritum sanctum: atti del Congresso teologico Internazionale di pneumatologia in occasione del 1600e anniversario del Concilio di Efeso, Roma, 22–26 marzo 1982*, 1359–80. Vatican: Libreria editrice Vaticana, 1983.

———. "La supreme logique de l'amour et la théologie." *Revue Thomiste* 83 (1983): 639–59.

Nicolas, Marie-Joseph. "Compte-rendu du livre de Febrer M., El concepto de persona y la union hipostatica." *Revue thomiste* 55 (1955): 186–88.

O'Connor, Jerome Murphy. "Péché et communauté dans le Nouveau Testament." *Revue biblique* 74 (1967): 161–93.

O'Neill, Colman E. "Extreme-Unction: Suffering in Christ." *Doctrine and Life* 12 (1962): 501–9.

———. *Meeting Christ in the Sacraments*. New York: Alba House, 1964.

———. *Sacramental Realism. A General Theory of the Sacraments*. Dublin: Dominican Publications, 1983.

Oechslin, R.-L. "Dimension ecclésiale de la penitence." *Vie Spirituelle* 117 (1967): 553–65.

Onate, J. A. "El discurso del 'Pan de Vida.'" *XXXV Congreso Eucarístico Internacional*, 2:402–12. Barcelona, 1953.

Onatibia, Ignacio. *La presencia de la obra redentora en el misterio del culto*. Vitoria: Editorial del seminario dio, 1954.

Optatus of Milevis. *De schismate donatistorum*. PL 11.

Origen. *Contre Celse*. Translated by Marcel Borret. SC 132. Paris: Éditions du Cerf, 1967.

———. *Homélies sur l'Exode*. Translated by P. Fortier. Introduction and notes by Henri de Lubac. SC 16. Paris: Éditions du Cerf, 1947.

Page, Jean-Guy. *Qui est l'Église? I. Le mystère et le sacrament du salut*. Montréal: Editions Bellarmin, 1982. *II. Qui est l'Église*. Montréal: Editions Bellarmin, 1979.

Paschasius Radbertus. *De corpore et sanguine Domini*. Edited by Beda Paulus. Turnhout: Brepols, 1969.

Patton, Hugh. *The Efficacy of Putative Attrition in the Doctrine of the Theologians of the XVI and XVII Centuries*. Rome: Herder, 1966.

Paul VI, Pope. *Ministeria Quaedam*. Apostolic Letter. August 15, 1972.

———. *Mysterium Fidei*. Encyclical Letter. September 3, 1965.

Périnelle, Joseph. *L'attrition d'après le concile de Trente et d'apreès Saint Thomas d'Aquin*. Kain: Revue des Sciences Philosophiques et Théologiques, 1927.

Perler, Othmar. "L'évêque représentant du Christ selons les documents des premieres siècles." In *L'épiscopat et l'Église universelle*, 31–66. Paris: Éditions du Cerf, 1962.

Peter, Carl. "Renewal of Penance and the Problem of God." *Theological Studies* 30 (1969): 489–97.
———. "L'intégrité de la confession et le concile de Trente." *Concilium* 61 (1971): 91–100.
Peter Lombard. *Sententiae in IV Libros distinctae*. Rome: Collegii S. Bonaventura ad claras aquas, 1971.
Pétré, Hélène. "Les leçons du Panem nostrum quotidianum." *Recherches des sciences religieuses* 40 (1951–52): 63–79.
Peuchmaurd, Réginald. "La messe est-elle pour Luther une action de graces?" *Revue des sciences philosophiques et théologiques* 43 (1959): 632–42.
Philips, Gérard. "Perspectives mariologiques: Marie et l'Église." *Marianum* 15 (1953): 436–511.
———. "La femme dans l'Église." *Ephemerides Theologicae Lovanienses* 37 (1961): 71–93.
———. *L'Église et son Mystère au deuxième concile du Vatican. Histoire, texte et commentaire de la constitution "Lumen Gentium."* Paris: Desclée, 1968.
Pinto de Oliveira, Carlos Josaphat. "Signification sacerdotal du ministère de l'évêque dans la Tradition apostolique d'Hippolyte de Rome." *Freiburger Zeitschrift für Philosophie und Theologie* 25 (1978): 398–427.
Piolanti, Antonio. *Il mistero eucaristico*. Florence: Libreria editrice fiorentina, 1955.
Pius VI, Pope. *Auctorem fidei* (Condemnation of the Pseudo-Council of Pistoia). August 28, 1794.
Pius XII, Pope. *Mystici Corporis*. Encyclical Letter. June 29, 1943.
———. *Mediator Dei*. Encyclical Letter. November 2, 1947.
———. *Sacramentum Ordinis*. Apostolic Constitution. November 30, 1947.
———. "Allocution aux participants du premier congrès de pastorale liturgique" (1956). *AAS* 48 (1956): 711–72.
Pius a Langonio. *De bulla innocentiana seu de potestate papae committendi simplici presbytero subdiaconatus et diaconatus collationem Disquisitio historico theoogica*. Rome, 1902.
Plé, Albert. "Pour une mystique des mystères." *Vie Spiritualle, Supplément* (1952): 377–96.
Poschmann, Bernhard. *Pénitence et onction des maladies*. Paris: Éditions du Cerf, 1966.
Potel, Julien. *D'autres prêtres? Leur place et leurs rôles*. Paris: Centurion, 1977.
———. *Les prêtres séculiers en France. Evolution de 1965 à 1975*. Paris: Centurion, 1977.
Potterie, Ignace de La. "L'impeccabilité du chrétien d'après 1 Jn 3, 6–9." In *La vie selon l'Espirit, condition du chrétien*, edited by Ignace de La Potterie and Stanislaus Lyonnet, 197–216. Paris: Éditions du Cerf, 1965.
———. "Naître de l'eau et naître de l'Espirit, le texte baptismal de Jn 3, 5." In *La vie selon l'Espirit, condition du chrétien*, 31–64. Paris: Éditions du Cerf, 1965.
Pourrat, Pierre. *La theologie sacramentaire, étude de théologie positive*. Paris: Gabalda, 1907.
"Pouvons-nous nous passer de symboles?" *Concilium* 31 (1968).

Prat, Ferdinand. *Théologie de S. Paul*, vol. 2. Paris: Beauchesne, 1938.
Prudentius. *Hymne XII en l'honneur des Saints Innocents, Livre d'Heures*. Paris: Belles-Lettres, 1943.
Quasten, Johannes. *Monumenta eucharistica et liturgica vetustissima*. Florilegium patristicum, Fasc. 7. Bonnae: Hanstein, 1935.
———. *Initiation aux Pères de l'Église*, vols. 1–2. Translated by Jean Laporte. Paris: Éditions du Cerf, 1955–56.
Quinot, Bernard. "L'influence de l'épître aux Hébreux dans la notion augustinienne de vrai sacrifice." *Revue d'études augustiniennes* 8 (1962): 129–68.
Rahner, Hugo. *Mythes grecs et mystères chrétiens*. Translated by Henri Voirin. Paris: Payot, 1954.
———. *Marie et l'Église*. Translated by Bernard Petit and Jean-Pierre Gérard. Paris: Éditions du Cerf, 1955.
Rahner, Karl. "Die Kirche der Sünder." *Stimmen der Zeit* 140 (1947): 163–77.
———. "Martyrium." In *Lexikon für Theologie und Kirche*, edited by Josef Höfer and Karl Rahner, 7:136–38. Second edition. Freiburg im Breisgau: Herder, 1957.
———. "L'appartenance à l'Église d'après la doctrine de l'encyclique Mystici Corporis Christi." In *Ecrits théologiques*, 2:9–112. Paris: Desclée de Brouwer, 1960.
———. "Quelques réflexions sur les principes constitutionnels de l'Église." In *L'épiscopat et l'Église universelle*, 541–64. Paris: Éditions du Cerf, 1962.
———. "Essai sur le martyre." *Ecrits théologiques*, 3:184–203. Paris: Desclée de Brouwer, 1963.
———. *L'eucharistie et les hommes d'aujourd'hui*. Translated by Charles Muller. Paris: Mame, 1966.
———. "Le péché dans l'Église." In *L'Eglise de Vatican II*, 373–94. Paris: Éditions du Cerf, 1966.
———. *Die vielen Messen und das eine Opfer*. Questiones disputatae 31. Freiburg: Herder, 1966.
———. "Parole et Eucharistie." In *Ecrits théologiques*, 9:41–91. Paris: Desclée de Brouwer, 1968.
———. "La presence du Christ dans le sacrament de l'eucharistie." In *Ecrits théologiques*, 9:95–124. Paris: Desclée de Brouwer, 1968.
———. "Sur la durée de la presence du Christ dans celui qui vient de communier." In *Ecrits théologiques*, 9:127–37. Paris: Desclée de Brouwer, 1968.
———. "Vérités oubliées sur le sacrament de pénitence." In *Ecrits théologiques*, vol. 2. Paris: Desclée de Brouwer, 1969.
———. *Église et sacrements*. Translated by Henri Rochais. Paris: Desclée de Brouwer, 1971.
Ramos-Regidor, José. "La 'réconciliation' dans l'Église primitive. Suggestions pour la théologie et la pastorale actuelles." *Concilium* 61 (1971): 25–34.
Ratzinger, Joseph. "Les implications pastorals de la doctrine de la collégialité." *Concilium* 7 (1965): 33–56.
———. "L'eucharistie est-elle un sacrifice?" *Concilium* 24 (1967): 67–75.

Riga, Peter J. "Penance: A New Orientation." *American Ecclesiastical Review* 163 (1970): 407–15.

Ritzer, Korbinian. *Le mariage dans les Églises chrétiennes*. Paris: Éditions du Cerf, 1970.

Rivière, Jean. "La messe durant la période de la Réforme et du Concile de Trente." In *Dictionnaire de théologie catholique*, edited by Alfred Vacant et al., 10.1:1085–99. Paris: Letouzey et Ané, 1928.

Robert Pulleyn. *Sententiarum*. PL 186.

Robeyns, Anselme. "L'idée du sacerdoce des fidèles dans la tradition, le concile de Trente et la théologie moderne." *La participation active des fidèles au culte*. Louvain: Abbaye du Mont César, 1933.

Roche, Eugène. "Pénitence et conversion dans l'évangile et la vie chrétienne." *Nouvelle revue théologique* 79 (1957): 113–34.

Roguet, Aimon Marie. "Les célébrations communautaires de la penitence." *Vie Spirituelle* 116 (1967): 188–202.

———. "Le à-peu-près de la prédication eucharistique." *La Maison-Dieu* 11:178–90.

Rondet, Henri. *Introduction à l'étude de la théologie du mariage*. Paris: Lethielleux, 1960.

———. "Esquisse d'une histoire du sacrament de penitence." *Nouvelle revue théologique* 90 (1968): 561–84.

———. *Pourquoi se confesser. Le sacrament de penitence et le sacrament des maladies*. Paris: Beauchesne, 1971.

Roo, William A. van. "A Survey of Recent Literature and Determination of the State of Question." *Gregorianum* 35 (1954): 406–73.

———. *De sacramentis in genere*. Rome: Apud aedes Universitatis Gregoriana, 1960.

Rouiller, Grégoire, and Marie-Christine Varone. "Saint Jean." *Les échos de Saint Maurice* 8 (1978): 181–91.

Rousseau, Olivier. "La descente aux enfers fondement du baptême chrétien." *Recherches des sciences religieuses* 40 (1952): 273–97.

———. "La vraie valeur de l'épiscopat dans l'Église d'après d'importants documents de 1875." In *L'épiscopat et l'Église universelle*, 709–38. Paris: Éditions du Cerf, 1962.

———. "Divorce et remarriage. Orient et Occident." *Concilium* 24 (1967): 107–25.

Ruch, C. "La messe d'après la Sainte Ecriture." In *Dictionnaire de théologie catholique*, edited by Alfred Vacant et al., 10.1:785–863. Paris: Letouzey et Ané, 1928.

Sagne, Jean-Claude. *Tes péchés ont été pardonnés*. Paris: Chalet, 1977.

Salaville, Sévérien. "Epiclèse eucharistique." In *Dictionnaire de théologie catholique*, 5.1:194–300. Paris: Letouzey et Ané, 1913.

Salmanticenses. *Collegii Salmanticensis cursus theologicus*. Paris: Palmé, 1897.

Scheeben, Mattias Joseph. *Le mystère de l'Église et de ses sacraments*. Translated by Augusin Kerkvoorde. Paris: Éditions du Cerf, 1956.

Schenker, Adrian. *Das Abendmahl Jesu als Brennpunkt des Alten Testaments*. Fribourg: Verlag Schweizerisches Katholisches Bibelwerk, 1977.

Schillebeeckx, Edward. *De sacramentele heilseconomie*. Antwerpen: H. Nelissen, 1952.

———. *Le Christ, sacrament de la rencontre de Dieu*. Translated by Augustin Kerkvoorde. Paris: Éditions du Cerf, 1960.

———. *Le mariage est un sacrament*. Brussels: La Pensée Catholique, 1961.

———. "L'Église et l'humanité." *Concilium* 1 (1965): 57–78.

———. *Le mariage, réalité terrestre et mystère de salut*. Paris: Éditions du Cerf, 1966.

———. *Le presence du Christ dans l'eucharistie*. Translated by Martin Benzerath. Paris: Éditions du Cerf, 1970.

Schleck, Charles A. "St. Thomas on the Nature of Sacramental Grace." *The Thomist* 18 (1955): 1–30 and 242–78.

Schlier, Heinrich. *Le temps de l'Église*. Tournai: Casterman, 1961.

Schlink, Edmund. "Écriture, tradition et magistère dans la constitution Dei Verbum." In *Vatican II, la Révélation divine*, 499–511. Paris: Éditions du Cerf, 1968.

Schmitt, Joseph. *Jésus ressuscité dans la prédication apostolique. Étude de théologie biblique*. Paris: Gabalda, 1949.

Schnackenburg, Rudolf. *L'Église dans le Nouveau Testament Réalité et signification théologique; Nature et mystère de l'église*. Translated by Raphaël Louis Oechslin. Paris: Éditions du Cerf, 1964.

———. "Taufe." In *Bibeltheologisches Wörterbuch*, 1086–95.

Schoonenberg, Piet. "Dans quelle measure la doctrine de la transubstantiation a-t-elle été déterminée à Trente?" *Concilium* 24 (1967): 77–88.

Schönborn, Christoph. "Evangélisation, celebration, et sacrement." *Communio* 3 (1978): 28–39.

Schüller, Bruno, ed. *Péché, penitence et confession*. Paris: Mame, 1970.

Seckler, Max. *Le salut et l'histoire*. Paris: Éditions du Cerf, 1967.

Selvaggi, Filippo. "Il concetto di sostanza nel dogma eucaristico in relazione alla fisica moderna." *Gregorianum* 30 (1949): 7–45.

———. "Ancora intorno ai concetti di sostanza sensibile e realtà fisica." *Gregorianum* 38 (1957): 503–14.

———. "Realità fisica e sostanza sensibile nella dottrina eucaristica." *Gregorianum* 37 (1956): 16–33.

Semmelroth, Otto. *L'Église, sacrement de la redemption*. Translated by Germain Varin. Paris: St. Paul, 1963.

———. *Marie archétype de l'Église*. Translated by Robert Givord. Paris: Fleurus, 1965.

———. "Pour l'unité de la notion d'Église." *In Questions théologiques aujourd'hui*, vol. 2, translated by Y-Cl. Gélébar, 161ff. Paris: Desclée de Brouwer, 1965.

———. "L'Église, nouveau people de Dieu." In *L'Eglise de Vatican II*, 2:395–409. Paris: Éditions du Cerf, 1966.

Sheedy, Charles E. *The Eucharist Controversy of the 11th Century Against the Background of Pre-Scholastic Theology*. Washington, D.C.: The Catholic University of America Press, 1947.

Smit, G. C. "Epiclèse et théologie des sacrements." *Mélanges de science religieuse* 15 (1958): 95–136.

Smulders, Pieter. "L'Église sacrement de salut." In *L'Eglise de Vatican II*, 313–38. Paris: Éditions du Cerf, 1966.

Solano, Jésus. *Textus eucharisticos primitivos (up to Gregory the Great)*. Madrid: BAC, 1947 and 1954.

Spicq, Ceslas. *L'epître aux Hébreux*, vols. 1–2. Paris: Gabalda, 1952–53.

———. "Médiation dans le Nouveau Testament." *Dictionnaire de la Bible*, 5:1040–41.

———. *Théologie morale du Nouveau Testament*. Paris: Gabalda, 1965.

———. "La revelation de l'enfer dans la Sainte Écriture." In *La Théologie du renouveau*, edited by Guy-Marie Bertrand and Laurence K. Shook, 91–143. Paris: Éditions du Cerf, 1968.

Spinsanti, Sandro. "La visite de Dieu dans le pardon." *Communio* 4 (1971): 11–25.

Stenzel, Alois. *Il battesimo, genesi e evoluzione della liturgia battesimale*. Translated by Mariano da Alatri. Alba: Edizioni Paoline, 1962.

Taille, Maurice de La. *Mysterium fidei. De augustissimo Corporis et Sanguinis Christi sacrificio atque sacramento*. Paris: Beauchesne, 1921.

Teetaert, Amédée. *La confession aux laïcs dans l'Église latine depuis le VIIIe siècle jusqu'au XIVe siècle*. Paris: Gabalda, 1926.

Tertullian. *De corona*. CSEL 2.

———. *De exhortation castitatis*. CSEL 2.

———. *De oratione*. CSEL 1.

———. *De pudicitia*. CSEL 2.

———. *De resurrection carnis*. PL 2.

———. *Traité de la prescription contre les hérétiques*. Translated by François Refoulé and Pierre de Labriolle. SC 46. Paris: Éditions du Cerf, 1957.

———. *Traité du baptême*. Edited by François Refoulé. Translated by François Refoulé and Maurice Drouzy. SC 35. Paris: Éditions du Cerf, 1953.

Theodore of Mopsuestia. *Homélies catéchétiques*. Edited by Raymond Tonneau and Robert Devresse. Studi e Testi 145. Vatican City: Biblioteca Apostolica Vaticana, 1949.

Thils, Gustave. *Primauté pontificale et prérogative épiscopale. "Potestas ordinaria" au concile du Vatican*. Louvain: Warny, 1961.

———. "Ceux qui n'ont pas reçu l'Évangile." In *L'Eglise de Vatican II*, 669–79. Paris: Éditions du Cerf, 1966.

———. *L'Église et les Églises*. Paris: Desclée de Brouwer, 1967.

Thomas Aquinas. *Expositio et Lectura super Epistolas Pauli Apostoli*. Turin: Marietti, 1953.

———. *Lectura super Ioannem*. Turin: Marietti, 1952.

———. *Saint Thomas d'Aquin. Somme théologique, Le baptême et la confirmation*: 3a, Questions 66–72. Edited and translated by Pierre-Thomas Camelot. Paris: Desclee & Cie, 1956.

———. *Saint Thomas d'Aquin. Somme théologique, L'eucharistie: 3a, questions 79–83*, vols. 1–2. Edited and translated by Aimon-Marie Roguet. Paris: Éditions du Cerf, 1967.

———. *Saint Thomas d'Aquin. Somme théologique, L'extême-onction. Suppl. questions 29–33*. Translated by Henri-Dominique Gardeil. Paris: Éditions du Cerf, 1967.

———. *Sancti Thomae de Aquino opera omnia*, Leonine edition. Rome, 1882– . Vols. 5–12, *Summa theologiae*; vols. 13–15, *Summa Contra Gentiles*; vol. 23, *Quaestiones disputatae De Malo*; vol. 40, *De forma absolutionis*; vol. 41, *Contra retrahentes*; vol. 42, *De articulis fidei*.

———. *Scriptum super Sententiis*. Edited by Maria Fabianus Moos. Paris: Lethielleux, 1933 and 1947.

Thornton, Lionel Spencer. *Confirmation, Its Place in the Baptismal Mystery*. Westminster: Dacre, 1954.

Thurian, Max. *La confirmation, consecration des laïcs*. Neuchâtel: Delachaux et Niestlé, 1957.

———. *L'eucharistie*. Neuchâtel: Delachaux et Niestlé, 1963.

———. *Le pain unique*. Taize: Les Presses de Taize, 1967.

Tillard, Jean-Marie-Roger. "A propos de l'intention du minister et du sujet des sacrements." *Concilium* 31 (1968): 101–12.

———. "Compte-rendu du livre d'Antonius Van Bruggen Réflexions sur l'adoration eucharistique." *La Maison-Dieu* 100 (1969): 196–98.

Tomasso de Vio Cajetan. *De missae sacrificio*. In *Opuscula Omnia*, vol. 3, opusc. 9. Venice, 1594.

———. *Quaestiones de Contritione*. In Thomas Aquinas, *Opera Omnia*. Leonine Edition, 12:341–46. Rome: Ex Typographia Polyglotta, 1906.

Torrell, Jean-Pierre. *La théologie de l'épiscopat au premier concile du Vatican*. Paris: Éditions du Cerf, 1961.

La Tradition sacerdotale. Paris: Mappus, 1959.

Trembelas, Panagiotis N. *Dogmatique de l'Église orthodoxe catholique*, vols. 1–3. Paris: Desclée de Brouwer, 1967–68.

Tromp, Sebastian. *Corpus Christi quod est Ecclesia*. Rome: Aedes Universitatis Gregorianae, 1946.

Vanneste, Alfred. "La théologie de la penitence chez quelques maîtres parisiens de la première moitié du XIIIe siècle." *Ephemerides Theologicae Lovanienses* 28 (1952): 24–28.

———. "Doctrina eucharistica, cap. VI ev. S. Joannis." *Coll. Burg. Et Gand.* 1 (1955): 215–24.

Vatican Council I. *Pastor Aeternus*. July 18, 1870.

Vatican Council II. *Ad Gentes*. December 7, 1965.

———. *Gaudium et Spes*. December 7, 1965.

———. *Lumen Gentium*. November 21, 1964.

———. *Nostra Aetate*. October 28, 1965.

———. *Sacrosanctum Concilium*. December 4, 1963.

———. *Unitatis Redintegratio*. November 21, 1964.

Vatja, Vilmos. *La théologie du service religieux chez Martin Luther*. Göttingen: Vandenhoeck & Ruprecht, 1959.

Vaux, Roland de. *Les sacrifices de l'Ancien Testament*. Paris: Gabalda, 1964.

Villette, Louis. *Foi et sacrement*. Vols. 1–2. Paris: Bloud et Gay, 1959 and 1964.

Vogel, Cyrille. *La discipline pénitentielle en Gaule des origines à la fin du VIIe siècle*. Paris: Letouzey et Ané, 1952.

———. "La discipline pénitentielle dans l'Église orthodoxe de Grèce." *Revue des Sciences Religieuses* 27 (1953): 374–99.

———. *Le pécheur et la penitence au Moyen-Age. Textes traduits et présentés par Cyrille Vogel.* Paris: Éditions du Cerf, 1969.

Vonier, Anscar. *La clef de la doctrine eucharistique.* Translated by Aimon-Marie Roguet. Lyon: Éditions de l'Abeille, 1943.

Vorgrimmler, Herbert. "Mathieu 16, 18s. et le sacrement de penitence." In *L'homme devant Dieu, Mélanges offerts au P. H. de Lubac*, 1:51–61. Paris: Aubier, 1963.

Wagner, Albrecht. "Reformatorum saeculi XVII de necessitate baptismi doctrina." *Divus Thomas* (Piacenza) (1942): 5–34.

Walty, Jean-Nicolas. "Controverses au sujet du baptême des enfants." *Revue des sciences philosophiques et théologiques* 34 (1952): 52–70.

Watteville, Jean-François Noël de. *Le sacrifice dans les textes eucharistiques des quatre premiers siècles.* Neuchâtel: Delachaux et Niestlé, 1966.

Webb, Douglas. "La liturgie nestorienne des apôtres Addai et Mari." In *Eucharistie d'Orient et d'Occident*, vol. 2. Paris: Éditions du Cerf, 1970.

Wenger, Antoine. *Vatican II. Chronique de la deuxième session.* Paris: Centurion, 1964.

Willems, Boniface. "La nécessité de l'Église pour le salut, aperçu bibliographique." *Concilium* 1 (1965): 101–11.

Williams, George Hunston. *Anselm: Communion and Atonement.* St. Louis, Mo.: Concordia, 1960.

Wilmart, D. A. "Transfigurare." *Bulletin d'ancienne littérature et d'archéologie chrétiennes* (1911): 282–92.

Winzen, Damasus. *Die deutsche Thomas-Ausgabe. Die Sakramente, Taufe und Firmung.* Salzburg: Pustet, 1935.

Scripture Index

Genesis
  1:18–24, 723n5
  1:27–28, 722n3
  2:23, 38n71
  24, 724n6
  28:17, 47n106

Exodus, 420
  19:6, 638
  34:15, 371n60

Leviticus
  2:2–3, 367n45

Numbers
  5:15, 366n44

Deuteronomy
  8:3, 362n25
  22:22–39, 724n9

1 Samuel
  9:12, 371n60

2 Kings
  10:19, 371n60

Tobit 8, 724n7

Psalms
  51:17, 423n9
  80:9–17, 41n85

Proverbs
  2:17, 724n8
  9:4–6, 362n25

Sirach, 41
  24:17–20, 41n87

Isaiah
  5:1–7, 41n85
  15:1–8, 42
  7:2–5, 41n85
  54:6, 582n25
  62:1, 370, 370n56
  62:6–7, 370, 370n57

Jeremiah
  2:21, 41n85
  4:4, 241n18
  9:25, 241n18
  12:10–11, 41n85
  31:31–34, 358n14
  31:31, 364

Lamentations
  5:21, 247n5

Ezekiel, 47
  15:1–8, 41n85
  16, 582n24
  17:5–10, 41n85
  19:10–14, 41n85
  47:1–12, 47n109

Hosea
  10:1, 41n85
  14:2, 367n47

Malachi
  1:10–12, 375, 375n68

Matthew
  3:11–12, 244n28
  4:4, 362n25
  9:2, 618n6
  12:6, 46n104
  12:31, 551n3
  13:11, 143n9
  16:18, 52n118
  16:19, 552
  18:19, 552
  19:1–9, 741n12
  19:3–12, 722n4, 723n5
  20:15–28, 692n25
  21:33–46, 41n86
  26:26–30, 356
  27:39, 46n103
  28: 18–20, 303, 304
  28:18–20, 245n29
  28:19, 245n31
  28:20, 52n119, 303

Mark
  3:5, 618n6
  4:11, 8n7, 143n9
  6:13, 616n2, 618, 625n13

Mark (cont.)
  9:23, 279n15
  10:1–2, 741n12
  10:2–12, 722n4
  10:42–45, 692n25
  12:1–12, 41n86
  14:22–26, 356
  14:57, 46n102
  15:21, 355n2
  16:15–16, 303, 304
  16:16, 245n29, 303

Luke
  4:4, 362n25
  7:20, 618n6
  8:9, 143n9
  16:18, 741n12
  17:21, 15n28
  20:9–19, 41n86
  22:15–23, 356
  22:25, 692n27
  22:28–30, 370, 370n58
  23:24, 355n1

John, 360–363
  1:18, 8n10
  1:25, 243n25
  1:33, 244n27
  1:51, 47n105
  2:18–22, 46n101
  3, 142
  3:3–10, 242
  3:5, 42n89, 303, 304
  3:16, 753n1
  3:21, 84n51
  4:20–25, 46n100
  4:32–34, 362n25
  6, 372
  6:22–48, 361
  6:22–71, 361n23
  6:41, 363
  6:49–51, 382
  6:49–59, 361
  6:56, 42n90
  6:60–70, 361
  6:62, 362
  6:63, 361, 362
  7:37–38, 47n108
  7:39, 274n63
  10:11–16, 56n126
  10:36, 47n107
  11:51–52, 528n42
  13:12–13, 692n26
  14:26, 55n124
  15:1–17, 41n83
  15:4, 42
  17:11, 14n27
  17:14, 14n26
  20:23, 599n61

Acts, 239–240, 278
  1:5–22, 243n26
  2, 133
  2:18, 240n2
  2:38, 240n6
  2:41, 240n4, 278n8
  2:41–44, 142n6
  2:41–47, 240n9
  3–5, 9
  3:17–19, 240n3
  4:4, 240n4
  4:12, 240n7, 249n8, 756n7
  5:5–21, 657n61
  5:14, 240n9
  5:31, 240n3
  6:7, 240n9
  8:4, 240n4
  8:4–20, 323n3
  8:12, 240n4, 278n8
  8:16, 240n6
  8:33–37, 278n8
  8:36–40, 117n9
  9:31, 240n9
  10:38, 110n96
  10:43, 240n4
  10:44–48, 240n8, 283n22
  10:48, 240n6
  11:18, 240n2, 240n5
  11:21, 240n9
  11:24, 240n9
  13:40–48, 240n5
  16:14–15, 278n8
  16:30–33, 240n4
  16:32–33, 278n8
  17:30, 240n3
  18:8, 240n4
  19:1–7, 323n3
  19:5, 240n6
  19:6, 330
  20:17–36, 647, 647n39
  20:28, 59n133, 694n31
  22:16, 240n2

Romans
  1:1, 693n30
  1:9, 214n121
  5:5, 70n20, 747n16
  5:12–25, 255n31
  5:20, 755n4
  5:22–24, 241n16
  6, 142n4
  6:1–4, 193
  6:1–12, 33n61
  6:3, 241n15
  6:3–7, 240n11
  6:5, 155n44
  6:5–11, 14n15
  6:11, 204n112
  6:23, 257n35
  6:29, 241n19
  7:14–25, 250n13
  8, 241n13
  8:10–11, 254n23
  8:15, 65n8
  8:19–20, 467n28
  8:21, 467n28
  8:23, 254n26
  8:30, 444n58
  11:2–8, 131n35
  11:15, 131n36
  11:23, 131n37
  11:25, 143n9
  11:28, 270n57
  12:1, 424n10, 638n12
  12:2, 424n11
  12:4–5, 33
  15:16, 214n121b
  16:25–26, 143n9

1 Corinthians, 644
  1:9, 260n41
  2:7–10, 143n9
  3:17, 47n111
  6:15–18, 33n61
  7:10, 692n23
  7:12, 692n23
  7:17, 692n23
  10:14–21, 363n31
  10:14–22, 142n5
  10:16, 517n14

Scripture Index

10:16–17, 33n61, 363, 389n133
10:17, 525n34
11:17–33, 142n5
11:17–34, 356
11:23–32, 363n30
11:26, 368
11:27, 539n60
12–13, 241n14
12:3, 124n22
12:9, 625n13
12:12–27, 33
12:28, 69n16
14:36, 700n39
15:14, 253n19
15:17, 253n20
15:20–29, 40
15:28, 758n9
15:29, 254n27

2 Corinthians
5:17, 259n38
6:15–18, 29n52
6:16, 48n112
10:8, 692n23
11:2, 90n59

Galatians
2:20, 14n25
3:23, 309n14
3:26–27, 241n17
3:27, 240n11, 241n15
3:29, 130n34
4, 241n13
4:4, 756n6
5:6, 303n1

Ephesians 33, 39–40
1:9–10, 40n82
1:10, 9n15, 38n74
1:14, 758n8
1:22, 35n69
1:23, 33n59, 34n68, 40n80
2:4–6, 253n22
2:12, 602n66
2:22, 48n112
3:1–12, 45n98
3:3, 8n8
3:6, 9n14

3:9, 143n9
3:17, 461n17
3:19, 33n59
4:1–13, 40n81
4:4, 69n18
4:13, 33n59
4:16, 34n67, 36
4:30, 344n44, 587n34
5, 725
5:21–32, 101n89
5:21–33, 724n10
5:22, 90n62
5:22–32, 37n70
5:23, 34n64, 34n68
5:25–26, 17n32
5:25–28, 81n48
5:26, 142n7
5:27, 88
5:28, 38n72
5:30, 34n65

Philippians, 692
2:6–7, 692n24
3:2, 241n19

Colossians 33, 35, 38–39
1:15, 9n13
1:18, 35n69
1:18–24, 34n68
1:18–29, 754n3
1:19, 33n59, 38n76
1:25–27, 8n8
1:26, 143n9
2:2, 8n8
2:9, 33n59, 39n77
2:10, 38n74
2:11–12, 241n20
2:11–15, 39n78
2:12, 240n11, 253n21
2:19, 34n67, 36
3:1, 254n24
3:1–4, 242n23
3:3–4, 254n25
3:15, 34n66
4:3, 8n8

1 Thessalonians
1:9, 121n18

1 Timothy
2:4, 115n5
2:5, 636n2
4:14, 716, 716n55

Titus
3:5–7, 241n12, 242n23
3:9, 694n32

Hebrews
5:4, 695n33
6:4, 277
6:4–8, 551n3
7:23–26, 636n1
9:12, 434n34b
9:24–10:21, 656n60
10:10, 433n29
10:19, 218n128
10:19–22, 638n11
10:22, 278n8
10:26, 551n3
12:16–17, 551n3
12:24, 358n15

James
5:14–15, 616, 616n3

1 Peter, 318–319
1:20, 754n2
2:1–10, 638
2:4–6, 48
2:9–11, 29n52
3:18, 55n123

1 John
1:3, 260n41
1:8, 250n14
2:29, 242n24
2:29–3:9, 242
3:1–2, 260n42
3:2, 15n29
3:9, 242n24
5:16, 551n3

Revelation, 757
1:6, 638
2:11, 624n12
20:6, 638
20:6–14, 624n12
22:1, 47n109

Name/Subject Index

Abelard, Peter, 149, 568, 569, 570
absolution: efficacy of priest's actions, 607–9; formula of, 591–92; relation to confession, 593–94
accidents: and Christ's there-being in Eucharist, 494; distinguished from substance, 161, 485–92; and nonlocal presence, 495–96
Addai (apostle), 507
Adnès, Pierre, 719n1
African bishops (3rd century), 286
agápē, 48–49, 530, 692
Alain of Lille, 403
Albert the Great, Saint, 570, 686
Alexander III (pope), 400
Alexander of Hales, 570, 868
Alexander VIII (pope), 580n20, 681n3
Alexandrian Fathers, 349, 383–84, 391
Alfrink, Johannes, 353
Alger of Liège, 397, 399–400
Allmen, Jean Jacques von, 112n97, 128, 249n9, 291n44, 296, 298, 300, 320, 322n2, 342, 701
Allo, Bernard, 353, 364n33
Althaus, Paul, 290n38
Alzeghy, Z., 610
Ambrose, Saint, 89, 96, 144, 349, 381, 384–85, 386, 388, 389, 458, 477, 510, 541n67, 549, 554
Ambrosius Catharinus, 509
amor Dei (universal good), 10
amor sui (individual good), 10
Anciaux, Paul, 566, 569n3, 581n23
Andriessen, Paul, 38n73

Andrieux, Michel, 635, 671n82
Anglican Church, 642
annunciation, 132, 133–34, 330
anointing (confirmation), 148
anointing of the sick, 615–29; Council of Trent, 621–22; instituted by Christ, 622–23; during Middle Ages, 619–21; and preparation for death, 627–29; and sacramental grace, 625–27; theology of, 623–29
Anomoeanism, 286
"anonymous Christians," 116, 120–21
Antiochian Fathers, 349
antitype, 380, 387, 503–4
Apollinarians, 63
apostles: apostolic college, 665; apostolicity, 13–14, 56–57; apostolic succession, 642, 643–47, 649; bishops as, 645–46; priestly consecration, 647–48
Apostolic Constitutions, 379
Apostolic Tradition (Hippolytus), 377, 716
appropriation and reception of Holy Spirit, 271–72
Aquarians, 378
Arianism, 286
Aristotle, 36, 335, 473
Armbruster, C. J., 701
Arnauld, Antoine, 541
Athanasian Creed, 62–63
Athanasius, Saint, 287, 383
atheists, 119–21
Athenagoras, 375
attrition, 572–73, 576–77, 580, 607–8, 609, 614

791

Audet, Jean-Paul, 353, 355n5, 364–65, 374, 375–76, 539n61, 554n5, 675, 698n36
augmentum, 331, 333
Augustine, Saint, 41, 89n57, 108–9, 136–37, 152n41, 155n46, 203n109, 258n36, 276n2, 284n24, 285n28, 287n34, 310n15, 313n20, 381nn96–98, 507n26, 529n45; on baptism, 268; on Church's unity, 526; *De baptismo*, 114; on Eucharist, 381, 389–91, 392, 393, 426; on infant baptism, 291, 293; on Judas, 386–87; on Limbo, 315; on martyrdom, 312; on penance, 554–56; sacramental reception vs. spiritual reception, 541; on sacraments, 146–48, 211, 537; sacraments as signs, 153; on sacrifice, 423–24, 436–37; on salvation history, 306; soul and body, co-extensive character of, 69–70; on spiritual struggle, 257–58; sun metaphor for God's love, 584; truth/fruitfulness of sacraments, 19, 287

Baciocchi, Joseph de, 415, 456, 458, 476
Balthasar, Hans Urs von, 88n53, 93, 116n8
Bandinelli, Roland, 400
baptism: children dying without, 314–20; command to baptize, 244–45, 304–6; components of, 144; effects of, 246–75; of Ethiopian, 117; "feigning," problem of, 283–90; and filial adoption, 241; in first Christian community, 239–40; as gift of Holy Spirit, 269–75; as illumination, 277, 280; infant baptism, 290–302; intermediary reality of, 21; law of, 303–9; minister's role, 179; and new birth, 260–63; in New Testament, 240–43; origins of Christian baptism, 243–45; and persistence of sin, 551–56; received by Jesus, 244; and redemptive death of Christ, 249–50; remission of sins, 246–59; repetition of, 552–54; and resurrection, 253–55; rite of, 265–69, 320–21; and sacramental order, 543–44; as sacrament of faith, 276–83; salvation prior to, 306–9; salvation through, 142; substitutes for, 309–20; Trinitarian formula, 245; truth vs. fruitfulness, 287, 289–90
Bardy, Gustave, 127–28, 635, 644n33

Barré, Henri, 214n124
Barth, Karl, 53, 290, 290n39
Barthélemy, Jean-Dominique, 358n16
Basil of Caesarea, Saint, 278n9, 280n19, 287, 502, 503
Battifol, Pierre, 354, 374, 396n148
Baum, Gregory, 130n33
Bavaud, Georges, 92, 267n53, 284n24, 285–86
Beatific Vision, 77, 190, 317
Begley, J. J., 701
Bellarmine, Saint Robert, 25n47, 50–51, 63–64, 411, 660
belonging to the Church, 27, 71, 116–17, 121–31, 206, 208, 739
Benedict XV (pope), 417n199, 660
Benoît, André, 276, 290n39
Benoît, Jean-Daniel, 290n38
Benoît, Pierre, 33n60, 34n62, 38–39, 130n33, 319, 354, 355, 356, 359n17, 360, 363n32, 369, 372, 390n134, 413n186, 514n4, 538n55, 694n31
Béraudy, Roger, 623
Berengarian controversy, 19, 20, 43, 168–69, 396–400
Berenger of Tours, 350, 395, 401–2, 464
Bernard, Saint, 568
Bertrand, Guy-Marie, 603n68
Bérulle, Pierre de, 653–54, 714
Besnard, A. M., 610
Betz, Johannes, 193n99, 354, 374
Betz, Otto, 358n13
bibliography concerning the Church, 4
Billot, Louis, 175–76, 350, 411, 412n183, 414, 419n1, 445, 472n35, 482
Billuart, Charles-René, 411, 667
bishops: as apostles, 645–46; and Church's unity, 655–56; episcopal collegiality, 661–65; priest/bishop distinction, 666–80, 689–91
Bobichon, Marius, 28
Bobrinskoy, Boris, 322n2, 503
Bock, Colomban, 666n75, 667n77, 668, 669n80
Body of Christ: Christ as head, 35–37; Church as, 11, 33–46, 269, 527–28, 628; cosmic Christ, 40–42; local churches and universal Church, 128–29; "Mystical Body," 42–46; Pauline

Name/Subject Index 793

image, 11, 28, 33–35; *plérôma*, 38–40; spousal image, 37–38, 66, 93; transubstantiation, 385–91, 395–96, 409, 465–67, 473–84, 490
Boelens, Wilm Luurt, 371n59, 413n188, 462n19, 531
Boismard, Marie-Émile, 241n21, 354, 363–64, 675, 767n90
Bonaventure, Saint, 570, 660, 686
Boniface VIII (pope), 660
Boniface IX (pope), 669–70
Boros, Ladislaus, 320n38
Bossuet, Jacques-Bénigne, 61
Botte, Bernard, 325, 374, 377n80, 541n67, 593n44
Bouëssé, Humbert, 193n99, 635, 675
Bouillard, Henri, 263n48
Boureau, Daniel, 296n53
Bouyer, Louis, 4, 24, 28, 44n95, 55, 56n127, 73n28, 84n52, 90, 112n97, 135, 152n40, 205n113, 262n46, 311n18, 313n21, 322n2, 326–27, 329, 332, 340n38, 341, 351, 355, 356, 357–58, 364, 367n46, 369, 429, 499, 502n13, 508, 510, 522n26, 641, 644n30, 645n34, 646n38, 647–48, 677n93
Braeckmans, Louis, 566
Brand, Paul, 701
Braun, François-Marie, 239n1, 354, 362n27
bread and wine, symbolism of, 359, 372, 409, 429, 465, 527. *See also* Eucharist; Eucharistic presence of Christ; Eucharistic sacrifice; Eucharistic theology, development of
"bread of life," 143, 361, 388, 391, 407, 530
bride of Christ, Church as, 45. *See also* spousal image of Christ and Church
Bruggen, Antonius van, 520–21n23
Buchen, Alphonse van, 331n25

Cabasilas, Nicolas, 504, 509
Cadier, Jean, 406n168
Cajetan, Saint Thomas (Tomasso de Vio), 74, 152n40, 223–24, 229, 316–17, 419n1, 430, 441, 469n32, 472n35, 475n41, 483n59, 573n7, 578–79
Calvin, John, 147, 405, 406–7, 408, 409, 411–12, 461n18, 523–24, 525, 541–42, 638, 722

Camelot, Pierre-Thomas, 276, 326n12, 331n25, 333, 334n33, 339n37, 390n131, 391n136
Camus, Albert, 590
Cano, Melchior, 738
canonical power of the Church, 84, 86, 738
Caperan, Louis, 113n1
Capharnaites, 399
Capreolus, John, 223, 229
Carle, Paul-Laurent, 701
Cartesian duality, 412
Casel, Odo, 193–94, 195, 205, 414, 419n1, 437–38
Catholic Reformation, 111
causality: efficient, 200; instrumental, 189, 198–99; and sacramental order, 218–20; of sacraments, 173–77
"causing grace," 18, 273
Cavallera, Ferdinand, 143n8, 562n15, 566, 617
Celestial Hierarchies (Dionysius the Areopagite), 655
celibacy of priests, 698–700
Cerfaux, Lucien, 9n12, 33n60, 127n26, 239n1, 527, 641, 644n31
Cerularius (Patriarch of Constantinople), 107–8, 504
Chaillet, Pierre, 3, 51n117, 650n48
Champollion, Claire, 193n99
change, nature of, 472–74. *See also* transubstantiation
Chardon, Louis, 73n28, 74
charity, 744–46; at aid of conjugal love, 747–50; of Church, 123; and conversion of heart, 582–86; Eucharist as sacrament of, 536–45; and sacrament of marriage, 747; and true penance, 567–68
Charlier, Louis, 639n21
Charue, André Marie, 128
Chavannes, Henry, 406n168, 408n176
Chavasse, Antoine, 617
Cheffontaines, Christophe de, 509
"Christian paradox," 253–54, 262
Christians: as priestly people, 638–41; temporal engagement in world, 534–35

Christ Jesus: anointing of the sick, 622–23; baptism of, 244; Beatific Vision of, 190; Body of Christ, 527–28; Church's obedience, 58–60; confession, institution of, 562–63; cosmic conception of, 40–41; Divine Personality, 196; earthly life of, 262–63; efficacy of salvific acts, 200–202; Eucharist, presence in, 370–73; external activities of the Church, 83–87; foundation of Christianity, 213; founder/head of Church, 35–37, 54–56; humanity of, 72–73; hypostasis of His Mystical Body, 74; imagery of temple, 46–49; immanent activities of the Church, 81–83; intercession of, 433; as master and servant, 692–93; "mystery of Christ," 9; and New Law, 146–47; power of words in Eucharist, 507–8; priesthood of, 214–15, 652–53, 673; resurrection, and believers' baptism, 253–55; role in sacraments, 188–90; sacramentality of, 7–8; sacraments, and encounter with, 157–58; sacraments, institution of, 169–71; sacrifice of and remission of sins, 249–50; and sanctification, 171–72; as "Savior" and "salvation," 11; as shepherd, 30, 656, 689–90; sole priest of New Covenant, 635–36; spiritual presence in Eucharist, 455–56; spousal image of Christ and Church, 37–38, 45; structure of, and Church's structure, 62–73; therebeing in Eucharist, 492–97, 513, 519–20; twofold (soul and body) nature of, 63–71; ultra-terrestrial and ultrahistorical conditions, 465–68; union with the Church, 724–25; universal nature of sacrifice, 115–16. *See also* Eucharistic presence of Christ

Church: apostolicity of, 56–57; apostolic succession, 643–47, 649; authority in, 665; baptism as rite of initiation, 265–69; as Body of Christ, 11, 33–46, 527–28; as Bride of Christ, 93, 101–2; Christ, relationship to, 18; Christ as head, 35–37; Church's faith and Eucharist, 349–51; collegiality and papal primacy, 661–65; collegiality of pastoral power, 657–61; as communion, 598–99, 658, 694–95; as community of believers, 23; community unity and Eucharist, 530–34; definitions of, 9; discovery of sacramental character, 210–14; and dissident churches, 532; division within, 267–69; earthly finality of sacraments, 208–9; earthly life and eternal life, 206; Eucharist and action of Church, 439–40, 445–48; Eucharist and spiritual nourishment, 389–93; Eucharistic conversion, 382–89; Eucharistic tradition after Nicaea, 379–81; Eucharistic tradition before Nicaea, 374–79; external activities of, and Christ, 83–87; false things said concerning, 112; hierarchy, 694–95; history and eschatology, 46; immanent activities of, and Christ, 81–83; juridical activities, 84–86; local Churches, 127–29; membership and participation, 212–14; obedience to Christ, 58–60; personality of, 73–81; place in theological synthesis, 1–2; and priesthood, 635–41; rejection of, 116; role in sacrament of pardon, 559–61; sacramental activities, 18, 83–84, 233–35; sacrifice and Eucharist, 426–27; and social authority, 557; as society and institution, 49–53, 115; soul and body, co-extensive character of, 68–71; spousal image of Christ and Church, 37–38, 45; structure of, and Christ's structure, 62–73; "time of the Church," 205–6; twofold (soul and body) nature of, 63–71; union with Christ, 724–25; unity and bishops, 655–56; unity of, 79–80; universal mediation of, 113–40; visible and invisible elements, 43–44, 62, 64; women's roles in, 703–4

Church and salvation: belonging to the Church, 121–31; communities' membership in the Church, 127–31; hidden and unconscious belonging, 125–27; implicit adherence to Church, 117–21; Mary's mediating role, 131–40; no salvation outside of, 113–21, 127

Church of Africa, 268

circumcision, 243, 308–9

"circumcision of the heart," 241

Name/Subject Index

Cistercian Order, 666–67
Citeaux, abbey of, 667
city, image of, 29
clemency (mercy) vs. strictness, 556–59
Clement of Alexandria, 143, 375, 391
Clement of Rome, Saint, 57, 57n128, 644
Clement XI (pope), 604n70
Coathalem, Hervé, 131n38
Colombo, Carlo, 490
Colson, Jean, 641, 675
Columba (saint), 558
communion: and Body of Christ, 390; Calvin on, 407; Church and baptism, 266–67; Church as society and community, 22, 45, 49–53, 598, 658, 694; of Churches, 128; Church's personality, 80–81; Church's soul and the body, 64–68; *communio sanctorum*, 95–96; epiclesis, 507, 512; "first communion," 342–43; intercommunion, 530–36; priest and bishop, 672, 688, 710; sacramental vs. spiritual, 541; separation from, 708; Wycliff on, 404
community: baptism and community of believers, 311, 317, 338; Christians as "cultic community," 638; Church and sacramentality, 32; Church as, 23–24, 25, 49, 50–51, 100–102, 176, 233–34, 678–80; *communis natura entis*, 476, 477, 479; *esse commune*, 474–75; Eucharistic, 446–48, 459, 467, 513–14, 523; Israel as first Christian community, 130–31, 243; *perfectio essendi*, 475–76, 477; and sacrifice, 640; unification and Holy Orders, 662
Condren, Charles de, 651
confession, 562, 564–65; contrition-confession-satisfaction, 590–91; St. Thomas on, 571–72. *See also* penance, sacrament of, theological problems
confirmation, 322–45; baptized persons who aren't confirmed, 338–40; character bestowed by, 343–45; and Eucharist, 340–43; and Holy Spirit, 333–40; intermediary reality of, 21; in *Lumen Gentium*, 322; maturation and passage to adulthood, 335–37; tendency to minimize, 329–31; theological problems and solutions, 323–33
Congar, Yves, 3, 4, 24, 28, 31, 32n58, 46n99, 51n116, 53n120, 56n127, 73n28, 77, 83, 84n52, 88n53, 89n54, 95n78, 96, 99–100, 104, 113n1, 119, 122–23n20, 129n30, 141n1, 149n25, 267n53, 269n56, 329n18, 333n32, 407n171, 524n31, 549, 641, 645n36, 650, 658, 660n67, 663n72, 667n77, 668, 691–92, 693
conjugal bond, 735–43
consubstantiality, 41, 752, 756
contrition: attritionist/contritionist controversy, 580; Cajetan on, 578–79; contrition-confession-satisfaction, 590–91; efficacy of penence, 607–14; God as inspiration of, 568, 569–70; as interior act, 586–88, 599; perfect contrition, 596–97; St. Thomas on, 571–75
conversion: and baptism, 553; Christ's "there-being" in Eucharist, 470–72; Eucharist and transubstantiation, 384–86, 400–401, 444–45; grace of, and penance, 574, 581–600; of the heart, 601
Cools, Jos., 193n99
Coppens, Joseph, 4, 239n1, 323, 354, 456n5
Corecco, Eugenio, 733n19
cornerstone of temple, Christ as, 48
Corvez, Maurice, 291n44
cosmic conception of Christ, 40–41
Cothenet, Édouard, 549
Council of Chalcedon, 688–89
Council of Constance, 350, 404
Council of Ferrara-Florence, 394
Council of Florence, 150, 403, 501, 615, 632, 681
Council of Jerusalem, 657
Council of Sens, 568
Council of Trent, 29, 150, 169, 211, 350, 400, 409–18, 450, 477, 482, 501–2, 524n32, 562, 563, 592–93, 603, 611, 632, 655n57, 667, 681nn1–2, 732n18; anointing of the sick, 615–16, 621–22; on created grace, 172; on Holy Orders and sacramental character, 656, 681, 682; on marriage, 732; and sacrament of penance, 579–80
Counter-Reformation theology, 411

Couturier, Charles, 143n8, 146n18, 147, 148n24, 387n120
Creedal statements of faith, 347–48, 751
Crouzel, Henri, 719n1, 741n11
Cullmann, Oscar, 15, 54n122, 128, 205n114, 239n1, 249n9, 255n30, 278, 290–91, 359–60, 362n27, 363n29
cultic acts, 194–95, 638; priest's role, 673, 675, 677, 682; sacrifices, 419–20, 525
Cyprian, Saint, 3, 113–14, 210–11, 268, 285–87, 294n51, 312–13, 378–79, 657, 659, 675
Cyril of Alexandria, Saint, 277n6, 384
Cyril of Jerusalem, Saint, 144, 277n5, 279, 280n16, 280n18, 349n5, 379–80, 383, 387, 514, 520n22, 521, 539n62

Dabin, Paul, 639n16, 651n49
Dalmais, Irénée-Henri, 263n47
Daly, Mary, 701
Daniélou, Jean, 193n99, 322n2, 323
Darlap, Adolf, 453n1
death: preparation for, 617–18, 622, 627–29; victory over through Baptism, 253–55. *See also* anointing of the sick
De baptismo (Augustine), 114
De captivitate babylonica (Luther), 681–82
de-Christianization, 114
De corpore et sanguine Domini (Paschasius Radbertus), 395
Decree for the Armenians, 615, 632, 681
Decree on the Sacrament of Orders, 632
Decretum de Sacramentis, 150
Decretum pro Armenis (Council of Florence), 150
Deferrari, Roy J., 566
Dejaifve, Gustave, 4, 128
Dekkers, Eligius, 194
De la fréquente communion (Arnauld), 541
Delhaye, Philippe, 701
"delocalization," 495–96
Deloupy, Jean-Paul, 635
Deluz, Gaston, 156n48, 193n99
De Montcheuil, Yves, 414, 415n193
De mysteriis (Ambrose), 144, 385, 389
Denis, Albert-Marie, 675
Denis, Henri, 152n40
Denzinger, Heinrich Joseph Dominicus, 88
De pudicitia (Tertullian), 552

D'Ercola, G., 566, 661
De Sacramentis (Ambrose), 386
Descartes, René, 412
Deschamps, Philippe, 540
de Vaux, Roland, 366n42, 419n1, 420
De veritate (Thomas Aquinas), 179
devotion, 443, 447–48, 628
diaconia, 691
Didache, 374–75, 390, 526, 527–28, 554
Didier, Jean-Charles, 193n99, 291, 394n146, 396n150, 419n1, 514n5, 617
Diekamp, Franz, 667
Dillenschneider, Clément, 635, 636n1, 639n16
Dionysius the Areopagite, 655
dissident Churches, 532
Divine Life, 64–68, 171–72, 260–61, 263–64, 295
Divine Omnipotence, 400, 458, 478
divinization, 263–65, 294
divorce, possibility, 739, 741, 742–43
Dix, Gregory, 326–28, 329–30, 364
Docetism, 349, 386
Dombes Group (1972), 413, 506n25, 642
Donatism, 145, 210–11
Dondaine, Hyacinthe François, 151n36, 566, 575n11, 577n13
Doronzo, Emmanuel, 419n1, 485n61, 499
Dostoyevsky, Fyodor, 590
Druthmar of Aquitaine, 396
duality (soul and body), 63–64
Dubarle, André-Marie, 38n73
Duby, Georges, 737n7
Duliscouët, D., 550
Dumont, Christophe-Jean, 38n73
Dupont, Jacques, 28, 354, 359n17
Dupuy, Michel, 639n18, 651n49, 653n54
Duquoc, Christian, 566
Durwell, François-Xavier, 416n197, 465, 468n29
Duval, André, 617, 675
Dyer, George, 316n28

Eastern churches: on apostolic succession, 642; Holy Chrismation, 323, 670; indissolubility, principle of, 741; marriage, sacrament of, 731, 738; married men as priests, 699; patriarchates, 657; Patristic tradition, 393–94; and

Name/Subject Index 797

reciprocal communion, 533–34; on transubstantiation, 502–5, 511, 512; and unity, 659
Eastern Fathers, 287
ecclesiology in theological synthesis, 1
ecumenicism, 126–27, 129–30, 321, 462
Ekklesiologie im Werden (Koster), 29–30
Eliade, Mircea, 336n36
Émery, Pierre-Yves, 267n53, 419n1
epiclesis, 394, 499, 501–4, 506–7, 509–12
Eppacher, Anton, 566
eschatological nature of Church, 14–15
Étienne of Tournai, 403
Eucharist, 347–52; Catholic doctrine, 510–12; charity, sacrament of, 536–45; Christ's presence in, 370–73; Christ's there-being, 492–97, 519–20; Church as separate from, 43; and confirmation, 340–43; and consecration, 163, 164; consecration and minister's role, 179–81; Council of Trent on, 169–70; epicletic character of, 506–7; episcopacy/presbyterate distinction, 671–72; eschatological meaning of, 368–70; as essence of worship, 217–18; Eucharistic community, 677–79; and faith, 522–24; instituted by Christ, 170–71; invisible sacrament, 518–21; manducation, 163, 409, 460–61, 472, 517–18; miraculous nature of, 187–88; *mysterium fidei* (mystery of faith), 347–51; as nourishment, physical/spiritual, 362–63, 389–93; "presence" and there-being, 453–61; as sacrament, 448–49, 514–24, 525–36; sacrificial character of, 448–49, 524–25, 528–29; sacrificial efficacy of, 441–48; salvation through, 142; signification, ultimate, 521–22; and sin, 538–40; substance of, 486–95; theology of, 351–52; unity of the sacrament, 517–18; vine and branches imagery, 42; and Word, 523–24
Eucharist, Church's beliefs regarding: after Nicaea, 379–81; Church's celebration of, 373; Eucharistic conversion, 382–89; Gospel of John, 360–63; Jesus' command to repeat His actions, 359–60; Last Supper, 354–73; memorial function, 364–68, 370; before Nicaea, 374–79; Paul's doctrine, 363–64; scriptural narratives of Last Supper, 356–64; spiritual nourishment, 389–93
Eucharistic presence of Christ: overview, 451–52; transignification and transfinalization, 453–61; transubstantiation, change undergone, 472–81; transubstantiation, Christ's there-being, 481–97; transubstantiation, necessity of, 461–72
Eucharistic sacrifice: believer's participation, 427–28; Church's sacrifice, 426–27; Eucharist as sacrifice-meal, 429; heavenly sacrifice, 433–35; identity of with Calvary, 425–26; memorial of the Passion, 436–49; overview, 419–25, 449–50; reiteration of sacrifice of Calvary, 430–32; and substitution, 421
Eucharistic theology, development of: dogmatic definitions, 401–3; Eucharistic controversies, 394–400; Patristic tradition, 393–94; Protestant theologians, 412–13; and reformers, 403–9; transubstantiation, 400–401; Trent, aftermath, 411–18; Trent, decrees of, 409–11
evangelical orientation of Church, 57, 553
evil: mystery of, 256–59; and sin, 604–5
Evrard, Jean, 28
excommunication, 108–9
ex opere operato formula, 203–4
Exposcit (Innocent VIII), 666–67
extra ecclesiam non est salus, 113–14, 121
extreme unction, 148, 616, 620–22

faith: of atheists, 119–21; baptism as sacrament of, 276–83; and Church membership, 125; and Eucharist, 522–24; implicit, 117–18; lack of true, 284–87; of non-Catholic Christians, 118; of non-Christians, 118–119; sacraments as signs of, 142, 156–57
The Fall (Camus), 590
faults: personal vs. collective, 99–100; personal vs. historical, 104, 105–7
Faustus of Riez, 331
fear, as motivation for repentance, 603–4
Feeny, Leonard, 114

Name/Subject Index

Feuillet, André, 9n12, 41, 115n7, 193n99, 354, 361–62, 549, 635, 637n10, 641, 648
Fidei Donum (Pius XII), 660
fidelity in marriage, 741
Filthaut, Theodor, 193n99
Fink, Karl August, 668n78
First Council of Constantinople, 286
First Vatican Council, 659, 660, 662
Fitzsimons, John, 566
Florand, François, 73n28, 74n29
Florus of Lyons, 396
forensic justification, 250–51
Foreville, Raymonde, 149, 403
foundation of temple, Christ as, 48
Fourth Lateran Council, 402n159
French School of spirituality, 434, 653
Funk, F., 550

Gaillard, Jean, 193n99, 196n102
Galileo, 107–8
Galot, Jean, 214n123, 419n1
Galtier, Paul, 550, 581n23
Gardeil, Henri-Dominique, 617
Garrigou-Lagrange, Reginald, 419n1
Garrigues, Jean-Miguel, 641, 645n36
Gaudel, August-Joseph, 419n1
Gaudium et Spes, 212
Gaullier, Bertrand, 315n26
Geremia, Francesco, 28
Gerentes ad vos (Martin V), 668
Gerlaud, Marie-Joseph, 669n80
Ghellinck, Joseph de, 143n8
gifts, supernatural, 70
gnostic theories, 38–39
God: Divine Omnipotence, 185–86, 188, 189–90, 191; divine pardon for sin, 255–56, 259; Divine Will and sacramental order, 305–6; God's Covenant and marriage, 724–25; pardon and remission of sins, 246–49; revelation of through sacrament, 5–6
Gonet, Jean-Baptiste, 667
good: individual *(amor sui)*, 10; universal *(amor Dei)*, 10
Goossens, Werner, 354
Gospel, 693; Divine Power for salvation, 154
Gouillard, Jean, 505n21
grace: and absolution, 608; and anointing of the sick, 625–27; of being a priest, 715–17; "causing grace," 18, 273; and character, 220–22; and Christ's passion, 443–44; conversion and penance, 574, 581–600; created grace, 67–68, 122, 172; and divinization, 263–65; and God's paternal love, 65–66; grace-being, 78–79; as immanent activity of the Church, 82–83; mystery of, 138; Protestant views of, 442; redemptive, and baptism, 280–83; and remission of sin, 601–2; reviviscence of baptismal grace, 289–90; sacramental contrasted with common, 710–17; sacramental grace, 192–93, 222–33; sacramental grace, universality of, 230–33; sacramental grace of Eucharist, 536–38; sacramental grace of Holy Orders, 705–9; sinner's preparation for, 602–7
Grass, Hans, 405n164
Gregorian reform, 111, 659–60, 693
Gregory of Nazianzus/Nazianzen, Saint, 144, 380
Gregory of Nyssa, Saint, 277, 349, 383
Gregory VII (pope), 350n7, 402n158
Grelot, Pierre, 29n51, 30n56, 550, 638n13, 641, 643n29, 644n31, 648nn42–43, 687n11, 688n15, 698–99n36, 699n38, 702, 703n45, 719n1
Gross, Jules, 263n47, 384n107
Group de Dombes, 413, 506n25, 642
Guillet, Jacques, 399n152
Guillou, Marie-Joseph Le, 413n186, 641, 645n36, 675
Guitmond of Aversa, 397, 398, 401n154
Gutwenger, Engelbert, 409n180
Guysens, D. G., 409n180
Gy, Pierre-Marie, 719n1

Hajjar, Joseph, 128
Hamer, Jérôme, 42n91, 51n116, 124n23, 268n53
Hamman, Adalbert, 239n1, 243, 276, 323n6, 330, 332–33, 354
Hänggi, Anton, 349n2, 373, 379n89, 386n116, 502n13
Häring, Hermann, 4
Hauret, Charles, 366n42
Haymon of Halberstadt, 396

Name/Subject Index

healing, bodily and spiritual, 624–25
Henry, A. M., 413n186
heresy/heretics, 124–25, 531–32
Héris, Vincent, 316n30
Hermas, 550
Hervé, Jean-Marie, 667
hierarchical priesthood, 650–53
Hilary of Poitiers, Saint, 384
Hippolytus of Rome, Saint, 291, 311n18, 324n7, 377, 619, 672, 706n50, 716
Hocédez, Eddgara, 419n1, 669n80
Höfer, Josef, 239n1, 311n18
holiness: objective vs. personal, 97–98; present holiness vs. holiness in the making, 101–2
Holiness of the Church, 88; as cause of holiness, 95; fair judgment of, 110–11; and faults committed by, 107–9; as mystery, 95; objective holiness, 103–4; objective holiness vs. holiness of members, 95–96; personal holiness, 104; problem of sin, data of, 97–102; problem of sin, suggestions for solution, 103–12; and problem of sin, 88–90; and purification, 111–12; solutions proposed to problem of sin, 90–96; as subject of holiness, 94
Holy Order, sacrament of, 631–33, 651–52, 655–60; grace of holy orders, 705–17; intermediary reality of, 21; priestly character, 681–83; priestly power, 683–91; priestly service, 691–95; priestly vocation, 695–704. *See also* priesthood
Holy Spirit: baptism vs. confirmation, 324–25, 326–29; and confirmation, 333–40; extrinsic personality of the Church, 75–78; and gathering of People of God, 32; gifts of and Baptism, 269–75; gifts of and confirmation, 330; God's grace as, 264; hypostasis of the Church, 74; indwelling, after Pentecost, 47–48; as love, 269–70; Pentecost, 17; as personified Divine Life, 66; role in sanctification, 507; as soul of the Church, 66–67
Homilies on the Mass, 380
homoousios, 401
Houssiau, Albert, 268n53
Huftier, M., 390, 390n131, 610

Hugh of Saint-Cher, 570
Hugh of St. Victor, 141, 148, 149, 151, 568–69
Huguccio (Hugh of Pisa), 403
Hulsbosch, A., 243, 245n30
Humbert (pope), 107–8
Humbert of Silva Candida, 401–2
Hurley, M., 290n39
Huss, John, 404
hylomorphism, 150, 158–62, 499–500, 589
Hypostatic Union, 56, 62–63, 72, 229, 653–54

Ignatius of Antioch, Saint, 127, 349, 374, 376, 382, 526, 531
illumination, baptism as, 277, 280
images: Christ as image of the Father, 8; sacraments as, 6
Immaculate Conception, 132
immolation, 421–22; of Christ, 431–32, 433–34, 440, 441; immolationist theories, 414
imperium, 184, 185, 186, 187–88, 189–90
Incarnation: Church as continuation of, 61; Church's prolongation of, 73; and God's free initiative, 56; and salvation, 7; universal and historical event, 12
indissolubility, principle of, 741–43
infant baptism, 290–302
Innocent III (pope), 150, 203, 403
Innocent VIII (pope), 666–67
Innocent XI (pope), 581n22
Inquisition, 105
instrumental causality, 177, 178
intention: of ministers, 163–67, 181–85; real-intentional causality, 175–77
intercommunion, problem of, 530–34
Interdonnato, F., 610
"invisible sacrament" in Eucharist, 518–21
Irenaeus of Lyon, Saint, 69, 349, 377, 426, 644, 687
Isidore of Seville, Saint, 148
Islam, 118
Israel: as chosen by God, 30–31; and the Church, 130–31; God's Covenant with, 724; Mary as spiritual personification of, 133–34; Passover meal, 429

Jacob's Ladder, 47
Jacquemont, Patrick, 535n51

Jaki, Stanley, 4
James, Saint: and anointing of the sick, 617–18; on baptism, 242
Jansenism, 315–16, 580, 612
Jatosz, Thomas Jude, 566
Javierre, Antonio M., 641
Jean-Nesmy, Claude, 610
Jedin, Hubert, 566
Jeremias, Joachim, 239n1, 243, 253n18, 254, 259–60n39, 290–91, 354, 355, 357, 360, 365, 369
Jerome, Saint, 287
Jerome of Souchère, 667
Jesus. *See* Christ Jesus
John, Saint: on baptism, 242; on sin, 250; vine and branches imagery, 41–42
John Chrysostom, Saint, 143–44, 278n10, 280, 380, 384, 502, 510, 514
John Damascene, Saint, 394, 503–4
John of St. Thomas, 152n40, 152n42, 224, 229, 411n181, 482
John Scotus Eriugena, 395
John the Baptist, 243, 245
Jonas of Bobbio, 558n9
Jong, Johannes Petrus de, 499, 514nn5–6
Jossua, Jean-Pierre, 550
Journet, Charles, 4, 14, 21n38, 24, 32n58, 51n115, 56n127, 61, 67, 68n15, 75, 77, 83, 84n52, 88n53, 92n68, 96, 99–100, 104, 108, 109, 122, 124n23, 125, 126n24, 130n32, 198, 315n25, 374–75, 376n77, 419n1, 427, 456n5, 468–69, 508, 531–32, 607n73, 663
Juan de Torquemada, 92
Judaism, 118; of Jesus' era, 702; Jewish antecedents to Last Supper, 354–56; Old vs. New Law, 307; priestly roles, 676; rites of purification, 243. *See also* Israel
Jüngmann, Josef Andreas, 374, 419n1, 499, 507n27, 517n16
Justin Martyr, Saint, 277, 374, 375n66, 508

Kaelin, Jean de la Croix, 413n187
katangellein, 368
Kelly, John Norman Davidson, 349n6, 386
"keys, power of," 552, 562, 568, 569, 574, 591, 593
King, Ronald F., 19n36, 150n32

kingdom, and People of God, 29
Korn, Ernest, 58n130
Koster, Mannes Dominikus, 29–30
Küng, Hans, 4, 28, 54, 60, 84n52, 90n58, 94n72, 127, 130n33, 251n15, 641, 653–54, 691, 737

Labourdette, Michel, 314n23, 719n1
Lagrange, Marie-Joseph, 41, 354, 362n27
Lambert, Bernard, 701
Lampe, Geoffrey, 329–30
Lanfranc, 396–97, 398n151, 399, 400
Langton, Steven, 403
language: hylomorphic, 159; and sacramental signification, 160; signs as, 153–54
Laporta, Jorge, 457
Larrabe, José Luis, 566
Larranaga, Victoriano, 354
Last Supper, 354–73
Laurent, B., 617
Laurentin, René, 132n41, 134n46, 703n45
Law, Old vs. New, 146–47, 171–92, 307, 451, 741
Le Bras, Gabriel, 719n1, 736, 738
Leclerc, Jean, 675
Lecordier, Gaston, 387n120
Lécuyer, Joseph, 322n2, 639n16, 661, 675
Leeming, Bernard, 152n40
Leenhardt, Franz "Francis," 291, 304n4, 354, 413, 419n1
Le Guillou, Marie-Joseph, 675
Leo, Saint, 561
Léon-Dufour, Xavier, 354, 358n16, 361
Leo XIII (pope), 61n1, 72n25, 660, 667
Lepin, Maurius, 405n164, 412n184, 419n1, 427, 430, 431n25, 432, 433, 435
Leroy, Marie-Vincent, 4
Lessius, Leonard, 667
"Letter of Miltiades," 331–33
L'Huillier, Pierre, 741n11
Liégé, Pierre-André, 296n53
life: Divine Life, 64–68; *motus ab intrinseco*, 65; transmission of, in marriage, 728–29
Ligier, Louis, 550, 687n13
Lilienfeld, André de, 38n73
Limbo, 315–17
local churches, 127–29

Name/Subject Index

Lombard, Peter, 19, 141, 148–49, 151, 331, 561, 569n4, 570, 620
Lombardi, Riccardo, 113n1, 119
Long-Hasselmens, Abbé, 650–51
Lossky, Vladimir, 61, 132, 133n43, 133n45, 134n49
love: conjugal, 744–46; and gifts of Holy Spirit, 269–71; God's gift of, 581–82, 605–7; mutual love in marriage, 729–30; parental, 746; penitential, 261–62; self-gift in marriage, 727
Lubac, Henri de, 3, 42–43, 47n110, 155n45, 205n113, 389n130, 390, 393n144, 396n149, 433, 438n48, 453n2, 457, 457n7, 646n37, 661, 701, 704, 705n48, 717n56; on Eucharist, 416, 427–28, 430
Lumen Gentium (Vatican II), 2–3, 10nn17–19, 16n30, 97n83, 114n4, 119n14, 132, 136n54, 139, 632n6, 639n20, 655n57, 656n59, 674n86, 675–76; Church as "People of God," 28–32; on confirmation, 322; res tantum of Church-sacrament, 22
Luneau, Auguste, 28, 306n7
Lunen-Chenu, Marie-Thérèse, 701
Luther, Martin, 53, 250–51, 406, 603, 620, 638; on Eucharist, 430; on priestly character, 681–82
Lyonnet, Stanislaus, 550

Magisterial power of the Church, 84–86
Malevez, Léopold, 205n113
manducation, 163, 409, 460–61, 472, 517–18
Mansi, Giovanni Domenico, 43n94
Marchal, L., 635
Marcion of Sinope, 386
Mari (apostle), 507
Mariology, 131–32. See also Mary
Maritain, Jacques, 4, 73n28, 75–77, 79, 99, 120, 438n48
Marliangeas, B. D., 550
marriage, 719–20; fidelity, 741; indissolubility, principle of, 741–43; matrimonial contract, 730; mixed marriages, 736–37, 738; monogamy, 740–41; religious vs. civil, 737–40; and sacramental order, 543; and sexual union, 725–30

marriage, sacrament of, 632, 721–33; and God's Covenant, 724–25; sacred character of, 721–24
marriage, sacrament of, effects of: *res et sacramentum*, 734–43; *res tantum*, 744–50
Marsili, Salvatore, 448n63
Martelet, G., 465n23, 476, 480
Martimort, Aimé Georges, 333, 333n31, 334n33, 377, 377n79
Martin V (pope), 668
martyrdom, 311–13, 376–77
Mary: annunciation, 133–34; Mariology, 131–32; member of the Church, 132–33; Mother of the Church, 139–40; spiritual maternity of, 135–39; spiritual personification of Israel, 133–34; Type or Icon of the Church, 133–35
Masi, R., 193n99, 490n66
Masterson, Robert Reginald, 222n134
Masure, Eugène, 152n40, 419n1, 432
Matthew, Saint, 245
Matthew of Aquasparta, 660
Maximum Illud (Benedict XV), 660
McClendon, James William, 290n39
McCue, J., 566
McSorley, Harry, 566
Mediator Dei (Pius XII), 632
Melanchthon, Philip, 406
memorials: Eucharist as, 364–68, 370; memorial and sacrifice, 366–68, 406, 429; memorial nature of redemptive death, 364–66; memorial of the Passion, 436–49, 461; theological meanings, 436–37
mercy vs. strictness, 556–59
Mersch, Émil, 29n53, 33n60, 384n109
metanoia (penitence), 247
Meyendorff, John, 499, 506n24, 531
Meyer, Charles, 566
Michel, Albert, 142n5, 170n70, 203n110, 419n1, 667
Minerd, Matthew, 485n61
ministers: efficacy of, 185–88; intention, 182–85; role in sacraments, 177–82; of sacraments, 166, 167–68
miracles, 186, 684–85
missionary activities, 31, 106, 300, 302, 320, 330, 675, 677

mixed marriages, 736–37, 738
Möhler, Johann Adam, 3, 4, 51, 61, 650–51
Mohrmann, Christine, 143n8, 144
Moingt, Joseph, 291n44, 531
Mollat, Donatien, 354
Möller, Johann Adam, 38n73
monogamy in marriage, 740–41
Montanism, 268, 638
Montcheuil, Yves de, 454
Montclos, Jean de, 306n150
moral causality, 174–75
Morin, Jean, 667
Mosaic law, 273, 275, 307–8
Mühlen, Heribert, 64n3, 73n28, 74
Müller, Alois, 131n38
musterion, 5, 16
mysteric presence of sacraments, 193–95, 202
mysterion, 143, 202; to *sacramentum*, 144–45
Mysterium Fidei (Paul VI), 417
Mysterium Salutis (Congar), 24
mystery of Christ, 7–8, 44; contrasted with mystery of Church, 61–62, 462–65. See also Mystical Body of Christ
mystery of the Church, 97
Mystical Body of Christ: and Church's role, 3, 11, 14; in Eucharist, 381; origin/value of expression, 42–46; power of, 687–91; sinners' participation in, 123
mystical spirituality vs. mysterical spirituality, 205
Mystici Corporis (Pius XII), 42, 52, 71, 97, 114, 126, 660

Natalis, Hervaeus, 660
Nestorian liturgy, 507
Neunheuser, Burkhard, 239n1, 322n2, 323, 394n145, 401n155, 405n164, 427n15
New Covenant, 30–31, 56, 357–59, 363–64, 632; Christ as sole priest, 635–36
New Law: and Christ, 307, 741; and efficacy of sacraments, 171–92; sacraments, 146–47
New Testament, 142; on baptism, 240–43
New World, discovery of, 114
Nicaea, Council of, 286
Nicholas II (pope), 402n157
Nicolas, Jean-Hervé, 25n46, 64n4, 66n10, 68n14, 71n24, 73n28, 74n29, 85n52, 113n1, 120n17, 122n19, 133n44, 135n51, 137n58, 155n45, 173n73, 175n75, 175n77, 205n113, 222n134, 233n140, 245n1, 247n3, 248n7, 259n37, 271n60, 281n20, 314n24, 438n47, 453n1, 456n5, 459n14, 475n42, 506n22, 531, 583n27, 585n30, 604n71, 605n72, 613n77, 635, 637n9, 654n56, 699n36, 728n11, 743n14, 755n5
Nicolas, Marie-Joseph, 42–43n93, 51n117, 132n39, 138n59, 685n7
Nolte, Josef, 4
Nostra Aetate (Vatican II), 119n11

obedience: Church's to Christ, 38, 58–60; grace of, 711
oblation, Christ's, 431–32, 433–34, 438–39
occasional causality, 173–74
Ockham, William of, 403–4
O'Connor, Jerome Murphy, 550
Oechslin, R.-L., 610
Oecolampadius, Johannes, 406
oikonomia (mercy), 741
oil, anointing with, 615–16, 619. See also anointing of the sick
Old Law, 451
Onate, J. A., 354, 361
Onatibia, Ignacio, 193n99
O'Neill, Colman E., 152n40, 193n99, 419n1, 445n62, 623
Optatus of Milevis, 145, 268, 287, 288, 289n36
order, subjective vs. objective, 164–65
Origen of Alexandria, 143, 291, 382, 391–92, 519
Orthodox Church, 24, 343. See also Eastern Churches
Oswald, Johann H., 3

Page, Jean-Guy, 4
Pahl, Irmgard, 349n2, 373, 379n89, 386n116, 502n13
papal primacy, 661–65
pardon: Church's vs. God's, 610; divine, fullness of, 255; divine, internal character of, 559–61; and penance, 567–68; remission of sins and baptism, 246–49
Parousia, 134, 306, 465–66, 644
Paschal day, 242

Name/Subject Index 803

Paschasius Radbertus, 395–96, 397
Passover and Last Supper, 354–56, 429
Patristics, 193–94, 393–94
Patton, Hugh, 566
Paul, Saint, 644; on baptism, 16–17, 240–41, 303; on Body of Christ, 33–34; Christ as head of Church, 35–36; Christ as temple, metaphor, 46; Church as bride of Christ, 101–2; on equality, 702, 704; Eucharistic doctrine, 363–64, 390; on grace, 263; letters and "mystery of Christ," 9; letters written from captivity, 34–35, 40; on local churches, 127; on Old Law, 308–9; as servant of Jesus Christ, 693–94; on sin and death, 255; on spiritual struggle, 257; spousal image of Christ's relationship with Church, 37–38
Paul of Samosata, 286
Paul VI (pope), 139, 417, 417n201, 455, 455n4, 655n57
Pelagianism, 247, 279–80
penance, 218; done by the Church, 94; efficacy of penitent's acts, 609; and sin, 100–101
penance, sacrament of, theological problems: Church's gradual awareness, 550–61; external vs. interior character, 559–61; historical development, 550; mercy vs. strictness, 556–59; sacramental nature of ecclesiastical penance, 561–65
penance, sacrament of, theology of: disposition required, 600–614; formation of, 566–80; grace of conversion, 581–600
Pentecost, 17; Church as new temple, 47–49; as foundation of Church, 54–55; Mary's role, 133
People of God: Church as, 28–32, 55–56, 86, 631; Israel as, 130–31, 309; priestly people, 638, 649
Périnelle, Joseph, 566, 580n19
Perler, Othmar, 128, 658n62
Person of the Church (Church-Person), 76–81
Person of the Incarnate Word, 63
Petavius, 74
Peter, Carl, 566

Peter, Saint, 110, 241–42
Peter of Palude, 660
Peter of Poitiers, 203, 401, 403
Pétré, Hélène, 392n138, 541n67
Peuchmaurd, Réginald, 405n164
Phèdre (Racine), 165
Philips, Gérard, 4, 22n39, 28, 132n39, 139n61, 701
Photius of Constantinople, 504
pilgrim character of Church, 31
Pinto de Oliveira, Carlos Josaphat, 641
Piolanti, Antonio, 419n1, 454n3
Pistoia, pseudo-council, 580, 612
Pius a Langonio, 666n75
Pius VI (pope), 315–16, 581n21, 604n70
Pius X (pope), 342, 343, 660
Pius XI (pope), 660
Pius XII (pope), 42, 44n97, 71, 122n20, 417, 445n62, 632, 660, 664, 702
Plato, 36
Plé, Albert, 205n113
plérôma (fullness) of Christ, 33, 38–40
pneumatology, 507
Polycarp, Saint, 376
Pontifical Biblical Commission, 107
Poschmann, Bernhard, 550, 552n4, 564, 570n5b, 574n9, 575n11, 617
The Possessed (Dostoyevsky), 590
Potel, Julien, 535
potestas passiva (passive power), 217
Potterie, Ignace de La, 239n1, 253n17, 304n5, 552n4
Pourrat, Pierre, 143n8
power: active vs. passive, 221; passive power *(potestas passiva)*, 217
Prat, Ferdinand, 115n6
presence: and Berengardian controversy, 396–400; Christ's, in Eucharist, 370–73, 390, 393–94, 402–4, 407–8; Christ's, in history, 46, 192; God's, in the righteous, 97–98; indivisible, 495; invisible, 496–97; mysteric, 193–95, 202, 462–65; new interpretations, 414–16; non-extensive, 495; nonlocal, 495–96; *per modum substantiae*, 494–95; spiritual, 395–96, 497; symbolic vs. real, 437–38; and transubstantiation, 453–61
"presence" and there-being, 453–61

Prevotin of Cremona, 403
priesthood; apostolic succession, 643–47; as calling, 695–700; celibacy of priests, 698–700; Church's participation, 635–41; collegiality and papal primacy, 661–65; collegiality of pastoral power, 657–61, 710–11; cultic function and pastoral function, 675–79; "desacralization" of, 679–80; fullness of, 655–56; hierarchical priesthood, 650–53; mediation of, 653–55; ministerial priesthood, 641–50; and personal destiny, 708–9; priest/bishop distinction, 666–80; priestly consecration, 647–48; priestly spirituality, 713–15; recognition of ministers, 648–50; twofold character of, 633; universal priesthood, 652–53; women, exclusion of, 701–4. See also Holy Order, sacrament of
prophecy, gift of, 684–85
Protestant Reformation, 53–54, 111
Proust, Marcel, 457
Pulleyn, Robert, 568n1
purification: of the Church, 111–12; Jewish rites of, 243

Quaestiones Disputatae de Veritate (Thomas Aquinas), 179
Quasten, Johannes, 374, 379nn88–89, 388n123, 392, 517n16
Quesnel, Pasquier, 612
"Quicumque" Symbol, 62–63
Quinot, Bernard, 381n98
Qumran community, 429

Rabanus Maurus, 396
Racine, Jean, 165
Raeder, M., 254
Rahner, Hugo, 132n39, 193n99
Rahner, Karl, 90n58, 113n1, 116, 118n10, 120–21, 124n23, 152n40, 239n1, 249, 311n18, 445n62, 456n5, 487n63, 519, 520, 591n41, 627n17
Ramos-Regidor, José, 610
Rancé, Armand Jean Le Bouthillier de, 603
Ratramnus, 395, 396
Ratzinger, Cardinal Joseph, 357, 632, 661
real-intentional causality, 175–77

rebaptism, 20, 169, 210, 286
reconciliation: with the Church, 598–99; grace of, 231; *impositio manuum*, 148; sacrament of penance, 561
redemption: baptism and, 249, 261, 292; Christ's, efficacy of, 157; and Christ's return, 155, 756; Christ's self-sacrifice, 637; earthly phase of, 207; Mary's role, 139; progressive nature of, 259; redemptive grace, 280–83; and salvation, 11
Refoulé, François, 324n7
regeneration, 144, 259–65, 291
Reiser, Beatus, 152n40
"relays" of the sacraments, 201–2
repentance: and anointing of the sick, 564, 576–79; charity as inspiration, 605–6; contrition, 587–88, 590–91, 594; motivation for, 603–5; necessity of, 586; and remission of sins, 246
Rerum Ecclesiae (Pius XI), 660
res et sacramentum, 150, 208–9, 215, 217–21, 227–32, 285, 515, 518, 530; sacrament of marriage, 719, 734–43; sacrament of penance, 597–600
res sacra, 58–59
res tantum, 20, 22–25, 168–69, 228–29, 515, 530; sacrament of marriage, 719, 744–50; sacrament of penance, 595–97
revelation: Christ as exegete of the Father, 8; divine, 84–85; sacrament as, 5–6
Riga, Peter J., 610
righteousness, state of, 65–66, 67–68, 204, 251, 254, 582
Ritzer, Korbinian, 719n1, 730n12, 731n14
Rivière, Jean, 405n164, 419n1
Robeyns, Anselme, 639n19
Rochais, Henri Marie, 28
Roche, Eugène, 550
Roguet, Aimon-Marie, 151n36, 152n40, 193n99, 419n1, 499, 502nn11–12, 512, 514n3, 530, 610
Rondet, Henri, 550, 610, 719n1, 736, 738
Rouiller, Grégoire, 354
Rousseau, Olivier, 242n22, 319n35, 661n70, 719n1, 741n11
Ruch, C., 419n1

sacramentality of Christ, 7–8
sacramentality of the Church, 5–60, 233–35; Christ as Lord, 53–60; comprehensive value of, 28–53; definitions and overview, 5–6; explanatory value of, 15–28; and mystery of Christ, 9; nature of the sacrament, 10–11; as organizing principle, 2–3; reason for, 12–13; and sacramentality of Christ, 7–8; sanctifying rites as expression of, 16–18; threefold signification of (past/present/future), 13–15; threefold structure of, 19–28
sacraments: as actions, not objects, 17; beneficiary's dispositions, 204; bringing about transubstantiation, 498–512; and causality, 173–77, 178, 218–20; character and grace, 220–22; charity, Eucharist as sacrament of, 536–45; Christ's role, 188–90, 200–201; and Church's life, 192–233; double finality and double effect, 206–10; efficacy of, 171–92; efficient causality, 200; Eucharist as, 448–49, 514–24; and faith, 142; and Holy Spirit, 334–35; as human act, 163–64; and human intention, 163, 164–67; initiatives, reversal of, 190–92; instituted by Christ, 169–71; "invisible sacrament" in Eucharist, 518–21; minister's role, 177–82, 592–93; mysteric presence, 193–95; of the Mystical Body, 11, 14; nature of Christian sacraments, 152–58; Peter Lombard on, 148–50; power to perform, 683–86; of redemption, 11; redemptive mystery, 192–206; "relays" of, 201–2; sacramental character, 210–18; sacramental doctrine of Augustine, 146–48; sacramental grace, 222–33; sacramental hylomorphism, 150, 158–62; sacramental order, 141–51; sacramental order, Eucharist's specificity, 543–45; sacramental order, unity of, 542–43; sacramental reception vs. spiritual reception, 541–42; sacramental theology, 2; sacrament-thing vs. sacrament-action, 162–63; of salvation, 11; seven distinct (septenary), 149–50, 224–25, 561–62, 631; as sign-symbols, 155; structure of, 158–69; symbolism of, 143; three structures of, 168–69; truth vs. fruitfulness, 284–85; twofold dimension of, 6; *votum sacramenti*, 231–32

sacramentum, 16
sacramentum et res, 20, 21, 25–28, 168–69
Sacramentum Ordinis (Pius XII), 632
sacramentum tantum, 19, 20, 22–23, 71, 150, 168–69, 215, 515, 530, 589; marriage, 719
Sacra Religionis (Boniface IX), 669–70
sacrifice: Biblical offering of first fruits, 423; efficacy of, 441–48; Eucharist, memorial function of, 366–68; Eucharist as, 448–49, 640; external vs. internal, 640; heavenly, 433–35; human, 421–22; sacrificial character of Eucharist, 524–25, 528–29. *See also* Eucharistic sacrifice
sacrilege, 145, 425–26, 510, 519, 532, 541, 724
Sagne, Jean-Claude, 610
Salaville, Sévérien, 499, 503–4
Salmanticenses, 667
Salvation: baptism, prior to, 306–9; Church as sign of, 14; and definition of sacraments, 21; efficacy of salvific acts, 200–204; faith and baptism, 116; by faith vs. by baptism, 241; historicity of vs. universality of, 192–93; Incarnation as primordial event, 7; and infant baptism, 293–94; sacraments and "redemptive mystery," 152; supratemporality of, 195–200; through baptism and Eucharist, 142. *See also* Church and salvation
sanctification: and Eucharist, 516; Holy Spirit's role, 507; and New Law, 146, 171–72; personal vs. collective, 631–32, 708–9, 717; progressive character of, 336–37; sacraments as signs of, 170
Sanseverino, Gaetano, 667
Scheeben, Mattias Joseph, 3, 4
Schenker, Adrian, 354
Schillebeeckx, Edward, 3, 5n1, 6n3, 12n20, 17nn33–34, 116n8, 152n40, 166n60, 415n196, 450n15, 458, 499, 500, 511, 720n1, 732
schism, 268, 288, 394, 531–32
Schleck, Charles, 222n134

Schlier, Heinrich, 9n12
Schlink, Edmund, 84n52
Schmitt, Joseph, 9n11
Schnackenburg, Rudolf, 9n12, 23n40, 28, 33n60, 115n7, 239n1, 304n3, 641
scholasticism, 330, 399, 400, 403–4; and sacrament of penance, 566–70
Schönborn, Christoph, 610
Schoonenberg, Piet, 409n180, 458, 459n13
Schüller, Bruno, 550
Scotus (John Duns Scotus), 174, 504, 575–78, 579, 686
Scriptum (Thomas), 151, 177
Scripture contrasted with sacraments, 154
Seckler, Max, 205n114
Second Council of Lyon, 403, 562
Second Council of Nicaea, 503
Second Vatican Council. *See* Vatican II
Selvaggi, Filippo, 490
Semmelroth, Otto, 3, 28, 30n55, 124n23, 132n39, 703n45
Sentences (Lombard), 148
sequela Christi, 57. *See also* apostles
service: to the Church, 707–8; Church functions as form of, 30; God's service, 423, 428; grace of, 711–12, 715–17; and priesthood, 633, 652, 693–94, 698
sexual union in marriage, 725–30
Sheedy, Charles E., 396n150
Shook, Laurence K., 603n68
sickness: and healing, 624–25; and sin, 623–24. *See also* anointing of the sick
signification: Christ as signifier, 563; as rationate relation, 158; and substance of sacrament, 500; transignification and transfinalization, 453–61
signs: form and matter, 500; sacraments as, 6, 152–55; sign-character and spiritual power, 215–17; "signing" (consignation) and baptism, 323–24, 325, 326; sign-power of baptism, 266–67; sign-symbols, 155
Simeon of Thessalonica, 504
Simon of Cyrene, 355
simul iustus et peccator formula, 251–52
sin: baptism and persistence of sin, 551–56; continuous confrontation of the baptized, 250–53; contrasted with fault, 105–6; detestation of, 586–87; and Eucharist, 538–40; liberation from, 207–8; *macula* and *reatus*, 567; mortal vs. venial, 612–13; and penance, 100–101; persistence of consequences, 255–56; remission of after baptism, 581–88; remission of in sacrament of penance, 588–600; remission of through baptism, 246–59; and separation from Christ, 104–5; and sickness, 623–24; sinners in Church body, 70, 122–24; sinner's preparation for grace, 602–7; unforgivable, 551–52
Smit, G. C., 499, 500, 502n11, 503, 511, 512
Smith, L., 458–59
Smulders, Pieter, 3n2
society: Church and baptism, 266–67; Church and communion, 45, 598, 658, 694–95; Church as, 25–27, 29, 49–53, 115–16, 265; Church's soul and body, 64; civil society and marriage, 737–38; mercy vs. strictness, 556–57; visible/invisible Church, 43–44
Solano, Jésus, 374
Soto, Peter de, 411, 578
soul: after death, 495–96; Christ as soul of Church, 62; co-extensive character of soul and body, 68–71; and created grace, 172; duality of soul and body, 63–68, 184, 227, 723; Holy Spirit as soul of Church, 104, 122–23; Hypostatic Union, 62–63, 74; nourishment of, 391; overview, 52–53, 264; vegetative soul, 331, 335
Spicq, Ceslas, 115n6, 246n2, 277n4, 278n8, 367n48, 433n28, 603n68, 636n1, 736n11
Spinsanti, Sandro, 610
spiritualism, 389, 392, 393
spirituality, priestly, 713–15
spousal image of Christ and Church, 37–38, 45, 66
Stenzel, Alois, 239n1, 240n10, 320
Stephen (pope), 286, 287, 288, 289
Stoic philosophy, 33, 36; *plérôma* (fullness), 39
strictness vs. mercy, 556–59
Suarez, Francisco, 411, 482, 667
substance: distinguished from accidents, 161, 485–92; of Eucharist, 486–95
substitution and sacrifice, 421

Name/Subject Index

Suenens, Leo-Joseph, 28, 128n29
Summa Sententiarum, 148–49
Summa theologiae (Thomas Aquinas), 1, 151, 177, 178, 179–80, 186, 479, 594, 626
"Super-Christ" (universal Christ), 61
"symbol" in sacramental theology, 437–38, 440
symbols: Creedal, 88; sacraments as, 6, 194, 305, 414; sign-symbols, 155
Synod of Arles, 286, 289–90
Synod of Pistoia (1786), 315–16

Taille, Maurice de La, 350, 411, 412n183, 419n1, 430, 432, 433, 472n35, 482, 499, 528n41, 530
Tanquerey, Adolphe, 667
Teetaert, Amédée, 564
Teilhard de Chardin, Pierre, 44, 61
temple, imagery of, 29, 46–49
Tertia pars (Thomas Aquinas), 490
Tertullian, 144–45, 268, 291, 325, 326, 379, 382, 386, 517, 519, 552, 558, 561, 638
Theodore of Mopsuestia, 380n92, 385, 388, 539n62
Theodoret, 349
Théologie de l'Église (Journet), 61
there-being: of Christ, 456–61, 484–97, 513, 519–20; and spiritual presence, 454–55
Thils, Gustave, 113n1, 128, 661
Third Lateran Council, 149
Thomas Aquinas, Saint, 1, 119–20, 124, 158n50, 207n115, 372n62, 600n63, 601n64; on absolution, 591–94; on acts of the penitent, 589–90; on anointing of the sick, 620–21, 626, 628; on authority of bishops/priests, 690–91; on baptism, 272–73; on Christ's humanity, 137; Church as *congregatio fidelium*, 51; on Church's sacramental action, 235; on Church's unity, 526; on circumcision, 308; on confirmation, 331, 335, 341; episcopacy/presbyterate distinction, 671–72; on Eucharist, 347–48, 442–43, 479, 481, 495, 496–97; grace and remission of sin, 601; on healing, 624; on infant baptism, 291–92, 293, 301–2; on "Letter of Miltiades," 331–33; on martyrdom, 312; ministers' role in sacraments, 166, 167, 177–82, 186–87; on miracles/prophecy, 684–85; on mystery of evil, 256–59; on occasional causality, 173–74; offering and sacrifice, 420; on papal authority, 670; priesthood/priestly roles, 675, 680; remission from sin, 207; on sacramental grace, 223; on sacramental hylomorphism, 159–60, 499; on sacramental nourishment, 537, 538; sacramental reception vs. spiritual reception, 541; on sacrament of holy orders, 656; on sacrament of penance, 570–75; on sacraments, 13, 151; on sacrifice, 424–25; on salvation and baptism, 319; on salvation history, 306–7; on spiritual power, 216; *Tertia pars*, 490; on Transubstantiation, 469–70, 474, 484–85; on universal priesthood, 639
Thomism, 411; and supra-temporality of salvation, 196–97
Thornton, Lionel, 330
Thurian, Max, 327n14, 365–66, 368, 369n54, 373, 408, 413, 428n17, 431, 433, 434, 436n41, 463n21, 464, 499, 511, 515n9, 531
Tillard, Jean-Marie-Roger, 163n56, 520–21nn23–24
time: Christ's universal scope, 192; end of time, 40, 46, 81, 192, 255, 299, 636; of the law of nature, 307; of Old Law, 307; supra-temporality of salvific acts, 195–97; temporal aspects of Eucharist, 438; threefold signification of sacraments, 13; "time of the Church," 205–6, 255
Tixeront, Joseph, 667
Traduction Oecuménique de la Bible, 214
transignification and transfinalization, 453–61
Transubstantiation, 385–86, 400–401; Catholic doctrine, 510–12; change undergone, 472–81; Christ's there-being, 481–97; Eastern Church position, 502–5; instantaneousness of, 508–10; Latin position, 501–2; necessity of, 461–72; sacramental action of "becoming," 498–512
Trembelas, Panagiotis N., 322, 323, 324n7, 362n26, 477–78n45, 499, 505n21, 731n13

Trent, Council of. *See* Council of Trent
Trinity, 751–58; faith in, 145–46; and grace, 65–66; Holy Spirit as Divine Life, 66; mystery of, 8; and salvation, 11
Tromp, Sebastian, 33n60, 43n93, 51n116, 88n53
Tübingen school, 52

unity: Eucharist as sacrament of, 525–36; of sacramental order, 542–43; and salvation, 10
universal mediation of Church. *See* Church and salvation
universal priesthood, 638–41, 652–53

Van Buchen, Léonard-Alphonse, 322n2
van den Eynde, Damien, 143n8
Van der Lof, L. J., 390, 392
van der Meer, Haye, 701
Van Iersel, B., 245n32
Vanneste, Alfred, 354, 566
van Roo, William A., 143n8, 314n23
Varone, Marie-Christine, 354
Vasquez, Gabriel, 666, 667
Vatican II, 661; on anointing of the sick, 616, 621–22, 627; on baptism, 287, 288; Church's presence in world, 212–13; on dissident Christians, 268; and ecumenicism, 129–30; on "faith" of non-Christians, 118–19; on Mary, 132, 135–36; Mystical Body of Christ, 42; on non-Christian religions, 308; priest/bishop relationship, 674; on priesthood, role of, 675–76; on religious liberty, 740; and sacramentality, 2–3, 16; sacrament of holy orders, 656; on salvation, 114; on universal priesthood, 639. *See also Lumen Gentium* (Vatican II)
Vatja, Vilmos, 405n164
verbum-elementum, 150
viaticum, 622
Villette, Louis, 142n2, 143n8, 146n18,

156n47, 276, 282n21, 287n33, 289n36, 291n45, 392n140
vine and branches imagery, 41–42
Virgin Mary. *See* Mary
vocations: monastic, 679; priesthood as calling, 695–700, 704, 716–17; and sacramental grace, 705, 708; universal Christian vs. particular, 78, 257, 658; unrealized, 622
Vogel, Cyrille, 550, 554n7, 556n8, 558n10, 560n11
von Gunten, A. F., 642n26
Vonier, Anscar, 153, 162, 419n1, 432
Von Rad, Gerhard, 366n42, 371n61
Vorgrimmler, Herbert, 550

Wagner, Albrecht, 290n38
Waldensians, 150
Walty, Jean-Nicolas, 290n39
water: and baptism, 244, 304, 310–12, 409, 452, 757; cleansing and healing, 624; living water, 47, 330; symbolism of, 143, 144, 147; into wine, 349, 477
Watteville, Jean-François Noël de, 374, 413n188
Webb, Douglas, 507n29
Wenger, Antoine, 132n40, 136n53
Willems, Boniface, 113n1, 114n3, 116n8, 124n23
William of Auvergne, 150, 570, 573
Williams, George Hunston, 566
Wilmart, D. A., 386, 388n128
Winzen, Damasus, 329n19
women, exclusion from priesthood, 701–4
Word of God, 523–24; authority of, 693; Christ as Divine Person, 7–8
words, *See* language
Wycliff, John, 43, 350, 404

Zachary of Besançon, 569
Zwingli, Ulrich, 406